Home, Work, and Play

Third Edition

Home, Work, and Play

Situating Canadian Social History

Edited by James Opp & John C. Walsh

Oxford University Press is a department of the University of Oxford.
It furthers the University's objective of excellence in research, scholarship,
and education by publishing worldwide. Oxford is a registered trade mark of
Oxford University Press in the UK and in certain other countries.

Published in Canada by
Oxford University Press
8 Sampson Mews, Suite 204,
Don Mills, Ontario M3C 0H5 Canada

www.oupcanada.com

Library and Archives Canada Cataloguing in Publication

Home, work, and play : situating Canadian social
history / edited by James Opp & John C. Walsh. — Third edition.

Includes bibliographical references.
ISBN 978-0-19-901086-8 (pbk.)

1. Canada—Social conditions—20th century. 2. Canada—
Social conditions—19th century. I. Walsh, John C., 1969–, editor
II. Opp, James William, 1970–, editor

HN103.H56 2015   971   C2015-900352-0

Cover image: CurvaBezier/iStockphoto

Oxford University Press is committed to our environment.
Wherever possible, our books are printed on paper which comes from
responsible sources.

Printed and bound in the United States of America

1 2 3 4 — 18 17 16 15

Contents

Part III: At Play   325

More online. Look for this icon at the end of the readings for additional material online.

Chronological Contents

Acknowledgements

When we were unexpectedly thrust together to teach a course in Canadian social history at Carleton University in the fall of 2003, we had no idea that many of the concepts we set out in class would evolve into this work. Although the readings and articles assigned in History 2304 have changed considerably, the students and teaching assistants have always been exceptional participants in sharpening our sense of purpose and clarifying how space could be used to structure and communicate the importance of social history. Their responses, their enthusiasm, and their generosity are constant reminders to us that the classroom is truly a two-way learning experience. It was the sharp eyes of Maja Villarroel, a standout student from our first social history class, who brought the Eveready battery ad to our attention. Another course alumna, Laura Jackman, introduced the "lady cyclist" both to our class and this book.

In taking on a third edition of this book, our debts to others have also grown. Doug Fischer from the *Ottawa Citizen* graciously shared digitized images. David Carr and Glenn Bergen from the University of Manitoba Press helped us to secure permission for work that was not quite published at the time of compilation. Research assistants Laura Lutes and Kathryn Boschmann combed collections from Ottawa to Winnipeg to identify new primary sources for this edition. Sara Spike's sharp eyes helped us to see this book in new ways at the proofing stage. The tremendous collections from the Canada Science and Technology Museum were accessed with invaluable help from David McGee. At Oxford University Press, Tamara Capar, Caroline Starr, Ian Gibson, and Cailen Swain moved mountains to accommodate our desire to launch this book "at home." It has been more than a decade, but we remain grateful for the faith and support that our first editor, Laura Macleod, extended to us in making *Home, Work, and Play* such an important part of our professional lives.

We also continue to receive a great deal of encouragement and feedback from instructors, students, and scholars from across the country. Our reviewers provided careful and constructive comments that helped us to refine this book. In particular, Todd McCallum offered us a considerable exposition on the "work" section that was greatly appreciated. As editors, we are always surprised and heartened by the variety of ways that our book is used, and we continue to urge historians to seek out new and innovative strategies for designing courses and delivering materials. We hope that this third edition will open even more doors and offer more options in relation to the themes, methodologies, and theoretical approaches that characterize the rich diversity of social history today.

The first edition of this book was developed at a time when we both found ourselves taking on new roles as fathers. Each subsequent edition has seen the steady expansion of our families to the point where we can now field a basketball team. Far too much of our work has followed us home, but Karen Reyburn and Pamela Williamson have seen us through many highs and lows. And finally, thanks to Emily, Hope, Henry, Nevan, and Celia for reminding us every day about the spectacular importance of play.

James Opp and John C. Walsh
Mike's Place
June 2014

Figure 1. "The Bright Way is the Right Way . . ." *Maclean's*, 15 Sept. 1952

Introduction
Situating Canadian Social History

James Opp and John C. Walsh

In a 1952 advertisement for Eveready batteries (Figure 1), the flashlight is heralded as an essential tool for Canadian consumers, whether at home, at work, or at play. Although the flashlight remains the same in each setting, the context for its use suggests dramatically different social and physical environments. From illuminating the inside of an oven for a housewife to exposing an ambulance's engine for a driver to lighting the way in a dark forest for a group of young adults, the social relations surrounding the device are depicted in specific ways that shift across space, gender, and age. In this example, the three fields of home, work, and play are deeply gendered; domestic labour is a feminine activity, while a masculine mechanical aptitude is required outside the home to accomplish paid labour. Leisure activities, such as camping, are characterized by young adults, who are at a stage in life when courtship and sexual relations are in flux and their own home and work lives have not yet been defined. The ad suggests that the flashlight is useful "from basement to attic," reinforcing the broad post-war middle-class conception of home ownership. Furthermore, the fact that all the actors in these images are white has the effect of normalizing a particular racial identity as typically Canadian. While the intention of this ad is clearly to sell batteries, it communicates a great deal more in evoking a set of cultural ideals that characterized Canada in the 1950s.

Such idealizations were not, of course, descriptions of reality as much as they were the projections of a comforting social order defined by an advertising agency. Nevertheless, the advertisement serves as a useful starting point for considering how historians situate history in terms of social and physical space, real or imagined. In bringing together a diverse selection of articles in recent Canadian social history, this volume calls attention to how historians, implicitly and explicitly, frame their work in relation to these spatial categories. The inclusion of visual primary sources offers readers an opportunity to go one step further, developing their own analysis of spatial meanings. Home, work, and play are not, as the battery advertisement suggests, self-evident or natural categories. Ultimately, our objective is to unsettle simplistic notions of how such spaces are constituted and made meaningful.

As spatial categories, home, work, and play operate in this collection in two different but complementary ways. First, the articles shed light on how these spaces were historically understood and experienced by various peoples in multiple contexts. For example, Franca Iacovetta and Valerie J. Korinek explore how the consumer choices and homemaking of immigrant mothers were viewed by authorities as agents of acculturation and assimilation in Cold War Canada. Making Jell-O was not only a way to put a smile on children's faces, it was also considered an important element of cultivating good citizenship. Andrew Parnaby explains how Aboriginal men were at the heart of labour organization and labour relations around Vancouver's Burrard Inlet. His article demonstrates how working for wages affected these men and how their experiences and identities were essential to broader local and regional patterns of working-class formation. Dan Malleck's article on the regulation of barrooms in Ontario shows how constructions of gender and respectability guided the regulation and inspection of drinking spaces, and how both men and women transgressed the codes of behaviour they were expected to conform to. Despite the different historical settings, all three essays demonstrate that the spatial context in which people lived, worked, and played was an active component of their identities and experiences. This theme can be observed in each essay in this volume through different sources and can be understood from a variety of methodological and theoretical positions. While this collection makes no pretense to being comprehensive, the selections reorient how we can and should think about home, work, and play.

Second, we have used the terms *home*, *work*, and *play* as an organizational framework. These categories operate as a map to help readers (most of whom we expect are newcomers to Canadian social history) navigate what might otherwise seem a dense and unmanageable field of study. Through our own teaching experience, we wanted to develop something more than a strictly chronological structure or an endless list of themes with little in common. At the same time, we understand that chronology is critical to historical understanding and that social history is as diverse as the peoples whose stories it tells. The organization of this text offers students an opportunity to see shifts in social relations over time within the broad spatial parameters of home, work, and play. Whether the reader is following the original thematic arrangement or adopting a more chronological approach through the alternative table of contents, locating these selections within a spatial context is a useful exercise for thinking about the historical contexts of everyday life.

Although we have organized our selections into three discrete categories, our intent is not to insist on their strict separation. Rather, this structure allows readers to challenge the very artificiality of such predetermined classifications. Many of the selections point to the permeability of these boundaries. The male patrons who frequented the high-end "supper clubs" of West End Vancouver or the working-class nightclubs of the East End might have viewed their activity as leisurely "play," but as Becki Ross and Kim Greenwell explain, the women dancing on stage were most certainly at work. While many readers may take it for granted that their home, work, and play lives are interconnected, thinking about these connections historically is unsettling because it compels us to embrace the messiness of the past.

The porous nature of the boundaries that surround home, work, and play also extends to the other types of borders that surround us. Social historians have long been interested in mobility and movement through space and across territory, but new studies of borderlands and border crossings are revitalizing how we think about where (and when) "Canadian" social histories were made and experienced. Colin D. Howell's analysis of sport in the Maritimes demonstrates the cultural exchanges that brought Boston and the northeastern United States closer to home than Montreal or central Canada. The connections between mobility, identity, and attachments to home are also noticeable in Merle Massie's analysis of migration within Saskatchewan during the Great Depression. Looking closely at how local communities tell their own stories, Massie recasts the historical narrative away from prairie devastation and onto parkland adaptation and sustainability. Similarly, Marguerite Van Die's analysis of a Victorian middle-class family points to the gendered nature of mobility and how domestic relations were formed through an increasing "sacralization" of the family. Whether the boundaries are political, social, or cultural, identities are formed and re-formed by our movements within and across spaces and places.

In designing and updating this collection, we deliberately sought out recent work. While new is not necessarily better, we wanted readers to have a clear sense of the diversity of interests, methodologies, and approaches that currently characterize the field. We were also aware that framing our volume in terms of social space shifted the focus away from other major themes such as immigration, industrialization, and urbanization.[1] These large-scale transformations and the dislocations they triggered are not absent from this collection, but they are positioned in relation to other concerns, reflecting new directions in social history that have emerged in the twenty-first century.

Along with the organizational structure, another innovative feature of *Home, Work, and Play* is the incorporation of visual primary sources. Historians tend to rely solely on textual sources, and images (when noticed at all) often serve as little more than inert illustrations. In recent years, however, visual culture has emerged as an important resource for scholars interested in how social spaces and bodies were represented. In paintings, photographs, advertisements, cartoons, maps, and architectural plans, social space is portrayed, reshaped, and given meaning by producers and consumers of such images. The inclusion of illustrations in this volume is therefore not a means simply to "visualize" the past—we want to encourage readers to "read" visual imagery critically in light of the historical context provided by the essays. We also want to engage with the historical imagination, and the visual source sections challenge readers to "see" both critically and creatively. For us as teachers, history is not simply about acquiring knowledge—it is as much about cultivating an informed and inspired engagement with the past. It is about learning how to pose questions and search for answers. In this book, these questions and answers have much to do with the intersections of people and social space and how they were represented visually. Indeed, as with the Eveready advertisement, we need to be aware of how visual images create and reinforce the social constructions of gender, class, race, and sexuality just as they represent the spaces of home, work, and play.

Our framing of social history in this way speaks to the wider historiographical landscape facing Canadian historians. In the 1990s, conservative critics lamented the loss of a national narrative in the face of multiple perspectives and the fragmentation of history into specialized subfields. In the twenty-first century, we have seen concerted attempts by governments to reconstruct a singular national narrative through commemorations, memorials, and statues, using war and military conflict as the centrepieces for how Canadians should understand themselves. Social history has always resisted such attempts to produce homogeneous stories of the nation. Indeed, far from ignoring politics, social history has arguably been at the forefront of reconsidering the meanings of power, the state, and governance. We would argue that the proliferation of perspectives and new areas of interest testifies to the continuing vitality of Canadian social history. Rather than return to the nation as the privileged framework for understanding Canada, this book charts a different path by using space to organize and arrange our histories. If the sheer variety of social history has made it difficult to synthesize, it is worth questioning why history demands a singular narrative, and perhaps considering the value of histories that disrupt, fragment, and force us to reconsider comfortable, unified stories of nationhood. Rather than assuming "the" story of Canada, social history encourages us to continue exploring what kinds of Canadian histories are possible to imagine, to know, and to make known.

Making Social Histories

When social history emerged on university campuses in the 1960s, it was often defined against the dominant tradition of political history. Self-consciously revolutionary, social historians declared that they were doing history "from the bottom up" or writing a more complete "total history." Over the past 50 years, however, the field has evolved. Perhaps a better way to define social history is as an attempt to relate the social experience of the lived past to the social structures that limit and define such experiences. Karl Marx famously said that individuals make their own histories (thus enacting what social historians often call "agency") but that they do so within parameters defined for them by others ("structure"). Most, if not all, Canadian social historians would agree with this basic proposition, although they would differ on the relative importance of agency and structure. Indeed, there is an enduring and underlying tension between the two in the broad landscape of Canadian social historical writing.

Agency and structure were central questions for social historians in the 1960s and 1970s who sought to restore a place for those marginalized by the traditional focus on national politics and the elite classes. For some, the path to recovering this history lay in a social science methodology that mined new and different types of sources, such as wills, baptismal and wedding registries, tax assessment records, city directories, and census returns. Like their colleagues in sociology and economics, historians became adept at statistical analysis and eventually produced a startling array of figures about the historical identities and behaviours of Canadians, from child-rearing to marriage patterns to kinship and community relations. This research was both interdisciplinary and international, as Quebec historians drew upon the work of the French Annales movement while English-speaking historians found inspiration in demographic studies of the Cambridge Group for the History of Population and Social Structure. The use of statistical analysis also owed much to the social scientific history emerging in the United States, which made an explosive entrance into Canada via the work of American-born and -trained Michael Katz and his well-funded project on Hamilton.[2] These works produced tables of data that spoke to large-scale economic structures related to industrialization, urbanization, and family strategies. For some historians, however, the social scientific approach offered little room for recovering the actual voices of the historically marginalized—the working class, immigrants, and women. A parallel, and occasionally overlapping, impulse within social history sought to go beyond these structures to explore how people were agents of history in their own right.

In particular, these scholars drew upon the work of British Marxist E. P. Thompson, whose classic *The Making of the English Working Class* (1963) is still regarded as the seminal text in the field. In his preface, Thompson famously remarked that his objective was to recover workers "from the enormous condescension of posterity."[3] For him, the key to recovering working-class agency lay in taking working-class culture seriously and in analyzing class-based organizations, customs, rituals, songs, and poems as expressions of political resistance that "made" the working class as much as it "was made" by the economic forces of capitalism and industrialization. Canadian working-class historians followed this lead, focusing on topics such as the organization and rituals of the Knights of Labor, the parades of the Orange Order, and the use of the charivari as markers of working-class culture.

Thompson's influence extended beyond his scholarly conclusions. In his political activism, most famously his campaigning for British disarmament in the 1980s, Thompson demonstrated a new type of critical social role for the intellectual in contemporary society. Social historians in Canada similarly engaged with Marxist, New Left, and feminist concerns. The creation of the journal *Labour/Le Travailleur* (later *Labour/Le Travail*) in 1976 reflected the interest in creating dialogue between intellectuals and Canada's working class, and the journal actively sought outside contributors and cultivated a broad readership. Social historians' pursuit of agency and voice was viewed as a meaningful contribution to present-day politics. Concerned over the apparent rising tide of subversive activity among historians, the RCMP even sent spies to observe what went on at the annual meetings of the Canadian Historical Association.[4]

In the 1980s and 1990s, the interests and approaches of social historians evolved, but agency and structure remained central. Increased interest in immigration, ethnicity, and women's lives raised questions about whose experience was being reconstructed by historians. Labour and working-class historians had acknowledged the role of ethnicity in shaping working-class experience, but immigration historians focused their efforts on family and community bonds, framing their work as part of a narrative of migration and relocation. Women's historians called attention to the public and private aspects of women's lives, but in turn discovered that women's experiences varied with class and ethnicity. This broad-ranging dialogue called attention to the complexity of peoples' identities, shaped by multiple and overlapping factors including sex, class, and race. Textbooks in Canadian history reflected these trends through titles such as *A History of the Canadian Peoples* and *The Peoples of Canada*, which implicitly rejected a single national narrative in favour of a more pluralistic perspective.

However, this embrace of multiple voices and identities produced new debates over the ethical position of historians and their unspoken assumptions. How accessible are past experiences, and who has the right to speak for those whose voices were denied or lost over time? How do we understand historic actions and events when the records preserved in archives were written by those in positions of authority, such as housing inspectors, Indian agents, and court officials? The claim to understanding the experience of others was critiqued particularly by historians who worked with First Nations, Métis, and Inuit. The representation of Indigenous voices produced heated debates at academic conferences, as Aboriginal peoples demanded a role in narrating their own histories. Social historians struggled to bridge a cultural divide between academic interests, collective memory, and the enduring legacies and practices of colonialism.

The search for agency raised troubling questions for historians in many fields and, drawing again on similar developments in the social sciences, new tools were developed to differentiate social realities from historically produced social constructions. In the late 1980s and early 1990s, gender historians rejected the too-common assumption that women's history could simply be appended to a mainstream, national narrative. Rather than divide history by biological "sex" into women's and men's stories, gender historians focused on the dynamic relations between masculine and feminine identities, binary social constructions that were fundamental in naturalizing the perceived "truth" of sex. Whereas women's history sought to give women a voice and narrate their experience, gender history examined the fluid representations of femininity and masculinity that infuse and structure our understanding of social actions, behaviours, and spaces.[5] For some women's historians, the movement toward gender history appeared to threaten the traditional focus on women's experiences and agency. In response, gender historians argued that we cannot grasp the full meaning of individual experience without first understanding the structures of gender that have historically surrounded and constituted women and men.

Such debates demonstrate that as a category of analysis, gender functions at a very different conceptual level, forcing historians to rethink how customs, conventions, language, and other forms of representation both affirm and confront historically produced identities. Jennifer A. Stephen's chapter explores the gendered assumptions and discourses of "employability" that surrounded women workers mobilized by the National Selective Service during World War II. Not only were certain tasks deemed to be "natural" extensions of women's innate characteristics, but women's biological potential for motherhood made them the subject of extensive moral regulation and inspection. In a similar vein, Donica Belisle's analysis of unionization drives for clerical staff at Eaton's suggests that labour leaders also held to the model of the "male breadwinner," producing gendered assumptions of work and consumption in the post-war period. And yet in both of these studies, women resist, challenge, and subvert gendered expectations. Understanding the underlying discursive formations recasts how historians view and perceive the agency of their subjects.

By the end of the twentieth century, other socially constructed categories of analysis had emerged. In particular, social historians turned their attention to the way perceptions of racial difference have changed over time. Writing about "race" is not simply a matter of narrating the story of various ethnic groups. Rather, it exposes how essentialized notions of "character" were produced and performed through racialized cultural codes. Unmasking particular racial stereotypes is only one aspect of critically engaging with the social construction of race; it is also important to recognize how "whiteness" operates as an implicit universal norm and serves as the standard by which other categories of race are measured. Franca Iacovetta and Valerie J. Korinek's analysis of Cold War food politics points to the absence of a "British" category in the nutritional guide *Food Customs of New Canadians*, published by the Toronto Nutrition Committee. Couched in objective language, the discourses of race permeated the descriptions of immigrant food habits, reinforcing unspoken middle-class white standards. For Becki Ross and Kim Greenwell, the ability of Vancouver burlesque performers to embody racial fantasies of the exotic varied. White dancers could appropriate the trappings of other cultures, but African-Canadian and African-American performers found that fewer venues would book them and the cultural repertoire they could draw upon was more limited. Nevertheless, the strategic redeployment of racial stereotypes was used to enhance such performances as truly "authentic." As both of these chapters illustrate, gender, race, and sexuality are not competing levels of analysis but need to be understood as overlapping and intersecting categories.

As with many other scholars in this volume, Ross and Greenwell's analysis is influenced by the emergence of postcolonial scholarship that seeks to unravel how power is embedded in the cultural knowledge of "others." Although the term *postcolonial* suggests a time period, the concept is better understood as a mode of critique that questions the continuing cultural legacies of colonialism and imperialism.[6] In their chapters, Sharon Wall and Gillian Poulter point to the appropriation of Indigenous cultures and identities in such disparate settings as Ontario summer camps and Montreal snowshoeing clubs. In both cases, it was the ability of white settler society to enact and embody knowledge of the "Other" that made such performances meaningful. Often Indigenous peoples had little control over their representations, but as Andrew Parnaby notes, Aboriginal dock workers employed strategies that played upon these very stereotypes as a form of economic resistance.

Underlying the historiographical shifts toward gender, the social construction of race, and postcolonial critiques is a wider engagement with questions of language, discourse, and power, prompted by the emergence of poststructural and postmodern theories. Broadly speaking, such postmodern approaches to history suggest that because words can never capture the past in a complete or neutral manner (whether embedded in primary sources or in the narratives of historians), we need to be aware of how the structures and conventions of language and discourse produce the texts and narratives we encounter. Since our access to the past is always mediated by language, the "linguistic turn" is also, in effect, a call to historicize our own understandings of how we come to know what we know. Such an approach opens up new methodologies, new ways of examining how discursive power operates, and new kinds of representational forms, including visual, spatial, and literary sources.

The postmodern critique cuts to the heart of the historical enterprise. Can historians truly claim to reveal how others experienced the past when we know "reality" only through layers upon layers of "discourse" and language?[7] Are the historical meanings we draw from these fragments representative of past experience or the product of our own present understandings? Critics warn that an exclusive focus on discourse leaves little room for analyzing experience or for recovering a sense of agency on the part of oppressed groups. They also worry that such a focus pushes us farther away from our historical subjects rather than bringing us closer to them.

While it may never be entirely possible to reconcile such oppositions, the types of questions that historians ask have been fundamentally reshaped by these important theoretical shifts. As historians became more attentive to the power embedded in discourses and the production of knowledge, they also identified the potential for transgressive acts and points of local resistance. For example, in Paige Raibmon's article, Aboriginal domestic space is put on display and carefully constructed as a spectacle of either "primitiveness" or "civilization." And yet Indigenous peoples themselves reconfigured their houses to suit their own needs, subverting the attempt to establish assimilation through domesticity. By viewing space itself as a form of language, Raibmon allows us to envision domesticity as a site where everyday life was both culturally constructed and materially contested. In understanding the surrounding context of representation and performance, agency is not lost but gains new meaning.

The question of language has been particularly important for historians of sexuality, who problematize the use of "homosexual" and "heterosexual" as nineteenth-century terms created to psychologize sexual behaviours. Rather than assume rigid categories of sexual identity, historians like Valerie Korinek are fashioning histories of same-sex desire that accommodate a wide range of sexual practices. This strategy allows Korinek to include people who openly identified as gay or lesbian, as well as those who did not see themselves in such terms but who nevertheless participated in an evolving queer culture. Like Raibmon, Korinek is attentive to issues of performance, space, and agency. While navigating the complex discourses of sexuality that shaped identity formation in Winnipeg, this chapter foregrounds local practices, subversive acts, and the reclamation of public spaces as sites of sexual encounter.

As social history comes to terms with new theories and new areas of research, it has also started to rethink the relationship between historians and the archive. In its ability to organize, arrange, and selectively preserve documentary materials, the archive itself is an expression of power. Social historians today are more willing to incorporate the archive and their archival experiences within their narratives as an essential part of the story rather than leaving such encounters buried in the footnotes. Telling stories about where our histories come from and how they are produced offers another strategy for destabilizing the hidden forms of knowledge and power that present "the archive" as a neutral and apolitical space.

For Stacey Zembrzycki, the archive was not housed in a government building but was rather an encounter at the kitchen table, talking to Ukrainian Canadians in Sudbury about their childhood memories. Her chapter and others in this volume point to a resurgence of interest in oral history as a methodology and as a way to explore issues of memory.[8] In the 1970s, social historians began conducting oral history interviews, but the results were often regarded as secondary or a supplement to the archival record, which stood as the "objective," verifiable site for serious historical analysis. Often, the goal was to separate historical "facts" from the fallibility of "memory." However, the questioning of the traditional archive and a rising interest in memory studies led to a reconsideration of the value and meaning of oral history. For Zembrzycki, the stories told to her at the kitchen table offer more than just insights about childhood; they are also memories that define individual and collective selves. Rather than looking for "bias" or falsehoods, Zembrzycki interrogates these narratives as a way to understand why men and women remember their Depression-era childhoods as they do.

In the 1970s and 1980s, social historians debated the value and meaning accorded to agency, to quantitative methodologies, to class, and to the role of women in Canadian history. In the following decade, the discussions shifted to questions surrounding power, discourse, gender, race, and sexuality. In the twenty-first century we see yet more scholarly "turns" as space, the body, memory, performance, and governance make their mark in the historiographical landscape. Even within this volume, different historians take up different and sometimes conflicting approaches and methodologies based on the questions they pose and the evidence they wrestle with. If the issue of "agency" has been with us since the work of E. P. Thompson in the 1960s, it certainly has not disappeared, as

Katherine M.J. McKenna's chapter on the Prescott Board of Police indicates in its very title, "Women's Agency in Upper Canada." The frictions between agency and structure, between experience and representation, challenge us to retrace our steps, question our assumptions, and think carefully about how we use our sources. One of the defining elements of social history has been a willingness to question itself—to ask difficult and sometimes discomforting questions about what social history is and should be.

Thinking about Space

By the end of the twentieth century, the interdisciplinary study of culture, power, and society had produced a "spatial turn" in humanities and social science research. Language, discourses, and their effects were not only historically constructed, but also had important geographical dimensions. Building on the linguistic turn, and inspired by important theoretical work from Henri Lefebvre, Michel de Certeau, and Michel Foucault, scholars investigated how discourses help "produce" space and place. They also demonstrated that space and place affect the making of discourses and their effects on social and political life. In a parallel but distinct development, the rise of environmental history in the 1990s similarly encouraged Canadian social historians in the early 2000s to consider how people's lives were circumscribed by the ecologies of place and region, to see both "nature" and the built environment as exercising agency rather than being an inert stage for culture. Certainly earlier generations of rural and urban history had considered these issues, but the spatial turn has spurred an even wider range of social historians to explore the interconnected histories of everyday life, space, culture, and power. The spatial turn has had a profound impact on this book as well. Since the first edition, we have used "situating" in the subtitle and curated primary source chapters that encourage reflection on and analysis of the intersection of the social and the spatial in Canadian social history.

Through this intersection, the spatial turn has inspired new ways of approaching traditional topics, as is the case with Nicolas Kenny's chapter in this volume. Kenny offers an evocative mapping of late nineteenth-century "industrial Montreal" with its self-consciously stylized factory architecture, streetcars clanging through crowded streets, and the seemingly ubiquitous chimneys billowing smoke into the sky. He then takes us inside the factory walls, describing the foul smells, the noise, the bodily pain of extended hours and on-the-job injuries, and even the perils of the factory bathroom. While earlier social histories focused on labour relations and worker regulation on the factory floor, Kenny turns his analysis to the competing ways in which workers and others made sense of industrialization's effect on space, the body, and health. While ostensibly concerned with workers' health, the governing class of factory inspectors, social reformers, and public health crusaders who observed, documented, and evaluated workers' bodies and workspaces were concerned as much or more so about order and discipline in the industrializing city. Fixing the "problems" of industrial workspaces and broken down workers' bodies was a means to help repair "polluted" Montreal.

These relationships between space, social life, and governance are a recurring theme in this collection. Russell Field's chapter on constructing Maple Leaf Gardens points to the disciplinary effects of such spaces. Lower-level seating was plush and opera-house like, the middle tier had wooden seats with backs and arms, while upper-level seating was simple (and inexpensive) long wooden benches, a classed landscape reproduced in the accompanying porcelain toilets in the lower levels and steel trough urinals for the upper. These design elements were accompanied by rules and a staff trained to cultivate "well-behaved spectators." While Kenny's chapter demonstrates how the state contributed to the production of space and to the construction of gendered and classed identities, in Field's chapter it is architects, businessmen, and ushers who acted as governing agents. If workers' bodies were deemed to be a threat in Montreal, in Toronto the question was how to attract and discipline the right kinds of bodies as paying spectators.

The ability of liberal governance to embed codes of conduct within space has also drawn the attention of social historians. Rather than rely on regulators or ushers to enforce respectability, the goal was for people to behave "correctly" on their own. In this volume, for example, Patrick Vitale shows how planners, neighbourhood associations, and neighbours in the post-war Toronto suburb of Thorncrest nurtured a landscape aesthetic to affect a set of experiences related to family, community, and place. Among other things, Vitale shows how residents in Thorncrest were educated and disciplined to internalize the rules of the suburb—such as keeping property neat, not leaving garbage cans unattended at the end of the day, and keeping garage doors closed—so that they would become self-governing residents. By policing themselves and one another, Thorncrest homeowners would be happy, fulfilled individuals much like the two-sided suburban man featured in the 1978 "Kanata: For the two of you" advertisement, reproduced as Figure 17 in "Visualizing Home."

From these examples it is apparent that the spatial turn provides social historians with fresh perspectives from which to explore questions of agency and structure, experience and representation. Spaces are never neutral or empty of meaning, especially those designated as proper sites of home, work, and play. In the very classification of certain activities as "naturally" belonging to these spheres, a multitude of historical assumptions are brought to bear in defining domesticity, labour, and leisure. Social spaces function materially and symbolically in shaping everyday life. In situating Canadian social history, we want to stress the active nature of these processes. Although not all the articles in this volume directly address the question of social space, they all point to the dynamic negotiation of power, whether imposed from above or resisted and restructured from below.

Visualizing Space

It is important to note the distance between experience and representation, especially when examining visual sources. Kate Boyer explores how the new "office girl" of the 1920s and 1930s was an essential element of advertising related to the new Remington typewriter. In comparing the depictions offered in these advertisements with other forms of evidence, such as company journals and employee records, Boyer reveals a significant by-product of new office technologies: in "saving" time and effort, as these advertisements claimed, new technologies actually tethered women to their desks, limiting their career choices and opportunities. Here the social space of the office is both "real" and "constructed," existing simultaneously as a sphere of lived experience and as a wider representation of waged labour and technology.

Cultural representations are not just passive reflections of existing discourses, but also function as active components in producing space. As Sean Purdy argues in his chapter on Toronto's Regent Park, films produced by the National Film Board recast the area first as a "slum" that required redevelopment and then later as a site of poor government planning dominated by crime and drugs. These filmic narratives were not only ideologically charged but also had very real effects on Regent Park's development and public perceptions of it. Purdy also notes how these spatial constructions were resisted by the voices of residents, who saw their community very differently. For Purdy, envisioning the problems of Regent Park as simply the logical outcome of poorly planned space ignores the deeper economic and social problems that lie beneath these representations.

Historically, the visualization of space has contributed to the production of space and the governing of social experiences and identities. Valerie Minnett and Mary Anne Poutanen's examination of the "swat the fly" campaign in 1910s Montreal emphasizes that public health officials and social reformers deployed various forms of visual culture, including photographs, illustrations, and maps, as part of their efforts to educate citizens about the dangers posed by disease-carrying flies. Through images and captions, officials and reformers made visible the spatial decay that they insisted resulted from disease. Such a strategy was endemic to public health campaigns across urban Canada in this era, and both maps and photographs were oft-used forms of visualization. Appearing in newspapers and in pamphlets, health officials published maps of the city that placed large circles around zones that had become "infected" and leaving untouched those that remained "healthy." Presented as modes of scientific representation, these visualizations legitimized a wide range of interventions and regulations of spaces where people lived, worked, and played.

Visual sources, like textual material, thus require an informed, critical eye. Even photographs, which appear to offer an objective view of the past, are subject to multiple interests and cultural constructions. The photographer selects what to include within the frame and what to leave out. The subjects may willingly pose, or they may resent the intrusion. Technological limitations and cultural aesthetics influence what is captured on film and what is not. Publishers routinely recrop images to suit other needs, often adding captions that may have little to do with the original intention. And, as with any form of representation, what the producer *intends* to portray is not necessarily what the audience takes from it.

Visual sources actively contribute to the construction of meanings that surround and infuse social space. Sometimes they explicitly reinforce existing ideologies, and sometimes they articulate unspoken assumptions and attitudes. What is clear, however, is that we cannot dismiss such sources as simply illustrations or "pretty pictures." For example, during the preparations of the first edition of *Home, Work, and Play* two major banks denied us permission to reprint advertisements that had appeared in *Maclean's* in the 1950s. At a time when the banks were facing lawsuits over past labour practices, the recirculation of these visualizations was not deemed to be in their corporate or legal interest. Visual sources matter, then as now, and by including images for readers to analyze, critique, and evaluate, we hope to encourage discussion of perspective, evidence, and methodology. Ultimately, there is no simple way to determine how such images were received or what their creators intended. However, the insight provided by the articles in this collection may help readers to think about the visual representation of social space in new ways.

Conclusion

The obstacles facing historians in recovering social experience and social structures in many ways mirror the difficulties inherent in drawing out meanings and understandings from images. Social historians face a daunting task in trying to produce historical narratives that capture the multiple voices, meanings, textures, and complexities of past social worlds. The choices we make as historians are not dissimilar to the choices a photographer makes in framing his or her subject. In selecting what to focus on, a great deal is left out. The picture, like history, is never entirely complete.

Social history has changed a great deal in the last 50 years. A field once dominated by a focus on labour and the working class has expanded to include issues of gender, race, and sexuality. Domesticity and home life are no longer marginal areas of concern but are viewed as fundamental elements of nation-building, colonization, and imperialism. A new interest in popular culture has led to wide-ranging studies in leisure, recreation, the environment, and spaces of play. New sources, including oral history, photographs, and advertisements, have led to new questions surrounding identity and representation. Yet, for all that is new, social historians remain committed to seeking understanding of and respect for the diversity of peoples who made Canada, a project that was as fundamental to scholars in the 1960s as it is today. *Home, Work, and Play* is a testament to the determination of social history to push the boundaries of our knowledge and understanding of the past while remaining unapologetically humane in its concerns.

Notes

1. For social history collections that explicitly approach these topics, see Franca Iacovetta and Robert Ventresca, eds., *A Nation of Immigrants: Women, Workers, and Communities in Canadian History, 1840s–1960s* (Toronto, ON: University of Toronto Press, 1998), and Ian Radforth and Laurel Sefton MacDowell, eds., *Canadian Working Class History: Selected Readings*, 3rd ed. (Toronto, ON: CSPI, 2006).

2. Michael B. Katz, *The People of Hamilton, Canada West: Family and Class in a Mid-Nineteenth-Century City* (Cambridge, MA: Harvard University Press, 1975), and Michael B. Katz, Michael J. Doucet, and Mark J. Stern, *The Social Organization of Early Industrial Capitalism* (Cambridge, MA: Harvard University Press, 1982).

3. E. P. Thompson, *The Making of the English Working Class* (London, UK: Penguin Books, 1980 [1963]), 12.

4. Steve Hewitt, "Intelligence at the Learneds: The RCMP, the Learneds, and the Canadian Historical Association," *Journal of the Canadian Historical Association* 8 (1998): 267–86.

5. Joan Wallach Scott, "Gender: A Useful Category of Historical Analysis," in J. W. Scott, ed., *Gender and the Politics of History* (New York, NY: Columbia University Press, 1988). See also Scott's response to a forum discussion of her seminal work in "Unanswered Questions," *American Historical Review* 113 (December 2008): 1422–30.

6. Edward Said, *Orientalism* (New York, NY: Vantage 1994 [1978]).

7. For an accessible introduction to postmodernism, see Callum Brown, *Postmodernism for Historians* (New York, NY: Routledge, 2004). For an early critique, see Bryan D. Palmer, *Descent into Discourse: The Reification of Language and the Writing of Social History* (Philadelphia, PA: Temple University Press, 1990).

8. Anna Sheftel and Stacey Zembrzycki, eds., *Oral History Off the Record: Toward an Ethnography of Practice* (London, UK: Palgrave Macmillan, 2013).

PART I

At Home

Before the 1970s, the question of the home rarely found its way into the pages of Canadian history. Even the earliest works in women's history tended to focus on the pioneering roles of women outside the home, instead of viewing the home itself as an important historical space. However, in the 1970s and 1980s, social historians interested in women, children, the family, household structures, immigration, and kinship placed the home and household at the centre of their analyses rather than treating domestic spaces as marginal to the larger narrative of national (and political) history. For many historians, researching and theorizing the "private" world of home and family offered a useful way of recovering the voices, work, and actions of women and children, which had been marginalized by historians' traditional understandings of the nation and citizenship.

As scholars delved into new issues such as domestic labour, child care, and women's property rights, the very distinction between public and private was called into question. The conceptualization of diametrically opposing social worlds, also known as the ideology of separate spheres, was itself a historical construction of the Victorian period (c. 1830–1900). In the shift from an agrarian society to an industrial economy, the middle classes physically separated home from work, as fathers no longer worked with or near their families but instead found employment in factories and offices. This separation produced new ideals of domesticity and new boundaries of gender. Women were viewed as naturally embodying domestic virtues such as fidelity, compassion, and moral strength. In contrast, men were seen as the breadwinners, more capable of rational thought, and uniquely suited to the public affairs of politics and work. Within this binary context, the home was idealized as a "haven in a heartless world," a moral centre that counteracted the ruthless competitiveness that marked nineteenth-century economics and politics. This middle-class, Victorian ideology was critical to the work of early feminist historians who focused on the home as the space where women lived and made history, where they were agents rather than passive spectators of historical change, and where the moral rhetoric of home played a significant role in historical struggles for political and legal rights.

Very quickly, however, historians realized that the ordering of society as naturally divided into public and private broke down in multiple ways. Studies of the Victorian era demonstrated that the waged labour of immigrant domestic servants betrayed the notion that work did not take place in the home, while the realities of working-class family economies compelled many women and children to work for wages, both inside and outside their homes. Apart from a few urban areas, the majority of Canadians continued to live in rural settings well into the twentieth century, and it was clear that the ideal of separate spheres had limited relevance for understanding the everyday experiences of rural families, where work and home often remained firmly intertwined. Historians even began to wonder if urban, middle-class women themselves fit the domestic ideal in light of their public activities, such as participating in religious societies and social reform movements. The conclusions drawn from this research understandably led to a new questioning of the boundaries between the spheres. The simple division of public and private could not be sustained, since most people have historically inhabited some portion of both worlds simultaneously.

The emergence of gender history in the 1980s and early 1990s, along with a rising concern over language and representation sparked by poststructuralist critiques, offered new avenues for analyzing home as a social space. Instead of viewing "public" and "private" as static categories, a new generation of historians started to unravel these binaries of social division as intertwined and dependent on the construction of masculine and feminine identities. The use of gender as an analytical tool allowed scholars to demonstrate the fluidity of the meanings that surround space, calling attention to the shifting representations of masculine and feminine attached to particular sites even within the home, such as the kitchen, the dining room, the study, and the parlour. Rooms occupied by both sexes could be gendered very differently. Further complicating the picture, gendered perceptions of domesticity also intersected class, race, and sexuality. As the following essays demonstrate, the home is not simply a physical place inhabited by people; it is also a space that has historically been embedded with contradictory social meanings.

Although social history was attacked in the 1990s for being too compartmentalized and disconnected from a national narrative, these historiographical developments actually brought the political sphere back to the doorstep of the home. Instead of viewing the public sphere as having a separate history from the home, historians raised new questions about how the expression of power was deeply gendered and why so much energy was invested in maintaining idealized conceptions of domesticity.

These themes run through many of the articles included in this section. The home as a space for raising families was seen as the key to the future of the nation, and domestic ideals were central to middle-class perceptions of Aboriginal peoples, immigrant communities, and the working class. As these essays illustrate, inside and outside the physical space of the home a broad range of domestic relations were infused with moral tensions, especially marriage, sexuality, and the family. The governance of public health, the inspection of boarding houses, and the missionary focus on "civilizing" the domestic spaces of Aboriginal peoples were all profoundly political acts of state regulation. The public surveillance directed at the domesticity of "others" points to the depth of anxiety that the white middle class felt about the future of Canada and the state of its "race." Urban planning, especially after World War II, also produced new ways for homeowners to police each other as suburbs expanded.

If the home has become more political in our histories, it has also become a more tangible and personal space as historians continue to explore the lived experience of domestic spaces. Oral history methodologies, the rise of memory studies, and expanding areas of research such as the history of food are casting the history of the home in a new light. This is especially the case for the post-war period, when growing suburban spaces and perceptions of home clashed with massive urban renewal projects. In an age of Cold

War anxiety, kitchens served as a new site of citizenship, and consumerism reshaped both the food and the technology used to prepare it.

In the articles that follow, some focus more on the representation of the home, some call attention to the lived experience of its inhabitants, and others move between these approaches. Collectively, they suggest that the home was far from being a marginal space with little influence. Rather, the home was central to the culture and politics of governance and state formation in the nineteenth and twentieth centuries.

Further Readings

Adams, Annmarie. *Architecture in the Family Way: Doctors, Houses, and Women, 1870–1900.* Montreal, QC: McGill-Queen's University Press, 1996.

Baillargeon, Denyse. *Babies for the Nation: the Medicalization of Motherhood in Quebec, 1910-1970.* Translated by W. Donald Wilson. Waterloo, ON: Wilfrid Laurier University Press, 2009.

Bradbury, Bettina. *Wife to Widow: Lives, Laws, and Politics in Nineteenth-Century Montreal.* Vancouver, BC: UBC Press, 2012.

Carter, Sarah. *The Importance of Being Monogamous: Marriage and Nation Building in Western Canada to 1915.* Edmonton, AB: University of Alberta Press, 2008.

Davies, Megan Jane. *Into the House of Old: A History of Residential Care in British Columbia.* Montreal, QC: McGill-Queen's University Press, 2003.

Dennis, Richard. *Cities in Modernity: Representations and Productions of Metropolitan Space, 1840–1930.* Cambridge, UK: Cambridge University Press, 2008.

Epp, Marlene, *Mennonite Women in Canada: A History.* Winnipeg, MB: University of Manitoba Press, 2008.

Fahrni, Magda. *Household Politics: Montreal Families and Postwar Reconstruction.* Toronto, ON: University of Toronto Press, 2005.

Iacovetta, Franca, et al., ed. *Edible Histories, Cultural Politics: Towards a Canadian Food History.* Toronto, ON: University of Toronto Press, 2012.

Gleason, Mona. *Small Matters: Canadian Children in Sickness and Health, 1900-1940.* Montreal, QC: McGill-Queen's University Press, 2013.

Harris, Richard. *Creeping Conformity: How Canada Became Suburban, 1900–1960.* Toronto, ON: University of Toronto Press, 2004.

Parr, Joy. *Domestic Goods: The Material, the Moral, and the Economic in the Postwar Years.* Toronto, ON: University of Toronto Press, 1999.

Perry, Adele. *On the Edge of Empire: Gender, Race, and the Making of British Columbia, 1849–1871.* Toronto, ON: University of Toronto Press, 2001.

1 Women's Agency in Upper Canada
Prescott's Board of Police Record, 1834–50

Katherine M.J. McKenna

Just before midnight on a dark, chilly November night in 1837 in Prescott, Upper Canada, Mary Greneau was startled out of her sleep by the sound of a mob outside her house. Male voices shouted, "Kill her" and "By God I'll fix her!" Her attackers pounded on her door, heaving against it until the hinges burst and her home was broken open. Spilling inside were six horrifying figures, dressed in grotesque imitation of Native Indians. Their faces were blackened and streaked with red and they wore blanket coats. As they whooped and hollered, they went on a destructive rampage, smashing her windows, breaking her furniture, and throwing her possessions out into the street. Mary and the two women living with her, Jane Craig and Elizabeth Brady, felt entirely defenceless and in real terror for their lives. Only when a neighbour threatened to shoot them if they did not desist did the six marauders depart.[1]

Although this incident bears some resemblance to the classic charivari, there are important differences. Mary Greneau was, it is true, a well-known local figure. She was a constant nuisance to those living near her, and in particular had an ongoing feud with her neighbours across the street, John and Catharine Kelleaugher. They were fed up with her running

what was then called a "disorderly house," a place of entertainment operating at all hours and outside the law. She sold liquor, employed a fiddler, and entertained drunken men with "dancing and indecent conduct."[2] Women of doubtful reputation were living there and going in and out at all hours, on at least one occasion fighting in the street. Catharine Kelleaugher later testified that, on one May evening, Bridget Savage and Margaret Doneghan disturbed the peace as they were coming out of Mary Greneau's house by engaging in a shouting match, calling each other "bitch," "whore," and "bastard" for all to hear.[3] The Kelleaughers took to displaying their displeasure in a nonviolent but pointed manner. Crossing to the drainage ditch in front of their disruptive neighbour's house, they emptied their slops and chamber pots there. When she complained to them, they replied with very "insolent answers."[4]

Earlier that November, Mary had clashed with some of her patrons as well. Late one Saturday night, she brought back three men to her home in a state of intoxication, giggling and laughing. One, William Glazier, called for four glasses of liquor, one for him, one for her, and one each for James Campbell and John Honeywell. The latter whispered to her, perhaps in jest, that because Glazier was a newcomer to Prescott from Glengarry "that she might skin him." When Mary tried to cheat William out of his change, he declared "he would have the change or the worth of it before he left the house." They scuffled, falling against the stovepipes with such violence that they were knocked over. She finally chased the men out of the house at gunpoint, firing a warning shot into the street in the wee hours of the morning.[5] This was too great an insult to the pride of John Honeywell, who promptly went to the authorities and charged her with firing the gun, and on the Sabbath, too, a double bylaw violation. Mary Greneau was duly fined, but was not prepared to take this passively. She counter-charged Campbell and Honeywell, perhaps angry with them for not defending her against Glazier, for having "abused her in her own house." The public testimony that resulted was not to her advantage. One witness asserted that "for some weeks past" she had "kept a very noisy house, after hours, Sunday evenings not excepted." The whole story about the evening's doings became a matter of public record. Samuel Indicott, who had been employed by Mary as "waiter and fiddler," tried to put a good face on it, testifying that he only "saw drunken people there occasionally, saw some dancing and indecent conduct sometimes, heard singing frequently." Pandering to racist sentiment, he asserted in her defence that he "never saw the coloured people use her familiarly." As for the accusation of carrying on such activities on Sunday, he assured his listeners that he had in fact seen "some say grace before drinking."[6] This did not persuade local authorities of the justice of her case. The charges against Campbell and Honeywell were dismissed, and Greneau was assessed steep costs of £1.3.6.[7]

This victory did not appease John Honeywell. A few days later, he and some others launched the attack on her house, wreaking revenge on a woman who they thought needed to be put in her place. Their intentions were well known locally. One witness had "heard it frequently said that she ought to be rid on a rail." Others had

been invited to join the raiding party but had declined. Honeywell's band hatched their plot at the store of Alexander Thomas, where they met to put on their costumes. A passerby heard them say, "damn the old devil, she'll not know us." They carried the charade to the point that they "spoke in imitation of the Indians" when spoken to on the street, responding "Chip, Chip, Chuck" in a crude mimicking of Native dialect. After the raid was over, they conveniently left their disguises at Thomas's store, where they were easily found and later presented as evidence. The men then repaired to Beale the barber's for a drink to celebrate their triumph over Mary Greneau.[8]

Charivaris were a not uncommon form of "rough justice" in Upper Canada.[9] This one deviated from the norm because it was not a political protest and was less an expression of community censure than the settling of a personal quarrel.[10] Even though it is clear that there were many in the Prescott community who objected to the behaviour of Mary Greneau, the raid on her premises was not accepted by her neighbours as "rough justice." After some initial delay in recognizing that the attack was something more than just the usual carousing heard from her home, they turned out in her defence. Surprisingly, it was the short-changed Glazier who finally drove the rioters off with the threat of shooting. Other members of the community, Mr. Deneau and Mr. Cavalier, had not only refused to join the party, but also testified against Honeywell's band.[11] Mary Greneau herself, as we have seen, was not one to accept attack passively, and she quickly sought her own revenge through legal means, successfully prosecuting Alexander Thomas, Thomas Meredith, and John Honeywell for disturbing the peace. As an expression of community censure, they were handed exceptionally punitive fines of £2.10 with costs of 17 shillings, 3 pence each.

Such a remarkable story about a woman of the popular class is rare in Upper Canadian history. That it has survived is due to the existence of an equally remarkable document—the Minute

Book of the Board of Police for Prescott, Ontario. For almost 150 years this record has sat virtually untouched in the vault of the municipal offices of Prescott.[12] What it reveals is an unparalleled source of social history on many aspects of Upper Canadian life. Standards for acceptable community behaviour on everything from control of livestock, health regulations, road maintenance, keeping the Sabbath, licensing alcohol and entertainment, and even what language was permissible to use in public space are recorded in the 400 densely written pages of this Minute Book. Of particular interest are the cases brought to the Board of Police that involved women as prosecutors or plaintiffs or were brought on their behalf by men during the 16 years it presided over Prescott life, from 1834 to 1850.

In the 1830s and 1840s Prescott was at the peak of its success, a rapidly growing small town of more than 2,000 persons.[13] Situated just above a section of the St. Lawrence River made unnavigable by rapids and with a natural, deep harbour, it was an important transfer point for goods and people arriving overland from Montreal en route to Ogdensburg to the south and points west such as Kingston and Toronto. This forwarding trade meant that merchants prospered, and associated activities such as shipbuilding and marine insurance developed.[14] During the 1837–8 Rebellion, the decrepit Fort Wellington was rebuilt, and from 1843 to 1854 it was garrisoned with a company of men from the Royal Canadian Rifle Regiment.[15] After the Montreal–Toronto railway was built in the 1850s, Prescott subsided in importance. The time covered by the Board of Police Record, then, coincided with the town's height of prosperity and activity.[16]

. . .

. . . [In] the 1830s a new governing model was implemented in eight rapidly developing communities across Upper Canada, incorporating them as towns and establishing local Boards of Police to take over the comprehensive duties of the Quarter Sessions. If the Quarter Sessions was flexible and well suited to frontier needs, so too

were the Boards of Police. They were also more democratic and more closely tied to their communities. In Prescott, presiding Board members were chosen from among local male property holders of at least £60 assessed value and elected by men who were British subjects owning a dwelling house and a plot of land or paying rent of at least £5 per annum within the boundaries of the corporation. . . . This system held sway until a new Municipal Act in 1849 called for the establishment of a mayor and council, with a separate Police Court.[17] . . .

. . . As Allan Greer has observed, early Upper Canadian justice was a "ramshackle affair" which "could not function as the instrument of an external and superior state power to anything like the degree that modern police forces later would."[18] Only after the change in government in 1850 do we see a few charges brought to trial on behalf of the Board as a corporate body, despite the fact that the Board often asked town officials to perform bylaw enforcement duties.

In keeping with this personalized model of justice, cases were summarily dealt with, often the same or the next day. There were no judges, lawyers, prosecutors, or police witnesses, only the members of the Board, sometimes the bailiff or constable, the plaintiff, defendant, and the witnesses whom they had brought. The Board members themselves were not remote from those who appeared before them. Although some professionals such as lawyers and physicians served, for the most part the members were practical men of business, local merchants and manufacturers.[19] In their daily affairs they rubbed shoulders with those brought before them, even if they did have the authority to impose taxes and fines and to imprison defaulters for up to 30 days. Despite the fact that many of the individuals who appeared in front of this informal tribunal were not able to elect its members, it was nonetheless a community-responsive and immediate form of justice.

As a record of the public activities of ordinary women, the Board record provides us with rare insight into their transgressive behaviour, as well as the gender-based and class-linked sanctions increasingly brought to bear on them by the Prescott town fathers throughout this period. There was a rough total of 139 cases involving women between 1834 and 1850. Only 12 of these were brought on behalf of women by men. Of the 139, more than half (about 76) were independently initiated by the women themselves as prosecutors. Overwhelmingly, these were ordinary labouring women of the popular class, most of whom did not skirt the boundaries of the law in their daily lives like Mary Greneau. More often, they appeared at the court to settle everyday disputes that arose in their community. To a greater extent than the more formal Court of Quarter Sessions or the Police Courts established after 1850, the Board of Police was a practical means of dealing with community problems. . . . It was not costly; it was informal and conveniently located in the town. . . . More often, it was a tool used by the local populace for their convenience, as a strategy for negotiating dissent within their neighbourhoods. . . .

On the other hand, it is worth underlining that the Board of Police was a coercive institution, ultimately representing the interests of the wealthier male members of the Prescott community. It was no idealized, democratic, grassroots body. Yet, since it did not always control the charges brought before it, but only sat in judgment, it was easily used by common citizens as a tool in negotiating social difficulties. Katz, Doucet, and Stern still see this occurring in the Hamilton Police Court of the 1870s. They observe, "To Hamilton's working class the Police Court was not remote. Rather, as the assault cases in particular show, it was used to settle disputes within families or between friends and neighbours and to resolve the tensions that resulted when the strains of everyday life erupted into minor incidents of violence."[20] Those who appeared before the court were not criminals, but were using the courts for their own private purposes.

Public records such as the Prescott Board of Police Minute Book, it has been argued, reveal at least as much about the institutions that created them as they show about the subjects whose histories are recorded in their pages. All too often the entries followed a prescribed script that undermines their value as authentic sources of information about people's lives.[21] Although this problem can never be totally removed, the Board of Police for Prescott is perhaps less prone to it, due to the Board's informality and the fact that in 1834 it was a new Upper Canadian institution with little in the way of established practice to follow. Although not totally unmediated, the Board record appears to provide a summary of actual testimony recorded by the Clerk, taken verbatim from the lips of those who testified, complete with grammatical mistakes and colloquialisms. It is likely to be as close as one is going to get to hearing the real voices of women of plebeian origin for this early nineteenth-century period. This is a record, then, that can provide us with rare insight into the public roles of ordinary Upper Canadian women.

Many of the women of Prescott who brought charges before the Board were married with their spouses still living, despite the fact that, according to British law, they were not supposed to act as legal entities apart from their husbands. Constance Backhouse's path-breaking work on women and the law in early Canada indicates that, in particular, married woman were legally subjected to patriarchal control.[22] Law and custom do not always coincide, however. Women in Prescott could and did take the law into their own hands, acting as full citizens in the eyes of the Board of Police, if not in any other capacity in Upper Canadian society. . . . There is even at least one recorded instance of a woman successfully charging her own husband with disturbing the public peace by striking her.[23] Married as well as single women in Prescott could and did have their day in court, acting independently of their husbands despite the fact that law might dictate otherwise.

In this public role, women of the popular class of Prescott differed from their bourgeois sisters. Throughout the nineteenth century in Upper Canada, a new consensus was emerging about middle-class gendered social and moral values.[24] "The Cult of True Womanhood" prescribed that women's role was in the private domestic sphere. Purity, chastity, delicacy, and retirement from the male world of politics, law, and business were requisite to this ideal of femininity.[25]

The chasm that separated the classes in Upper Canada is dramatically revealed in the pages of the Board of Police Record. Middle-class ladies were not to appear in public unescorted and were never to raise their voices. Compare this to the behaviour of Mrs. Hannah Ahern and Mrs. Catharine Murphy, screaming insults at each other in the street in a dispute over a pig. This fracas was concluded by Hannah's employment of a favourite contemporary insult, placing, as the record shows, "her hand upon her hind parts" and inviting her neighbour to kiss her there.[26] Contrast the ideal of the "domestic angel" with the behaviour of Mrs. Thursbay and Mrs. Chamber toward Mr. Reynolds, Mrs. Chamber's former landlord. Mrs. Chamber had departed without paying her rent, so Reynolds was holding as security a box of her possessions. The two women arrived at his door one day, in the company of "one or two" soldiers, to reclaim her property. According to the court record, "Chamber pretended to offer him 3/—being the balance due . . . but would not let him see the money. He refused to give up the box without the same." The two women then left the house and "commenced breaking his Windows" with their umbrellas. "Both then made great confusion in the street cheering as they broke the glass crying out whores thiefs and villains." Not many women behaved as outrageously as these two, and the stiff fines of 25 shillings each with costs of 2 shillings, 6 pence ensured that they would most likely have been sent to jail for 30 days in default of payment.[27] Still, their case

and those of other women in the Board of Police Record of Prescott show the striking differences between the genteel ideal to which the colony's social leaders aspired and the rough and ready nature of small-town street life. It is rare to locate such information about women of the popular class for this early period of Canada's history.[28]

The records of the Board of Police may have been dominated by the lower-class citizens of Prescott, but it was not a criminal court. It merely tried bylaw infractions, however broadly defined. . . . Although the behaviour that brought individuals to the Board of Police was deviant, it was not deviant enough to lead to exclusion from society. There are even accounts of prominent male citizens who appeared before the Board without seriously damaging their social position.

. . .

. . . The illustrious Jessup family, staunch Loyalists and founders of Prescott, were represented locally by two male descendants in the 1830s and 1840s. One, Hamilton D. Jessup, was a local physician who was a respectable pillar of his community and elected to the Board in 1837, 1843–5, and 1848. The other headed a decaying branch of the family tree. Henry James Jessup came up before the Board on many occasions, caused by either his hot temper or by his predilection for frequenting houses of "disorder." In 1844 Jessup was rumoured to be "keeping a bad woman" at the house of Mrs. Black, by the name of Mary Delany.[29] Two years later he had tired of her, but Mary was not taking his abandonment without protest. She took to following him around, accosting him in public barrooms, and calling him a "damned whoremaster." This got to be too much for him, and he charged her with "annoying, insulting and abusing" him. The members of the Board were all too aware of the pair's former relationship and they sought to mediate the dispute. The matter was finally concluded when "defendant agreed with Prosecutor that if he would give two pounds ten shillings and give up her cloths and she to give up his they were to part. He gave up her cloths, gave her the money. She gave up his cloths, they appeared to be satisfied at parting." This settlement did not prevent the Board from fining Mary Delany 15 shillings plus court costs, however, which made a substantial dent in her £2 from Jessup.[30]

Henry Jessup may have already taken up with a new woman by this time, by the name of Marian or Mary Lang or Lane. She was living in Mrs. McLean's house, which earlier that summer of 1846 had been such a nuisance to the neighbourhood. Jane McLean, Mary Lane, Mary Keating, and Bridget Wood were "brought before the Board for a violation of the By-Laws" by their neighbour and later Board member, merchant Robert Headlam, for a "Breach of Public Decency and good order and for intoxication." Witnesses testified that they had been "annoyed by these prisoners for a long time," but, on one particular night, "a large party of drunken men [were] in and about the house creating a riot and disturbance in the door of the house where the prisoners live." One "saw men passing and repassing with Bottles in their hands, drunk . . . saw one man pulling Mrs. Lane by the arm outside the house."[31] This may have been the same woman who, like Mary Delany, began shouting abusive names at Jessup in the street a year later. The first time Jessup charged her, the case was dismissed, but a month later, when she added threats to throw stones through his window to her insults, she was fined 5 shillings plus costs.[32] The comparatively light fine that she received may have been an acknowledgement by the Board of Jessup's role in provoking such behaviour from two different women.

Perhaps Jessup should have followed the lead of railway engineer Walter Shanley, who was always on the lookout for sexual prey, but concluded that Prescott was a dead loss in this respect.[33] "There is a sad deficiency of anything *safe* in these diggings," he complained to his brother in 1851.[34] Shanley had a highly tuned sense of what was appropriate to what he considered his station as an educated professional man. For example, he was shocked when he heard that his brother had entered a public bar frequented by some railway labourers. "Nothing I had heard for some time 'put me out' so much as your confession of swilling porter in a public bar with my serfs," he complained. "I keep all my staff at an immeasurable distance. How they must have laughed in their sleeves at the porter drinking and in what utter contempt . . . must hold you . . . but the subject is an unpleasant one to dwell on."[35] Shanley preferred not to "slum it" with women like Mary Delany and Marian Lang, but sought out the more respectable elements of the popular class. He particularly was attracted to innkeepers' daughters. When he stayed for a while at Gilman's Hotel in Prescott, he complained that he was not allowed access to "those sisters-in-law of Gilman's" who were "really very fine girls—but so 'severely proper' you can scarcely approach them. . . . Mrs. Gilman, who is as fine a looking woman as I ever saw, keeps strict watch & ward over them, & it is not easy even to see them."[36] . . . Yet, for all his frequent preoccupation with sexual adventure in his letters to his brother, Shanley scorned the society of women who kept and frequented disorderly houses. After renting a room in Prescott at Torr the baker's, he found it to be "a most Bawdy-house place" and determined to move at the first opportunity.[37] Although some men were able to get away with crossing the class barrier, for the most part the women who turned up in the Board records for disturbing the public peace were consorting with men of their own class or nearly so. They most certainly did not aspire to be middle-class angels of domesticity.

Still, in the earlier years of the Board of Police records, even if disorderly houses were not appreciated, neither were they especially condemned. Mary Anne Poutanen has observed a similar tolerance in Montreal neighbourhoods, provided the peace was not disturbed.[38] The line between them and houses of prostitution was not sharply delineated. Katz, Doucet, and Stern note this later in the century as well. "In fact," they observe, "little distinction was made between houses in which prostitution took place and ones where loud, uninhibited behaviour annoyed the neighbours or attracted the attention of the police."[39] Selling a little bit of sex on the side was rarely a specialty for most popular-class woman, who adopted a number of strategies of survival, which in Prescott included, as Bettina Bradbury has noted for Montreal, keeping pigs and other livestock and taking in boarders.[40] Selling liquor and providing entertainment, as did Mrs. Greneau, was an easy way of augmenting one's income. Certainly a ready clientele would be found among the soldiers at Fort Wellington and the sailors and traders who passed through Prescott. Such women did not consider themselves to be prostitutes and might even have had other occupations such as needlework or laundering that did not pay them enough to survive.[41] Catherine Curry, for example, who appeared before the Board on three occasions on charges related to keeping a disorderly house, was listed on the 1851 census as a dressmaker, with two female "servants" living with her.[42] Mary Keating, Mary Lane, Bridget Wood, and Jane McLean, when charged with public drunkenness, were all women on their own who had combined their households to stretch their limited means. Although they may very well have been providing sexual services to their patrons, they were not charged with prostitution.

In fact, there was no bylaw that specifically referred to prostitution, only a vaguely worded general ordinance that called for penalties for any breach of public decency or order, which included, among other things, breaking the Sabbath, cutting down shade trees, and defacing buildings.[43] Most of the charges against disorderly houses came under this bylaw. Although in testimony it was often mentioned that the defendants were keeping disorderly houses, on only three occasions before 1848 were women actually charged with this offence, and one of these charges was dismissed. In 1841, perhaps alarmed by the military presence of British soldiers at Fort Wellington after the Upper Canadian Rebellion, the Board for the first time brought in two bylaws dealing specifically with keeping bawdy houses and "vagrant public Prostitutes loitering about the streets."[44] No charges were ever brought under these new bylaws, however, and they were not renewed the following year.

Indeed, although almost all of the charges involving women included some element of public disorder, most were not for offences related to providing entertainment. A significant number—about 32 cases of the 139 involving women—were related to violence against women committed by men, in particular between husbands and wives. A much smaller number—about nine—involved violence against women committed by women. Often alcohol abuse was implicated, as when Henry Hughes disturbed the public peace by striking Mrs. Anne Crowthers in the street outside the Dog and Duck tavern.[45] When labourer Jonathan Houlihan was charged by Constable Cavalier "for being drunk on Sunday night and for abusing his wife" Teresa he admitted his guilt, but blamed it on the drink.[46] One case of wife assault complicated by racial discrimination involved a Black man, Lewis Beale, the local barber. He first appears in the record when involved in a barroom brawl. Witnesses said that he had "ushered himself into some company he had no business with" and was accordingly refused service. Beale asserted in response "that he was a Gentleman & would flog all the englishmen in the place" along with a number of other threats. When Joseph Wood called him "a fool and a drunkard," Beale responded that "if he could have the chance to shave him he would cut his throat," hardly a statement that would be good for business. He was evidently a large man, too strong to be removed by those present. Later Beale's wife and child took the brunt of his anger and fled to the home of Obadiah Dixon and his wife in fear for their lives. When Dixon refused to deliver up Beale's wife, Beale drew a dagger. In the process of disarming him, Dixon suffered a bite on his thumb and a fight ensued. Although only charged 5 shillings for the first offence, this second time Beale was given a fine of £2.10 with costs, a serious deterrent. He did not appear on charges again, although he was living in Prescott until at least 1842, when a reference in another case was made to the "nigger barber."[47]

Sometimes violent cases involved some element of sexual coercion, as when Charles Gray and Joseph Webb were charged in 1848 "for disturbing the public peace, and abusing Mrs. Webb this day and previously and for keeping a house of ill fame."[48] One particularly disturbing case involved William Lee, who had been charged before for public intoxication and using profane language, and the young daughter of Mrs. Keating. Lee was charged by Alexander MacMillan, a well-off farmer who had been a Board member for 10 years, "for committing a breach of public decency." Witnesses testified that, although "Mrs. Keating's daughter desired Lee to leave her Mother's residence," he refused. Passersby heard the "child cry murder" and call Lee "a blackguard." The record implies that perhaps she had resisted Lee's sexual advances. Apparently he beat her severely; others heard "screeches from Mrs. K's child, went there and saw the child almost breathless and in a state of suffocation from the ill treatment of Lee, and her face was covered with blood." Lee was given a heavier fine than normal, 15 shillings, but it was still nothing close to what Beale had been fined for biting a white man's thumb.[49]

Popular-class women were not simply passive victims as these cases of assault have implied. More typical was the behaviour of Dorothy Erringy toward her husband Thomas, a local hotelkeeper. Their marriage was in crisis in the summer of 1850. Thomas had moved into the home of Minerva Coons (alias Finley, according to the record), who was considered to be keeping a house of ill fame. Rather than accept this abandonment, Dorothy went to the house, broke the windows, and "called Mrs. Finley a whore." She then publicly berated her husband, calling him a "whoremaster," and ended up in a violent argument which ended with him hitting her. Even

though Dorothy had started the altercation, the neighbours charged Thomas and Minerva with disturbing the peace, and they were fined 25 and 20 shillings respectively. Thomas launched his own complaint against his wife for her role in disturbing the peace, but such was the community censure of his behaviour that, when the Board convened, he did not show up and was charged costs. In the 1851 census, Dorothy and Thomas were listed as occupying the same premises and Minerva Coons Finley had evidently moved out of town, so it appears that Dorothy's aggressive action had reclaimed her husband.[50]

Such violent cases were not typical of the charges brought to the Board, however. By far the greatest number, about 78 of the 139 cases involving women, had to do with name calling. In any public dispute involving women, such as with Minerva and Dorothy, far and away the favourite insult was some variant of whore. Men, in contrast, were called a variety of names such as scoundrel, thief, villain, or blackguard, which more generally reflected on their character or integrity rather than their sexual behaviour.[51] Ethnic insults were relatively rare, according to the Board record. Cases of name calling often involved women from the "respectable" part of the popular classes, as well as the obvious easy targets of such insults. Anna Clark has studied defamation cases involving women from 1770 to 1825 in the Church of England London Consistory Court. She argues that the frequency of cases involving insults to the sexual reputation of lower- and middle-class women reveals tensions and anxieties surrounding changing social values about women's honour. Prior to the development of a middle-class ideology of female domestic purity, being seen in public did not automatically mean that a woman was suspected of being a prostitute. Defamation charges were both examples of conformity and resistance to a new moral standard. The insult of whore served to restrict a woman's public life, for to be truly respectable a woman had to remain in the home. Clark argues that, when women called each other whore, "they were succumbing to the reality of the importance of sexual reputation in women's lives, drawing upon the moral vocabulary of the dominant class to carry out their own vendettas. But they were also defying the linguistic constraints of ladyhood by being loud and aggressive and by refusing to accept the newly defined private domestic sphere."[52] This was, then, a discourse of both repression and resistance. . . .

Insults which called into question a woman's moral honour could be used to put her in her place, as when Mr. Desordie responded to Hannah Ahem's attempt to collect payment for bread by calling her a "drunken woman."[53] They could also be a way in which a woman whose reputation had been maligned might counterattack, by discrediting her critics. When William Dove accused Christina Brogan of keeping a disorderly house, she replied by calling his wife a whore and a bitch.[54] . . .

It is important to note that these cases were not defamation charges, but usually complaints brought under the bylaws for disturbing the peace. It was a matter of utmost indifference to the Board whether the charges were justified or not, simply whether or not the breach to the public peace had occurred. Just calling a woman a whore in public was considered inappropriate, whether or not she actually was one. It was very likely that the size of the fines given reflected the Board's opinion of the woman's respectability, but only in exceptional circumstances was more than 5 shillings assessed for public insults. Although the many women who brought charges for name calling obviously must have felt they were defending their honour, they did not have to prove it. Thus Catherine Curry was able, for example, immediately following a conviction for keeping a house of ill fame, to charge Henry James Jessup successfully with using insulting and improper language to her.[55]

Since it was so easy to obtain convictions, and the consequences for being found guilty were usually so minor, the women of Prescott came to use the Board more and more

for settling personal disputes. This peaked in 1840–1, when about twice as many cases involving insults against a woman's reputation were heard by the Board than in the previous five years; this number was about the same as that of similar cases heard over the next eight years. Anxiety about the increased complaints may have been another reason that motivated the Board to enact the bylaws concerning streetwalking and keeping bawdy houses in 1841. It may have also been behind a stern warning issued in June 1840 reminding citizens "that anyone after the date hereof entering complaint" should be aware that "the Board will not hold themselves responsible for whatever costs the said complaint may incur to the Clerk or constable for said complaint."[56] . . .

Particularly after 1848, however, the use of the Board changed. The steady drop in charges brought to it by women may have had to do with a growing sense that such public displays were damaging to female reputation. From a peak of 25 cases involving women in 1840, the number steadily dropped to only three by 1844. Then the numbers slowly began to rise, hitting a smaller peak of 13 by 1850. The cause of the second rise, however, was not more women themselves bringing charges, but rather more aggressive action by the town fathers, particularly aimed at reducing the incidence of disorderly houses.

In the mid-nineteenth century, a wave of evangelical reform was sweeping over North America as well as Britain. Historians such as Jan Noel, in her study of temperance movements, documented a striking change in social values in Upper Canada in the 1840s and 1850s.[57] In Prescott, this may have also been fuelled by concern over the number of destitute Irish immigrants who were arriving after 1847. In the summer of that year, the Board had been ordered by the Governor General to take steps to prepare to deal with an expected onslaught of the ill and the desperate.[58] Nonetheless, although such steps were taken, in 1849 the Board responded to complaints about "the occupation of a dilapidated house in the main street by emigrants, that said house being in a filthy state." Orders were given to "abate the aforesaid nuisance by ejecting the parties living in said premises and cleaning and securing the same from further annoyance to the Neighbourhood."[59]

The same urge to clean up was directed toward alcohol consumption and public morality. After 1848 there are cases of applications for liquor permits being turned down, something that was unheard of before this time. Certainly a very large amount of alcohol was manufactured in Prescott. According to the 1851 census, 30,937 gallons of spirits, wine, and fortified wine were sold annually, as well as 1,500 gallons of beer. Although some of this was surely sold away, it still is a remarkable amount produced in a town of 2,156 persons. J. O'Sullivan, who took the census, was a stonemason and a temperance man. He could not resist editorializing about this amount of alcohol. "The Enumerator begs leave," he wrote in an extraordinary notation concerning this use of grain products, "to draw the Hon. Inspector General's attention to this large amount of the people's food [being] consumed into poison and prays that his noble efforts may be employ[ed] either in Council or in the legislature to suppress the crying evil of intemperance."[60]

The Board was equally concerned about the "crying evil" of female immorality and the public disorder it caused. In 1848 a new bylaw specifically prohibited prostitution and houses of ill fame occupied by "loose" women.[61] The first three charges brought under this bylaw, however, were dismissed for lack of evidence. It is not clear who brought the charges, but obviously people were not willing to testify against their neighbours under the new law.[62] The local authorities then became increasingly involved in pressing charges, as when Constable Benjamin Cavalier charged Bridget Agar with "riotous conduct," "scolding," and keeping a "bad house." He actually entered her home and, when he "saw part of a man's pantaloon stuck out of a hole,"

he pulled out the half-undressed Patrick Griffin. Fines also became stiffer, and thus imprisonment more likely. Bridget Agar was fined 20 shillings and sent to [the] Brockville jail in default of payment for 21 days, although Griffin was not charged.[63] A local lock-up was also built, so that miscreants such as Mary Hutton could be imprisoned locally while they awaited trial. Both she and her husband were found drunk and arguing in the street, but only Mary was locked up until the Board assembled on Monday.[64] Obviously this would send a strong message to women who were fond of drinking. Increasingly, women of the popular class stopped laying charges, and several charges before the court were delayed and then quietly died. Accordingly, the Board stepped up its role in prosecution. In late 1849 the Corporation took it upon itself to charge William Sanders with keeping a bawdy house. Even though he confessed, he was fined 10 shillings and had his liquor licence revoked.[65] Half a dozen other successful charges were brought after 1848 against women for keeping disorderly houses, the most notable of which was that against Catherine Curry, brought by none other than Henry James Jessup. Her neighbours turned out in force to defend her, asserting that they never saw men there, that the house was always quiet by 9:00 p.m., and that she did not allow gambling. Jessup, they said, was having a quarrel with her and had said publicly that "he would perjure himself to have Mrs. Curry turned out of town." Jessup alone testified against her, and on that basis she was convicted. This was quite a departure from the judgments of earlier boards.[66] Still, as we have already noted, Catherine Curry successfully countercharged Jessup the following day and was not run out of town. She was still in Prescott the next year and shows up on the census as a dressmaker.

In conclusion, it is illustrative to look at the career of one particularly notable user of the Board's services, Mrs. Ann Black. She appeared before the Board for many different reasons a total of 15 times between 1839 and 1850. . . .

In 1843 Ann charged Mary McMannus with accusing her of "bringing up bastards for Bill Johnston." This had occurred in the context of an argument over whether Mary was entitled to stay in the room she was renting from Ann. Ann told her "that two women had been looking at the house," and Mary replied that "she would keep the key until her month was up . . . that no one should come in as long as she paid the rent." During the course of this dispute, Ann had also insulted Mary by alleging that she lay in bed all day drunk. The Board fined them each 5 shillings and split the costs between them.[67] Obviously, Ann could give as good as she got, and in 1844 she was charged by Louisa Fortier, as one witness attested, for saying "that Mrs. Fortier was taken out of a whore house in Quebec and was a whore to all the Canadians in Quebec" and for "throwing stones into her house." Although Ann was charged with using abusive language, her neighbours volunteered much more evidence. One witness said that she had heard "noise throughout the night" from Ann's house, "which from all circumstances the Witness considers . . . an indecent house. . . . [T]he defendant keeps a woman who is not a decent woman in her opinion, her house is open at all hours of the night." The woman who was not decent was none other than Mary Delany, at that time the kept mistress of Henry James Jessup. Jane Wilson even alleged that she had "lived in Mrs. Black's house five months and caught a man in bed with Mrs. Black." Ann was given double the usual fine, 10 shillings plus costs.[68]

Between 1843 and 1850, Ann was involved in seven other cases in the record, one as witness, two as complainant, and four as defendant. She won both her cases, one in which the defendant had called her a "poxed bitch" and the other in which the defendant had spit on her in the street.[69] Two of the charges against her were dismissed, and she was convicted and fined the standard 5 shillings on two others involving abusive language.[70]

Finally, in 1850 the respectable men of Prescott decided that Ann Black had troubled them enough. Thomas Gainford, MD, took it upon himself to charge her with keeping a house of ill fame. His testimony was recorded in detail:

> Dr. Gainford sworn, Says that ever since she came to the neighbourhood, that her conduct was a specimen of depravity a little short of Murder. Debauched females are harboured in said house and incendiary conduct carried on therein. Says that Mrs. Black did curse & swear on the night & morning as aforesaid & continued so doing for about the space of two hours—calling out infernal liars, Damn liars, and it would be impossible to repeat all that she said in the way of Cursing and Swearing, even said God Damn liars to some persons outside the door. . . .[71]

This language actually sounds fairly tame for Ann, but perhaps Gainford could not bring himself to repeat the full extent of her profanities. She was fined the incredible sum of 50 shillings, which of course she could not pay, and so was sent to Brockville prison for 30 days. . . . The most remarkable case, however, was the last recorded about her. In 1850 John Bodry assaulted Ann. She testified that "she was in her house and [he] asked her if he would be allowed to lye down awhile, she would not allow him to lye down in her house then he commenced breaking several articles in said house and insisted that Complainant should go to bed with him, witness says that he used violence to effect his purpose."[72] Bodry did not succeed in subduing the indomitable Ann Black. She fought him off, and, even though he offered to settle with her by paying $1 in damages, she insisted on her day in court. He was fined 20 shillings and costs of 7 shillings, 6 pence. The mayor was paid 2 shillings, 6 pence; the court 8 shillings, 9 pence; and 8 shillings, 9 pence went to Mrs. Black. This was a truly incredible result since, as a convicted keeper of a house of ill repute, she could not possibly have obtained a judgment against Bodry for attempted rape in a higher court.[73]

Although women like Catherine Curry and Ann Black could still have their day in court, by 1850 the Board of Police was playing a very different role in the Prescott community than it had in 1834. From a peak of cases brought by women in 1841, women's use of the Board declined as it became increasingly the instrument for a gendered and class-based agenda of social control and moral reform, led by professional men of the bourgeois class. The character of the record changes as well, and we no longer hear as much from the voices of the women themselves as we do from their accusers.[74] From 1850, municipal enforcement bodies such as the police and police courts were established, which were much more effective in asserting the power of local authorities. Throughout the latter part of the nineteenth century, the process of establishing the hegemony of gendered middle-class values of appropriate female behaviour was well advanced. By the late nineteenth and early twentieth century, if a women was raped or assaulted, she was the one on trial, and her male attacker's crime was mitigated by any failure on her part to live up to the domestic and moral ideal of "True Womanhood."[75] We still struggle with this legacy today.

What Ann Black's story, and those of the other women who used the Board of Police, can tell us today is that, despite the dictates of law, class status, and convention, they were publicly active in the pursuit of their interests. The Board of Police Record gives us a glimpse of women's transgressive behaviour and shows that they could choose not to be compliant with the restrictive ideology of "True Womanhood." Women of the popular class of Prescott in this early period could and did take the law into their own hands and use institutions run by male community leaders for their own purposes, as agents in their own lives.

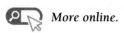 *More online.*

Notes

1. Board of Police Records, Prescott, Ontario, 28 November 1937 (hereafter referred to by date).
2. 6 November 1837.
3. 15 May 1836.
4. 2 November 1835.
5. 6 November 1837.
6. November 1837.
7. 20 November 1837.
8. 28 November 1837.
9. On charivaris, see Allan Greer, "From Folklore to Revolution: Charivaris and the Lower Canadian Rebellion of 1837," *Social History* 15 (January 1990): 25–43; J. I. Little, *State and Society in Transition: The Politics of Institutional Reform in the Eastern Townships, 1838–1852* (Montreal, QC: McGill-Queen's University Press, 1997), 92–101; Bryan Palmer, "Discordant Music: Charivaris and Whitecapping in Nineteenth-Century North America," *Labour/Le Travailleur* 3 (1978): 5–62. . . .
10. The attack also differed from usual Upper Canadian charivaris in the adoption of Indian dress. This suggests that one or more members of the raiding party may have come from the United States, where the assumption of Indian dress had a long tradition, dating as far back as the Boston Tea Party. See Philip J. Deloria, *Playing Indian* (New Haven, CT: Yale University Press, 1998).
11. Deneau, Cavalier, and Greneau are names that suggest a common French Canadian background, which may have been a reason why these men would not attack Mary Greneau.
12. I am indebted to the generosity of town officials for granting me access to this resource. In particular, I would like to thank Andrew Brown, Prescott town clerk. There is also now a microfilm copy of the Board of Police Record in the Queen's University Archives in Kingston, Ontario.
13. Toronto, Archives of Ontario (hereafter AO), 1851 Prescott Census.
14. Douglas McCalla, *Planting the Province: The Economic History of Upper Canada, 1784–1870* (Toronto, ON: University of Toronto Press, 1993), 118–21, 158.
15. Katherine M. J. McKenna, *Family Life in a Military Garrison: History of the Routines and Activities of the Royal Canadian Rifle Regiment at Fort Wellington, Prescott, 1843–1854* (Ottawa, ON: Canadian Heritage Parks Canada. Microfiche Report Series No. 533, 1995).
16. Ruth McKenzie, *Leeds and Grenville: Their First Two Hundred Years* (Toronto, ON: McClelland & Stewart, 1967), 188.
17. On the history of municipal government and policing in Upper Canada, see James H. Aitchison, "The

Development of Local Government in Upper Canada, 1783–1850" (Ph.D. thesis, University of Toronto, 1953); Paul Craven, "Law and Ideology: The Toronto Police Court," in David H. Flaherty, ed., *Essays in the History of Canadian Law*, vol. II (Toronto, ON: University of Toronto Press, 1983), 248–307. . . .

18. Allan Greer, "The Birth of the Police in Canada," in Allan Greer and Ian Radforth, eds., *Colonial Leviathan: State Formation in Mid-Nineteenth-Century Canada* (Toronto, ON: University of Toronto Press, 1992), 19.

19. Information on the occupations of Board members and of citizens who appeared before the Board has been obtained by checking names against the 1848 and 1851 Prescott censuses.

20. Michael Katz, Michael J. Doucet, and Mark J. Stern, *The Social Organization of Early Industrial Capitalism* (Cambridge, MA: Harvard University Press, 1982), 228–9.

21. Karen Dubinsky, "Afterward: Telling Stories About Dead People," in Franca Iacovetta and Wendy Mitchinson, eds., *On the Case: Explorations in Social History* (Toronto, ON: University of Toronto Press, 1998), 359–66; Franca Iacovetta and Wendy Mitchinson, "Introduction: Social History and Case Files Research," in *On the Case*, 3–21; Annalee Golz, "Uncovering and Reconstructing Family Violence: Ontario Criminal Case Files," in Iacovetta and Mitchinson, eds., *On the Case*, 289–311.

22. Constance Backhouse, *Petticoats and Prejudice: Women and the Law in Nineteenth-Century Canada* (Toronto, ON: Osgoode Society, 1991). . . .

23. 7 September 1841.

24. On the development of these new ideas about the gendered public and private spheres propagated by the middle class, see Andrew C. Holman, *A Sense of Their Duty: Middle-Class Formation in Victorian Ontario Towns* (Montreal, QC: McGill-Queen's University Press, 2000); Lynne Marks, *Revivals and Roller Rinks: Religion, Leisure, and Identity in Late-Nineteenth-Century Small-Town Ontario* (Toronto, ON: University of Toronto Press, 1996); Katherine M. J. McKenna, *A Life of Propriety: Anne Murray Powell and Her Family, 1755–1849* (Montreal, QC: McGill-Queen's University Press, 1994). . . .

25. On the genesis of the new ideal of middle-class womanhood in eighteenth- and early nineteenth-century England, see Leonore Davidoff and Catherine Hall, *Family Fortunes: Men and Women of the English Middle Class, 1780–1850* (London, UK: Croom Helm, 1987). . . .

26. 12 June 1840.

27. 8 February 1841.

28. One exception is the information on women's work that Jane Errington has gleaned from newspaper sources

in her book, *Wives and Mothers, School Mistresses and Scullery Maids: Working Women in Upper Canada, 1790–1840* (Montreal, QC: McGill-Queen's University Press, 1995). . . .

29. 29 April 1844.

30. 4 August 1846.

31. 26 May 1846.

32. 30 June and 6 July 1847.

33. A recent book on the Shanley brothers discusses their professional careers and their class status as "gentlemen" in some detail, but not their views on women. Richard White, *Gentlemen Engineers: The Working Lives of Frank and Walter Shanley* (Toronto, ON: University of Toronto Press, 1999).

34. AO, Shanley Papers, Box 68, Walter Shanley to Frank Shanley, Prescott, 23 June 1851.

35. Ibid., 6 October 1851.

36. Ibid., 16 June 1851.

37. Ibid., 23 November 1851.

38. Mary Anne Poutanen, "The Geography of Prostitution in an Early Nineteenth-Century Urban Centre: Montreal, 1810–1842," in Tamara Myers, Kate Boyer, Mary Anne Poutanen, and Steven Watt, eds., *Power, Place and Identity: Historical Studies of Social and Legal Regulation in Quebec* (Montreal, QC: Montreal Public History Group, 1998), 102.

39. Katz et al., *The Social Organization of Early Industrial Capitalism*, 231.

40. Bettina Bradbury, "Pigs, Cows and Boarders: Non-Wage Forms of Survival among Montreal Families, 1861–91," *Labour/Le Travail* 14 (1984): 9–46.

41. Judith Fingard has also seen this type of practice of prostitution in Halifax; see *The Dark Side of Life in Victorian Halifax* (Porter's Lake, NS: Pottersfield Press, 1991), 95–113.

42. 24 February 1848; 29 January 1849; 8 May 1850.

43. See bylaws for April 1834.

44. 7 June 1841.

45. 26 July 1839.

46. 1 July 1850.

47. 6 July and 7 October 1837; 26 September 1842. Beale, as noted earlier, does not appear in the 1848 and 1851 censuses.

48. 15 September 1848.

49. 5 September 1844.

50. 1 July 1850.

51. S. M. Waddams observes the same gendered pattern in name calling in English ecclesiastical courts in his book, *Sexual Slander in Nineteenth-Century England: Defamation in the Ecclesiastical Courts, 1815–1855* (Toronto, ON: University of Toronto Press, 2000). . . .

52. Anna Clark, "Whores and Gossips: Sexual Reputation in London, 1770–1825," in Arina Angerman, Geerta Binnema, Annemieke Keunen, Vefie Poels, and

Jacqueline Zirkzee, eds., *Current Issues in Women's History* (New York, NY: Routledge, 1989), 238–9. . . .

53. 12 July 1837.
54. 26 August 1850.
55. 9 May 1850.
56. 15 June 1840.
57. Jan Noel, *Canada Dry: Temperance Crusades before Confederation* (Toronto, ON: University of Toronto Press, 1995), 123–39. . . .
58. 7 June 1847.
59. 4 June 1849.
60. AO, 1851 Prescott Census, 75.
61. Mary Anne Poutanen also sees a sharp rise in the number of women arrested for prostitution in the 1840s in Montreal. "'To Indulge Their Carnal Appetites': Prostitution in Early Nineteenth-Century Montreal, 1810–1842" (Ph.D. dissertation, Université de Montreal, 1996), 233.
62. 28 February 1848.
63. 13 July 1850.
64. 28 April 1849.
65. 3 December 1849.
66. 8 May 1850.
67. 12 May 1843.
68. 29 April 1844.
69. 23 March 1846; 30 November 1848.
70. 20 July 1849; 9 November 1849; 8 September 1846; 12 August 1848.
71. 25 June 1850.
72. 3 October 1850.
73. On the difficulty of getting convictions related to rape, see Constance Backhouse, "Nineteenth-Century Canadian Rape Law, 1800–92," in David Flaherty, ed., *Essays in the History of Canadian Law*, vol. II (Toronto, ON: University of Toronto Press, 2011), 200–47. . . .
74. Lykke de la Cour, Cecilia Morgan, and Mariana Valverde see this trend more generally in what they call a "masculinization of public power" after the rebellions in Upper Canada. See "Gender Regulation and State Formation in Nineteenth-Century Canada," in Greer and Radforth, eds., *Colonial Leviathan*, 163. . . .
75. On women's supposed responsibility for crimes committed against them, see especially Karen Dubinsky, *Improper Advances: Rape and Heterosexual Conflict in Ontario, 1880–1929* (Chicago, IL: University of Chicago Press, 1993); Golz, "Uncovering and Reconstructing Family Violence."

2 Nurture and Education
The Christian Home

Marguerite Van Die

In March 1871, when despite her husband's [Charles] frantic mining efforts the fear of bankruptcy began to loom, Hattie [Child Colby] reminded him, "The quiet way we live now brings us all very near to each other, and I have great comfort in mother & Charley and our good little girls. It never can be just home without you but it is a duty to make it and feel it as pleasant as we can."[1] Much has been written about the ways in which the Victorian home, presided over by the mother as the ministering angel of light, increasingly became a haven for businessmen caught up in the loneliness and frenetic activity of the commercial "outside world."[2] In this way, historians have seen it taking on a religious function, replacing the institutional church in a secularizing society by being a private site of Christian socialization and moral formation. As one historian has succinctly summarized the development, "The outer world had become destitute, but the home was still endowed with the old, positive values; it had not relinquished tested standards and Christian morals; it was the place of the old order; it was the sanctuary of traditional principles. It was separated from the outside world and better for it."[3]

On the surface, Hattie's comments to her husband fit well into this typology, as does his frequently reiterated desire to spend more time with his family. But the candour that surfaces at times in her letters, when referring to her shortness of temper and the long hours spent in housework, suggests that the lives of real mothers often failed to live up to the prescriptive literature. Similarly, the prototype of the hard-pressed businessman exiled to the amoral marketplace has come under significant revision as gender historians such as John Tosh have drawn attention to the value that middle-class Victorians placed on paternal domesticity.[4] As the old patriarchy of [Charles's father] Moses Colby's day began to crumble and as the burden of providing a family livelihood shifted from land to the marketplace, fathers found that spending time with their children could be emotionally gratifying as well as giving them "the satisfaction of fulfilling a critical role of adult masculinity—the ability to feed, clothe and shelter children."[5] For Charles Colby, this found expression in a wide range of activities, from carrying out requests of his wife and daughters for purchases in the various urban centres to which his work took him, to assuring his children frequently by letter of his constant love, and, as they grew older, by taking them along when his travels allowed visits to distant relatives.[6]

Citation: Marguerite Van Die, "Nurture and Education: The Christian Home," in *Religion, Family, and Community in Victorian Canada: The Colbys of Carrollcroft* (Montreal, QC: McGill-Queen's University Press, 2007): 101–24.

For men as well as women, this domesticity was rooted in a livelihood derived from the marketplace. The form of patriarchy that Moses Colby had tried to ensure in his will by basing his family's security on land no longer worked for his sons. Having lost the land, they had to find other means to achieve economic security for their families. "Do not think I had no feeling at parting with our old home the walls of which I had reared under great difficulties and around and through which cluster so many associations of happiness and sorrow," Charles wrote to Hattie two days after the sale of the stone house. Valuable as a house might be to a middle-class family's self-worth, other less tangible but more enduring forms of security had to be found in a world in which fortunes could be lost as quickly as they were acquired. As Charles elaborated, "All the means which we are likely to have over and above the bare cost of living are needed to educate and fit out the children—and as they grow older they need more of our personal care."[7]

At the time, the children consisted of Abby, age 12; Jessie, age 10; and Charles William, who had just turned five. As Charles intimated in his letter, education and self-formation had taken on new importance in the family's straitened circumstances, calling for careful distribution of their financial resources. This held true not only for his sons (John would be born the following year) but also for his daughters, whose only dowry would be their family name and reputation, their physical attributes, and their ability to excel in the graces of a developing middle-class society. As it turned out, Abby did not marry until the age of 28 and Jessie remained single. The two sons spent considerable time in postgraduate studies as preparation for careers in, respectively, university teaching and medicine. Paternal provision was therefore a lengthy process and fell entirely on the male head of the household—unlike the case with their parents and William's [Charles's brother] two daughters, all of whom worked briefly as school teachers to help with family finances.

Although practical in their purpose, education and formation were also, according to Victorian domesticity, to be shaped by love and order, two qualities that were notably absent in the unpredictable marketplace. Here religion, especially the domesticated heart religion of evangelical Protestantism, had much to offer, and historians have drawn attention to the close fit between evangelical family religion and the home as its most perfect location.[8] How this fit took place, however, is less well understood. Did religion turn the home into a "haven in a heartless world," into a surrogate church, as was argued above? Or—following the lead of research that has questioned the explanatory value of such dualisms as sacred and secular, material and spiritual, male and female, private and public—did religion in the home help the middle-class family adapt to the socio-economic order . . .?[9]

As this chapter will explore more fully, the Colbys, like many other Victorian families, did place very high expectations on the home. And as a businessman who in 1858 had experienced a "new birth," which led him to exchange his understanding of a righteous, awe-inspiring God for a loving father, Charles Colby tried to work out its implications for domestic life, just as he did for the marketplace. Meanwhile Hattie, drawing on her childhood formation, her training as a teacher, and her literary tastes, found her own ways of making religion a meaningful element in the nurture of their children. And though at times—as when the family's material fortunes plummeted—she wrote appreciatively of their quiet home life, the home emerges in many of the family letters not as a retreat but as the place of integration, from which gender, school, church, community, and nation ultimately assumed their significance. This was also the intention of evangelical ministers and educators. But as laypeople, the Colbys found their own ways of integration, which were sometimes at variance with the official tenets of religion. Through such means, their story enters into a much larger narrative of social and religious change in which the symbolic universe of religion begins to merge with the family as a source of ultimate meaning.

Since the seventeenth century, when the first Colbys and Childs emigrated to the New World, Puritan teaching had underscored the importance of the home as a "nursery of virtue" in preparing children to take up their adult responsibilities in church and state. By law, the heads of the Colby and Child households in the Massachusetts Bay colony had been required to catechize their children and servants at least weekly and to instruct them in the Scriptures.[10] The subsequent separation of church and state and the shift to revivalism had the potential to undermine this tradition, and ministers unrelentingly continued to emphasize the importance of family religious instruction by the head of the household.[11] Rather than seeing the eternal safety of their offspring depending on the experience of a "new birth," or conversion, many clergy as well as laypeople such as [Charles's parents] Moses and Lemira Colby had chosen to uphold the old tradition of religious instruction in the home. This had been supported by the increasing prevalence of the Sunday school.[12] Even such revivalist denominations as Canada's Wesleyan Methodists, though equivocating on the need for the conversion of children raised in the faith, were beginning by the 1860s to emphasize the importance of childhood religious instruction.[13]

Roman Catholic priests in Quebec were equally zealous in pointing out to parents their duty to begin instructing their children in the truths of the Christian faith the moment the children's intelligence "awakened." Where Protestants relied on the Scriptures and a flood of tracts and moral publications, Roman Catholic parents had the *petit catechisme*. About 15 per cent of this was devoted to the sacrament of penance, which was the chosen vehicle for training the child's conscience by seeking God's forgiveness through repentance and monthly confession of sin.[14] In their theological stance on infant depravity, Roman Catholics, despite their

many differences from Protestantism, held to a view of the human condition that was significantly closer to the Puritan understanding than the view beginning to hold sway among many middle-class Protestants. The liberalizing shift in Protestant theology from an emphasis on the atonement to the incarnation affected not only a businessman's self-understanding but also had profound implications for the religious nurture which parents provided for their children.

Officially, in their baptismal liturgies, mainline Protestant denominations continued to uphold the view that every infant entered the world tainted with the sin of Adam and was thus in need of regeneration. In the Wesleyan Methodist liturgy, for example, which was followed when baptizing Charles and Hattie's children and which faithfully reflected its Anglican predecessor (derived in turn from the Roman Catholic form), the minister, while sprinkling water on the newborn infant, solemnly intoned, "All men are conceived and born in sin" and "None can enter into the kingdom of God, except he be regenerate and born anew of water and of the Holy Ghost."[15] How this rebirth was to take place, however, became a matter of theological controversy. Was it through the breaking of a child's will in order to experience a conversion by accepting God's forgiveness through the atonement, as the revivalists preached? Or could such a rebirth occur naturally and slowly, within the confines of a Christian home? In his highly influential book *Christian Nurture*, published in 1847, Horace Bushnell, Congregationalist minister in Hartford, Connecticut, argued that evangelical conversion, with its emphasis on sin, provided a negative model for the religious formation of the child and had every chance of turning the child away from religion as an adult. Instead, the child should be surrounded by loving parental influences from the time of its birth, enabling it to experience religion as part of the normal process of growth. Bushnell did not reject the belief in original sin, but his remedy placed a new emphasis on the role of parents to become positive agents of grace in the lives of their children.[16] Although its impact among mainline evangelicals was slow initially, in retrospect *Christian Nurture* has been seen as a critical turning point—away from revivalism and towards religious socialization. "In its entirety," historian Margaret Bendroth has succinctly summarized, "Bushnell's theology brought God closer to human reach, an emphasis that places him at the forefront of an emerging liberal strain within Protestant Christianity, emphasizing divine immanence in human reality."[17]

. . .

Hattie held similar views, as a result of the religious nurture given her by her father, her interest in romantic poetry, and no doubt some of her reading as a teacher. Improvements in communication through train travel, mail service, and increased choice in periodicals and newspapers ensured that even in such villages as Stanstead, people were kept abreast of developments in social and religious thought. Although there exists no record of Hattie reading Bushnell's *Christian Nurture*, there were many other likeminded treatises. One that she did read enthusiastically described marriage and family as the earthly foretaste of the bliss of heaven. Since "God we are told is love," the author asserted, "it is but reasonable to suppose that he would establish between his children a relation designed to inspire universal and eternal love."[18]

In the course of the couple's economic woes, Hattie reassured her husband that their love for one another constituted the one certainty in life.[19] Implicitly endowing the family with an absolute value formerly reserved only for religion, she reflected the belief of Bushnell, Beecher, and other liberal Protestant writers that the love of family members for one another was truly the nursery of religion. The love that Charles and Hattie expressed for their children was indeed unconditional, total, and exuberant. "Papa sends Charley three kisses—one on his two lips, each of his red cheeks and a Scotch kiss beside," wrote Charles to his daughter Jessie after she and

Charley had been sent to Weybridge during the fatal illness of their baby sister, Alice.[20] Cleaning up after a birthday party for one of the children, Hattie commented to her husband, "Certainly nothing is wasted that tends to make home happy for children."[21]

Although Bushnell had argued the importance of environment as a redemptive force and thus had cleared the ground for romantic views of childhood innocence, he had not rejected the Calvinist view of total depravity. Where his peers were critical of such theological inconsistency, laypeople were less troubled. Among Hattie's papers, for instance, can be found a poem, written by a friend but preserved in her own handwriting, entitled "Little Hattie."[22] Intended as comfort for a mother who is about to lose an infant daughter (and thus possibly written in 1871 during Alice's terminal illness), the lines place the new emphasis on childhood innocence side by side with an older belief in the inscrutable ways of God described in the hymn that Lemira had sung at the funeral of her daughter Emily. The updated poem was a humanized (and feminized) confession, in which a loving Saviour welcomes the "gem . . . borrowed from Paradise":

> Yea! thy cherished babe will slumber there
> On the holy Saviour's breast
> Perchance long years of woe mother
> May be spared thy little one
> For our Father sees not as we see,
> His will not ours be done.

Although in Methodist circles the theological debate about infant depravity continued to rage for another 20 years, long before that, middle-class women such as Hattie had already rewritten official doctrine in ways that reflected their own experience.[23]

. . .

Middle-class evangelical families had at their disposal a number of ways in which "gloomy piety" could be replaced by a religious nurture that was more in tune with the optimistic spirit of the age. Although the religious press continued to stress the role of the father when reminding readers of the importance of family devotions, the shift in responsibility for leadership from the father to the mother was part of a wide and well-documented pattern.[24] In the Colby household, since the father was often away and since Hattie had been a teacher as a young woman, it was the mother who took on the task of religious instruction. Early in her marriage, to mark Charles's infrequent periods at home, and reflecting the new interest in quality "family time," Hattie had instituted a special Sunday domestic ritual after the usual church and Sunday school attendance.[25] Known as "dressing and combing father's whiskers," the practice (and its much-regretted absence when he was away) surfaced regularly in family correspondence in the 1860s.[26] Juxtaposed with this family ritual, rich in its potential for physical intimacy, was an hour each Sunday afternoon when the children systematically read aloud to their mother a chapter of Scripture and committed to memory selected verses for Sunday school. Changed into "prayers and psalms" once the children had ceased attending Sunday school, the practice continued well into the 1890s, with their father becoming a more frequent participant after his retirement from political life.[27]

Sunday Bible-reading in the home was a long-established Puritan tradition in children's lives, but in the nineteenth century the growing trade in inexpensively published books and Bibles offered a new context.[28] Gifts for the Colby children drew on the growing religious consumerism that by the nineteenth century was fuelling both Protestant and Roman Catholic piety.[29] To prudent parents, the educational purpose of religiously inspired children's gifts justified the monetary outlay.[30] When money was at its scarcest during the year of the bankruptcy, Hattie was able to justify the one-dollar purchase of a Noah's Ark, which delighted Charley during a visit to her friends, the Cowles. Birthday gifts for Jessie, who from an early age showed an

interest in religion, included a gilt little Wesleyan hymnal from her Uncle William, followed some years later by the gift of the Bible that had once belonged to her grandfather Moses.[31] Whether handed down or newly purchased, Bibles became coveted children's gifts in the religiously charged culture of the period; their contents were considered essential to furnishing a child's mind with a wealth of imagery, which later would inform an understanding of literature and poetry. Charles William, the eldest son, precociously already reading at age three, was given an illustrated copy of *Pilgrim's Progress* by his grandmother and a Bible by his mother on his sixth birthday. "He is pleased as can be with each gift, but regards the Bible, all his own, as most too good to be true," Hattie proudly informed her husband. "He returns to it again and again: reading now in the Old Testament and now in the New: finding alone the places he is familiar with."[32] Thanks to such encouragement, a child's mind became richly furnished with biblical imagery, some of which could be put to remarkable use. When, for example, his careless playing with matches set the barn on fire and he was faced with a rare paternal use of the switch, young Charley was able to deflect his well-deserved corporal punishment by pointedly comparing his situation to the New Testament martyr Stephen, thereby seeing his solicitous and largely female audience dissolve into laughter.[33]

The fact that none of the children required encouragement in reading can in large part be attributed to their mother's example. A favourite family pastime, reading aloud to one another, was begun by the couple in the first months of their marriage, and it was transmitted to the children, the two eldest daughters taking it upon themselves to read to their brothers, and all four later taking turns to read to their grandmother [Lemira] in her final years. Since their father had ready access to the parliamentary library in Ottawa after his election in 1867, requests for books surfaced regularly in the family letters. These included a request from

Hattie for *Moods* by Louisa May Alcott, *Robinson Crusoe* for Charley, and a biography of the evangelical hymn writer Frances Havergal, which in 1883 was read aloud to Lemira and other household members, including Rosalie, the Roman Catholic servant. By his own account Charles Williams was "a boyish bookworm." At seven he was deeply enamoured of Richard the Lionheart and soon developed an admiration for the novels of Sir Walter Scott. By the age of 12 he had completed the extensive *Commonplace Book of Shakespeare*, and extending beyond the Anglo-Saxon corpus he read the Quran to his grandmother.[34] Thanks to this steady fare of books, literary and biblical images fuelled the children's imagination, as well as providing subject matter for games such as charades and their own theatrical productions.

Poetry and song, like reading aloud, especially when presented from a mother's lips, were seen by educators as ideal ways of inculcating early childhood religious influences. Hearth, home, and song figured prominently in the nostalgia of the later Victorians, and among Hattie Colby's happiest experiences was an evening of singing around the piano when her brother Jack made an unexpected visit with his young son.[35] Jessie and Abby were both given piano lessons, and their mother took every opportunity to have them display their musical talent before admiring house guests. Such accomplishments, in tandem with the family's exposure to literature, refined the taste of both adults and children.

In a society that placed a high value on self-formation, these also became an essential component to religious nurture. Here, too, historians have pointed to the influence of Horace Bushnell who, in addition to his interest in child nurture, expressed strong views about the difference between what he called "fashion" and "taste." While fashion marked the values of an effete aristocracy, taste was a God-given quality through which people participated in God's creative work of beautifying the universe. Thus, the moral for middle-class evangelical Americans was, as

historian Richard Bushman has pointed out, "to cultivate taste and avoid fashion."[36] Others have gone further, seeing in this "refinement" of religion a new secular understanding of the process of sanctification, a practical updated expression of Christian perfection—the "second blessing" (as Charles Colby called his 1858 experience of divine love). Given the social value placed on self-improvement, moral formation came to be seen as a religious duty, no longer the preserve of a small number of male intellectuals, as it had been in the eighteenth century, but a popular ideal available to all. Since the literary culture of the period was polite, evangelicalism began to take on accents of this broader culture, aided by the availability of inexpensive printed material and its own emphasis on individual transformation. The true Christian was not only someone whose sins were forgiven but was also a person who was refined, balanced, and had benefited from the increasingly available opportunities for self-development.[37]

The marriage between good taste and religion inevitably challenged some forms of evangelical expression, and in the Colby household not all of the didactic material available to a juvenile audience received approval. A travelling panorama of *Pilgrim's Progress*, for example, performed at the Stanstead town hall, to which Hattie took the children, left her profoundly disappointed. Its pictures seemed "fearful daubs," the angels' wings reminded her of "half-worn store wings from the goose," and "the pearly gates anything but what a fine faith sees."[38] In like manner, the moralistic children's literature that flooded the evangelical book market and was highly favoured by adults as gifts did not escape the criticism of the Colby children (and, no doubt, other juvenile readers). "Charley's book is beautifully illustrated," Hattie wrote in a letter to Abby, "but he doesn't care much about the story. It is written in the 'goody-goody' style. Jess began reading it aloud to me, but would say every other sentence 'now it's going to moralize.'"[39] This literary form of self-development, redolent of an earlier gen-eration and still solemnly extolled in children's literature, resonated little with the lives of well-read middle-class youth.[40]

An aversion to moralization did not mean that children should not be exposed to moral influences. In fact, such influences were seen to lie at the heart of the new understanding of reli-gion, whereby children were socialized into the faith rather than being brought to conversion as had been the practice a generation earlier. Since refinement was no longer a capitulation to fash-ion but was seen as a desirable characteristic, it was to be cultivated like other virtues, such as courage and kindness. And it was the task of the mother, as the central figure in family reli-gious nurture, to impart to the next generation the importance of good manners and good taste. Manners and morals went together. "Charley waits upon me elegantly everywhere I go, and he did last night," Hattie informed her daugh-ters when describing a recent Methodist social, whose "first rate" entertainment had included several duets, a violin solo, and sundry readings and declamations by Stanstead youth.[41]

This refinement assumed that religion was not simply a spiritual concern but also had an important material dimension. Nineteenth-century evangelical religion was a religion of the heart and could endure only if it remained sensitive to the changing material culture of its adherents.[42] "All this material scene is but the homestead, the playground, the workshop and schoolhouse, of human nature," one contempor-ary writer reminded his readers as he impressed upon them the value of childhood religious nur-ture.[43] In a Christianity that stressed the incar-nation of God's love, high-toned poetry, literature, and tastefully manufactured religious commod-ities all became part of "the material scene" of family religion. Since religious beliefs are in large part transmitted through image and language, refinement may well have been more instru-mental than the well-publicized theological dis-putes of the period in bringing about the shift in

evangelical Protestantism from an emphasis on the atonement to the incarnation.[44]

Studies of the Victorian middle-class home, with a few notable exceptions, have focused on the nuclear family—a claustrophobic unit com-prising father, mother, and children—and they have devoted little attention to the wider context of kinship and community.[45] However, as social workers and psychologists emphasize, these net-works play an indispensable role in child forma-tion.[46] Victorian educators were no less assiduous in reminding parents of the importance of sur-rounding children and youths with sound moral influences. "The family is not a unit, cast alone into space," Mrs. Julia McNair Wright, author of *The Complete Home*, told her readers. "It is one of many which make up the grand sum-total of the race; in every department of life we touch on our fellows: we were born social animals, and we will exercise our social instincts."[47] Not every family had a resident grandmother and an assortment of cousins and family friends living with them for extended periods, as was the case with the Colbys. But nineteenth-century children, like their parents, were part of larger communal net-works. Hattie and Charles Colby were therefore no less assiduous than Mrs. Wright in ensuring that their children's social instincts were well shaped.

In their youth, the burden of moral forma-tion had rested on the immediate family, on the church, and on whatever rudiments of a public/private system of education happened to be in place in the area. By the 1860s and 1870s, their children were able to benefit from a greatly wid-ened circle, thanks to the large output of the reli-gious presses, a host of material refinements, and an increase in voluntary societies such as Sunday schools and Bands of Hope directed at the young. As a result, decisions concerning formal education, the selection of marriage partners, and a career now took place in an environment permeated by religious and moral influences. Like the older custom of seeking patrons, the new emphasis on refining influences meant that young people needed to be part of a wide network of social interaction. Although not always borne out in practice, ministerial families were considered specially endowed to extend such refinement. "It is good to get a little out of the commonplace talk of weather, health and servants which makes up the staple of our talk usually, and hear governments and aristocracy and literature," Hattie appreciatively commented, with her daughters in mind, after a visit by the recently appointed Methodist minister and his wife.[48]

Leisure activities of a communal nature provided the children with opportunities for self-development unavailable a generation earlier. In a village such as Stanstead with a population of 575, rural and urbanized life frequently intersected, but for its children aged 14 and under . . . activities associated with rural life predominated.[49] The letters of the Colby children abound with such traditional events as sugaring and taffy pulling, buggy rides in the area, and bathing in the region's large cool lakes. As well, there were family and community picnics, fishing and hunting for the boys, visits to the homes of local residents, and a steady stream of children's parties. Depending on the age and gender of the guests, such gatherings included long-established games such as blind-man's bluff, hide-and-go-seek, and charades, but the children also had the opportunity to learn dancing and card playing, whist being a favourite.[50]

Lemira, Charles, and Hattie had grown up in the shadow of a middle-class society whose evangelical ministers had frowned on moral "dissipations" such as dancing and cards (though this had not prevented Hattie from enjoying a game of whist). By the 1870s, Stanstead claimed a number of prominent Universalists, and while Hattie tended to decline invitations from members of this more "worldly" religious denomination, the children mixed freely and attended one another's parties. For children, dancing consisted largely of hopping in step with the music, but by the time the two Colby daughters had

reached their early teens and were ready to learn more formal dancing, they encountered no parental opposition to what had become a general peer practice in Stanstead.[51] Nor, as long as one was not a church member, was there much ministerial opposition.[52] In 1886, implicitly acknowledging the prevalence of dancing, the Methodist denomination prohibited members from taking part not only in the "buying, using, or selling" of liquor, but also in "the dance, gambling games, the theatre, the circus, and the race course."[53] Long before this effort to regulate the behaviour of the laity in an increasingly worldly society, Stanstead's ministers, like some of their colleagues elsewhere, had already quietly accepted for adherents such "refined" activities as dancing in homes and attending the theatre.[54] This was facilitated by the fact that Stanstead's Methodists, by then the most influential Protestant denomination in the region, usually managed to ensure that only ministers who shared their values were sent to them by the denominational stationing committee. There were evangelical families who resisted dancing, but in the eyes of the Colby children this made the socials they put on rather dull affairs.[55]

While there was some disagreement on the matter of dancing, this was not the case with "dry socials," which were the prevalent form of entertainment among all the region's Protestants, young as well as old. Within the evangelical framework of individual moral responsibility, intemperance represented the greatest threat to family harmony and unity; but also, happily, it offered the greatest opportunity for social reform. The cold winters of the Eastern Townships and the availability of beer and rye whisky (as the cheapest way of marketing hops and wheat in the early days) continued to be a formidable challenge to the temperance movement.[56] By the 1870s and 1880s, when the Colby children were reaching adolescence, support for Prohibition had become strong and widespread, especially among women, children, and civic leaders. Few families seemed to be immune from the ravages of alcohol—including, at one point, Stanstead's Anglican rector, whose wife's black eye and children's neglected state did not go unnoticed.[57] Closer to home, where the Colby children's own beloved Uncle William sometimes went on an extended spree, it was his wife Melvina who took forceful charge of the village's juvenile temperance organization, which was known as the Band of Hope. Whether they liked it or not, children were often harnessed into the good causes promoted by their parents. When, on her niece Mary's birthday, she had been requested to bring bread and butter to a parlour meeting which Melvina was holding to talk up the Band of Hope to the young guests, Hattie noted, tongue in cheek, "I hope Mary will like that form of celebration."[58] In Hattie's approach to nurture, this was putting Prohibition ahead of the children's need to enjoy themselves.

A major reason for juvenile involvement in Protestant voluntary societies was their role in character building and nation building.[59] In a world where evangelicals presented public duties as part of convivial pleasures and where a father's role in civic life was a way of impressing his children of his importance in the wider world, even the political picnics of the 1870s, with their endless speech making, were of interest.[60] "It was a treat," 15-year-old Jessie enthusiastically told her sister when describing 12 successive speeches (including two by her father, who "spoke *splendidly*") delivered one fine July day in 1877 when Sir John A. Macdonald and his entourage visited Stanstead.[61] No less political, but more tuned to juvenile participation, was the temperance movement. During a temperance picnic held at Derby, a visiting niece (also called Hattie) decided to join the Temperance Lodge, and as the older Hattie confided to Jessie, joining the lodge in this small American border community would enable young Hattie to enter into contact with "all the best portions" of its population.[62]

. . .

By the mid-1880s, the major Protestant denominations had become more concerned with attending to the social needs of young women and men by forming young people's societies.[63] Stanstead's Methodist Young People's Association, established in 1884, like many others, reflected the tastes and skills of its membership by offering such entertainment as piano duets, recitations, and related fundraising for church-related causes. These societies with their expected etiquette, like the ritualized entry of denominational youth into full church membership, were indicative of a pattern of carefully planned stages in religious socialization informed by commitment to family and community. In turn, young people who had been socialized into religion took it upon themselves, through church groups, to transmit to the next generation some of the influences that had shaped their own outlook.[64] Nineteen-year-old Jessie's efforts through study and activities at "children's meetings" evoked from her mother the approving comment: "Grown people are what they are and cannot (generally) be materially changed—but youth is plastic and can be moulded to good purpose."[65] In a variety of ways, therefore, the new ideals of Christian nurture were extended beyond the home to a younger generation and a wider community.

. . .

Abby's fragile health made her the first to embark on what became a female family tradition of travel in search of improved well-being. Accompanying her father on one of his western business trips in the spring of 1875, she spent some time with a great aunt's family in Chicago (where her mother, with an eye on the future, sent her a strong encouragement to "get a taste of dancing").[66] . . . Hattie, who joined Abby in January 1880, found herself two months later faced with the delicate task of having to deal with the first of three western suitors for her daughter's hand. Regretting profoundly her husband's absence when his advice was so needed, she confided in a letter home, "The fact is as you and I know, that Abby is qualified to adorn *any* position, the higher the better, and it would seem a sad waste, for her to accept anything or anybody who was second rate. With her good head and good heart and her very rare social qualities she is fairly entitled to the best."[67] Although Hattie noted the family background of the suitors, including denominational affiliation, for her husband's information, she did not have to make a decision. Abby, who agreed with her mother's assessment of her attributes, decided that "the best" was to be pursued not in the West but in the nation's capital, through the connections of her politician father. By the spring of 1881, therefore, she began to spend time in Ottawa, boarding with her father at the Russell Hotel, and after 1883 Jessie often accompanied her.[68] Marriage did not appear to be a priority for Jessie, but spending increasing amounts of time in Ottawa allowed her to perfect her musical training, and her letters home gave detailed accounts of the fun available in the national capital for two attractive young women of marriageable age.[69]

Their mother, at home in Stanstead, accompanied them vicariously, unable to restrain either her enthusiasm or her inclination to offer advice: "Isn't papa lovely and elegant at the parties tho? I knew you w'd find it out. I think he w'd have been willing to see you dance a few times (I would just—) after supper and not disappoint the partners on your list."[70] Abby, who as the more attractive and coquettish seems to have been especially receptive to her mother's coaching, received several proposals. Two of these were refused, one resulted in a brief but brilliant engagement to a Winnipeg business partner of her father, and a fourth, at first refused, ultimately led to marriage.[71] Concerned that her daughter's tempestuous road to engagement might have led to gossip in Ottawa and elsewhere, Hattie sought to reassure herself while giving her daughter a subtle reminder of the standard of true womanly behaviour: "I am thankful to know that in every instance, where you have declined 'the highest compliment,' it has been through no fault of yours that it was offered—on the contrary that it has been

[offered] notwithstanding very guarded conduct on your part."[72]

The final choice, Somerset Aikins, was everything a mother could desire in a son-in-law. He was the second son of James Cox Aikins, a Conservative MP from Winnipeg, who had recently been appointed lieutenant governor of Manitoba and was an active Methodist.[73] Initially refused by Abby, the suitor had briefly transferred his affections to Jessie, but by the spring of 1887, upon the termination of Abby's earlier engagement, he was encouraged to make a second proposal. It was a time of major change in the lives of the Colby family. That May, thanks to improved material circumstances and the death of the previous owner of the stone house, Charles was able to buy back the family home, henceforth to be called Carrollcroft. In addition, his son Charles William graduated from McGill with first-class honours and the Shakespeare gold medal in English. The final thread was tied down when Somerset Aikins arrived in Stanstead, stayed nine days, proposed to Abby, and in the words of Jessie's journal, "went away happy."[74] The next few months, in anticipation of Abby's wedding on 13 October, saw furious activity around the stone house before the family reentered it in August. Since the bride was "not strong" and her mother was "very poorly," the decision was made to have a private wedding. As evidence of the extent to which a private family was also part of a larger public network, 800 invitations were sent out, but fortunately only 200 guests were able to attend. Conducted in Stanstead's small Anglican church, it was followed by a reception at Carrollcroft, which reflected in every way that taste and refinement had become well-entrenched evangelical values.[75]

As evidenced by this highly acclaimed wedding, the expanding marketplace of the 1880s and Charles Colby's growing success therein had indeed brought a remarkable change in the opportunities for self-definition available to at least some young people, when compared with those of their parents and grandparents. To the earlier emphasis on self-control, self-development had been added as an important way for members of the middle class to advance in a commercial society shaped by expanding economic opportunity. In this process, polite culture which, as a number of historians have observed, had earlier begun to shape the values of "the middling sort" in Britain, had also begun to permeate the domestic life of middle-class evangelicals in North America.[76] Having proudly informed his mother that his costs in his first year at McGill had been significantly lower than those of his housemates, Charles William promptly received a stinging rebuke: "Never sponge in any way— but take your share in paying for treats. To be prudent is one thing and to be 'mean and small' is quite another. The family tradition & practice will warrant you in spending all you need to *spend*, and in doing it frankly like a man."[77] Although Charles and John Colby's financial circumstances as students remained cramped, the concept of character had undergone a sea change since the days when their father as a student at Dartmouth had carefully noted his expenses in order to assure his parents that he was making every possible economy.

By the 1880s, frugality, which had once been seen as a commendable character trait in the middle class, had come to be equated with unmanly behaviour. Liberality in spending was no longer a trait that evangelicals associated with a wasteful upper class; it had become the noblesse oblige of upper-middle-class Methodists. Thus, the wedding of the older Colby daughter, her elaborate trousseau, and her lifestyle as a newlywed member of a prominent Winnipeg Methodist family were far removed from the experience of her mother. The latter's wedding had been noteworthy only in its soberness, and as a young bride she had had to defer material purchases and remind her husband that "costliness is not happiness." Abby, through her marriage, and Jessie, in her single life as a companion to her parents, had entered a way of life reminiscent of that of late eighteenth-century English gentlewomen, so well described by Amanda Vickery and others.[78]

By the latter part of the nineteenth century, Canadian Methodists as a group had become solidly middle class, respectable, and in many cases, "refined." . . . In a world in which God was seen to be immanent, the Christian family became the site where self-improvement and religious nurture worked together to prepare a child for this life as well as for eternity. From the time of the Puritans to that of Moses Colby's generation, the family had been seen as "a little church" in which the child was taught the eternal truths of salvation. Evangelicals took a distinctive turn when they went further and added to their concern for salvation "the conviction that the particular arrangements of family life could have eternal consequences," to cite historian Margaret Bendroth.[79] It is not surprising, therefore, that some have seen the Victorian fascination with domestic religion as an important step in the gradual disenchantment of western society.[80]

For late nineteenth-century evangelicals, however, the equation was precisely the reverse: instead of the family replacing religion, religion sacralized the family. As Hattie Colby had reminded her husband during the nadir of their economic fortunes, in the unpredictable world of industrializing North America, family was the one constant that promised stability and security. Taken together, family and religious moral formation provided security, order, and practical assistance, and it is not surprising that both were seen to be of divine origin and universal. . . . In the words of an 1865 publication, "As the family is a divine institution and a type of the church and of heaven it cannot be understood in its isolation from Christianity; it must involve Christian principles, duties and interests; and embrace in its educational functions, a preparation not only for the State, but also for the church."[81]

. . .

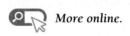 *More online.*

Notes

1. Hattie Child Colby (HCC) to Charles Carroll Colby (CCC), 1 March 1871, HCC Papers, Series 1, Box 1:2, Fonds Colby (FC), Stanstead Historical Society.

2. For an early example, see Anne L. Kuhn, *The Mother's Role in Childhood Education: New England Concepts, 1830–1860* (New Haven, CT: Yale University Press, 1947), and Barbara Welter, "The Cult of True Womanhood, 1820–1860," *American Quarterly* 18 (1966): 151–74.

3. Maxine Van de Wetering, "The Popular Concept of 'Home' in Nineteenth-Century America," *Journal of American Studies* 28 (1984): 1, 5–28.

4. John Tosh, *A Man's Place: Masculinity and the Middle-Class Home in Victorian England* (New Haven, CT: Yale University Press, 1999), 79–86, and Leonore Davidoff, *The Family Story: Blood, Contract, and Intimacy, 1830–1960* (New York, NY: Addison Wesley Longman, 1999), 151–7.

5. Tosh, *A Man s Place*, 101.

6. See, for example, his description of purchases in anticipation of a trip to Vermont with his wife and youngest daughter; CCC to HCC, 4 April 1870, CCC Papers, Series 4:A, Box 2:4, FC.

7. CCC to HCC, 30 April 1872, CCC Papers, Series 4:A, Box 2:5, FC.

8. Davidoff, *The Family Story*, 109; Colleen McDannell, *The Christian Home in Victorian America, 1840–1900* (Bloomington, IN: Indiana University Press, 1986); and Margaret Bendroth, *Growing Up Protestant: Parents, Children, and Mainline Churches* (New Brunswick, NJ: Rutgers University Press, 2002), 1–80. . . .

9. This has been well argued for Victorian England in Leonore Davidoff and Catherine Hall, *Family Fortunes: Men and Women of the English Middle Class, 1780–1850* (Chicago, IL: University of Chicago Press, 1987), 76–148. For the United States, see Mary P. Ryan, *Cradle of the Middle Class: The Family in Oneida County, New York, 1790–1865* (Cambridge, UK: Cambridge University Press, 1981). In both, however, the relation to the institutional church has received little attention.

10. Edmund S. Morgan, *The Puritan Family: Religion and Domestic Relations in Seventeenth-Century New England* (New York, NY: Harper and Row, 1944), 87–108.

11. J. I. Little, "The Fireside Kingdom: A Mid-Nineteenth-Century Anglican Perspective on Marriage and Parenthood," in Nancy Christie, ed., *Households of Faith: Family, Gender, and Community in Canada, 1760–1969* (Montreal, QC: McGill-Queen's University Press, 2001), 77–100. . . .

12. The most informative study on the Sunday school movement (for the United States) is Ann Boylan, *Sunday School: The Formation of an American Institution, 1790–1880* (New Haven, CT: Yale University Press, 1988). . . . [F]or Methodism in Canada, see Neil Semple, *The Lord's Dominion: The History of Canadian Methodism* (Montreal, QC: McGill-Queen's University Press, 1996), ch. 14. . . .

13. In Canada the official resolution of the theological dispute about whether a child's eternal safety rested on conversion, rather than on baptism and childhood nurture, took significantly longer than in the United States; see Marguerite Van Die, *An Evangelical Mind: Nathanael Burwash and the Methodist Tradition in Canada, 1839–1918* (Montreal, QC: McGill-Queen's University Press, 1989), 25–37. See also Neil Semple, "'The Nurture and Admonition of the Lord': Nineteenth-Century Canadian Methodism's Response to Childhood," *Histoire Sociale/Social History* 14 (1981): 157–75.

14. Serge Gagnon, *Plaisir d'amour et crainte de Dieu: sexualité et confession au Bas-Canada* (Sainte-Foy, QC: Presses de l'Université Laval, 1990), 79.

15. *Liturgy or Formulary of Services in Use in the Wesleyan-Methodist Church in Canada* (Toronto, ON: S. Rose, 1867), 7.

16. For a succinct summary of Bushnell's thought, see Gary Dorrien, *The Making of American Liberal Theology: Imagining Progressive Religion, 1805–1900* (Louisville, KY: Westminster John Knox Press, 2001), 111–78. . . .

17. Bendroth, *Growing Up Protestant*, 25.

18. George S. Weaver, *The Christian Household: Embracing the Christian Home* (Boston, MA: Tompkins and Musey, 1856), 36. The reference to its reading is in Journal, 10 March 1861, HCC Papers, Series 2, Box 1, FC.

19. HCC to CCC, 1 April 1873, HCC Papers, Series 1, Box 1:3, FC.

20. CCC to Jessie Maud Colby (JMC), 7 July 1872, CCC Papers, Series 4:A, Box 1:5, FC.

21. HCC to CCC, 26 March 1875, HCC Papers, Series 1, Box 1:5, FC.

22. "Little Hattie," HCC Papers, Series 2, Box 2, FC.

23. For the debate on infant depravity in Canadian Methodist circles, including recent historiographical controversy, see Van Die, *An Evangelical Mind*, ch. 1.

24. McDannell, *The Christian Home*, 108–16, and Bendroth, *Growing Up Protestant*, 14–16.

25. Tosh, *A Man's Place*, 84.

26. See, for example, HCC to CCC, 22 September 1867, HCC Papers, Series 1, Box 1:1, FC.

27. HCC to CCC, 20 and 23 March 1873, HCC Papers, Series 1, Box 1:3, FC; and Diary, 5 April 1903, JMC Papers, Series 2, Box 1, FC.

28. See the fine study on Victorian Bibles as commodities in Colleen McDannell, *Material Christianity: Religion and Popular Culture in America* (New Haven, CT: Yale University Press, 1995), 67–102.

29. McDannell, *The Christian Home*, 77–107.

30. Insightful commentary on the moral dimension of consumer choice, though for a later period, is found in Joy Parr, *Domestic Goods: The Material, the Moral and the Economic in the Postwar Years* (Toronto, ON: University of Toronto Press, 1999).

31. HCC to CCC, 12 November 1868, HCC Papers, Series 1, Box 1:1, FC.

32. HCC to CCC, 25 March 1873, HCC Papers, Series I, Box 1:3, FCM.

33. Charles William Colby (CWC), "Garrulities of an Octogenarian" (typescript), 21, CWC Papers, Series I:C, Box 11:3, FC.

34. Ibid. See also HCC to CCC, 2 March 1883, HCC Papers, Series 1, Box 1:6, FC.

35. HCC to CCC, 31 August 1874, HCC Papers, Series 1, Box 1:4, FC.

36. Richard L. Bushman, *The Refinement of America: Persons, Houses, Cities* (New York, NY: Vintage, 1993), 326–31.

37. Daniel Walker Howe, *Making the American Self: Jonathan Edwards to Abraham Lincoln* (Cambridge, MA: Harvard University Press, 1997), 118–19.

38. HCC to CCC, 27 March 1873, HCC Papers, Series 1, Box 1:3, FC.

39. HCC to Abby Lemira Colby Aikins (ALCA), 11 April 1875, HCC Papers, Series 1, Box 2:4, FC.

40. This did not seem to deter the evangelical press. See David Paul Nord, "Religious Reading and Readers in Antebellum America," *Journal of the Early Republic* 15 (Summer 1995): 241–72.

41. HCC to girls, 23 February 1883, HCC Papers, Series 1, Box 2:1, FC.

42. As argued in William McLoughlin, *Revivals, Awakenings, and Reform: An Essay on Religion and Social Change in America, 1607–1977* (Chicago, IL: University of Chicago Press, 1978), which analyzes the close fit between nineteenth-century experiential religion and its cultural expression.

43. Weaver, *The Christian Household*, 104.

44. This is also briefly noted in Bushman, *Refinement of America*, 351–2 . . .

45. For an example of the former, see Van de Wetering, "The Popular Concept of 'Home' in Nineteenth-Century America." Notable exceptions include Davidoff and Hall, *Family Fortunes*, and Françoise Noël, *Family Life and Sociability in Upper and Lower Canada, 1780–1870: A View from Diaries and Family Correspondence* (Montreal, QC: McGill-Queen's University Press, 2003).

46. Peter N. Stearns and Timothy Haggerty, "The Role of Fear: Transitions in American Emotional Standards for Children," *American Historical Review* 96, no. 1 (1991): 63–94.

47. Julia McNair Wright, *The Complete Home: An Encyclopedia of Domestic Life and Affairs* (Brantford, ON: Bradley, Garretson, 1879), 289.

48. HCC to JMC, 28 Aug. 1872, HCC Papers, Series 1, Box 2:7, FC.

49. Census of Canada, 1871, Stanstead (microfilm) C-10089-90, Library and Archives Canada (LAC).

50. A good entry into these varied activities can be found in CWC, "Garrulities of an Octogenarian" (typescript), 22–4, CWC Papers, Series 1:C, Box 11:3, FC.

51. See, for example, HCC to JMC, 5 July 1874, HCC Papers, Series 1, Box 2:7, FC, in which she notes that Abby had been "invited to a little dance on account of Johnny Foster's friends."

52. Hattie told her husband of a female church member's announcement of a Ladies' Aid meeting at the parsonage for the purpose of arranging suitable entertainment "for the young people who are church members want some kind of party that they may go to: and as they are so to speak forbidden to accept the invitations they do receive, they call for something suited to their case." She did not attend. See HCC to CCC, 20 January 1875, HCC Papers, Series 1, Box 1:5, FC.

53. This was done by adding a footnote to paragraph 35 of its official Doctrine and Discipline. For the wider context, see William H. Magney, "The Methodist Church and the National Gospel, 1884–1914," *Bulletin* (Committee on Archives, United Church of Canada), 20 (1968): 3–95.

54. Charles William Colby (who married Emma Cobb, granddaughter of Wilder Pierce, member of another prominent Stanstead Methodist family) recounts that the dancing at his outdoor wedding in 1897 was witnessed by six ministers, who, though they did not participate, did not . . . object; see Diary, 23 June 1897, CWC Papers, Series 1:C, Box 12, FC.

55. HCC to ALCA, 31 January 1875, HCC Papers, Series 1, Box 2:4, FC.

56. Jean-Pierre Kesteman, Peter Southam, and Diane Saint-Pierre, *Histoire des cantons de l'Est* (Sainte-Foy, QC: Presses de l'Université Laval, 1998), 396–8.

57. HCC to CCC, 3 August 1873, HCC Papers, Series 1, Box 1:3, FC.

58. HCC to CCC, 21 October 1884, HCC Papers, Series 1, Box 1:7, FC.

59. Bendroth, *Growing Up Protestant*, 39–50.

60. On the relationship between public duty and paternal domesticity, see Tosh, *A Man's Place*, 124–41.

61. JMC to ALCA, 9 July 1877, JMC Papers, Series 1, Box 7:2, FC.

62. HCC to JMC, 10 and 14 August 1874, HCC Papers, Series 1, Box 2:7, FC.

63. For the wider context, see Semple, *The Lord's Dominion*, ch. 14, and Christopher Coble, "The Role of

Young People's Societies in the Training of Christian Womanhood (and Manhood), 1880–1910," in Margaret Lamberts Bendroth and Virginia Lieson Brereton, eds., *Women and Twentieth-Century Protestantism* (Urbana, IL: University of Illinois Press, 2002), 74–92.

64. Young Canadian Methodists in urban centres applauded the move away from the old barnlike buildings, characteristic of their denomination's earlier architecture, and displayed their aspirations to taste and gentility in their fundraising and social activities.

65. HCC to JMC [early 1880s], HCC Papers, Series 1, Box 2:7, FC.

66. HCC to ALCA, 30 April 1875, HCC Papers, Series 1, Box 2:4, FC.

67. HCC to CCC, 10 and 25 February 1880, HCC Papers, Series 1, Box 1:6, FC.

68. Although they were very different in temperament, the two daughters were extremely close and, when not together in Ottawa or Stanstead, they shared a lively correspondence. . . . It may have been [Jessie's] attraction to the more interesting male world that led her, at the age of 12, to announce that she would "never marry anyone, because there wouldn't be *another* man *just like papa*"; HCC to CCC, 2 April 1873, HCC Papers, Series 1, Box 1:3, FC.

69. JMC to HCC, and JMC to family, JMC Papers, Series 1, Boxes 1:1, 2 and 2:1, FC.

70. HCC to ALCA, 26 February 1881, HCC Papers, Series 1, Box 2:5, FC.

71. By the spring of 1883, with both daughters well established in the Russell Hotel, letters between Ottawa and Stanstead began to make frequent mention of Abby's engagement with a certain K. N. McFee. K. N., as he was generally known, was a Winnipeg entrepreneur who had won the confidence and admiration of her father, as well as the approval of her mother. A frequent visitor in Stanstead, McFee took up a number of business partnerships with Charles Colby in the Northwest.

72. HCC to ALCA, 24 March 1883, HCC Papers, Series 1, Box 2:5, FC.

73. Upon hearing of Abby's engagement to McFee, Aikins had immediately transferred his affections to Jessie, the younger daughter. . . . See HCC to ALCA and JMC, 26 March 1883, HCC Papers, Series 1, Box 2:1, FC.

74. Diary entries, 11 and 29 May 1887, JMC Papers, Series 2, Box 1, FC.

75. See also description in Diary, 31 January 1881, JMC Papers, Series 2, Box 1, FC. The wedding notice in the *Stanstead Journal* stated that the couple were married on Thursday evening at 7 o'clock, Christ Church, Stanstead, followed by an At Home at 8 o'clock, Mr. and Mrs. C. C. Colby, Carrollcroft.

76. Amanda Vickery, *The Gentleman's Daughter: Women's Lives in Victorian England* (New Haven, CT: Yale University Press, 1998), 161–94, and Marjorie R. Hunt, *The Middling Sort: Commerce, Gender, and the Family in England, 1680–1780* (Berkeley, CA: University of California Press, 1996), 193–218. . . .

77. HCC to CWC, 23 July 1883, HCC Papers, Series 1, Box 3:1, FC. . . .

78. See note 76 above.

79. Bendroth, *Growing up Protestant*, 14.

80. "It is the tie between parents and children which has been imbued with ever more poignancy as people's relationship to the transcendental realms of religion, folk belief and magic has gradually disappeared." Davidoff, *The Family Story*, 81. John R. Gillis, *A World of Their Own Making: Myth, Ritual, and the Quest for Family Values* (New York, NY: Basic Books, 1996), esp. ch. 4.

81. S. Phillips, *The Christian Home as It Is in the Sphere of Nature and the Church* (New York, NY: Gurdon Mill, 1865), 23, donated to the Archives of the Stanstead Historical Society.

3 Living on Display
Colonial Visions of Aboriginal Domestic Spaces

Paige Raibmon

Notions of domesticity were central to colonial projects around the globe. They were part of the fray when metropole and colony collided and transformed one another. As Jean and John Comaroff put it, "Colonialism was as much about making the center as it was about making the periphery. The colony was not a mere extension of the modern world. It was part of what made the world modern in the first place. And the dialectic of domesticity was a vital element in the process."[1] The colonial desire to order domestic space had its correlate in broader attempts to impose discipline in the public sphere.[2] On the late nineteenth-century Northwest Coast, this process took shape for Aboriginal people who increasingly lived not only overseas from, but within, the society of the colonizing metropoles. Aboriginal people experienced extreme pressure to bring their lives into conformity with Victorian expectations about private, middle-class, bourgeois domesticity. This pressure came not only from isolated missionaries posted in lonely colonial outposts but also from a broad swath of colonial society. So intense was the interest in Aboriginal domestic arrangements, however, that colonial society brought Aboriginal domestic space into the public domain as never before, even as it urged Aboriginal communities

to adopt the Victorian values of the domestic private sphere. While missionaries and government officials pressured Aboriginal families to replace multifamily longhouses with Victorian-style nuclear family dwellings, anthropologists and tourists invaded Aboriginal homes, alternately in search of a rapidly receding ("savage") past or a slowly dawning ("civilized") future. Missionaries encouraged such voyeuristic investigations in the hope that the object lessons of everyday Aboriginal life would generate a flow of funds from Christian pocketbooks into missionary society coffers. Anthropologists such as Franz Boas fed their own form of economic necessity with these displays, which they hoped would encourage benefactors to provide funding for additional anthropological fieldwork and collecting. In a sense, as they transformed Aboriginal domestic spaces into spectacle, all of the members of these non-Aboriginal groups became sightseers.

Domestic space was transformed into spectacle, and attempts to effect greater separation between private and public spaces simultaneously blurred the two, creating a hybrid public/private domain. Colonialism is riven with such invariably ironic contradictions. But the importance of such contradictions runs deeper than postmodern

Citation: Paige Raibmon, "Living on Display: Colonial Visions of Aboriginal Domestic Spaces," *BC Studies* 140 (2003): 69–89.

irony. While with one hand colonial society held out the promise of assimilation, with the other it impressed upon Aboriginal people its lack of good faith. The history of Aboriginal people in North America is replete with "sweet" promises gone sour; with "final" promises turned final solutions.[3] How did colonizers reconcile these contradictions, these "tensions of empire"?[4] A review of their views of Aboriginal domestic space provides an opportunity to address this question.

When curious, often nosy, sometimes aggressive members of colonial society entered Aboriginal homes, they brought the things they needed to make sense of the room around them. The significance of cultural practice may lie in the story we tell ourselves about ourselves, but the insight that the metropole has been defined by the colonies, and the "self" by the "other," forces us to acknowledge that culture is also the story we tell ourselves about others.[5] The colonial preoccupation with the domestic spaces of Aboriginal people provides a window onto stories that worked in both of these ways simultaneously. The stories that members of colonial society told themselves about Aboriginal people were also stories they told themselves about themselves. The stories that Canadians and Americans told themselves differed, as did specific policies and conditions on both sides of the border. However, during the late nineteenth century, public interest in "authentic" Indians and pride in successful Indian policy were important components of both countries' sense of nationalism. Differences in policy did not preclude continuities in attitudes and assumptions. Colonizers' fascination with the domestic spaces of Aboriginal people offers us an important moment of cultural convergence.

The colonial narration of Aboriginal domestic space as spectacle generated a multiplicity of stories about, among other things, Aboriginal savagery, white civilization, colonial legitimacy, and modernity. Two assumptions of colonial thought recur in these stories. First, from their various, and admittedly diverse, vantage points, members of late nineteenth-century colonial society cast domestic spaces and domestic goods as material markers of civilization. But this alone cannot explain the sway that these markers of domesticity held over the colonial imagination. The second assumption takes us this additional step. The evidence suggests that members of colonial society assumed that the significance of these markers was more than skin deep. They assumed that the markers were straightforward reflections of the inner state of the individual's soul and the family's moral state. They extrapolated from fixed material form to fixed immaterial self. If the space was civilized, then likewise its inhabitants; if the space was uncivilized, then so were its inhabitants.

Aboriginal domestic spaces were put on display in a variety of contexts and along a continuum of consent. Some Aboriginal people willingly participated in the public performance of their private lives, while others submitted somewhat more grudgingly to the public gaze. Sometimes Aboriginal people did not have the opportunity to grant or withhold consent at all, when non-Aboriginal viewers invaded their private homes without bothering to ask permission. All of these interactions were infused with relations of power. Whether they suffered public scrutiny willingly or not, most Aboriginal families could ill afford to forgo the material benefits that accompanied submission to the colonial view. Some form of direct or indirect remuneration usually accompanied the performance of everyday life. This sometimes came as wages, at other times it came from the sale of souvenirs to sightseers hoping to commemorate their excursions into Aboriginal domestic space.

In this article, I explore a selection of domestic spectacles that fall along various points of the aforementioned continuum of consent, and I also address the nature of some of the stories that these spectacles enabled colonizers to tell themselves. I conclude with some brief considerations of the quite different stories that Aboriginal people told themselves about domestic spaces.

The transformation and narration of everyday life were central to colonial policy and culture alike. This article takes preliminary steps toward considering why this may have been so.

Exposition Space

The world's fairs and expositions of the late nineteenth century provide some of the clearest examples of Aboriginal people voluntarily submitting to living on display. Beginning with the Paris Exposition in 1889, colonized peoples became important attractions at world's fairs and expositions. In many respects, exhibit organizers intended these so-called "live exhibits" to display and legitimate colonial narratives of modernity and progress. Early examples of mass advertising that helped generate public support for foreign and domestic policies, the expositions were themselves grand stories that members of colonial society told themselves about themselves.[6] While live exhibits at European fairs tended to come from distant overseas colonies, North American fairs, beginning with the 1893 Chicago World's Fair, featured displays of internally colonized Aboriginal people. While most of these performers spent at least some time in scripted song and dance performances, the bulk of their time as live exhibits was given over to the performance of everyday life.

The live exhibits at the 1893 Chicago World's Fair invariably revolved around domestic dwellings. Millions of tourists flocked to see Aboriginal people supposedly living "under ordinary conditions and occupying a distinctive habitation."[7] These dwellings fed into the fair's organizational theme: progress. They offered a relief against which visitors could measure the architectural achievements not only of the rest of the fair but also of dominant society in general. As one reporter wrote, the Aboriginal dwellings stood "in amazing contrast to the white palaces stretching away to the north, that evidence[d] the skill and prosperity of their successors in this western domain."[8] Against this backdrop of

modernity, the Aboriginal dwellings lent themselves to a social evolutionist narrative that legitimated colonial endeavours.

Anthropologists and other exhibitors erected a "great Aboriginal encampment,"[9] consisting of the living spaces of Aboriginal people from across North America. While newspaper reporters might concede that Aboriginal people lived in "stone, brick and frame houses"[10] when they were at home, they imagined "authentic" Aboriginal dwellings as something quite different. For the duration of their time at the fair, Inuit families lived in skin tents; Penobscot families in birchbark wigwams; Navajo families in hogans; Menominee families in skin tepees; Winnebago families in "sugar-loaf" woven reed mat wigwams; Chippewa families in birchbark longhouses; Iroquois families in elm and birchbark huts and longhouses; and Kwakwa̲ka̲'wakw families in cedar plank longhouses.[11] Anthropologists simultaneously created and fulfilled expectations of authenticity among visitors to the fair by carefully stage-managing the forms of dwelling put on display.[12]

The Kwakwa̲ka̲'wakw performers from northern Vancouver Island were, in several respects, typical of the live exhibits. Frederic Ward Putnam, Harvard professor and organizer of the anthropology display, explained that the 16 Kwakwa̲ka̲'wakw participants would "live under normal conditions in their natural habitations during the six months of the Exposition."[13] In order to reinforce the aura of ordinary life, Putnam and his assistants worked to ensure that the Kwakwa̲ka̲'wakw troupe consisted of family units. This principle was applied to most of the live exhibits, although the definition of "family" in this context was a non-Aboriginal one. Organizers attempted to limit the performers to couples and their children, even when would-be performers expressed a desire to travel in larger groups.[14] The coordinator of the Kwakwa̲ka̲'wakw troupe, George Hunt, arranged for his brother and his brother's wife to join the group, although his own wife did not come to Chicago.[15] Hunt's son and father also came. The group included two other couples and two small children. Another performer came with his brother. Hunt seems to have made an effort to meet the desires of his employer, anthropologist Franz Boas, by recruiting people in such a way as to approximate nuclear families. While the final group was not quite a Victorian nuclear family unit, neither was it an extended family of the kind that would have lived in a cedar longhouse.

Putnam's fixation with producing authentic, "normal" conditions extended to his insistence that the domiciles be originals rather than faux reproductions. Thus, when the Kwakwaka'wakw from Vancouver Island arrived at the Chicago World's Fair, they reassembled the planks of a cedar longhouse that had been disassembled at a Nuwitti village on the northern coast of Vancouver Island before being shipped by rail to Chicago. The house's authenticity was heightened by the report that, when it was chosen for the exhibit, it had actually been occupied by a Kwakwaka'wakw family.[16] The house may even have been the property of one of the performers, which would have added an extra layer to the exhibit's patina of everyday life. The Kwakwaka'wakw house was situated alongside the fairground's South Pond, which stood in for the waters of the Johnstone, Queen Charlotte, and Hecate Straits. The houses faced a sloping "beach" upon which canoes were pulled ashore.

The display of everyday life was about domestic goods as well as domestic space. "Traditional" domestic goods completed the tableaux of Aboriginal domesticity presented by the familial scenes. Visitors could see the Kwakwaka'wakw living among items representative of everyday and ceremonial life, including canoes, house poles, totem poles, masks, and regalia. And if they strolled past the dairy exhibit to the nearby anthropology building, visitors could inspect hundreds of other implements integral to Northwest Coast Aboriginal life. Like other human performers, the Kwakwaka'wakw were living appendages of the vast displays of ethnographic objects, many of them drawn from domestic life.

The Kwakwaka'wakw exhibit in Chicago was an explicit realization of the colonial assumption that the "normal"—that is, "traditional" and "authentic"—state of these so-called savages was most visible in their "everyday life." The enormous trouble and expense that exhibit organizers took to ensure that the mock villages consisted of "real" houses, filled with "real" goods, was emblematic of their belief that inner meaning was inherent within outward form. They knew that the live exhibits did not "normally" live beneath the intrusive eyes of millions of visitors. But they nonetheless assumed that the more subjective characteristics of everyday life could be held stable as long as outward conditions and characteristics were replicated as precisely as possible. This assumption was apparent in a number of other settings.

Migrant Space

The Kwakwaka'wakw who travelled to Chicago did so voluntarily and earned lucrative wages for their efforts. Less consensual examples of the performance of everyday life abound. When the domestic spaces of migrant labourers became spectacles, the degree of Aboriginal consent was much more ambiguous. In the late nineteenth century, thousands of Aboriginal people from British Columbia and Washington converged on Puget Sound for the fall hop harvest. Workers harvested a cash crop that was sold on a volatile world market. Yet while employers may have seen Aboriginal pickers as an emerging proletariat, many non-Aboriginal consumers of spectacle cast the labourers as remnants of a vanishing, authentic Aboriginal past, inexorably dying off to make way for the region's non-Aboriginal future. The migrant labour camps to which the influx of workers gave rise became tourist destinations for non-Aboriginal inhabitants of urban and rural Puget Sound. Entrepreneurs and sightseers converged to transform the migrants' temporary living quarters into spectacles. Although the migrant hop pickers had not set out with the intention to perform commodified versions of Aboriginal culture, their experiences in the migrant camps around Puget Sound bore striking resemblances to those of the Kwakwa̲ka̲'wakw in Chicago's "great aboriginal encampment."

The workers were sights of interest even before they reached the hop fields. Local newspapers commented on them when they travelled through urban areas on their way to and from the fields.[17] The appearance of the hop pickers in Seattle was said to be as "regular as the annual migration of water fowl or the rotation of the seasons, and . . . ever a source of attraction and interest."[18] The most commonly referred to centre of Aboriginal activity in Seattle during the hop season was the waterfront area known as "Ballast Island." Aboriginal migrants began fashioning makeshift camps atop this pile of rocks and rubble in the 1870s, and by 1892 *Harper's Weekly* informed readers that Ballast Island was the place to go to see the pickers.[19] Other sites in and around Seattle and Tacoma also became known for the appearance of seasonal Aboriginal camps.[20]

Rural Aboriginal camps in the hop fields themselves provided an even greater spectacle for curious tourists. During the harvest season in late August and early September, each day hundreds of tourists descended on rural towns like Puyallup and the surrounding hop fields, travelling from Seattle or Tacoma in carriages and on the frequent interurban passenger trains.[21] In the late 1880s and early 1890s, day trippers turned into vacationers as businessmen opened hotels at or near the hop farms.[22]

These urban spectators converged around the domestic lives of the Aboriginal hop pickers. Local papers touted the temporary villages as being "always worth a visit and study."[23] John Muir found "their queer camps" more striking than even the natural setting of "rustling vine-pillars."[24] When 400 Cowichan camped in the Puyallup Valley in 1903, visitors and residents alike flocked to watch the "mode of life and habits of these fish-eating aborigines from Vancouver island."[25] For tourists, these "queer camps" were colourful spectacle with a measure of ethnographic education thrown in.

Physical conditions at these urban and rural encampments varied. Tents made of a variety of materials, ranging from cedar bark or rush mats to canvas sheeting, were common in city- and field-side camps alike. Along the urban waterfronts, some migrants erected structures on the ground, while others used their canoes as the foundation over which to hang canvas or mats.[26] At the fields, workers located wood with which to frame the canvas or mats that they had brought with them. Some farmers built houses or temporary huts for seasonal labourers.[27] Cabins, and even "wooden houses, built after the style of the white man,"[28] could also be found along urban waterfronts. Some Aboriginal people found the living arrangements substandard—even uncivilized. Twana subchief Big John visited the Puyallup hop fields and commented that the people living there had "small huts, not like our houses, or even barns, but more like chicken coops, while we have houses and are civilized."[29] For Big John, as for colonial viewers, domestic form and domestic character were interlocking.

For the non-Aboriginal viewer, the fact that these were migrant labourers living in temporarily erected tents did not detract from the attraction of the spectacle. The notion that they were viewing "real" everyday life rather than reproductions (as they would at a world's fair) likely appealed to many. In the hop fields, they could believe that they were one step closer to the real thing than even Putnam, with all his attention to authentic details, could offer.

The transitory quality of the structures themselves also corresponded with common assumptions about Aboriginal people, who were presumed to be shiftless and wandering by nature. The assumption that Aboriginal people were incapable of permanently possessing property shrouded the self-congratulatory stories immigrants told themselves about the improvements they wrought with their transformation of the Pacific Northwest landscape from primitive (Aboriginal) to modern (non-Aboriginal). As railway investor, amateur ethnographer, lawyer, and (later) judge James Wickersham put it, "the Indian doesn't care [about retaining reservation land]—clams, a split cedar shanty on the beach, a few mats and kettles, leisure and a bottle of rum once in a while are all he wants— anybody can have the land that wants it. Really why should our govt [sic] go to such enormous expense in trying to make a white man out of an Indian?"[30] Wickersham's bluntness may have been somewhat unusual, but his sentiment was not. North of the border, in British Columbia, newcomers applied a different land policy than that used in Washington, but it, too, systematically deprived Aboriginal people of the land base required to remain self-sustaining.[31] The scene that Wickersham described was much like the ones that non-Aboriginal viewers in Washington and British Columbia, or at the Chicago World's Fair, found when they sought out spectacles of Aboriginal domestic space: picturesque object lessons featuring the notion of the vanishing Indian. The hop pickers reinforced several dearly held assumptions for tourists who ventured forth to view the workers en route or in camp: Aboriginal people used land and resources sporadically and unsystematically; they were inevitably disappearing in the face of civilization and modernity; and investment in an Aboriginal future was an oxymoron.

These assumptions were apparent in popular assessments of how the pickers spent their hard-earned wages. Here again, domestic goods as well as domestic space came under scrutiny. Although Indian agents commented that Aboriginal pickers often returned with "useful" goods such as furniture, harnesses, sewing machines, and stoves, tourists and reporters focused on items they deemed ridiculous and frivolous.[32] The belief that outer form mirrored an inner subjective state informed these assumptions as well. It

elevated the brief glimpses non-Aboriginal viewers had of Aboriginal lives from anecdotal evidence to generalized and authoritative judgment.

Casual viewers who made afternoon or weekend excursions to the hop fields or waterfront did not see the rough migrant labour camps as a component of a hardworking and highly flexible Aboriginal economy, which is what they were. They read the seasonal itinerancy of the migrant workers as evidence of an underlying lack of connection to any fixed locale. The notion that Aboriginal people had no use for land or resources was a fiction; however, in the hands and minds of a growing non-Aboriginal population, it was a powerful one. As in Chicago, spectacles of Aboriginal domestic space provided a jumping-off point for the stories viewers told themselves about themselves.

Home Space

As migrant labourers, the hop pickers faced constraints on the level of privacy they could maintain over their domestic spaces. The circumstances of travel would have subjected their spaces and processes of domestic life to a degree of public view, even without tourists' obsession with "vanishing Indians." Their presence as travellers was noticeable to local residents. As in Chicago, it had been temporary structures that were on display at the hop fields. Yet, along the late nineteenth-century Northwest Coast, even inhabitants of Aboriginal villages who remained at home had to deal with the intrusions of non-Aboriginal viewers. With the advent of tourist steamship routes along the Inside Passage in the early 1880s, adventurous non-Aboriginal travellers could now journey along the coasts of British Columbia and southeast Alaska. As Sitka, Alaska, became one of the prime ports along the Inside Passage tourist route, the Tlingit residents faced one of the most intrusive forms of assault on Aboriginal domestic space. For tourists the "performances" of everyday life in Sitka seemed among the most "authentic" to be found; the

Tlingit, meanwhile, found themselves cast in the role of involuntary "performers." This latter point is of course not unrelated to the former. In Sitka the Aboriginal people stayed put; thus, the display of Tlingit lives falls among the least consensual examples of "living on display."

Sitka's tourist industry provided visitors with a dual view of Tlingit domestic life: (1) the "civilized cottages" inhabited by Presbyterian mission school graduates and (2) the Tlingit village. The "Ranche," as the latter was dubbed, was both the figurative and literal antithesis of the mission cottages located at the far end of town. Tourists arrived by steamer, and, as they disembarked, they had the choice of turning left toward the Ranche or right toward the mission school and cottages. This dichotomous division of domestic space was not unique to Sitka. Farther south, along the coast in British Columbia, missionary Thomas Crosby made the same distinction between what he called "Christian street" and "Heathen street."[33]

Publications for visitors to Sitka invariably featured the Ranche as a "must-see" sight. The local newspaper encouraged visitors to "get off the beaten track" and, if possible, to find a local guide: "Get some one who knows the village to conduct you through, as many places of interest will be otherwise overlooked. Don't confine your attention to the front row only, go in among the houses and see those on the back street." This reporter urged visitors to penetrate the inner reaches of Tlingit domestic life, claiming that "generally the natives do not object to visitors entering their houses."[34] At least some visitors took this advice to heart. As Sir John Franklin's niece wrote of her visit in 1870, "We went into several [houses], not merely to inspect, but in search of baskets & other queer things."[35] Glimpsing the interior was important because this was sometimes the most distinctive aspect of the building: "In exterior appearance [the houses] do not differ from those of the white man, but usually there is only a single room within on the ground floor."[36] Although some

Tlingit residents undoubtedly chafed at such intrusions, many took advantage of the situation that literally came knocking on their door. Pine doorplates appeared above the lintels of certain houses, directing visitors toward homes that gained renown in the tourist literature.[37]

Tourists carried their assumptions about domestic space as women's space with them to the Ranche. Although male residents such as "Sitka Jack" and the hereditary chief, Annahootz, put up such doorplates, the "palace of Siwash Town" had a matriarch on the throne.[38] Mrs., or "Princess," Tom was the most sought-after resident of the village and was renowned throughout southeast Alaska. Visitors never failed to scrutinize her domestic situation. In some respects, her home sounded like the epitome of domesticity: "a painted cabin with green blinds, and a green railing across the front porch."[39] But it was other elements of her domestic situation that attracted the most attention from visitors in search of a savage authenticity: her excessive wealth in gold, silver, blankets, and furs; and her multiple husbands, one of whom was reported to have been her former slave.

While male and female visitors alike focused their travel writings on Mrs. Tom, they told different stories about her. While female visitors used stories of Mrs. Tom to argue obliquely for women's economic independence and sexual freedom, male writers decried Mrs. Tom's behaviour. Eliza Ruhamah Scidmore's 1885 description of Mrs. Tom was the basis for subsequent writers' accounts, and its transfiguration over time is telling. Scidmore wrote that Mrs. Tom had "acquired her fortune by her own ability in legitimate trade."[40] Later male writers cast aspersions on her moral and sexual conduct, characterizing her as "a disreputable Indian woman" who used "doubtful methods" to amass her large fortune.[41] Female writers, on the other hand, viewed Mrs. Tom's accomplishments of domestic economy in a more positive light. In 1890 a female traveller emphasized that this wealth allowed Mrs. Tom to support two husbands and to still live in greater luxury than Chief Annahootz.[42] The "regal splendor" in which she reputedly lived included silk, satin, and lace dresses; carpeted floors; a mirror; pictures; and a "Yankee" cooking stove.[43] While female writers, beginning with Scidmore, stressed the neatness of Mrs. Tom's home and self, Frederick Schwatka characterized her as a "burley Amazon of the Northwest."[44] When these visitors stepped inside Mrs. Tom's house, they brought with them the narrative framework of the story they would tell.

Nearly a mile through and then beyond town, at the mission cottages, visitors could investigate the lives of the "civilized," "modern" Indians. They lived in two rows of neat, frame cottages built by Aboriginal labour but paid for by donations from American churches. The local, Presbyterian-aligned newspaper articulated the purpose of the cottages: "With their neat and inviting appearance, they are an object lesson which strongly contrasts with the filth and squalor of the Indian huts in other parts of the town."[45] Not only were the Ranche houses presumably dirty, they were also said to "cause trouble"; that is, to encourage uncivilized, tribal behaviour and relationships.[46] Missionaries worried that tourists' romanticization of "uncivilized" Aboriginal life would hinder their missionary endeavours, but they also saw the money that the tourists spent on curios in the Ranche.[47] The mission came to rely on displays of domestic space in order to convince potential donors that mission work could be successful and that mission graduates had a future other than "back-sliding" into Ranche life. By putting the object lesson of the cottages on display, missionaries hoped to elicit donations for their work.

The object lesson among object lessons was the Miller cottage (named for the pastor of the Pennsylvania church that donated the funds), in which the mission's star graduate, Rudolph Walton, lived. According to Presbyterian missionary Sheldon Jackson, the Miller cottage was "a better and more comfortable house" than those of 90 per cent of the Americans in Sitka,

"one of the best dwelling houses in the place."[48] But the donors were disappointed. When Walton sent them a sketch of the finished cottage, they complained that the structure did not look to have the character of a $500 house.[49]

The donors' concern with appearances makes sense in the context of the assumption that outer form reveals inner state. This non-Aboriginal assumption was as apparent in Sitka as it was at the Chicago World's Fair and in the Puget Sound hop fields. Visitors invariably subjected the domestic arrangements of cottage residents to close scrutiny and paid close attention to the bourgeois furnishings. When the mission doctor wrote an article about the Miller cottage he detailed everything from the furniture to the behaviour of the children. He commented on "the neat board walk and gravel walks around the side"; the "parlor and sitting room, about twelve feet square—carpeted, sofa at one side, rocking chairs, table and book case, as we should find in any comfortable home." Continuing, he noted, "in a small room adjoining this sitting room we find a cabinet with some pretty china and a few odd trinkets treasured by the family. The dining room and kitchen in the rear though less pretentious are neat, while upstairs the two bedrooms are furnished with bedsteads and the usual furniture."[50] Such details were evidence that the family within had escaped the "contaminating influences of the Ranch."[51] Other cottages received similar evaluations by visitors. "In many of their homes are phonographs, pianos, and sewing machines," wrote local schoolteacher Dazie M. Brown Stromstadt in her promotional book on Sitka.[52] For Stromstadt, these items were evidence that their Tlingit owners were "living a 'civilized life.'"[53] The cottage settlement was meant to stand as objective material proof of the subjective spiritual transformation that had taken place in the lives of the resident Tlingit. The material circumstances of the cottages were critical measurements of civility and modernity. Missionaries and tourists alike assumed that the geographical and structural opposition between

Ranche and cottages extended to the inner lives of the residents.

Needless to say, reality was not as simple as this idealized picture would have it. Close attention to the written descriptions of Ranche and cottage life reveals that some of the similarities are as striking as the differences. Much like the cottage settlement, the Ranche, too, had neat boardwalks and a general tidiness about it.[54] Ranche homes also contained modern domestic goods such as furniture and stoves (often of the "modern type").[55] The cottages, too, were less severed from Ranche life than many missionaries liked to admit. While living in the cottages, Rudolph Walton and other Tlingit residents sustained familial ties with Ranche residents and participated in important Tlingit ceremonies and community events.[56] They also followed similar cultural practices. The family unit within Miller cottage was not a nuclear one but, rather, included Rudolph Walton's widowed mother and grandmother, who spoke Tlingit to Walton's children.[57] Moreover, it was not just Ranche residents who were likely to offer baskets, carvings, or "curios" for sale to visitors but also cottage residents.[58] However, in the minds of white observers, the larger context—either Ranche or cottage—of each domestic interior seemed to carry overriding importance.

The notion that outside mimicked inside was less a statement of the status quo than it was a wishful prescription—an interpretation that observers attempted to impose, against the natural grain of the evidence before them. It was the story they *wanted* to tell themselves. Not surprisingly, the contradictions inherent within such an exercise frequently broke through to the surface, rending the oppositional social fabric of Ranche versus Cottage. At such times, observers worked hard to repair the damage and to restore the impression of easy opposition. Visitors might attribute the "civilized" signs of cleanliness and order in the Ranche to the influence of white discipline (through the police and military) or white blood (through interracial sex).[59] Either

way, they countersunk their narratives in the common plank of domestic space as social text.

The stakes of sustaining domestic space as transparent social text become clearer when we realize that challenges to the Ranche–Cottage dualism came not only from Aboriginal people but also from white frontier residents. While interracial sex and marriage might explain signs of civilization found within Tlingit homes, they might just as easily engender new contradictions when white "squaw-men" adopted the domestic habits of their Aboriginal wives. In places remote from white settlement such behaviour could be attributed to the poverty that prevented the men from travelling to find white wives.[60] Such rationalizations were less tenable in busy settlements like Sitka. There, the Russian fur trade had given way to American settlement, and the domestic choices of "squaw-men" became increasingly difficult to reconcile with the standard colonial dualisms of Indian and white, primitive and modern, savage and civilized. Too many white men failed to enact the bourgeois values that middle-class society worked to impress upon Aboriginal people. The narrative power of domestic space could justify the marginalization of men whose race ostensibly should have ensured them a measure of colonial privilege. It could likewise broadcast the price that would-be "squaw-men" faced if they failed to conform to the bourgeois values of the modern settlement frontier.

Non-Aboriginal viewers used Aboriginal domestic spaces as a trope through which to tell themselves stories about themselves. Even when Aboriginal people did not intentionally or willingly place their homes and goods on display, non-Aboriginal viewers sought them out, often penetrating the inner reaches of Aboriginal home life. The contradictions of such a situation run deep. While the forces of colonial society urged Aboriginal people to adopt bourgeois values of privacy and domesticity, they simultaneously transformed Aboriginal homes and private spaces into public spectacles. Even missionaries, who were among the most aggressive proponents of bourgeois domestic values, encouraged the public to view the Aboriginal domestic space of "civilized" Christian converts. The homes of families who became mission success stories were as subject to inquiring eyes as were those who resisted missionary overtures. While missionaries promised that Aboriginal converts could earn equality through outward conformity to colonial, Victorian values, they broke this promise from the very start. Aboriginal homes—whether civilized or uncivilized—were *always* subject to different rules than were non-Aboriginal ones. Voyeurs implicitly judged *all* Aboriginal domestic space as savage when they subjected it to a degree of scrutiny that they would never have tolerated in their own homes. The display of domestic space became not just a story white people told themselves but also a story they told *to* the Aboriginal spectacles.

Aboriginal Stories

Non-Aboriginal viewers were not the only ones who narrated domestic space. They were not the only ones telling stories. While the display of domestic space did not always begin with Aboriginal consent, Aboriginal people invariably took advantage of the situation when they could, catering to tourists' desire for souvenirs and "curios," thus creating added income opportunities for themselves. "Traditional" Aboriginal domestic goods circulated as commodities, the returns from which sometimes allowed the vendors to purchase "modern" domestic goods that tourists would later judge, depending on the context, as either material markers of civilization or laughable markers of pretense.

Aboriginal people did not tell themselves the same stories as non-Aboriginal people told themselves. Aboriginal transformations of domestic spaces, and the adjustments they made to nineteenth-century colonialism, suggest a storyline out of keeping with any straightforward correlation between outward form and inner nature. Sometimes cottage life was literally a facade concealing traditional practices. For residents of Sitka's cottage community, the outer trappings of civilization fit easily over sustained hereditary obligations and practices. Similarly, the Christian homes in Metlakatla, British Columbia, looked, from the street, like workers' cottages. Past the door, however, they opened up into large communal spaces with sleeping areas to the sides, just like the interiors of old longhouses.[61] Sometimes, when the main floors of houses were conjoined (with only the second storey separate), the communal space extended to more than one "house."[62] The model Christian Indians of Metlakatla also refused to relinquish the longhouses they kept at Port Simpson.[63] The outward forms of Christian life at Sitka and Metlakatla distracted missionaries from the continuities of practice and value within cottage walls. Cottage residents could live in accord with Aboriginal values and simultaneously placate missionaries, thus reaping the material and spiritual benefits that accrued to converts.

It seems likely that chiefs mimicked Victorian architecture in order to speak to both colonial and Aboriginal society. When Christian Tsimshian chief Alfred Dudoward built himself a Victorian mansion, he moved in with a large lineage-based group and continued to fulfill his hereditary obligations.[64] His wife, Kate, confused missionary women with her syncretic domestic habits. On one occasion, she concluded a respectable afternoon gathering with a slightly suspect biscuit giveaway. When the white women returned the following day, they watched, shocked, while Kate and other Tsimshian women performed in front of them, "painted and dressed in their skins blankets and other old fixtures," before sending them off with more tea biscuits.[65] Like Dudoward, Musqueam chief Tschymnana built a colonial house; his was in imitation of Colonel Moody's residence. When Bishop George Hills visited the house in 1860, he found the chief's *three* wives at home.[66] These prominent chiefs' houses engaged colonial notions of form and content as well as indicating Aboriginal awareness of colonial scrutiny. They also demonstrate a degree of confidence and flexibility that culture inheres not in the post-and-beam structure itself but in something else: the idea that form can change without foreclosing continuity. Indeed, the forms of these houses may have offered an added measure of prestige within Aboriginal communities.

With the advent of colonialism, high-ranking individuals sought new ways of displaying power and status.[67] Engaging with "modern" colonial culture is one example of this. Shingles, hinged doors, milled lumber, and windows functioned as status symbols.[68] They marked new forms of expression within an age-old system. This hybrid facility extended to domestic goods as well as to structure. Nineteenth-century photographs reveal Aboriginal interiors to be "contents displays" of status items of both Aboriginal and non-Aboriginal origin.[69] These new styles and objects joined older symbols of wealth and power that marked the status of Aboriginal homes and their residents. Crest art painted on house fronts or carved on house posts has long asserted the status and hereditary rights of the inhabitants.[70] A house's size, materials, and position relative to other houses rendered the intravillage hierarchy visible—a pattern dating back over 4,000 years on the Fraser River.[71] The spatial distribution within pre-contact longhouses designated the relative status of the family units within,[72] and, similarly, the styles of pit houses can be correlated to wealth and status.[73] Such examples hint at the contours of Aboriginal narratives of domestic space.

Present Space

Through the twentieth century, agents of colonial policy continued to target Aboriginal homes for transformation. Reserve houses constructed by the Department of Indian Affairs continued in the "cottage" tradition of attempting to reshape Aboriginal domestic life socially as well as architecturally.[74] At the same time, twentieth-century

Stó:lō families who had the means continued to build European-style frame homes that could accommodate the large extended family and community gatherings of Stó:lō social tradition.[75]

The preoccupation with "traditional" Aboriginal domestic space has likewise survived. The "Indian house" has remained the ethnographic artifact par excellence, somehow imbued with an unstated yet assumed ability to speak for Aboriginal culture and history writ large. When the Civilian Conservation Corps of the New Deal looked to define a project in Alaska in the 1930s, it chose, at the urging of the local non-Aboriginal population, to undertake a meticulous and authentic restoration of Chief Shakes's house at Wrangell.[76] Some members of Wrangell's Tlingit population initiated a further restoration of four house posts in 1984.[77] When the Canadian Museum of Civilization designed its Grand Hall, which opened in 1989, it decided to construct a composite Northwest Coast "village" with houses and totem poles from various nations placed side by side, although still in geographical order.[78] The similarity in form with Chicago's "great Aboriginal encampment" is too striking to ignore. However, unlike the world's fair, the Grand Hall intends to celebrate rather than to condemn Northwest Coast culture. The difficult question comes in deciphering the relationship between this colonial form and its postcolonial message. To pose a familiar question: Can new meanings transcend old forms?

Conclusion

More than just an ironic contradiction of private turned public, an analysis of the spectacle of Aboriginal domestic space reveals some underlying colonialist assumptions. The audiences of Aboriginal people living on display defined themselves as modern through a dialectic of stories: stories they told themselves about themselves; stories they told themselves about others; and stories they told others about themselves.

Colonial society presumed that civilization and modernity were as easy to read as an open book. This assumption, although false, shaped myriad interactions. Various groups, Aboriginal and non-Aboriginal alike, have had an interest in the spectacle of Aboriginal domestic life, with money and prestige always at stake. Missionaries' and anthropologists' interests dovetailed in the contrasting displays of uncivilized and civilized domestic spaces. For missionaries, the former demonstrated that reform was needed while the latter demonstrated that it was possible. Anthropologists focused on the former to display the ethnographic strangeness and value of their work and on the latter to establish that such work was urgent because Aboriginal disappearance was imminent. For many other non-Aboriginal members of colonial society, the display of domestic spaces reinforced comfortable stories about themselves and their position in a colonial world. The souvenirs they brought home to their "curio-corners" played a role of their own in bringing middle-class status to Victorian homes.[79]

Aboriginal people also linked domestic and social space to individual and group identity. Traditional elites might manipulate domestic forms to shore up their personal power and status over other Aboriginal people as well as in relation to colonial society. Ambitious nouveaux riches might play with old and new markers of domestic space in their move to climb the social status ladder. It seems certain, however, that Aboriginal people conceived of the connections between domestic space and identity in a radically different manner than did colonizers. The form and content of domestic spaces did not obviously offer the key to the interior of residents' sense of self and community responsibility. The links that existed were not clearly visible to outsiders. Looks could indeed be deceiving, at least for those with colonial eyes.

Colonial society from the nineteenth century through to the present has focused on houses as representative material forms of culture—as culture in practice. And Aboriginal people have consistently inhabited their houses in ways that prove the simplistic nature of this assumption. Still, scholars today continue to find it remarkable that Aboriginal people can proceed with traditional values and practices in "untraditional" contexts. Twentieth-century Tlingit potlatches held in "Western-style buildings" indicate to one writer, for example, that "the presence of proper joinery and other architectural devices that refer to past form, the 'classic building blocks,' are not required for traditional practice."[80] The history of Aboriginal domestic spaces suggests that we should not be taken aback by the realization that the presence of "knowledgeable people" and witnesses from other clans is more important than are the specifics of a particular architectural form.[81]

The endurance of domestic space as a trope for the narration of Aboriginal culture gives rise to many questions. Why has domestic space proven such a powerful symbol? What is it that imbues domestic spaces with the power to shape judgments about inner selves? How did the fixed material forms of houses and household goods come to signify fixity of character and culture? Perhaps we are more prone to naturalize the values and arrangements of domestic spaces because they are the most familiar environments we have. The intimacy with which bourgeois domestic space has been experienced since the Victorian age may set off the alleged strangeness of other ways of living. And perhaps it is the very changelessness of material form that lends itself to rendering accessible the otherwise amorphous concepts of self and culture.

Members of colonial society have been searching for the location of culture since they first arrived on the Northwest Coast. Just when we think we have it cornered, it escapes out the back door. Maybe what these stories of domestic space tell us is that we should begin looking somewhere other than architectural plans.

 More online.

Notes

I wish to acknowledge SSHRC, whose support made this research possible. I would also like to thank Kathy Mezei, who encouraged me to present this as a conference paper and then to write it up as an article; Tina Loo, who offered editorial suggestions; and Jean Barman and Susan Roy, who pointed the way to useful primary sources.

1.   John and Jean Comaroff, *Ethnography and the Historical Imagination* (Boulder, CO: Westview Press, 1992), 293.

2.   Dipesh Chakrabarty, "Postcoloniality and the Artifice of History: Who Speaks for 'Indian' Pasts?" *Representations* 37 (1992): 13.

3.   J.R. Miller, *Sweet Promises: A Reader on Indian–White Relations in Canada* (Toronto, ON: University of Toronto Press, 1991); Frederick E. Hoxie, *A Final Promise: The Campaign to Assimilate the Indians, 1880–1920* (Lincoln, NE: University of Nebraska Press, 1984).

4.   Frederick Cooper and Ann Laura Stoler, eds., *Tensions of Empire* (Berkeley, CA: University of California Press, 1997).

5.   Clifford Geertz, *The Interpretation of Cultures* (New York, NY: Basic Books, 1973), 448.

6.   Robert W. Rydell, *All the World's a Fair: Visions of Empire at American International Expositions, 1876–1916* (Chicago, IL: University of Chicago Press, 1984), 6, 8; E. A. Heaman, *The Inglorious Arts of Peace: Exhibitions in Canadian Society during the Nineteenth Century* (Toronto, ON: University of Toronto Press, 1999), 7.

7.   "The Man Columbus Found," *New York Press*, 28 May 1893, Scrapbook, vol. 2, Frederic Ward Putnam Papers (hereafter FWPP), Harvard University Archives (hereafter HUA).

8.   *The Dream City* (St. Louis, MI: N.D. Thompson Publishing Co., 1893), n.p.

9.   "All Kinds of Indians," *Daily Inter Ocean* (Chicago), 20 June 1893.

10. See, for example, *Daily Inter Ocean* (Chicago), 9 July 1893, Scrapbook, vol. 2, FWPP, HUA.

11. Clipping, 8 February 1893; *Daily Inter Ocean* (Chicago) 9 July 1893; *Pioneer Press* (St. Paul, MN), 15 March 1893, Scrapbook, vol. 2, FWPP, HUA.

12. In a strange wrinkle in the authentic fabric of the fair, the Midway included Sitting Bull's "log cabin." The presence of the log cabin was unusual, as all other Aboriginal performers lived in dwellings that fair organizer's deemed "traditional." Perhaps Sitting Bull's fame imbued the cabin with the necessary aura of authenticity that, in other cases, only a teepee could have offered. Or perhaps the log cabin conveyed a grudging respect for the Sioux chief. *Official Catalogue of Exhibits on the Midway Plaisance* (Chicago, IL: W.B. Conkey Co., 1893), box 38, FWPP, HUA; Gertrude M. Scott, "Village Performance: Villages at the Chicago World's Columbian Exposition, 1893" (Ph.D. dissertation, New York University, 1991), 329–30.

13. Rossiter Johnson, ed., *A History of the World's Columbian Exposition Held in Chicago in 1893* (New York, NY: D. Appleton and Co., 1897), I: 315.

14. See, for example, Antonio, an Apache, to F. W. Putnam, 25 July 1892, box 31, FWPP, HUA; F. W. Putnam to Antonio, 4 August 1892, box 31, FWPP, HUA.

15. For the most complete account of the identities of the Kwakwa̱ka'wakw performers that I have been able to compile, see Paige Raibmon, "Theaters of Contact: The Kwakwa̱ka'wakw Meet Colonialism in British Columbia and at the Chicago World's Fair," *Canadian Historical Review* 81, no. 2 (June 2000): 175.

16. Clipping, July 1893, Scrapbook, vol. 2, FWPP, HUA. Organizers went out of their way to apply this principle to other Aboriginal groups at the fair as well. On the Navajo performers, for example, see F. W. Putnam to Antonio, 4 August 1892, box 31, FWPP, HUA.

17. "Siwashes Again Seek the Street," *Seattle Post-Intelligencer*, 31 May 1904, 9; "Great Influx of Indians," *Seattle Post-Intelligencer*, 10 September 1899, 6; "Indians Returning from Hop Fields," *Seattle Post-Intelligencer* 1 October 1906, 16.

18. J. A. Costello, *The Siwash: Their Life, Legends and Tales, Puget Sound and Pacific Northwest* (Seattle, WA: The Calvert Company, 1895), 165.

19. W. H. Bull, "Indian Hop Pickers on Puget Sound," *Harper's Weekly* 36, 1850 (1892): 546.

20. "Indians Returning from Hop Fields," *Seattle Post-Intelligencer*, 1 October 1906, 16; photo NA–698, Special Collections, University of Washington (UW); Paul Dorpat, *Seattle: Now and Then* (1984), 45; photo NA–897, Special Collections, UW; photo 15,715, Museum of History and Industry, Seattle, Washington (MOHI); "Indian Life on Seattle Streets," *Seattle Post-Intelligencer*, 10 December 1905, 7; "Siwash Village on Tacoma Tide Flats," *Seattle Post-Intelligencer*, 15 April 1907, 20.

21. "Hop Picking," *Washington Standard*, 24 September 1886, 2; *Puyallup Valley Tribune*, 3 October 1903, 6.

22. "A Western Hop Center," *West Shore* 16, 9 (1890): 137–8; "Meadowbrook Hotel Register," Snoqualmie Valley Historical Society, North Bend, Washington.

23. "Picturesque Hop Pickers," *Puyallup Valley Tribune*, 10 September 1904, 1.

24. John Muir, *Steep Trails* (Boston, MA: Houghton Mifflin, 1918), 257.

25. "At the Indian Village," *Puyallup Valley Tribune*, 19 September 1903, 1.

26. Photos 2561 and 6123–N, MOHI; photos NA–1508,

NA–1501, NA–1500, NA–698, NA–680, Special Collections, UW.

27. "Hops in Washington," *Pacific Rural Press*, 3 January 1891.

28. "Indian Life on Seattle Streets," *Seattle Post-Intelligencer*, 10 December 1905, 7; "Siwash Village on Tacoma Tide Flats," *Seattle Post-Intelligencer*, 15 April 1907, 20.

29. Myron Eells, *The Indians of Puget Sound: The Notebooks of Myron Eells*, ed. George Pierre Castile (Seattle, WA: University of Washington Press, 1985), 270.

30. Quoted in George Pierre Castile, "The Indian Connection: Judge James Wickersham and the Indian Shakers," *Pacific Northwest Quarterly* 81, 4 (1990): 126.

31. Cole Harris, *Making Native Space: Colonialism, Resistance, and Reserves in British Columbia* (Vancouver, BC: University of British Columbia Press, 2002), 88, 109, 111.

32. Canada, Department of Indian Affairs, Annual Report, 1886 (Sessional Papers 1887, no. 6), 1x; W. H. Lomas to J. Johnson, Commissioner of Customs, 3 November 1886, Cowichan Agency Letterbook, 1882–7, vol. 1353, RG 10; Bull, "Indian Hop Pickers," 545–6; E. Meliss, "Siwash," *Overland Monthly* 20, 2nd ser. (November 1892): 501–6.

33. Susan Neylan, "Longhouses, Schoolrooms, and Workers' Cottages: Nineteenth-Century Protestant Missions to the Tsimshian and the Transformation of Class through Religion," *Journal of the Canadian Historical Association* 11 (2000): 76.

34. *The Alaskan*, 5 June 1897, 1. See also "Sitka and Its Sights," *The Alaskan*, 7 December 1889, 1.

35. Sophia Cracroft, *Lady Franklin Visits Sitka, Alaska 1870: The Journal of Sophia Cracroft, Sir John Franklin's Niece*, ed. R. N. DeArmond (Anchorage, AK: Alaska Historical Society, 1981), 24.

36. George Bird Grinnell, *Alaska 1899: Essays from the Harriman Expedition* (Seattle, WA: University of Washington Press, 1995), 157.

37. E. Ruhamah Scidmore, *Alaska: Its Southern Coast and the Sitkan Archipelago* (Boston, MA: D. Lothrop and Company, 1885), 176.

38. Ibid.

39. Ibid.

40. Ibid., 177.

41. H. W. Seton Karr, *Shores and Alps of Alaska* (London, UK: Sampson, Low, Marston, Searle and Rivington, 1887), 59.

42. "Journal of a Woman Visitor to Southeast Alaska, ca 1890," fol. 4, box 7, MS4, Alaska State Historical Library (ASHL), 20. See also Anna M. Bugbee, "The Thlinkets of Alaska," *Overland Monthly* 22, 2nd ser. (August 1892), 191.

43. Bugbee, "The Thlinkets of Alaska," 191; "Journal of a Woman Visitor," 20.

44. Scidmore, *Alaska: Its Southern Coast*, 176; "Journal of a Woman Visitor," 20; Bugbee, "The Thlinkets of Alaska," 191; *New York Times*, 3 October 1886. Quoted in Frederica de Laguna, *Under Mount Saint Elias: The History and Culture of the Yakutat Tlingit* (Washington, DC: Smithsonian Institution Press, 1972), 191.

45. *The Alaskan*, 23 January 1891, 4. See also "A Visit to the Cottages," *The Alaskan*, 30 October 1897, 2.

46. Brady to Rev. J. Gould, 30 December 1905, J. G. Brady, *Letters Sent*, vol. 9, November 1905–May 1906, files of the Alaska Territorial Governors, roll 7, microcopy T–1200, National Archives Microfilm, AR25, ASHL.

47. "The Orthodox Indian Temperance," *The Alaskan*, 10 July 1897, 1.

48. J. Converse to W. H. Miller, 30 August 1888, Sheldon Jackson Correspondence, reel 97–638, Sheldon Jackson Stratton Library.

49. J. Converse to W. H. Miller, 25 July 1888, Sheldon Jackson Correspondence, reel 97–638, Sheldon Jackson Stratton Library.

50. B. K. Wilbur, "The Model Cottages," *The North Star* 6, 8 (1895): 1.

51. Ibid.

52. Dazie M. Brown Stromstadt, *Sitka, The Beautiful* (Seattle, WA: Homer M. Hill Publishing Co., 1906), 9. See also *The North Star* 5, 8 (August 1892) in *The North Star: The Complete Issues*, 228.

53. Stromstadt, *Sitka, the Beautiful*, 9.

54. "President's Message," *The Alaskan*, 9 December 1905, 3; Bertand K. Wilbur, "Just about Me," box IB, no. 8, MS4, ASHL, 220–1.

55. Wilbur, "Just about Me," 220–1; J. G. Brady to Geo. C. Heard, Attorney at Law, Juneau, 19 June 1905, fol. 86, box 5, John G. Brady Papers, Beinecke Library, Yale University.

56. For examples, see Rudolph Walton, "Diaries," 1900–4, 1910, 1919. Private possession of Joyce Walton Shales.

57. *The North Star*, 6, 1 (1895): 1.

58. Wilbur, "The Model Cottages," 1.

59. Scidmore, *Alaska: Its Southern Coast*, 175; "Journal of a Woman Visitor," 24; E. Ruhamah Scidmore, *Appleton's Guide-Book to Alaska and the Northwest Coast* (New York, NY: D. Appleton and Co., 1896 [1893]), 120; Francis C. Sessions, *From Yellowstone Park to Alaska* (New York, NY: Welch, Fracker Co., 1890), 92; Wilbur, "Just about Me," 221.

60. *The Alaskan*, 5 August 1893, 2.

61. Neylan, "Longhouses, Schoolrooms, and Workers' Cottages," 81.

62. Ibid.

63. Ibid., 82.

64. Ibid.

65. 28 and 29 January 1884, Kate Hendry, Letterbook, 1882–9, EC/H38, British Columbia Archives.

66. Roberta L. Bagshaw, ed., *No Better Land: The 1860 Diaries of Anglican Colonial Bishop George Hills* (Victoria, BC: Sono Nis Press, 1996), 75. Even allowing for the distinct possibility that Hills misinterpreted the exact nature of the relationship between the women and the chief, this domestic space clearly housed an extended rather than a nuclear family.

67. Judith Ostrowitz, *Privileging the Past: Reconstructing History in Northwest Coast Art* (Vancouver, BC: University of British Columbia Press, 1999), 31.

68. Neylan, "Longhouses, Schoolrooms, and Workers' Cottages," 79–80; Ostrowitz, *Privileging the Past*, 32.

69. Ostrowitz, *Privileging the Past*, 30. See also Tony Bennett, "The Exhibitionary Complex," in David Boswell and Jessica Evans, eds., *Representing the Nation: A Reader* (London, UK: Routledge, 1999), 333.

70. Neylan, "Longhouses, Schoolrooms, and Workers' Cottages," 79; Ostrowitz, *Privileging the Past*, 9.

71. Keith Thor Carlson, ed., *A Coast Salish Historical Atlas* (Vancouver, BC: Douglas & McIntyre, 2001), 36, 41.

72. Ibid., 43.

73. Ibid., 46.

74. Ibid., 44.

75. Ibid., 43, 45.

76. Ostrowitz, *Privileging the Past*, 33–9.

77. Ibid., 39–43.

78. Ibid., 51.

79. As one writer put it, "every well-appointed house might appropriately arrange an Indian corner." George Wharton James, "Indian Basketry in House Decoration," *Chautauquan* (1901): 620. See also Lloyd W. MacDowell, *Alaska Indian Basketry* (Seattle, WA: Alaska Steamship Company, 1906).

80. Ostrowitz, *Privileging the Past*, 39.

81. Ibid.

4 Swatting Flies for Health
Children and Tuberculosis in Early Twentieth-Century Montreal

Valerie Minnett and Mary Anne Poutanen[1]

Introduction

Responding to an appeal by city physicians and sanatoria to destroy a prodigious disease carrier, the housefly, the *Montreal Daily Star* launched an island-wide contest in July 1912, offering $350 in prizes to children who collected the most dead flies. First prize was $25, a princely sum for most households. Nearly a thousand children, largely from working-class families, participated in the three-week-long "Swat the Fly" competition. As sponsor, the newspaper diligently covered the event, publishing participants' photographs, keeping running tabs of the amounts collected, reminding contestants that there were "Lots of Flies So Do Not Get Discouraged,"[2] and providing instructions on the most efficient method to hunt flies with traps and fly swatters. Altogether, Montreal children collected more than 25 million flies. The *Star* was self-congratulatory; not only had Montreal contestants "learned a valuable lesson in hygiene" but they handily trounced 30 other North American cities that offered similar contests. Children elsewhere, it would seem, did not have the same exuberance for fly swatting; in Toronto, they managed to kill fewer than 1.5 million flies; in Washington, 7 million.[3] But then, no other city on the continent had been referred to as the "Calcutta of the West."

Montreal had an abysmal infant mortality rate as well as an extraordinary level of childhood morbidity and mortality owing to infectious diseases such as tuberculosis. Engaging children in anti-tuberculosis campaigns with contests such as "Swat the Fly" underscores a popular idea at the time that the best way to improve public health and combat the ignorance of a generation was to arm a new one with knowledge. "Children have no prejudices," a member of the Publication Committee of the Montreal League for the Prevention of Tuberculosis asserted, "and remember the hygienic training received in their youth all their life."[4] While historians recognize that children's participation in campaigns to promote public health measures was pivotal to their success,[5] youngsters are often rendered as passive recipients of reformers' travails. Historian Robert McIntosh reminds us that the history of children "is the account of action undertaken by others to improve their condition. Implicitly, children are impotent; their welfare is the object of others' efforts. They are mere victims of history."[6] We argue that children were active agents in these campaigns both as consumers and as advocates.

Citation: Valerie Minnett and Mary Anne Poutanen, "Swatting Flies for Health: Children and Tuberculosis in Early Twentieth-Century Montreal," *Urban History Review* 36, no. 1 (Fall 2007): 32–44, 60.

By deconstructing children's contests associated with the housefly and the environment that spawned them, we highlight their agency.

. . .

This study begins in the first decades of the twentieth century when public health reformers became increasingly convinced that the housefly was a conduit for spreading diseases such as typhoid fever, infant diarrhea, and tuberculosis. This preoccupation with the *Musca domestica* resulted in a flurry of literature warning the public of its dangers and contests that encouraged its destruction as well as the eradication of environmental factors that engendered the fly's proliferation. Notwithstanding the white plague's threat to the urban population, public health authorities constructed a link between the housefly and the dissemination of the *tubercle bacillus*, based on selective scientific evidence. The vilification of the housefly had, according to Naomi Rogers, occurred by the turn of the twentieth century and was an important part of the shift from the practice of sanitary science to the New Public Health. While the public readily associated the presence of filth and garbage with disease, it was more difficult for reformers to "show" people that microscopic germs were to blame for spreading infection. Rogers argues that scientists transformed the fly from a familiar plaything, an insect of beauty and grace, and at worst a pest, to "germs with legs," in order to perpetuate acceptance and understanding of the germ theory of disease.[7] The flight of the odious fly explained how invisible microbes travelled and spread infection, . . . but also alerted the public that personal action and vigilance, such as fly swatting and screening windows, was necessary to stem the flow of disease. This fetish with the disease-spreading capacity of the housefly lasted nearly three decades.

To investigate the role that Montreal children played in public health campaigns, we consider the visual culture of contests in conjunction with textual historical sources. Information gleaned from photographs, maps, posters, and drawings complement data collected from the city's Catholic and Protestant school board archives, the municipal health board, annual reports of anti-tuberculosis groups and health-care facilities, and public health journals. Equally important is the media coverage of Montreal contests. We consulted both French-language and English-language newspapers of the period.

Tuberculosis in Montreal

By the turn of the twentieth century, Canada's largest urban centre was the most unhealthy city in North America. Montreal's tuberculosis rates were reportedly the highest on the continent and caused more deaths than all other contagious diseases combined and second only to infant diarrhea.[8] Class and ethnicity played a critical role in determining who would most likely become tubercular. Since the vast majority of francophone Montrealers, who represented nearly two-thirds of the city's population, were concentrated in the lowest-paid factory jobs and occupied the most unhealthy neighbourhoods, they were more susceptible to tuberculosis than their anglophone and Jewish counterparts who made up 25 per cent and 10 per cent of the population respectively.[9] Yearly statistics published by the municipal health department consistently recorded the highest rates of infection among French Canadians of all ages. For example, in 1911, 489 francophone Montrealers died of consumption, compared to 72 anglophones, and 12 from the city's Jewish community.[10] Two years earlier, childhood tuberculosis accounted for 135.1/1,000 deaths of children between 5 and 14 years of age, and for those above the age of 14, the number of deaths increased more than threefold (446.2/1,000 deaths of ages 15 to 24).[11] These statistics were likely underrepresented; many of the children dying from pneumonia, meningitis, peritonitis, or sequelae of childhood diseases such as measles and whooping cough may have had tuberculosis. Moreover, public health workers were unaware how widespread childhood consumption was, since the disease affected joints, bones, and glands more than lungs. Nonpulmonary tuberculosis was often transmitted to children in milk and meat that had been infected with bovine tuberculosis.

Living in Working-Class Wards

The city's working-class environments were characterized by widespread filth, ineffective public infrastructure, inadequate green space, and wretched living conditions associated with rampant poverty. Industrial workers and their families lived in these insalubrious neighbourhoods to be within walking distance of their jobs. As early as 1897, Herbert Ames,[12] in his well-known sociological study of Montreal *The City below the Hill,* drew public attention to the fact that the working class largely inhabited overcrowded and polluted wards located in the shadow of Mount Royal. By contrast, the Golden Square Mile, which lay upon the slopes, was home to some of Canada's richest industrialists and businessmen. Largely an Anglo-Protestant enclave, its inhabitants lived in mansions or grey stone townhouses with spacious gardens, on wide streets, far above the factories they owned and the homes of the working class who laboured in them.

Ames reported that the death rates in the wards below the hill were double the city's average and in certain areas equalled the birth rate.[13] Infant mortality rates were especially high, owing to the prevalence of untreated water and unpasteurized milk, and tuberculosis was rampant, a result of widespread poverty and living in too close proximity. Municipal inspectors identified common defects in many residential buildings: dirty, damp, and smelly houses; filthy and inadequately drained backyards; and overflowing privies.[14] These homes of labouring families, characterized by poor ventilation and dark rooms, became a lightning rod for reformers such as Dr. Elzéar Pelletier, secretary of the Quebec Provincial Board of Health. His 1908 essay, "Our

Unhealthy Dwellings," drew attention to the dismal household conditions that many of the city's residents were forced to inhabit. Pelletier noted that rooms "without any windows opening into the external air" were ubiquitous in these wards.[15] Inadequate airflow was understood to be a significant risk to good health. Without continual aeration, tuberculosis and other contagious diseases were thought to breed and multiply at will. A 1911 study published by the Royal Edward Institute echoed these concerns: 60 per cent of those who sought treatment for pulmonary tuberculosis came from homes with medium to bad ventilation. Reformers argued that tenants, ignorant of basic principles of hygiene, willingly occupied these buildings, and that landlords' greed surpassed any guilt aroused by letting tenants live in these unhealthy circumstances.[16] In reality, such abysmal conditions reflected the narrow range of choices available to industrial workers who sought affordable rentals close to sites of employment. It also spoke to the need for and implementation of hygienic building codes, in addition to better enforcement of those measures that were already in place.

These popular wards, or "hives of sickness,"[17] comprised both tenements and factories, in addition to dirty, dusty streets and laneways. The stench of sewage, manure boxes, overflowing garbage receptacles, offal, and decomposing dead animals mingled with the smoke and effluvium emanating from nearby factories. More than half of the households were not equipped with indoor plumbing and depended upon an outdoor privy as the sole means to dispose of human waste. Herbert Ames referred to the pits as "insanitary abominations" and "a danger to the public health and good morals."[18] Flies fed and laid eggs at these insalubrious sites. Ames's dogged but successful eight-year campaign to rid the city of outdoor privies earned him the moniker "Water Closet Ames."[19] By the end of 1916, most of the privies in working-class wards situated "below the hill" had been eliminated. The majority of those still in existence—officially 1,315—were reported in areas that had been annexed by Montreal's municipal government.[20] As an example Rosemont had 250 reported privy pits.[21] Located in the east end of the city, bordering the northern-most limits of Hochelaga and Maisonneuve, Rosemont's sizable territory had hardly been touched by urbanization, thus likely accounting for the high number of reported outhouses. Only Rosemont's southern section had been developed before World War I for the workers who laboured in the Angus Yards, its largest employer. Flies were also drawn to the piles of manure produced in the city's livery stables and in the much more numerous horse stables maintained by carters and milkmen at their places of residence. Before the interwar period, horse-drawn carts were a common feature of Montreal streets. The average city horse in the early twentieth century produced 10 kilograms of manure a day; the horse dung left lying in city streets became another vector where flies bred and subsequently spread disease. Some scientists posited that an effective method to eradicate the disease-carrying housefly was to rid American cities of horses.[22] While Montreal health officials did not advocate an end to horsepower, they sought improved street cleaning and more rigorous inspection of work sites, schools, milk, meat, and housing to ensure a healthier urban environment.

Reformers and Public Health

Public education was thought to be an effective and inexpensive way to contain and prevent disease. William Osler's well-known maxim that [tuberculosis] is a social disease with a medical aspect embodied the attitude of social reformers in this period.[23] It also reflected a public health morality, which posited that the working class had to take responsibility to guard itself, families, and neighbours against infection.[24] By eradicating the unhealthy habits of an uneducated working class, middle-class reformers, influenced by both the social gospel and Catholic social action, believed that it would renew society through healthy living practices.[25]

The 1910 report of the Royal Commission on Tuberculosis had much to say about childhood consumption, and suggested that school inspections, hygiene instruction in schools, open-air schools, legislation against child employment, and inspection of meat and milk would help to prevent tuberculosis. Campaigns for clean water, pasteurized milk, and compulsory immunization, the establishment of fresh-air camps for inner-city children, public health nurses to visit the homes of the working poor to promote children's health, and the construction of children's hospitals also occupied reformers. In the inter-war period, urban reformers recognized that healthy children were a nation's asset, when substantial numbers of working-class men were rejected from combat during World War I on the basis of chronic poor health. Montreal's health department responded by establishing a separate division of child hygiene in 1918. Public health crusaders and medical authorities demanded that the provincial government force municipalities to institute preventive measures to control disease, believing that it was the responsibility of the Quebec Board of Health to improve the city's dismal public health. Quebec City refused to finance public health, leaving it to municipalities—usually private charities and other organizations—to raise the necessary funds to enact programs.[26] This neglect was problematic, especially in the case of tuberculosis. Despite its high mortality rates, lack of a cure, and the recommendations of the 1909–10 Royal Commission on Tuberculosis, the state remained impassive about financing a network of badly needed clinics, preventoria, and sanatoria,[27] or even ensuring that Montreal's milk supply was safe.

. . .

Children's sites of play in working-class neighbourhoods also came under reformers' scrutiny. The parks and playground movement, modelled on American efforts to create wholesome spaces within the city, found recruits in Montreal as the streets, back alleys, and courtyards where children played became more

Figure 1. *"A human rookery." Bulletin Sanitair* 12, 1–13 (1912): 80.

visible. The emphasis on appropriate sites of play coincided with a vigorous campaign to promote child welfare, culminating in the 1912 Child Welfare Exhibition. A chief concern among philanthropists and reformers involved in this endeavour was the housing conditions of the working class, as described above. Photographs played a critical role in promoting reformers' points of view and exemplified the social documentary style that pervaded reform efforts during the late nineteenth and early twentieth centuries.[28] Historian James Opp has argued that urban reformers and proponents of the social gospel used this mode of photography as a strategy to draw viewers' attention away from the bodies, often children, posing in the images to the urban environment. This strategy, to illustrate spatial dominance, was an effective means to both highlight middle-class anxieties and deliver

persuasive messages about the moral and physical decay of urban life.[29] The photograph entitled "A Human Rookery" (Figure 1) was displayed in both the 1908 Montreal Tuberculosis Exhibition and the 1912 Child Welfare Exhibition. The image is an example of the social documentary method, complete with its own title, and reveals the squalid and filthy conditions under which many working-class Montreal families lived and children played. This site lacked adequate access to sunlight, fresh air, and green space. The eight small children are engulfed, even enslaved, by their surroundings; the photograph renders them victims of their environment. Those in the upper left-hand corner of the image are barely distinguishable from the structural entanglement that surrounds them. This photograph, and others like it, delivered a forceful message that rates of tuberculosis were substantially higher in these spaces and that affirmative action was needed to rectify the situation.

Children were encouraged to exert control over aspects of their environment by swatting flies to reduce the spread of disease and by cleaning up their homes, yards, courtyards, alleys, and neighbourhoods to instill a sense of responsibility and civic pride. Moreover, motivating youngsters to assume this kind of leadership situated them as active participants in the anti-tuberculosis public health strategies that urban reformers promulgated.

Flies and Public Health

When the *Montreal Daily Star* proposed a fly contest for children, it was responding to the widely held belief among entomologists, physicians, and educators that the *Musca domestica* played a significant role in transmitting diseases such as typhoid fever and even tuberculosis.[30] The *Montreal Daily Star*'s sister newspaper, the *Toronto Daily Star*, reported, "Tuberculosis . . . is carried by the pesky fly. The fly that alights on you everywhere you go may be carrying germs of this disease. The bulk of the germs of tuberculosis are carried directly from the sputum of tubercular people."[31] Scientists postulated that the insect spread tuberculosis by ingesting the *tubercle bacillus* from infected sputum "with the greatest avidity"[32] or from feces and then regurgitating or defecating the micro-organism onto food, milk containers, baby bottles, or pacifiers. Others asserted that the fly wreaked public health havoc when it landed on food with its bacteria-laden hairy legs, feet, and body.[33]

If that was not enough to convince *Star* readers of the fly's threat to society and the expeditious need to go to war with the insect, New York physician Woods Hutchison equated the fly with moral as well as physical danger: "[A] fly in a house is as dangerous as a rattlesnake, as filthy as a louse, and as disgraceful as a bedbug."[34] And flies were everywhere. Professor Hodge, of Clarke University, Worcester, Massachusetts, calculated

that a pair of flies that began to breed in May would produce 143,675 bushels of offspring in just four months.[35] In light of the growing alarm over the housefly's penchant for transmitting infectious diseases to an unsuspecting citizenry, the Montreal health department asked that the medical health officer report on "the best method of exterminating flies."[36] Citing the lessons learned at the Panama Canal—to reduce the incidents of malaria and yellow fever it was imperative to remove the sources where mosquitoes bred—he recommended that the city cover garbage cans and interest schoolchildren "in the work of destroying flies . . . and they should be encouraged by being supplied free with those special brushes invented for the purpose."[37] Across Canada and the United States, children's anti-fly campaigns received kudos from urban reformers, municipal health authorities, and physicians. . . . In Toronto, tuberculosis and typhoid specialist Dr. Hanley of the Toronto General Hospital wholeheartedly backed a "Swat the Fly" contest. Ridding the world of flies, he claimed, would make it easier to eliminate typhoid fever and tuberculosis: "In the case of tubercular sores or septic conditions, the possibility of flies lighting upon such spots is obvious. Imagine what it would be if we allowed flies free ingress to the hospitals. They would spread disease all over the city."[38] And in Montreal, hygiene expert Dr. T. A. Starkey supported such an initiative: "I consider that there is plenty of room for an educational campaign among the children. So far as I know nothing definite has yet been done in the schools in this direction. If teachers made a point of impressing upon their pupils the danger of the fly to the community, and the best means of preventing and exterminating the pest, I am sure a vast amount of good would soon result."[39]

Given Montreal's high infant mortality rate, reformers understood that children needed to learn about the threat of the housefly not only to their own health but to the health of family members, especially baby sisters and brothers.[40] The housefly appeared in public health campaigns, often playing a feature role in "moving pictures." University Settlement, for example, organized 30 public health instruction sessions in green spaces across the city during the summer of 1912. Children watched health films about milk, tuberculosis, and the dangers associated with the fly in Parc Lafontaine, Fletcher's Field, Dufferin Square, Haymarket Square, and Hibernia Road.[41] The head worker of University Settlement, Miss E. Helm, publicly supported the "Swat the Fly" contest, which ran concurrently with the film series. The housefly also made an appearance at the Child Welfare Exhibition, which opened just a few months after the *Star* contest. Pauline Witherspoon, an organizer of the event, described its appearance in one of the exhibition's films: "[It] shows a place from which the fly comes—a manure heap, a garbage heap, or a heap of rotting fish—and afterwards its journey to a house and its subsequent attentions to the food are depicted in the most marvellous and instructive fashion."[42] Similar disturbing images of the fly travelling from garbage pile or dung heap to supposedly hygienic sites was published in both the *Montreal Daily Star* and the provincial health journal, the *Bulletin Sanitaire*. The tryptic . . . pictured the pesky fly alighting on a pile of discarded fish heads, then stopping for a break atop an infant's pacifier. The last movement in this visual composition shows the baby sucking its soother, blissfully unaware of the disease and filth with which it had been contaminated.[43] The face of the contented baby exemplified the hidden dangers of the fly, its role in cross-contamination, and revealed the unseen hygienic transgressions that just one insect could perpetrate. This image surely rallied support for war against the "loathsome" insect.

"Swat the Fly" Contest

Any child under 17 years of age and living on the island of Montreal was eligible to participate in the fly competition; French-speaking children were disadvantaged because "Swat the Fly" was promoted by an English-language newspaper.

With respect to gender, it was an equal opportunity contest. The sponsor put forward that boys and girls were every bit as skilled in fly catching and would receive the same number of prizes of the same value. To sustain enthusiasm, additional prizes were awarded biweekly, and contestants were repeatedly reminded in newspaper accounts that waging war on houseflies was saving the lives of babies and young children—indeed brothers and sisters—and even a patriotic act. Local stores distributed fly swatters to contestants free of charge. The newspaper offered to pay the public transportation costs of any contestant who brought in 500 or more flies. Despite these compelling incentives, children decided not only to participate but how long they would do so. The obvious enjoyment of a contest, the prizes, and the public attention they received notwithstanding, such a three-week contest required discipline and sustained activity to win. One of the newspaper articles noted that some children were "too busy catching flies" to collect their prizes. Courtland Auburn's mother went to the *Star* offices on her son's behalf, telling reporters that "he's at it all day, and says he hasn't a moment to spare, even to fetch his prize."[44] By contrast, the 1908 Tuberculosis Exhibition essay-writing contest, which also included monetary prizes, attracted approximately 325 children.

"Swat the Fly" participants transported their treasure trove of dead flies in pails, jars, boxes, and cans to the newspaper's office, where they were carefully weighed and tabulated by special *Star* staff. . . . Curiously, the *Star* encouraged children's increased contact with the housefly at the same time that it raised the dangers of the insect to the health of youngsters. The irony of the situation was not lost on public health officials of London, Ontario, who complained that fly contests put children's health at risk.[45] Local health authorities rejected these concerns. When M. H. McCrady of the Chemical Department of the Provincial Board of Health was asked to respond to the criticism he stated, "I don't think there is anything in it . . . I have never heard of any danger to the children engaged in the campaign being alleged by any authority on the subject." McCrady went on to say, "Children in hunting flies are very unlikely to go to the places where the flies are most dangerous—that is where there are faecal discharges . . . In Montreal there is no need for the children to go far afield to catch their flies."[46] The abundance of these insects meant that even toddlers could join in the contest without leaving home. Two-year-old Augustina Parsons brought in over 9,000 flies to the *Star* office. Her comments to *Star* reporters confirm that children indeed were in close contact with the "pests." The tot complained that she "'tan't tatch' any more, as her 'tingles' are sore."[47] Perhaps responding to the publicity, the prizes, or prompting from peers and family, but in the midst of the summer school break with no school authorities to encourage their participation, working-class children were abuzz about the contest.

Figure 2[48] reveals that most of Montreal's juvenile fly swatters lived in inner-city wards such as Pointe-Ste-Charles, on or near Boulevard St-Laurent, also known as the Main, or in working-class suburbs such as Verdun. An analysis of the contestants' addresses (which the *Star* published) provides clues as to the demographic characteristics of participants. As the map shows, contestants came from predominately blue-collar families (determined by the medium grey denoting household rents of between $61 and $100 per annum) and that friends in the same neighbourhoods entered the contest together (symbolized by the clusters of black triangles). As an example, David Devine of Hermine Street had been appointed the president and director of a "fly trust" that he and friends had established.[49] By contrast, children from households paying the lowest rents (represented by the dark grey indicating rents less than $60 a year) usually did not participate in the contest. Extreme poverty

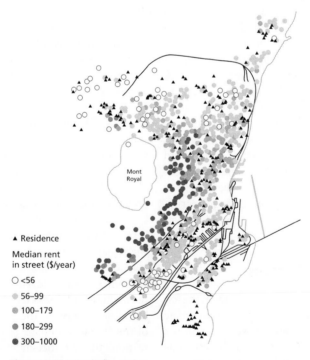

Figure 2. Montreal's fly catchers.

and limited contact with local newspapers meant that they were disadvantaged. Similarly, middle-class children often passed the summer in the countryside and inhabited more wholesome neighbourhoods (indicated by the light grey).

Youngsters from working-class homes, on the other hand, could finally benefit from the mounds of horse manure, heaps of rotting garbage, decomposing dead animals, unfenced wastelands, and outdoor privies in their locality, which spawned flies by the thousands. The contest's winner, eight-year-old Eddie Kavanagh, took advantage of the proximity of his family's shed to one such site to trap flies. He enticed nearly 1.5 million of them into the shed by a window that opened onto the Boyer Street garbage dump. Others used traps, fly swatters, even their own hands to kill flies at local stables, abattoirs, fish shops, bakeries, and restaurants. Two young girls decided that neighbourhood restaurants furnished the best hunting grounds: "We go into the restaurants, one said, and they let us catch all their flies. We got just heaps of them and the people are glad for us to help them. Flies are horrid, buzzing around on your food and we may always go in and catch all we want."[50] Home was another. Neighbours allowed Ethel Reyes of Verdun to catch flies in their homes: "The kitchen is the best place and tea-time keeps us busy, for they all seem to love the butter and bread and jam."[51] All agreed—contestants, sponsor, and supporters—that with fewer flies at home, it made eating and sleeping easier

City Clean-Up Competitions

The relationship between Montreal's dirty environment—as a breeding ground for both germs and insects—and children's compromised health was not lost on reformers. Thus, the "Swat the Fly" contest was part of a larger local strategy aimed at not only killing houseflies but preventing their spawning by cleaning up the environment. The same year that the *Montreal Star* hosted the fly contest, the City Improvement

League established a Clean-Up Day; the following year, it had been transformed into an annual Clean-Up Week, usually held the beginning of May when Montrealers traditionally moved households. The housefly once again played an important role; it topped a list of insects that necessitated extermination:

> Science proved conclusively that the common, ordinary fly, in summer time, was even more dangerous, as it carried in its poisoned fangs the deadly germs of typhoid fever, consumption and other intestinal diseases. To destroy this deadly foe is the greatest civic duty one can accomplish. If there were no more dirty breeding pools, no more pestilential garbage, no more flies, there would be no more epidemic to decimate our homes and the whole of mankind.[52]

. . . The city's health department welcomed the anti-fly campaign associated with Clean-Up Week and encouraged Montrealers to wage war all year round: "Swat the Fly, even in winter. The cold weather will not kill it but will simply numb it and it will awaken in the spring and continue to multiply itself by millions."[53]

In 1915, Clean-Up Week organizers distributed 50,000 pamphlets, "Health First," to city homes, developed an education program and pledge campaign, and designed a home-garden competition. The City Improvement Campaign Committee also coordinated a series of meetings with youngsters in mind. It promoted public and personal hygiene through lantern slides, lectures, and film: "In order to vary the interest, moving pictures of a general character were shown together with those of educational value, and in this manner the minds of the children were improved in a way, calculated to have a permanent effect."[54] To enlist the support of students, health authorities encouraged elementary and secondary school teachers to make Clean-Up Week the theme of short lectures and to emphasize the co-operative spirit of such an endeavour. Its message was that cleanliness not only "begets health" but "makes life worthwhile even with the poor."[55] At the urging of both Protestant and Catholic school boards, 3,000 children entered the home-garden competition, making them eligible to win $1,250 in prizes. Figure 3 is a promotional poster used by the committee in its campaign. *Les écoliers* or students are among the helping hands that grasp the handle of the great broom that was to sweep the city clean.[56] By including children on this public flyer or poster, members of the Civic Improvement League made a direct appeal to Montreal youngsters to take responsibility for their city's public health.[57]

To compete in the contest, participants filled out pledge cards promising to clean up their neighbourhoods, plant flowers, keep gardens and maintain lawns, refrain from littering, vandalizing property, or spitting, encourage others to keep Montreal clean, protect animals and birds, and be a loyal citizen.[58] The City Improvement League divided Montreal into five districts, each of which would distribute prizes amounting to $250. The grand prize was $25. The committee planned two contests: The first one ran from the beginning of May to the end of June; the second one focused on contestants who could keep up their efforts until the end of summer. Participants were awarded points for tidy back and front yards, painted house exteriors, vegetable and flower gardens, and the overall appearance of buildings. Children who lived in houses without yards earned extra points if they placed flower boxes and hanging baskets in and around their dwellings.[59]

During World War I, the home-garden competition had much broader implications. By awarding prizes for the cultivation of vacant lots or backyards, the committee tied its

Figure 3. "Clean up, Nettoyons!" *The Montreal Clean-up Campaigns 1912–1916* (Montreal: City Improvement Campaign Committee, 1916).

clean-up campaign to the war effort being mobilized in Protestant schools and communities on the island and elsewhere.[60] Montreal's children were transformed into soldiers of dust, dirt, and disease:

> Some are called upon to fight with the usual arms of war, but others can only help by using other weapons: the plough, the hoe and the spade to cultivate every inch of soil for food for ourselves and our brave allies; the broom, the mop, the paint pot and the water pail and their good strong arms to wage the war against Dust, Dirt and Disease, the enemies which menace the Health of the Community and impair its strength.[61]

The campaign tapped into the patriotic fervour of the city's English-speaking population by linking civic pride to citizenship and effectively contrasting its war effort with French Canadian ambivalence about the war.

Since planting vegetables and flowers entailed some expense, the Health Committee of the Local Council of Women distributed seeds to impoverished children attending public schools. Nonetheless, the committee's obvious middle-class standard of environmental cleanliness must have made the task for working-class children daunting, given that their neighbourhoods were characterized by a lack of gardens and lawns and by dense and dilapidated housing. Moreover, these "city beautiful" contests had limited effect in most working-class wards. Health authorities, for example, reported that the 1914 Clean-Up Week provided a "clean city at least for some weeks."[62]

Children's Contribution to Anti-Fly Campaigns

Children's involvement in public health campaigns were explicit, as members of the Junior Red Cross with its authoritative motto, "I Serve," and implicit, as role models in the fly contest.

Referred to in the *Montreal Daily Star* as "a great awakening," the "Swat the Fly" contest provided an important example of what could be accomplished for only $350 in prizes and donations from local businesses without disturbing the status quo. The fervour with which Montreal children embraced the contest, their success in killing over 25 million flies, and their subsequent coronation as North American (even world) champions impressed the *Star*:

> They can walk about with their heads in the air and their prizes in their pockets, and when they are grown up and have children of their own, they can tell them of the great anti-fly crusade and of all the ways in which they rid the city of the pests. It would be twice as interesting as the story of the Pied Piper of Hamelin and the rats![63]

It must have fascinated onlookers as well. Children's frenzied participation provided compelling role models for adult observers and is exemplified by contestants such as Harold Brookwell: "I caught nearly all of them in my daddy's abattoir, he said, and once I caught 47 flies with one swat. I counted them just for fun. I catch them in buckets with some molasses smeared inside, and heaps I've swatted in the house and of course in the abattoir, and some I got in cages of wire netting."[64] Courtland Auburn of Liverpool Street was too busy hunting flies to pick up a special prize he had won, and Christopher Mair of Verdun was too ill. Having to undergo an emergency appendectomy, he gave his flies to his older brother Stephen, who recounted the dramatic events to a *Star* journalist: "And just as he was being taken along the passage to the operation, he said, tell Stephen that he can go on catching flies for me till I come out. He seemed to think more of the magic lantern he had won, and the fly competition than being cut with a knife."[65] Contestants reminded adults that flies bred in proportion to the amount of filth and garbage deposited in city streets, back alleys, and in public buildings, and they conveyed disease from these sites to the food that Montrealers consumed. In a flurry of newspaper articles and letters to the *Star* editor during the fly contest, writers insisted that to prevent this contamination, shopkeepers screen food from flies and that the municipal government rigorously enforce regulations, institute a better system of garbage collection and drainage around local stables, and prohibit privy pits. In this way, youngsters served as active agents in anti-fly health campaigns.

. . . The crusade against the housefly persisted until well into the 1920s.[66] The Canadian Red Cross and Junior Red Cross presented the fly as an impediment to good health, and appealed directly to children to help stop its menace. A "Health Alphabet" published in the November 1927 issue of *The Canadian Red Cross Junior* reminded youngsters that

K means to Kill
Every fly with a swat,
For living, they're dangerous;
Dead, they are not.[67]

Members of the Junior Red Cross in Montreal also spread the message that the insect was most pestilent by staging a play, titled "The Land of the Lollypop." One of the main characters in the drama was Jack, the Fly Killer. Brandishing a fly swatter, this palace guard's chief task was to keep flies (which he describes as a mortal enemy) away from the king. In the 1920s, the exploits of flies were depicted in the *Canadian Red Cross* magazine in very graphic detail:

After walking on filth, corruption and, as likely as not, infection; does he manicure? Not a bit of it. With feet clogged with foulness, he is seen on the spoons, on the forks, on the butter, the sugar, the rim of the drinking vessel, the meat, the edge of the milk pitcher. And be sure that as muddy boots will leave a track across a crimson Persian carpet so the fly will leave his tracks on everything he touches.[68]

. . . Children were urged to take an active role in eliminating house flies by setting traps and then killing those they caught with boiling water or burning sulphur. Fly swatting was also advocated as an effective method of their destruction. The article, perhaps drawing on the success of earlier campaigns, claimed that "boys and girls can do a great deal to control the fly nuisance by swatting every fly they can find . . . 'Swat the Fly' is an excellent motto."[69] In the 1930s, Walt Disney included the same "Swat the Fly" message in one of his animated shorts. The 1938 Disney rendition of the Grimm Brothers classic tale "The Brave Little Tailor" has Mickey Mouse going head to head with the pest, killing "Seven with one blow!"[70]

Children played an important and essential function in spreading health propaganda among their peers, in their communities, and at home. Their role as ambassadors of public health was not without conflict. In light of widespread poverty and the lacklustre performance of city hall when it came to improving Montreal's infrastructure, tensions between children advocating anti-tuberculosis measures and their parents who could do little to ameliorate the family's living conditions must have risen. Thus, the process of imbuing children with health standards that could not be met at home gave messages that contradicted those of many parents, created stress, and left children, according to historian Mona Gleason, both empowered and frightened.[71]

Conclusion

Reformers identified the fly as a serious impediment to the public's health at the same time it provided a convenient scapegoat and simple solution to complex public health problems associated with widespread poverty and inadequate city services. The City Improvement League sought lofty, inexpensive, and largely ineffective solutions to complex public health problems that required costly interventions. Historian Terry Copp maintains that such a quixotic program diverted attention from building an infrastructure that would provide basic civic services such as clean running water, indoor toilets, and building inspection to all of its citizens. An investment of this type entailed costs that the municipal government was eager to avoid and regulatory measures that were anathema to economic liberalism.[72]

Undoubtedly, "Swat the Fly" had little effect on tuberculosis rates. The contest, however, was an important opportunity for little Montrealers to assume individual responsibility for public health. The legacy of "Swat the Fly" forever tainted the housefly as a harbinger of dirt and disease, yet the *Star* reported several positive outcomes as well. Following the contest, food inspectors more stringently enforced regulations on the screening of commercial food and charged store owners with exposing food to contaminants.[73] The *Star* also claimed that the competition had alerted all Montrealers to the danger of the fly and the conditions that engendered its propagation and highlighted the fact that all citizens were responsible for keeping streets and lanes free of filth. The *Star*'s most emphatic pleas, however, were directed at city health authorities. It resolved that the city must "do away with the open privy-pits that still exist, they must insist on the proper draining of the numerous stables whose filth is now allowed simply to ooze away into the ground, and they must inaugurate a much more cleanly and effective system of garbage collection than the crude methods now in force."[74] Naomi Rogers argues that in New York, the anti-fly campaign served health authorities well: to reinforce the importance of popular education as a solution to ensuring public health; link science with everyday life; strengthen the idea that mothers had to keep their houses free of flies to maintain family health; and, at the very least, to give the impression that officials were acting aggressively against the spread of disease.[75] One merely had to "Swat the Fly"; even children could go to battle against the *Musca domestica* and claim success 25 million times over. Notwithstanding a range of motivations that included empathy, an earnest desire to do good, and real health concerns, reformers did not recommend transformations in social relations that would have resulted in better housing, healthier neighbourhoods, or equal access to medical services. Rather, they urged public education to reduce rates of tuberculosis.

Targeting youngsters with contests such as "Swat the Fly" and city improvement was understood to arm a new generation with knowledge that parents allegedly resisted. Thus, the prescription for improving the public's health stood in sharp contrast with the lives of most children and simply could not be met. Although Montreal's death rate from tuberculosis was higher than Toronto's, by the end of the Depression the numbers began to drop, as a consequence of a higher standard of living, the widespread use of tuberculin tests and chest X-rays to detect insipient disease, and the eradication of bovine tuberculosis.[76] Nonetheless, children were receptive to public health campaigns and acted as health ambassadors in the anti-tuberculosis crusades. They served as role models and joined the Junior Red Cross, spreading health propaganda to their peers, family, and community. Their decision to embrace and participate in these contests speaks to their autonomy. Locating children's agency in Montreal's anti-tuberculosis campaigns—despite adult attempts to implement and regulate their activities, as well as the problematic nature of historical documents—is critical to writing a history of children and represents new theoretical considerations of childhood at work.

 *More online.*

Notes

1. We wish to thank Sherry Olson for her helpful critique of an earlier version of the paper and for making the map of "Montreal's fly catchers," as well as Annmarie Adams and the anonymous readers for their astute comments. . . .

2. "Swat the Fly, Then Do It Again," *Montreal Daily Star*, 25 July 1912.

3. "*Star*'s Fly Campaign Breaking All Records with 9,356,361 Flies," *Montreal Daily Star*, 1 August 1912.

4. Publication Committee Meeting, 22 October 1903, Library of the Montreal Chest Institute.

5. See, for example, Cynthia R. Commachio, *Nations Are Built of Babies: Saving Ontario's Mothers and Children, 1900–40* (Montreal, QC: McGill-Queen's University Press, 1993); Norah Lewis, "Physical Perfection for Spiritual Welfare: Health Care for the Urban Child, 1900–39," in *Studies in Childhood History: A Canadian Perspective*, ed. Patricia T. Rooke and R. L. Schnell (Calgary, AB: Detselig, 1982), 135–66; Neil Sutherland, *Children in English-Canadian Society: Framing the Twentieth-Century Consensus* (Toronto, ON: University of Toronto Press, 1976) . . .

6. Robert G. McIntosh, *Boys in the Pits: Child Labour in Coal Mining* (Montreal, QC: McGill-Queen's University Press, 2000), 10.

7. Naomi Rogers, "Germs with Legs: Flies, Disease, and the New Public Health," *Bulletin of the History of Medicine* 63 (1989): 599–604.

8. Terry Copp, *The Anatomy of Poverty: The Condition of the Working Class in Montreal 1897–1929* (Toronto, ON: McClelland & Stewart, 1974), 100.

9. Paul-André Linteau, *Histoire de Montréal depuis la Confédération* (Montreal, QC: Boréal, 2000), 318.

10. 1911 Annual Report, 121, Bureau of Health, Archives de la Ville de Montréal (hereafter AVM).

11. Royal Commission on Tuberculosis, *Report, Province of Quebec, 1909–10* (Quebec: s.n., 1909–10), 22.

12. Ames was born in Montreal in 1863 to American parents. His father established the highly successful Ames-Holden Company, a shoe and boot manufacturing plant that Ames inherited after his father's death. . . . Elected to the municipal council in 1898, Ames maintained his position as alderman until 1906, when he ran in the constituency of Montreal-St-Antoine and won a seat in the House of Commons as a Conservative in 1904, serving in federal politics until 1920. . . . Despite this prolific career in politics, Ames is still best known for *The City below the Hill*. See Mélanie Méthot, "Herbert Brown Ames: Political Reformer and Enforcer," *Urban History Review* 31, no. 2 (2003): 18–31.

13. Herbert Brown Ames, *The City below the Hill: A Sociological Study of a Portion of the City of Montreal,* *Canada* (Toronto, ON: University of Toronto Press, 1972), 80–6.

14. 1901 Annual Report, 94–5, Bureau of Health, AVM.

15. "Our Unhealthy Dwellings," *Bulletin Sanitaire* 8, nos. 1–4 (1908): 15.

16. Ibid.

17. See David Rosner, "Introduction: 'Hives of Sickness and Vice,'" in *Hives of Sickness: Public Health and Epidemics in New York City*, ed. David Rosner (New Brunswick, NJ: Rutgers University Press, 1995), 1–21.

18. Ames, *The City below the Hill*, 45.

19. Copp, *The Anatomy of Poverty*, 15.

20. Between 1905 and 1914, Montreal annexed 26 territories, 16 of which were municipalities. Linteau, *Histoire de Montréal*, 202.

21. 1916 Annual Report, 128, Bureau of Health, AVM.

22. Joel A. Tarr, *The Search for the Ultimate Sink: Urban Pollution in Historical Perspective* (Akron, OH: University of Akron Press, 1996), 323–31.

23. Katherine McCuaig, *The Weariness, the Fever, and the Fret: The Campaign against Tuberculosis in Canada, 1900–50* (Montreal, QC: McGill-Queen's University Press, 1999), xvii.

24. Nancy Tomes, "Moralizing the Microbe," in *Morality and Health*, ed. Allan M. Brandt and Paul Rozin (New York, NY: Routledge, 1997), 272.

25. Valerie Minnett, "Inside and Outside: Pathology, Architecture, and the Domestic Environment at the Montreal Tuberculosis Exhibition, 1908" (Master's thesis, McGill University, 2004), 4.

26. Copp, *The Anatomy of Poverty*, 88–93.

27. Ibid., 102–3.

28. American Studies scholar Maren Stange has proposed that "the documentary mode [of photography] testified both to the existence of painful social facts and to reformers' special expertise in ameliorating them, thus reassuring a liberal middle class that social oversight was both its duty and its right." (Maren Stange, *Symbols of Ideal Life: Social Documentary Photography in America 1890–1950* [Cambridge, UK: Cambridge University Press, 1989], xiii–xiv).

29. James Opp, "Re-Imaging the Moral Order of Urban Space: Religion and Photography in Winnipeg, 1900–14," *Journal of the Canadian Historical Association* 13 (2002): 83–4.

30. The correlation between the presence of the fly and the spread of contagious disease was relatively new at the time. In 1905, for instance, British entomologist Frederick V. Theobald claimed that though the common housefly was exposed to widespread disease, it appeared to be "relatively harmless" to humans. See Theobald, *Insect Life: A Short Account of the Classification and Habits of Insects* (London, UK: Methuen, 1905), 166.

31. "Swat the Fly and Sell Them to Us for Cash!" *Toronto Star*, 6 July 1912.

32. Rogers, "Germs with Legs," 614.

33. See, for example, the publications of Canadian civil servant and entomologist C. G. Hewitt, *House-Flies and How They Spread Disease* (Cambridge, UK: Cambridge University Press, 1912), and *The House-Fly Musca Domestica Linn: Its Structure, Habits, Development, Relation to Disease and Control* (Cambridge, UK: Cambridge University Press, 1914).

34. "One Fly Can Carry over Six Million Microbes at a Time," *Montreal Daily Star*, 16 July 1912.

35. "'Swat the Fly,' and So Help Humanity: Specialist Endorses the New Crusade," *Toronto Daily Star*, 11 July 1912.

36. Minutes of the Meetings, vol. 23 (11 May 1911–2 February 1920) 11 May 1911, Board of Health, Health Committee (City Council of Montreal), VM21, AVM.

37. Minutes of the Meetings, vol. 23 (11 May 1911–2 February 1920), 22 May 1911, Board of Health, Health Committee (City Council of Montreal), VM21, AVM.

38. "'Swat the Fly,' and So Help Humanity: Specialist Endorses the New Crusade," *Toronto Daily Star*, 11 July 1912.

39. "Kill the Flies, Yes, But Remove the Cause Too, Say Physicians," *Montreal Daily Star*, 15 July 1912.

40. Nancy Tomes has argued that reformers criticized people's routine and everyday activities, profoundly affecting what she calls "public health morality": the responsibilities that ordinary people assumed to guard themselves, their families, and their neighbours from infection. See Tomes, "Moralizing the Microbe," 272.

41. "Moving Pictures in Parks to Be Repeated Next Year," *Montreal Witness*, 21 November 1911; and "What Authorities on Health Think of the Anti-Fly Campaign," *Montreal Daily Star*, 24 July 1912.

42. "One Fly Can Carry over Six Million Microbes at a Time," *Montreal Daily Star*, 16 July 1912.

43. "Attention Is Called to the Dangerous House-Fly," *Bulletin Sanitaire* 10, nos. 2–3 (February–March 1910): 19.

44. "Too Busy Catching Flies," *Montreal Daily Star*, 30 July 1912.

45. "Star's Fly-Swatting Campaign Is Defended by Board of Health," *Montreal Daily Star*, 29 July 1912.

46. Ibid.

47. "Scores by Little Tots," *Montreal Daily Star*, 7 August 1912.

48. For information about the spatial dimensions of contestants to the city as well as the social and economic characteristics of the families of children who participated in the "Swat the Fly" contest we made use of the databases assembled by *Montreal Avenir Passé*

or MAP located at McGill University's Department of Geography.

49. "The Little Contestants Tell Some of Their Experiences," *Montreal Daily Star*, 22 July 1912.

50. "Ten Prize Winners in First Day's Count Show Large Figures," *Montreal Daily Star*, 23 July 1912.

51. "Flies by Hundred Thousand Swatted by Boys and Girls," *Montreal Daily Star*, 26 July 1912.

52. "Exterminate the Fly and Other Parasites," *Montreal Spring Clean-Up Campaigns* (Montreal, QC: City Improvement Campaign Committee, 1917).

53. Ibid.

54. The City Improvement Campaign Committee, *The Montreal Spring Clean-Up Campaigns: A Record of Certain Phases of Civic Improvements, 1912–16* (Montreal, QC: The City Improvement Campaign Committee, 1916), 14.

55. *Sanitary Bulletin of the Department of Hygiene and Statistic City of Montreal / Bulletin Sanitaire du Bureau Municipal d'Hygiène et de Statistique Cité de Montréal*, no. 7 (May 1915): 1.

56. Note that several dead flies are among the debris caught by this broom.

57. The City Improvement League, *Clean Up, Nettoyons!*

58. The City Improvement Campaign Committee, *The Montreal Spring Clean-Up Campaigns* (Montreal, QC: The City Improvement Campaign Committee, n.d.), 17.

59. The City Improvement League, *Record of Civic Pride* (Montreal, QC: The City Improvement Campaign Committee, n.d.).

60. For more on this, see Rod MacLeod and Mary Anne Poutanen, "Daughters of the Empire, Soldiers of the Soil: Protestant School Boards, Patriotism, and War," in their book, *A Meeting of the People: School Boards and Protestant Communities in Quebec, 1801–1998* (Montreal, QC: McGill-Queen's University Press, 2004), 223–43.

61. Clean Up Committee of the City Improvement League, *Clean Up Week May 19th to May 25th 1918: A Pamphlet Issued by the Clean Up Committee of the City Improvement League on Life, Health, Sanitation and Conservation Containing Also Other Useful Information for the Home and the Citizens of Montreal* (Montreal, QC: Clean Up Committee of the City Improvement League, 1918).

62. 1914 Annual Report, 47, Bureau of Health, AVM.

63. "Swat The Fly, Then Do It Again," *Montreal Daily Star*, 25 July 1912.

64. "Last Count in Fly-Killing Competition Breaks All Previous World's Records," *Montreal Daily Star*, 7 August 1912.

65. "Competitors Coming in with Fly Catches Receive Their Prizes," *Montreal Daily Star*, 30 July 1912.

66. Issues of both the *Canadian Red Cross* and the *Canadian Red Cross Junior* present articles relating to flies and

their effect on health and the transmission of disease until at least 1928. See, for example, A. E. Berry, "The House Fly," *Canadian Red Cross Junior* 7, no. 5 (1928): 8–9, and "Following the Fly," *Canadian Red Cross* 4, no. 5 (1925): 9.

67. "Health Alphabet," *Canadian Red Cross Junior* 6, no. 9 (1927): 19.

68. "Following the Fly," *Canadian Red Cross* 4, no. 5 (1925): 9.

69. Berry, "The House Fly," 9.

70. Walt Disney, *The Brave Little Tailor* (Toronto, ON: Random House, 1974), 3. *The Brave Little Tailor* was originally released as a Walt Disney animated short on 29 September 1938.

71. Mona Gleason, "'Don't Feel Today Like Speaking': Children, Experts, and Conceptions of Health in English Canada, 1900 to 1950" (paper presented at the conference Comparative and Interdisciplinary Approaches to Child Health in the 20th Century, 29–30 October 2004, Montreal, Quebec).

72. Copp, *The Anatomy of Poverty*, 85–6.

73. "Health Officials Aroused," *Montreal Daily Star*, 5 August 1912.

74. Ibid.

75. Rogers, "Germs with Legs," 600–1.

76. McCuaig, *The Weariness, the Fever, and the Fret*, 148.

5 "There Were Always Men in Our House"
Gender and the Childhood Memories of Working-Class Ukrainians in Depression-Era Canada

Stacey Zembrzycki

When Bill Semenuk recently shared his memories about growing up in Depression-era Sudbury, Ontario, as one of seven children born to a Ukrainian immigrant worker employed at the International Nickel Company (INCO) and his wife, he highlighted a number of personal narratives. One was a happy narrative of how, when the family moved from a neighbouring farm to "the Donovan" area of Sudbury, Bill always had "places to play," stating "there were ball fields, [we played] cowboys in the rock mountains . . . [and in] the winter there was a lot of sliding [and] we used to crawl up the telephone poles and then drop ourselves into snow piles underneath." Another was a moving narrative about his mother's illness and eventual death. When his mother, Mary, became sick, he told me, "I used to ask to leave school early to take care of her." Sadly, Mary died in 1932 when Bill was 9 years old. "It was very hard for a while after mother died," Bill explained, noting that often the family was "just glad to eat" and that "sometimes us kids would fight over potatoes."

Bill also pointed out that his "father always worked day shift" and thus he marvelled at the thought of how this man had looked after the whole lot of them: "He would leave at six in the morning and return at six at night. Father would

do everything. I remember him sewing clothes, [and putting] patches upon patches." In addition, since many men could not find jobs in the Depression, there were always Ukrainian men who would come to Sudbury, a place where job opportunities actually existed, and stay with Bill's family. "These men," Bill said, "were good friends of my father [and they] looked after us when mother died." He added: "I remember the kitchen being the main room of the house where everyone congregated and told stories. We [children] would sit around and listen."[1]

Bill Semenuk's childhood narrative, which takes place against the backdrop of a family home that became a boarding house for Ukrainian male workers during the 1930s, is not an abstract discussion about the general conditions of the Great Depression. As we sat at his kitchen table and he recounted his childhood years, Bill, a member of Sudbury's Ukrainian Catholic community, structured his narrative around what he considered to be his most important Depression-era memory: the death of his mother. Her death, he makes clear, dramatically affected his life and that of his father and siblings. By turning the history of this period into a biographical memory, Bill acted as a subjective and central historical actor in his narrative. In elucidating his general experiences in

Citation: Stacey Zembrzycki, "'There Were Always Men in Our House': Gender and the Childhood Memories of Working-Class Ukrainians in Depression-Era Canada," *Labour/Le Travail* 60 (Fall 2007): 77–105. Reprinted by permission of the publisher.

deeply personal terms, Bill's narrative provided a means by which he could both order and validate his childhood experiences and understand the meanings of his life.[2]

It is also entirely possible that the gender dynamics of our kitchen table interview, in which a now elderly man shared his boyhood memories with a much younger Ukrainian–Canadian female researcher, affected how Bill told his tale. As oral historians note, the interviewer and the interviewee both participate, although perhaps to varying degrees, in the making of an oral history and/or memory text.[3] Taking this insight one step further, and explicitly gendering it, feminist labour and immigration historian Franca Iacovetta has demonstrated how when female historians interview older immigrant male workers about their pasts, asking gendered questions, they may well encourage their male informants to reflect more fully on the women in their lives and on their gendered understandings of their pasts.[4] The gendered character of female narratives of the past has also been well demonstrated by feminist scholars, including labour and immigration historians, but perhaps most forcefully by those who have probed the silences and gaps in women's recollections of such deeply traumatic events as wartime rape and internment; such silences can represent coping strategies to protect fragile memories.[5]

Of course, Bill was not alone when it came to constructing biographical memories about growing up ethnic and working class in Sudbury during the thirties. Specifically, there were plenty of other Ukrainian working-class men and women who also lived out their boyhood and girlhood years in Depression-era family homes that doubled as boarding houses. In significant respects, both Ukrainian men and women who grew up in the Sudbury region during this period understood and viewed the Depression in similar ways. Many of them, for example, did not focus on the economic crash of 1929, an event that few children appreciated before they reached adulthood, but rather remembered the personal difficulties that their families faced during the Depression era as well as the years that preceded and followed it. As recent immigrants of humble and/or poor rural backgrounds, many working-class Ukrainians in Canada were accustomed to subsistence living and penny capitalism and thus the collapse of the wider economy in the thirties did not have as great an impact on their daily lives as was the case for many middle- and upper-class Anglo-Canadians.[6]

Still, the Depression years were trying ones, and my informants generally filtered their narratives into personal stories about struggle and despair. Their accounts of the difficulties, however, went hand in hand with memories that spoke to the issue of immigrant and working-class pride as well as stories about coping strategies and ultimately survival. At the same time, it must be noted that there were significant gender differences in how boys and girls lived and remembered their daily lives during this period, especially in regard to social relationships with male boarders, household work, and leisure pursuits that took place inside and around their immigrant boarding houses. To paraphrase the European oral historian Alessandro Portelli, all of these subjective—and gendered—narratives "tell us not just what people did, but what they wanted to do, what they believed they were doing, and what they now think they did."[7]

As an exploration of the childhood memories of working-class Ukrainians who grew up in Depression-era boarding houses (or houses with a few boarders) in a heavily immigrant northern Ontario town, this paper treats the oral histories as the subject, not merely the method, of analysis and highlights, in particular, the gendered differences that emerge in the narratives of the men and women that I interviewed. Moreover, this article argues that even within a politically polarized immigrant group such as the Ukrainians, where left/right, progressive/nationalist, and secular/religious splits were so pronounced, and thus central to shaping the histories and historiographies of both camps, it was the influence of dominant gender roles rather than politics, religion, or ideology that most directly informed the differing memories of experience that men and women had of growing up Ukrainian and working class in Sudbury.[8] The political egalitarianism professed by progressive Ukrainians, for instance, did not transgress the boundaries of their households and thus traditional gender roles were assumed by inhabitants. This article therefore focuses on my informants' recollections regarding three areas of activity that were part of everyday boarding-house life: children's relationships with male boarders, their domestic chores, and leisure activities.

. . .

When it came to conducting the interviews for this project, I was both an outsider and an insider to Sudbury's Ukrainian community. Although I grew up in the city, I neither participated in any community-sponsored activities, nor joined any Ukrainian organizations. My paternal *Baba* (grandmother), however, was very active in the organized life of the community, devoting much of her spare time to St. Mary's Ukrainian Catholic Church. While *Baba*'s stories about the community undoubtedly provided me with an insider perspective about the narratives which had shaped its history, I also struggled to understand and clarify aspects of the narratives which I found unclear as an outsider.[9] With *Baba*'s help—she often telephoned Ukrainian men and women that she knew and convinced them to grant me an interview—I interviewed 82 of her friends and acquaintances in English using a life story approach.[10] It must be noted that *Baba*'s connection to the church did not hinder my ability to interview Ukrainians who belonged to other institutions; my informants had Catholic, Orthodox, nationalist, and progressive affiliations. Moreover, my relationship with *Baba* was something that could be discussed with the men and women that I interviewed, opening up the conversations because it provided a level of trust in the interview spaces.

While I certainly consider social and material conditions when turning to childhood memories of the Depression, my main intention is to "communicate with the past more directly."[11] Childhood is a separate and socially constructed stage of existence which complicates the creation of a memory text; in terms of age, all of my interviewees were under the age of 13 prior to 1939. Since as Neil Sutherland notes, adults tend to use childhood memories that are "really a reconstruction of what is being recalled rather than a reproduction of it," this article will pay particular attention to the form, content, and silences of these Ukrainian narratives.[12] In making the act of remembering just as important as the memories themselves, we will be able to explore and evaluate how Sudbury's Ukrainians used memory, experience, and history to construct their subjective Depression-era narratives.[13] . . .

My interviewees tended to couple their childhood memories about financial instability with those that recalled the many men in their lives, namely the boarders with whom they shared their private domestic spaces. . . . As one of the most common survival strategies during the Depression years, boarding was a normal occurrence in this heavily masculine resource town and thus directly and indirectly touched the lives of most working-class residents. This is reflected in my sample: a majority of my interviewees, roughly 66 per cent, recalled having boarders or roomers living in their houses at this time. Together, these domestic working-class childhood narratives shed light on the collective and shared experiences as well as the noteworthy gender differences experienced by Ukrainian men and women. Different political or religious affiliations, for example, did not produce dramatically different memories. Whether they frequented the Ukrainian Labour Farmer Temple Association (ULFTA) hall, St. Mary's Ukrainian Catholic Church, St. Volodymyr's Ukrainian Greek Orthodox Church, or the Ukrainian National Federation (UNF) hall, the Ukrainians who shared their stories with me recalled the boarding-house or rooming-house culture in which they grew up in a similar fashion. . . .

In considering the economic importance of boarding among Sudbury's Ukrainians, we must also understand it as part of a wider family economy and as a strategy, among others, for surviving in a particular set of economic conditions. As an ethnic entrepreneurship most often managed by my interviewees' mothers, it was a way for the family to earn extra money during these difficult years, improving its ability to pay the mortgage as well as the bills at the local grocery store. In addition to supplementing a father's wages, boarding was also an informal insurance policy when a father lost his job. Since Ukrainians with foreign surnames, or alleged links to communism, were the first to be fired during this period, a wife's boarding business ensured some steady income that allowed the family to survive such a disaster.[14] Moreover, since most fathers' days were spent at work or looking for extra work if they lost their jobs or had their shifts cut back, the mothers were the dominant figure in their children's lives.[15] Heavily male resource towns offered women few opportunities for earning incomes and this, of course, affected the gendered family strategies employed by those who lived in these kinds of environments. . . . Ukrainian women may have had few formal job opportunities, but they were able to create their own economic opportunities at home. By taking in boarders, they either supplemented their husbands' incomes or managed to be financially independent, supporting themselves and their children if their husbands had either lost their jobs, or abandoned them, or died prematurely. In many cases, women were the primary breadwinners and housewives in these spaces. By placing memories at the heart of this analysis it is thus possible to illuminate the ethnic and gendered roles performed by Ukrainian women in these boarding houses. Since these memories belong to children who grew up in these spaces, getting "inside" these boarding houses also enables a discussion of the gendered contributions girls and boys made to these family economies.

It is also important to note that Sudburians had a unique Depression experience. In contrast to other parts of the country, this region remained relatively unscathed because of its nickel and the global demand for it. As Carl Wallace shows, the local market nearly collapsed in 1931 and 1932 but it quickly recovered between 1933 and 1937, stumbling in 1938 and then exploding with the outbreak of war.[16] Sudbury thus became a "destination city" during this period.[17] . . .

Those men who made the decision to come to Sudbury during the 1930s, both single and married men with children, settled in a variety of working-class neighbourhoods, both multicultural and ethnically homogeneous; the majority of my interviewees recounted what it was like to grow up on the streets of the Donovan, the West End, the East End, and Polack Town, in the INCO company town of Coniston. It must be noted that these neighbourhoods were not ideologically, religiously, or politically ordered; it was not unusual for a Ukrainian Catholic to live down the street or next door to a Ukrainian who was a member at the local ULFTA hall.

. . .

Boarding was always a risky business but during the Depression it was particularly precarious.[18] A successful business depended upon reliable and employed clientele who paid their bills regularly, and this was made difficult with the uncertainty of the times.[19] Boarding either eliminated the effects of the Depression or it brought them right into the home, adding yet another challenge for the immigrant family to overcome. Nick Evanshen, a Ukrainian with no organizational affiliations, recalled the ways that his life changed when his parents, Steve and Mary, moved from their house on Whittaker Street to their new one at 268 Drinkwater Street; this was a large boarding house that had enough space for 30 boarders and roomers. Before undertaking this business, Nick remembered how his "mother went for days with very little food so she could scrape up enough to feed all five children," remarking "it wasn't very pleasant during the . . . [early days of the] Depression." After moving into the boarding house, he recalled how his mother would wake at three or four o'clock in the morning to make lunch pails and then she would spend her day cooking, cleaning, and doing laundry. He also understood that her labours mattered: the boarding fees "helped the family income, [and] improved the situation," and it meant that they "always had enough food [to eat] when they lived on Drinkwater [Street]."[20]

For others, boarding proved to be more of a hassle than a solution to their family's economic difficulties. Olga Zembrzycki (née Zyma), a lifelong member of St. Mary's Ukrainian Catholic Church, stated: "If times were tough some roomers left father holding the bag. They would leave to look for work elsewhere and never pay their rent. They always said that they would come back to pay [but] they never did." . . .[21] Pauline Kruk's (née Mykoluk) parents, both of whom were members of Holy Trinity Roman Catholic Church, faced a similar fate, nearly losing their only house in the Depression because of the pressures of providing for a large family which included 10 children and sometimes up to three Ukrainian boarders who were often unable to pay their fees. Had it not been for one boarder who was particularly close to Pauline's parents, and paid regularly, Malanka and Jacob would have lost their home. . . .[22] Engaged in a difficult and sometimes uncertain venture, especially during the Depression, boarding-house keepers could not always find reliable boarders.

One way of trying to ensure more trustworthy boarders was to have relatives, such as uncles, cousins, or grandfathers, stay in the home. This proved to be a better arrangement for some interviewees. Financially, these family members helped to pay the bills; splitting the cost of living made it possible for more families to buy homes rather than rent them. Their presence could also ease the emotional difficulties that came with immigrating to a new country.

For example, those who knew their *Gidos* (grandfathers) and *Babas* (grandmothers), even if only for a brief period before they sojourned back to the old country, considered themselves lucky.[23] Still, some relatives took advantage of the situation. Bernice Crowe (née Haluschak) had a vivid childhood memory of the four uncles (her father's brothers) who came to live with her family after getting jobs at Falconbridge Mine. When her mother, who spent some of her "leisure" time cooking in the ULFTA kitchen, got angry about this arrangement and confronted the men, they replied: "well he's our brother and we don't have to pay."[24] Taking on family members, then, could also involve considerable economic risk.

. . . Unless they had family in the region, most of my interviewees' parents came to Sudbury only after they settled in another part of the country and failed to obtain the standard of living that they had envisioned. Men saw advertisements for jobs in Sudbury or they learned about them from co-workers. John Stefura's father, Alec, one of the founding members of Sudbury's UNF hall, received a letter from friends in the region who told him that "if you wanted a job INCO was hiring for 25 cents an hour and you could work for 6 1/2 or 7 days a week."[25] If the men had family or friends in the region, they usually stayed with them until they could get settled and send for any immediate family members who were living in other parts of Canada or in Ukraine. In contrast, those men without a connection to anyone living in Sudbury would ride the rails to the town and when they arrived they would either hear about a boarding house from the men that they encountered or they would visit the local Ukrainian church, the ULFTA hall, or the UNF hall where they would be welcomed and recommended to a boarding-house operator. Thus, in contrast to the mixed neighbourhoods of the town, these boarding houses tended to be ethnically, ideologically, politically, and religiously homogenous; a progressive Ukrainian would not have boarded with a Catholic family for instance. Unless one of the operators was familiar with the men recommended to them, they always took a chance when taking in boarders. The desperation of the times meant that one could not be particularly fastidious.

Children who grew up in these kinds of households thus recalled that there were always men in the house, usually eating or sleeping. This was especially true for Paul Behun's family, all of whom were devout members of St. Michael's Ukrainian Catholic Church. When his father, John, died in 1932, his mother collected $30 a month in mother's allowance to raise Paul and his older brother Bill. To supplement that income, Anna took in three boarders, one for every shift at the nearby INCO smelter. While one man slept, the second man worked, and the third man remained awake. Anna had to do this in order to qualify for mother's allowance, rotating the men to prove to officials that she did not have a constant breadwinner in the house.[26] It is significant to note that although Anna's strategy was meant to help her evade officials, other Ukrainian women also employed bed rotation schedules to accommodate more men. By having the men sleep in shifts, a three-bedroom home with two beds in each room, for instance, could then meet the needs of 18 men who worked the day, afternoon, and night shifts at the local mines. According to Anne Matschke, "the beds were always warm."[27]

In these childhood memories, the boarders occupy different ranks with respect to the family. Some male interviewees elevated the men to the status of "uncles" while others could rarely remember the names of those with whom they had shared their domestic space. As the opening story tells us, after Bill Semenuk's mother, Mary, died in 1932, his father, John, a devoted member of St. Mary's Ukrainian Catholic Church, had to raise seven children alone. Luckily he worked steady day shift at INCO's Frood Mine and so he could come home in time to meet the children when they arrived from school. In those instances when he needed a babysitter, the male boarders looked after the children, congregating in

the kitchen where they would play cards and tell stories that the children would sit around and listen to. For Bill these men were like family.[28] Taciana, who frequented St. Mary's and the UNF hall, also remembered the men who lived in her parent's home fondly; she reminisced about the many Ukrainian holidays spent with them at her mother's kitchen table, eating traditional Ukrainian dishes and listening to stories about the old country.[29] It is, in this case, important to stress that adult memories about childhood are fallible and thus these now nostalgic stories may have been transformed with the passage of time.[30]

Other interviewees had very different memories of the boarders who had lived in their homes. These stories do not move toward a "happy ending," but rather interviewees remembered these men as simply strangers who had shared their space. For instance, Mary Brydges (née Ladyk), who took mandolin lessons at the ULFTA hall, stated that the men "used to come through the back door, through the kitchen and go straight upstairs," eating with her family but otherwise living separately. Mary left school at the age of 13 to help her mother run the family's boarding house, and although she vividly recalled waking every morning to make 13 or 14 lunch pails to send to work with the men, she could not remember any particular man.[31] . . . Angela Behun (née Bilowus), a member of St. Michael's Ukrainian Catholic Church, echoed this sentiment, emphasizing that there were always different men staying with her family. Her house was like a "temporary stop-over," a place where the men would stay before switching to another boarding house or getting married.[32]

If a child developed a relationship with a boarder, he was usually the son, not the daughter, of the family. The girls spent a significant amount of time helping their mothers, while boys usually had few domestic chores. Nellie Kozak (née Tataryn), one of five daughters in her Ukrainian Catholic family, remembered that when the one boy, her brother, Steve, arrived

". . . God was born. For Ukrainian people, the son was everything and the girls were nothing. The girls would just have to work."[33] Lynne Marks has well documented the different gendered dimensions of working-class leisure and certainly there were important gender distinctions in Sudbury as well.[34] Boys like Steve tended to have more spare time than their sisters. Consequently, some boys spent much of their leisure time with the men who lived in their homes, often getting to know these men better than their own fathers who worked long 12-hour shifts at the local mines. It must be noted that boarders, with whom boys formed bonds, often did not work at the mines. Rather they worked odd jobs and thus had more time to spend at home. Peter Chitruk remembered developing close relationships with many of the men living in his home, but one particular man, "Bill," stood out; Bill worked odd jobs in and around the region. They had a close bond and a special Sunday morning routine: Bill would buy the *Toronto Star* and read it to Peter while he sat next to him and looked at the pictures.[35] Nick Evanshen developed a similar bond with two brothers who boarded at his house, John and Peter Buyarski. When they were not working at the nearby East End Bakery, a job which took them away from home in the morning, John and Peter would babysit Nick, taking him swimming in the summer and skating in the winter. Nick admitted to seeing these men more often than his father, fondly recalling that they bought him his first pair of skates.[36] . . .

While girls may have had less time to spend with male boarders because their workload in the home was heavier than that of their brothers, we must also address the other ways in which parents regulated these relationships. Parents subtly limited the time their daughters spent with these men and monitored any interaction they may have had with them to ensure that relations did not turn sexual. For instance, girls often ate at different times from the men and slept in bedrooms that were located on separate floors. I say that these measures were subtle because when

asked about their relationships with boarders, my interviewees noted that their memories contained no recollections of undue sexual anxiety about having had men living in their homes. Although these silences seem to indicate that sexual anxiety was not a part of my interviewees' experiences, it is important to recognize that the Ukrainians with whom I spoke may have suppressed, transformed, and/or chosen not to reveal these kinds of incidents to me when asked about boarding-house culture.

We must, as [Donna] Gabaccia and Iacovetta argue, nevertheless view boarding houses as sexualized spaces of pleasure and danger. Although the childhood memories of the Ukrainian men and women that I interviewed downplayed the fear and/or alarmism expressed by social reformers who argued that crowded domestic spaces threatened girls' sexuality, there is no doubt that sexual tensions and sexual misconduct of various types did occur in some of these households.[37] Instances of boarders guilty of sexually assaulting the girls with whom they lived can be found within the written record even if they were not reported by my informants.[38] Despite their silences on the issue of sexual assault, some intriguing stories did emerge in these interviews which give us insight into some of the sexual tensions which occurred in these homes. One woman recalled that certain boarding-house keepers treated the younger men as a pool of potential husbands for their daughters, in some cases making their choices very clear to the community so as to avoid unnecessary competition for their daughters.[39]

. . . Although we may not be able to determine whether my interviewees' houses were sexually charged places, some of the men and women were forthcoming when it came to telling negative stories about other boarding houses and their operators; gossip is therefore essential to shedding light on those issues which my interviewees refrained from discussing. . . . While stressing that their parents' boarding houses had been filled with respectable men, they referred to certain Ukrainian boarding-house operators as "floozies" who had left their husbands for boarders. These women became outcasts in the Ukrainian community because in leaving their husbands they also often left their children. At least this was the case with religious Ukrainians; no one from the progressive community raised this matter. Those Catholics who did share their memories of "bad" women stressed that these women never returned to church. Living in a common law situation, or as Ukrainians negatively referred to it, living *na bushwel*, was unrespectable. If a Ukrainian woman married, then the belief was that she had chosen a life partner. Regardless of whether a woman's husband abused her or their children, drank excessively, or lost his job, divorce was not considered to be an option. . . . The immigrant generation believed that there was no right or wrong reason for a woman to divorce, let alone abandon, her husband. Stories such as these therefore remind us that we need to study the silences that occur when doing oral history. Memories about boarders who became "uncles" need to be read alongside those of men who were cunning or abusive; memories of boarding houses as sites of pleasure alongside those that spoke to danger.

Although the sexual dynamics within boarding houses varied, all successful boarding businesses required thriftiness and this was especially true during the Depression. This burden fell upon the woman of the household. In performing this type of paid labour in the home, the boundaries between a woman's public and private spheres were inevitably blurred. Despite this compromise and the fact that boarding created more work for women and led to extra expenditures and infringements on their private spaces, this domestic business, as Bettina Bradbury reminds us, offered women a source of income comparable to a wage.[40] During the Depression, this wage came with a catch. . . . The boarding-house keeper had to prepare enough food for her boarders and, at the worst of times, try to financially break even.

Not surprisingly, this was often difficult to do when boarders did not have enough money to pay their boarding fees. Ukrainian women responded to this challenge by preparing ethnic food. . . . Ukrainian women, like most immigrant women feeding families on tight budgets, took their role as food providers seriously and drew on customary ways of stretching meals to feed their households.[41] A pot of borscht or a roast pan of perogies or cabbage rolls fed many hungry mouths and these foods could be made in large quantities for a relatively low price; it must be noted that these dishes were often made with seasonal ingredients. Such ethnic foods were a staple, made at least once a week to satisfy the boarders' hunger as well as the family's budgetary constraints. Boarding-house operators also made a variety of soups. Like perogies made with flour and potatoes, and cabbage rolls made with cabbage and rice, large quantities of soup made with water, a small portion of meat and some kind of vegetable could be made quite inexpensively. Anne Matschke (née Kuchmey), a member at St. Mary's Ukrainian Catholic Church, remembered her mother preparing a different pot of soup for her boarders almost every day, especially during the Depression. If she did not have enough food to feed her boarders as well as her seven children, her mother, Malanka, would just "add more water to the soup."[42] Like perogies and cabbage rolls, soup was a cost-efficient answer for those struggling to feed many hungry mouths on a small budget.

. . . Interestingly, the children said that taste was never compromised; nearly every one of my interviewees made sure to report that their mothers had been exceptional cooks. Preparing ethnic food was an economically efficient way for women to provide their boarders with the calories that they needed to work underground for 12-hour shifts. Ethnic food may have helped to preserve Ukrainian traditions but it was above all a way for women to ensure that their boarding businesses were successful in tough times.

Boarding was also a labour-intensive business and thus many mothers asked for assistance.

While some hired single or married women looking to make some extra money, most relied on their children, whose labour was free and often readily available. In addition to managing their boarding businesses and overseeing their family's finances, mothers supervised their children, assigning them tasks to be done in and around the home.[43] Although mothers and their children conversed in Ukrainian, the tasks assigned to them were not ethnic but gendered: girls undertook domestic tasks within the household while boys performed masculine chores and errands outside of the home.

After Bernice Crowe's (née Haluschak) father passed away in the late 1930s, her mother, Stella, a member of the ULFTA, decided to take in boarders to support her family. Although six men lived with them at a time, Stella cooked for about 25 to 30 men a day, serving as a type of restaurant cook for those who were rooming in the area. In speaking about the ways that she helped her mother, Bernice explained: "Every Saturday I would help mother with the cleaning, and I would sweep and then scrub those darn wood floors. It was hard. [During the week] I was going to school and I would have to come home and do the afternoon dishes and set the table."[44] Helen Cotnam (née Cybulka), who attended a French Catholic school and had no Ukrainian organizational affiliations, also helped her mother with her rooming business. They did not cook meals for the men but every week Helen had to help her mother clean the rooms that they had rented. Although they were lucky enough to have indoor plumbing, she emphasized that this was a mixed blessing because she had to clean the bathrooms the men had used. As she vividly recalled, it only took her a few dirty toilets to issue an ultimatum, insisting that her mother buy her a toilet brush before she would clean another toilet.[45] . . .

Running a boarding business was always hard work. Those girls who helped their mothers often undertook daily domestic chores, mainly cleaning. Surprisingly, few of them learned to cook from their mothers. Cleaning was a task that could be assigned to a child. If not done properly, it would not send the business into disarray. But as the women interviewed explained, cooking was a greater responsibility—while men may not have minded coming home to a house with dirty floors and unmade beds, they would have been upset to find that a meal was not waiting for them at the end of a 12-hour shift—and so it was left up to the older women in the household. . . . In addition to these domestic duties, girls were also responsible for caring for their younger siblings. When the oldest daughter in the household married—they often did so at a young age to alleviate the financial strain placed on the family—the next oldest female sibling would take over her domestic and child-rearing responsibilities. This familial female cycle was another essential ingredient for a successful boarding business.

Boys' chores often took them outside of the home. Whenever Paul Behun's mother needed wood for the stove, he and his brother Bill would go into the bush, cut logs, and then haul them home, splitting them before stacking them close to the house.[46] If boys were not splitting firewood, they were collecting coal and shovelling it through the chute which carried it into the basement. Many mothers also kept a number of farm animals in the backyard, including cows, pigs, and chickens. Most often it was the boys in the home who were responsible for milking the cows and cleaning the chicken coops and then delivering milk or eggs to customers in the neighbourhood. Blueberry picking was another way for a Ukrainian family living in northern Ontario to supplement its income and it was usually the boys in the household who were responsible for picking them. It was laborious and hot work, usually done during late July and early August.[47] Although he now enjoys picking blueberries, Stanley Hayduk, a Roman Catholic who attended St. John the Evangelist Church, remembered when he hated doing this task, recalling that he would only be allowed to play ball after he had filled a basket.[48] Like Stanley, Bill Semenuk spent many mornings during the 1930s picking blueberries to earn extra money. He looked forward to it though, as a morning of picking often went hand in hand with an afternoon of swimming at Ramsey Lake.[49] Boys rarely helped their mothers when it came to domestic chores although many, including Frank Makarinsky, have fond memories of watching their mothers cook, waiting for such things like fresh bread to come out of the oven.[50] In highlighting memories like those recalled by Frank, I am not trying to deny that boys worked less than their sisters. Certainly chopping wood, shovelling coal into the house, and picking blueberries were difficult tasks. However, it is important to note that these chores were done less frequently than the daily domestic tasks assigned to girls.

As this description of the gendered division of child labour suggests, Ukrainians, like other immigrant and Canadian parents, had gendered expectations of their children, and those expectations reflected a response to economic realities as well as cultural and ideological factors. Daughters were trained to be future wives while boys emulated their fathers and learned what it took to be a successful breadwinner. By sending their boys to deliver milk or pick blueberries, parents gave them not only independence but also financial responsibility, teaching them the value of a dollar at an early age. Ukrainian immigrants who arrived in early twentieth-century Canada brought a distinct peasant culture with them. This baggage, as Frances Swyripa shows, included a set of clearly defined gender roles and stereotypes: "They [women] were essential to the functioning of the family as the basic unit of production and consumption, yet they were regarded as inferior beings subject to the authority of their menfolk."[51] But this view was not limited to Ukrainians or even immigrants more generally. In Denyse Baillargeon's study about the Depression experiences of French Canadian women who lived in Montreal, one of her informant's comments was similar to the one made by

Nellie Kozak (née Tataryn): "Little boys were like little kings. Very few homes made the boys work. They couldn't be touched. If there was something to be done, the girls did it."[52] Within the wider Anglo-Celtic society, an enduring Victorian ideology of separate spheres (which in practice were never separate) did not necessarily justify male privilege (the point was that boys and girls were to be trained for separate but complementary worlds) but it could and did lead to a double standard. Boys were encouraged to undertake roles that would train them to be breadwinners while girls were trained for the domestic roles that they would eventually assume. Economic factors led many working-class families to make strategic decisions about children's work. If a boy could make more money than a girl in the public sphere then he was sent to work, not his sister.[53] These gendered roles, then, reflected the interplay of a number of economic and cultural factors, including the dynamics of the mining town and the differing job opportunities available to men and women. But transplanted Old World ideas about what it meant to be a "Ukrainian man" and a "Ukrainian woman" reinforced such gender roles.

Accounting for the situation and living it are two different things. It must be stressed that in reflecting upon their childhoods, my interviewees, especially females, were well aware of the gender dynamics that ordered their households.[54] In the women's opinions, boys were valued more than girls and were treated accordingly. Indeed, decades later there is still a great degree of bitterness in the voices of women who recall the broken dreams and the many limitations placed on them. Some remain upset that their parents did not encourage them to stay in school; they are haunted by the memory of the rhetorical question that their father had put to them: "Why go to school [when] you are going to scrub floors and do housework anyway?"[55] Most of them, however, shrugged off their feelings and subtly warned me not to stress these gender inequalities because "this was normal" for that time. As Michael Frisch warns, we must be sensitive to such differences when doing oral history or we risk creating a "discursive disconnect," essentially causing us to lose touch with the people we interview and the narratives we hope to reconstruct.[56] While we should listen attentively and read our interview transcripts carefully for trends and silences, we must not pass judgment on the opinions of past generations. Rather it is vital to note that these gendered notions structured the ways in which boarding houses operated and therefore they are central to the collective experience of Sudbury's Ukrainians. Moreover, these gendered notions of work are vital to understanding the child-rearing practices of most parents, not just Ukrainian parents, who struggled to raise a family during the first half of the twentieth century.

When it came to reminiscing about their pasts, Ukrainian men and women used deeply personal biographical memories to understand their boyhood and girlhood experiences. In particular, boarders and boarding-house culture left indelible marks on the memories of Sudbury's Ukrainians. Regardless of their Catholic, Orthodox, nationalist, or progressive affiliations, my informants recounted similar working-class experiences, uniting an otherwise ideologically, politically, and religiously divided community in a collective struggle to survive.[57] There is no doubt that Sudbury's Ukrainians had very different experiences when they stepped onto the streets of their neighbourhoods or into their halls or churches; however, an examination of their domestic spaces reveals that boarding-house culture was a gendered, working-class experience shared by all those who lived it. Catholic girls who were chased down their streets by May Day protesters and progressive girls who were called communists in their schoolyards at recess both washed floors when they went home at night. Progressive boys who learned to speak Ukrainian and play the mandolin at the ULFTA hall and Catholic boys who spent their Sunday mornings as altar boys

both ran errands for their mothers and spent their leisure time telling jokes to the boarders who lived in their houses. Mothers who sang in the church choir or slaved over the ULFTA stoves all prepared perogies and cabbage rolls to satisfy their boarders. In noting such similarities, I am not denying that difference is important; indeed, it is quite central to the story of Sudbury's Ukrainians. It is however meant to bring attention to an underdeveloped but ever-present theme in the stories of men and women who grew up working class and Ukrainian in one northern Ontario town.

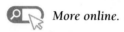 *More online.*

Notes

This article is based in part on a chapter of my doctoral dissertation. I would like to thank Franca Iacovetta, John Walsh, Steven High, Marilyn Barber, Rhonda Hinther, Myron Momryk, Kristina Guiget, Andrew Burtch, and Bryan Palmer for their comments on this article. An earlier draft of this article was presented at the Oral History in Canada Conference and therefore I would also like to thank all of the people who offered astute comments throughout the proceedings of that conference. These insights, along with those of *Labour/ Le Travail*'s anonymous reviewers, have enhanced this article. Above all, however, I am indebted to those who shared their stories with me.

1.   This article is based upon 82 oral history interviews conducted with Ukrainians who were . . . born or raised [in Sudbury] or came to the Sudbury region prior to 1945; 50 of these interviewees were women and 32 were men. These interviews took place between October 2004 and June 2005. Those interviewees who wished to remain anonymous were given the opportunity to choose an alias. When quoted, an interviewee's alias will be followed by an asterisk. Moreover, interviewees' maiden names have been included in the body of this article as well as in the footnotes. Many female interviewees married men who descended from other ethnicities and thus they now have non-Ukrainian surnames. This inclusion is meant to denote their Ukrainian heritage. Bill Semenuk, interview by author, Sudbury, 11 November 2004.

2. . . . Michael Frisch, *A Shared Authority: Essays on the Craft and Meaning of Oral and Public History* (Albany, NY: SUNY Press, 1990), 12–13.

3. See, for instance, Paul Thompson, *The Voice of the Past: Oral History* (Oxford, UK: Oxford University Press, 1988), 271–5; Alessandro Portelli, "The Peculiarities of Oral History," *History Workshop* 12 (Autumn 1981): 103–4; Virginia Yans-McLaughlin, "Metaphors of Self in History: Subjectivity, Oral Narrative, and Immigration Studies," in Virginia Yans-McLaughlin, ed., *Immigration Reconsidered: History, Sociology, and Politics* (Oxford, UK: Oxford University Press, 1990), 261–2; Joan Sangster, "Telling Our Stories: Feminist Debates and the Use of Oral History," *Women's History Review* 3 (March 1994): 10–13. . . .

4. Franca Iacovetta, "Post-Modern Ethnography, Historical Materialism, and Decentring the (Male) Authorial Voice: A Feminist Conversation," *Histoire Sociale/Social History* 32 (November 1999): 286.

5. For a Canadian discussion about the silences which result when informants are asked to recall events that have been deeply traumatic, see, for instance, Marlene Epp, *Women without Men: Mennonite Refugees of the Second World War* (Toronto, ON: University of Toronto Press, 1999), 48–63; . . . Paula Draper, "Surviving Their Survival: Women, Memory, and the Holocaust," in Marlene Epp, Franca Iacovetta, and Frances Swyripa, eds., *Sisters or Strangers? Immigrant, Ethnic, and Racialized Women in Canadian History* (Toronto, ON: University of Toronto Press, 2004), 399–414; . . . [and] Pamela Sugiman, "'These Feelings That Fill My Heart': Japanese Canadian Women's Memories of Internment," *Oral History* 34 (Autumn 2006): 78–80.

6. For a discussion about the ways in which Ukrainian immigrants structured their daily lives see Frances Swyripa, *Wedded to the Cause: Ukrainian-Canadian Women and Ethnic Identity, 1891–1991* (Toronto, ON: University of Toronto Press, 1993), 20–62. It must be noted that Denyse Baillargeon makes a similar point about working-class housewives in Montreal, noting that they were already used to unemployment, low wages, and frugal living before the Depression crippled the economy. Baillargeon, *Making Do: Women, Family, and Home in Montreal During the Great Depression*, Yvonne Klein, trans., (Waterloo, ON: Wilfrid Laurier University Press, 1999), 107. . . .

7. Alessandro Portelli, *The Death of Luigi Trastulli and Other Stories: Form and Meaning in Oral History* (Albany, NY: SUNY Press, 1991), 50.

8. . . . For a more sophisticated discussion about these contrasting identities, see, for instance, Frances Swyripa, *Wedded to the Cause*; Rhonda Hinther, "'Sincerest Revolutionary Greetings': Progressive Ukrainians in the Twentieth Century" (Ph.D. Dissertation, McMaster University, 2005); and Orest Martynowych, *Ukrainians in Canada: The Formative Period 1891–1924* (Edmonton, AB: Canadian Institute of Ukrainian Studies Press, 1991).

9. Paul Thompson and Sherna Berger Gluck discuss the ways in which insider/outsider relationships can impact the interview space. Unlike Thompson, Gluck also highlights the important roles that gender, class, and ethnicity play during an interview. See Thompson, *The Voice of the Past*, 140–1; and Gluck, "What's So Special About Women? Women's Oral History," in Susan Armitage, Patricia Hart, and Karen Weathermon, eds., *Women's Oral History: The Frontiers Reader* (Lincoln, NE: Frontiers Publishing, 2002), 3–26.

10. See Robert Atkinson, *The Life Story Interview* (Thousand Oaks, CA: Sage, 1988). It is significant to note that all of my interviewees were of working-class status. . . .

11. Frisch, *A Shared Authority*, 8.

12. Neil Sutherland, "When You Listen to the Winds of Childhood, How Much Can You Believe?" in Nancy Janovicek and Joy Parr, eds., *Histories of Canadian Children and Youth* (Toronto, ON: Oxford University Press, 2003), 23. . . .

13. For a discussion about the subjective nature of oral history and the importance of interpreting the silences which result in oral history narratives, see, for instance, Luisa Passerini, *Fascism in Popular Memory: The Cultural Experience of the Turin Working Class*, Robert Lumley and Jude Bloomfield, trans., (Cambridge, UK: Cambridge University Press, 1987), 67–70; and Sangster, "Telling Our Stories: Feminist Debates and the Use of Oral History," 7–10.

14. See, for instance, "Coniston—Letter from Maksym," *Ukrainski robitnychi visti*, 20 February 1930; "Sudbury," *Ukrainski robitnychi visti*, 8 July 1930, articles translated by Larissa Stavroff.

15. This was a generalized statement made by the majority of my interviewees. Ukrainian men and women regarded their mothers as dominant figures because in addition to running their households, they handled most of the disciplining that occurred in these spaces. Nick Evanshen, for instance, recalled that his mother, Mary, was very strict: "If I did something that wasn't right she would make me go outside, get a handful of rocks, and then I would have to kneel in the corner on the rocks with a broom over my head. . . . She was too busy to chase me around or spank me [and] that punishment stuck." See Nick Evanshen, interview by author, Sudbury, 14 May 2005.

16. C. M. Wallace, "The 1930s," in C. M. Wallace and Ashley Thomson, eds., *Sudbury: Rail Town to Regional Capital* (Toronto, ON: Dundurn Press, 1993), 143. . . .

17. Wallace, "The 1930s," 139.

18. Although working-class Ukrainians who lived in

Sudbury used boarding as a coping strategy, it must be noted that working-class families living in other parts of the country did not have the means to follow suit. In particular, Denyse Baillargeon notes that because of small and often crowded urban living spaces, boarding was not an option for working-class housewives living in Montreal during the thirties. See Baillargeon, *Making Do*, 97.

19. It is unclear how much men paid for boarding arrangements. Children were not involved in the financial end of these businesses and thus interviewees could not comment on these fees.

20. Nick Evanshen, interview.

21. Olga Zembrzycki (née Zyma), interview.

22. Pauline Kruk (née Mykoluk), interview by author, 20 January 2005.

23. Anonymous interview, interview by author, Sudbury, 18 May 2005.

24. Bernice Crowe (née Haluschak), interview by author, Sudbury, 17 May 2005.

25. John Stefura, interview by author, Sudbury, 24 January 2005.

26. Paul Behun, interview by author, Coniston, 12 May 2005. For a discussion about mother's allowances and the moral regulation of women, see Margaret Jane Hillyard Little, '*No Car, No Radio, No Liquor Permit': The Moral Regulation of Single Mothers in Ontario, 1920–1997* (Toronto, ON: Oxford University Press, 1998). . . .

27. Anne Matschke (née Kuchmey), interview by author, Sudbury, 7 May 2005. . . .

28. Bill Semenuk, interview. Employing the work of preindustrial British historian Naomi Tadmor, it is important to broach the term "like family" critically, noting that the boundaries of Ukrainian families were quite fluid at times and thus emanated from relationships of co-residence and authority. See Tadmor, "The Concept of the Household-Family in Eighteenth-Century England," *Past and Present* 151 (May 1996), 113 and 120–5.

29. Anonymous interviewee, interview by author, Sudbury, 16 November 2004.

30. Sutherland, "When You Listen to the Winds of Childhood, How Much Can You Believe?" 20.

31. Mary Brydges (née Ladyk), interview by author, Sudbury, 28 October 2004.

32. Angela Behun (née Bilowus), interview by author, Coniston, 12 May 2005.

33. Nellie Kozak (née Tataryn), interview by author, Sudbury, 6 June 2005.

34. See Lynne Marks, *Revivals and Roller Rinks: Religion, Leisure, and Identity in Late-Nineteenth-Century Small-Town Ontario* (Toronto, ON: University of Toronto Press, 1996).

35. Peter Chitruk, interview.

36. Nick Evanshen, interview.

37. For an examination about the ways that social reformers depicted the moral boundaries of urban space and, in particular, the boarding house, see James Opp, "Re-imaging the Moral Order of Urban Space: Religion and Photography in Winnipeg, 1900–1914," *Journal of the Canadian Historical Association* 13 (2002), 86. . . .

38. See, for instance, Archives of Ontario (AO), Record Group (RG) 22–392, Box 151, File: Swerda, John, Sudbury, 1920, Carnal Knowledge of Girl Under 14.

39. Olga Zembrzycki (née Zyma), interview.

40. Bettina Bradbury, *Working Families: Age, Gender, and Daily Survival in Industrializing Montreal* (Toronto, ON: McClelland & Stewart, 1993), 175–8.

41. Food is central to understanding the narratives of immigrants, especially immigrant women. See, for example, Franca Iacovetta, *Gatekeepers: Reshaping Immigrant Lives in Cold War Canada* (Toronto, ON: Between the Lines, 2006), 137–69; Franca Iacovetta and Valerie J. Korinek, "Jell-O Salads, One-Stop Shopping, and Maria the Homemaker: The Gender Politics of Food," and Marlene Epp, "The Semiotics of Zwieback: Feast and Famine in the Narratives of Mennonite Refugee Women," in Epp, Iacovetta, Swyripa, eds., *Sisters or Strangers?* 190–230, 314–40. . . .

42. Anne Matschke (née Kuchmey), interview.

43. For a discussion about the ways in which women were financially responsible for budgeting the family income, see, for instance, Bradbury, *Working Families*.

44. Bernice Crowe (née Haluschak), interview.

45. Helen Cotnam (née Cybulka), interview by author, Sudbury, 2 May 2005.

46. Paul Behun, interview.

47. Generally, interviewees stated that blueberry picking lasted about three weeks a year and supplemented the family income nicely. Although many interviewees recalled that this extra income helped to pay for groceries others, like Ernie Lekun's mother, Mary, saved the money they earned. Mary, who made about 50 cents a basket, spent a number of years saving and, in the end, purchased her first refrigerator with the money around 1947. Ernie Lekun, interview. Also see "88,000 Quarts of Blueberries Are Harvested," *Sudbury Star*, 20 July 1932; and "4,500 Baskets Sent to Toronto Each Day from District Points," *Sudbury Star*, 12 July 1933.

48. Stanley Hayduk, interview by author, Garson, 19 May 2005.

49. Bill Semenuk, interview.

50. Frank Makarinsky, interview by author, Sudbury, 4 May 2005.

51. Swyripa, *Wedded to the Cause*, 26. Rhonda Hinther also draws on Swyripa's argument and provides a convincing discussion pertaining to the ways in which this

gendered cultural baggage was a part of the Ukrainian left. See Hinther, "'Sincerest Revolutionary Greetings': Progressive Ukrainians in the Twentieth Century," 128–9. . . .

52. Baillargeon, *Making Do*, 42.

53. See Bradbury, *Working Families*; and "Gender at Work at Home: Family Decisions, the Labour Market and Girls' Contributions to the Family Economy," in Gregory S. Kealey and Greg Patmore eds., Canadian and Australian Labour History (Australian-Canadian Studies, Sydney, 1990), 119–40.

54. Although the Ukrainian men that I interviewed openly admitted to being treated in a more superior manner than their sisters, they did so in more hesitant and guarded ways than women, making sure to indicate that they had contributed to the family economy nevertheless. See, for instance, Joseph Maizuk, interview by author, Sudbury, 25 January 2005.

55. Olga Zembrzycki (née Zyma), interview. Nellie Kozak's (née Tataryn) mother echoed this sentiment, stating ". . . you don't need to go [to school] to wash dishes and diapers." See Nellie Kozak (née Tataryn), interview.

56. Michael Frisch, "Working-Class Public History in the Context of Deindustrialization: Dilemmas of Authority and the Possibilities of Dialogue," *Labour/Le Travail* 51 (Spring 2003), 153–64.

57. Despite the egalitarian views that progressive Ukrainians maintained in the public sphere, especially in their ULFTA hall, they did not transfer these beliefs to their homes. "Equality," as Swyripa notes, "often remained an elusive and contentious ideal." See Swyripa, *Wedded to the Cause*, 151.

6 What to Do with the "Tubby Hubby"?
"Obesity," the Crisis of Masculinity, and the Nuclear Family in Early Cold War Canada

Deborah McPhail

Introduction

On Thursday, 13 March 1952, the first page of Canada's national newspaper, the *Globe and Mail*, announced a new serial by regular columnist Josephine Lowman: the "Tubby Hubby Diet." The "Tubby Hubby Diet," which ran every few days until 8 July and was again serialized in 1953 and 1954, pronounced obesity as a "top killer" and "one of [Canada's] top national health problems."[1] The "Tubby Hubby Diet" was new territory for this women's column.

As the accompanying illustrations made explicit,[2] Lowman's serial targeted fat, white, heterosexual men, seemingly counteracting feminist arguments that fat phobia has been historically and primarily directed toward women.[3] Yet, even as Lowman spoke *of* men, she continued to speak *to* women, as the following titles attested: "Slim him 7 to 12 lbs in just 12 short days,"[4] "Don't let him on scales until 12 days are over,"[5] and "Doesn't need to know he's on a diet."[6] Therefore, while to some extent supporting the feminist theory that "fat is feminine,"[7] this example illustrates that there is a need for a more nuanced reading of gender in relation to fatness, and for theoretical work which explores how and why the collapse of fat and feminine differs over

time, across space, and together with shifting notions of gender, race, and class. Focusing in particular on anti-obesity regulatory measures regarding the atrophying physical fitness of male Canadians in the early Cold War[8] and on the increased consumption and availability of new foods in this era, I argue that obesity cannot be divorced from the gendered, raced, and classed political economy from which it emerges.

This paper is a historically and geographically specific analysis of feminized fat, in which I place primary texts in conversation with theories of abjection in order to question why obesity concerns circulated in a particular place, at a particular time, despite a lack of statistical and scientific evidence about the prevalence of fat. Drawing upon and extending the growing literature, both within and outside the discipline of geography, that understands obesity as a culturally or discursively produced mode of embodiment as opposed to a purely biological or epidemiological problem,[9] this paper explores how discourses of fat and obesity emerged in early Cold War Canada to define and police borders between public and private spheres. In doing so, I argue that Lowman's "Tubby Hubby Diet" reflected a more general Cold War concern with white male obesity in Canada, as "tubby

Citation: Deborah McPhail, "What to Do with the 'Tubby Hubby'? 'Obesity,' the Crisis of Masculinity, and the Nuclear Family in Early Cold War Canada," *Antipode* 41, no. 5 (2009): 1021–50. © 2009 *The Author Journal* compilation © 2009 Editorial Board of *Anntipode*..

hubbies" were defined and mobilized to assuage anxieties created by shifts in racialized gender relations necessary to the post-war economy, and by beliefs about impending nuclear war. The fat male body, and in particular the *removal* of encroaching fat from white, middle-class men's bodies, therefore functioned symbolically to rearticulate the breadwinner husband, home-maker wife division of labour and to repos-ition Canada as a nation of white, middle-class nuclear families. This discussion is of contem-porary as well as historical significance since, if the problem of growing obesity in Cold War Canada was more about social anxieties created by shifting power relations and less about sci-entific and medical facts,[10] then similar critiques can be made of the seemingly unquestionable Truths about the current-day obesity epidemic.

. . .

Embodying the Apocalypse: Obesity and the Cold War

During the 1950s and 1960s, Canadian discus-sions of male obesity occurred in the context of three overarching anxieties. First, concern proliferated regarding the possible, if not prob-able, attack on Canadian cities by commun-ist Russia.[11] Second, economic shifts requiring middle-class men to perform more "relational" or service-based paid labour and increasing numbers of women working for wages induced a post-war Canadian "crisis of masculinity."[12] Last, worries surfaced regarding the influx of post-war immigrants who, along with Aboriginal peoples, challenged the supposed universality of the patriarchal, white, middle-class nuclear family form in Canada.[13] In this section I will explore in further detail the role of these anxieties in the production of racialized gender relations within which white male fatness came to constitute abject embodiment. To do so, I first outline the production of obesity concerns in Canada dur-ing this time before discussing the economic and political context which underlay them.

Obesity served as a general seat of anx-iety during the Cold War period in Canada. Spurred by medical, government, and insur-ance company research that claimed obesity to cause everything from cardiovascular disease to varicose veins, from appendicitis to cancer, from depressive psychosis to diabetes, and from accidents to suicide, medical journals, the *Globe and Mail*, and *Maclean's* expressed concern about a country growing too big.[14] To support these claims, reports surfaced declaring that any-where from one-fifth to one-half of Canadians were too fat.[15] Yet, despite such confident and rather dire proclamations about the effects of obesity, the evidence of obesity's prevalence was far from consistent during the 1950s and 1960s. The lack of dependable obesity sta-tistics was discouraging for some, including S. S. B. Gilder who, in a rather defeated tone, stated in his *Canadian Medical Association Journal* (*CMAJ*) column that ". . . in spite of much research, we know little about the prevalence of obesity, [and] its measurement . . ."[16]

Gilder was exactly right on both counts: The prevalence of obesity in Canada was not known because the category of obesity had yet to be definitively measured and determined. During the early Cold War, there was no estab-lished agreement over categories such as obes-ity, overweight, and fat, and such terms were used interchangeably throughout the 1950s and 1960s. Medical experts defined obesity any-where from 20 per cent to 30 per cent above the ideal weights listed on insurance company height/weight charts.[17] The *Globe and Mail* illus-trated similar disagreement, with some reports defining obesity as 10 per cent above the ideal,[18] and some as 25 per cent.[19]

This lack of consensus about obesity's defin-ition, and hence prevalence, can be understood in part as a result of competition between insur-ance companies, employees of the federal govern-ment's Department of Health and Welfare, and the medical establishment and must be context-ualized within a changing Canadian healthcare system. Since 1948, the federal government had considered government-funded healthcare for all Canadians regardless of income, which eventually became a reality between 1968 and 1970.[20] During the years leading up to public medicare, the Canadian Medical Association and insurance companies expressed serious resistance to the health plan, both believing that a state-funded health system would impede the selling of their services in a supposedly free market.[21] The struggle for power between insurance companies and doctors on the one hand, who were aligned by their disdain for state-funded medicare, and the state on the other, surfaced in disagreements regarding the etiology of obesity. Specifically, debate raged relating to the use of insurance company height/weight charts in the classification and definition of obesity. For example, the federal government's Nutrition Division's Chief, L. B. Pett, did not hide his skepticism of the charts in his correspondence or his publications.[22] Pett challenged the notion that heights and weights alone should define obesity and advocated for the additional measurement of subcutaneous fat with skin calipers, eventually devising his own charts based on the height, weight, and skin measurements of Canadians.[23] However, the dominant measure for obesity continued to be height/weight, evident in the proliferation of the BMI as a measure today.[24] . . .

It should be noted that dissent about obesity measurement did not necessarily follow a neat opposition of insurance companies and doctors versus the state. Some medical practitioners writing in the CMAJ also critiqued insurance company charts citing similar reasons to Pett's,[25] and, though Pett's height, weight, and skin caliper charts were rarely cited in the same journal, they were published there in 1955.[26] Pett's research was also used by the insurance industry, and the American Society of Actuaries cited the Canadian data in its *Build and Blood Pressure Study* of 1959.[27] The fact that insurance companies could incorporate Pett's study, which was conceived and carried out as a counterweight to

ineffective insurance company classifications, points to the companies' tradition of "[resisting] the call for better statistics . . . in order to preserve the standard insurance practice of equalizing risk."[28] The wider range of weights and measurements insurance companies could characterize as "obese," the better for their profit margins.[29]

Conflicts about the measurement of obesity did not preclude state officials and writers in the popular press and medical journals from declaring obesity a national problem of vast proportions. For example, in a 1957 CMAJ article, Dr. Rosario Robillard named obesity "undoubtedly the most frequent disease encountered" by Canadian physicians;[30] in a 1960 CMAJ article, LeRiche stated that "[t]he commonest form of malnutrition in North America is obesity";[31] and in 1967, Dr. J. V. G. A. Durnin called obesity "one of the great disabling conditions of modern civilization."[32] Indeed, obesity was considered such a problem for Canada that in 1967, the editor of the CMAJ went so far as to describe it, along with accidents, smoking, and alcoholism, as one of the "four horsemen [of the Apocalypse]."[33] Such declarations were also made by the state. For example, at a 1965 meeting of the Canadian Public Health Association, J. E. Monagle, chief of the Canadian government's Nutrition Division and successor to L. B. Pett, called obesity ". . . a problem of increasing proportions" and "a matter of major public health concern."[34] Monagle also devised "The Civil Service Obesity Study" together with his colleague E. L. Davey, chief of the Civil Service Health Division in 1960 (Nutrition Division 1960–3). Unfortunately for the two men the study, which had the intent of slimming down the civil service and increasing the division's knowledge about the causes of and cures for obesity, failed to get off the ground due to poor design.

The continued assertion of obesity as a problem despite disagreement over its classification in early Cold War Canada has clear similarities to current practices in the discursive production of an "obesity epidemic" critiqued by many critical obesity scholars.[35] Given this lack of consensus regarding how fat was "too fat," it seems important to question why obesity was declared a Canadian problem and to explicate why, indeed, it was pronounced a sign of the apocalypse. In order to understand this, I argue that it is necessary to situate obesity within the wider economic and political context of the early Cold War period.

Of "Missiles and Muscles"[36]: Abjection and the "Tubby Hubby"

Even as obesity was considered a national problem during the Cold War, and was therefore supposedly applicable to every Canadian, some Canadians more than others were singled out for concern. Chief among these "problem populations" was the otherwise seemingly "normal" white, heterosexual, middle-class man who mainstream discursive agents anxiously noted was becoming "soft" as a result of his growing body weight.[37] Much of the worry about men's "atrophying muscle" and "expanding pot-bellies" was rooted in Cold War crises of impending war, the feminization of the economy, and challenge to white, middle-class nuclear family typicality engendered by post-war immigration.

Impending War

The explosion of two atomic bombs heralded the end of one war and the beginning of another. During this new "Cold War" successive Canadian governments, in the main, aligned themselves politically and ideologically with other western nations, and especially with the United States.[38] With its northern stores of uranium essential to the United States's nuclear arsenal and its Arctic region so close to enemy shores,[39] Canada became an important, though admittedly unequal, American ally, as well as a potential communist target. The vulnerability created by Canada's close affiliation with and proximity to the United States gained frightening plausibility

following the Gouzenko affair of 1945, in which a Russian spy working at the Soviet embassy in Canada, Igor Gouzenko, admitted to gathering intelligence on Canada's atomic program and claimed that other Soviet spies were doing the same.[40] The unease created by the Gouzenko affair gave rise to conversations regarding a full-scale attack on Canadian cities. For its part, the Canadian state took up a rhetoric of civil defence similar to that of the United States,[41] encouraging individual citizens to prepare themselves for nuclear war.[42]

The spectacle of the normative man's supposedly atrophying muscle was sensationalized in the context of civil defence discussions, as it was argued that everyday male civilians would be required not only to fight in case of communist attack, but to rebuild the nation during nuclear fallout. In the early 1950s, the Canadian press, both popular and medical, continued to worry about Canada's campaign in World War II which, though obviously successful, had revealed a disturbing fact about the fitness of the nation: 44 per cent of army recruits called up for duty during conscription proved unfit for immediate service, otherwise known as a "C-3" classification.[43] While a "C-3 nation" could win World War II, concern was that World War III would be very different, and the ostensible climb of male obesity seemed to demonstrate that men were not up for the challenge. For example, *Globe and Mail* reporter James Senter connected the army's worries regarding the softness of the nation's men to a probable war, stating: "Army concern over the standard of physical fitness prevailing in this country is a direct result of the increased need for mobility in this era of atomic war."[44] Indeed, fears regarding men's abilities to fight World War III seemed validated by the Canadian army's estimated recruitment rejection rate during the Korean conflict which, though not as high as World War II, was 30 per cent.[45] Referring to the "abhorrent" physical fitness of Korean armed forces rejects, the editor of the *Globe and Mail* made cryptic links between men's increasing fat and the potential fall of the nation, noting that "history deals harshly with nations which go soft."[46]

The Feminization of the Workforce

Reports decrying Canada's dilapidating manhood were not only concerned with national defence, but also the nation's gendered economic relations. The Cold War created and required an economy which evoked worries about the feminization of both men and the public sphere, which Mona Gleason and Mary Louise Adams have named a post-war "crisis of middle-class masculinity."[47] This crisis was precipitated by three main economic phenomena, including the feminization of male labour, the increase of women's paid labour in the public sphere, and the belief that men's sedentary labour was, ironically, making men too ill to work.

According to Gleason and Adams, the concomitant post-war expansion of the social welfare and corporate bureaucracies created an explosion of white-collar work for middle-class men.[48] White-collar jobs at the civil service or in corporate offices were relational jobs requiring the "organization man."[49] This new male worker had a feminized personality "concerned with the thoughts of others, tuned to the needs of others," which was the "antithesis of the 'rugged individualism' that grounded . . . [ideals of] white, middle-class masculinity."[50] At the same time that middle-class men's jobs were becoming feminine, single and married women were entering the paid workforce with increasing frequency.

During World War II, women had taken up the call of government and industry to fill previously male jobs, thus proving productive labour was not a "naturally" male prerogative. Moreover, the post-war economy required the cheap-yet-paid labour of women who continued to participate in the labour force although initially in smaller numbers and in different capacities than during the war.[51] Women did jobs that men would not do, due to the labelling of

such work as "women's work" or the low payment offered. Indeed, Armstrong notes that the expansion of both the social welfare state and corporations was facilitated in part by women's clerical labour.[52]

While women were increasingly winning their own bread, men were reportedly becoming less physically able to work for theirs. The Canadian government's nationwide Sickness Survey, commissioned in 1948, had shown that more men were beginning to take "disability" or "sick" days, a fact that commentators were beginning to relate to a lack of physical fitness.[53] Over and above any other type of men's labour, there was a palpable Cold War concern about the physical fitness of white-collar workers, or businessmen, who, due to post-war shifts in labour, were increasingly required to carry out sedentary work sitting at desks. Such concerns about insalubrious sedentary male office workers were reflected in a 1958 newsletter published by the Royal Bank of Canada, called the *Monthly Letter*:

Business men, alas, are among the world's worst practitioners of health habits. They may be able administrators, well-informed about company operations, excellent in work systems, and towers of strength in production, but they tend to be careless and thoughtless with regard to their own fitness . . ."[54]

Worries like these expressed by the Royal Bank were echoed in the popular press. In a 1959 article in the financial section, the *Globe and Mail* reported a growth in fitness clubs and classes designed exclusively for male businessmen.[55] This same article noted that some firms were beginning to require their male desk workers to take fitness classes. In a *Globe and Mail* pictorial, a line of white men were shown undertaking various physical fitness tests for upper arm and abdominal strength. The tests, conducted at the Central YMCA in Toronto, and to be repeated at YMCAs across Canada, "showed that those examined, like most Canadian businessmen, [were] not at their peak of physical fitness."[56] The YMCA, in addition to testing the fitness of businessmen's bodies, also suggested exercises for them. The YMCA's Jim McVicar, for instance, advised a program of "desk exercises" to a Rotary Club in Toronto, a men's service organization.[57] The *Globe and Mail* quoted McVicar: "Every time your phone rings pull your stomach in against your backbone and hold it there until you find out who it is."[58]

Due to their purportedly larger waist lines and soft muscles, men, and specifically white, middle-class office workers, were said to be less able both to defend their country in war and to work for wages during a time of Canadian capitalist expansion. Additionally, as Adams and Gleason note, the sedentary jobs in which middle-class men were increasingly engaged were themselves highly feminized, so much so that even if men were not chronically absent due to illness, their work engendered a middle-class crisis of masculinity.[59] The fact that this relational labour was also said to be making men obese was an inflection of this crisis. As writers about men's fat argue of other periods,[60] male fat in the Cold War era became an embodied stand-in for anxieties about men's intensified femininity and inability to fulfill their male roles—a fact which rang clear in a 1958 *Globe and Mail* editorial in which the editor, decrying male softness, declared Canadian men an "effete people."[61]

The codification of male body fat as "effete" and "soft" recalls Longhurst's description of the abject as a form of feminized and malleable embodiment.[62] Considering men's body fat as abject is helpful in explaining the almost obsessive degree to which discursive agents were interested in producing obesity as a problem, despite conflicting evidence regarding its prevalence. Convinced that men were becoming, to paraphrase Kristeva, "swamped" by feminized fat,[63] medical, state, and popular figures organized slim-down campaigns for men that generally took the form of physical fitness and dieting

regimes. Such regimes, which can be characterized as processes of abjection, expelled the feminine from the bodies of subjects, allowing the "recuperation" of men's masculinity.[64] As Longhurst and McClintock lead me to suggest, however, these processes of fat abjection were not only levelled at the bodies of individual men, but also at the social body, redeploying the public/private split through the recitation of weight loss rituals.[65] In large part, the reification of the border between public and private was accomplished through narratives of the nuclear family which, in response to shifts in gender and race relations, were already in heavy circulation.

Fighting Fat in the Nuclear Family

The Cold War period was a troubling time for the white, middle-class nuclear family in Canada. Not only were more and more women, and even mothers, working for wages in the public sphere, not only were breadwinner husbands keeling over at their desks and becoming emasculated by their sedentary labour, but post-war Canada was witnessing an influx of immigration that was worrisome to a nation supposedly of Western European descent.[66] Feminist historians have shown, however, that anxieties regarding the state of the white nuclear family were as productive as they were repressive, re-creating the normative nuclear family through the very narratives of its demise.[67]

For example, immediately following World War II, a large population of immigrants originating from Southern and Eastern Europe landed on Canada's shores who, although white-skinned, elicited a racial panic in mainstream Canadians.[68] This panic increased as numbers of immigrants of colour to Canada began to grow with the "liberalization of immigration policy and citizenship in the 1960s and 1970s."[69] Ideals of the nuclear family, and especially of the heterosexual breadwinner/homemaker duo upon which the family supposedly depended, became important both as tools of assimilation and as means of reprimand used against immigrants, who did not or could not organize themselves into the type of families mainstream Canadians had in mind.

In *Gatekeepers*, Franca Iacovetta details how public health workers, social workers, state agents (like nutritionists), and the popular press worried that ever-increasing populations of immigrant women did not know Canadian housewifery techniques, and advised "new Canadian" women in the proper ways of the bourgeois nuclear family.[70] Through cooking classes held at local social work agencies, government-published booklets, and articles in magazines, these women were admonished for everything from bad hygiene to unscientific cooking, and were particularly villainized as "un-Canadian" if they worked outside of the home for wages.[71] Indeed, rising numbers of working mothers were characterized as immigrant and working class, despite the fact that white, middle-class women were also working for wages in growing numbers.[72] Similar practices were carried out by agents of the colonial–capitalist state, who impressed nuclear family norms and middle-class housewifery practices upon Aboriginal women.[73]

The exclusion, assimilation, and punishment of immigrants and Aboriginal peoples with nuclear family discourse reaffirmed the supposed superiority and prevalence of the patriarchal, bourgeois nuclear family while it also rendered white, middle-class families, and those who composed them, as "normal" and "Canadian." The notion that the nuclear family was common was integral to Cold War Canada, not only because it reassured Canadians that the nation remained white, but also because it calmed the fears of nuclear annihilation. As scholars of the Cold War era have shown,[74] the reproductive labour of women in the home was touted as intrinsic to the survival of the Canadian nation in case of nuclear attack. In this context, women were positioned as the stalwarts of democracy in the home, responsible for keeping their families strong and healthy through their cooking, cleaning, and general child-rearing practices, and for instilling the values and norms of the Free World in their children. The nuclear family was thus imagined as the "secret weapon" of the Canadian nation; the place, in the end, where democracy was spawned and the war would be won. In *The Trouble with Normal*, Mary Louise Adams describes this popular argument, proliferated by psychologists, the popular press, and state agents alike, that if everything was alright with the nuclear family, then everything was alright with the nation. Thus, as Adams writes, "the nuclear family came to operate as a symbol of safety—not just on the individual level, but on the national level as well."[75]

Given the discursive milieu wherein the coherence of the race-based national identity, and indeed the very existence of the nation, depended in part upon the recitation of the nuclear family form, antidotes for male obesity played an important role. These cure-alls recited nuclear family normalcy through texts and pictorials that positioned the soft Canadian man as a family-waged husband surrounded by his white, heteronormative, middle-class nuclear family. Unlike Iacovetta's study of cookery advice, anti-obesity regimes focusing on both physical fitness and men's diets were mobilized to construct the normative nuclear family through exclusion, and were less used to admonish directly the embodied practices of immigrant and Aboriginal peoples.[76] Physical fitness manuals for men provide an example, as they positioned immigrant and Aboriginal families as "abnormal" and "un-Canadian" through their continued representation of the Canadian family as white and middle class.

The YMCA's fitness classes for businessmen were not the only fitness plans available to male white-collar workers, as the 1950s and 1960s witnessed a veritable explosion in physical fitness regimes for this specific group. Fitness guru Lloyd Percival, for example, was a virtual fitness industry all to himself. As host of a regular Canadian Broadcasting Corporation (CBC) radio program called *Sports College*, "Head Coach Lloyd Percival" dispensed fitness advice and broadcast physical fitness regimes. In addition to his radio show, Percival published numerous $1 "how-to" manuscripts and films, which included *Fitness Is Easy* along with such titles as *How to Keep Your Body Young* and *How to Keep Lean and Healthy*.[77]

Percival's fitness research and advice, when not directed at adolescent boys, was often intended for the sedentary male desk worker. Reporting on the results of a fitness test conducted in Don Mills, a Toronto suburb, which began in 1949 and spanned six years, Percival argued that the male middle-income businessman was the most fat and physically unfit of all Canadians.[78] And no wonder. In *Fitness Is Easy*, Percival described, in chart form, the normal day of a man working a desk job. The chart, which Percival called "Typical daily caloric burn-up of sedentary urban male" included the time and calories spent by such activities as "shaving, etc.," "reading paper, talk," "looking for briefcase, etc.," "driving to work," "parking, walk to office, etc.," "getting settled, working at desk," "drive home," "waiting for dinner," and "television."[79] Evident here is men's participation in office labour and concomitant lack of contribution to domestic chores, as physical fitness regimes like those provided in Percival's *Fitness Is Easy* and his *Fitness for All the Family* were marketed to combat such a sedentary lifestyle elicited by the desk job.[80] Indeed, even though fitness may have been "for all the family," it is apparent by Percival's illustrations of white men doing push-ups, sit-ups, chin-ups, running on the spot, and so on that his regime was in fact designed for the "hardening-up" of sedentary white-collar men.

The state via the Royal Canadian Air Force [RCAF] was also involved in selling physical fitness manuals to sedentary middle-class men. Originally designed for RCAF personnel, the *5BX Plan for Physical Fitness* was a graduated

regime designed specifically for men, intended to counteract the "[m]echanization, automation, and work-saving devices designed to make life easy" that were depriving men of "desirable physical activity."[81] Noting that "Canadians . . . [were] in danger of deteriorating physically,"[82] the *5BX* provided charts to record one's progression through increasingly strenuous activities, and illustrations and instructions for such exercises as the stationary run and "semi-spread eagle" jump which consisted of 75 stationary runs, a squat, and a jump in the air with the legs split to each side.[83] The *5BX* program took off, becoming hugely popular in both the Canadian and American civilian populations and in other countries' armies and air forces, including those of the United States, Australia, New Zealand, and Thailand.[84] One copy of the *5BX* had been purchased by none other than John Wayne, as reported in a *Globe and Mail* interview with the actor.[85] In addition to Hollywood icons and foreign armed forces, the *5BX* program was also intended in part to shape up Canadian sedentary office workers, as demonstrated by its illustration of a tired-looking white man wearing a business suit being dragged into action by another white man in exercise garb, a copy of the RCAF's plan in hand (see Figure 1).

Reflecting what theorists and sports historians argue more generally about the conflation of masculinity and physical fitness,[86] physical fitness during the Cold War period was primarily regarded by state agents and writers in the medical and popular presses as a male prerogative. While there were some physical fitness regimes for women, they had quite different emphases. For example, the Air Force also produced the popular *XBX* program for women, consisting of a series of exercises like toe touching, leg raises, and arm circles.[87] Unlike the *5BX* for men, the *XBX* program did not purport that physical fitness was necessary to counteract the "physical deterioration" of the nation, but rather included a page-long section on how physical fitness could help appearance. The "Your Appearance"

Figure 1. Preventing sedentary men's obesity without delay. Source: Royal Canadian Air Force, *5BX Plan for Physical Fitness*, 3rd ed. (Ottawa, ON: Queen's Printer, 1965), 5. Amicus No: 10085790 National Defence.

section, which was not printed in the *5BX*, noted that the muscle toned through the *XBX* could "perform the same function as a girdle,"[88] pulling in the fat which accumulated on women's stomachs. "The *XBX*," the plan assured readers, was "designed to firm . . . muscles—not to convert [the participant] into a muscled woman."[89] The *XBX* also advocated physical fitness for the sake of housewifery, as a picture of a happy white housewife, ironing clothes with one hand, playing tennis with the other indicated, the caption reading: "Lead a balanced life" (see Figure 2). Similarly, in an article entitled "Scrub to keep fit," the *Globe and Mail* quoted physical fitness consultant to the federal government, Dr. Doris Plewes, as encouraging women to "get down on hands and knees and scrub the kitchen floor" to keep physically active and attractive to men.[90] When dominant discursive agents did encourage women to become fit, then, they often did

not advocate physical activity for women's own sakes, but rather for men's, as fitness plans for females were almost always designed to produce better-rested, better-looking, and sometimes even larger-busted housewives.[91]

At the same time that physical fitness programs were beginning to hit their zenith, restricted menu plans for men also surfaced. Many writers in the popular and medical presses believed that while exercise was fine, the battle of the bulge would inevitably fail if food intake was not restricted. In the words of Josephine Lowman, selling the benefits of the diet that opened this paper: "Exercise won't save you men, if you are greatly overweight. Join the Tubby Hubby Diet."[92] Even as medical interest in physical fitness increased after the Canadian Medical Association's honorary president, HRH Prince Philip, criticized Canadian sloth in his 1959 presidential address,[93] articles in the

Figure 2. "Lead a balanced life." Source: Royal Canadian Air Force, *XBX: XBX Plan for Physical Fitness* (Ottawa, ON: Queen's Printer, 1962), 46. Amicus No: 32617834.

medical press focused less on fitness than they did on the study of nutrition, dietary changes, or appetite-reducing drugs for weight loss purposes.[94] Though skepticism about exercise was not shared by everyone, least of all such fitness experts as Lloyd Percival, the focus on food and food restriction charged women not only with slimming their already-obese husbands but also with keeping them slim in the first place. It was women in this scenario, not men, who were to blame for obesity, and wives were charged with the task of slimming their "tubby" husbands.

Cooking tips for women with fat husbands like the kind Josephine Lowman gave in her "Tubby Hubby Diet" were intended to help those women who were cooking nutritionally unbalanced meals. For example, Lowman's serial included menu plans at the end of every article which were "scientifically planned to give him the right number of calories and necessary food elements."[95] A typical menu read as follows:

Breakfast
One cup of orange juice
Generous helping of oatmeal (with cup skimmed milk and two teaspoons of sugar)
Two pieces of toast, lightly buttered
Two pieces of crisp bacon
Coffee

Lunch
Two grilled hamburgers
Green salad, lemon juice for dressing
One green or yellow vegetable
One slice of bread or roll, little butter
One glass of butter milk or skimmed milk

Dinner
Clear soup
One helping of lean meat
One-half cup of squash
One cup of string beans
One piece of bread

Gelatine, moderate helping
One glass of buttermilk or skimmed milk[96]

The notion that housewives were making husbands fat because they failed to balance calories "scientifically," and therefore required such menus as the one reproduced above, was combined with worries about the explosion of food availability which had occurred after World War II. Not only was more food obtainable at more times of the year, but so, too, could Canadians afford to buy more of the stuff. As Sidney Katz reported in a 1955 *Maclean's* article called "A Report on Eating," "sales of twenty or thirty dollars" had "become routine" in Canada's shiny new supermarkets, and "one supermarket cashier recall[ed] watching a customer stagger off with ninety-five dollars worth of groceries."[97]

Connecting post-war Canadian affluence, increased food choice and consumption, and obesity, a number of texts provided anti-obesity nutrition education for housewives who were said to be fattening up their families at an alarming rate. Lowman's "Tubby Hubby Diet" series was one example of anti-obesity nutrition for housewives—and there were others. "The Kitchen Demon," as Percival called the "wife and mother who prides herself on her cooking, on her special recipes and special desserts," required guidance in order to keep her husband and family from becoming "super-fatty" in a time of heightened food affluence.[98] Percival provided such guidance with menus and charts for the housewife in his fitness guides,[99] as did the federal government's Nutrition Division in its publication *Healthful Eating*. *Healthful Eating* used the science-based Canada Food Guide to help women avoid nutrition problems, including obesity, when feeding families and "working" husbands.[100] A revision of a publication originally printed in 1943,[101] the pamphlet was produced for "teachers . . . health workers, high school students, and housewives," and made links between increasing food choice and obesity.[102] In a section called "Other Foods" the pamphlet warned the reader that too many

calories derived from bad food choices, in this case referring to food with high fat content, "may contribute to undesirable weight gain (obesity) and should be avoided."[103]

. . . [T]he attempted expulsion of fat from the bodies of men through fitness and dieting functioned, in part, as a social curative. By picturing the corpulent as exclusively white in all instructive texts including the 5BX, *Healthful Eating*, and the "Tubby Hubby Diet" series, and by narrating men as ailing white-collar workers and women as housewives who could potentially purchase any and all food without thought as to its cost, discourses of food excess and obesity reified the white, middle-class nuclear family as normative through a sheer and almost total denial of non-nuclear families, people of colour, the working class, immigrants, or Aboriginal peoples. Despite the belief that the gendered practices associated with the normative nuclear family had to be taught to immigrant and Aboriginal families, and even though middle-class families with working mothers were on the rise, physical fitness plans and diets for men touted the nuclear family as natural, common, and Canadian.

In addition to reiterating raced and classed norms, physical fitness and diet plans served to recite gendered ones, as well. Physical fitness manuals established the masculinity of individual men through hardening their soft and feminized bodies, a particularly important task during a time of impending war; it was probably no coincidence that a fitness plan published by the Royal Canadian Air Force was a Canadian bestseller. While more feminine and relational jobs were making middle-class men soft, ill, and unprepared for war, highly masculinized and militarized routines like the 5BX could make men muscular, taut, and masculine again even while they remained white-collar workers. Diet plans also alleviated worries about men's feminizing labour. By claiming that women had to adjust their cooking to cure male obesity, discursive agents were, in effect, shifting the blame for obesity from middle-class men's increasingly sedentary jobs to their wives. While fat could be exacerbated or even caused by sedentary labour in the public sphere, it was really in the private sphere where obesity spread. If husbands were fat, women were charged with doing something about it. If men were slim, the kitchen demon could easily make them fat. The "tubby hubby" scenario thus soothed the post-war crisis of masculinity caused by economic shifts, in that the need for female instruction indicated no failure in masculinity, but certainly one in femininity.

Thus, physical fitness plans and diets for "tubby hubbies" that reified the nuclear family did more than remove the abject feminine from the bodies of men, but also from the public sphere as a whole, containing it in the private through representational means. As pictures of men in suits and women ironing showed, physical fitness narratives served to reiterate the gendered division of labour as if it were typical and universal. Confidently reified were the notions that men were in the public sphere, sitting at their desks and sucking in their abdomens when answering the telephone, while women were happily "down on their knees and scrubbing the floor" for physical fitness purposes. Like those regarding physical fitness, discussions of increased food availability and the obesity created by it served to reposition women in the private sphere—the "kitchen demon" was, most importantly, *in the kitchen*. Moreover, in maintaining that fat originated or at least proliferated at the hands of wives, obesity was placed in what McClintock calls the feminized "abject zone" of the private sphere, the place, as Longhurst notes, where bodies are put to leak.[104] Such reification of public/private split through processes of fat abjection were both a corollary of and necessary to a time in which worries about the raced identity of the nation, disruptions in the gendered division of labour, and nearing apocalypse were tied to the proliferation of the nuclear family form. Promoting the normalcy of the nuclear family by cordoning off coherent public and private spheres, men's slim-down projects reassured Canadians that

men were still men, women still women, and the nation was safe.

Conclusion

As the examples in this paper illustrate, anxieties regarding obesity in Cold War Canada had less to do with the actual growing girth of bodies which had yet to be proven unequivocally, and more about the psychic trauma elicited by the impossibility of the necessary feminization of the public sphere. . . . In rearticulating the gendered division of labour through discourses of obesity, early Cold War Canada could be positioned and repositioned as a patriarchy, a nation composed of white and middle-class breadwinner husbands, homemaker wives, and as a country ready and willing to fight and win a nuclear war, should that awful need arise.

By considering obesity as a discourse which functioned, through the abjection of fat on the bodies of white, middle-class men, as a balm for early Cold War social crises, my study has called into question the common-sense "naturalness" of the fat body. Further, this paper demonstrates how relations of power produce fat embodiments in specific spaces in a particular time. Analyzing obesity in such a way interrupts epidemiological imaginings of obesity as a static biological category easily pathologized by medical, physiological, or nutritional models of analysis. Obesity is not biologically self-evident, but a historically articulated, worked-through, and worked-on category infused by power, politics, and positioning.

With the use of historical data, it is my intent to open up possibilities for understanding how fat works to assuage contemporary psychic crises. In Cold War Canada, the abjection of fat from the bodies of white, middle-class office workers acted to reassert the autonomy and independence of the masculinized public sphere from the feminized private during a time of threatening war. Presently, Canada is again aligned with the United States in a globalized war—the War on

Terror. Additionally, the Canadian economy, like those of other western states,[105] rests upon feminized service-based employment, performed by both women and men, with women of colour undertaking the least-desirable and lowest-paid jobs.[106] It remains to be seen, or at least studied, if Canada's current "obesity crisis" is related to the political–economic agendas of war and globalization. A study of the Cold War period suggests, however, that if fat phobia flowed from larger and overarching national agendas and anxieties, then so too might current worries about fat be grounded in something other than Canadians' supposedly growing girth.

 More online.

Notes

I would like to thank four anonymous reviewers for their very helpful comments and suggestions. I am extremely grateful to Bethan Evans, Rachel Colls, Stephanie Rutherford, and Jocelyn Thorpe for their numerous careful readings and recommendations. Research for this paper was undertaken with funds from the Social Science and Humanities Research Council of Canada.

1. J. Lowman, "Tubby Hubby Diet: Obesity Top Killer, Watch Your Weight," *Globe and Mail*, 1 October 1953.

2. Illustrations for the "Tubby Hubby Diet" depicted: an angry white woman wagging her finger at her portly husband during suppertime ("Tubby Hubby Diet: Obesity Top Killer, Watch Your Weight," *Globe and Mail*, 1 October 1953); a large white man losing his wife to a thinner man ("Tubby Hubby Diet: Women Prefer Slim Males to Those Who Add Weight," *Globe and Mail*, 28 September 1953); a fat white man attempting, and failing, to touch his toes ("Tubby Hubby Diet: Weight Charts Not Ideal of Persons of All Build," *Globe and Mail*, 29 September 1953); an insurance agent warning his large, white male client about the dangers of obesity ("Tubby Hubby Diet: Good Nutrition Helps in Weight-Cutting," *Globe and Mail*, 30 September 1953); a portly white man sitting in an arm chair, the belly fat spilling over his belt precluding his son from climbing onto his lap ("Tubby Hubby Diet: If Son Can't Find Dad's Lap It's Time to Take Action," *Globe and Mail*, 3 October 1953); a tuxedoed white man too winded to dance with his gowned wife ("Tubby Hubby Diet:

320-Pound Man Sheds 10 in 7-Day Trial of Course," *Globe and Mail*, 5 October 1953); and a white woman, in housecoat and slippers, enraptured by her new and improved, less-tubby hubby ("Tubby Hubby Diet: Look Out, Wives Warned Tubby Hubby Cuts Pounds," *Globe and Mail*, 8 October 1953).

3. S. L. Bartkey, "Foucault, Femininity, and the Modernization of Patriarchal Power," in D. Meyers, ed., *Feminist Social Thought: A Reader* (New York, NY: Routledge, 1997), 93–111; S. Bordo, *Unbearable Weight: Feminism, Western Culture and the Body* (Berkeley, CA: University of California Press, 1993); J. E. Braziel, "Sex and Fat Chicks: Deterritorializing the Fat Female Body," in J. E. Braziel and K. LeBesco, eds., *Bodies out of Bounds: Fatness and Transgression* (Berkeley, CA: University of California Press, 2001), 231–54; K. Chernin, *The Obsession: Reflections on the Tyranny of Slenderness* (New York, NY: Harper, 1981); C. Hartley, "Letting Ourselves Go: Making Room for the Fat Body in Feminist Scholarship," in J. E. Braziel and K. LeBesco, eds., *Bodies out of Bounds: Fatness and Transgression* (Berkeley, CA: University of California Press, 2001), 39–73; S. Orbach, *Fat Is a Feminist Issue: The Anti-Diet Guide for Women* (New York, NY: Berkeley, 1978); C. Rice, "Out from under the Occupation: Transforming Our Relationships with Our Bodies," in A. Medavarsky and B. Cranney, eds., *Canadian Woman Studies: An Introductory Reader*, 2nd ed. (Toronto, ON: Inanna, 2006), 411–23; C. Rice, "Becoming the Fat Girl: Emergence of an Unfit Identity," *Women's Studies International Forum* 30, no. 2 (2007): 158–72; and N. Wolf, *The Beauty Myth* (Toronto, ON: Vintage Books, 1991).

4. J. Lowman, "Tubby Hubby Diet: Slim Him 7 to 12 lbs in Just 12 Short Days," *Globe and Mail*, 17 March 1952.

5. J. Lowman, "Tubby Hubby Diet: "Don't Let Him on Scales until 12 Days Are Over," *Globe and Mail*, 24 March 1952.

6. J. Lowman, "Tubby Hubby Diet: Doesn't Need to Know He's on a Diet," *Globe and Mail*, 18 March 1952.

7. Braziel, "Sex and Fat Chicks," 241.

8. As R. Whitaker and S. Hewitt note, the Cold War lasted for "more than four decades, from the latter half of the 1940s to the end of the 1980s." (*Canada and the Cold War* [Toronto, ON: James Lorimar & Company, 2002], 5). My study encompasses only two of those four decades; I begin in 1950 and end in 1970.

9. P. Campos, *The Obesity Myth: Why America's Obsession with Weight Is Hazardous to Your Health* (New York, NY: Gotham Books, 2004); P. Campos, A. Saguy, P. Ernsberger, E. Oliver, and G. Gaesser, "The Epidemiology of Overweight and Obesity: Public Health Crisis or Moral Panic?" *International Journal of Epidemiology* 35 (2006): 55–60; R. Colls, "Outsize/

Outside: Bodily Bigness and Emotional Experiences of British Women Shopping for Clothes," *Gender, Place and Culture* 13 (2006): 529–45; B. Evans, "'Be Fit Not Fat': Broadening the Childhood Obesity Debate beyond Dualisms," *Children's Geographies* 2 (2004): 289–91; B. Evans, "'Gluttony or Sloth': Critical Geographies of Bodies and Morality in (Anti)Obesity Policy," *Area* 38 (2006): 259–67; M. Gard and J. Wright, *The Obesity Epidemic: Science, Morality and Ideology* (New York, NY: Routledge, 2005); R. Longhurst, "Fat Bodies: Developing Geographical Research Agendas," *Progress in Human Geography* 29 (2005): 247–59; L. F. Monaghan, "Big Handsome Men, Bears and Others: Virtual Constructions of 'Fat Male Embodiment,'" *Body & Society* 11, no. 2 (2005): 81–111; and L. F. Monaghan, "McDonalidizing Men's Bodies? Slimming, Association (Ir)rationalities and Resistances," *Body & Society* 13, no. 2 (2007): 67–93.

10. I am guided, here, by feminist critiques of scientific and medical objectivity. See D. J. Haraway, *Primate Visions: Gender, Race and Nature in the World of Modern Science* (New York, NY: Routledge, 1989); D. J. Haraway, *Simians, Cyborgs and Women: The Reinvention of Nature* (New York, NY: Routledge, 1991); S. Harding, *The Science Question in Feminism* (Ithaca, NY: Cornell University Press, 1986); S. Harding, *Whose Science? Whose Knowledge? Thinking from Women's Lives* (Ithaca, NY: Cornell University Press, 1991); E. Martin, *The Woman in the Body: A Cultural Analysis of Reproduction* (Boston, MA: Beacon Press, 1987); M. Poovey, *Uneven Developments: The Ideological Work of Gender in Mid-Victorian England* (Chicago, IL: University of Chicago Press, 1988); and N. Shah, *Contagious Divides: Epidemics and Race in San Francisco's Chinatown* (Berkeley, CA: University of California Press, 2001).

11. R. Whitaker, *Cold War Canada: The Making of an Insecurity State* (Toronto, ON: University of Toronto Press, 1994).

12. M. Gleason, *Normalizing the Ideal: Psychology, Schooling, and the Family in Postwar Canada* (Toronto, ON: University of Toronto Press, 1999).

13. M. L. Adams, *The Trouble with Normal: Postwar Youth and the Making of Heterosexuality* (Toronto, ON: University of Toronto Press, 1997).

14. S. Katz, "A Report on Eating," *Maclean's*, 11 June 1955: 86–91; W. Leith and J. C. Beck, "The Use of Phenmentrazine Hydrochloride (Predulin) in the Obese Diabetic," *Canadian Medical Association Journal* [hereafter *CMAJ*] 79 (1958): 897–8; H. LeRiche, "A Study of Appetite Suppressants in a General Practice," *CMAJ* 82 (1960): 467–70; Metropolitan Life Insurance Company of Canada, *How to Control Your Weight* (Ottawa, ON: Metropolitan Life Insurance Company of Canada, 1958); L. B. Pett and G. F. Ogilvie, "The Canadian

Weight–Height Survey," *Human Biology* 28 (1956): 177–88; Society of Actuaries, *Build and Blood Pressure Study: Volume 1* (Chicago, IL: Society of Actuaries, 1959); and Society of Actuaries, *Build and Blood Pressure Study: Volume 2* (Chicago, IL: Society of Actuaries, 1959).

15. Katz, "A Report on Eating," 90; *Globe and Mail*, "Form of Malnutrition: One-Fifth of Canadians over 30 Said too Fat," 18 June 1953.

16. S. S. B. Gilder, "The London Letter," *CMAJ* 100 (1969): 1109.

17. D. Capon, "Review Article: Obesity," *CMAJ* 79 (1958): 568–73; J. A. Leis, "Hypertension: A Problem of Growing Importance," *CMAJ* 64 (1951): 26–9; and D. E. Rodger, J. G. McFetridge, and E. Price, "The Management of Obesity," *CMAJ* 63 (1950): 265–7.

18. *Globe and Mail*, "Please Be Kind: Fat People Get Thinner by Sympanthy," 11 September 1950; and *Globe and Mail*, "Block that Whipped Cream, It Could Kill You: Doctor," 19 October 1952.

19. *Globe and Mail*, "Plan Review of Rejected Students," 30 October 1959.

20. K. McPherson, "Nursing and Colonization: The Work of Indian Health Service Nurses in Manitoba, 1945–70," in G. Feldberg, M. Ladd-Taylor, A. Li, and K. McPherson, eds., *Women, Health and Nation: Canada and the United States Since 1945* (Montreal, QC, McGill-Queen's University Press, 2003), 223–46.

21. C. D. Naylor, *Private Practice, Public Payment: Canadian Medicine and the Politics of Health Insurance, 1911–66* (Montreal, QC: McGill-Queen's University Press, 1986).

22. L. B. Pett, "A Canadian Table of Average Weights," *CMAJ* 72 (1955): 12–14; L. B. Pett, Department of Health and Welfare, Nutrition Division, "Letter from L. B. Pett to Florence Swan," 24 July 1959, available from Library and Archives of Canada [(hereafter LAC)] RG 29 vol. 922, file 385-6-3, "Nutrition Services Liaison & Co-operation with Province—New Brunswick," Ottawa, Canada; L. B. Pett, Department of Health and Welfare, Nutrition Division, "Letter from L. B. Pett to Florence Swan," 2 October 1959, available from LAC RG 29 vol. 922, file 385-6-3, "Nutrition Services Liaison & Co-operation with Province—New Brunswick," Ottawa, Canada.

23. Pett and Ogilvie, "The Canadian Weight–Height Survey."

24. B. Evans and R. Colls, "Measuring Fatness, Governing Bodies: The Spatialities of the Body Mass Index (BMI) in Anti-Obesity Politics," *Antipode* 41, no. 5 (2009): 1051–83.

25. W. I. Morse and J. S. Soeldner, "The Non-Adipose Body Mass of Obese Women: Evidence of Increased Muscularity," *CMAJ* 90 (1964): 723–35; and C. Young, "Body Composition and Body Weight: Criteria of Overnutrition," *CMAJ* 93 (1965): 900–1000.

26. Pett, "A Canadian Table of Average Weights."

27. Society of Actuaries, *Build and Blood Pressure Study: Volume 2*, 216.

28. T. Alborn, "Insurance against Germ Theory: Commerce and Conservatism in Late-Victorian Medicine," *Bulletin of History of Medicine* 75 (2001): 444.

29. I would like to thank an anonymous reviewer for pointing me to Alborn's article.

30. R. Robillard, "Predulin Treatment of Obesity in Diabetes Mellitus: Preliminary Report," *CMAJ* 76 (1957): 938.

31. LeRiche, "A Study of Appetite Suppressants," 467.

32. J. V. G. A. Durnin, "The Influence of Nutrition," *CMAJ* 96 (1967): 717.

33. *CMAJ*, "Editorials and Annotations," *CMAJ* 96 (1967): 1382.

34. J. E. Monagle, "Nutrition and Health—A Critical Evaluation," *Canadian Journal of Public Health* 56 (1965): 490.

35. See, for example, Evans and Colls, "Measuring Fatness, Governing Bodies"; . . . Campos, *The Obesity Myth*; Gard and Wright, *The Obesity Epidemic*; and L. F. Monaghan, *Men and the War on Obesity: A Sociological Study* (London, UK: Routledge, 2008).

36. The subtitle is borrowed from the title of a *Globe and Mail* article, "Editing the Editors: Missiles and Muscles" by Herbert Sallans (22 February 1958).

37. Certainly, privileged men were not the only ones subject to anti-obesity rhetoric during the 1950s and 1960s. See P. Stearns, *Fat History: Bodies and Beauty in the Modern West* (New York, NY: New York University Press, 1997). Women, for example, were the targets of slim-down campaigns launched by government, medicine, and popular publications in Cold War Canada. For the purposes of this paper, however, I will concentrate exclusively on white, middle-class men.

38. This was more true of some governments than others. For example, the government of John Diefenbaker fell after the 1963 federal election due to the (soon-to-be-former) prime minister's disdain of John F. Kennedy's, and NATO's, nuclear weapons program. (A. Finkel, *Our Lives: Canada after 1945* [Toronto, ON: J. Lorimer, 1997], 110–18).

39. S. Grant, *Sovereignty or Security? Government Policy in the Canadian North, 1936–50* (Vancouver, BC: UBC Press, 1988); and M. Zaslow, *The Northward Expansion of Canada 1914–67* (Toronto, ON: McClelland & Stewart, 1988).

40. Adams, *The Trouble with Normal*, 22; Grant, *Sovereignty or Security?* 178; and F. Iacovetta, *Gatekeepers: Reshaping Immigrant Lives in Cold War Canada* (Toronto, ON: Between the Lines, 2006), 16, 271.

41. E. T. May, *Homeward Bound: American Families in the Cold War Era* (New York, NY: Basic Books, 1988).

42. Whitaker, *Cold War Canada*; and Whitaker and Hewitt, *Canada and the Cold War.*

43. J. T. Marshall, Department of Health and Welfare, "Armed Forces Medical Rejections Civil Defense," memo to J. J. Heagerty, 20 September 1942, available from LAC RG 29, vol. 34, file 30-2-3, Ottawa, Canada; A. McCallum, "Is Canada Healthy?" *CMAJ* 63 (1950): 294–8.

44. J. Senter, "National Defense: Fitness of Canadians Is Causing Concern," *Globe and Mail*, 5 August 1957, 11.

45. J. Vipond, "Jim Vipond's Sports Editorial," *Globe and Mail*, 4 September 1958.

46. *Globe and Mail*, "Stop and Look," 15 November 1952, 6.

47. Adams, *The Trouble with Normal*, 33; Gleason, *Normalizing the Ideal.*

48. Adams, *The Trouble with Normal*; Gleason, *Normalizing the Ideal*; see also P. Armstrong, *Labour Pains: Women's Work in Crisis* (Toronto, ON: Women's Educational Press, 1984), 49–66.

49. Gleason, *Normalizing the Ideal*, 54.

50. Adams, *The Trouble with Normal*, 33–4.

51. Adams, *The Trouble with Normal*; Armstrong, *Labour Pains*; Gleason, *Normalizing the Ideal*; and J. Sangster, "Doing Two Jobs: The Wage Earning Mother," in J. Parr, ed., *A Diversity of Women: Ontario: 1945–80* (Toronto, ON: University of Toronto Press, 1995), 98–134.

52. Armstrong, *Labour Pains*, 52.

53. D. Spurgeon, "Philip Urges Get-Fit Drive for Canada," *Globe and Mail*, 1 July 1959.

54. Royal Bank of Canada, "In Search of Physical Fitness," *Royal Bank of Canada Monthly Letter* 39, no. 1 (1958): 1.

55. *Globe and Mail*, "Businessmen's Health Clubs Are Booming," 16 May 1959.

56. *Globe and Mail*, "30 Grunt, Perspire in 2-Hour Physical," 10 March 1958, 5.

57. During the 1950s and 1960s, Rotary Clubs were fraternal organizations. (J. A. Charles, *Service Clubs in American Society: Rotary, Kiwanis, and Lions* [Urbana, IL: University of Illinois Press, 1993]).

58. *Globe and Mail*, "4-Mile-an-Hour Walk Suggested for Fitness," 4 August 1962, 5.

59. Adams, *The Trouble with Normal*; Gleason, *Normalizing the Ideal.*

60. S. L. Gilman, *Fat Boys: A Slim Book* (Lincoln, NE: University of Nebraska Press, 2004); Monaghan, "Big Handsome Men"; Monaghan, "McDonalidizing Men's Bodies?"; Monaghan, *Men and the War on Obesity*; and J. Mosher, "Setting Free the Bears: Refiguring Fat Men on Television," in Braziel and LeBesco, eds., *Bodies out of Bounds: Fatness and Transgression* (Berkeley, CA: University of California Press, 2001), 166–96.

61. *Globe and Mail*, "Brains and Muscle," 10 July 1958.

62. R. Longhurst, *Bodies: Exploring Fluid Boundaries* (New York, NY: Routledge, 2001).

63. J. Kristeva, *Powers of Horror: An Essay on Abjection*, trans. L. S. Roudiez (New York, NY: Columbia University Press, 1982), 64.
64. Monaghan, *Men and the War on Obesity*, 182.
65. Longhurst, *Bodies*; A. McClintock, *Imperial Leather: Race, Gender and Sexuality in the Colonial Contest* (New York, NY: Routledge, 1995).
66. Finkel, *Our Lives*; Iacovetta, *Gatekeepers*; F. Iacovetta and V. J. Korinek, "Jell-O Salads, One-Stop Shopping and Maria the Homemaker: The Gender Politics of Food," in M. Epp, F. Iacovetta, and F. Swyripa, eds., *Sisters or Strangers? Immigrant, Ethnic, and Racialized Women in Canadian History* (Toronto, ON: University of Toronto Press, 2004), 190–230; Whitaker and Hewitt, *Canada and the Cold War*.
67. Adams, *The Trouble with Normal*; Gleason, *Normalizing the Ideal*.
68. Iacovetta, *Gatekeepers*; Iacovetta and Korinek, "Jell-O Salads, One-Stop Shopping and Maria the Homemaker."
69. S. Thobani, *Exalted Subjects: Subjects in the Making of Race and Nation in Canada* (Toronto, ON: University of Toronto Press, 2007), 144.
70. Iacovetta, *Gatekeepers*.
71. See also Gleason, *Normalizing the Ideal*; and Iacovetta and Korinek, "Jell-O Salads, One-Stop Shopping and Maria the Homemaker."
72. Adams, *The Trouble with Normal*, 27; see also V. J. Korinek, *Roughing It in the Suburbs: Reading Chatelaine Magazine in the Fifties and Sixties* (Toronto, ON: University of Toronto Press, 2000); and Sangster, "Doing Two Jobs."
73. H. Sewell, *"Enough to Keep Them Alive": Indian Welfare in Canada, 1873–1965* (Toronto, ON: University of Toronto Press, 2004); F. J. Tester and P. Kulchyski, *Tammarnit (Mistakes): Inuit Relocation in the Eastern Arctic, 1939–63* (Vancouver, BC: UBC Press, 1994).
74. Iacovetta, *Gatekeepers*; Iacovetta and Korinek, "Jell-O Salads, One-Stop Shopping and Maria the Homemaker"; Korinek, *Roughing It in the Suburbs*.
75. Adams, *The Trouble with Normal*, 23.
76. Iacovetta, *Gatekeepers*.
77. L. Percival, *Fitness Is Easy* (Toronto, ON: Sports College, 1957), 65.
78. L. Percival, "Our Flabby Muscles Are a National Disgrace," *Maclean's*, 15 April 1953, 20–1, 71–3.
79. Percival, *Fitness Is Easy*, 37.
80. Percival, *Fitness Is Easy*; L. Percival, *Physical Fitness for All the Family* (Winnipeg, MB: Harlequin, 1959).
81. Royal Canadian Air Force, *Royal Canadian Air Force Exercise Plans for Physical Fitness: XBX and 5BX Plans* (Ottawa, ON: Queen's Printer, 1962), 54.
82. Ibid.
83. Ibid., 77.
84. Z. Cherry, "After and Exercising Fashion," *Globe and Mail*, 30 June 1961; and E. Dowd, "RCAF Fitness Plan Best Seller: While US Does Knee Bends, Canada Rubs Hands in Glee," *Globe and Mail*, 5 April 1962.
85. G. Walker, "RCAF Fitness Pamphlet Helps to Shape Frame of Wayne," *Globe and Mail*, 26 June 1962.
86. M. A. Hall, *The Girl and the Game: A History of Women's Sport in Canada* (Peterborough, ON: Broadview Press, 2002); B. Kidd, *The Struggle for Canadian Sport* (Toronto, ON: University of Toronto Press, 1996); and Monaghan, "Big Handsome Men."
87. Royal Canadian Air Force, *Royal Canadian Air Force Exercise Plans for Physical Fitness: XBX and 5BX Plans*.
88. Ibid., 6.
89. Ibid.
90. *Globe and Mail*, "Scrub to Keep Fit," 2 December 1957. It is important to note one exception to the fitness for housewifery regime suggested by the XBX and other sources that was a 1950 publication from the federal government's Fitness Division called *Daily Does It . . . Daily Does It . . .* provided a set of exercises for a sedentary male office worker named "Slim," and one set for his sister "Sue," a young, white woman who was pictured hunched over a typewriter. Sue, "so tired after a long, hard day of sitting at the office," was "for once in her life . . . willing to take brotherly advice," and begin an exercise regime consisting of lunges, toe touches, and knee lifts. Canada, National Physical Fitness Division, *Daily Does It . . .* [Ottawa, ON: King's Printer, 1950]). . . .
91. J. Callwood, "She Wants to Be the World's Strongest Woman, but . . . She Keeps Hoping It Won't Show," *Maclean's*, 16 April 1955, 22–5, 50–5; Cherry, "After and Exercising Fashion"; and J. Strong, "Morning Coffee Club: Fitness Boring, Laziness Blissful," *Globe and Mail*, 8 October 1964.
92. J. Lowman, "Tubby Hubby Diet: Weight Charts Not Ideal for Persons of All Build," *Globe and Mail*, 29 September 1953.
93. HRH Prince Philip, "Presidential Address," 20 June 1959, available from the Archives of the Canadian Medical Association, Ottawa, Canada, 112–13.
94. B. N. Berg and H. S. Simms, "Nutrition, Onset of Disease, and Longevity in the Rat," *Canadian Journal of Public Health* 93 (1965): 911–13; I. Gogan, "The Role of the Hospital in the Prevention of Disease," *Canadian Journal of Public Health* 52 (1961): 431–6; W. W. Hawkins, "Some Medical and Biological Aspects of Obesity," *Canadian Journal of Public Health* 54 (1963): 477–81; W. Leith, "Experiences with the Pennington Diet in the Management of Obesity," *CMAJ* 84 (1961): 1411–14; E. W. McHenry, "Public Health Nursing: Nutritional Requirements in Pregnancy," *Canadian Nurse* 48, no. 5 (1952): 404–8; B. McLaren,

"Nutritional Control of Overweight," *Canadian Journal of Public Health* 58 (1967): 483–5; Robillard, "Predulin Treatment of Obesity"; A. Royer, "Problems in Infant Feeding," *Canadian Nurse* 58, no. 11 (1962): 991–2; and J. F. Webb, "Maternal Nutrition and Prenatal Mortality," *Canadian Journal of Public Health* 47 (1956): 482–4.

95. Lowman, "Tubby Hubby Diet: Slim Him 7 to 12 lbs in Just 12 Short Days."

96. Lowman, "Tubby Hubby Diet: Doesn't Need to Know He's on a Diet."

97. Katz, "A Report on Eating," 86.

98. Percival, *Physical Fitness for All the Family*, 100.

99. Percival, *Fitness Is Easy*; Percival, *Physical Fitness for All the Family*.

100. Canada, Nutrition Division, *Healthful Eating* (Ottawa, ON: Queen's Printer, 1963), 13–21.

101. In addition to 1963, *Healthful Eating* was reprinted in 1949, 1950, 1952, 1961, and 1967.

102. Canada, Nutrition Division, *Healthful Eating*, 4.

103. Ibid., 13.

104. McClintock, *Imperial Leather*; Longhurst, *Bodies*.

105. L. McDowell, "Learning to Serve? Employment Aspirations and Attitudes of Young Working-Class Men in an Era of Labour Market Restructuring," *Gender, Place and Culture* 7 (2000): 389–416; and L. McDowell, "Transitions to Work: Masculine Identities, Youth Inequality and Labour Market Change," *Gender, Place and Culture* 9 (2002): 39–59.

106. C. Gabriel, "Restructuring the Margins: Women of Colour and the Changing Economy," in E. Dua and A. Robertson, eds., *Scratching the Surface: Canadian Anti-Racist Feminist Thought* (Toronto, ON: Women's Press, 1999), 127–66.

7 Jell-O Salads, One-Stop Shopping, and Maria the Homemaker
The Gender Politics of Food

Franca Iacovetta and Valerie J. Korinek

Food is about more than recipes, cooking, nutrition, and eating. The practices surrounding its purchase, preparation, and consumption have long been a matter of conflict and contest. Food campaigns have been the site of clashes and accommodations between health professionals and beleaguered mothers told to forsake folk routines to "scientific" regimes; between food fashion-makers and discerning or ostentatious culinary consumers; and between gatekeepers of receiving societies and immigrants bearing allegedly exotic or offensive cuisine and smells. Forced to consider our own food habits, many might see them as a matter of personal choice, yet such claims overlook the ways in which food tastes and customs are informed, prescribed, or mediated by government, education, social services, multinational food corporations, and mass media. In short, food and its attendant practices are also about power. Food traditions evolve in social and cultural contexts that are shaped by economic conditions and class politics, racial–ethnic relations, and other factors.

Food can also act as a signifier of difference. Historically, "ethnic" foods have been relegated to the margins of receiving societies, dismissed as unhealthy or inappropriate, or pilloried by

food experts in search of new ideas to pick up the palates of bored eaters. Bastardized versions of "foreign" recipes, with most of the chili peppers or other pungent spices removed, are one aspect of the homogenizing process that comes from adapting ethnic cuisine to mainstream culture. Yet, immigrants have also transformed (albeit unevenly) the cuisine of mainstream cultures even as their own food habits were modified. Though hardly a new phenomenon, the current allure of "multicultural" dining has brought some immigrant and minority food cultures into the forefront, where, ironically, they have become middle- and upper-middle-class demarcators of status and taste.[1]

Here, we grapple with the complex politics of food through the prism of early post-1945 Canada, a period marked by a mix of social optimism and Cold War hysteria; economic expansion and persistent poverty; heightened domesticity and social and sexual nonconformity.[2] These tensions coincided with another major trend, mass immigration; by 1965, 2.5 million newcomers, many of them women and children, and members of young families, had entered Canada.[3] The Canadian context thus permits us to explore how the dominant gender ideologies

Citation: Franca Iacovetta and Valerie J. Korinek, "Jell-O Salads, One-Stop Shopping, and Maria the Homemaker: The Gender Politics of Food," in Marlene Epp, Franca Iacovetta, Frances Swyripa, eds., *Sisters or Strangers? Immigrant, Ethnic and Racialized Women in Canadian History* (Toronto, ON: University of Toronto Press, 2003): 190–230. Reprinted with permission of the publisher.

of capitalist democracies in the Cold War—including a middle-class model of homemaking and North American–defined standards of food customs and family life—influenced reception work and social service activities among immigrant and refugee women. Did efforts to reshape the culinary and homemaking skills of female newcomers overlap or diverge from the wider campaigns aimed at transforming all Canadian women into efficient shoppers, expert consumers, nutrition-wise cooks, and nurturing wives and mothers? Did Canadian and New Canadian women respond in similar ways to popular postwar campaigns designed to teach women the benefits of modern homemaking, meal planning, and nutritional guides? . . . In tackling such themes and questions, we adopt a comparative approach that probes the varied situations and responses of Canadian- and foreign-born women and of middle- and working-class women from both dominant and immigrant cultures in English Canada. So doing, we hope also to help bridge the continuing gap between what is generally seen as Canadian women's history and the history of immigrant and refugee and racialized women in Canada.[4]

Canadian "Affluence" in a World of Hunger

. . .

Canadian propagandists promised immigrant and refugee women a better life. Their promotional materials, including films made by the National Film Board [NFB] in conjunction with the federal Citizenship Branch, featured enticing images of the modern conveniences and range of choices that helped define Canadian ways. The film *Canadian Notebook* presented the modern store and mail-order catalogue as products of Canadian post-war affluence now within the reach of the New Canadian homemaker. A Maritime rural scene sings the praises of the mail-order catalogue, which brings "the largest city shopping centres" to the homemaker's

"fingertips." Greater praise was reserved for the urban department store (a "meeting place" with a "wide range of items and variety of styles") and the one-stop, self-serve "groceteria." As the following sequence featuring a white, slim, and attractive "Mrs. Sparks" indicates, depictions of the modern Canadian supermarket emphasized convenience and order, abundance of items, and quality and cleanliness of food. It also delivered messages about the sort of priorities that should preoccupy the Canadian homemaker:

Mrs. Sparks finds cellophane-wrapped meats in different quantities and grades on the refrigerated shelves. And now for some things for the picnic tonight! Prices, grades, and weights are all clearly marked, and Mrs. Sparks can finish her shopping very quickly. As all her food needs are here, Mrs. Sparks usually buys her whole week's groceries at one time. If she wishes, she can get a few other articles here too: magazines, cigarettes, and candies. When finished, Mrs. Sparks leaves through the cash register aisle, where the cashier totals her bill and gives her an itemized receipt.

Canadians, the narrator concludes, "find the self-service store well-suited to the faster pace of city life, where a busy housewife has to buy the week's groceries, go to the bank and the hairdresser's and still get home in time to prepare supper."[5] Another NFB film enthused over that "newest" trend in post-war merchandising, "the suburban Shopping Centre, with its 'one-stop' buying, and ample parking space for several hundred cars."[6]

While the Cold War alone cannot explain its renewed popularity as post-war ideology, the homemaker ideal, in that it symbolized the stability and superiority of western democratic families, took on great political import. That it reflected a misplaced or cultivated nostalgia for a bourgeois ideal that never entirely reflected most people's lives, and a conservative reaction to women's wartime gains, has been well documented.[7] It was also part and parcel of contemporary debates over women's roles engendered by the growing presence of working mothers, daycare lobbies, increasing divorce rates, and other signs of women's changing status in post-1945 society.[8] That many war-weary immigrants and refugees quickly married or remarried and started families does not negate the argument that dominant definitions of family and gender, well encapsulated by the phrase *breadwinner husband and homemaker wife*, privileged middle-class, heterosexual, Christian, and North American ideals.[9] The large presence of immigrant wives and mothers in paid labour did not stop reception workers from encouraging eventual domesticity. Indeed, the greater emphasis now placed on parents' obligations to produce mentally fit as well as socially productive children[10] made not only working mothers (whether Old or New Canadian), but also stay-at-home immigrant mothers allegedly cut off from mainstream (English) Canadian society, highly vulnerable to professional scrutiny. However, being "othered"—or marginalized as social problems to be resolved—hardly meant being ignored. Immigrant women, who were part of a wider campaign to reform Canadian women and elevate post-war family life, were isolated for special attention. As women, female immigrants were considered essential to modifying the social habits of family members. As front-line English teachers in Toronto put it, the most effective way to encourage the newcomers' adaptation was to target "the key person" in the immigrant family, "the housewife and mother," and ensure that she was sufficiently exposed to Canadian ways.[11]

. . .

Canada's racist restrictions on the admission of "not-white" peoples were post-war nation-building devices intended to keep Canada (mostly) white. It is thus not surprising that most early post-war newcomers before the 1970s were white Britons, Europeans (led by Italians and Germans), and white Americans, all of whom came in the hundreds of thousands.[12] Canadian officials restricted the number of Jewish refugees largely by bureaucratic means, but Jewish-Canadian lobbies helped secure safe passage for tens of thousands of them. Newcomers settled across Canada but Ontario attracted a majority of them. And while countless villages, towns, and cities felt the impact of their presence, Toronto became home to most of them.[13]

Canada's early post-war female newcomers were thus largely "white ethnics" who shared a British or European heritage but they were not a homogenous group. . . . These women would be joined by a continuing mix of peoples, including West Indians and South Asians,[14] but in the early post-war decades, white newcomers, considered far better suited for Canadian citizenship, garnered the lion's share of attention. Indeed, all this handwringing on the part of reception workers reflected the centrality of these immigrants to the remaking of the post-war Canadian nation.[15]

. . .

Nutritional Experts, Food Fashion-Makers, and Women

. . .

Food and health campaigns aimed at immigrant women and their families were varied and numerous. Early efforts began in European refugee camps, where Canadian relief workers taught "Canadian ways" with Canadian magazines, newspapers, school texts, films, and, most popular of all, Eaton's and Simpsons's catalogues.[16] The British war brides, whose integration was closely defined in homemaking terms, were the target of better organized culinary campaigns designed to ensure that "when [they] set up their new homes in the Dominion, they will have a good idea of what's expected of them in the cooking line."[17] As part of a state-funded and chaperoned scheme to resettle the wives of Canadian servicemen, cooking classes and health lectures for British war brides dominated orientation programs delivered in London; professional dieticians like Canadian Red Cross officer Ruth Adams stressed the importance that Canadians attached "to well-balanced diets." "Time spent in planning meals," she also advised "would payoff in saving doctor and dentist bills." Adams counselled the women "not to forget their own specialties such as scones and Yorkshire pudding" but "urged" them "to get busy and practise on pancakes and Canadian-style salads." To demonstrate what Canadians "like to eat," she brought along "a real apple pie, tea biscuits, a white cake with fudge icing, several types of salads, [and] the biscuit part of a strawberry shortcake."[18]

This training continued in Canada. In Ontario, Red Cross staff in North Bay, St. Catharines, and elsewhere gave courses in cooking (where women made muffins, tea biscuits, cream sauces, salads, and cakes, and learned to cook vegetables), canning techniques, nutrition, and participated in Department of Health home visits for meal planning and budgeting. One war bride evidently prompted local staff to begin a pastry-making class with her declaration that "the ambition of every British bride was to make a good lemon pie."[19] In these records, favourable assessments abound (though other sources, especially oral testimonies, tell more complicated stories).[20] "The girls," declared their teachers, gained "practical experience in actual cooking," grew familiar with Canadian equipment (including wooden spoons),[21] and enjoyed the chance to socialize over tea and cookies or cigarettes. Graduates received an appropriately Canadian gift—a set of plastic measuring spoons. Beyond specialized cooking courses, many reception programs for immigrant women included nutrition and food lessons as part of a larger orientation program. English classes in settlement houses, for instance, could become forums for discussing children's food needs and shopping trips.[22]

Chatelaine and Canadian Culinary Ways

For nutrition experts, the first priority was to teach all Canadians, especially mothers, sound nutritional advice and healthy food habits. (They never tired of praising the Canada Food Guide as a simple and flexible teaching tool for raising nutritional awareness.)[23] A good diet, they stressed, improved children's growth rate and physique, resistance to disease, and meant longer lives; a faulty diet established early in life might not show immediate results but could produce far greater damage than a vice such as adult drinking. In dispensing advice, food editors and health experts often prioritized middle-class food customs and efficiency regimes derived from capitalist time-management principles, and emphasized cleanliness. Descriptions of the family meal, especially dinner, invariably assumed (or pictured) a nuclear family, its well-groomed members assembled around an attractively set table in a dining room, happily engaged in conversation while eating mother's nicely presented and healthy meal. Their awareness of the myriad of "families" inhabiting inner-city flats, boarding houses, and suburban bungalows, did not alter their pitch.

. . . An excellent source of Canada's postwar health and homemaking campaigns is the country's premier women's magazine, *Chatelaine*. Although usually dismissed as a bourgeois women's magazine, *Chatelaine* was an affordable, mass-market periodical that by the late 1960s enjoyed the largest circulation of any Canadian magazine in the country. Circulation figures, surveys, and letters to the editor show that its audience came from across Canada and included urban and rural as well as working- and middle-class women and some men and children. The primarily female readership was English-speaking and Anglo-Celtic but included some ethnic Canadian and immigrant women. . . .

The magazine's food features were largely the creations of the Chatelaine Institute kitchen staff or recipe entries in the annual Family Favourites Contests that had been adjudicated and tested by the Institute staff. Founded in 1930 and modelled after the US-based *Good Housekeeping* Test Kitchen, the Chatelaine Institute was staffed by professional home economists whose white robes and laboratory-style kitchen lent a scientific air to the departmental features. Efficient and economical meal preparation, with a focus on nutrition, was their central message. As female professionals operating in the overlapping worlds of health and fashion, they took their job seriously: taste testings on in-house recipes, inspection visits to factories, and product test runs to determine which items would receive the *Chatelaine* Seal of Approval (again mimicking the *Good Housekeeping* Seal of Approval). . . . The particular gender dynamics that gave Chatelaine Institute nutritionists a degree of autonomy not enjoyed by their counterparts in the United States are also noteworthy. In contrast to the United States, where male editors vetted materials submitted by female writers, *Chatelaine*'s editorial and advertising departments were separate, sundering the usual cozy relationship between editorials and advertising. *Chatelaine*'s male publishers complained about women editors who refused to be dictated to. In the budget features, women food editors who, theoretically, should have been promoting the advertiser's products (many of them processed goods) refused, on the grounds that they were too expensive.[24]

While undergoing some transformations in the two decades under review, *Chatelaine*'s food features remained remarkably consistent. Even amid the changing food fads that appeared, the Canadian way was most commonly represented by images and texts extolling the virtues of affordable abundance. As in the NFB films, recurring images of attractive . . . WASP women pushing overflowing grocery carts or posed near well-stocked freezers and store shelves attested to the Canadian homemakers' good fortune. So did recipe and cooking contests. Proud contest winners photographed alongside their prize-winning

Jell-O-mould salad, carrot medley, casserole, or dessert parfait promised women readers ease of preparation and family fun. The come-on ads of brand-name food corporations of prepared products, such as canned soups and vegetables, stressed how convenience foods offered maximum return for minimal preparation. By contrast, the advertisers of baking supplies preferred labour-intensive treats to enchant husbands and children. Invariably, their ads drew on women's supposed virtues for self-sacrifice, sending out the message that a mother's proof of her devotion to husband and family was literally in the pudding, or in homemade bread and pies. Indeed, despite the prominence of convenience food corporate advertisers, the majority of recipes in *Chatelaine*'s departmental pages (as opposed to those in name-brand advertisements) involved cooking "from scratch." As to economical eating, the magazine increasingly featured frozen foods as a cheaper and healthy alternative to fresh items, though the higher price of frozen goods compared to the tinned variety, and the limited freezer space of the older refrigerators that most fridge-owning Canadian homes had, could put even frozen food beyond the grasp of many struggling families. Not so with canned foods, which were consistently promoted as the cheapest way of attaining the well-balanced meal. Particularly in winter, women were encouraged or cajoled to buy tinned foods instead of more expensive fruit and vegetable imports.

. . . Only infrequently did *Chatelaine*'s food articles acknowledge that many Canadian wives worked outside the home, and some of them offered less than solid advice. "Seven Dinners on the Double" tantalized working wives with this appealing fantasy: "You're home at six and dinner's on the table in thirty minutes. Here's how you do it in a small apartment kitchen: work to plan and let your husband help." The accompanying photo essay depicts a cheerful heterosexual couple, both wearing aprons, preparing food in a tiny kitchen. Some examples from the 1960s highlighted working women who made ends meet by preparing meals the night before or shopping at a well-stocked deli counter. The affordable meals in *Chatelaine*'s sixties repertoire were also slightly more glamorous than their fifties counterparts, though casseroles remained popular. One of the quickest ways of interjecting novelty was to feature "ethnic" ingredients and food—a process, that as Harvey Levenstein and others have described for the United States, usually meant modifying "foreign" fare for more timid North American palates. *Chatelaine*'s examples of this homogenizing process include the following 1960 recipe for Easy-to-Make Pizza Pin Wheels: biscuit mix, tomato soup and ketchup, pressed meat, cheese wafers, cheddar cheese, and modest amounts of oregano, green pepper, and onion. Clearly, authenticity was not a hallmark of such recipes.[25]

. . .

Greater attention to ethnic foods—both inside the pages of women's magazines and beyond— . . . reflected an increasing interest on the part of North Americans in the sort of "gourmet" cuisine associated with such successful food writers as Julia Child (who sparked interest in French cuisine with the publication of her cookbooks in the early 1960s) as well as a greater degree of culinary experimentation and the internationalization of foods more broadly speaking. Whether dubbed as hippies, radicals, bohemians, or brown-ricers, many middle-class youth were enticed by the alternative tastes of global foods. Their rebellion against the standard "meat-mashed-potatoes-and-peas" family fare was part of a larger interest in cultural and for some political and sexual experimentation. It suggests the need to pay more attention to what Levenstein aptly referred to as people's growing appreciation of the "sensuality" of food.[26]

Changes were also taking place in mother's kitchen. A summary of the recipes submitted for *Chatelaine*'s 1965 Family Favourites Contest suggests that many Canadian housewives were incorporating ethnic cuisine into the meal plans. "Chinese food" was "the most popular dish, followed by Italian"[27]—though such nods toward multicultural eating should not be exaggerated. Even by the end of the 1960s, the "Canadian way" was best exemplified by the homemaker who had the major burden of food preparation, and the food standard usually meant updated classics like "hamburgers with class" or "ten ways with a pound of hamburg," rather than experimental cuisine.[28]

From the Point of Nutrition?

Other sources, including a popular postwar nutritional guide, *Food Customs of New Canadians*,[29] speak more directly to the concerns and practices of health and food experts serving immigrant communities. Produced by an organization of nutritionists and dieticians (Toronto Nutrition Committee [TNC]), the guide appeared in 1959 and was revised and expanded in 1967. A part of a cookbook project launched by the International Institute of Metropolitan Toronto, the city's largest immigrant aid society, the guide's claims to be objective and social scientific, like its rejection of an overtly assimilationist approach, reflects the general approaches of postwar reception activists like those who staffed the Institute. The TNC's liberal perspective is clearly evident in their counselling of flexibility when assessing immigrant food customs—"From the viewpoint of nutrition, some food habits may be better than our own, and changes may not be necessary"—but the committee's presumption of expert authority is equally evident. Notwithstanding its constant reference to immigrant groups and New Canadians, the guide's main target is the homemaker whose schooling in Canadian ways was seen as crucial to affecting desired changes in the whole family.

The guide profiled the food customs of 14 of Toronto's significant ethnic groups,[30] with the British conspicuous by their absence. The data collected (from published texts, military surveys, international agencies, and interviews with immigrants) was organized into categories.

For each group, there is a detailed table of food customs both in the Old World setting and in Toronto, with the relevant information broken down into subcategories: food groupings (milk, fruits and vegetables, bread and cereals, meat and fish), meal patterns, and cooking facilities, Vitamin D, fats, sweets, beverages, and condiments. Another category, Food for Special Ages, dealt mainly with prenatal education for mothers, child-feeding patterns, and public health facilities. Conclusions and recommendations were then grouped together under Teaching Suggestions. With two exceptions,[31] the guide used national groupings (Chinese, Portuguese), but was careful to document regional and rural/urban variations in Old World contexts, to highlight patterns in areas of out-migration, and to note changes (for better or worse) in food habits that pertained in Toronto. In most cases, however, stark contrasts are drawn between the more "primitive" and time-consuming cooking facilities of rural homes, where running water is scarce and women operate charcoal, wood stoves, or clay stoves, and the "modern" urban homes equipped with gas, electricity, and running water. Although such differences undoubtedly reflected class as much as city residence, only the West Indian entry draws explicit class distinctions.[32] The desire to be precise and comprehensive makes for some very terse summaries, as indicated by the following German–Austrian entry:

> German and Austrian food habits are combined since differences are more regional than national. North Germans like sweet soups and sugar on salads, serve potatoes and vegetables regularly, and drink beer with meals. South-West Germans and Bavarian-Austrians do not eat sweet soups and salads; South-West Germans replace potatoes with noodles and use less vegetable while Bavarian-Austrians use dumplings and fewer vegetables except for sauerkraut. Although South-West Germans replace beer

with wine at meals, the Bavarian-Austrians do not.

The guide's claim to neutral assessments of immigrant food customs and liberalism was inexorably mingled with the presumption of scientific, even cultural, authority to define standards for newcomers. Indeed, the guide was designed precisely to inform health and social service personnel "helping" newcomers "adapt the familiar food patterns of their homelands to the foods and equipment available in Canada." The aim was to gradually change the food and eating habits of immigrants so as to bring them in line with Canadian ways and standards. . . .

The wisdom encoded in *Food Customs* was meant to be objective, yet the advice involved an act of cultural imperialism: advising conformity to North American health regimes meant deliberately bringing about changes in the daily habits, and social and cultural values, of those being counselled. It might be unfair to equate this guide with the blatantly assimilationist intentions of nineteenth- and early twentieth-century domestic science professionals or residential school staff who taught African-American, Native, and immigrant children to reject their mother's cooking and customary foods in favour of mainstream choices.[33] Still, definitions of health and nutrition can be culturally constructed. Despite its scientific language, the guide reflected a shared normative discourse regarding dominant bourgeois definitions of Canadian "ways" and "standards" that were as much about class and capitalist notions of efficiency and budgeting as about nutrition and food. For instance, it held the North American pattern of three meals per day as sacrosanct. "Canadians," it said, "follow a pattern of three meals a day which fits into school and working hours." That newcomers had to adapt to this industrial pattern was not in dispute.

. . .

The nutrition committee's preoccupation with the shopping habits of immigrant and refugee women also reflected the experts' class and cultural bias. In short, they pathologized this behaviour, seeing it as the consequence of poverty (lack of storage, refrigeration) or rural underdevelopment, and all but ignored its cultural and social significance. In the bakeries, butchers, fish shops, and other specialty stores of Old World towns and villages, women developed important lines of trust and credit with shopkeepers, and maintained critical gossip networks of information and support. For Canadian nutrition experts, however, efficiency concerns predominated: access to clean, well-stocked stores meant shopping less frequently and more efficiently. Such practices were equated with modernity, as suggested by a German–Austrian entry: "Shopping is done less frequently than before, mostly at neighbourhood stores, but supermarkets are increasing." Such views also ignored the fact that many thousands of working-class immigrants would live for years in inner-city flats and basement apartments without modern stoves or fridges, and thus rely on daily shopping of perishables. Equally important, the modern supermarket being promoted—large chain stores such as Dominion, Loblaws, and Power—were hardly places where immigrant women well versed in marketplace "haggling" could practise their craft. Ethnic shops and open markets made greater economic sense than urban or suburban supermarkets. Frequency of contact helped women to forge bonds of trust with local shopkeepers, who often extended credit to families in financial straits.

Harsher professional judgments accompanied discussion of nursing mothers and child-feeding regimes. These evaluations, usually grouped under Food for Special Ages, noted child-feeding practices (breastfeeding or artificial) in each country, availability of specialty foods for children, level of public instruction for mothers, and the state of prenatal health services.[34] Again, immigrant mothers were evaluated in terms of their conformity to "modern" health regimes. As in the past, post-war nutrition experts showed little respect for the folk traditions and mothering remedies of Europe, Asia, and elsewhere. Rural Chinese women's supposed inadequacies on the child-feeding front, for instance, was attributed to their devotion to folk practices. The entry in *Food Customs* reads:

> No special foods prepared. Mothers increase only their starch intake during pregnancy and, although prenatal health services are improving, the authorities recognize that there is still a need for education of mothers in the kinds of foods required for an adequate pregnancy diet. Following birth of the baby, mother does not eat fruits or vegetables or drink cold water for a month. She eats as much meat, poultry, and eggs as the family can afford. Eggs coloured red are sent to the mother to celebrate the birth.

Women of other countries were depicted as more closely resembling Canadian or North American standards. Of women in Czechoslovakia, the guide observed: "In rural areas, breast feeding is prevalent although increasing attention is paid to modern methods" (presumably, use of baby formula). . . . Highest praise of all went to Dutch women whose child-feeding patterns—which followed a progression from formula feeding to gradual introduction of solid foods—were decidedly modern. In Holland, "formula feeding is generally accepted" and "a variety of evaporated milk formulae and canned infant foods," as well as vitamin supplements, were widely used. . . .

Amid the details emerge some broad patterns. First, the nutrition experts were careful not to give any group an entirely negative evaluation. They commended most groups for varied diets that combined in-season fruits and vegetables, meat, and fish. Here, Chinese food customs scored well because of the "economical use of meat, varieties of fish, crisp-tender method of cooking vegetables and consistent use of fruit." They also acknowledged the fine-honed skills of women from modest rural backgrounds accustomed to stretching economical cuts of meat with starches and vegetables or producing one-dish meals using meat alternatives such as fish. The assessment of the Polish homemaker in Toronto echoed that of most European women under review. She could make "a small amount of inexpensive meat" go "a long way in soups and stews," and she often substituted "legumes, eggs and fish in all forms" for meat. She had adapted easily to new foods, such as citrus fruits, that had been prohibitively expensive back home, though she did need to learn to cook vegetables for a shorter time and to cook a "more substantial breakfast."

Nor did any group receive an entirely positive evaluation; there was always room for improvement, and the experts identified precisely where. Since immigrant children "become very fond of candy and sweet carbonated beverages," social service personnel were told to discourage "the increasing use of sweet fruits" among all newcomers. The TNC also insisted that most immigrant women had to be taught the value of canned or frozen fruits, vegetables, and fruit juices as substitutes for expensive, out-of-season fresh imports.

The guide established a food customs hierarchy of immigrant groups, and it closely resembled Canada's historic racial–ethnic preference ladder. The basis of ranking was the comparative ease with which newcomers made the transition to Canadian foods and customs. Without exception, the most positive evaluations were of Canada's more "preferred" groups of Europeans: North and West European whites. The "similarity of foods in the home countries and Canada," the guide observed of Germans and Austrians, for instance, "makes adjustment relatively easy."[35] . . .

By contrast, women and families belonging to Canada's "less preferred" immigrants—Chinese, southern Europeans, and West Indians—appear in the guide as less equipped to adopt modern culinary standards. . . . Chinese

hygienic standards needed serious upgrading. Serious adjustments were required of Italians, particularly southern Italians (who regularly use "strong spices and hot peppers" and "highly seasoned meats like salami"), before they would better conform to Canadian food ways. This, even though Italians, like other Europeans, earned good marks for a varied diet, use of fresh foods, and a three-meals-a-day pattern. Still, serious adjustment problems plagued Italian newcomers, a low-income group, in part, the nutritionists claimed, because they preferred expensive, imported goods, such as olive oil, meats, and cheeses, when cheaper Canadian alternatives (such as corn oil) were available. Hence, the TNC counselled social service personnel to encourage Italian women to forgo familiar items, now dubbed expensive luxury foods, in favour of affordable Canadian products. . . .

Culinary Pluralism from the Bottom Up?

Historically, food customs have offered some racial minorities, such as First Nations, African-Americans, and urban immigrants, a resource, albeit limited, in resisting the forces of cultural hegemony. Although wary of intruding middle-class professionals, working-class immigrant mothers might more willingly heed the advice of nutrition experts because good health, especially in a child, reflects certain universal qualities.[36] The capacity for choice or resistance greatly differed among Canadian and New Canadian women and, as recently documented for Toronto's post-war inner-city neighbourhoods, low-income women from humble or impoverished rural regions bore the greatest brunt of Canadian professional discourses and front-line practices that singled out immigrant women for special attention or blame. In the late 1950s and 1960s, for example, Portuguese and Italian mothers were branded as too ignorant, isolated, backwards, stubborn, and/or suspicious to access "modern" healthcare facilities or to trust the school nurses and visiting homemakers who dispensed advice.[37] Still, neither group should be treated as monolithic categories, and within each group, women displayed a differing willingness and/or capacity to embrace or resist professional interventions. New and Old Canadian women responded in selective and varied ways to external and internal pressures to recast themselves in ways promoted by bourgeois image-makers.

. . .

Refugee and immigrant women . . . responded selectively to post-war health and homemaking campaigns. Like surviving written sources, oral testimonies, including our sample of 28 taped interviews,[38] reveal patterns that defy easy categorization: immigrant mothers who steadfastly stuck to "traditional" meals at home and those keen to experiment with Canadian recipes or convenience foods; refugee husbands who pressured wives to stick to familiar meals and those who encouraged wives to incorporate some Canadian foods; and endless permutations of hybrid diets in the households of working- and middle-class immigrants who increasingly combined familiar and Canadian foods and "ethnic" foods from elsewhere.

Post-war immigrant and refugee narratives contain their own versions of the theme homeland scarcity and Canadian abundance. Hunger and fears of starvation dominate the wartime stories of early post-war arrivals, including Holocaust survivors. Female survivors recall the smaller rations of food given to women in the camps, and of the courage of Jews and Gentiles who sneaked food into Nazi-created ghettos and camps. When English soldiers arrived to liberate Bergen-Belsen, recalled Amelia S-R., they found "everyone running to the planted areas to dig beet roots and potatoes out with their hands." English soldiers helped them to find food, and she and others suffering from typhus and other illnesses were slowly nursed back to health by Red Cross personnel in quarantined hospitals in Sweden. But even there, Amelia added, the fear that they might yet starve never subsided.

A Dutch war bride describing the days before Holland's liberation spoke of "starving under German occupation." The anti-Soviet DPs had also endured prolonged hunger and inadequate sanitation facilities in the refugee camps, forcing many to take up jobs or begin families in Canada while still suffering from malnourishment and related diseases.[39]

No wonder, then, that many newcomers reacted with astonishment to the comparative abundance of food in Canada. Some, including Dutch newcomer Maria B., marvelled at the stock in Canadian "self-serve" grocery stores. Many recalled their first taste of new foods, such as "Canadian-style" bread or cereals, and the joy of eating fresh fruits in scarce supply back home. A German woman, Helga, who arrived with her husband in 1952, swore the apples and oranges "tasted just like heaven"; they lived on McIntosh apples for months, she added, while her husband, a former electrician, looked for work. A Czech refugee who settled in Hamilton in 1949 recalled her excitement at tasting cornflakes and at once again eating eggs. Financially strapped, she also learned how to bargain shop at the market.[40]

Not everyone enthused over Canadian food, however. Some much preferred their dense dark bread to the light and airy Canadian fare and complained about unappetizing meat. As an East European refugee woman declared "only the immigrants . . . brought good taste in food to Canada." Whether Baltics from the post-war DP camps, Hungarian 56ers, or Iron Curtain escapees, many refugees expressed their disgust with what they considered Canadian wastefulness, especially in restaurants, where, they noted, people were served an appalling amount of food and an evening's leftovers could have sustained several refugees for weeks at a time.[41] As most volunteer immigrants arrived with little cash or capital, they too could endure a spartan diet— something that worried Canadian nutritionists. Yet, as the example provided by the Portuguese couple who lived for several years on bread and coffee, bean soup, and pigs feet while saving money to start a small family business indicates, the diets were not outrageously unhealthy.[42] Still, illness or injury could cut into a modest food budget, creating yet more pressures for women.

. . . The evidence does suggest that some East European refugees who eventually found work in former or alternative professional or white-collar jobs more quickly moved into suburbs and integrated Canadian foods and customs into family meals and holiday celebrations. . . . But other women put up greater and longer resistance, and shopped in their "old" city neighbourhoods to get the necessary ingredients. Working-class immigrants such as Italians, Portuguese, and West Indians could largely reproduce their homeland diets precisely because they relied on low-budget food items such as rice and pasta and comparatively little meat though this kind of cultural continuity, at least early on, was more easily attained in large cities like Toronto, which already had a wide range of ethnic foods, or in smaller cities like Sudbury, which had established Ukrainian, Finnish, and other ethnic businesses.

Women's efforts to negotiate a complex culinary terrain emerge clearly from oral testimonies. Our sample also underscores the importance of individual choice and of differing family and household dynamics. For example, while many mothers experimented with tinned soups, tuna fish sandwiches laden with mayonnaise, hot dogs and hamburgers, and Jell-O in response to their children's persistent requests, others resisted, even for years. An East German refugee woman who liked to supplement her "mostly German" diet with various foods also recalled the "tensions" between her and her children over her husband's domineering approach to maintaining "strict" German standards in food and child-rearing.[43] By contrast, Austrian-born Susan M., who married an Italian immigrant she met in Toronto, said she never cooked "in any particular style" for her family. . . . For Nazneed Sadiq, a young and recently married upper-caste Pakistani woman who emigrated with her accountant husband in the early 1960s,

learning to cook in her North Toronto apartment building (where everyone else was white) meant experimenting with both "Indian" and North American foods. The resulting weekly meal pattern: Pakistani food two to three times a week, a lot of salads, and the occasional Canadian-style barbeque.[44] Such experimentation led to many multicultural family diets, of which holiday food customs are perhaps most emblematic: Italian households that combined antipasto and lasagna with turkey for Thanksgiving, Ukrainian mothers who added Canadian cakes and hams to the family favourite, perogies, and so on.[45]

The *Chatelaine* stories dealing with immigrants devoted considerable space to culinary customs or reactions to Canadian patterns of consumption and domestic images. Published in 1957, when the plight and arrival of the Hungarian 56ers had captured the imagination of many Canadians, Jeannine Locke's "Can the Hungarians Fit In?" about Frank and Katey Meyer illuminates key themes under scrutiny.[46] Like other Iron Curtain "escape" narratives, Locke's article drew a sympathetic and compelling portrait of the young refugee couple as freedom fighters who fled the Hungarian revolution, spent some harrowing time "crouched in a ditch" near the Hungarian–Austrian border, and now looked forward to a "good" life in Canada. The caption that accompanies the cover photograph of an attractive, smiling Katey declares: "[She] resembles that mythical creature, the average young Canadian housewife. In a straight-cut skirt, soft sweater and low-heeled shoes, her brown hair and eyes healthily bright, her skin rosy as a schoolgirl's, she is inconspicuously attractive." Although she and her engineer husband occupied a small flat in Toronto, Locke added that Katey, "could fit into any setting from St. John's to Saanich." The domestication of Katey is all the more telling given that she was a professionally educated woman who first worked in Canada as a hospital cleaner and then a bank teller.

. . . Under the provocative subtitle "Katey Discovers Supermarkets and Limps to Mass in

Red Leather Shoes"—Locke describes Katey's first exposure to a modern Canadian household and then grocery store. In Budapest, the couple had shared a three-room apartment with three other family members; they had had no electrical household appliances and endured a "perpetual chill" due to the scarcity and high cost of fuel. By contrast, their Toronto patrons, a doctor and his large family, had given the couple commodious accommodations: a suite of two rooms, a new refrigerator and stove, and their own bathroom. While living there, Katey discovered the wonders of the Canadian supermarket: one day "she came home staggering under a load of newly discovered delicacies—sardines, instant coffee, canned soups, ham and chicken legs," and "so much ice cream that they used it in great scoops even in their coffee." In a statement that would have pleased Canadian boosters, Katey, wrote Locke, told her husband: "There is everything you could want to buy in the supermarket . . . not like the little shops at home where there was little to buy and what we wanted we could never afford." Next came department stores. When husband Frank told Katey to buy herself a present, Katey had decided on a pleated nylon slip but on impulse bought high-heeled red leather pumps that cost about $35 (nearly a week's salary for Frank), and then "limped, painfully but persistently around their rooms in her tall, thin pumps until she was accomplished enough to manoeuvre them, for the first time in public, to Sunday morning mass." "Katey's new red shoes," added Locke, "were part of their celebration of three most happy events": mail from home; Frank's (and brother Louis's) acceptance, with scholarship, into the University of Toronto engineering school; and Katey's bank job.

Canadian nutritionists might have disapproved of Katey's culinary indiscretion (all that ice cream!) but enjoyed the depictions of a Canadian paradise of goods and the Meyers's eagerness to become Canadian consumers. Locke spelled out the stages of their acculturation: learning English, landing a job, one-stop shopping, plans to purchase a suburban home, and their first car. The couple's enthusiasm for all things Canadian was tempered by wistful memories of Hungarian food and gypsy music—which, much to their delight, they rediscovered in a Hungarian restaurant, the Csarda, in downtown Toronto. "Transported home by the smells and sounds" of Csarda, the Meyers, writes Locke, "eat goulash and cheese strudel" and "believe they are back in their favourite restaurant" at the lakeside resort near Budapest where they spent vacations. Although the couple never enjoyed the traditional gypsy music back home (a sign of their class status), Katey is "amused" to find that the same songs heard here please her very much. So do the Hungarian cafe's slightly tart desserts that remind her of mother's cooking. Katey has even absorbed North American women's obsession with weight: at home, she yearned for expensive cream-fllled eclairs but, here, where she can and, at first, did buy them, "[she] is suddenly calorie conscious."

The role played by food in the Meyers's tale of escape and redemption is a complex one, at once signifying Canadian abundance, novelty, and satiety, while in the couple's obvious enjoyment of "traditional" Hungarian cuisine a romanticization of their "older" ways. As with most public articulations of post-war cultural pluralism, the tension between assimilation and acculturation is never completely resolved, yet its success at weaving a compelling Cold War narrative of a Canadian democratic paradise is suggested by the positive letters the article engendered.[47]

. . .

Conclusion

In adapting ethnic cuisine to mainstream culture, food fashion-makers drew, explicitly or implicitly, on liberal notions of celebrating diversity—a theme that post-war Canadian officialdom encouraged, within limits—but early post-war culinary pluralism also produced uneven and contradictory results: Canadians were encouraged to appreciate immigrant customs while newcomers themselves were often transformed into (or, rather, reduced to) colourful folk figures bearing exotic foods and quaint customs but never accorded an equal status with "real" Canadians. The emergence in these years of "multicultural" cookbooks with a "unity in diversity" theme were financed with some federal government funds because officials considered them "an excellent medium to further the idea of Canadian unity."[48] Such texts reflect the contradictory features of post-war cultural pluralism: celebrating ethnic customs and encouraging "multicultural" cuisines while at the same time perpetuating cute and patronizing stereotypes of immigrants as static folk figures. By stripping immigration of its more threatening aspects, they reduced ethnic diversity to entertainment and novelty.[49]

When post-war Canadian health and welfare experts, food fashion-makers, and mass-market magazines promoted a Canadian way of cooking and eating, they prioritized pro-capitalist, middle-class food practices, household regimes, and family values. Approved patterns included careful meal planning, strategic shopping in "modern" stores, three nutritionally balanced meals per day—all washed down with countless glasses of milk. The bourgeois experts encouraged all Canadian women, and particularly low-income and immigrant mothers, "to get the most for their food dollar" through planned grocery shopping trips using a seven-day menu plan, taking advantage of grocers' specials, and following the casseroles and roasted-meat diet favoured by Canadians. The Canadian way held centre stage while ethnic dishes were relegated to the margins as novelty items to entice North American palates (and often bastardized in the process) or as a source of economical meals.

We should be wary of imputing too much influence on the prescriptive literature, however. The different kinds of evidence mined for this paper indicate a range of responses to post-war food and homemaking campaigns. For those eager to embrace all facets of Canadianism . . .

eating Canadian was very important. In contrast . . . many other adult newcomers expressed their desire to be Canadian but drew the line at Canadian food, while for others, incorporating Canadian food customs meant neither abandoning their previous food culture nor a passive acceptance of "modern" child-feeding regimes that front-line health and welfare workers tried to impose on them. The differing capacities of both Canadian and New Canadian women to incorporate, ignore, or modify the suggestions of experts should not be overlooked. Indeed, it suggests that the relationship between food experts and newcomers is perhaps best understood as a series of negotiations and encounters that transformed both food cultures, though not equally. Anglo-Canadian experts had the power and position to define "ethnic" food as un-Canadian, while the *Food Customs* guidebook and other projects for newcomers suggest that nutrition experts and food fashion-makers, like other experts involved in immigrant and refugee reception work, sought to modify, not obliterate, the food (and other) cultures of emigrating groups, but liberal intentions did not eliminate cultural chauvinism. In turn, the vast number of post-war immigrants and refugees actually transformed Canadian cuisine even as they incorporated Canadian foods into their own diets. Through *Chatelaine*, some, perhaps many, post-war Anglo-Canadian housewives experimented with their first Italian, Chinese, Indian, and Caribbean dishes. If the recent allure of multicultural dining experiences and conspicuous dining has brought immigrant food cultures into the forefront of North American bourgeois standards of "taste," the 1950s and 1960s were more tentative, contested contexts. Still, current food wars—including the recent "wok wars" in Toronto sparked by an Anglo-Canadian couple who complained about their Chinese neighbours' food smells—remind us that class and cultural conflict continue. . . .

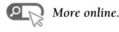 *More online.*

Notes

1. Our discussion draws on the emerging literatures on food and accompanying practices and issues, such as Stephen Mennell, Anne Murcott, and Anneke H. van Otterloo, *The Sociology of Food: Eating, Diet and Culture* (London, UK: Sage, 1992). On social histories of food, see, for the United States, Harvey Levenstein's pioneering works, *Revolution at the Table: The Transformation of the American Diet* (New York, NY: Oxford University Press, 1988) and *Paradox of Plenty: A Social History of Eating in Modern America* (New York, NY: Oxford University Press, 1993), and more recently Donna Gabaccia, *We Are What We Eat: Ethnic Food and the Making of Americans* (Cambridge, MA: Harvard University Press, 1998). A comprehensive survey of the Canadian scene remains to be written, but worthwhile forays into the field are Margaret Visser, *Much Depends on Dinner* (Toronto, ON: McClelland & Stewart, 1986) and *The Rituals of Dinner* (Toronto, ON: HarperCollins, 1991), and Anne Kingston, *The Edible Man: Dave Nichol, President's Choice and the Making of Popular Taste* (Toronto, ON: Macfarlane Walter & Ross, 1994). . . .

2. For a sample of the emerging social and gender history of post-1945 Canada, see Gary Kinsman, *The Regulation of Desire*, 2nd ed. (Montreal, QC: Black Rose Books, 1996); Franca Iacovetta, *Such Hardworking People: Italian Immigrants in Postwar Toronto* (Montreal, QC: McGill-Queen's University Press, 1992); essays in Joy Parr, ed., *A Diversity of Women: Ontario 1945–80* (Toronto, ON: University of Toronto Press, 1998) and in Gary Kinsman, Dieter K. Buse, and Mercedes Steedman, eds., *Whose National Security? Canadian State Surveillance and the Creation of Enemies* (Toronto, ON: Between the Lines, 2000). . . .

3. The literature on post–World War II immigration to Canada is extensive, but useful studies include the relevant chapters in Donald H. Avery, *Reluctant Host: Canada's Response to Immigrant Workers, 1896–1994* (Toronto, ON: McClelland & Stewart, 1995) and in Irving Abella and Harold Troper, *None Is Too Many: Canada and the Jews of Europe 1933–1948* (Toronto, ON: Lester and Orpen Dennys, 1982); and, on the impact of Cold War policy on immigration, Reginald Whitaker, *Double Standard: The Secret History of Canadian Immigration* (Toronto, ON: Lester and Orpen Dennys, 1987).

4. Marlene Epp, Franca Iacovetta, Frances Swyripa, eds., *Sisters or Strangers? Immigrant, Ethnic, and Racialized Women in Canadian History* (Toronto, ON: University of Toronto Press, 2004), 3–19. On this topic and on recent efforts at such integration see the discussion in the introduction.

5. National Film Board Archives (hereafter NFBA), Montreal, file 51-214, *Canadian Notebook*, produced by NFB for Department of Citizenship and Immigration, Information Sheet (April 1953). On the NFB and Cold War, see Reg Whitaker and Gary Marcuse, *Cold War Canada: The Making of a National Insecurity State, 1945–1957* (Toronto, ON: University of Toronto Press, 1994).

6. NFBA, file 57-327, *Women at Work*, produced for Department of Citizenship and Immigration (Gordon Sparling, producer and director) 1958 . . . .

7. The vast international literature on the professionalization and medicalization of "mothercraft" and on "homemaking" in the pre-1945 period includes valuable Canadian studies such as Cynthia Comacchio, *Nations Are Built of Babies* (Montreal, QC: McGill-Queen's University Press, 1993) and Kathryn Arnup, Andrée Lévesque, and Ruth Pierson, eds., *Delivering Motherhood* (London, UK: Routledge, 1990). For studies that deal more explicitly with immigrants and minorities, including First Nations, see J. R. Miller, *Shingwauk's Vision: A History of Native Residential Schools* (Toronto, ON: University of Toronto Press, 1996); Gabaccia, *We Are What We Eat*; and Levenstein, *Paradox of Plenty*. On post-1945 trends, see, for example, Parr, *A Diversity of Women*; Mary Louise Adams, *The Trouble with Normal* (Toronto, ON: University of Toronto Press, 1997); and Mona Gleason, *Normalizing the Ideal* (Toronto, ON: University of Toronto Press, 1999).

8. For Canada, see, for example, Susan Prentice, "Workers, Mothers, Reds: Toronto's Postwar Daycare Fight," *Studies in Political Economy* 30 (1989); and Veronica Strong-Boag, "Home Dreams: Canadian Women and the Suburban Experiment," *Canadian Historical Review* 72, 4 (1991). . . .

9. Doug Owram, *Born at the Right Time: A History of the Baby Boom Generation* (Toronto, ON: University of Toronto Press, 1996), chs 1 to 3; Franca Iacovetta, "Remaking Their Lives: Women Immigrants, Survivors, and Refugees," in Parr, ed., *Diversity of Women*; Marlene Epp, *Women without Men: Mennonite Refugees of the Second World War* (Toronto, ON: University of Toronto Press, 2000).

10. Gleason, *Normalizing the Ideal*.

11. City of Toronto Archives (hereafter CTA), Social Planning Collection (SPC), SC 40, box 56, file 9 – c "Immigrants, Migrants, Ethnic Groups – English Classes – West Toronto, 1954, 1959–1962, 1966," *Report of the Committee on English Language Instruction*, June 1961.

12. Not until the 1970s did migration streams from "non-white" nations reach significant numbers. Government recruitment policies of Caribbean women for domestic service brought only handfuls of these women into Canada before 1965. A modest number of Chinese

women arrived by 1965, but their presence was significant: in 1947, Canada rescinded the racist Chinese Immigration Act (1923) (and that had been preceded by the infamous Chinese head taxes dating back to 1895).

13. For details, see Avery, *Reluctant Host*; Abella and Troper, *None Is Too Many.*
14. Iacovetta, "Remaking Their Lives"; Epp, *Women without Men*; Joyce Hibbert, *The War Brides* (Toronto, ON: PMA Books, 1978); Agnes Calliste, "Canada's Immigration Policy and Domestics from the Caribbean: The Second Domestic Scheme," in Jesse Vorst et al., eds., *Race, Class and Gender: Bonds and Barriers* (Toronto, ON: Between the Lines, 1989) . . .
15. On race, racialized women, and nation building—an important theme in recent multidisciplinary work on immigrant and refugee women and women of colour—see, for example the essays in the special theme issue "Whose Canada Is It?" of *Atlantis*, co-edited by Tania Das Gupta and Franca Iacovetta.
16. Jean Huggard, "From Emigrants to Immigrants: Hungarians in a European Camp," *Canadian Welfare* 33 (February 1958). On women in South Korean refugee camps, for example, see Pierre Berton, "The Ordeal of Mrs. Tak," *Maclean's*, 15 June 1951.
17. On this and other examples, Canadian Red Cross (CRC), Ontario Division, *News Bulletin*, Special Issue on the British War Brides (September 1946). Thanks to Frances Swyripa for this source.
18. CRC, Ontario Division, *News Bulletin* (Ruth Adams) (September–October 1945). No doubt strawberries were not easily obtained in post-war London; see also ibid. (May 1946).
19. CRC, Ontario Division, *News Bulletin* (September 1946).
20. For contrasting examples of war-bride experiences, including women's stories of intense loneliness, conflicts with Canadian in-laws, and difficult marriages, see, for example, Iacovetta, "Remaking Their Lives"; Hibbert, *The War Brides*; and Estella Spergel's collection of oral testimonies (including her own) in her "British War Brides, World War Two: A Unique Experiment for Unique Immigrants—The Process that Brought Them to Canada" (Master's thesis, University of Toronto, 1997). With thanks to Estella for sharing her material.
21. The British measured liquids by weight, North Americans by volume.
22. For examples, consult: YWCA, MU3527, *Annual Reports*, 1941–9; *Annual Report*, 1949 Weston Branch; University Settlement, Social Planning Council, vol 24, Nl, box 1, Staff Meeting Minutes 1948–65, 4 June 1957 report.
23. Rather than specifying foods, the Canada Food Guide listed food groupings based on their nutritional value—vegetables, and meat and fish, and so on—and

then offered general guidelines for their consumption while allowing for choice and variety. In 1950, a revised guide was issued.

24. For more details, see Korinek, *Roughing It in the Suburbs: Reading Chatelaine in the Fifties and Sixties* (Toronto, ON: University of Toronto Press, 2000).
25. Marie Holmes, "Meals off the Shelf" (February 1955); Elaine Collett, "98 Cent January Specials" (January 1960); "Seven Dinners on the Double"; and "Easy-to-Make Pizza Pin Wheels" (1961), all in *Chatelaine*. Levenstein, *Paradox of Plenty*; see also Gabaccia, *We Are What We Eat.*
26. Levenstein, *Paradox of Plenty*, 218. We also thank the members of the Toronto Labour Studies Group, the faculty at several universities where we delivered this talk (individually or collectively), and other colleagues "of a certain age" who shared their stories of culinary (and other forms of experimentation) in the 1960s and 1970s!
27. Editors, "What's New with Us" (March 1965).
28. For example, see Elaine Collett, "Ten New Ways with a Pound of Hamburg" (September 1961).
29. This and the following references are from the AO, International Institute of Metropolitan Toronto, MU 6410, file: Cookbook Project, booklet: Toronto Nutrition Committee, *Food Customs of New Canadians.* Published with funds from the Ontario Dietic Association.
30. The revised guide profiled Chinese, Czechoslovakian, German and Austrian, Greek, Hungarian, Italian, Jewish, Dutch, Polish, Portuguese, Spanish, Ukrainian, and West Indian "food customs."
31. The entries for Jewish and German–Austrian.
32. Although the guide does not explicitly state it, these class distinctions, in turn, overlapped with racial distinctions between wealthier whites and poorer Blacks more likely to emigrate.
33. Miller, *Shingwauk's Vision*; Gabaccia, *We Are What We Eat*; Comacchio, *Nations Are Built of Babies.*
34. Another entry noted the availability and use of vitamin D for mothers and children.
35. As for improvement, it stated: "If income low the use of more poultry might be encouraged" and "The cost and relative value" of sugar-coated cereals and milk was explained.
36. For a valuable discussion see Comacchio, *Nations Are Built of Babies.*
37. Franca Iacovetta, "Recipes for Democracy? Gender, Family and Making Female Citizens in Cold War Canada," *Canadian Woman Studies* 20, no. 2 (Summer 2000).
38. The sample is of 28 interviews conducted in the 1970s with immigrant women and couples asked to comment on food customs and with the following national,

regional, and ethnoreligious breakdown: European (18), including European Jewry (4), Asian (2), Caribbean (1), and South Asian (mainly from India) (3). This sample was selected from Iacovetta's database of more than 60 interviews with post-1945 immigrants culled from the Oral History Collection, Multicultural History Society of Ontario (hereafter MHSO), Toronto.

39.   MHSO sample, interviews with Amelia S-R. and Maria B. Similar reports come from POWs, including Lotta B., a Polish Gentile woman who fought in the Polish Resistance until her arrest during the Warsaw insurrection in 1944. For her, the Germany POW camp meant lack of food, poor sanitary conditions, and total isolation from world events.

40.   MHSO sample, interviews with Maria B., Helga A., and Dagmar Z.

41.   MHSO sample; the theme also comes up repeatedly in the recordings of reception workers.

42.   MHSO sample, interview with Iusa D.

43.   MHSO sample, interview with Annemarie H.

44.   MHSO sample, interviews with Susan M., Helga A., and Nazneed S.

45.   For one example, see Franca Iacovetta, "From Jellied Salads to Melon and Prosciutto, and Polenta: Italian Foodways and 'Cosmopolitan Eating,'" in Jo Marie Powers, ed., *Buon appetito!* (Toronto, ON: Ontario Historical Society, 2000).

46.   Jeannine Locke, "Can the Hungarians Fit In?" May 1957.

47.   All were favourable though for varied reasons. . . . Mrs. M. Filwood, Toronto to Editors, "Letters to *Chatelaine*" (July 1957); Letter from a new reader, Halifax, to Editors (August 1957); Rev. G. Simor, SJ, St. Elizabeth of Hungary Church, Toronto, to Editors (September 1959).

48.   For example, see NA, MG31, Citizenship Branch, D69, col12, file: 1950, Liaison Officer, Dr. V. Kaye, Report of Trip to Toronto and Hamilton, 27 September–2 October 1950.

49.   For example, AO, IIMT, file: Cookbook Project, *Special Greetings in Food Christmas 1963* (homemade pamphlet). A more detailed discussion of this theme is in Iacovetta, *Making New Citizens in Cold War Canada* (in progress).

8 A Model Suburb for Model Suburbanites
Order, Control, and Expertise in Thorncrest Village

Patrick Vitale

Today, travelling north from Islington station on a number 37 bus, it is difficult to imagine the rural landscape that greeted Marshall Foss in 1945. Newly returned from service as a wing commander in the Royal Canadian Air Force in the autumn of 1945, Foss began to develop the subdivision of Thorncrest Village at the corner of Islington Avenue and Radburn Road in the township of Etobicoke, just west of Toronto (see Figure 1). Now subsumed by the condo towers and traffic of metropolitan Toronto, a small nondescript shopping plaza marks the spot where Foss began his development. When Foss first visited this corner in 1945, it was occupied by rolling farmers' fields, which seemed the optimal site on which to build a "modern community" dedicated to "country living."

Foss developed a community devoted to the central ideals of suburban living: conformity, community, privacy, stability, and a careful mixture of nature and city. These ideals clearly motivated Thorncrest Village's design and development and had a substantial, albeit lesser, impact on suburban design in Toronto and other cities. In the late 1940s, Thorncrest Village was a model for other suburban developments, and newspapers and magazines highlighted it frequently. . . . Its planner, Eugene Faludi, would

go on to have a prominent career, developing plans for cities and suburbs across Canada.[1] The national attention focused on Thorncrest Village may have been unusual, but its design and social life were not. Thorncrest Village exemplified the clichés of suburbia, and the principles applied there are apparent throughout suburban Canada. Thorncrest Village and hundreds of other Canadian suburbs provide ample evidence to support Robert Fishman's claim that the residential suburb was an "archetypical middle-class creation."[2]

This paper focuses on Thorncrest Village as a key location and moment for the genesis of modern suburban planning in Canada. By understanding the search for order and control that motivated the designers, developers, and residents of Thorncrest Village, we can better understand the broader forces that shaped post–World War II Canadian cities. During the postwar period, the middle class invested increasing faith in professionals' abilities to solve a wide range of problems from war to famine to sickness. The problems of the city were in no way different, and in Thorncrest Village and throughout Toronto, professional planners, with the support of the middle class, went to work rationally clearing old neighbourhoods and creating new

Citation: Patrick Vitale, "A Model Suburb for Model Suburbanites: Order, Control, and Expertise in Thorncrest Village," *Urban History Review / Revue d'histoire urbaine*, 40, no. 1 (2011): 41–55.

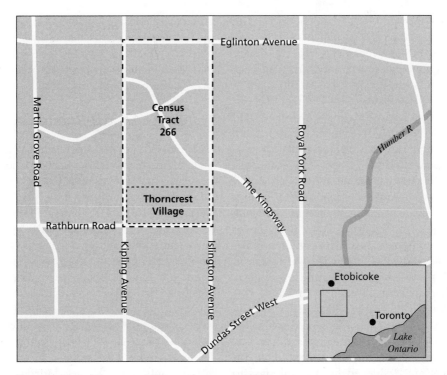

Figure 1. Map of Thorncrest Village and census tract 266.

ones.[3] The development of Thorncrest Village was a key moment and place where middle-class Torontonians invested not only their savings, but also their identities in the modern project of developing a more orderly city. The developers and residents of Thorncrest Village saw themselves as suburban pioneers who would demonstrate to all of Canada a modern and more rational way of living.

. . .

History of Post-War Suburbanization in Canada

Most recent writing on suburbanization in Canada takes two distinct, yet parallel approaches, focusing on either the history of women and domesticity in suburbia or the history of working-class and industrial suburbanization.[4] Most of this work has focused on pre-1945

ones suburbanization, rather than the massive tide of suburbanization that followed World War II.[5] Much of it can be broadly categorized within the framework of new suburban history. New suburban historians are a disparate group who question traditional meta-histories of suburbanization.[6] They argue that prior studies of suburbia, particularly classic syntheses by Fishman and Jackson, have concentrated exclusively on white middle-class residential suburbanization and have ignored the presence of working-class, industrial, and nonwhite suburbanization.[7] They also question the classic trope of the suburban dupe—the middle-class suburbanite who is drawn to a place of conformity, consumerism, and affluence. These scholars provide an important reformulation of suburban history in Canada and the United States. They show, on one hand, that suburbanization was diverse and did not involve merely the middle class. On the other hand, they provide a more humane account of suburbia in the face of a long history of elite intellectual critique that described the dreary lives of suburbanites who succumbed to false consciousness and became "organization men."

There is good reason to embrace the critiques of these new suburban historians and their understanding of suburbanization from the bottom up, but it is also essential to question the power relations that they tend to overlook. While suburbanization in Canada was and remains very diverse, a certain type of suburb has been and remains dominated by the white middle class. The suburban myth of the lawn-obsessed, conformist, exclusive, white middle-class community, like any myth, was rooted in material processes and everyday experience. The suburban myth resulted from a long history of white middle-class flight from the city and the pursuit of more ordered and controlled residential space. Mary Corbin Sies argues that suburbanization is united by certain suburban ideals that are "fashioned by a social class to serve its own needs, pleasures, and interests as a group." Suburbanization is an "ideology" that "represents a historically specific set of built forms and values as the best universal approach to the housing needs of the citizenry."[8] These suburban ideals are rooted in a specific history of white middle-class residential suburbanization. When new suburban historians do not acknowledge these ideals and the particular suburbs that they correspond to, they overlook the power relations that produce and structure much of suburban life.

. . . This paper makes a small contribution to the enormous gap in the scholarly literature on post-war and middle-class Canadian suburbs. It focuses on Thorncrest Village, as a quintessentially middle-class suburb, in order to understand how developers, planners, and residents actively created a community devoted to the central suburban ideals of conformity, security, order, and control. They did so in order to create residential spaces that would help to reproduce

their power and prestige. Thorncrest Village is representative of many middle-class suburbanites' long pursuit of a bourgeois utopia of their own. This pursuit is an integral aspect of the history of suburbanization in Canada.

Building a Model Suburb

Thorncrest Village was the product of the combined efforts of several developers, among them Marshall Foss, the principal developer; E. G. Faludi, the planner of the village; and E. S. Cox, the architect of many of the Village's homes. Several early documents point to the outlandish potential that the developers envisioned for the Village. The most interesting of these documents is a mimeographed paper titled "Home Horizons." While the authorship of this paper is unclear, its presence in a TVHA [Thorncrest Village Homes Association] file titled "Copy Materials" suggest that Thorncrest Village's developers were its authors. . . .

The author of "Home Horizons" claimed that most suburban developments in Canada left aspiring suburbanites with neighbourhoods that differed little from the cities they were moving away from. These potential homebuyers faced "problems and pitfalls" and "want the one best of every component, and there is naught but contradiction available to them."[9] The designers of Thorncrest Village hoped to meet suburbanites' "dream of dreams" by both mechanizing and organizing suburban development within a corporate structure. Identifying the department store as a model, they argued that vertical and horizontal integration would have the dual effect of providing suburbanites with an ordered and desirous residential community and developers with windfall profits. The efficiencies brought about by mass production and comprehensive urban planning would allow for the expansion of suburban living to a wider segment of the population. More was at stake than corporate profits. As "Home Horizons" noted, "The opportunity offered . . . to a corporation geared to produce really modern complete living units in well planned development areas on a parity with present day production of other items for living enjoyment, with a sales organization on par with the product, can reap a golden harvest while making a unique contribution to human welfare, peace and the happiness of the middle classes, the backbone of our civilization."[10] . . .

While the designers of Thorncrest Village were well aware of its potential, they claimed that prospective suburbanites needed to be educated through a flurry of advertisements and brochures. An emphasis on potential suburbanites' lack of sound insight into the principles of orderly suburban planning was implicit in much of the advertising and planning literature created by the designers of the Village. The developers argued that the "common man" would ultimately learn to value the experience of living in a planned community, but first had to be taught the benefits of modern suburban planning. Reflecting on the experience of planning the Village, Faludi wrote, "The 'common man,' for whom we intended this community, was against everything. He disapproved the design of the houses in general. He disliked the free placement in relation to lot lines and neighbouring houses. He utterly rejected the idea of the living room being oriented towards the south and not towards the street. He did not believe that curved streets would slow down the speed of cars."[11] According to Faludi, as a result of this innate ignorance, most suburbanites needed to be taught the values of modern suburban living.
. . .

In educating suburbanites about the value of Thorncrest Village's design, the developers often maligned the speculative development that was predominant throughout metropolitan Toronto.[12] They noted that developers created dense suburban neighbourhoods that differed little in density or form from urban Toronto. In an "Introduction to Country Club Community," Foss argued that most subdivisions in Etobicoke Township were composed of "small lots, over

exploiting the countryside in this potential country home paradise, and despite the high price, offer only the same front and back yard, crowded row house plans of the central city."[13] Unlike these developers, Foss described himself as a "slightly modest pirate" who realized that home purchasers would "pay a premium for this type of home location, with its added protection of property values and its invaluable community co-operative services."[14] Foss walked a fine line between describing Thorncrest Village as profitable and as a project with social benefits that were far more important than mere money-making. He aimed to signal to potential buyers that Thorncrest was not just another speculative housing development; it was a place that was carefully engineered, not mass produced. This engineering offered residents a stable financial investment and secure social status. . . .

Advertisements described Thorncrest Village as a place where modern planning principles would paradoxically allow for country living—a carefully orchestrated blend of city and country. Thorncrest Village offered its residents "a 'country home,' true—yet one with not only the most modern conveniences of city living but with the added advantages of planned recreational and community facilities and services."[15] Thorncrest provided "the warmth of the sun . . . the whispers of leaves in the breeze . . . the song of birds and the beauty of a graceful countryside," all within a 20-minute commute to downtown Toronto.[16] Advertisements proffered the aesthetics of country life along with the fellowship of small-town life and access to shared modern facilities like a shopping plaza, pool, and clubhouse. Homebuyers purchased a carefully constructed hybrid of country and city.
. . .

Thorncrest Village's developers repeatedly argued that the "common man" needed to be taught the value of modern, expertly planned communities. Residents were not urban planners or architects, but if they could appreciate the expertise and methods applied in the design of the Village, this would reflect well on both their own status and that of the wider community. In other words, the stature of the community was intrinsically tied to a strong faith in expertise. In order to maintain this status, residents had to develop at least a partial appreciation of principles used in its design. A reciprocal relationship developed between the neighbourhood's status as expert designed and residents' status as people who could comprehend this expertise. The developers and fellow residents encouraged Thorncrest Villagers to develop at least a pedestrian appreciation of the methods used to develop the community. Local resident Larry Dack urged residents to read E. G. Faludi's article in the *Journal of the American Institute of Planners*, and the Thorncrest Village Homes Association provided copies at its office. Dack wrote to residents, "We are used to hearing our Village made the subject of debate. After all it is rather unique in Canada and decided pro and con views are to be expected. But when we extol the virtues of Thorncrest living are we quite sure we know 'whereof we speak'? How many of us, for instance, are acquainted with the original objectives of the planner or have any conception of the tremendous problems facing them in putting this experiment in community living to work?"[17]

. . .

One basic principle of the modern, planned subdivision was that it offered a controlled environment and a secure investment for its residents.[18] Thorncrest Village advertisements contrasted this control and security to the uncontrolled space and financial risk of housing in downtown Toronto or in speculatively built suburbs. As various advertisements and brochures repeatedly pointed out, "Home is what you make it . . . and where you place it."[19] Another ad described Thorncrest as "the stabilized community" and informed potential residents that "no house and lot has any real independent existence, permanent quality, or even monetary value apart from its neighbourhood. Modern planning

ensures good neighbourhoods."[20] The protection afforded by Thorncrest Village was one of the neighbourhood's key selling points. The developers explained the link between the lifestyle of the community and the financial value of the home. As they told prospective tenants, Thorncrest Village was a place where "your property values and your living values are secure and stabilized."[21] The security of property values in Thorncrest resulted from two mutually reinforcing protections. First, residence in Thorncrest was restricted and "all owners must be approved by vote as in an exclusive club."[22] Second, the comprehensive nature of Thorncrest's planning ensured that noxious uses could not be placed in close proximity. The possibility of noxious uses and noxious residents was eliminated. The security of investment offered by Thorncrest was a product of its "sensible restrictions" and the ability of its planners to scientifically account for potential threats. This all stood in contrast to the uncontrolled city characterized by "noise . . . smoke . . . and ceaseless traffic." . . .

From the beginning, the developers of Thorncrest Village imagined it as a model community, a place brought into being by the best of scientific planning and supported from within by residents' commitment to the planners' designs. Unlike most suburban communities, two of the developers, architect E. C. S. Cox and principal developer Marshall Foss, were the first residents of Thorncrest Village. The developers sought residents who were committed to the ideals of modern suburban living. In fact, the first point of a section of "Home Horizons" entitled "How to Proceed" suggests that developers "form a group of kindred spirits."[23] This group was to develop the neighbourhood gradually, accumulating capital along the way. This is the model that Foss and his partners followed, and Thorncrest developed slowly from 1945 until its completion in 1960. Recruitment of kindred spirits ensured that the status of the neighbourhood was maintained, and this status ensured the security of property values. The Village thrived by incorporating its residents into the daily reproduction of its value, status, and exceptionality. As Faludi recounted in his evaluation of the Village's planning, "The community belongs to them and they belong to the community."[24] The key question is who they were, how they were selected, and what was at stake for them in Thorncrest Village.

Selecting "Kindred Spirits"

Thorncrest Village's developers put in place several restrictions to ensure that the neighbourhood maintained its bucolic and middle-class character.[25] The most rigorous was a careful vetting of all potential residents. The Thorncrest Village Homes Association approved all homeowners and tenants before granting them the right to live in the community. This process began with a detailed two-page application that the prospective homebuyer submitted to the association. The application explained to the applicant that it aimed to protect "the heart of a neighbourhood," which is "the people, not the homes or grounds." The application was necessary to ensure an "advanced type of neighbourhood," because "it is imperative that the members be congenial in the sense that they have similar aspirations in regarding their home and home life and a consciousness of the importance of the locale on their family's welfare."[26] Applicants were assured that the process was for their own protection, as well as the community's. The application simply aimed to determine whether the applicant's aspirations were compatible with the community's. As it explained, "The following questions are intended solely to aid the membership committee formed of present members, in selecting new residents. This is at once obviously the greatest protection from every point of view, for the stability of the community as a whole and the individual home, the owner's investment and the happiness of the family."[27] The application went on to ask a page's worth of questions, among them the applicant's present address and type of home, cash available for home purchase,

occupation and employer, banker, number of children, address prior to marriage, spare time activities, and what features attracted them to Thorncrest Village.[28]

Following completion of the application and the submission of a $100 application fee, the name of the prospective resident, occupation, employer, and present address were posted in the community's newsletter, the *Bulletin*. The posting of all potential residents was mandatory, in accordance with paragraph 4 of Article 3 of the By-Laws, which stated, "The directors shall make . . . a diligent investigation of the applicant. The Secretary of the Corporation shall cause all regular members to be notified of each application, and if any Regular Member has any objection . . . he shall within three days . . . deliver to the Secretary of the Corporation written notice of such objection."[29] The final decision lay with the Board of Directors, who reviewed the application and any objections and then determined whether to give the resident status as a waiting member. If waiting members did not purchase a home within three months, their status would expire and they would be forced to reapply.

The files of the TVHA provide no evidence that residents or the Board of Directors ever exercised their ability to restrict residence in the community. There was probably rarely an objectionable applicant, as the potential residents listed in the TVHA *Bulletin* reveal a roster of professionals and executives working for downtown-based Toronto corporations.[30] In the late 1950s and early 1960s most prospective residents hailed from the Toronto metropolitan area and already resided in suburban neighbourhoods. Fourteen per cent of those surveyed by S. D. Clark were transplants from outside of Toronto, mostly from Montreal, Ottawa, and the United States. He likened these highly mobile residents to "organization men" who "moved from city to city" but stayed in the same "social world" wherever they lived. . . . Clark collected comments from residents about why they moved from Toronto to Thorncrest Village. One told him he moved because their previous home was not in a "good area" and "foreigners were starting to get in." Another, "We were driven out by immigrants." Other residents described their previous neighbourhoods as "a working man's district," "working and lower middle class," and "average."[31]

Despite certain residents' racist perceptions of their previous neighbourhoods, the ability to restrict residence was a little-used safeguard that was probably redundant, given the $100 application fee and the cost of purchasing a home in the Village.[32] Nonetheless, the application process surely discouraged some potential residents from applying. The application process is indicative of the emphasis that the community's designers and residents placed on limiting access, as well as the participatory process through which existing members granted entry to the community.

Membership in the TVHA was mandatory in order to purchase or rent a home in the community. However, the association's control of residents did not end with their admission into the neighbourhood. The bylaws of the TVHA enumerated "schedules, stipulations, restrictions, and provisions" that governed life in the neighbourhood, including prohibitions of signs, apartment buildings, duplexes, and fences and walls. All plans and renovations had to be approved by the TVHA. All utilities had to be placed in the rear of the lots. The bylaws required residents not to oppose public utilities if they were made available to the community. And the bylaws included a mechanism for expulsion of any nonagreeable residents if they engaged in conduct "injurious or prejudicial to the best interests of the corporation."[33] In such a case, the Board of Directors could call for a general meeting with 10 days' notice, and if two-thirds of residents approved, the resident would be forced to sell their home within one month to either a waiting member or the corporation. There is no evidence from the records of the TVHA that this expulsion mechanism was ever used, but it was consistently included in the bylaws.

The *Bulletin* also reminded residents that they must notify the corporation if they intended to sell or rent their home. This restriction exposed a consistent conflict at the crux of life in a "modern planned community." While residents appreciated the security provided by the bylaws, they often found them stifling when they inhibited their own ability to sell, rent, or make a modification to their home. This was the central conflict of life in a suburban planned community—a conflict between suburbanites' emphasis on their freedom and independence and the need to rein in this freedom in order to ensure the security and stability of their community.[34] This contradiction would be alleviated only if the residents began to identify with and enforce the disciplinary mechanisms put in place by the developer. Restrictions seemed less onerous to residents when they were mutually agreed upon norms, rather than infringements imposed on residents by an external force. . . .

"Men of the World"

Before moving to a discussion of the systems of social control and normalization that the residents of Thorncrest Village developed, it is useful to briefly consider the social characteristics of the residents of the Village. It is difficult to carry out this task with absolute certainty, given the changing shape of census tracts and the imperfection of existing data. However, on the basis of analysis of census tract and enumeration area (EA) data, it is incontrovertible that the Village's predominant adult residents were white, middle-class professionals who were employed in business or worked in highly educated professions like medicine, law, and academe. This point is easily validated using 1961 census data for census tract 266, which encompassed all of Thorncrest Village and the much larger affluent subdivision of Princess Anne Manor to the north (see Figure 1 for the boundaries of tract 266).[35] . . .

. . . Residents had substantially higher levels of home and automobile ownership than other Torontonians. The income differences between tract 266 and the rest of Toronto are equally stark, with an average man's income in tract 266 more than double that of the average in Metro Toronto ($9,811 versus $4,330). Even more impressive is the proportion of men who worked in managerial positions: 60 per cent in census tract 266 and 57.4 per cent in the EAs. The percentage of professionals in the EAs (19.1 per cent) was even higher than that of census tract 266 (16.6 per cent). Tract 266's low level of women's participation in paid labour suggests a number of factors, including the difficulty of accessing work on the suburban fringe, the proportion of families with children, and the overall high earnings of male income earners. Census and qualitative data confirm that Toronto's business and professional elite and their families were the predominant residents of Thorncrest Village. These figures are validated by S. D. Clark's 1964 study of suburbanization in Toronto, in which he describes the residents of Thorncrest Village as middle-class "men of the world" who were a "status conscious social group."[36] E. G. Faludi argued that the residents of Thorncrest Village, like its developers and designers, were visionaries "who always supported progress and advanced thought."[37] . . .

. . . [M]ost residents of the EAs (80.2 per cent) and Etobicoke (70.9 per cent) were of British origin. A higher percentage of Thorncrest Village residents identified as Protestants, compared to the rest of Toronto and Etobicoke. Thorncrest Village's design was not the only aspect of the neighbourhood imported from the United States. A greater proportion of the residents of tract 266 (7.2 per cent) and the EAs (7.3 per cent) than the city (1.2 per cent) or the metropolitan area (1.3 per cent) were born in the United States. This concentration was likely the result of the significant presence of American managers in the branch plants and offices of American corporations based in Toronto. While

the census does identify the presence of a small number of respondents who identified as Italian and Asiatic, these proportions were significantly lower than for Toronto as a whole. No residents of the EAs identified as Jewish. In sum, the average adult male resident of Thorncrest Village was significantly more likely to be white, wealthy, employed in a professional or managerial occupation, be of British or American origin, and worship at a Protestant church, than Toronto-area residents.

. . .

Normalizing the Neighbourhood

Thorncrest Village developed as a quintessentially middle-class suburban space, and residents worked hard to maintain its status as such. Reminders of how to properly behave and maintain one's home appeared regularly in the neighbourhood's newsletter, the *Bulletin*.[38] My analysis of extant copies of the *Bulletin* reveals several key aspects of life in Thorncrest Village. First, there were frequent discussions of conditions in the neighbourhood and attempts to prescribe proper behaviour for residents. Many of these discussions hinged on how individual decision making violated communal aspects of the neighbourhood. Through the *Bulletin*, residents attempted to create norms that mediated their often-contradictory desires to respect the rights of property owners and to develop an orderly and controlled community. Second, the *Bulletin* provides evidence of Thorncrest Villagers constructing norms based on their shared identities as residents of the subdivision. Thorncrest Villagers saw the neighbourhood as an essential aspect of their identities as, what S. D. Clark called, "men of the world." In order to fulfill the neighbourhood's potential, residents needed to believe in the shared expertise and prestige of fellow residents. Residents needed to see themselves and their neighbours as contributing to and identifying with this great experiment in community planning. While residents' expertise and prestige were undoubtedly complicated and multifaceted, they in part took a racialized form in which Thorncrest Villagers's whiteness allowed them to navigate and perform a variety of ethnic identities. In sum, the *Bulletin* shows the integral connections, in post-war Toronto, between the dual project of constructing modern suburbia and white middle-class identities.

In the early years, some of the TVHA's clearest directives on how to keep Thorncrest Village orderly arrived in the form of bulletins from Harvey the rabbit. Harvey was the pet of Village residents the Despards and was so beloved that he attended the Home Association's 1947 annual meeting in a black velvet box. At this meeting, the residents decided to name Harvey the Thorncrest mascot, and he began to adorn signs, as well as helpful "Harvey Says" and "Harvey Suggests" bulletins.[39] The TVHA's Information Committee and the Improvement and Maintenance Committee distributed these index-card-sized flyers to residents' homes. While many flyers contained innocuous announcements of "symphonic concerts," movies at the tennis courts, and changes to bus service, others spoke to more controversial issues concerning home maintenance and residents' behaviour. These flyers often bore a slogan along the bottom of the card, "Issued by your 'Improvement and Maintenance' committee in the interest of a tidy, orderly, well-kept Thorncrest."[40] On the flyers Harvey repeatedly asked residents to close their garage doors— "Your garage doors are gaping"—because "garage doors left open make the Village ill-spoken." He also requested that people not pick flowers, bring in their garbage cans promptly—"Pails left out . . . spoil a neighbour's view"—and restrain their dogs. For residents who spotted drivers violating the Village's "Drive Slowly" campaign, Harvey suggested that they "warn a thoughtless person and report them to the directors."[41]

Harvey's heyday was from 1948 to 1950 prior to the start of regular mail service in the community. As a brief history of Harvey remembered, "His suggestions continued until mail delivery

and other modern things invaded Thorncrest, but his ghost just won't lie down."[42] Always attuned to tradition and history, the authors of the *Bulletin* frequently resurrected Harvey in times of moral crisis. Harvey's ghost re-emerged in November 1961 to suggest that residents "be thoughtful of your neighbours—don't hang your washing on Sundays."[43] In May 1967, he issued an "Annual Spring Plea" that asked, among other things, that people "take mercy on soft lawns" by restraining their dogs and children, "Be kind to your neighbours who don't have dandelions and spray yours," and "Be considerate and don't cut your lawn on Sunday."[44]

While Harvey served as a useful proxy for moralizing and disciplining the neighbourhood, the authors of the *Bulletin* managed to carry on without him, and helpful reminders on home maintenance and other matters appeared frequently throughout the fifties and sixties, including pronouncements that all tennis players were required to wear white and that pool goers were to wear "proper dress" to and from the pool.[45] The *bête noire* of suburbanites everywhere, clotheslines, came under particular scrutiny, and residents were reminded to remove them when not in use.[46]

One of the more contentious and long-running debates in the *Bulletin* concerned the preservation of private property rights that conflicted with the communal design of the development. Residents used the newsletter to mediate the contradictions implicit in the designer's attempt to leave "room for both privacy and neighbourliness."[47] E. G. Faludi intentionally designed the community without fences in order to maximize the site's rolling country aesthetic. As he described it, one primary goal was to provide "the loose appearance of a village" in which the "houses fitted into the countryside."[48] As a condition of the bylaws, all residents had to seek approval from the Property Control Committee before erecting any fences and walls. The committee almost never approved them, and the neighbourhood remains fenceless today.

The inadvertent result of the restriction on fences and walls was free access to neighbours' yards for marauding children and dogs. Throughout the 1960s, the TVHA issued editorials in the *Bulletin* and distributed Resident Information Services (RIS) *Bulletins* in mailboxes calling on residents to not transgress the rights of property owners. The TVHA continually attempted to enforce a norm that was not being impressed upon neighbourhood children and dogs. The September 1960 *Bulletin* asked residents to "please restrain your dogs and warn your children not to cut through our neighbours' property."[49] Months later, an RIS *Bulletin* again noted that residents needed to "respect your neighbour's property" and that dogs were damaging "valuable shrubs" and children were taking shortcuts that damaged lawns and flowerbeds.[50] By June 1961, the TVHA began to declare that aggrieved residents might need to take "drastic action" against roaming dogs.[51] In March 1962, another RIS *Bulletin* again called on residents to "please be kind to neighbours, come on, let's curb our children and restrain our pets."[52] In April 1963 the *Bulletin*, clearly invoking the law, described children who crossed yards as "trespassers."[53] The discussion of lawn crossing slowed for a few years, only to re-emerge with renewed vigour in 1967. In March, the TVHA again described the "annoying" problem of "trespassing" and called on residents to self-police and "report on the trespassers and discourage this habit."[54] Weeks later, an extended editorial appeared in the *Bulletin*, noting that trespassers wilfully violated the norms of the neighbourhood: "Offenders today have in most cases grown up in the Village, and know its rules." It declared, "Property and privacy must be respected" and went to a new level to deter potential "offenders." It noted that the TVHA was collecting their names and, "unless this practice ceases forthwith, your board may authorize the publication of the names concerned, and if this fails other steps will be taken."[55]

The ongoing discussion about lawn crossing in the *Bulletin* reveals several aspects of the limits of communal thinking in the community. While the TVHA readily defended the fenceless design of the neighbourhood, it also worked to ensure that residents shared the norm of not entering another's property without permission. Physical property demarcation would be unnecessary if this norm was widely respected. In instances when the norm was not shared, the TVHA resorted to two measures. It attempted to publicly police and shame offenders, describing lawn crossing as a transgressive act that violated the deeply held ideals of the neighbourhood. When internal policing failed, the TVHA resorted to the threat of official police power, whether in the form of citing trespassers or having the dogcatcher apprehend roaming dogs. Like many communities of homeowners, the TVHA's ultimate resource was the power of the state.

The struggle over lawns was not limited to the fight against lawn crossers. The lack of a clean demarcation between neighbouring lawns resulted in frequent conflicts about weeds and lawn conditions. This is a point well made by Paul Robbins in his analysis of the power of the lawn as a social force in suburban life. He notes that lawn care is part of a "normative communitarian practice" that partially results from weeds' abilities to travel from yard to yard. As a result, those who care for their lawns are seen as contributing to a "civic good," and those who do not, exhibit "a form of free riding, civic neglect, and moral weakness."[56] The *Bulletin*'s authors did not shy away from pressing residents to take proper care of their yards. One announcement described how many residents were complaining about their neighbours' long grass and lack of watering, which was upsetting to residents, it explained, because "many . . . are entertaining their guests and . . . it is discouraging to have a burnt out, weedy neighbour's yard to look at." Another notice observed that some residents "have allowed weeds to overtake their backyards." This was "unsightly" and "not very thoughtful towards adjoining neighbours who have tended their properties all summer and are now faced with the spreading of weeds in their own yards."[57] The authors of the *Bulletin* told residents that if they required help, the TVHA's office would gladly provide the names of "reliable weed sprayers and lawn maintenance men."[58] As always, the TVHA placed faith in experts' abilities to address any lawn care problem.

Lawn maintenance was one of numerous neighbourhood affairs in which it was essential for residents to participate if Thorncrest Village was to maintain its reputation as an ideal middle-class community. The TVHA implored residents to partake in myriad activities, from swimming to sewing with the Village's chapter of the Red Cross to attending meetings, exercise classes, and stag parties. Residents were expected to support neighbourhood institutions financially and with their participation. In the early years of the subdivision, there were several attempts to develop communal services in the neighbourhood, such as snowplowing and lawn mowing, but these attempts failed for lack of participation. Frustrated calls in the *Bulletin* for residents' full participation in the life of the community came to a head in residents' multiyear battle to finance the construction and maintenance of a clubhouse and swimming pool . . . The first attempt to finance both failed in 1948 but passed in 1949, and the pool and clubhouse officially opened a year later. Some residents, who made less use of the pool and clubhouse, complained about their contribution to maintenance costs. Typical of the communitarian spirit of the neighbourhood, a response appeared in the *Bulletin* arguing that "democratic rights is a phrase used too glibly" and that in Thorncrest it is an "individual's responsibility to comply with the majority." The article went on to argue, "Coming to live in Thorncrest Village is . . . a personal approval of this experiment in community living and carries with it the responsibility of graciously accepting commitments approved by the majority."[59] Throughout the *Bulletin*, there are constant

references to the importance of resident participation in order for the Thorncrest experiment to succeed. In November 1959, during his annual president's address, Mr. Douglas called on residents to not become complacent, because if they did, Thorncrest would "become just another average community."[60] In her monthly "Norm's Notes," Norma Despard asked residents why participation at the Annual Meeting had been so low and told them that "to lose interest would be a great catastrophe."[61]

. . . Participation and a sense of belonging were essential to Thorncrest Village's success. "Identification of people in the community was readily maintained . . . There developed highly effective techniques to bring people together, make them acquainted, and weld them into a social group."[62] Such techniques ranged widely, from the *Bulletin* itself to welcome tea parties to the Thorncrest Village crests that the TVHA offered to attach to residents' cars.[63] In Thorncrest Village, suburbia was not a place of anonymity, but rather one where the viability of the community rested on the active participation and shared identities of neighbours. The viability of the neighbourhood rested on residents' ability to ensure each other's willingness to adhere to and identify with the established norms of the community.

. . . [I]n comparison to metropolitan Toronto, the population of Thorncrest Village was overwhelmingly of British ancestry, native born, white, and Protestant. A prevalent thread running across much of critical race theory is the notion that whiteness is an unspoken, invisible, and taken-for-granted identity. Whiteness seems identifiable only as an absence, which is constructed in relation to visible and exoticized others. In other words, whiteness appears as an invisible norm that is constructed in relation to those whose racialized identities are made visible.[64] In a classic essay, bell hooks argues that whiteness is both a position of subjugation and domination. This sense of white subjugation— that whiteness is representative of absence and lifelessness—results in a white desire to "eat the other" in order to "enhance the bleak landscape of whiteness." At the same time, white peoples' ability to wilfully transcend, identify, and consume varied racial identities (other than their own) is an obvious assertion of power and privilege.[65] In the case of Thorncrest Village, residents' privilege was in part the product of their whiteness and their ability to assert control over their own and others' racial identities.

Throughout the 1950s and 1960s, while never referring to their own racial identities, Thorncrest Villagers made frequent reference to those who did not live in the neighbourhood, most commonly through references to the exoticism of other ethnicities at parties held at the clubhouse. These parties were consistently organized around an ethnocultural theme, including Hungarian, Italian, Chinese, Hawaiian, Mexican, Québécois, and a Calypso Party with West Indian dancers. The invitations for the parties often called on residents to dress and perform a racialized part. The flyer for the Chinese party requested that attendees "Dress Occidental or Accidental."[66] An article recounting the tropically themed "Narcissus Festival" described "ingenious decorations," including "sea shells, netting with a Hawaiian flare, Chinese gods." "Gaily costumed guests" attended dressed in "sarongs, hula skirts, mandarin kimonos, and Chinese dresses." One attendee wore a green Buddha costume.[67] Another article described attendees at a party as "all those original looking Thorncrest Mexicans."[68] The announcements for these parties, as well as later summaries that appeared in the *Bulletin*, reveal how the residents felt the authority to play with and perform a variety of ethnic and racialized identities, other than their own.

Ethnicity was not the only theme explored at the parties held at the clubhouse. At a hillbilly party, attendees dressed in "Dogpatch style" and dined on "Hush Puppies, Corn Pones and Turnip Greens," as well as a mysterious drink called "Kickapoo Joy Juice."[69] Worth quoting at length,

a summary of the "Beatnik Ball" described it as "a *real gasser!* Man, a howlin' success, cute chicks all decked out in leotards, black pony tails, cigarette holders and each having a sultry air of mystery behind dark, real dark sunspecks. Dad—dig those cool cats, beards, berets, sandals, turtle neck sweaters, and to top it all off—poetry, flutes and bongas [sic] to send those chicks. Dig the hall—there was art for all, plenty of crates for those cats to sit with their mates, and how can you forget the real gone abstract painting that everyone had their mitt in, enough to make you flip your lid."[70] The author of this passage adopted a caricatured version of the slang of the Beat generation and, by extension, urban African-Americans. The description of people sitting on crates was clearly intended to invoke images of urban idleness.

Through their parties, Thorncrest residents positioned themselves as worldly people of power and white privilege, who had the ability to access and perform a wide variety of identities. This performance was a complicated product of their class and white privilege and their corresponding ability to move through space via travel, education, and status.[71] The residents were able to peer into other identities and strip them down to their stereotyped and visible parts. Thorncrest Villagers's obsession with publicly enacting race and ethnicity (other than their own) suggests that historians of suburbanization in Canada must focus greater attention on the importance of whiteness, even in the absence of large-scale white flight like that in the United States. Toni Morrison argues that for white Americans, "there is no escape from racially inflected language."[72] A similar argument could be made for American and Canadian suburbanites. Through the performance of ethnic and racialized others, Thorncrest residents intentionally defined themselves as people of privilege. The legitimacy to engage in such performances was the product of their class and white privilege and their ability to move freely throughout metropolitan Toronto, North America, and the globe.

Conclusion

New suburban historians have pointed out the diversity of forms of suburbanization and interesting exceptions to the suburban myth, but the example of Thorncrest Village validates many of the clichés that we associate with the suburbs. The designers, developers, and middle-class residents of the subdivision all envisioned it as a model community—a place that embodied their faith that expert planning could deliver control and order. Residents and the developers put in place a series of controls that limited who could live in the neighbourhood and the design and appearance of its homes. As a result of these controls, the Village developed as a racially and economically exclusive community that policed the appearance of homes and the behaviour of residents.

Developers did not subject residents to these controls; rather, residents participated in their reproduction. Residents served on committees that approved house designs, used the *Bulletin* to police behaviour, and fostered a sense of belonging through the activities of the TVHA. Residents developed a shared belief that their community was an important experiment in suburban living and that their own participation was vital to its continued success. They and the developers proclaimed the neighbourhood as a model for all of Canada—an expertly designed suburb that represented the best of modern urban planning. Residents shared the developers' vision of a stable and controlled modern suburban community and believed in the expertise of the planners and architects who designed it. In Thorncrest Village, a faith in the power of modern expertise and the development of a suburban middle-class identity developed hand in hand. Thorncrest Village suggests many similarities to both the clichéd conformist suburb of literature and film and the exclusive white, middle-class suburbs of the post-war United States. White middle-class Canadians fled the city during the period following World War II. This flight may have been less dramatic and racially inflected than it was in cities like Detroit and Chicago, but white suburbanites in Canada also sought out race and class privilege in the suburbs. Suburbs in Canada, like those in the United States, were specifically designed to reproduce the privilege and power of the white middle class. They offered the middle class control and order, and the security of their investment and social status. In turn, the residents of Thorncrest Village helped create an orderly and controlled model suburban community. Their efforts were no doubt typical of many suburbanites throughout post-war Canada.

. . .

  More online.

Notes

My thanks to Harold Bérubé, Robert Lewis, Katie Mazer, and the anonymous reviewers for their helpful comments on an earlier draft of this paper; to the archivists at the Toronto City Archives for their assistance; to Berenica Vejvoda of the University of Toronto's Map and Data Library for help obtaining EA data; and to Elizabeth Lord for help with translation.

1.   Faludi was the lead author of Master Plans for Toronto in 1943 and Hamilton in 1947. . . . [S]ee Stephen Bocking, "Constructing Urban Expertise: Professional and Political Authority in Toronto, 1940–70," *Journal of Urban History* 33, no. 2 (2006): 51–76. For an overview of Faludi's career, see John Sewell, *The Shape of the City: Toronto Struggles with Modern Planning* (Toronto, ON: University of Toronto Press, 1993).

2.   Robert Fishman, *Bourgeois Utopias: The Rise and Fall of Suburbia* (New York, NY: Basic Books, 1987), 1.

3.   See Bocking, "Constructing Urban Expertise"; Sewell, *Shape of the City*. Of course middle-class faith in expertise dates well prior to the 1940s and at least to the Progressive Reform era. See Sean Purdy, "Industrial Efficiency, Social Order and Moral Purity: Housing Reform Thought in English Canada, 1900–50," *Urban History Review* 25, no. 2 (1997): 30–40" . . .

4.   . . . Richard Harris, "From 'Black-balling' to 'Marking': The Suburban Origin of Redlining in Canada, 1930s–50s," *Canadian Geographer* 47, no. 3 (2003): 338–50; . . . Franca Iacovetta, "Gossip, Contest, and Power in the Making of Suburban Bad Girls: Toronto, 1945–60," *Canadian Historical Review* 80, no. 4 (1999):

585–623; V. Korinek, *Roughing It in the Suburbs: Reading Chatelaine Magazine in the Fifties and Sixties* (Toronto, ON: University of Toronto Press, 2000); . . . V. Strong-Boag, "Home Dreams: Women and the Suburban Experiment in Canada, 1945–60," *Canadian Historical Review* 72, no. 4 (1991): 471–504; . . . For an overview, see Richard Harris, *Creeping Conformity: How Canada Became Suburban, 1900–60* (Toronto, ON: University of Toronto Press, 2004).

5. The literature on pre–World War I residential suburban-ization includes Richard Harris and Matt Sendbuehler, "The Making of a Working-Class Suburb in Hamilton's East End, 1900–45," *Journal of Urban History* 20, no. 4 (1994): 486–511; L. D. McCann, "Planning and Building the Corporate Suburb of Mount Royal," *Planning Perspectives* 11 (1996): 259–301. . . .

6. For typical examples of this approach, see the intro-duction and essays in Kevin M. Kruse and Thomas J. Sugrue, eds., *The New Suburban History* (Chicago, IL: University of Chicago Press, 2006).

7. Fishman, *Bourgeois Utopias*; Kenneth Jackson, *Crabgrass Frontier: The Suburbanization of the United States* (Oxford, UK: Oxford University Press, 1985).

8. Mary Corbin Sies, "North American Cities and Suburbs, 1880–1950: Cultural and Social Considerations," *Journal of Urban History* 27, no. 3 (2001): 313–346.

9. "Home Horizons," box 119034–7, Toronto City Archives. The records of the Thorncrest Village Homes Association are located at the Toronto City Archives (TCA). Totaling four boxes, they include photographs, newsletters, correspondence, clippings files, original plans, and other sources. The fonds number is 55; the series numbers are 251, 252, 253, and 254; and the box numbers are 117682, 119033, 119034, and 119035. Subsequent references to this collection will provide only the box number and document details.

10. Ibid.

11. E. G. Faludi, "Designing New Canadian Communities Theory and Practice," *Journal of the American Institute of Planners* 16 (1950): 77.

12. The attack on less-planned suburbs was not unique to Foss and Faludi. Marc Weiss shows that large-scale "community builders" often organized within trade associations and through the state against the interests of "curb stoners" and "speculative" developers. Weiss, *The Rise of the Community Builders: The American Real Estate Industry and Urban Land Planning* (New York, NY: Columbia University Press, 1987).

13. M. Foss, "Introduction to *Country Club Community*," box 119034–7.

14. Ibid.

15. Thorncrest Development Company Ltd., "Thorncrest Village: A Country Home Community," box 119034–1.

16. Ibid.

17. *THVA Bulletin*, April 1951, 4–5, box 117682–1.

18. See Weiss, *Rise of the Community Builders*.

19. Advertisement, *Toronto Globe and Mail*, 21 November 1947.

20. Advertisement, *Toronto Globe and Mail*, 28 February 1948.

21. Advertisement, *Toronto Globe and Mail*, 13 March 1948.

22. See below for a more detailed description of this process. "Thorncrest Village: A Country Home Community," box 19034–1.

23. "Home Horizons."

24. Faludi, "Designing New Canadian Communities," 78.

25. Such restrictions were not uncommon in earlier Canadian suburbs, including Hamilton's Westdale, Toronto's Lawrence Park, and Victoria's Upland. For a comprehensive account of property restrictions and residential covenants, see R. Fogelson, *Bourgeois Nightmares: Suburbia, 1870–1930* (New Haven, CT: Yale University Press, 2005). For Canadian examples, see Harris, *Creeping Conformity*, 85–9.

26. "Thorncrest Development Company Ltd.: 1947–1950," box 119034–3.

27. Ibid.

28. Ibid.

29. "By-Laws: 1963, 1975, 1982," box 119032–15.

30. Data are not available to complete an exhaustive sur-vey of all residents who moved into Thorncrest during the 1940s, 1950s, and 1960s. However, I did review all bulletins that are available from January 1959 to November 1970 and recorded all applicants' names, former addresses, employers, and occupations. The following descriptions of applicants are drawn from this imperfect but convenient sample.

31. S. D. Clark, *The Suburban Society* (Toronto, ON: University of Toronto Press, 1966), 92, 34, 51, and 60.

32. Of course, there were many moments prior to the application process in which the THVA could have discouraged Jews and those of Southern and Eastern European ancestry, for example, from applying. While I cannot provide documentation of racial and ethnic exclusion, in the early years, people of British ancestry were an overwhelming majority of the residents and there were no Jewish residents. See the section below for a discussion of the ethnic and racial composition of the neighbourhood.

33. "By-Laws."

34. . . . See Catherine Jurca, *White Diaspora: The Suburbs and the Twentieth-Century Novel* (Princeton, NJ: Princeton University Press, 2001).

35. Tract 266 was bound by Rathburn Road, Kipling Avenue, Richview Side Road (now Eglinton Avenue West), and Islington Avenue, encompassing an area much larger than just Thorncrest Village. In 1961 the population of the tract was 4,575. At that time, all 180

lots in Thorncrest Village were occupied, except for a small addition called The Woods that was developed in the late 1960s. Dominion Bureau of Statistics, *1961 Census of Canada, Population and Housing Characteristics by Census Tracts, Toronto, Bulletin CT-15* (Ottawa, ON: Minister of Trade and Commerce, 1963).

36. Clark, *Suburban Society*, 94 and 105.
37. Faludi, "Designing New Canadian Communities," 77.
38. The following discussion is based on an extensive but incomplete collection of past issues of the *Bulletin*. . . . The content and form of the *Bulletin* bears marked similarities to a similar newsletter published by working-class residents of the suburb of Westwood Hills, Pennsylvania. See Patrick Vitale, "Learning to Be Suburban: The Production of Community in Westwood Hills, Pennsylvania, 1952–8," *Journal of Historical Geography* 35 (2009): 743–68.
39. "How Harvey Happened," *THVA Bulletin*, April 1961, box 117682–3.
40. Numerous "Harvey Says" and "Harvey Suggests" flyers are collected in box 119032–19.
41. Ibid. According to the *Bulletin*, speeding and reckless driving were frequent problems in Thorncrest Village, and at one point it published a "note of appreciation" for two "courageous Villagers" who appeared as witnesses against two boys who drove through a stop sign on Pheasant Lane. *Resident Information Services (RIS) Bulletin*, 16 February 1961, box 119034–4.
42. "How Harvey Happened." Norma Despard, Harvey's owner, also wrote a monthly gossip column called "Norm's Notes" for the *Bulletin*. Harvey's frequent reappearances are probably a result of her long participation with the newsletter.
43. *RIS Bulletin*, 9 November 1961, box 119034–4.
44. *RIS Bulletin*, 19 May 1967, box 117682–9.
45. *RIS Bulletin*, 16 July 1959, box 119034–3; *THVA Bulletin*, June 1959, box 119034–3.
46. *RIS Bulletin*, 29 November 1960, box 119034–4.
47. Faludi, "Designing New Canadian Communities," 74.
48. Ibid., 77.
49. *THVA Bulletin*, September 1960, box 119034–4.
50. *RIS Bulletin*, 13 April 1961, box 119034–4.
51. *RIS Bulletin*, 16 June 1961, box 119034–4.
52. *RIS Bulletin*, 16 March 1962, box 119034–5.
53. *RIS Bulletin*, 26 April 1963, box 119034–5.
54. *RIS Bulletin*, 2 March 1967, box 117682–9.
55. *RIS Bulletin*, 29 March 1967, box 117682–9.
56. As both Robbins and Kristoffer Whitney demonstrate, the pressure to keep a verdant lawn has serious environmental ramifications. See Paul Robbins, *Lawn People: How Grasses, Weeds, and Chemicals Make Us Who We Are* (Philadelphia, PA: Temple University Press, 2007), 99; Kristoffer Whitney, "Living Lawns, Dying Waters: The Suburban Boom, Nitrogenous Fertilizers, and the Nonpoint Source Pollution Dilemma," *Technology and Culture* 51 (2010): 652–74.
57. *RIS Bulletin*, 25 August 1959, box 119034–3.
58. *THVA Bulletin*, September 1960, box 119034–4.
59. *THVA Bulletin*, December 1952, box 117682–1.
60. *THVA Bulletin*, November 1959, box 1190343.
61. *THVA Bulletin*, December 1957, box 117682–1.
62. Clark, *Suburban Society*, 177.
63. In an article in the *Toronto Star*, one resident, H. R. Despard, claimed that she nearly "die[d] of loneliness" when she lived in North York, but when she moved to Thorncrest Village it was, what the *Star* called, an "answer to a housewife's prayer." She cited the series of four welcome teas as particularly helpful in integrating new residents into the community. As she told the *Star*, the Village was "like living in a big clubhouse, only instead of having a room, you live in your own home." "First Planned Community in the Land, 'Prayer Answered,'" *Toronto Daily Star*, 7 January 1949, 24.
64. See A. Bonnet, *White Identities: Historical and International Perspectives* (Harlow, UK: Prentice Hall, 2000); Richard Dyer, "White," Screen 29 (1988): 44–64; Toni Morrison, *Playing in the Dark: Whiteness and the Literary Imagination* (Cambridge, MA: Harvard University Press, 1992).
65. bell hooks, *Black Looks: Race and Representation* (Boston, MA: South End, 1992), 29.
66. *THVA Bulletin*, April 1960, box 119034–3.
67. *THVA Bulletin*, February 1962, box 117682–4.
68. *RIS Bulletin*, 5 August 1967, box 117682–9.
69. *THVA Bulletin*, February 1964, box 117682–6.
70. *RIS Bulletin*, 7 November 1959, box 119034–3.
71. Described as the "traveling Thorncresters" in the *Bulletin*, many residents took frequent trips abroad, particularly to New York City and Europe.
72. Morrison, *Playing in the Dark*, 13.

9 Framing Regent Park
The National Film Board of Canada and the Construction of "Outcast Spaces" in the Inner City, 1953 and 1994

Sean Purdy

. . . down came the verminous walls, the unclean, the unhealthy buildings and down came the fire hazards, the juvenile delinquency, the drunkenness, the broken marriages and up rose, something new, the nation's first large public housing project.[1]

In 1953 and 1994 the National Film Board of Canada (NFB) produced two documentary films about Canada's first and largest public housing project, Toronto's Regent Park. *Farewell to Oak Street* charted the dramatic "before" and "after" effects of public housing on the family, social, and cultural life of the inner-city dwellers whose "slum housing" was demolished in the late 1940s and early 1950s to make way for the pioneering housing scheme. The film was didactically scripted and shot to highlight the striking shift in the built and social environment from the untidy, rundown, row housing of the working-class "slum" to the spotless modernism of the houses and walk-up apartments of Regent Park. *Farewell* would be widely trumpeted by the City of Toronto until the late 1960s to publicize the triumph of its urban renewal campaign. Forty years later, the NFB made a *Return to Regent Park*. This time round, the film centred on the abject failure of public housing and urban renewal in

Toronto and the efforts of activists to combat drugs, crime, and the physical/social stigma of the project. Using interviews with activists, local politicians, and planners, and deftly punctuating its narrative with clips from its 1953 predecessor, it offers a much more subtle portrait of a state-created "ghetto" and its residents.

I argue in this article that both NFB films contributed to the powerful *territorial stigmatization* of inner-city workers and public housing tenants as social and cultural deviants. Such stigmatizing renderings were not free-floating ideological and spatial representations, but reflected and reinforced real spatial and social divisions in the city and had concrete political, economic, and social consequences for tenants. . . . The NFB reflected and reproduced a symbolic external representation of the old slum area and the new housing project as modern-day Babels, perilous problem areas full of dysfunctional families and cultural misfits. In a concluding section, I underscore how this powerful place-based stigma, brought to national prominence by Canada's influential state film agency, would complement the damning and pervasive characterizations of Regent Park residents by social workers, academics, and the media. In general, therefore, I aim to open up critical windows on

Citation: Sean Purdy, "Framing Regent Park: The National Film Board of Canada and the Construction of 'Outcast Spaces' in the Inner City, 1953 and 1994," *Media, Culture & Society* 27, no. 4 (July 2005): 523–49 and Society 27, 4 (July 2005): 523–49. Copyright © 2005, SAGE Publications.

the politics and ideology of urban redevelopment in Canada's premier metropolis.

Reading and Mapping the Documentary Film in Historical Context

Scholars of film studies have long paid attention to nonfiction films as important cultural artifacts of society. At the risk of simplifying a diverse and complex literature, film studies specialists have focused their research on three key areas involved in the documentary form: technological factors, sociological dimensions, and aesthetic concerns. . . . Historians, on the other hand, have tended to view nonfiction films uncritically, as rich repositories of primary sources. As Robert Rosenstone aptly notes, historians frequently accept documentaries as "a more accurate way of representing the past, as if somehow the images appear on the screen unmediated." Documentaries, of course, may reveal previously unknown facts about places, people, and events. Taken as a whole, however, it is crucial to remember that we do not see in the documentary film "the events themselves, and not the events as experienced or even as witnessed by participants, but selected images of those events carefully arranged into sequences to tell a story or to make an argument."[2] . . . Cultural geographers, too, have studied both the industrial geographies of the film industry and the depictions of places and people within documentaries and fiction films. They have focused on mapping the "representational" spaces of these particularly prominent media texts.[3]

. . . In this article, I adopt an interdisciplinary approach, drawing on elements of film criticism as well as historical and geographical studies. . . .

The Documentary, the City, and the NFB

Numerous studies have revealed the poignant effects of photographs in the popular construction of the "slum" in the late nineteenth and early twentieth century.[4] Yet surprisingly few researchers have highlighted the potent role played by film in shaping popular attitudes toward the inner city and the urban poor. Yet from its origins in the late nineteenth century, film has frequently utilized the city as its subject. . . . [I]t was in the 1930s with the rise of John Grierson and the British documentary movement that film most pointedly engaged with the "urban" for a mass audience.

Grierson, a one-time director with experience in Hollywood, founded and administered the semi-state agencies, the British Empire Marketing Board's Film Unit (1930–4), and the General Post Office Film Unit (1934–9). From 1939 to 1945, he headed the NFB in Canada and later tackled similar assignments in Australia and New Zealand.[5] From 1929 to 1952, he "gave impetus to a movement" that resulted in the production of over 1,000 films and helped shape the technical, social, and aesthetic elements of documentary filmmaking for more than a generation.[6]

. . .

Grierson would put his ideologically charged ideas on "slums" and the necessity of public housing to good use in the 1930s. Numerous films he oversaw in Britain charted the decrepit state of working-class housing and its effects on "slum" dwellers. The slum clearance and public housing movement was seen as a panacea and symbol "of progress that provides hope for the future."[7] As Gold and Ward emphasize, however, what is left out is equally important. There is little attention to the causes of overcrowded and dilapidated housing: They are just regarded neutrally as the "result of history and unenlightened practices."[8] Filmmakers also purveyed a simplistic environmental determinism that portrayed blighted areas and their residents as rife with social pathologies. Moreover, working-class residents are always seen as unequivocally welcoming the new public housing developments even though we know that many communities were uprooted and destroyed with little input or consent from the actual residents. In some cases, they openly resisted the destruction of their neighbourhoods.[9] In general, "slum dwellers" are seen purely as objects of state social policy, which downplayed structural explanations for poverty and ignored the agency of the poor.

Historians of the Grierson-founded NFB tell a similar story in the Canadian context. They have demonstrated that both management and the creative staff were imbued with a social mission to highlight the trials and tribulations, diversity and achievements, of post-war Canada. . . . While it may have been largely free from direct political intervention by its government paymasters and willing to engage with more controversial issues, it nevertheless depicted a middle-class view of the world with hackneyed images of women, workers, and the poor. It celebrated a rational and efficient ordering of the tumultuous post-war capitalist world, advocating modernizing social change within gradualist boundaries.[10] Part and parcel of this vision was the rigorous advocacy of the "advantages of democracy" to counter the ever-present threat of Communism. . . .

The NFB of the early 1990s was, of course, a different organization than the one founded by Grierson in 1939. Highly acclaimed over the years for its innovative approaches to animation, short films, and documentary, it has received over 70 Oscar nominations. It continued to engage with a wide variety of politically controversial topics in the 1960s and in 1974 created Studio D, a production unit dedicated solely to films on women's issues by women filmmakers. It has gained a reputation for producing socially critical material and has continued to engage with themes unpalatable to the mainstream commercial studios. . . .

Regent Park and Post-War Reconstruction

Public housing in Canada emerged as part of the broader reform impulse of governments at all levels during the post–World War II reconstruction period. The federal government constructed some dwellings for war workers and established a veterans' housing program but shortages remained severe in most urban centres throughout the 1940s and early 1950s.[11] During the war, unions, veterans' organizations, the Communist Party of Canada, and other socialists were instrumental in organizing mass demonstrations, occupations of public buildings, and militant defences of homeowners and tenants threatened with foreclosure and eviction—all of which were effective in pressuring the state for more action on the housing front.[12] . . .

Unlike the tumultuous "Red Years" of the post–World War I era, during this time the government could count on an "evangelistic" middle-class housing reform movement as a key ally in the 1940s and 1950s.[13] Composed of Keynesian-influenced social scientists, intellectuals, and community activists, reformers believed that comprehensive urban revitalization programs could allay the impact of post-war economic and social volatility. . . . These "public housers" envisioned the project as a spatially and socially ordered community, free from the debilitating vagaries of "slum life." From the 1930s onwards, they made a successful financial and moral case for the benefits of slum clearance and rebuilding and won the local government over to an interventionist policy. The City of Toronto put a question on the 1947 municipal election ballot asking voters (at this time, only property owners and long-term leaseholders) for financial and political support for a large-scale public housing project; 62 per cent of the voters answered in the affirmative.[14] Two years later, Regent Park North, the ground-breaking effort in Canadian public housing, would open its doors amid much fanfare and celebration by City Hall and the reform lobby.

Regent Park was constructed in the working-class neighbourhood of Cabbagetown in downtown Toronto. The majority of inhabitants were descendants of English, Scottish, and

Irish immigrants who worked in local factories and businesses. The area had long been characterized as a blighted area by what Seán Damer aptly calls "slumologists."[15] The northern section was composed largely of three-storey walk-up apartments and row houses; it began accepting low-income families and some senior citizens in 1949 and was completed by 1957. Regent Park South, completed in 1959, exclusively housed families and comprised a mix of townhouses and five large apartment buildings. By 1960, the two sections of the development contained approximately 10,000 people, a figure reduced to approximately 7,500 residents by the 1990s. . . .

Constructing "Outcast Spaces"

. . . Considerable historical research has been conducted on external, often racialized, depictions of "slum" neighbourhoods, for instance, showing that the substance and rhetoric of slum representations revealed more about distinctly white, middle-class notions of what constituted a proper neighbourhood and requisite behaviour than they did about the actual physical, social, and cultural environments of the poor and minorities.[16] From the disorderly, Victorian slums of the nineteenth century to the dangerous "no go" neighbourhoods of today, these slum representations have had a tenacious hold on the imaginations and practices of twentieth-century urban reformers, the media, state officials, and the wider public in both developed and developing nations.[17]

The Cabbagetown area razed to build Regent Park, and its residents, were subject to such a nefarious representation from the 1930s onward, which assisted the state and the reform movement in making their case for slum clearance and public housing. Most historians have overlooked the spatial dimensions of these brutalizing images of the poor. Identity and place were firmly entangled, nonetheless, in the minds of the growing cadre of slumologists. "Deviant" spaces—frequently the urban conglomeration itself, but more particularly, disreputable slum areas of the city—produced "deviant" people.[18] For urban reformers, as David Ward contends, slums expressed "the presumed causal links between social isolation, and adverse environment and deviant behaviour."[19] Thus, the urban reform campaign constructed a powerful slum narrative of Cabbagetown punctuated by exotic images of social pathology and "dangerous spaces," such as back alleys and streets where people congregated in a disorderly and often sexually licentious fashion. Images of poor housing conditions, poverty, filth, and moral wickedness were condensed into one striking picture of abject misery that was propagated en masse by the reform lobby, state officials, and the main media outlets in Toronto and nationally. Exoticizing the physical shabbiness of dwellings and neighbourhoods and the troublesome behaviours ostensibly produced by them was not only an instrument of moral indictment, it was also a rhetorical technique intended to sufficiently unsettle the social imagination of the public to acquire support for slum clearance and public housing.[20]

For a short period in the 1950s, the discourse of housing betterment focused on how the residents of the newly built Regent Park had been economically, socially, and morally transformed due to the new public housing environment. These arguments essentially centred on how residents had adopted "decent" ways of living in line with the norms of post-war middle-class notions of family and community. From the 1960s to the 1990s, however, a series of economic, political, and social shifts within public housing and the larger socio-economic context shaped a new slum discourse. By the late 1960s, the project itself would increasingly be characterized as a "slum," similar in many respects to the Cabbagetown neighbourhood that was destroyed to build it. Condemned as too large and badly designed by academics, as a haven of single mothers, welfare families, and deviants by governments and the media, a magnet for crime and drug problems by police and law and order advocates, and the site of potentially explosive "racial" problems by many popular commentators, it had come full circle in the public mind from the "ordered community" of the 1940s.

The media played a crucial role in constructing Regent Park as a dangerous problem area. As a number of scholars have established, the mainstream media tends to cover poor working-class, immigrant, and/or Black neighbourhoods in such a way as to stress anything that runs counter to the accepted social, economic, and moral order.[21] In such a way, Regent Park was almost always characterized in all forms of the local and national media as solely a site of poverty, behavioural problems, and crime.[22] The wider public, with little or no direct experience of the project or its tenants, only received the "bad" and the sensational from the media, significantly distorting their opinions on the project and its tenants. . . . Such harmful portrayals reinforced stigmatization by obscuring structural explanations for poverty and concealing the agency of tenants in contesting these brutalizing characterizations.[23] It is in this context that we need to situate the spatial representations of Regent Park in documentary films.

A Farewell to Oak Street

. . .

Farewell to Oak Street[24] enjoyed a mass audience markedly larger than the specialist expositions of social workers and academics. Conceived as part of an ongoing project boasting of the resilience of the country in the post-war era, the Canada Carries On series, it was mainly shown across the country as an introduction to popular films in the theatre. With the advent of television, it was probably rebroadcast on television numerous times, as was the custom with NFB shorts. The Housing Authority of Toronto (HAT), which managed Regent Park North, used it as one of its key propaganda tools. In 1949, Henry Matson, secretary of HAT, heeded the advice of his counterpart in the Detroit Housing

Authority, J. H. Inglis, to overcome opposition to slum clearance by using visual images such as films and photographs "to illustrate the dilapidated character of the buildings you propose to demolish" and therefore win over a sometimes reluctant public.[25] HAT personnel would play a close collaborative role in the making of the film, making suggestions for scenes and delighting in the positive publicity the film offered.[26] Throughout the first 20 years of Regent Park's history, Farewell to Oak Street would be shown regularly to university and high school audiences as well as diverse community groups. In 1965, it was running twice weekly to "interested" groups in the community and was compulsory viewing for nurses in Toronto-area hospitals on their annual field trips to the development.[27] . . .

The film was written and produced by Gordon Burwash and directed by Grant Maclean, seasoned staffers at the NFB. Extraordinarily, it was made over a five-year period and, for a 17-minute short, its $29,000 price tag was remarkably costly at the time, demonstrating the NFB's commitment to constructing well-wrought images of the progress of the nation. Shooting of the exteriors of existing houses slated for demolition and the beginnings of construction began in the summer of 1948. Filming of the interior of "slum" habitations commenced in the spring of 1949, and editing and voiceover narration was completed over the next four years. . . .

Burwash continued the tradition of the wartime NFB founder, John Grierson, in didactically scripting the film to make a crystal-clear propaganda statement about the physical and social depravity of the Cabbagetown slums and the modern promise of public housing. In 1949, he wrote to Matson that for the interior shots "we would like to shoot a family in its old residence (the more slum-like the better), the family's moving activity (van, wheelbarrows, or what have you), and the family joyfully taking possession of the new home" (author's emphasis).[28] As in the classic documentary film, it aimed to project "a generalized reality or social truth"[29] which, in the eyes of the filmmakers and contemporary reformers, consisted of the shameful contrast between the decrepit disorder of Cabbagetown and the efficiency of the new housing development.[30] To accomplish this, it mixed a real contemporary development—the ground-breaking urban renewal scheme of Canada's largest city—with fictional vignettes of the frustrations of the "old" and the joys of the "new" juxtaposed throughout the film to emphasize the striking contrast.

Despite its extensive use of fictionalized dramatic scenes, therefore, it was crucial that the film convey an air of authenticity and realism.[31] Each of the scenes was carefully crafted, acted, sequenced, and narrated to construct this "realist" vision. Locations were used rather than studios; the majority of actors were either residents themselves or non-professionals, which was intended to drive home to the viewers that what they were seeing was the genuine thing; the voiceover narration by well-known veteran of CBC radio and later American television star, Lorne Greene, aimed to express the "authority" of pro-urban renewal commentary. The NFB's press release gave viewers a hint of what to expect in the screening:

> This is the story of how many Toronto families, jam-packed in the squalor of the city's slums, were transplanted to a new spacious life in the homes of Canada's first large public housing project, the Regent Park development. The film depicts the corrosive misery of six families, 19 persons in all, sharing one bathroom, one source of running water and the common shame of a life where home is a place to get out of, and tavern, movie-house and street are refuge from substandard living. But the Brown's, the Bennett's and the Biggs's of the film, like 5,000 other Cabbagetown dwellers of Toronto's East End, were fortunate. The camera follows them from their Oak Street shambles to the comfort and dignity of four and five room apartment units in the 42 acres of Regent Park.

There, paying rent according to their income, they find life has a new face and home is a place in which to live.[32]

Above all, the images in the film would be depicted as if they were real scenes in real lives. In this way, the filmmakers meant to emphasize the overriding social and political necessity to do away with slums and construct efficient dwelling units for the urban poor and working class.

The film opens with a conspicuous still photograph of a dilapidated Cabbagetown house. The accompanying classical music is sombre and the dreary scene is enveloped in dim and eerie light. Immediately, the vista brightens as the first buildings of Regent Park are shown in the backdrop of the project's wide-open spaces as a grocer's delivery boy makes his rounds on his bike. While Lorne Greene authoritatively announces "not a trace" of the slum "remains, except its people. They're still here, still occupying the same stretch of space but in a different way. Everything is sparkling, and new, and tidy and kept that way," the camera pans to a set of clean windows and a woman sweeping the floor. The documentary switches back and forth in this way, contrasting the daily irritations and larger pathologies produced by slums with the virtues of modern project living.

The boost to social life within the home is strongly emphasized in *Farewell*, reflecting the widespread concern about inharmonious relations between husbands and wives, parents and children. One scene shot in the cramped slum home shows a family sitting down for supper, everybody strangely quiet and morose. "Supper time for the Browns," Lorne Greene narrates, "is the high point of any families' day. School behind, rest and relaxation ahead, the day's adventures to talk about. Hardly a time for silence. Trouble was, the Oak Street day was often best forgotten. There weren't many good days." The frustration of the slum existence also exacerbated domestic disputes. Another section of the film depicts a husband and wife verbally sparring against the backdrop of a dark and dreary room. The narration continues, "Not all tempers flared, some were diverted and dulled by escape" as the camera switches to an equally lifeless and dark tavern. By contrast, project life is bright and cordial. Families moving into their new units are smiling and curious. One young boy gleefully jumps into the shiny, new bathtub and the accompanying music reaches a crescendo as the whole family watches the bathwater run. The film cuts to the "brighter and more interesting and friendlier" kitchen with its well-placed, modern, and efficient appliances. The husband puts his arm around his wife as they contemplate their new surroundings. The new supper table shows the family excitedly conversing. Other scenes tell a similar story: the father relaxing in the living room, reading the paper, and the mother joyfully carrying out domestic chores.

The film especially accentuates women's enhanced roles as mother and housewife. Yvonne Klein-Matthews has shown that NFB films of the 1940s–50s only validated women's roles as mothers and housewives, celebrating their natural homemaking virtues and warning against the perils of joining the male-dominated workplace.[33] *Farewell to Oak Street* was no exception. The flaking paint, grimy walls, filthy floors, and crowded rooms are distinguished conspicuously from the spacious rooms, new-fangled appliances, and hardwood floors of Regent Park. Domestic work by women is duly celebrated: "A great deal of washing and scrubbing goes on nowadays. The Maclean kitchen has a new modern look as do the Maclean ladies." In Cabbagetown, on the other hand, "keeping clean was a daily battle and a lost cause." One dramatized scene shows a woman futilely attempting to kill a cockroach, expressing symbolically the frustration of women's life within the slums. Disorder and confusion are represented in the slum housing by showing six separate families trying to use the same bathroom: "Things mislaid, everyone getting in everyone's way."

Farewell to Oak Street prominently engages with the question of children's lives as well. Kids playing happily in the new project are juxtaposed in the same scene with a group of boys playing road hockey in an area not yet demolished. The message is that the orderly play spaces of "trees, grass, playground" are better than the "cars [and] pavement" that plague disorderly road hockey games. Greene adds that there are "backyards too and private entrances to homes," emphasizing the privatized orderliness of Regent's row houses. Even children's physical and sexual health is dealt with in the film. One shot portrays a teacher or nurse bringing kids home with lice in their hair. Boys and girls are shown sleeping in the same bed in the slum house, a taboo frequently condemned in the contemporary literature on housing reform. And, in probably the first depiction of sexual abuse in Canadian film, a young girl is assaulted in old Cabbagetown by a neighbour.[34] Greene gravely states: "Sometimes the vermin was human and the shame was secret," playing on the widespread, if false, notion that children were more vulnerable to sexual abuse in poor neighbourhoods. Such a sensationalist tactic was also a useful means to attract wider support for public housing.[35]

The documentary also deliberates on the practical difficulties of finding affordable housing and how the rental system works at Regent Park. It ends on a shot of residents industrially going about their business while Greene sounds off on the NFB's liberal modernization appeal that there are "too many Oak Streets for such a resourceful nation." The soundtrack ends on a triumphal note as the camera displays an impressive aerial view of the vast development.

The NFB joined contemporary sociologists, social workers, and the media in contributing to the powerful stigmatization of inner-city workers. Even if the slum environment itself was largely to blame in these accounts, working families in Cabbagetown were portrayed as dirty, disreputable, and prone to various pathologies, a condition only redeemed in the eyes of the national film agency and reformers by the top-down modernization of urban renewal and public housing. Only public housing, moreover, could reinstall women in their valid roles as housekeepers and mothers, and families to their central role as the bedrock of society and nation. Children, too, would benefit from a safe and orderly setting within the home and the neighbourhood, free from the lures of delinquency and sex. The medium of film with a mass, popular audience was a convenient and effective means to get across this message of the urgent necessity of social engineering.

The very tenants whose homes and lives were maligned were the first to respond to the documentary. A tenants' and homeowners' political association had been active since the outset of the Regent Park development, demanding a say in the process, criticizing high rents and other HAT policies, and the low compensation offered for their houses. They particularly resented the "slum" label and, on the release of the film, communicated their disgust to their Conservative Member of Parliament, Charles Henry. They were upset because they had no chance to view the film beforehand or make suggestions, a right reserved only for housing officials. In the House of Commons, Henry criticized the negative portrayal of Cabbagetowners and requested that the film be withdrawn from circulation.[36] It is difficult to gauge the reception of the film among the wider population but certainly the weight of the modernizing reform impulse and its support by the media suggests that the film's central message was accepted as authoritative. The *Toronto Telegram* and the *Ottawa Citizen* defended the portrayal of the "slums" and, even though some members of the NFB board of governors were sympathetic to Henry's appeal, the NFB soldiered on with the marketing and distribution of the film.[37] . . . In the process, it contributed to negative characterizations of inner-city workers and the poor in Cabbagetown, a set of harmful assumptions and ideas that would soon be applied to Regent Park dwellers themselves.

Return to Regent Park

Since this film was made only a decade ago, we have no archival records about *Return to Regent Park*;[38] I will rely on a reading of the film in the context of public housing in the 1990s. Directed by Bay Weyman, the film was financed and produced by the NFB, Weyman's Close-Up Productions, and the Canadian Broadcasting Corporation (CBC), Canada's public broadcasting network. It first aired on 6 May 1994 on CBC Newsworld's *Rough Cuts*, a weekly program that brings new national and international documentaries to the small screen. We have no viewing figures for the documentary, but it has been replayed periodically on public television in Canada and is widely available in university, public, and community libraries. In 1995, NFB head Sandra Macdonald told a federal parliamentary committee on Canadian Heritage that she was particularly proud of Weyman's film. In her nationalist vision of the NFB's role, she opined that, "We dream of the day when . . . *Central Park West* [a popular American show] will be replaced by a broadcast of *Return to Regent Park*."[39]

The film's promotional blurb gives a good introduction to the themes of the film and deserves full citation:

Ten thousand people live in Toronto's Regent Park, Canada's first large-scale housing project. Built in a spirit of post-WWII optimism that social problems could be corrected through urban renewal, Regent Park replaced a working-class neighbourhood with a modern, park-like community of apartment buildings.

But, forty years later, it has become a paradigm of city planning failure. The physical isolation of Regent Park from the surrounding community has created a unique ghetto-like environment. Within its confines, many residents feel as if they are under siege by an army of outsiders who are using the Park as a haven for drugs, prostitution and violent crime.

Frustrated by the apparent "benign neglect" of the Metro Toronto Housing Authority, groups of Regent Park residents have banded into committees organized by residents-turned-social activists. They are now persuasive advocates of the concept that Regent Park requires radical physical redevelopment in order to be successfully reintegrated within the larger social community.

Bay Weyman lets the people of Regent Park tell their own story of desperation and hope. Featuring interviews with residents, activists, community organizers, local politicians, academic planners, and the police, the film compresses three stories into one: the failure of traditional urban renewal schemes, the impact of drugs and crime on an enclosed environment, and the positive effects of social redevelopment in which people are empowered with a newborn self-respect, changing the way they think about themselves and their community.[40]

Unlike its 1953 predecessor, then, the film provides substantial room for (some of the) residents themselves to discuss life in what tenants nickname "Regent" or simply the "Park." In a narrative quite similar to *Farewell to Oak Street*, however, *Return to Regent Park* sets out to engage in social criticism, directing its fire at the superblock public housing design that enclosed the project's buildings within its own discrete borders. While its techniques are more subtle and elegant, the latter film also relies on the theme of the contrast between the "old" and "new" to tell its story. Reflecting a common technique in socially critical documentary filmmaking,[41] it constantly juxtaposes interviews with talking heads and residents and shots of the project with old archival footage from newsreels, television, and *Farewell to Oak Street* itself, contrasting the overly optimistic and top-down planning of 1940s–50s urban reformers with the drug and crime problems in the project today and the efforts of activists to sell a physical redevelopment plan to the City of Toronto.

The "outcast space" narratives of the 1940s and 1950s are evident in *Return to Regent Park* even if the pathologies have changed. The problem of drugs and crime in Regent Park take up a good portion of the documentary, although residents also intersperse positive comments about living in the project. In one of the first scenes, a teenage crack dealer is interviewed on the street, expressing his frustration about the lack of economic opportunities: "Police don't care. Government don't care. They're just trying to get elected." Yet he concludes by saying, "Despite all the bad publicity we get, I love this park." Betty Hubbard says, "My old man is from the States and lived in a ghetto and he says this is heaven compared to a ghetto." She goes on to say she's from a middle-class family and, as the camera pans out over the park from her balcony, she relates, "When I first come here the place was great and then when the crack came out it got really bad and we started having beatings, shootings, robberies . . ." Visibly weak and sullen, Tina Thibeault, a prostitute and crack addict who grew up in the project, talks about the nice times she had when she was a kid and contrasts it to the problems now, seeing her own history as illustrative of the change, "I'm to blame because I'm involved, right?"

Interspersed with the interviews are clandestine shots of drug dealing happening on the public streets and dark lanes of the development, and brutal police arrests of alleged traffickers. In one scene, one young Black man threatens to break the camera and orders the crew to stop filming. Perhaps the most revealing scenes of the drug problem in the film involve George Burkle, an ex-crack addict, who was one of the key activists in the North Regent Park Residents Steering Committee (NRPRSC). As he speaks in his apartment, the camera (again clandestinely) surveys the street below showing a fistfight and the brutal beating of a Black suspect by the police. Burkle explains that it is "welfare night" when social assistance cheques are delivered and, according to him, it regularly sparks drinking, drug-taking, and fighting until the money from the cheques is all gone. In another scene, he discusses how his life has changed and how activism has given him a focus. While we listen, the viewer is shown shady scenes of drug dealing, limousines pulling up to buy drugs, and prostitutes plying their trade on the project's many narrow laneways and courtyards. The themes of hope and despair are continually emphasized as the camera juxtaposes the "bad" with the "good."

As in the slum images of *Farewell to Oak Street*, much of the film focuses on the physical deterioration of the built environment. "The buildings are falling apart," one resident says early on in the film. One scene shows a family moving out, quoting the father as saying, "The people and the place you can adapt to but the housing seems to deteriorate so much. Nothing gets done too much about it." Close-up shots of graffiti ("Fuck the Police"), "tagging," holes in the walls, and overflowing garbage bins are revealed as the police and members of the redevelopment committee take the filmmakers on a tour of the project. While searching the corridors of one of the buildings for drug dealers, one policeman exclaims, "If only the camera could pick up the smell." The documentary actually aims in this scene to reveal the tangible sensual experience of physical deterioration.

As the promotional blurb emphasizes, great effort is expended in the film to highlight the role of resident activists involved in the NRPRSC. In conjunction with a new breed of urban reformers, the tenant committee rallied around a plan to physically redevelop a section of the project, which proposed to combine private-market rental units and various new commercial outlets with the traditional subsidized units. . . . Some of the most poignant scenes show the palpable frustrations of activists as they are stonewalled in their earnest efforts by the Metropolitan Toronto Housing Authority and Toronto mayor June Rowlands. The mayor misses an important meeting with the redevelopment committee and the homemade lasagna that residents had prepared for the gathering sits uneaten on a table. The sense of let-down on the part of activists is palpable as they express their anger and frustration.

. . .

One of the most remarkable scenes of the documentary actually comes near the beginning. In a suitably postmodern twist on representing the represented, the filmmakers shoot a scene of a local Toronto television station reporting in the project. Speaking from one of the internal streets of the project, the reporter comments on the crime rates, the drug problem, and the lack of jobs. Then he interviews a woman, who argues sharply,

> They should get the truth before they start reporting. I was watching it at home and it made me angry. The dark-haired reporter saying that we're "ridden." We're not "ridden"! Where's the shooting going on in Regent Park if we're so ridden? Where's the drug dealing going on right now? It's not that bad. Yes, we do have it bad in the Park. But it's outsiders coming into the Park. We're not bad. I love living in Regent Park. I'm raising my kids in Regent Park, I'm raising my grandchildren in Regent Park. You've been in the Park, have you been shot yet?

A raucous debate follows between the tenants gathered on the street about the problems of the project with one woman focusing on poverty and another arguing that these problems are everywhere, showing the contested nature of the causes of stigmatization among tenants. Unfortunately, this sense of debate among tenants and alternative arguments about the problems of project living (e.g., media stigmatization, poverty) is never revisited in the documentary. From then on, the focus is on how physical redevelopment will transform the project.

Return to Regent Park offers a more stylish and less preachy look at Regent Park than *Farewell to Oak Street*. Its inclusion of the voices of the tenants themselves is a welcome addition to the documentary form. However, it also (unintentionally) produces a damning characterization of the homes, neighbourhood, and residents of Regent Park by what it focuses on and what it omits. Drugs and crime, for example, are not discussed in any kind of social or historical context. As in its predecessor, the viewer gets little sense of the whys. Why are public housing residents so poor? Why does Regent Park have a drug problem? Many of the socio-economic and ideological developments that have shaped material misery and driven a minority of residents to drug dealing and anti-social behaviour in public housing are never discussed in the film. Yet it is in this context of bitter despair that we need to place the widely publicized rise in violence and drugs in the project and elsewhere in the 1990s.[42] As the state increasingly cut funding and programs, material deprivation intensified, and a related increase in hard drug dealing has plagued the project. Drug dealers, many of whom live outside the project, have sunk roots in the project,[43] providing much-needed monetary and social benefits to young people with no futures. Despite the long-standing propensity of the Toronto media to sensationalize and blow crime figures out of proportion, particularly in regard to public housing, it is apparent that the problems of violence and drugs had increased to worrying proportions for many tenants in the early 1990s. The film leaves us with no explanation for this, lending credence to the common-sense idea that tenants themselves are individually responsible.

The image of criminality in the project, increasingly racialized in the 1980s and 1990s, was nevertheless always more powerful than the reality. Social geographers have demonstrated the powerful spatial associations of racialized representations, which link race, crime, and neighbourhood. They have argued persuasively that racialized depictions of minority groups and criminality are enhanced when linked with certain identifiable places.[44] This is only hinted at in *Return to Regent Park* when one of the (largely white) activists in the redevelopment committee claims that the "multicultural" atmosphere of the project has impeded the establishment of law and order due to the fears of the police of being labelled racist. The film otherwise neglects the lengthy history of tensions between Black tenants and the police, which has centred on allegations of police brutality and other forms of unfair "racialized" policing.[45] As numerous studies of police culture have commented, many police officers perceive certain parts of the "public" to be their enemy, especially those populations labelled as problematic and dangerous—the poor, communities of colour, and ethnic minorities.[46] The activists cited in the film complained of a lack of security in the project and police ineffectiveness in patrolling the project. We are not told that this same group of tenants has persistently lobbied for a firmer police presence based on a mix of "hard-nosed zero tolerance" and "community policing" with extensive foot patrols, an approach that has put it at odds with many Black tenants.[47] Indeed, frustration with the police had reached an explosive boiling point by the mid-1990s. It came as little surprise that soon after social assistance rates were savagely chopped by 21.6 per cent by the Ontario Conservative government in 1995, pent-up frustration with police brutality and desperation with living conditions led to a riot against police in Regent Park involving several hundred residents and 100 police officers.[48] Yvonne Beasley, mother of Sydney Hemmings, a young Black man murdered in the project on 5 July 2001, angrily expressed these frustrations when confronting the police in a public forum: "My question to you is, how exactly do the youth of Regent Park trust the police in the neighbourhood, when all it is to them is niggers killing niggers?"[49] *Return to Regent Park* gives us little sense of the tensions and frustrations lying beneath the surface of daily life in the project in the early 1990s.

The frequent resort to juxtaposing historical archival footage of urban planners from the 1950s and 1960s with contemporary "experts" to show up the "naiveté of the past"[50] also implicitly comes down on the side of the new "experts" without acknowledging that they too have their own political axe to grind. Structural deterioration of the buildings has been a mainstay of recent criticism but the housing form and site design of Regent Park have long been the target of academic and popular criticism. Almost all commentary on the built environment of the project highlights the "ugliness" of the buildings, the unsuitability of high rises for children, the segregation of the development from the surrounding neighbourhood, and the lack of individually definable and private space within the project. Much of this criticism takes as its starting point Jane Jacobs's 1961 book, *Life and Death of Great American Cities*, which argues that urban design elements themselves can enable healthy and safe social interaction by providing spaces that encourage natural meetings and other friendly interactions. She believed that modernist planning, especially public housing projects, had destroyed this "natural" urban fabric.[51] . . . *Toronto Star* reporter Christian Cotroneo describes Regent Park as sprawling "in all its Soviet sameness, flanked by anonymous apartment blocks."[52] . . . The only solution to Regent Park's problems, these authors conclude, is wholesale redevelopment of the built environment to create safe and orderly communities.

Such arguments, echoed in the Regent Park redevelopment proposal discussed in the film, tread dangerously close to the same "environmental determinism" of post-war planners and the state. Physical form does influence human life and behaviour, but it cannot be treated as an independent phenomenon or factor. . . . Environmental determinist arguments not only deflect attention away from the wider socio-economic problems of poor project dwellers, they discourage, as Keith Jacobs and Tony Manzi argue, "new possibilities and alternative visions" to deal with the crisis of affordable housing.[53]

It also stretches belief to argue . . . that the problems of crime in public housing can be solved by mere changes to the built environment. Design changes making it less easy for drug dealers to hide or escape from the police, or to integrate living with public spaces, may enhance some tenants' sense of well-being, but it does nothing to deal with the root problems of economic misery, which fuel the drug trade and other security concerns. . . . David Harvey makes a similar point in arguing that such general design approaches falsely contend "that the shaping of spatial order can be the foundation for a new moral and aesthetic order"[54] bringing us back to the authoritarian utopianism of 1950s urban renewal.

. . . Certainly Regent Park needs substantial renovations due to the aging buildings and infrastructure. Improving design may be worthwhile but it does not provide jobs or adequate funding for local schools. Nor does it tackle police brutality against Black youth. These are the key reasons for socio-economic marginalization and it is this lack of power in society that leads to the often exaggerated but nevertheless real antisocial and harmful behaviour that is wrapped up with drugs and violence. In *Return to Regent Park*, we are told that redevelopment may promise a sense of stability and social order in a time of rapid socio-economic change. Yet it also "serves to legitimize the ideological shift presenting the problems of housing as attributable to individuals rather than a failure of government" as Jacobs and Manzi argue for the similar British case.[55]

Conclusion

. . .

Farewell to Oak Street meshed neatly with the housing reform, social work philosophy, and media attitudes of the 1940s and 1950s, which prescribed that the poor needed to live in "efficient" and "harmonious" communities purportedly like the rest of society. The film envisioned that this desired homogeneity and social cohesion could only obtain within a profoundly middle-class paradigm of private family life and responsible conduct in line with the social order. Neither the NFB nor public housing observers ventured structural explanations for the social problems of poor families, such as unstable employment, pitiful social services, a biased educational system, and sheer lack of socio-economic opportunities for those falling outside the accepted norms of suitable family and social life such as single parents. In the tumultuous post-war social and economic context, however, the scientific legitimacy of liberal modernization plans and the popular saliency of "realist" documentary film ensured that it sold well to the public. In this respect, Paula Rabinowitz's argument that, "documentary films provide a stability to an ever-changing reality, freezing the images for later instructional use" is particularly pertinent.[56] The "visual ideological" arguments in *Farewell to Oak Street* helped paint a nefarious portrait of the inner-city poor that would be used for two decades to bolster the arguments of the urban renewal movement.

In contrast with its 1953 counterpart, *Return to Regent Park* allows some residents of Regent Park to speak themselves directly about their problems and hopes for the future. Nevertheless, its steadfast concentration on the physical design deficiencies of the project provides only a very partial understanding of the problems that tenants face. Lacking any sense of social, economic, and political context concerning why Regent Park and its residents were territorially stigmatized, the documentary leaves the viewer with the impression that marginalization stems largely from the individual problems of tenants themselves. Moreover, we get little indication in the film that tenants contested this stigmatization in various ways. The film, therefore, unwittingly assists in the social construction of the project as an "outcast space," contributing to the

damning social and economic exclusion faced by project dwellers.

 More online.

Notes

This article was first presented at the International Geographical Union Conference, Commission on the Cultural Approach in Geography, Rio de Janeiro, June 2003. The author would like to thank conference participants and organizer, Mauricio Abreu, the editors of *Media, Culture & Society*, Bryan D. Palmer, and Richard Harris for helpful suggestions. Special thanks to Philip Alperson, Richard Immerman, and members of the Department of History at Temple University for a welcoming and stimulating intellectual atmosphere.

1. National Film Board of Canada (NFB), *Farewell to Oak Street*. Directed by Grant Maclean. Narrated by Lorne Greene, 1953, 17 minutes.

2. Robert Rosenstone, "History in Images/History in Words: Reflections on the Possibility of Really Putting History onto Film," *American Historical Review* 93, no. 5 (1988): 1179–80.

3. Chris Lukinbeal, "Reel-to-Reel Urban Geographies: The Top Five Cinematic Cities in North America," *The California Geographer* 38, no. 1 (1998): 64–78.

4. Peter B. Hales, *Silver Cities: The Photography of American Urbanization, 1839–1915* (Philadelphia, PA: Temple University Press, 1984). . . .

5. Erik Barnouw, *Documentary: A History of Non-Fiction Film*, 2nd ed. (New York, NY: Oxford University Press, 1993), 87–99.

6. John R. Gold and Stephen V. Ward, "Of Plans and Planners: Documentary Film and the Challenge of the Urban Future, 1935–52," in David B. Clarke, ed., *The Cinematic City* (London, UK: Routledge, 1997), 63.

7. Ibid., 65.

8. Ibid.

9. Kevin Brushett, "Blots on the Face of the City: The Politics of Slum Housing and Urban Renewal in Toronto, 1940–1970" (Ph.D. thesis, Queen's University, 2001), and Sean Purdy, "From Place of Hope to Outcast Space: Territorial Regulation and Tenant Resistance in Regent Park Housing Project, 1949–1999," (Ph.D. thesis, Queen's University, 2003).

10. A list of all NFB films dealing with urban issues over a period of 50 years can be found at the NFB English Language Collections Website, Urbanism—Housing and Public Housing, www.nfb.ca (consulted 10 November 2003).

11. Richard Harris and Tricia Shulist, "Canada's Reluctant Housing Program: The Veterans' Land Act, 1942–75," *Canadian Historical Review* 82, no. 2 (2001): 252–83.

12. John Bacher, *Keeping to the Marketplace: The Evolution of Canadian Housing Policy* (Montreal, QC: McGill-Queen's University Press, 1989); and Brushett, "Blots on the Face of the City."

13. "Evangelistic" was the word used to describe the efforts of the reformers of the period by one of their leading members, Humphrey Carver, in his memoirs (*Compassionate Landscape* [Toronto, ON: University of Toronto Press, 1978], 82). For a fuller treatment, see Sean Purdy, "Scaffolding Citizenship: Housing Policy and Nation Formation in Canada, 1900–1950," in Robert Menzies, Dorothy Chunn, and Robert Adomski, eds., *Canadian Citizenship: Historical Readings* (Peterborough, ON: Broadview Press, 2002), ch. 6.

14. Albert Rose, *Regent Park: A Study in Slum Clearance* (Toronto, ON: University of Toronto Press, 1958).

15. Seán Damer, *From Moorepark to "Wine Alley": The Rise and Fall of a Glasgow Housing Scheme* (Edinburgh, UK: University of Edinburgh Press, 1989).

16. Kay J. Anderson, *Vancouver's Chinatown: Racial Discourse in Canada, 1875–1980* (Montreal, QC: McGill-Queen's University Press, 1991).

17. Gerry Mooney, "Urban Disorders," in Steve Piles, Christopher Brook, and Gerry Mooney, eds., *Unruly Cities?* (London, UK: Routledge, 2000), 54–99.

18. Mariana Valverde, *The Age of Light, Soap, and Water: Moral Regulation in English Canada, 1900–1920* (Toronto, ON: McClelland & Stewart, 1991), 132.

19. David Ward, "The Progressives and the Urban Question: British and American Responses to Inner-City Slums, 1880–1920," *Transactions, Institute of British Geographers* 9, no. 4 (1984): 304.

20. Purdy, "From Place of Hope to Outcast Space," and Judith Walkowitz, *City of Dreadful Delight: Narratives of Sexual Danger in Late-Victorian London* (Chicago, IL: University of Chicago Press, 1992).

21. Robert M. Entman, "Blacks in the News: Television, Modern Racism and Cultural Change," *Journalism Quarterly* 69, no. 2 (1992): 341–61, and Patricia M. Evans and Karen J. Swift, "Single Mothers and the Press: Rising Tides, Moral Panic, and Restructuring Discourses," in Sheila M. Neysmith, ed., *Restructuring Caring Labour: Discourse, State Practice, and Everyday Life* (Toronto, ON: Oxford University Press 2000), 73–92. . . .

22. Purdy, "From Place of Hope to Outcast Space."

23. Sudhir Venkatesh, *American Project: The Rise and Fall of a Modern Ghetto* (Cambridge, MA: MIT Press, 2000), and Rhonda Y. Williams, "Living Just Enough in the City: Change and Activism in Baltimore's Public Housing, 1940–1980" (Ph.D. thesis, University of Pennsylvania,

1998). It is important to emphasize that Regent Park residents were not ill-fated spectators of their own futures or empty recipients of the ideological messages conveyed by outside critics. Stigmatization was contested at all levels over the years (see Purdy, "From Place of Hope to Outcast Space," . . . and Purdy, "By the People, For the People: Tenant Organizing in Toronto's Regent Park Housing Project in the 1960s and 1970s," *Journal of Urban History* 30, no. 4 (2004): 519–48.

24. NFB, *Farewell to Oak Street*, 17 minutes.

25. James H. Inglis, "To Henry Matson," City of Toronto Archives, Housing Authority of Toronto Papers, NFB 28, B, Box 33, File: "Regent Park Rate Payers and Tenants' Association, 1947–1954," 1 June 1949.

26. Henry Matson to Donald Mulholland, City of Toronto Archives, Housing Authority of Toronto, NFB 28, B, Box 41, File: Central Mortgage and Housing Corporation, 1947–1949, 7 February 1949.

27. Robert Bradley and Gordon Noble, City of Toronto Archives, Housing Authority of Toronto Papers, NFB 28, B, Box 41, File: "1965–1968 N," 1 June 1965.

28. Gordon Burwash, "To Henry Matson," City of Toronto Archives, Housing Authority of Toronto Papers, NFB 28, B, Box 41, File: "CMHC Progress Reports, 1947–1945," 29 April 1949.

29. Peter Morris, "After Grierson: The National Film Board, 1945–1953," *Journal of Canadian Studies* 16, no. 1 (1981): 7.

30. Donald Mulholland, "To H. L. Luffman," City of Toronto Archives, Housing Authority of Toronto Papers, RG 28, B, Box 41, File: "CMHC Progress Reports, 1947–1945," 27 April 1949.

31. Morris, "After Grierson," 7–9.

32. NFB, Press Release for *Farewell to Oak Street*, City of Toronto Archives, Housing Authority of Toronto Papers, RG 28, B, Box 36, File: "Regent Park North: Statements by Mayor, 1949–1955," 1953.

33. Yvonne Klein-Matthews, "How They Saw Us: Images of Women in the National Film Board Films of the 1940s and 1950s," *Atlantis* 4, no. 1 (1979): 20–33.

34. Gary Evans, *In the National Interest: A Chronicle of the National Film Board of Canada from 1949 to 1989* (Toronto, ON: University of Toronto Press, 1991), 37.

35. Brian Low, *NFB Kids: Portrayals of Children by the National Film Board of Canada, 1939–1989* (Waterloo, ON: Wilfred Laurier University Press, 2002), 85–6.

36. Brushett, "Blots on the Face of the City," 97.

37. Evans, *In the National Interest*, 37, n29, 346–7.

38. NFB, *Return to Regent Park*. Directed by Bay Weyman. 1994, 55 minutes.

39. Parliamentary Committee on Canadian Heritage, URL (consulted April 2003): http://www.parl.gc.ca/committees/heri/evidence/114_95–12–14/heri114_blk101.html. 1995.

40. NFB, *Return to Regent Park*.

41. Dan Georgakas, "Malpractice in the Radical American Documentary," *Cinéaste* 16 (1987–8): 46–9.

42. Iain Ferguson and Michael Lavalette, "Postmodernism, Marxism and Social Work," *European Journal of Social Work* 2, no. 1 (1999): 27–40. . . .

43. Don Gillmor, "The Punishment Station," *Toronto Life* (January 1996): 46–55.

44. Peter Jackson, "Policing Difference: 'Race' and Crime in Metropolitan Toronto," in Peter Jackson and J. Penrose, eds., *Constructions of Race, Place and Nation* (London, UK: University College Press, 1993), and Peter Jackson, "Constructions of Criminality: Police–Community Relations in Toronto," *Antipode* 26, no. 2 (1994): 216–35. . . .

45. *Toronto Star*, "Treatment Differs by Division," 19 October 2002, URL (consulted January 2003): www.thestar.com.

46. Neil Websdale, *Policing the Poor: From Slave Plantation to Public Housing* (Boston, MA: Northeastern University Press, 2001), ch. 6.

47. Jim Ward Associates, *The Report on a Study to Identify and Address Police–Community Issues in Regent Park* (Toronto, ON: Jim Ward Associates, 1996).

48. Gillmor, "The Punishment Station."

49. CBC (Canadian Broadcasting Corporation), "Making Peace, Ending the Violence," Town Hall Discussion, CBC Toronto; URL (consulted 3 June 2002): http://www.cbc.ca.

50. Paula Rabinowitz, "Wreckage Upon Wreckage: History, Documentary and the Ruins of Memory," *History and Theory* 32, no. 2 (1993): 133.

51. Jane Jacobs, *Life and Death of Great American Cities* (New York, NY: Bantam Books, 1964), Introduction.

52. Christian Cotroneo, "Dynamic Duo Delivers Christmas," *Toronto Star*, 16 December 2002, URL (consulted 2 March 2003): www.thestar.com.

53. Keith Jacobs and Tony Manzi, "Urban Renewal and the Culture of Conservatism: Changing Perceptions of the Tower Block and Implications for Contemporary Renewal Initiatives," *Critical Social Policy* 18, no. 2 (1998): 170.

54. David Harvey cited in Peter Marcuse, "The New Urbanism: Dangers So Far," *DISP Online* (2000), URL (consulted 2 March 2003): www.orl.arch.ethz.ch/disp/pdf/140_1.pdf.

55. Jacobs and Manzi, "Urban Renewal and the Culture of Conservatism," 167–8.

56. Rabinowitz, "Wreckage Upon Wreckage," 120–1.

10 Visualizing Home

Since the nineteenth century, domestic spaces have been a site of moral concern, political regulation, and a point of contestation for many competing interests. Presented here are three forms of visual culture in which the ideals of home were cultivated: floor plans, photography, and advertisements. Of these three, it is perhaps easiest to acknowledge the subjectivity of advertisements, for they were intended to convince audiences that they "needed" to fill their homes with consumer goods. Yet it is important that we do not privilege floor plans and photographs simply as objective images of domestic space-as-it-was; each played active roles in the societies that produced and used them. Indeed, it is hardly coincidental that the advertisements included here used both photographs and floor plans to sell their wares.

While we can "read" these images to better appreciate how Canadians have historically ordered their domestic spaces, we learn even more from these images about the ideals of domestic space dominant in the period. Keep in mind, then, the content, the form, and the intended audience of these visual materials.

Series 1: Domestic Visions

Figure 1 is a floor plan of a Kwakw̲a̲ka̲'wakw (Kwakiutl) longhouse, and Figure 2 is a photograph of a Kwakw̲a̲ka̲'wakw village, both produced in the late nineteenth century. The photograph was taken in 1881 by Edward Dossetter, travelling through by ship. The floor plan was sketched by anthropologist Franz Boas (1858–1942), who spent much of his professional life studying the First Nations of Canada's west coast and, like many of his fellow anthropologists, was very interested in Indigenous domestic spaces. In the name of science, Boas used rigorous schematic plans, photographs, and material specimens to produce an "objective" representation of everyday Kwakw̲a̲ka̲'wakw life. However, the cultural context of nineteenth-century anthropology indelibly shaped these scientific views, as noted in Paige Raibmon's chapter. Therefore, such sources require a careful reading, set against the cultural perspective of the fieldworker.

The legend and symbols on the floor plan are from the original, and the language in the legend is also that of Boas. Terms in quotation marks, such as "middle forehead," represent Boas's translation of the Kwaka̲'wala term. Also, only the exterior lines on the plan represent walls. The other lines represent beams that were used to frame the longhouse as well as the embankments that were built around the interior to create a separate level in case of flooding.

1. What would social reformers and missionaries approve and disapprove of in the ordering of domestic space in the longhouse (Figure 1) and in the organization of the village (Figure 2)?
2. How has Boas sought to "prove" the cultural worth of the Kwakwa̱ka'wakw? Why, for example, does his diagram suggest the presence of walls around the "bedrooms"?
3. How does this arrangement of domestic space relate to questions of family, kinship, and community? How might Boas's reading of the Kwakwa̱ka'wakw interior space be shaped by an understanding of "civilized" domesticity?

By the twentieth century, the "civilizing" influence of domesticity was no longer simply a moral issue, it had also become a scientific one. Figures 3, 4, and 5 are drawings produced by architect R. A. Abraham. In an April 1913 article for *Farmer's Magazine*, Abraham offered layouts and architectural tips that attempted to bring "scientific" principles to bear on the modern farmer, who was by this time presumed to be engaging in "scientific agriculture." As opposed to traditional farming methods handed down through the generations, scientific agriculture was the application of new, modern techniques and technologies assumed to be based on rational, expert knowledge. In other words, it was a self-defined "modern" pursuit of "traditional" farming goals. The text for Abraham's article is worth quoting at length to understand the context for these drawings:

> [T]he planning for the country home should be most carefully prepared, seeking to incorporate in all the latest ideas of labor-saving and healthful devices. . . . The farm-house today does not need to be large, as recent developments on the farm lead to the erection of smaller houses for married helpers . . .

less space is needed and the country home is coming to be what it ought to be, a real privacy for the farmer and his family. . . .

The farmer to-day is a reading farmer and he ought to have a library wherein he has an office desk with the farm data always on file at his elbow. This room ought to be convenient to the front entrance. . . .

One of the most important features is the bath-room. It is too often the case that the farm houses of our land do not know the luxury of a bath-tub and depend upon a basin, or a pail to do service . . . it should be considered before other luxuries, such as the purchase of a carriage, or of a piano. By attaching the pipes to the kitchen range there will always be hot water convenient. It will then be quite easy for the tired and soiled farmer to enter by the back stairs to the bath-room and there, reviving himself, improve his appearance and add to the comfort and dignity of the farm home. It is just such things as these that will hold the farm boys and girls to the good country life. . . .

1. How are notions of "privacy" reinforced by the spatial ordering of Abraham's farm house? How do these concerns for privacy relate to Stacey Zembrzycki's chapter on boarding houses?
2. How are the assumptions of "scientific agriculture" embedded within these architectural plans? What does this suggest about the boundaries of home and work in agrarian settings?
3. Contrast this idealized farm house with the layout of the Kwakwa̱ka'wakw longhouse. How do these spaces reflect different kinds of social interaction and relationships?

Series 2: Exhibition and Surveillance

In early twentieth-century Canada, the surveillance of homes went beyond Indigenous communities. Facing rapid urbanization and immigration, expanding cities across Canada struggled to manage and regulate chronic poor housing conditions. The rise of public health facilitated a new infrastructure of governance that mapped, inspected, and surveyed urban spaces. In different forms, the practice of "experts" deploying visual evidence to construct dangerous urban spaces has continued up to the present, as Sean Purdy demonstrates in his chapter on two National Film Board (NFB) films about Toronto's Regent Park.

The photographs included in this series (Figures 6–7) were taken by Arthur Goss, a photographer employed by Toronto's Department of Public Works. Goss's images were used by the city's Department of Health in its efforts to produce a wide-ranging social survey. Filed alongside photographs of the working poor were promotional advertisements from Mott's Ironworks, a New York–based manufacturer of plumbing fixtures that offered illustrations of ideal domestic spaces (Figures 8–9). The gap between these two sets of images is not one of "ideal" versus "reality"; both should be regarded as social constructions of space, projecting middle-class assumptions of how health, environment, and cleanliness relate to each other. Such images were staples of multiple exhibits of public health that toured the country, including the annual Canadian National Exhibition (CNE) in Toronto.

1. The images here focus on kitchens and bathrooms, but the moral concerns outlined in Valerie Minnett and Mary Anne Poutanen's chapter are still evident. Why would social reformers consider these spaces as areas of concern?
2. Analyze the compositional elements of the images, especially noting the use of light and darkness. How do these images reflect middle-class assumptions?
3. How could such images have been put on display as part of a public education

campaign? What kind of narrative would this visual evidence suggest?

Series 3: Food for Thought

Between World Wars I and II, the value of "healthy" food drew upon a wide range of factors. First were the broad societal and political concerns for bodily health, including the worrisome state of Canadian men's health revealed during the screening of World War I volunteers. In this context, healthy children were perceived as critical both for their own well-being as individuals and also as an index of the health of the "Canadian race" and the nation. Second, the economic upheavals of World War I and the interwar period (especially the Depression years) meant that consumers were sophisticated and strategic when it came to identifying value for their grocery budgets. "Value" in this case meant calculating a balance for sustenance, taste, nutrition, and cost. Third, while the "New Woman" of the interwar years was occupying new and more visible public roles in social spaces of work and play, at home she was cast as applying "modern" practices and technologies to fulfilling her obligations as a mother and wife. These obligations included understanding the basic science of nutrition and bodily health.

In the advertisements presented in this series (Figures 10–12), all three themes appear and intersect with one another in different ways. As advertisements, however, these images were very much about cultivating consumer desire by defining what meanings ought to be attached to their products. This was done through the marriage of visual imagery and text, as the words function to explain to viewers what the images signify. These advertisements thus strove to sell specific foodstuffs and also a better way of living that would come with their consumption.

1. How do these advertisements try to define their products as "healthy" food? Which

bodies are deemed in most need of this food and its nutritional benefits?

2. How are domesticity, food, and health gendered in these advertisements?

3. How is the eating of this "good food" at home related to the improvement of life away from home?

Series 4: Suburban Landscapes

The post-1945 era gave rise to a new form of suburban living. Empowered by the creation of new financing options, government programs, and a general boom in the economy, a generation who had lived through a massive depression and another world war enthusiastically made their way into the hundreds of thousands of new homes being built on the peripheries of Canada's major cities. As Patrick Vitale's chapter explains, those who designed and managed these suburbs valued "conformity, community, privacy, stability, and a careful mixture of nature and city."

One of the trends of domestic life that connected all of these elements was the promotion of a return to "normal" gender relations. Looking back at the turbulence of the Depression era and the upheavals of World War II, many felt that women's roles had strayed too far from the traditional Victorian ideals of home and family. Set against the backdrop of the Cold War, by the mid-1950s a suburban, nuclear family was celebrated as the epitome of the democratic west's

superior way of living, a bulwark against the threat of communism. The food, kitchens, and consumerism associated with western abundance were, according to Franca Iacovetta and Valerie J. Korinek's chapter, key ingredients in facilitating the assimilation and acculturation of immigrants in the post-war era. When examining the images in this series (Figures 13–17), carefully read the text in the advertisements and consider the following questions:

1. Examine the floor plans of Figures 13 and 14. What has been the most significant shift in domestic space compared to the Edwardian period (Figures 3 and 4)? What room(s) are located most centrally and would receive the most traffic?

2. How are these houses designed to fit a "suburban" lifestyle? What are the expectations of the builders in relation to the people who might occupy these homes?

3. How do the advertisements in Figures 15, 16, and 17 produce gendered assumptions regarding domestic space? How do they define or reinforce the proper social roles occupied by men and women? How did representations of masculinity shift from the 1950s to the 1970s?

4. Carefully examine the representations of children in the advertisements. How are the expectations for children gendered? What roles do children play in defining suburban spaces?

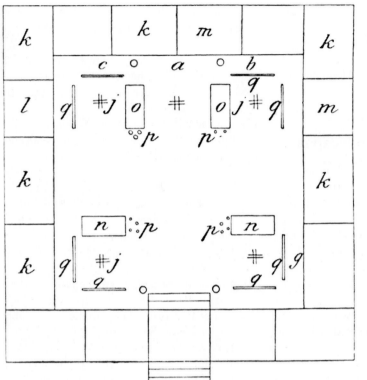

Figure 1. Plan of a Kwakwa̱ka'wakw longhouse, from Franz Boas, *The Jesup North Pacific Expedition*, vol. V, part II (Leiden: E. J. Brill Ltd, 1909; reprint, AMS Press, 1975), 415.

Legend
a – 'middle forehead'
b – 'right forehead'
c – 'left forehead'
f – 'upriver'
g – 'downriver'
j – 'house fire' (which Boas also
j – uses '#' to signify)
k – bedrooms (on embankments)
l – firewood
m – boxes containing provisions
n, o – seat of the housewife
p – cooking utensils
q – other seats

Note: Some information has been removed from Boas's original image for the sake of clarity.

Figure 2. Edward Dossetter, photograph of Humdaspe, Vancouver Island, 1881. Image 42298, courtesy the Library, American Museum of Natural History.

FRONT ELEVATION

The front elevation of this farm house.

Figure 3. Farm house elevation drawing. Illustration from R. A. Abraham, "That New Farm House," *Farmer's Magazine* 5, no. 6 (April 1913): 27.

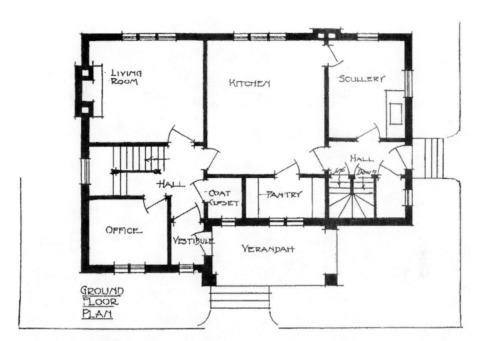

Figure 4. Farm house floor plan, ground floor. Illustration from R. A. Abraham, "That New Farm House," *Farmer's Magazine* 5, no. 6 (April 1913): 29.

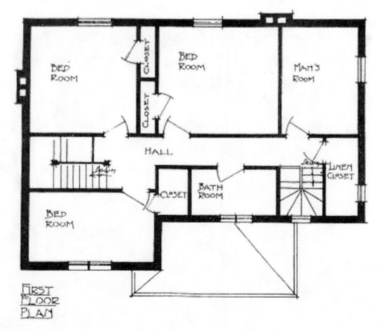

Figure 5. Farm house floor plan, upper floor. Illustration from R. A. Abraham, "That New Farm House," *Farmer's Magazine* 5, no. 6 (April 1913): 28.

Figure 6. Arthur Goss, photograph, 1913. City of Toronto Archives, Series 372, ss0032, it0247.

Figure 7. Arthur Goss, photograph, 1913. City of Toronto Archives, Series 372, ss0032, it0251.

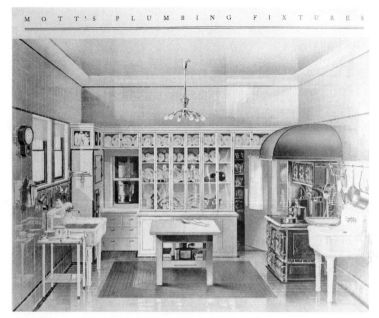

Figure 8. Illustration from catalogue, Mott's Ironworks, 1912. City of Toronto Archives, Series 372, ss0032, it0124.

Figure 9. Illustration from catalogue, Mott's Ironworks, 1912. City of Toronto Archives, Series 372, ss0032, it0127.

Figure 10. Advertisement for Shredded Wheat, "First in School and Sports, Too!" *Montreal Gazette*, 17 September 1935, 3.

Figure 11. Advertisement for Shredded Wheat, "Ready for a Good Day's Work and Play!" *Montreal Gazette*, 28 May 1935, 5.

For Fag
of Brain or Body~
natural Bran

IF hot summer days leave you draggy and fagged—if you have not energy to work or even to play—you should eat *natural* bran at least once a day.

Most cases of low vitality and drowsiness are due to faulty digestion and irregular and incomplete elimination of the body's waste. The digestive tract must function naturally and regularly and it must have roughage to do so. No other roughage is so good as Tillson's *natural* Bran.

The coating of soft winter wheat, clean and sterilized. Its fibrous texture ensures mastication and an efficient massage of the gums. Its bulk stimulates stomach and intestinal muscles to sweep waste and poisons out of the system—regularly, *naturally*, completely.

It gives you, as well, iron, lime and phosphorus and the important vitamin "B" which is not found in other wheat foods.

Eat Tillson's *natural* Bran in delicious muffins, gems and bran bread. Or sprinkle it on other cereals or on fruits. It will help you to get back your vim and it will banish needless fatigue of body and brain.

Tillson's
natural Bran
Not cooked — Not treated

THE QUAKER OATS COMPANY, PETERBOROUGH AND SASKATOON

Figure 12. Advertisement for Tillson's Natural Bran, "For Fag of Brain or Body—*natural* Bran," *Chatelaine*, July 1928, 36.

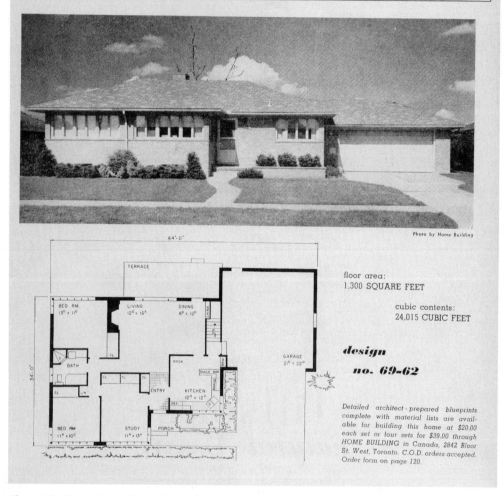

CONVENIENCE-PLANNED
for lasting satisfaction

THIS home is sure to be a favourite with SH readers for it meets just about every planning requirement of the average Canadian family. Attractively landscaped with well placed foundation shrubbery, the exterior combines bark face buff brick (veneer), brown-and-grey shaded roof, and very light mist green for trim and garage door.

The centre hall arrangement provides ex-

cellent traffic circulation. While the room to the left of the entry hall is indicated in the sketch plan as a study, most families will of course use it as a third bedroom. The vanity-equipped bathroom is much above-average in size—boasts a separate shower in addition to the bath.

The 145 square foot kitchen is brought up to the front and comes complete with built-in snack bar, corner sink, broom closet and dining nook. Notice its excellent placement in relation to basement stairs and the garage. A full basement is provided. Plans give full details for all built-ins.

Photo by Home Building

floor area:
1,300 SQUARE FEET

cubic contents:
24,015 CUBIC FEET

design
no. 69-62

Detailed architect - prepared blueprints complete with material lists are available for building this home at $20.00 each set or four sets for $39.00 through HOME BUILDING in Canada, 2842 Bloor St. West, Toronto. C.O.D. orders accepted. Order form on page 120.

Figure 13. "Convenience-Planned for Lasting Satisfaction," *Home Building in Canada: Small Homes,* 1960 edition (Toronto, ON: Walkers Publishing, 1960), 100.

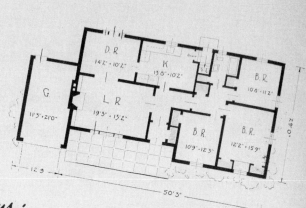

J. E. HOARE, Architect

Owner S. J. Reid of North Toronto, Ontario, is full of praise for this new ranch-style home. His only regret was that our picture was taken before a flagstone terrace had been added, and the landscaping completed!

We agree that the plan is particularly good, and the exterior most attractive. Outer walls are red brick, combined with white vertical boards. Roof is black. House was erected by H. A. Hoare, builder, and contains 25,600 cubic feet, without garage.

Figure 14. "The Home Owner Says: 'It's Comfortable and Convenient,'" *Home Building in Canada: Small Homes*, 1951 edition (Toronto, ON: Walkers Publishing, 1951), 140.

"To the King's Taste!"

...AND THAT PRACTICAL *CRANE* SINK IS TO THE LADY'S!

IT'S JUST the kind she wanted for *her* step-saving kitchen—a flat rim, lightweight, stain-proof Porcelain-on-Steel model that's installed flush with a continuous counter top. Low in cost, it has enduring easy-to-clean finish—handy swinging spout faucet and finger-tip "Dial-Ese" controls.

Your plans may call for something a little different and more elaborate—for a sink-and-drainboard combination, perhaps. If so, you'll find it, too, in the complete Crane line—which includes dozens of modern types, with single or double basins, single or double drainboards—

from which you can select the right sink for your particular needs, with the size, depth and work area you desire—to fit your taste, your space and your budget.

For complete information ask your Plumbing and Heating Contractor. He'll be glad to tell you all about Crane-quality sinks, built for endurance, convenience and easy cleaning.

For every home... For every budget

The Preferred Plumbing   1-5224

CRANE LIMITED • GENERAL OFFICE: 1170 BEAVER HALL SQUARE, MONTREAL • 6 CANADIAN FACTORIES • 18 CANADIAN BRANCHES

Figure 15. Advertisement for Crane Ltd (Montreal), "To the King's Taste!" *Canadian Homes and Gardens*, September 1952.

This floor is composed of Dominion Jaspé Linoleum tiles, Patterns J-720 and J-723

This floor reflects a thoughtful husband!

The kitchen above *and breakfast nook here say a cheery "Good morning" 365 days a year. Let us have your name and address so that we can send you colourful FREE literature which will open your eyes as to what is being done to create individual, delightful, durable floors for every room in the house. Sixty-five colours and patterns to choose from.*

"The floor in your kitchen," said my husband when we were planning it. "must be the kind that will save you work. I want you to have lots of leisure to enjoy yourself."

That's how linoleum came in. Our dealer told us it was the only answer — easy to keep colourful and clean even on the muddiest days, easy on the feet and — this really pleased my husband — easy on the budget!

I'm delighted with the result. Linoleum has everything!

If *you* are planning to build or renovate, consult your dealer or flooring contractor. Ask for comparative prices of linoleum and other floors. And keep in mind that linoleum is colourful, resilient, easy to keep clean . . . and that its durability has been time-tested by forty year's wear on Canadian floors.

DOMINION *Jaspé* **LINOLEUM TILES**

BEAUTIFUL · RESILIENT · TIME-TESTED

Also Marboleum · Battleship (plain) in tiles or by the yard . . . products of

DOMINION OILCLOTH & LINOLEUM COMPANY LIMITED
MONTREAL

1952 is our 80th Anniversary

Figure 16. Advertisement for Dominion Oilcloth and Linoleum Co. (Montreal), "This Floor Reflects a Thoughtful Husband!" *Canadian Homes and Gardens*, September 1952.

Figure 17. Advertisement for Campeau Corporation, "Kanata: For the Two of You," *Ottawa Citizen*, 4 July 1978. Also reprinted in Doug Fischer and Ralph Willsey, eds., *Each Morning Bright: 160 Years of Selected Readings* (Ottawa Citizen eGroup Inc., 2005), 382. Material reprinted with the express permission of: *Ottawa Citizen*, a division of Postmedia Network Inc.

 *More online.*

PART II

At Work

Work is the most thoroughly studied subject in Canadian social history, and it has also been central to the debates that have swirled around and within the field. In part, this is a reflection of the subject matter. The challenges of everyday life, as well as many of its opportunities, have historically involved questions of labour in one form or another. It is hardly surprising, then, that historians concerned with the study of social life—both its experiences and the structures that shape them—should spend so much time researching, thinking, and writing about the historical conditions of work. Labour, work, and the working class have been and remain among the most vibrant and innovative fields of social historical scholarship.

Historians of work have reshaped our historical understanding of Canada's transition in the late nineteenth and early twentieth centuries from a mostly rural, agrarian country to a mostly urban, industrial country. Until the 1970s, the study of this "great transformation" usually focused on broad economic patterns, various government trade policies, and the accomplishments of merchants and businessmen. After 1970, however, historians increasingly called attention to the experience and identities of workers and argued that their blood and sweat had made possible a more industrial Canada. Epitomized by the now classic studies by Bryan D. Palmer and Gregory S. Kealey, historians were especially interested in understanding how workers organized themselves into craft guilds, fraternal orders, and unions. They explored how workers accommodated and resisted such things as the deskilling of labour through new technologies and the reorganization of factory work under the scientific management theories of Frederick W. Taylor. At the heart of these analyses was an argument that a distinct working-class culture was produced in Canada that owed much to worker organizations and to the often tense relationships that existed between workers, their bosses, and a government that was often little more than a handmaiden to the interests of capitalists.

The 1980s and 1990s brought some change to the historical study of work. The convergence of this early social history of labour with other areas of social historical research, especially the history of women, the history of families, and the history of education, deepened our understanding of the impact of industrialization in all sectors of everyday life. Feminist scholarship was particularly important in calling historians' attention to the waged work of women and children, and their unwaged labour within the home. Immigration historians demonstrated how work could function as a form of social currency, reinforcing and delimiting community boundaries as new arrivals turned to earlier generations of immigrants for assistance in the settlement process. Education historians showed us how the decision to send or not to send children to school was contingent on their contribution to the family economy. Other studies sought to explore not only the political relationship between organized labour and the state, but also the ways in which forms and practices of governance at work were adopted and codified by various levels of Canadian state formation. By the end of the 1990s, the social history of work had not only become more aware of the complexity of "workers" as a historical category, but had also become essential to a wide range of Canadian historiographies.

In the twenty-first century, the social history of waged work has continued to evolve as it has become more consistently integrated into scholarly conversations with histories of colonialism and environmental histories. For example, while an earlier generation of scholarship called much-needed attention to the importance of Indigenous and Métis labour to the commercial successes of fur trade companies, we now appreciate more fully how work relations in the fur trade from the mid-eighteenth to mid-nineteenth century, both in the canoe and at forts, were also systems of colonial governance. Environmental historians have inspired social historians of work to listen more carefully to what their evidence says about not only the impact of work on ecosystems, but also how ecosystems have historically affected workers. Along with important contributions from social histories of medicine and the body, this has inspired a renewed and enriched historical interest in the health of workers' bodies. What impact on workers' health resulted from working in mines, factories, or even fast-food restaurants? How did workers understand and navigate the risks involved with "unhealthy" work? How did factory inspectors and medical practitioners perceive and understand "healthy" workers and work spaces?

Recent Canadian historiography more broadly has shown a pronounced concern with the second half of the twentieth century, and this also resonates in the research conducted by social historians of work. Scholars have explored the restructuring of a "post-industrial" economy and traced its impact on Canadian workers and workspaces. As reflected in Katharine Rollwagen's chapter, one of the most significant dimensions of these economic changes was and remains deindustrialization, a process of closures and shutdowns of traditional industrial worksites. Another fact of the post-1945 Canadian economy has been the expansion of the service sector, the focus of chapters by Donica Belisle and Becki Ross and Kim Greenwell. In addition to teaching us about the power relationships that swirled around these workers, these chapters also raise important questions about the regulation and disciplining of service labour, especially since this work was often gendered feminine and thus (de)valued accordingly. By remapping Canadian workspaces, these recent trends in social history are helping to puncture the myth of widespread post-war abundance and prosperity while also providing important insight into processes and experiences very much part of our present condition.

Over the course of this historiographical evolution, there remains an enduring interest in the importance of regulation to the historical experiences of work. While the sources of regulation have been multifaceted, including shop foremen, union stewards, co-workers, family members, consumers, and factory inspectors, the overall effect has been similar. Consistently, historians have demonstrated that workers' bodies and experiences have been subjected to various practices and technologies of discipline. Equally important, though, historians have shown how confronting, resisting, and accommodating discipline have been central to the experiences of work and the formation of workers' identities.

Disciplining work time and work space, however, took many different forms. It could be overt and sometimes brutal, including beatings, whippings, and other forms of corporal punishment, as well as verbal abuse or the threat of withholding wages. Discipline could also be covert. It might include codes of worker conduct, uniforms, punch clocks, scheduled washroom breaks, or an unspoken threat of social isolation. While such practices were common between bosses and workers, many of the chapters in this section demonstrate that workers themselves also disciplined and regulated their own work, workspaces, and other workers. In situations such as the docks of early twentieth-century Vancouver, where jobs were parcelled out among a large body of workers on a near-daily basis, or in the fractious efforts at unionizing sales staff in post-war department stores, the relationships among workers could be as important as those between workers and employers in even getting paid work. Whether it was voyageurs spending their first winter north and west of Lake Superior, stenographers and clerks in Montreal office buildings, or women factory workers, discipline and work were strongly affected by the formation of class cultures on the job.

Readers might be well served to keep some questions in mind as they explore the readings and documents in this section. What historical situations have existed where a person worked for reasons other than a wage? Whether people worked for a wage or not, what was this work environment like? What rules did one follow? How was the labour divided among the workers? How were individuals identified at work? How did those at work identify themselves as workers? How did work experiences affect other areas of everyday life? Such questions connect these diverse stories and documents of work, but they also allow us to see what has historically connected coal miners from early nineteenth-century Nova Scotia to Depression-era farmers in Saskatchewan to African-Canadian and African-American burlesque performers in post–World War II Vancouver. In doing so, perhaps we also learn a little bit more about ourselves and our ideas and assumptions about what it means to work.

Further Readings

Burley, Edith I. *Servants of the Honourable Company: Work, Discipline and Conflict in the Hudson's Bay Company, 1770–1870.* Toronto, ON: Oxford University Press, 1997.

Craig, Béatrice. *Backwoods Consumers and Homespun Capitalists: The Rise of a Market Culture in Eastern Canada.* Toronto, ON: University of Toronto Press, 2009.

Craven, Paul, ed. *Labouring Lives: Work and Workers in Nineteenth-Century Ontario.* Toronto, ON: University of Toronto Press, 1995.

Danysk, Cecilia. *Hired Hands: Labour and the Development of Prairie Agriculture, 1880–1930.* Toronto, ON: University of Toronto Press, 1995.

Desbiens, Caroline. *Power from the North: Territory, Identity, and the Culture of Hydroelectricity in Quebec.* Vancouver, BC: UBC Press, 2013.

Heron, Craig and Steven Penfold. *The Workers'*

Festival: A History of Labour Day in Canada. Toronto, ON: University of Toronto Press, 2005.

High, Steven. *Industrial Sunsets: The Making of North America's Rust Belt, 1969–1984.* Toronto, ON: University of Toronto Press, 2003.

Kealey, Gregory S. and Bryan D. Palmer. *Dreaming of What Might Be: The Knights of Labor in Ontario, 1880–1900.* Cambridge, UK: Cambridge University Press, 1982.

Khouri, Malek and Darrell Varga, eds. *Working on Screen: Representations of the Working Class in Canadian Cinema.* Toronto, ON: University of Toronto Press, 2006.

Llewellyn, Kristina R. *Democracy's Angels: The Work of Women Teachers.* Montreal, QC: McGill-Queen's University Press, 2012.

Mathieu, Sarah-Jane. *North of the Color Line: Migration and Black Resistance in Canada, 1870-1955.* Chapel

Hill, NC: University of North Carolina Press, 2004.

McIntosh, Robert. *Boys in the Pits: Child Labour in Coal Mines*. Montreal, QC: McGill-Queen's University Press, 2000.

McPherson, Kathryn. *Bedside Matters: The Transformation of Canadian Nursing, 1900–1990.* Toronto, ON: Oxford University Press, 1996.

Palmer, Bryan D. and Joan Sangster, eds. *Labouring Canada: Class, Gender, and Race in Canadian Working-Class History.* Toronto, ON: Oxford University Press, 2008.

Palmer, Bryan D. *Working-Class Experience: Rethinking the History of Canadian Labour, 1800–1991*, 2nd ed. Toronto, ON: McClelland & Stewart, 1992.

Parnaby, Andrew. *Citizen Docker: Making a New Deal on the Vancouver Waterfront, 1919–1939.* Toronto, ON: University of Toronto Press, 2008.

Ramirez, Bruno. *On the Move: French-Canadian and Italian Migrants in the North Atlantic Economy, 1860–1914.* Toronto, ON: McClelland & Stewart, 1991.

Sangster, Joan. *Transforming Labour: Women and Work in Postwar Canada.* Toronto, ON: University of Toronto Press, 2010.

Srigley, Katrina. *Breadwinning Daughters: Young Working Women in a Depression-Era City, 1929–39.* Toronto, ON: University of Toronto Press, 2010.

Sugiman, Pamela. *Labour's Dilemma: The Gender Politics of Auto Workers in Canada, 1937–79.* Toronto, ON: University of Toronto Press, 1994.

11

The Theatre of Hegemony
Masters, Clerks, and Servants

Carolyn Podruchny

At sunset we put ashore for the night, on a point covered with a great number of lopsticks. These are tall pine-trees, denuded of their lower branches, a small tuft being left at the top. They are generally made to serve as landmarks, and sometimes the voyageurs make them in honour of gentlemen who happen to be travelling for the first time along the route, and those trees are chosen which, from their being on elevated ground, are conspicuous objects. The traveller for whom they are made is always expected to acknowledge his sense of the honour conferred upon him, by presenting the boat's crew with a pint of grog, either on the spot or at the first establishment they meet with. He is then considered as having paid for his footing, and may ever afterwards pass scot-free.[1]

The "conspicuous objects" that HBC officer Robert Ballantyne described in the mid-nineteenth century while travelling to Norway House, variously called *lopsticks*, *lobsticks*, *mais*, and *maypoles* in the documentary record, could be found along the most travelled fur trade routes. These stripped trees, which in the subarctic were probably most often spruces, not pines, were reminiscent of poles erected to honour captains of militia in Lower Canada and of maypoles in Europe. They perhaps resonated with sacred poles or trees in some Aboriginal communities, such as those of the Iroquois, Mohican-Munsees, and Omahas.[2] During canoe journeys voyageurs created maypoles for some bourgeois and passengers in their company, usually those perceived to be wealthy or of high social rank. In return the person honoured was required to treat voyageurs to a drink of rum, wine, or whatever alcoholic beverage was available. The bourgeois and passengers were usually pleased to receive such a striking honour from voyageurs, and in turn voyageurs were glad to acquire a treat. The ceremony of constructing maypoles and the lasting symbol of the maypole itself reflected the delicate negotiation of power that characterized relationships between masters and servants. In the fur trade the maypole ritual allowed masters to claim authority and permitted servants to demand material rewards, as well as providing markers along routes.

This chapter turns to voyageurs' relationships with their masters, both clerks and bourgeois. Once they signed engagements, or contracts, they entered into a master–servant relationship that was typical of indentured

Citation: Carolyn Podruchny, "The Theater of Hegemony: Masters, Clerks, and Servants," in *Making the Voyageur World: Travelers and Traders in the North American Fur Trade* (Lincoln, NE: University of Nebraska Press, 2006): 134–64. © Board of Regents of the University of Nebraska 2006; published in Canada in 2006 by University of Toronto Press. Reprinted with permission of the publisher.

servitude in New France and other colonial settings. This system was based on masters asserting authority over their servants and servants obeying masters' orders. However, the organization of the labour system and the particulars of the fur trade workplace made the master–servant relationship more flexible than did many other early modern settings. In the fur trade voyageurs were able in limited ways to shape their workplace and control the pace of their work through forms of resistance that ranged from acts of minor disobedience to large-scale strikes. Although the master–servant relationship was based on inequality, its flexibility provided voyageurs with agency, or the ability to shape their working lives.

Fur trade servants vastly outnumbered their masters and worked far away from colonial structures of rule and policing. Masters depended heavily on their servants not only for the successful functioning of the trade but also for their very survival. How did this system of inequality and hierarchy sustain itself? How did the bourgeois rule over voyageurs without physical might? The Italian Marxist philosopher Antonio Gramsci argued that the ruling classes were able to maintain their domination over lower classes without the use of physical coercion through the dominant ideologies of inequality that were promoted by cultural institutions, such as schools, the media, and religions, and thus became normative.[3] Although Gramsci was building on Marxist theories to explain the consent of proletariats to subordination by the bourgeoisie in capitalist settings, the theory has become widely applicable to explaining many contexts of hierarchical rule.

Masters and servants accepted their positions as rulers and ruled. Voyageurs could challenge the substance and boundaries of their jobs to improve their working conditions without contesting the fundamental power dynamics. Voyageurs' acceptance of bourgeois (and sometimes clerk) domination was based on a deeply held belief in the legitimacy of paternalism. Voyageurs certainly became discontented, resisted the authority of bourgeois and clerks, and sometimes revolted, but it was outside their conception of the world to challenge the system of paternalism.[4] Thus cultural hegemony was not inconsistent with the presence of labour strife. Although voyageurs challenged the terms of their employment and contracts, they did not fundamentally challenge their position in the power relationship because they participated in constructing the system. Voyageurs, bourgeois, and clerks engaged in a dialogue of accommodation and confrontation as a means of constructing a workable relationship.[5] Hegemony did not prevent voyageurs from creating their own modes of work and leisure or from forming their own rituals. Hegemony offered, in the words of E. P. Thompson, writing of the eighteenth-century English plebeians, a "bare architecture of a structure of relations of domination and subordination, but within that architectural tracery many different scenes could be set and different dramas enacted."[6]

. . .

The Short Arm of the Law

At the centre of the master–servant relationship was the legal compact of voyageurs' engagements . . . The principal tenet of the contract dictated that servants obey their masters in exchange for board and wages. To enforce the terms of the legal contracts, the bourgeois tried to regulate their servants through legal and governmental sanctions. In January 1778 the NWC [North West Company] sent a memorandum to the Quebec governor Sir Guy Carleton requesting "that it be published before the Traders and their Servants that the latter must strictly conform to their agreements, which should absolutely be in writing or printed, and before witnesses if possible, as many disputes [arose] from want of order in this particular."[7] The memorandum goes on to ask that men be held to pay their debts with money or service and that traders hiring men already engaged to another company should purchase their contracts. Lower Canadian law eventually recognized the legality of notarial fur trade contracts, and a 1796 ordinance forbade voyageurs from transgressing the terms or deserting the service.[8] In Lower Canada, the legislature empowered justices of the peace (JPs) to create and oversee the rules and regulations for master–servant relations in the Montreal trade.[9]

In addition to seeking governmental support, the bourgeois and the clerks turned to courts of law to enforce the terms of voyageur contracts and charged voyageurs for breaking contracts through desertion, insolence, and disobedience.[10] The files of the Court of Quarter Sessions in the District of Montreal reveal a range of cases: Voyageurs accepted wages from one employer while already working for another, they obtained advance wages without appearing for the job, and they deserted the service.[11] Cases of voyageur desertion and theft can also be found in the records of the Montreal civil court.[12] In 1803 the British government passed the Canada Jurisdiction Act stipulating that criminal offences committed in the "Indian territories" could be tried in Lower Canada. The five JPs named were all prominent fur trade bourgeois.[13] The effectiveness of court actions to control workers is obscured because prosecution rates have not survived in most of the records. Presumably the bourgeois would not continue to press charges if their efforts did not pay off. On the other hand, pressing charges against voyageurs did not seem to deter them from continuing to desert, cheat on contract terms, and steal from their employers. It is difficult to imagine bourgeois and clerks chasing a deserter, arresting him while in the Pays d'en Haut, and keeping him in bondage until he could be jailed in Montreal, while crews were racing against time to deliver their cargoes. If a bourgeois decided to file against a deserting voyageur, how would the courts deliver notification to the voyageur, who was probably still in the Pays d'en Haut?

The difficulties of apprehending and transporting contract breakers to Montreal led fur trade companies and partnerships to seek alternative methods of worker control. Fur traders sometimes co-operated to prevent voyageurs from jumping among different companies by compiling blacklists of deserters. In 1800 NWC officer William McGillivray wrote to Thomas Forsyth of Forsyth, Ogilvy, and McKenzie: "I agree with you that protecting Deserters would be a dangerous Practice and very pernicious to the Trade and fully sensible of this when any Man belonging to People opposed to The North West Company have happened to come to our Forts, we have told the Master of such to come for them and that they should not be in any way wise prevented from taking them back."[14] McGillivray assured Forsyth that he was not protecting deserters and that he would always contact their masters should any come to him looking for work. . . .

Concurrently voyageurs often sued their bourgeois for wages by filing petitions with courts.[15] Cases of this kind were widespread in all sorts of labour contracts in New France and Lower Canada. Most voyageurs would have had some exposure to the power of courts while they lived in the St. Lawrence valley. Voyageurs were not usually successful, however, in claiming wages for jobs they had deserted or where they had disobeyed their masters.[16] Even in courts where the JPs were not all fur traders, the Montreal middle-class establishment supported the fur trade merchants, who belonged to their own social class.

The Beaver Club

The fur trade bourgeois were able to prevail in the Canadian court systems because they belonged to the ruling classes of colonial society. The fur trade masters created their own niche by founding the Beaver Club, one of many dining clubs for Montreal's merchant class. Membership in this all-male club was restricted to NWC bourgeois who had spent at least one winter in the Pays d'en Haut. But members frequently brought guests, who included militia officers, government officials, businessmen, and professionals, such as judges, lawyers, and doctors, and distinguished visitors to Montreal, such as John Jacob Astor, Washington Irving, and Thomas Moore. The Beaver Club dinners were part of a large continuum of vigorous socializing among fur traders and Montreal's bourgeoisie. Fraternization among men was formalized in clubs and associations, many of which had overlapping memberships. Other men's dining clubs in Montreal included occupationally defined groups, such as the Brothers-in-Law Club; clubs based on family status, such as the Bachelors' Club; clubs based on hobbies, such as the Montreal Hunt Club; and clubs of volunteer community service, such as the exclusive Montreal Fire Club. During these club dinners, the bourgeois mingled with other merchants and colonial elites to forge business alliances, exchange information, share ideas, and cement social ties.[17]

. . .

The [Beaver] Club served as a forum for retired merchants to reminisce about the risky and adventurous days of fur trading and for young fur traders to enter Montreal's bourgeois society. In this setting elder fur trade masters could teach new masters how to assert authority over their servants. Virtually no fur trade labourers (and very few clerks) were ever invited to the Beaver Club. In the mid-eighteenth century some men were able to rise from the rank of worker to manager, but by the time of the emergence of the NWC in the 1780s, the social and occupational hierarchies were firmly in place. Attitudes toward the lower orders, however, covered a complex and contradictory range, especially for fur traders who had lived and worked alongside their labour force in isolated and dangerous settings for long periods. Although fur trade bourgeois often admired voyageurs for their strength and skill and established relationships with them built on trust and interdependence, they also considered voyageurs to be thoughtless, irrational, and rude.[18] Club rituals

imitating voyageurs helped the bourgeois to distance themselves from their workers. One of the most frequently mentioned amusements was the singing of voyageur songs.[19] Club member James Hughes told stories of the men arranging themselves on the floor, imitating the vigorous paddling of a canoe, and mounting wine kegs to "shoot the rapids" from the table to the floor.[20] The romanticization of voyageurs' activities cast them as exotic curiosities. At the same time, bourgeois appropriated voyageurs' experiences in the fur trade. The bourgeois reminisced about paddling canoes and running through rapids, even though this was the work of the voyageurs. The bourgeois did not regularly risk their lives in rapids and portages, carry back-breaking packs, paddle at outrageous speeds, nor survive on minimal food, as did the voyageurs. Rather, bourgeois directed crews, managed accounts, distributed food, and had better rations than their voyageurs. The bourgeois distanced themselves from their men in the Pays d'en Haut to assert their superiority, and yet in Montreal they appropriated voyageurs' rugged behaviour to bolster their sense of manhood in the eyes of urbane Montreal merchants.

Scenes of Rule in the Pays d'en Haut

The bourgeois also tried to distance themselves from their servants while actually working in the trade. Junior clerks in particular, whose authority in isolated wintering posts was threatened by experienced labourers, were encouraged by more senior masters to establish firm lines of control. When the NWC clerk George Gordon was still a novice, he received advice from a senior clerk, George Moffatt, to be independent, confident, and very involved in the trade; Moffatt also advised: "[You should] Mixt. very seldom with the Men, rather retire within yourself than make them your companions.—I do not wish to insinuate that you should be haughty—on the contrary—affability with them at times, may get

You esteme, while the observance of a proper distance, will command respect, and procure from them ready obedience to your orders."[21] In 1807 John McDonald of Garth was sent out as a novice to take over the NWC's Red River Department, which was notorious for its corruption and difficult men. A French Canadian interpreter named Potras, who had long been in the district and had great authority among voyageurs and Aboriginal people, had to be reminded by McDonald: "You are to act under me, you have no business to think, it is for me to do so and not for you, you are to obey."[22]

Masters also enacted a "theatre of authority" in material ways. The bourgeois and the clerks performed less physical labour than the voyageurs. They were usually passengers aboard canoes and only helped their men paddle and portage in cases of extreme jeopardy. At times the rituals of travel situated masters at the head of great processions. In his reminiscences of his fur trading career, Alexander Ross described how the light canoe, used for transporting men and mail quickly through the interior, clearly positioned the bourgeois as a social superior: "The bourgeois is carried on board his canoe upon the back of some sturdy fellow generally appointed for this purpose. He seats himself on a convenient mattress, somewhat low in the centre of his canoe; his gun by his side, his little cherubs fondling around him, and his faithful spaniel lying at his feet. No sooner is he at his ease, than his pipe is presented by his attendant, and he then begins smoking, while his silken banner undulates over the stern of his painted vessel."[23] HBC surveyor Philip Turnor both envied and criticized the Montreal traders: "[They] give Men which never saw an Indian One Hundred Pounds pr Annum, his Feather Bed carried in the Canoe, his Tent which is exceeding good, pitched for him, his Bed made and he and his girl carried in and out of the Canoe and when in the Canoe never touches a Paddle unless for his own pleasure all of these indulgences I have been an Eye Witness to."[24] Likewise, the bourgeois did not participate in the vigorous round of activities that kept the post functioning smoothly, such as constructing and maintaining houses; building furniture, sleighs, and canoes; gathering fire wood; hunting; and preparing food. Rather, they kept accounts, managed the wares and provisions, and initiated trade with Aboriginal peoples.

. . .

Probably the greatest challenges the bourgeois and the clerks faced in asserting authority and controlling their workers came from the circumstance of the fur trade itself—the great distances along fur trade routes and between posts and the difficulties of transportation and communication. Thus, the further they penetrated the interior, away from the larger fur trade administrative centres, the more the bourgeois had to rely on inexpensive symbols and actions to enforce their authority, such as carefully maintained social isolation, differential work roles, control over scarce resources, reputation, and ability.[25]

. . .

Obligations

In paternalist contexts the masters' material advantages came with a symbolic and substantive price. As in maypole ceremonies servants expected that masters share the scarce resources of drink and food. On a symbolic level servants insisted their masters perform the paternalistic obligations that went hand in hand with authority.

Masters commonly met paternalistic obligations by providing voyageurs with drams (shots of alcohol) or regales (treats of alcohol, food, or tobacco). The frequency of providing drams or treats varied among masters and was affected by the availability of resources and the morale of a crew. Masters provided regales when settling accounts with servants and signing new engagements.[26] Voyageurs were awarded drams when they completed significant duties, such as building houses or erecting flagstaffs, the last task in constructing a post.[27] Drams marked arrivals to and departures from posts.[28] Masters were inclined to reward exhausting tasks such as the constant travel in winter between posts, hunting camps, Aboriginal peoples' lodges, and traps. Travelling in the company of Aboriginal people was often perceived as hazardous or risky, and masters frequently provided these travellers with drams as extra incentive, especially to those who were camping at Aboriginal lodges.[29]

Historian Craig Heron observes that in pre-industrial Canada "booze was obviously intended to fortify the manual worker for heavy toil, or to sustain him in carrying it out."[30] Likewise, in the fur trade masters incorporated routine "rewards" into the tedious and trying aspects of fur trade work, such as portaging.[31] Voyageurs also rewarded themselves after difficult portages by saving their regales for such occasions.[32] Constructing furniture or snowshoes could be rewarded with a dram.[33] Sometimes the giving of gratuities was self-interested, such as when Alexander McKay gave his men moose skins to make themselves shoes, mittens, and blankets to last them through the winter, warning them that they had "a strong opposition to contend with" that year and they must be ready to go at a moment's notice.[34] He apparently believed his gift would help the voyageurs to perform their duties more effectively.

As part of this general encouragement, masters treated their men with drams at the end of a day of hard work.[35] Masters also could provide drams at the start of a day or of a difficult task as added incentive.[36] The promise of a dram as a reward was often made explicitly to coax voyageurs to work harder and faster.[37] In one case during a particularly gruelling canoe journey, Alexander Mackenzie became fearful that his men would desert, so he cajoled them with a "hearty meal, and rum enough to raise their spirits," before resorting to threats and humiliation.[38] While on the Columbia River in the early nineteenth century, Ross Cox's party encountered

hostile Aboriginal people. The bourgeois in charge, Stuart, gave "each man a double allowance of rum, 'to make his courage cheerie.'"[39] Masters also gave the Aboriginal wives and families of voyageurs gifts.[40] Including families in gift giving was a tacit acknowledgement of their importance at interior posts. Maintaining the goodwill of Aboriginal wives was essential to traders dependent on their knowledge and skill. Providing men with drams and regales seemed to mirror the custom of gift giving in trading with Aboriginal peoples.[41]

. . .

Scenes of Resistance

Despite these points of accommodation, the fur trade workplace was infused with voyageur resistance to their masters' authority. Although voyageurs rarely challenged the structure of power, they constantly tried to shape the workplace to improve their lot. Voyageurs' discontents focused sharply on unsuitable working and living conditions, such as poor rations or unreasonable demands by bourgeois or clerks. They employed a number of tactics to initiate change, ranging from the relatively mild strategy of complaining to the extreme of deserting the service.

Voyageurs' complaining became a form of countertheatre that contested the masters' performances of their hegemonic prerogatives. Just as masters asserted their authority in a theatrical style, especially in canoe processions, voyageurs asserted their agency by "a theatre of threat and sedition."[42] In one illuminating example, in the summer of 1804 while trying to travel through low water and marshes, Duncan Cameron's men ceaselessly complained about the miserable conditions and difficulty of constantly portaging. They cursed themselves as "Blockheads" for coming to that "Infernal Part of the Country," as they called it, damning the mud, damning the lack of clean water to quench their thirst, and damning the first person who attempted that road. Cameron tried to be patient and cheerful with them, as he knew that complaining was their custom.[43] Voyageurs sometimes chose to limit their resistance to complaining to their bourgeois or clerk in private, so that they would not appear weak in front of the other men. During a difficult trip from Kaministiquia to Pembina, Alexander Henry the Younger commented that little or nothing was said during the day when the men had "a certain shame or bashfulness about complaining openly," but at night everyone came to gripe about bad canoes, ineffective co-workers, and shortages of gum, wattap, and grease.[44] But depending on the attitude of the bourgeois, voyageurs could also restrain their complaining in front of their master in order to avoid losing favour. In many cases their demands were more likely to be met if they approached their master individually with strategic concerns rather than openly abusing their masters for unspecified grievances. . . .

When labour was scarce, men often bargained for better wages, both individually and collectively. In a large and organized show of resistance in the summer of 1803, men at Kaministiquia, on the western tip of Lake Superior, refused to work unless they received higher pay.[45] Group efforts to increase wages were much rarer than the relatively common occurrence of men individually bargaining for better wages. Daniel Sutherland of the XYC [XY Company] instructed his recruiting agent in Montreal, St. Valur Mailloux, to refuse demands made by a couple of *engagés* for higher wages and to appease the men with small presents. One *engagé* named Cartier caused turmoil by telling the XYC wintering partners that Mailloux was hiring men at significantly higher wages and asking for his pay to be increased to that amount. Sutherland became angry with Mailloux, warning him: "Always [offer more to] oarsman and steersman, but never exceed the price that I told you for going and coming [pork eaters]."[46] Voyageurs could refuse to do tasks outside the normal range of their duties without extra pay as another means of increasing their wages.[47] . . .

Voyageurs had a reputation among all fur trade companies in North America as very skilled canoemen, and Montreal companies and the HBC often competed for voyageurs' contracts.[48] In a letter to the governor and the committee of the HBC, Andrew Graham, master at York Fort, wrote: "The Canadians are chosen Men inured to hardships & fatigue, under which most of Your Present Servants would sink, A Man in the Canadian Service who cannot carry two Packs of eighty Lbs. each, one & an half League losses his trip that is his Wages. But time & Practice would make it easy, & even a few Canadians may be got who would be thankful for Your Honours Service."[49] Their reputation made it easy for voyageurs to switch fur trade companies if they wanted to increase their wages or change their posting or if they were angry with their master.[50] Alexander Henry the Younger was disgusted by some men's lack of loyalty:

> [T]he voyageurs southward, about Michilimackinac, the Mississippi, etc., are in the habit of changing employers yearly, according to wages offered, or as the whim takes them, which, with the spirit of competition in the South trade, and the looseness and levity they acquire in the Indian country, tends to make them insolent and intriguing fellows, who have no confidence in the measures or promises of their employers. Servants of this description cannot be trusted out of sight; they give merely eye service, and do nothing more than they conceive they are bound to do by their agreement, and even that with a bad grace.[51]

Voyageurs who had worked in the service for some time often became expert bargainers, frustrating bourgeois and clerks who expected to be obeyed without hesitation. Clerk George Nelson expressed his frustration with servants: "The common men of all companies, places, who, or whatever they are, are always fretful, jealous, discontend & gluttonous, let the places or country be what it may, rich or poor, be the master ever so kind & indulgent, unless he be prudent & severe, not a little, the men will be always found the same, men; and only want an opportunity for shewing themselves so:—it is still worse where the country is hard."[52] The fretful, jealous, discontented, and gluttonous voyageurs were most likely those who negotiated for the best terms in their contracts and knew their worth. Their loyalty to their masters did not extend past their contract, and some of the men who went to work for the HBC did not hesitate to apprise HBC officers of the business plans of the NWC to please their new masters.[53] Men with uncommon skills and knowledge, such as interpreters and guides, were in the best position to bargain for better working conditions and more pay.[54] Because fur trade labour was often scarce, and the mortality rate was high, skilled men were valued. Masters often overlooked servant transgressions and met servant demands in an effort to maintain their services.

Another common strategy voyageurs employed to improve their working conditions was to deceive their bourgeois or clerk by pretending to be ill or by lying about resources and Aboriginal peoples in the area in order to evade work. It is difficult to judge the extent to which voyageurs tried to trick their masters, especially when they were successful. However, hints of this practice and suspicions of masters appear frequently in fur trade journals, suggesting that the practice was widespread. In December 1818 George Nelson, stationed near the Dauphin River, became frustrated with one of his men, Welles, who frequently sneaked in "holiday" time by travelling slowly or claiming to be lost.[55] Less-suspicious bourgeois and clerks probably did not catch half of the "dirty tricks" more careful voyageurs regularly played on them. Some masters, however, questioned their men's dubious actions and sent out "spies" to ensure that voyageurs were working honestly.[56] Other deceptions were more serious. Alexander Mackenzie was suspicious that his interpreters were not telling

Aboriginal people what Mackenzie intended, which could have had serious repercussions for the trade.[57]

When efforts to deceive their masters were frustrated, voyageurs could become sullen and indolent, working slowly and ineffectively, and even openly defying their masters' orders. In one case in the fall of 1800, while trying to set out from Fort Chipewyan, James Porter had to threaten to seize the wages of a man who refused to embark. When the voyageur reluctantly complied, he swore that the devil should take him for submitting to the bourgeois.[58] More serious breaches of the master–servant contract included stealing provisions from cargo. Though Edward Umfreville kept a constant watch over the merchandise in his canoes, a father and son managed to steal a nine-gallon keg of mixed liquor.[59] George Nelson described the pilfering of provisions as routine.[60] Men stole provisions to give extra food to their girlfriends or wives.[61] For the Orcadians working in the HBC service, Edith Burley characterizes this type of countertheatre—working ineffectively and deceiving masters—as both a neglect of duty and an attempt to control the work process.[62] The same applies to the voyageurs.

. . .

If voyageurs became frustrated with small acts of daily resistance, they engaged in direct action against their masters' rule. Deserting the service was an outright breach of the master–servant contract.[63] Voyageurs deserted the service for a variety of purposes. Temporary desertions could provide a form of vacation, a ploy for renegotiating terms of employment, and an opportunity to look for a better job. The act of deserting the service shows that voyageurs had a clear notion of their rights as workers, which was instilled by the reciprocal obligations of paternalism. This may be one of the more significant differences between voyageurs and labourers from the Scottish Orkney Islands who worked for the HBC. Orcadians did not desert very often because they had nowhere to go once they left the service. It was virtually impossible to find passage on a ship back to Great Britain because most ships belonged to the HBC. Orcadian labourers had fewer opportunities to form close ties with Aboriginal peoples in the Northwest because the fur trade officers conducted most of the trade, and HBC employees mainly lived within the confines of trading posts. Possible refuges for deserting Orcadians were posts of competing traders, such as the NWC and XYC, where they could look for alternative employment or find passage to the Canadian colonies.[64] Conversely, voyageurs working in the Montreal trade had the options of becoming freemen, joining Aboriginal families, or returning to the St. Lawrence valley.

Discipline

As part of the continual negotiations between masters and servants, the bourgeois responded to voyageurs' acts of resistance with intense performances of authority. The bourgeois and the clerks disciplined their men for transgressions of the master–servant contract and as a means of encouraging voyageur obedience. They withheld servant privileges, such as regales, drams, and liquor for purchase.[65] They frequently humiliated and intimidated their men. In one case during a journey to the Peace River in the summer of 1793, Alexander Mackenzie was confronted with a man who refused to embark in the canoe. He wrote: "This being the first example of absolute disobedience which had yet appeared during the course of our expedition, I should not have passed it over without taking some very severe means to prevent a repetition of it; but as he had the general character of a simple fellow, among his companions, and had been frightened out of what little sense he possessed, by our late dangers, I rather preferred to consider him as unworthy of accompanying us, and to represent him as an object of ridicule and contempt for his pusillanimous behaviour; though, in fact, he was a very useful, active, and laborious man."[66] Mackenzie also confronted the chief canoe

maker during the same trip about his laziness and bad attitude. The voyageur was mortified by being singled out.[67] This kind of ritualized public shaming reinforced masculine ideals of effectiveness and skill. On an expedition to the Missouri in 1805, one of Antoine Larocque's men wished to remain with Charles McKenzie's party. Larocque became angry and told the voyageur his courage failed him like an old woman, which threw the voyageur into a violent fit of anger.[68] On occasion a voyageur was whipped for delinquency. For example, at Fort Alexandria Archibald McLeod became frustrated with voyageurs La Rose and Ducharme for leaving part of a cargo of meat and some blankets behind at an Aboriginal lodge. McLeod recorded in his journal: "La Rose being the only one I saw, got Seven reprehensions for his carelessness, in respect of the Blanket & their leaving a part of the meat, I told him I Should charge the Blanket to his At [account] untill I learned whether it is lost or not. he means to return tomorrow, to learn the fate of the Blanket, & fetch the remainder of the meat."[69] Bourgeois and clerks sometimes played on the fear of starvation as a means of asserting authority over their men.[70]

In cases of severe dereliction bourgeois had the power to fire their employees.[71] In some cases voyageurs were happy to be dismissed because they desired to become freemen, as in the case of Joseph Constant, whom Nelson fired for his "fits of ill humour without cause."[72] It was a very serious matter when voyageurs decided to quit. Masters made efforts to recoup deserters and could punish deserters with confinement. In 1804 in the Rainy Lake area, NWC clerk Hugh Faries spotted a deserter named Gâyou from the Athabasca River brigade at an XYC post. Faries reported that the principal NWC clerk of the Rainy Lake District, Archibald McLellan "sent Jourdain [a voyageur] up with a note, desiring Lacombe [the head of the XYC post] to send [Gâyou] down. he told him, he might go if he pleased, but the fellow would not come down. Mr. McLellan went himself, & Richard [a voyageur] and [Faries] followed him. the fellow made no resistance but came down immediately. Mr. McLellan put him into a cellar swarming with fleas for the night."[73] Relations between masters and voyageurs were often tense, and on rare occasions the relationship could become violent. The usual difficulties of the weather, accidents, and the constant challenge of the strenuous work could lead to high levels of stress and anxiety. Voyageurs' blunders, lost and broken equipment, and voyageur insolence often resulted in tense situations.[74] Alexander Henry the Younger grew frustrated with one of his men, Desmarrais, for not protecting the buffalo he had shot from wolves. He grumbled: "My servant is such a careless, indolent fellow that I cannot trust the storehouse to his care. I made to-day a complete overhaul, and found everything in the greatest confusion; I had no idea matters were so bad as I found them. . . . Like most of his countrymen, he is much more interested for himself than for his employer."[75] Mutual resentments could lead to brawls between the masters and the servants. . . .

More typically tensions between masters and servants were expressed in unfair treatment rather than violence. Motivated by the desire to save money and gain the maximum benefit from their workers, the bourgeois and the clerks pushed their men to work very hard, which could result in ill will. Most serious cases of ill will and injustice concerned bourgeois selling goods to voyageurs at inflated prices and encouraging voyageurs to go into debt as soon as they entered fur trade service. It is difficult to find many cases of "bad faith" in the bourgeois' own writings, as they would not likely dwell on their cruelty as masters or reveal their unfair tricks. However, travellers, critics of fur trade companies, and disgruntled employees provided clues. The French Duke de La Rouchefoucauld Liancourt and Lord Selkirk charged that the NWC deliberately tried to ensure that their men went into debt by encouraging them to drink and throw their money away on "luxeries" and then charging their men highly inflated prices for these goods.[76]

Insurgency

Voyageur responses to masters' cruelty could reach intense levels of resistance. Ill will between servants and masters usually impeded work. Sometimes the tensions were so strong that voyageurs refused to share with masters the food they obtained hunting and fishing.[77] The more outrageous instances of masters abusing servants could lead to collective resistance among the voyageurs in the form of strikes or mass desertion. When a voyageur named Joseph Leveillé was condemned by the Montreal Quarter Sessions to the pillory for having accepted the wages of two rival fur trading firms in 1794, a riot ensued. A group made up largely of voyageurs hurled the pillory into the St. Lawrence River and threatened to storm the prison. The prisoner was eventually released, and no one was punished for the incident.[78] Voyageurs seemed to have developed a reputation for mob belligerence in Lower Canada. Attorney General Jonathan Sewell warned in a 1795 letter to Lieutenant Colonel Beckworth that officers in Lower Canada should be given greater discretionary power to counter the "riotous inclinations" of the people, especially of the "lawless band" of voyageurs.[79] Mass rioting and collective resistance sometimes occurred in New France and Lower Canada.[80] However, the small population, diffuse work settings, and not too unreasonable seigneurial dues usually restricted expressions of discontent to individual desertions or localized conflicts.[81] Yet instances of collective action created a precedent for mass protest.[82] On occasion voyageurs deserted en masse during cargo transports or exploration missions. In these cases their tasks were difficult and dangerous, and men worked closely together in large groups, performing essentially the same type of work. Communication, the development of a common attitude toward work, and camaraderie fostered collective consciousness and encouraged collective action. In the summer of 1794 a Montreal brigade at Lac La Pluie attempted to strike for higher wages. Duncan McGillivray explained: "A few discontented persons in their Band, wishing to do as much mischief as possible assembled their companions together several times on the Voyage Outward & represented to them how much their Interest suffered by the passive obedience to the will of their masters, when their utility to the Company, might insure them not only of better treatment, but of any other conditions which they would prescribe with Spirit & Resolution."[83] When they arrived at Lac La Pluie, the brigade demanded higher wages and threatened to return to Montreal without the cargo. The bourgeois initially prevailed upon a few of the men to abandon the strike. Soon afterward most of the men went back to work, and the ringleaders were sent to Montreal in disgrace.

Efforts at collective action in the Northwest did not always end in failure. In his third expedition to Missouri Country in the fall of 1805 and the winter of 1806, Charles McKenzie's crew of four men deserted. They had been lodged with Black Cat, a chief in a Mandan village, who summoned McKenzie to his tent to inform McKenzie of their desertion. The men had traded away all of their property to the Mandans and intended to do the same with McKenzie's property, but Black Cat secured it. When McKenzie declared he would punish his men, Black Cat warned that the Mandans would defend the voyageurs. McKenzie tried to persuade the men to return to service, but they would not yield.[84] As this shows, men who spent their winters in the Pays d'en Haut became a skilled and highly valued labour force; they felt entitled to fair working conditions and were not afraid to work together to pressure the bourgeois.[85]

Despite the occasions of mass action, voyageurs acted individually more often than collectively, like the Orcadians working for the HBC.[86] Their most powerful bargaining chip in labour relations was the option of desertion. Although the bourgeois took voyageurs to court for deserting their contracts, the measure had little effect because voyageurs continued to

desert anyway. The option to desert acted as a safety valve, relieving pressure from the master–servant relationship. If voyageurs were very unhappy with their master, they could leave to work for another company, return to Lower Canada, or become freemen. Collective action was also hindered because voyageurs seemed to idealize freedom and independence.[87] Desertion of individuals worked against a collective voyageur consciousness.

Some permanent deserters maintained a casual relationship with fur trading companies, serving the occasional limited contract or selling furs and provisions. One man, Brunet, was pressured to desert because his Aboriginal wife wanted to join her relatives rather than stay at the post. George Nelson negotiated with Brunet to provide him with a more informal contract and allowed Brunet and his wife to leave if they helped the company make trading contacts with her family.[88] Conversely, another man named Vivier decided to quit his contract in November 1798 because he could not stand living with Aboriginal people, as he was ordered to do by his bourgeois, John Thomson, who noted: "[H]e says that he cannot live any longer with them & that all the devils in Hell cannot make him return, & that he prefers marching all Winter from one Fort to another rather than Live any Longer with them."[89] Thomson refused to give him provisions or equipment because in the fall he had provided him with enough to pass the winter. Thomson had been frustrated with the man's behaviour all season, as he had refused to return to the fort when ordered. Vivier had become so disenchanted with the trade that he offered his wife and child to another voyageur so he could return to Canada, but his wife protested. Thomson finally agreed to provide him with ammunition, tobacco, and an axe on credit, and Vivier left the post. A month and a half later Vivier returned to the post to work.[90] Voyageurs may have returned to work for fur trade companies because they could not find enough to eat or desired the protection that a post provided. Fear of starvation and the dangers of the Northwest may have discouraged voyageurs from deserting in the first place. In one case Alexander Henry the Younger came across a pond where Andre Garreau, a NWC deserter, had been killed in 1801 with five Mandans by a Swiss party.[91]

Despite the efforts of the bourgeois to impose a system of organization on the Montreal fur trade, the terms of work for voyageurs were not fixed. The changing needs of the fur trade companies and the habitants led to fluctuations in recruitment, engagements, and wages. The instability in the system was probably key to providing the flexibility necessary to the growth of the fur trade companies, especially in the context of the fierce competition for furs in the interior.

Although it is difficult to quantify the occurrence of turbulence and accommodation in the relations between masters and servants, negotiations over acceptable labour conditions dominated the Northwest fur trade. Masters tried to exert control over the workforce by encouraging men to become indebted to their company and by being the sole providers of European goods in the interior. Masters also capitalized on risk taking and the tough masculine ethos to encourage a profitable work pace. However, their most successful way to maintain order was to impress their men with their personal authority, generated by a strong manner, bravery, and effective management of servants and limited resources. Formal symbols, such as dress, ritual celebrations, access to better provisions, and a lighter workload, reminded voyageurs of the superior status and power of masters. This theatre of daily rule helped to construct the hegemonic structure of paternal authority. Masters also turned to the courts to prosecute their men for breaches of contract and attempted to co-operate with other companies to regulate the workforce, but these methods were far from successful in controlling their voyageurs. The most effective means of asserting authority was through rituals and symbols. In turn voyageurs resisted master authority in their own countertheatre in an effort

to shape their working environment. Voyageurs generally had very high performance standards for work, which were bolstered by masculine ideals of strength, endurance, and risk taking. Nonetheless, voyageurs created a space to continually challenge the expectations of their masters, in part through their complaining. They set their own pace, demanded adequate and even generous diets, refused to work in bad weather, and frequently worked to rule. When masters made unreasonable demands or failed to provide adequate provisions, voyageurs responded by working more slowly, becoming insolent, and occasionally free-trading and stealing provisions. More extreme expressions of discontent included turning to the Lower Canadian courts for justice, but, like the bourgeois, voyageurs found that their demands were better met by negotiating for a better lot off the legal record. Their strongest bargaining chip proved to be deserting the service, which they sometimes did en masse. Overall voyageurs tended to act individually more than collectively, as the option to desert the service discouraged the development of a collective voyageur consciousness. . . .

  More online.

Notes

1. Robert M. Ballantyne, *Hudson Bay; or, Every-Day Life in the Wilds of North America during Six Years' Residence in the Territories of the Honourable Hudson's Bay Company* (London, UK: William Blackwood & Sons, 1848; reprint Edmonton, AB: Hurtig, 1972), 191–2.

2. See Allan Greer, *The Patriots and the People: The Rebellion of 1837 in Rural Lower Canada* (Toronto, ON: University of Toronto Press, 1993), 107–13; Robert L. Hall, *An Archaeology of the Soul: North American Indian Belief and Ritual* (Urbana, IL: University of Illinois Press, 1997), 107–8; and Robin Ridington and Dennis Hastings, *Blessing for a Long Time: The Sacred Pole of the Omaha Tribe* (Lincoln, NE: University of Nebraska Press, 1997), 1–3, 53–54, 66–67, 68–106.

3. Antonio Gramsci, *Selections from the Prison Notebooks*, ed. and trans. Quintin Hoare and Geoffrey Nowell Smith (New York, NY: International Publishers, 1971); John Thurston, "Hegemony," in *Encyclopedia*

of *Contemporary Literary Theory: Approaches, Scholars, Terms*, ed. Irena R. Makaryk (Toronto, ON: University of Toronto Press, 1993), 549–50.

4. For a discussion of cultural hegemony and the consent of the masses to be ruled, see T. J. Jackson Lears, "The Concept of Cultural Hegemony: Problems and Possibilities," *American Historical Review* 90, no. 3 (1985): 568–70.

5. Edith Burley also found that the relationship between masters and servants in the HBC was constantly subject to negotiation. Edith I. Burley, *Servants of the Honourable Company: Work, Discipline, and Conflict in the Hudson's Bay Company, 1770–1879* (Toronto, ON: Oxford University Press, 1997), 110–11.

6. E. P. Thompson, *Customs in Common* (London, UK: Merlin, 1991), 85–6.

7. Library and Archives Canada (LAC), MG21, Add. MSS-21661–21892, cited by Harold Adams Innis, *The Fur Trade in Canada: An Introduction to Canadian Economic History* (Toronto, ON: University of Toronto Press, 1956), 221.

8. *Ordinances and Acts of Quebec and Lower Canada*, 36 George III, chap. 10, 7 May 1796. See also G. W. Wickstead, *Table of the Provincial Statutes and Ordinances in Force or Which Have Been in Force in Lower Canada* (Toronto, ON, 1857).

9. Grace Laing Hogg and Gwen Shulman, "Wage Disputes and the Courts in Montreal, 1816–35," in *Class, Gender and the Law in Eighteenth- and Nineteenth-Century Quebec: Sources and Perspectives*, eds. Donald Fyson, Colin M. Coates, and Kathryn Harvey (Montreal, QC: Montreal History Group, 1993), 129.

10. For one example, see Montreal, McCord Museum of Canadian History, M17607, M17614, Deposition of Basil Dubois, 21 June 1798, and Complaint of Samuel Gerrard, of the firm of Parker, Gerrard, and Ogilvie against Basil Dubois.

11. Archives nationales de Québec, dépôt de Montréal (ANQM), TL32 SI SSI, Robert Aird vs. Joseph Boucher, 1 April 1785, JP Pierre Foretier; Atkinson Patterson vs. Jean-Baptiste Desloriers dit Laplante, 21, April 1798, JP Thomas Forsyth; and Angus Sharrest for McGillivray & Co. vs. Joseph Papin of St. Sulpice, 14 June 1810, JP J-M. Mondelet. . . .

12. ANQM, TL16 S4/00005, 37, 27 March 1784, JPs Hertelle De Rouville and Edward Southouse; and TL16 S4/00002, no page numbers, 2 April 1778, JPs Hertelle De Rouville and Edward Southouse.

13. The JPs were William McGillivray, Duncan McGillivray, Sir Alexander Mackenzie, Roderick McKenzie, and John Ogilvy. Marjorie Campbell, *The North West Company*, (Toronto: Macmillan, 1957), 136–7.

14. LAC, MG19 BI, 131, William McGillivray to Thomas Forsyth, Esq., Grand Portage, 30 June 1800.

15. ANQM, TL16 S3/00001, 41, 314–25, 3 July 1770, and 3 July 1778, JPs Hertelle De Rouville and Edward Southouse; and TL16 S3/00008, no page numbers, 13 January 1786, JPs Hertelle De Rouville and Edward Southouse; 6 October 1786 (followed by several other entries later in the month), JPs John Fraser, Edward Southouse, and Hertelle De Rouville; 27 October 1786, JPs Edward Southouse and Hertelle De Rouville; and Henry (the Younger), *New Light*, 27 March 1814, 2: 860–1.

16. Hogg and Shulman, "Wage Disputes," 128, 132, 135–40, 141–3.

17. See Carolyn Podruchny, "Festivities, Fortitude and Fraternalism: Fur Trade Masculinity and the Beaver Club, 1785–1827," in *New Faces in the Fur Trade: Selected Papers of the Seventh North American Fur Trade Conference*, eds. William C. Wicken, Jo-Anne Fiske, and Susan Sleeper-Smith East Lansing, MI: Michigan State University Press, 1998), 31–52.

18. For example, see Daniel W. Harmon, *Sixteen Years in Indian Country: The Journal of Daniel Williams Harmon, 1800–16*, ed. W. Kaye Lamb (Toronto, ON: Macmillan, 1975), 197–8.

19. Montreal, McCord Museum of Canadian History, M144450, *Rules and Regulations*, 3; and Reed, *Masters of the Wilderness*, 68.

20. Charles Burt Reed, *Masters of the Wilderness* (Chicago, IL: University of Chicago Press, 1914), 68.

21. Ontario Archives (OA), MU 1146, Moffatt, Fort William, to George Gordon, Monontagué [sic], 25 July 1809. See also James Scott Hamilton, "Fur Trade Social Inequality and the Role of Non-Verbal Communication" (Ph.D. dissertation, Simon Fraser University, Vancouver, 1990), 135–6. . . .

22. LAC, MG19 A17, 119–21.

23. Alexander Ross, *Fur Hunters of the Far West: A Narrative of Adventures in the Oregon and Rocky Mountains*, 2 vols. (London, UK: Smith, Elder, 1855), 1: 301–2.

24. J. B. Tyrrell, ed., *Journals of Samuel Hearne and Philip Turnor*, journal 3, "A Journal of the Most Remarkable Transactions and Occurrences from York Fort to Cumberland House, and from said House to York Fort from 9th Septr 1778–15th Septr 1779 by Mr. Philip Turnor," 15 July 1779 (Toronto, ON: Champlain Society, 1934), 252.

25. As described by Hamilton, "Fur Trade Social Inequality," 137–8, 261–3.

26. For examples, see Henry (the Younger), *New Light*, 23 July 1800, and 6 May 1804, 1: 10, 243; Harmon, *Sixteen Years*, 19 July 1807, 105; and Ross Cox, *Adventures on the Columbia River, including the Narrative of a Residence of Six Years on the Western Side of the Rocky Mountains, among Various Tribes of Indians Hitherto Unknown: Together with a Journey across the American Continent*, 2

vols. (London, UK: Henry Colburn & Richard Bentley, 1831), 19 September 1817, 304–5.

27. For an example of completing a house, see Toronto Metropolitan Reference Library Baldwin Room (TBR), S13, George Nelson's Journal, 29 August 1805–8 March 1806, 10 October 1805. For examples of erecting flag-staffs, see LAC, MG19 CI, vol. 14, 11 November 1799, 3a; LAC, MG19 CI, vol. 6, 11 October 1800, 54. . . .

28. LAC, MG19 CI, vol. 7, 10 February 1799, 30; LAC, MG19 CI, vol. 6, 28 and 29 February, 7 April, and 16 May 1800, 1, 2, 12, 21; Henry (the Younger), *New Light*, 4 September 1800, 1: 78; McGill University Libraries (MRB), Masson Collection (MC), C.26, 11 January, 7 and 22 February 1801, 20, 22, 25; and MRB, MC, C.28, 2 and 3 October 1807, 8. . . .

29. LAC, MG19 CI, vol. 7, 12, 18, and 27 October 1798, 8, 11–12, 15; and LAC, MG19 CI, vol. 14, 19 October 1799, 3. . . .

30. Craig Heron, *Booze: A Distilled History* (Toronto, ON: Between the Lines, 2003), 34.

31. In 1797 Charles Chaboillez commented at a portage that "after they had finished according to custom gave the People each a Dram." LAC, MG19 CI, vol. I, 11 August 1797, 3. . . .

32. Henry (the Younger), *New Light*, 23 July 1800, 1: 10.

33. MRB, MC, C.26, 5 and 24 February 1801, 22, 27. . . .

34. Ca. 20 June 1807, described in TBR, S13, George Nelson's journal "No. 5," 186.

35. LAC, MG19 CI, vol. I, 29 August 1797, 6; Henry (the Younger), *New Light*, 26 September 1800, 2: 98; LAC, MG19 CI, vol. 13, 9 October 1804, 22; and Fraser, "First Journal," 8 July 1806, 140.

36. MRB, MC, C.26, 10 October 1798, 6; and Henry (the Younger), *New Light*, 9 and 10 September 1800, 1: 91, 93.

37. LAC, MG19 CI, vol. 13, 12 October 1804, 22.

38. Alexander Mackenzie, *Voyages from Montreal on the River St. Laurence through the Continent of North America to the Frozen and Pacific Oceans in the Years 1789 and 1793 with a Preliminary Account of the Rise, Process, and Present State of the Fur Trade of That Country* (London, UK: R. Noble, Old Bailey, 1801), 13 June 1793, 322–6.

39. Cox, *Adventures on the Columbia River*, 111–13, 173–6.

40. MRB, MC, C.26, 1 January 1801, 19. . . .

41. For some examples see Arthur J. Ray, *Indians in the Fur Trade: Their Roles as Hunters, Trappers and Middlemen in the Lands Southwest of Hudson Bay, 1660–1870* (Toronto, ON: University of Toronto Press, 1974), 137–42. . . .

42. E. P. Thompson, *Customs in Common*, 67.

43. MRB, MC, CI, 38–9.

44. Henry (the Younger), *New Light*, 28 July 1804, 1: 247–8.

45. Mentioned in Henry (the Younger), *New Light*, 1 July 1804, 1: 247.

46. LAC, MG19 A7, D. Sutherland to Monsr. St. Valur Mailloux, Montreal, 10 November 1802, 29 November 1802, and 20 December 1802, 18–19, 2572 6. My translation.

47. For one example of men demanding their pay be doubled for extra duties, see LAC, MG CI, 20 March 1798, 49.

48. MRB, MC, C.29, 42–4; TBR, S13, George Nelson's journal, 30 November 1815–13 January 1816, 31 December 1815, 1 and 7 January 1816, 92–4, 97; LAC, MG19 BI, William McGillivray to Murdock Cameron, Montreal, 10 May 1799, and 23 May 1802, 44–5, 183; and R. McKenzie, "Reminiscences," Alexander Mackenzie to Roderick McKenzie, Rivière Maligne, 1 September 1787, 1: 20.

49. Extracts from a Letter of Andrew Graham, Master at York Fort, to the Governor and Committee of the HBC, dated York Fort, 26 August 1772, in W. Stewart, Wallace, ed., *Documents Relating to the North West Company*, 26 August 1772 (Toronto, ON: Champlain Society, 1934), 43.

50. TBR, S13, George Nelson's journal, 1 April 1810–1 May 1811, 18 and 20 June 1810, 13–14 (my pagination); TBR, S13, George Nelson's journal and reminiscences, 13 September 1836; and MRB, MC, C.13, 31 July 1800, 60–1 (my pagination).

51. Henry (the Younger), *New Light*, Sunday, 17 April 1814, 2: 890.

52. TBR, S13, George Nelson's journal, 29 January–23 June, 7 February 1815, 3.

53. Hudson's Bay Company Archives (HBCA), B.89/a/2, 15 and 21 June 1810, fols. 2, 3.

54. LAC, MG19 CI, vol. 3, 8–15; and TBR, S13, George Nelson, 29 January–23 June 1815, 8 April 1815, 30–2.

55. See entries 2 November and 1–30 December 1818, OA, MU 842, 10–11, 18–23.

56. LAC, MG19 CI, vol. 15, 26 June 1800, 7.

57. MRB, MC, C.8, 5 March 1806, 125. See also Lloyd Keith, ed., *North of Athabaska: Slave Lake and Mackenzie River Documents of the North West Company, 1800–21* (Montreal, QC: McGill-Queen's University Press, 2001), 228.

58. On a trip from Athabasca to the Mackenzie River, see LAC, MG19 CI, vol. 6, 29 September 1800, 50. . . .

59. OA, MU 2199, Edward Umfreville. . . .

60. George Nelson, *My First Years in the Fur Trade: The Journals of 1802–4*, eds. Laura Peers and Theresa Schenck (St. Paul, MN: Minnesota Historical Society Press, 2002), 34–5.

61. Henry (the Younger), *New Light*, 6 August 1800, 1: 25.

62. Burley, *Servants of the Honourable Company*, 139–44.

63. For an example see MRB, MC, C.7, 5 and 6 December 1793, 4.

64. Burley, *Servants of the Honourable Company*, 153–4; and R. C. Harris, *The Resettlement of British Columbia: Essays on Colonialism and Geographical Change* (Vancouver, BC: UBC Press, 1997), 45–6.

65. For example, see MRB, MC C.24, 2 January 1801, 15.

66. Mackenzie, *Voyages from Montreal*, 15 June 1793, 329.

67. Mackenzie, *Voyages from Montreal*, 29 June 1793, 373–4.

68. MRB, MC, C.12; the account is published in W. Raymond Wood and Thomas D. Thiessen, *Early Fur Trade on the Northern Plains: Canadian Traders among the Manelan and Hidatsa Indians, 1738–1818; The Narratives of John Macdonell, David Thompson, François-Antoine Larocque, and Charles McKenzie* (Norman, OK: University of Oklahoma Press, 1985), 221–95.

69. MRB, MC C.24, 22 November 1800.

70. Nelson mentioned that fear of starvation bolstered clerks' limited authority with voyageurs. TBR, S13, George Nelson's journal "No. 1," 17 November 1809, 43.

71. TBR, S13, George Nelson's journal, 29 January 29–23 June 1815, 10 February 1815, 8; and Faries, "Diary," 2 April 1805, 235.

72. TBR, S13, George Nelson's coded journal, 17 April–20 October 1821, 10 May 1821, 14–15. . . .

73. Hugh Faries, "The Diary of Hugh Faries," in *Five Fur Traders of the Northwest*, ed. Charles M. Gates, 26 August 1804 (St. Paul, MN: Minnesota Historical Society, 1965), 206.

74. Henry (the Younger), *New Light*, 9 October 1800, 1: 114.

75. Henry (the Younger), *New Light*, 18–19 September 1800, 1: 100.

76. Duke de la Rochefoucauld Liancourt, *Voyages dans les États-Unis d'Amérique, fait en 1795, 1796 et 1797 par La Rochefoucauld-Liancourt Paris*, 2 vols. (Paris, FR: Chez Du Pont, Imprimeur-Librarire, 1799–1800), 2: 225; and Thomas Douglas, *A Sketch of the British Fur Trade in North America; with Observations Relative to the North-West Company of Montreal*, 2nd ed. (London, UK: James Ridgway, 1816), 32–47.

77. TBR, S13, George Nelson's journal, 29 January–23 June 1815, 9 March, 23 and 24 May 1815, 17–18, 40–1.

78. LAC, RG7 G15C, vol. 2, CO42, vol. 100, Sheriff Edward Gray to Attorney General James Monk, 9 June 1794; J. Reid to same, 12 June 1794; T. A. Coffin to James McGill, 21 July 1794; cited in F. Murray Greenwood, *Legacies of Fear: Law and Politics in Quebec in the Era of the French Revolution* (Toronto, ON: University of Toronto Press, 1993), 80, 285.

79. LAC, MG23 GI110, vol. 9, 4613–14, Jonathan Sewell to Lieutenant Colonel Beckworth, 28 July 1795. Donald Fyson brought this reference to my attention.

80. For example, in late December 1744, French and Swiss soldiers at Louisbourg on Isle Royale mutinied because they were dissatisfied with poor rations and meagre pay. Allan Greer, *Soldiers of Isle Royale*, Parks Canada History and Archaeology 28 (Ottawa, ON: Minister of Supply and Services Canada, 1979), 41–51.

81. Terrence Crowley, "'Thunder Gusts': Popular Disturbances in Early French Canada," *Canadian Historical Association Historical Papers* (1979): 11–31, 105–6, 114–17; and Jean-Pierre Hardy and David-Thiery Ruddel, *Les Apprentis Artisans à Québec, 1660–1815* (Quebec, QC: Les Presses de l'Université du Québec, 1977), 74–80.

82. Jean-Pierre Wallot, *Un Québec qui Bougeait: Trame socio-politique du Québec au tournant du XIXe siècle* (Montreal, QC: Boréal, 1973), 266–7.

83. Duncan McGillivray, *The Journal of Duncan McGillivray of the North West Company at Fort George on the Saskatchewan, 1794–5*, ed. Arthur S. Morton (Toronto, ON: Macmillan, 1929), 6–7.

84. MRB, MC, C.12, 72, 77–8.

85. MRB, MC, C.S, 26 July and 7 August 1806.

86. Burley, *Servants of the Honourable Company*, 118–20.

87. Ross, *Fur Hunters*, 2: 236–7.

88. Nelson, *My First Years*, 31 January, 14, 15, and 17 February 1804, 143, 148.

89. LAC, MG19 CI, vol. 7, 18–20 November 1798, 19–20.

90. LAC, MG19 CI, vol. 7, 4 January 1799, 23–4.

91. MRB, MC, C.S, 23 July 1806, 50.

12 A Colony of Miners

Daniel Samson

Albion Mines stood out from the surrounding [Nova Scotia] countryside. Writers of travel accounts routinely paused to describe the village, and several contrasted the red brick houses, smoke, and blackened landscape with the neighbouring farms. George Wightman, a Windsor-born engineer sent from Halifax by the House of Assembly to investigate the operations of the General Mining Association (GMA), described the village as "a colony of miners." His comment was meant to highlight the village's difference. Pointing to the workplace in particular, he attempted to show how the miners' work habits were inappropriate to the colony: Their wages were too high ("more than is accordant with the current prices of labour in this country"), and the company's business strategy was "not on a par" with local practice. The company's owners, managers, and workers were "applying the maxims and practices of England to a country under different circumstances."[1]

Wightman was an improver. Trained as an engineer, the friend and ally of Joseph Howe applied his utilitarian ideals to plans to bureaucratize road construction, cost overruns on the Shubenacadie Canal, and reforms to the land system in Prince Edward Island.[2] Like John Young, Captain John Macdonald, and the many others who focused their attention on agricultural practices, Wightman trained his eye on inappropriate activities and sought to apply better systems. His report on Albion Mines attempted to portray an anomaly, one that could be changed given the appropriate technique and patience. Certainly, there were differences in the ways that things were done at Albion Mines, and at Sydney Mines too, compared with elsewhere in Nova Scotia, and we should not be surprised that Wightman picked up on them. After all, looking for difference was the stock approach of the travel writer, and of the missionary, as it accounted for the peculiar—and usually aberrant—ways of the natives. Whether one was selling one's book or raising money to spread the Gospel, illustrating difference best conveyed the perceived problems. . . . [T]he coal towns at Sydney Mines and Albion Mines were planted with specific intentions that required specialized tasks and that produced fairly obvious differences compared with the surrounding countryside. Their inhabitants were digging coal, not potatoes. But how different? Can we view the mining societies as separate enclaves within the colonial countryside? Or can we detect more uniformity with their agricultural neighbours than the term "enclave" might suggest?

Citation: Daniel Samson, "A Colony of Miners," in *The Spirit of Industry and Improvement: Liberal Government and Rural–Industrial Society, Nova Scotia, 1790–1862* (Montreal, QC: McGill-Queen's University Press, 2008): 164–86.

Ordered Towns

It is difficult to "see" the miners in either of the mining towns; it is even difficult to locate miners in the census manuscripts. The major problem relates to how individuals were identified and categorized. In the period under discussion [1830–62], only the 1851 census is of much assistance, but there was no category for coal-miners, and the manuscripts for Cape Breton are missing.[3] Outside of a few professions (clergyman, lawyer, and school teacher), the census used only generic categories: One was either a merchant, a farmer, or a mechanic. The following discussion risks conflating colliers with any independent artisan in the area, as well as with most labouring employees of the GMA. Nevertheless, at least one-third of these men were skilled colliers, and at least half would have been underground employees of some sort.[4] We can learn a fair bit by briefly turning to their census returns.

. . .

So what did it mean that mining households so heavily populated this district? . . . The most obvious difference from farmers was the miners' weaker ability to provide their own food. Some, perhaps even most, of the mining households probably kept small gardens either outside their homes or in a common field behind the row houses. These would have been a vital component of these people's lives, an effort to reduce their spending on food and defer something of their reliance on wages. None of these gardens, however, were deemed worthy of note by the census enumerators. There were no formal instructions to enumerators on this point, but it was common to mark a single acre as the lower limit in the nineteenth-century census; none of these gardens would have been close to one acre. Nevertheless, despite the small gardens, a number of other "rural" practices were maintained. Almost 40 per cent of Albion Mines's miner-headed households owned one or more cows, while one household in eight reported producing

anywhere from 40 to 96 pounds of butter. About 40 per cent also reported cloth production, averaging about 26 yards of fulled and unfulled cloths and flannel. By way of comparison, East River farm households produced an average of 49.8 yards each year, and the proportion of households producing was much higher at 88.5 per cent.

Some of these figures may be surprising. That Albion Mines was composed mostly of miners should not surprise us. Nor should it surprise us that "urban" workers employed "rural" tactics such as gardening and raising animals to supplement their waged income.[5] Alan Campbell describes Lanarkshire miners as "incompletely proletarianized" and notes that mid-nineteenth-century mine officials worked hard to "erode the rural trappings" (particularly animals and firearms for hunting) of life in the district's Scottish mining towns.[6] But the extent of the "rurality" in the industrial village of Albion Mines might nonetheless seem startling. Certainly, the cloth production seems higher than we might expect, if only because the raw material would not have been easily accessible. There were also more cows roaming the backfields and laneways of Albion Mines than we might have expected. The common pattern was for households to have one milk cow and one "neat" cow (for meat). With limited storage possibilities, we must presume that they purchased a beef cow in the spring for slaughter in the fall and sold, shared, or somehow exchanged what they did not consume themselves. It also gives us a slightly better sense of the contribution of women and younger children in these households. If we can presume that women tended the cattle and the garden and made the cloth and butter, in addition to tending to the children, the cooking, the washing, the stove, and the house itself, it is evident that while this work was not as dangerous as mining, it was at least as demanding. It was also important from a simple (household) finance perspective. . . . There was nothing inherently "rural" about weaving cloth or having a cow or two. But we might also note that one commonly assumed difference between rural and urban households is the latter's greater use of and access to consumer products. It is certainly worth noting that these women, whether migrants from the surrounding countryside or Staffordshire, did not fully immerse themselves in the possibilities of the "Big Store" (the company store at Albion Mines, where it was said anything could be had).[7] Whether this was by choice or necessity is not clear, but as with poor farmers and small-holders, domestic production lessened reliance on wages, cash payments, and merchant credit.

One major difference between farm households and mining households stood out on the census forms. Enumerators were asked to note both the assessed and "probable" values of each household's holdings. It is entirely possible that, in Albion Mines, the enumerators simply never bothered asking about property values while going through a village dominated by company-owned red brick houses, but if the figure offered us is accurate, home ownership was very low. In Albion Mines only two "mechanics" in our sample were listed as having holdings with any "probable value"—an average of less than £1 per household. . . . In a colony where capital was increasingly important to anyone's betterment, this difference mattered. A few years later, a Cape Breton County farmer observed that the material life of miners compared favourably with that of poor farmer-fishers; the miners, he commented, "work well . . . are never in want, and always well clad."[8] Cash wages might allow one to be "well clad," but apparently remuneration was not substantial enough for one to purchase property. Thus miners could look forward to little security or independence.

. . .

Before 1858 and the expansion of the coal industry, the miners did therefore form something of a cultural enclave within the countryside. But were they, as some have assumed, isolated—that is, were they apart from the broader world of culture, politics, and even their

more immediate neighbourhood? To be sure, there was intercourse between the miners and everyone else, but it was limited and the miners often stood apart, consciously, to protect their hold on their workplaces and, less consciously although not unknowingly, through their beliefs and practices. In the early years of the mines, almost all of the skilled men—the colliers—were imported from Great Britain. Some had probably worked in several mines before emigrating, and the steady stream of workers arriving kept them well abreast of goings on at home.[9] And not all the Britons working in the mines had come straight from another isolated coal town. These were men who came from the south of Scotland and the north of England, and they continued to correspond with people in the old country as well as with others who had moved on to the United States. Take, for example, Peter Barrett's account of his own life. He was one of three brothers who arrived in 1866, the sons of a couple who alternated between farm labour and Methodist preaching. The three young men left their employ as farm labourers to work in coalmines in Staffordshire in order to earn the money for the crossing. Over the next 10 years, all three would continue to live their lives centred on coalmining, moving from Nova Scotia to Pennsylvania and then briefly to Upper Canada before returning to Nova Scotia; they also purchased land and farmed to the best of their abilities. Barrett, like millions before and after him, travelled the routes of the transatlantic labour market. When he was in Philadelphia, three shysters whose scam preyed on newcomers tried to take his money. As Barrett quickly figured out, many had been robbed before him, and plenty more would follow.[10]

. . .

But having had worldly experiences does not guarantee maintaining one's worldliness. . . . Were the "enclaves" so insular as to make these towns isolated? Coalminers have always been regarded as a "breed apart." They were the archetypal proletarian,[11] the extreme in nineteenth-century social relations. Historians and contemporary social commentators alike drew from a rich base of mining stereotypes when they represented coalminers and the coalmining family as a separate and notoriously fertile breed. One mid-nineteenth-century English observer commented that migration was neither a necessary nor a useful component of the coalmining labour market because "Pitmen must be bred to their work from childhood," adding that there was little need for either training or recruitment in this "notoriously prolific section of the population."[12] We have only poor figures for Nova Scotia miners' vital statistics before 1865, but we do know that in some ways they were segregated. In Pictou one commentator described the village of Albion Mines as an island of skilled workers who "fix their prices and will not consent to admit any other persons into the works."[13] Clearly, this was a comment on the workplace, not the community, but the two locations were vitally linked. In the mining villages, the workplace and many broader cultural activities intermeshed.

Economic life in the coal towns centred almost exclusively on the coalmines. There was little else. The mines provided a market for merchants, farmers, and traders from around the province as well as for shipping interests. Stores, homes, and wharves were built, and businessmen were drawn by the lure of coal and coastal trading vessels. What set the coal villages apart was their planted, town-like atmosphere. Within two years the brick manufactory at Albion Mines had produced enough bricks to build several rows of houses for miners at all four mines, and several log-framed houses were built as well. The company also built lavish homes for the managers: Mt. Rundell, at Pictou, and Beech Hill, at Sydney Mines.[14] Mt. Rundell, built for Richard Smith, overlooked the works in appropriate paternalist fashion, while Beech Hill still commands the entrance to Sydney harbour. Both were very impressive homes for their day, rivalling most anything in Halifax, and outside the

capital they were matched by very few. The presence of these orderly villages, characterized by patent hierarchies that extended from managers' mansions down to workers' red brick houses and log huts (a distinction that almost certainly represented status within the mine), was a real mark of difference. Anyone visiting the East River after about 1830 could not possibly have failed to observe the works, the village attached, and the manner in which they were organized.

The GMA treated its employees quite differently than most other employees of the time were treated. In many ways, this was good. Certainly, in terms of pay, the company's well-experienced managers treated their employees as the valuable and skilled workers that they were. It was not out of chauvinism that the GMA brought miners from Britain but because it knew the value of skilled employees.[15] Coal cutters, the men most responsible for the quality and quantity of coal removed, could earn 10s per day, while even loaders earned 4s. Boys, very often the sons of the colliers, could earn anywhere from 1s6d to 3s depending on their age. Outside the mines, few skilled workers could obtain more than 4s per day; farm labourers typically received 2s or 2s6d, and this rarely in cash. The company also provided housing at a low fixed rent, and coal was either free or available at minimal charge.[16] The housing was inexpensive, although variously described as "neat [and] well furnished" or as "low Dirty, dingy houses."[17] The drawback, however, was that Nova Scotia's export season (especially at Pictou) was limited to the period from April to January. Thus few men were paid such high wages year round. Even in summer, the peak shipping season, if demand was down, the need to produce for the next year was minimized, and even regularly employed men might obtain only a few days per month.[18]

The managers ran their operations, including their men, tightly. Discipline was emphasized. All employees were expected to produce to their best abilities and also to conduct themselves well above ground. At Sydney Mines, Richard

Brown "mustered" his men twice a year as lieutenant colonel of the militia. When faced with a poor showing, as in 1834, Brown promised the provincial secretary that in future those who did not attend would be "severely punished" and that he would "preserve order" among his men. Indeed, failure to muster would be punished in the same way that he punished insubordinate employees: Offenders would be dismissed.[19] At the same time, he could be a protector and could "lecture" an underground manager "on his conduct toward the men."[20] Typically, such paternalist actions cut both ways. On a range of day-to-day concerns, the miners were very often able to fix their own terms of employment without resorting to a strike. Brown's diaries from the early 1830s to the late 1840s record a consistent pattern of men setting their own days and hours of working. In 1849 Brown recorded that the "pits [were] idle" on 10 separate days. Three were because of poor shipping and one because of a mechanical problem, but the remainder, save for one on "account of the races," were due to St. Patrick's Day, a meeting of the "friendly society," the procession of the Temperance Society, and a "fast day."[21] Even the lieutenant colonel had to give a little slack.

Individually, the GMA and the managers exercised a substantial power over the day-to-day lives of the men from their wages to their housing conditions, the number of helpers that they could obtain, and the safety of the workplace itself. Yet the miners, with their high skills and relative scarcity, maintained a strong bargaining position. The company was, in many ways, held captive by the skill of its employees—the only explanation for the tremendously high wages that they were offered. Few incidents relate the two-sidedness of the relationship between master and men better than Richard Smith's recollection of the early days of Albion Mines. After returning to England, Smith recalled that the gas at Albion Mines, and thus the danger of explosions, was greater than anything he had witnessed before. Smith described his first few

times in the Nova Scotia mines and the experience of entering a seam where the gaseous emissions were so great that they sounded "like a hundred thousand snakes hissing."[22] Although the miners were all well experienced, none had ever worked in such strong gas before—but they knew exactly what it meant. While Smith's work was on the surface, he understood that he had to be the first down the shaft every morning: "It [the gas] was very alarming and I had to go every morning with the men . . . as I would not ask them to go where I would not go myself."[23] Smith, Brown, and the underground managers set many of the conditions, but the miners could set some too. A few years later the *Colonial Patriot* waxed lyrical about the strength of the relationship between Smith and the miners and about the "parental care" that he offered them: "He seems to look upon them as his own children," the newspaper observed, "and they upon him as a kind protector."[24] Parental, paternal, perhaps even kind—the metaphors seem to fit. But few children insist that their parents put their lives on the line as a condition of consent.

Paternalism characterized most employment relations in early nineteenth-century North Atlantic societies.[25] What marked these Nova Scotia paternalisms, however, was the effects of insular work in the industrial plantation, most notably the advantage exercised by the men through their unusual positions as highly skilled men in a highly regulated labour market, and the effects of a segregated life in the industrial plantation. Two miners' parades, one in 1833 and another in 1841, give us some sense of the clear cultural differences and similarities between the inhabitants of the industrial villages and their neighbours. They also reveal something of how the miners both understood and appreciated their place in their new home.

In December 1832 a fire shut down Albion Mines for almost six months. A year later the miners of the village staged a parade in commemoration of the incident, which had killed 14 horses.[26] The circumstances of the fire were suspicious. Believed to be the work of "incendiaries," the fire remained a mystery. A two-month local investigation and an additional inquiry by the solicitor general had been unable to find the guilty parties. On Monday, 31 December 1833,[27] a few hundred residents assembled outside the main shaft. The men had constructed, on top of a coal sled, a tableau with "a mixture of the coal charred by the conflagration, and a quantity of the bones of the horses suffocated in the pits." Standing amid the ash and bones were "two Effigies, and on a board attached . . . the characters INCENDIARIES was [sic] written large." Fourteen horses were harnessed as a team to pull the sled, with a man alongside each horse and boys mounted and carrying flags. The parade then marched off in 14 "orders," each with a flag and a horse. The first flag read "Anniversary," followed by "Fire," "Starvation of 500 persons," "Indignation," "14 Horses Murdered," and "Cruelty," and the seventh advertised the "£300 Reward." These were followed by a silent group of three carrying identical black mourning flags "bearing the skeletons of horses," followed by "Justice," "Punishment," "Pillory," and "Gridiron." The parade made the circuit of the GMA's property, "slowly [and] a large concourse of people then assembled in an orderly and peaceable manner on the spot immediately over where the fire had been below." After the parade the people reassembled with Richard Smith and some unnamed government officials, turning from the condemnation of past acts to a celebration of what had been good, and of the new year to come, with a meal of "roast Beef and plumpudding and Beer." After offering three cheers for the king, the president, the council, the House of Assembly, the GMA, the solicitor general (who had investigated the fires), and the coal trade, they offered "3 deep groans of abhorrence of the vile incendiaries and their abettors, if it be possible that such there be." Having cast the light of suspicion into the wider community, they then made clear their general goodwill by offering cheers for the success of the "surrounding

neighbourhood . . . the general prosperity of the land we live in [and] the Ships Trade and Commerce." All they desired, as they noted in their cheer for "the Constitution," was rights to the protection of "its laws and justice."[28]

It was a remarkable display. Clearly, their anger was most evident. Although they did not burn the effigies (Smith had asked them not to), the display of charred coals and bones, the black flags with skeletons, and the text ("Justice," "Punishment," "Pillory," and the delightfully medieval "Gridiron") made certain that any viewers would understand the magnitude of this crime and the colliers' complete support for the charges made by their superiors. Indeed, in some ways the parade seemed to have been as much for their superiors as for themselves. The miners also offered cheers "for the success of the Albion Mines," "the coal trade," and "Richard Smith, Esq." That they should wish their own industry well is by no means surprising—indeed, we might expect that they should be strong advocates of anything conducive to their industry's prosperity.[29] It is also in this context that we can understand the inclusion of Smith, who, like the trade and the GMA, assumed the role of provider. In a similar expression of dependence, they also exhorted their "comrades in Sydney and Bridgeport" to "treat with equal indignation, every attempt to injure and destroy the property of their employers, and to deprive themselves of honest labour and daily bread."[30] Here, the messages became more complex, and we can begin to see the multiple strategies contained in their actions. That there was condemnation and moral outrage is certain. That there was a slightly defensive edge is also evident, a sense that they were, especially in their comment on the abettors but also in the message to their "comrades" in Cape Breton, asserting their own complete innocence in the matter. Although the investigation never turned toward any of them,[31] the men seem to have felt it necessary to at least reassert their loyalty and remind their employers of the ties binding employee to employer. In this sense, then, the parade would seem to have been for the benefit of Smith and the board of directors, and perhaps the sheriff too, as much as anyone. Indeed, that the parade was confined to company property seems rather more insular than such a public display might have warranted. Parades were common public displays in both town and country.[32] It seems odd that on this occasion they confined their display to themselves and their masters, literally under the gaze of Mt. Rundell. In the paternalist order of the mine village, many actions were both acts of self-expression and paternal performances.

Another parade, six years later on the opening of the South Pictou Rail Road, suggests a broader public presence, a greater scope for worker self-activity, and a clearer assertion and affirmation of the miners' own importance. Although remaining within the bounds of paternalist performance, the mineworkers seem to have constructed a stronger place for themselves within the company's celebratory representation of itself.[33] The parade was but one element in a daylong celebration to mark the opening of the railway. Starting at 6:30 in the morning, the steamship *Pocahontas* travelled back and forth between New Glasgow, Pictou, and the Loading Ground, below the mines where the railway ended, carrying what appears to have been half the county to the site of the celebrations: "Ladies . . . *rigged* [original emphasis] out in their finest attire," together with their "gallant beaus," paraded down the main street, while the Volunteer Artillery Company marched and fired regular volleys across the river. The major show, after the parade, was the first run of the trains. The *Samson*, the *Hercules* (appropriately strong names), and the *John Buddle* (in due respect for his assistance)[34] were on display for the entire morning and afternoon, before they were "cleared of the vulgar throng [and] filled with those to whom the gentlemen of the Association had sent tickets of admission." . . .

The parade, to be sure, was part of the company-sponsored affair. But this parade suggests that the miners had a much greater role in organizing it than the previous one. Again, the procession was organized into orders, this time 10. Each of these represented a group of workmen. First came 100 horses "mounted by their respective drivers—horses and men decorated, [and] carrying flags." They carried two "devices" (i.e., banners) and a flag: The first was a large crown surrounded by a rose, a shamrock, a thistle, and a mayflower, with the motto "Long life to Queen Victoria"; the second was a depiction of "2 horses with 2 wagons coming out to the pit bottom, meeting 2 Colliers going in to their work, with picks under their arms," with the motto "Success to the coal trade; as the old cock crows the young one learns." The parade continued, with each order representing similarly the enginemen, the colliers, the freemasons, the foundrymen and blacksmiths, the bricklayers and stone masons, and the carpenters, followed by bagpipers and, finally, the Albion Mines Band.

Each device carried its own message, and in most we see the same play between an assertion of self and an ultimate dependence on the GMA. The enginemen's motto, for example, was:

Long may the Company flourish,
And their servants rejoice;
May Steam Navigation never fail
To burn our Coal and send us sail.

The carpenters' device simply read, "The Albion Mines and Joseph Smith, Esq.," while the bricklayers' said, "Success to Locomotive Engines, and All the Trades belonging to the Albion Mines." We also see the sense of craft pride found wherever we examine craftworkers in the North Atlantic world. The foundrymen and blacksmiths did not look to the coal trade so much as assert their common ties with other engineers and knowledge workers; their device represented Archimedes and James Watt with the motto "Ours and for Us; Knowledge is Power." All the mottos and devices contained the common symbols of their trades (engines, trowels, and the square and compass) and expressed their connection to a broader Atlantic world of trades.

While expressions of craft and collective pride poured from these texts, they contained only weak assertions of class solidarity. Only the colliers articulated an explicit expression of solidarity with their motto, "United we stand, when divided we fall, Unanimous as Brethren." The parade itself may have recognized some intercraft solidarities, but there was little sense that anything beyond this was binding the crafts. The issue here was more corporate than particular—that is, while the paraders separated themselves within their particular crafts, their point of unity seemed to be less their affinity as workers, or even workingmen, than their affinity as workmen in the coal trade. To be sure, there was an expression of working-class independence here, but it is doubtful that these men would have recognized it as having political consequences beyond their immediate audience. The newspaper account also noted as remarkable the "good order" with which the men conducted themselves; both in the parade and in seating and unseating themselves from dinner, they moved with an apparently military-like precision. This should not be surprising. Both Joseph Smith and Richard Brown were militia leaders, and as we have already seen, Richard Brown routinely paraded his miners.[35] In some sense, then, the parade may have been very well rehearsed.

This is not to argue that these workers were wholly subservient to a coercive paternal order. The following summer (1840) there would be a major display of independent action—a strike to protest a wage cut. And two years after this strike, there would be another, during which the colliers and their families would turn the paternal order on its head, threatening violent confrontations and terrorizing the residents of Mt. Rundell.[36] Nevertheless, we need to recognize the context of workers' dependency and the limits of even those strongly positioned within the lower end of a paternal social hierarchy. The same scarcity of workers that leveraged their wage-bargaining position also entailed their own limited access to new employments; although there was the possibility of moving elsewhere for work, such movement was not as easy in the monopolized coal industry as it would have been in Britain or in other industries within the colony. For miners in Nova Scotia, protesting with one's feet meant finding a berth aboard a train bound for New York or Philadelphia and the money to transport one's entire family. As we have already seen, this was common enough, but it was perhaps one upheaval too many for most families. Whatever their skills, whatever their pride, whatever forms of resistance they might engage in, they were employees, not independent artisans; they were proletarians whose workplace allowed them to act as artisans, hire their own men, and apprentice boys, but they were still employees whose craft position relied on foreign trade, international duties, and the economic prosperity and stability of the industrializing US northeast. . . .

On another level, the parades were assertions not only of the miners' identity but also of their place within these rural societies. It is interesting, for example, that they made the gestures they did to the broader community. The second parade—celebrating the opening of the railway—was an unambiguously public event in a way that the earlier one was not; this time they explicitly made common cause with the farmers, shipping interests, and "the land" upon which they both trod. They recognized a shared fate; upon the prosperity of one depended the prosperity of the other. On this level, then, it may be true that there was some sense of commonwealth here, although not the kind of republicanism (or even proto-republicanism) that Sean Wilentz sees in New York City parades in the same period.[37] However unequal the relationship may have been, the miners were reminding their neighbours of the GMA's benefits and constructing a common producers' cause with a success that often eluded their masters. However this reflects their politics, it seems clear that the miners were not so isolated that they lacked either awareness or an appreciation of their surrounding communities.

Part of this, undoubtedly, was because there was much more engagement between the people of the mines and those from the surrounding towns and countryside than we might think. As most of the miners were Scots, many quickly joined the major Scottish churches and became active participants. In the 1830s and 1840s Presbyterian missionaries in Sydney Mines, who were often quicker to describe irreligiosity than piety, were "touched" to observe the number of collier-laymen reading at service as well as the common sight of "coal stained fingers" holding prayer books in the pews.[38] Catholics too seem to have supported their church at Sydney Mines, despite not having their own priest until the 1840s. The Presbyterians and Catholics built their own churches in the late 1830s. In a display of tolerance remarkable for schismatic eastern Nova Scotia, Catholic and Presbyterian workmen volunteered their labour in the construction of both churches.[39] . . . Identity, religious, and class solidarities were not always harmonious, so from the outside (where almost all accounts originated) the mining villages could simultaneously appear to be both rough and respectable. Just like in the countryside, improvement's hold in the mining towns was uneven. But the existence of activists addressing temperance, unions, self-help, and other issues of working-class self-government suggests that improvement was finding a place.

Most critically, the integration of mining towns into local society could be seen in the increasing numbers of people born in the area (but not of mining parents) who came to work in the mines. . . . Outside of roadwork, the best opportunities for waged employment could be found in coasting vessels, the fishery, the timber trade, and shipbuilding. Wages were always important for struggling farm households, but those in search of employment were now willing to travel great distances, often on foot, to obtain good wages. Almost all of these men came from the poorer squatters' farms, where their labour was absolutely crucial. . . . After 1858, when the GMA's monopoly was broken and the number of coalmining companies expanded quickly, there was a virtual explosion in the number of Nova Scotia–born males entering mine work and Nova Scotia–born females marrying miners. By the 1860s over two-thirds of the young men entering mining were born in the province, and over half came from the countryside, not the mine villages. These data would certainly suggest that if two separate populations—miners and farmers, village and countryside—had existed in the 1830s and 1840s, by mid-century the ties between them were growing stronger. . . .

The Strikes of the 1840s

If the GMA's miners were dependent, they were not servile. During the early 1830s there were numerous indications of what appear to have been brief (one- to three-day) work actions in which the men "refused to go down" because another worker had been discharged or sometimes because of a safety issue.[40] By the early 1840s the market for coal was changing, and the miners faced the company's first attempt to deal with its own precarious position by reducing the men's wages. The coal market thrived through the late 1830s and into 1840 but came to a quick halt that summer when the men struck for a pay increase. With production below demand, prices up, ships waiting in the harbour, and little coal in reserve, it was an ideal time to strike, and the miners won a quick and relatively easy victory.[41] But the combination of the recession of the early 1840s, an increased US tariff on coal, and increased competition from Pennsylvania anthracite put tremendous pressure on the GMA's markets, and their US sales fell off. The company attempted to enforce the "strictest economy" in its operations in order to recover some of its profitability. Part of this was an attempt to roll back the advances that the colliers had earned a year and a half earlier, a move that resulted in a three-month strike in the winter of 1841–2.[42] As we shall see, the 1842 strike was the object of much comment for the "disorder" that it occasioned and had near-devastating consequences for the mines, the community, and especially the miners and their families.

The strike succeeded in preventing part of the rollback, but it was long and difficult. This was partly due to the tactical error of striking in February, but it was also due to the ruthlessness of Samuel Cunard, who handled all the negotiations.[43] The wage reductions were calculated by [J. B.] Foord and Cunard and announced in October 1841—that is, near the end of the shipping season. The timing was carefully selected. The new scale would see a collier's earnings reduced by 20 per cent.[44] There would be little immediate need for production at this time of the year, as not many ships risked the North Atlantic after 1 December, and the few that did could be handled from the stored coal on hand. Details are sketchy until early February,[45] but it appears that after the company announced its intention to bring in English strikebreakers the following spring, the men offered to return to work at the old rate of wages until the new men arrived. Cunard, of course, refused this offer, knowing fully well that the men would strike again in the spring and that the new colliers might support them; downtime in February was much easier to deal with than downtime in the peak shipping season. The managers also recognized their employees' vulnerability at this time of the year, so they cut off both coal supplies and credit at the company's sublet store.[46] The *Mechanic and Farmer*, showing neither the miners' nor Cunard's savvy, condemned both: the miners for striking in the first place and the company's agent for not allowing the men to return to work "at their former rate of wages until other men could be procured, as the loss otherwise resulting to the company (to say nothing of its effects upon the community) will be much more than if the highest rate of wages had been paid

until the spring." The publication's argument made sense in the short term, but Cunard (and eventually, although too late, the miners as well) knew that whatever the effect on the community, the long-term interests of the company were best served by maintaining the strike, now effectively a lockout. For its part, the *Pictou Observer* simply noted that it was "not right" that these "unfortunate men whom [the GMA] brought here from their distant homes . . . are now to be seen daily stretched on the ice spearing smelts to keep their families alive."[47] The paper's sympathy, however, was limited. Although the *Observer* called for the company to "furnish the labourers with employment at the usual rate of rates, and in accordance with their agreement," it was not the sanctity of contracts, the plight of families, or even honour between masters and servants that was emphasized here but the demand that they "not inflict an injury on the people of New Glasgow by throwing the families of the Miners on the Township of Egerton." The issue was simply about keeping miners off poor relief.

In addition to this public and more visible "disorder," the strikers made clear their willingness to risk damage to the mines and possibly even imprisonment for their cause. The "negotiations" were protracted and quite irregular. The strike appears to have been what later would be called a "100 per cent" strike, where not only the colliers struck but also the boys, the surface workers, and even the maintenance crews, forcing the managers to remove the horses from underground.[48] More dramatic still, however, was the terrorizing of manager Henry Poole and his family in Mt. Rundell on the night of 25 January 1842.[49] Poole claimed that over 100 of the "wives and children of the colliers" surrounded his house that night while the men "during all the time remain[ed] in the bushes." Most of the terrorizing came from the women, who spent the evening "shaking the shutters," "using abusive language to [Poole], heaving mud and dirt at the windows . . . and remaining about the house for about an hour" before going away "threatening to return before daylight." Poole offered to meet the men the next day, but it was the women who appeared, "insist[ing] upon getting their coal free of charge as they were accustomed." As later events confirmed, and as the striking families undoubtedly knew, the strike leaders would not likely retain employment. The women, then, were able to act as the men's proxy, effectively negotiating, hiding their partners' faces, protecting their families' interests, limiting the response of the managers, and adding a touch of masculine humiliation. The manager relented somewhat, offering to sell the coal. Three days later, on 29 January, the women's actions having effectively made clear the strength of their resolve, Poole agreed to meet a "deputation" of three miners, the first face-to-face meetings since the strike had begun. Following the "first outrage," the men were "quiet, without any apparent disposition to commit any further outrage."[50]

The men went back to work less than two weeks after Cunard's arrival on the scene, "they and the employer having 'split the difference.'" The magistrates arrested some of the "ringleaders," but the threatened replacement workers did not arrive, and some sense of normality returned to the village and the workplace.[51] Clearly, however, the strike was not good for the men or the community. It was not only ill-planned but also divisive. A number of men, perhaps recognizing the folly of the timing, attempted to go back to work during the strike but were prevented from doing so, their effigies burned outside their houses at night. Some, it was said, had "set off for the United States, leaving their wives and children behind them, presuming, no doubt, that they will be provided for from the Poors' fund." Indeed, they were, but those who had been "turned adrift by the Association" consumed all the township's poor-relief money, and the township was not pleased.[52] Once again, the residents of Pictou County were being asked to pay for the privilege of having this new industry in their backyard. This time, feeling called upon by "duty and humanity," they did. But the

following spring they successfully petitioned the legislature "for setting off the Albion Mines as a separate poor district."[53] It was the biggest and roughest strike that Nova Scotia or the GMA had yet witnessed, although much worse were to come. There would be more strikes, but for the next 15 years the GMA's major difficulties would be with the provincial government and local elites, not its own workers. During these years the provincial government increased its efforts to break the company's monopoly. Ironically, the strike would form a part of the attack on monopoly.

Conclusion

The evidence from this period leaves us with an incomplete, and contradictory, view of this colony of miners planted on the western side of the Atlantic. If in many ways the towns' inhabitants were starkly different from their farm-family neighbours, there were already some indications that the lines were blurring. Ironically, as industry grew around the mine villages and New Glasgow, the connections to the countryside in some ways grew stronger. The miners themselves were part of this transformation, most notably as a second generation began to marry local farm-born women and as some farm-born men found work in the mines. Clearly too, all sides appear to have been cognizant of the differences, and some at least made an effort to bridge the divide. Here, the miners appear at the forefront. Although isolated and dependent, they were not sheep. Their variously expressed gestures of defiance and deference to their employers, and to the broader community, indicate something infinitely more complex. And their clear connectedness to the broader movement of labour across the North Atlantic reminds us that more than capital was transforming the New World.

The defiance of these men, who some days would muster and parade, came back to haunt them and the GMA. As the parade devices proclaimed, the miners understood well that their fate was closely tied to the success of the company. The board's response to the changes in the Atlantic coal market was to attempt to shift much of this economic burden onto the miners. The mining communities' abilities to resist part of this change may have pushed the company to grow more cautious in its larger plans. Moreover, at least in the longer term, the "disorder" of the strike undercut part of the company's legitimacy. Industrial colonization had been premised in part on the GMA's ability to bring order to the mining frontier. Building mines, housing workers, and constructing railways was one thing. Strikes, riots, and draining a township's poor monies was quite another. Here was clear evidence that the GMA could not police its own affairs. . . .

 More online.

Notes

1. Report of George Wightman, 10 March 1842, no. 37, vol. 3, RG 21, Nova Scotia Archives and Records Management (NSARM).
2. J. M. Beck, *Joseph Howe*, vol. 1, *Conservative Reformer, 1804–48* (Montreal, QC: McGill-Queen's University Press, 1984), 236–9; Ian Ross Robertson, *The Tenant League of Prince Edward Island, 1864–67: Leasehold Tenure in the New World* (Toronto, ON: University of Toronto Press, 1996), 34–5, 301–2.
3. The first census that we might use (1827) is missing for both Sydney Mines and Albion Mines. The 1838 census nicely identifies miners for us but sadly does not tell us much more than that they were there and the size of their families.
4. These approximate proportions are based on the description supplied by H. S. Poole, "Cost of Raising Coal at Albion Mines," 7 February 1842, file: "Correspondence, 1842," vol. 7, "A," RG 21, NSARM.
5. Bettina Bradbury, "Pigs, Cows, and Boarders: Non-Wage Forms of Survival among Montreal Families, 1861–91," *Labour/Le Travail* 15 (Spring 1985): 7–22. . . .
6. Alan Campbell, *The Lanarkshire Miners: A Social History of Their Trade Unions, 1775–1974* (Edinburgh, UK: John Donald, 1979), 108–9.
7. Robert Grant, *East River Worthies* (New Glasgow, NS: Scotia Printers, 1895), 23; *Pictou Observer*, 14 October 1834.
8. W. Ouseley, quoted in C. B. Fergusson, ed., *Uniacke's Sketches of Cape Breton and Other Papers Relating to Cape Breton Island* (Halifax, NS: Public Archives of Nova Scotia, 1958), 173.
9. Campbell, *Lanarkshire Miners*, 20–1; Robert Colls, *The Pitmen of the Northern Coalfield: Work, Culture, and Protest, 1790–1850* (Manchester, UK: Manchester University Press, 1987), 123–33. . . .
10. See Peter Barrett, "Twelve Years in North America, Containing a Brief Sketch of the Life, Trials and Persecutions of Peter Barrett, an English Immigrant, in Nova Scotia, Canada, Written by Himself," unpublished manuscript, 1879, PANS; and Allan C. Dunlop, "Peter Barrett's Pictou County: From the Fenian Scare to the Drummond Colliery Explosion," *Nova Scotia Historical Review* 14, no. 1 (1994): 135–52.
11. Royden Harrison, ed., *The Independent Collier: The Coal Miner as "Archetypal Proletarian" Reconsidered* (New York, NY: St. Martin's, 1979).
12. Arthur Redford [c. 1860], quoted in Michael R. Haines, *Fertility and Occupation: Coal Mining Populations in the Nineteenth Century and Early Twentieth Centuries in Europe and America* (Ithaca, NY: Western Societies Program, Occasional Papers, Cornell University. 1975), 9.
13. Report of George Wightman, 10 March 1842, no. 37, vol. 3, RG 21, NSARM.
14. See H. B. Jefferson, "Mount Rundell, Stellarton, and the Albion Railway of 1839," *Collections of the Nova Scotia Historical Quarterly* 34 (1966): 81–120; Mt. Rundell was destroyed late in the century.
15. Richard Brown, *The Coal Fields and Coal Trade of the Island of Cape Breton* (London, UK: Sampson, Low, Marston, Low and Searle, 1871), 50–2, 62–8.
16. Some ships carpenters near Pictou were reportedly earning as much as 7s6d per day. On local wage rates, see "Return Showing the Average Wages of Mechanics and Others in Pictou, Nova Scotia, for the Three Months ended 10 October 1842," enclosure no. 7 in Viscount Falkland to Lord Stanley, 3 February 1843, reprinted in "Correspondence Related to Emigration," in Great Britain, *Parliamentary Papers*, vol. 16, 483. Data on colliers' wages and the employment of sons are from Henry Poole, "Cost of Raising Coal at Albion Mines," 7 February 1842, vol. 7, "A," RG 21, NSARM. Data on housing and coal are from George Smith, "Report on Riots at Albion Mines," 19 November 1841, Report, vol. 35, "R," RG 5, NSARM. Coal was usually free for employees.
17. "Report on Riots at Albion Mines" 19 November 1841, Report, vol. 35, "R," RG 5, NSARM; Barrett, "Twelve Years in North America," 6; Frederic S. Cozzens, *Acadia, or A Month with the Blue Noses* (New York, NY: Derby and Jackson, 1859), 186.
18. George Smith, for example, noted that although the men were well paid by the day, this might not amount

to much by the month. Two miners told him that although they earned 10s per day, they might earn as little as £2 per month. See George Smith, "Report on Riots at Albion Mines," 19 November 1841, vol. 35, "R," RG 5, NSARM.

19. "Diary, Richard Brown," 5 and 6 July 1830 (mustering); 8 September 1830 (fired miner for refusing an order); 13 September 1830 (fired cooper for misconduct); 28 September 1830 (fired someone for "not working more industriously"); 15 November 1830 (fired three men for "bad treatment of some strangers"); and 8 and 9 July 1831 (mustering), no. 8, vol. 38, "A," RG 21, NSARM. On the incident in 1834, see Brown to Sir Rupert George, 3 September 1834, no. 111, vol. 458, RG 1, NSARM.

20. "Diary, Richard Brown," 29 April 1845, no. 8, vol. 38, "A," RG 21, NSARM.

21. R. H. Brown Sr., Diary, 29 April 1845, 16 and 17 March, 26 and 28 June, 13–15 and 29 August, and 15 November 1849, no. 8, vol. 38, "A," RG 21, NSARM. . . .

22. Richard Smith, quoted in "Report of the Select Committee of the House of Commons on Accidents in Mines," in Great Britain, *Parliamentary Papers*, vol. 5 (1835), 223–37, 249–53, 276–84, quotation at 276. . . .

23. Smith, quoted in "Report of the Select Committee," 276–7.

24. *Colonial Patriot*, 31 December 1833.

25. Bryan D. Palmer, *Working-Class Experience: Rethinking the History of Canadian Labour, 1800–1990* (Toronto, ON: McClelland & Stewart, 1991), 41–8, 76–8.

26. *Colonial Patriot*, 31 December 1833.

27. It is worth noting that Sunday, 30 December 1833, was the anniversary, but the commemoration occurred on Monday.

28. *Colonial Patriot*, 31 December 1833.

29. Many parades in New York were explicitly supportive of the politics of economic expansion; see Sean Wilentz, *Chants Democratic: New York City and the Rise of the American Working Class, 1788–1850* (New York, NY: Oxford University Press, 2002), 87–91.

30. *Colonial Patriot*, 31 December 1833.

31. "Report on the Fire at Pictou," 1833, vol. 1625, "S," RG 5. NSARM.

32. *Colonial Patriot*, 11 January 1828; *Mechanic and Farmer*, 25 September 1839; *Cape Breton Advocate*, 13 January 1841; *Spirit of the Times*, 21 June 1844 and 11 January 1845; "Diary, Richard Brown," 28 June 1849, no. 9, vol. 38, "A," RG 21, NSARM.

33. The following description of the celebration and the parade is taken entirely from *Mechanic and Farmer*, 25 September 1839.

34. "Mr. Buddle's Report on The Sydney Mines Railway," no. 32, vol. 39, "A," RG 21 NSARM, original emphasis. See also Jefferson, "Mount Rundell."

35. "Diary, Richard Brown," 5 July 1830 and 8 July 1831, no, 8, vol. 40, "A," RG 21, NSARM. . . .

36. These strikes are discussed later in the chapter.

37. Wilentz, *Chants Democratic*, 87–91.

38. Reports from *The Home and Foreign Missionary Record for the Church of Scotland*, July 1839 to December 1841, quoted in Laurie Stanley, *The Well-Watered Garden: The Presbyterian Church in Cape Breton, 1798–1860* (Sydney, NS: University College of Cape Breton Press, 1983), 137–8; and in Alexander Farquharson, *Sketch of the Missionary Proceedings at Cape Breton from August 1833 to October 1834* (Edinburgh, UK: s.n., 1835), 8–10.

39. *Spirit of the Times*, 24 May 1844; Mrs. Roderick G. Bain, compiler, "History of Sydney Mines," unpublished manuscript [1951], 29–30, Beaton Institute. Farquharson, *Sketch of the Missionary Proceedings*, 8, estimated that the mining population was 60 per cent Presbyterian and 40 per cent Catholic.

40. "Diary, Richard Brown," 4 April, 14 April, 21 April, 3 May, and 1 September 1831, no. 8, vol. 40, "A," RG 21, NSARM.

41. I have found no contemporary description of the 1840 walkout. This description is based on commentary comparing the 1841–2 strike with that of two summers earlier; see *Mechanic and Farmer*, 2 February 1842. The tactic, however, was the same used six years later in another strike at Pictou, during which "several masters of the vessels protested against the Company," presumably out of their own interest, not that of the miners; see *Novascotian*, 12 October 1846. See also Walter R. Johnson, *The Coal Trade of British America, with Researches on the Characters and Practical Values of American and Foreign Coals* (Washington, DC: Taylor and Maury, 1850), 20.

42. On the GMA's economizing, see "Cost of Raising Coal at Albion Mines" 7 February 1842, file: "Correspondence, 1842," vol. 7, "A," RG 21, PANS; and Petition of the GMA [authored by Cunard], 22 December 1842, no. 104, vol. 459, RG 1, NSARM. The length of the strike is not clear. The *Mechanic and Farmer* described it as 10 weeks old on 2 February 1842, two weeks before it ended, while George Wightman, who was sent to investigate for the province, described it as two months.

43. *Mechanic and Farmer*, 26 January 1842.

44. Henry Poole, cited in George Smith, "Report on Riots at Albion Mines" 19 November 1841, vol. 35, "R," RG 5, NSARM.

45. We might know a fair bit more if the *Pictou Observer* had published a letter that it received from "A Miner" sometime in January. The editor agreed that the "Association's agents are pursuing an erroneous course towards the unfortunate men" but felt that they should delay publication of the letter "until we learn the result

of Mr. Cunard's next visit to the mines." Unfortunately (for us), the strike was settled the day of the next issue, so the letter was not published. See *Pictou Observer*, 25 January and 3 February 1842.

46. Henry Poole, cited in George Smith, "Report on Riots at Albion Mines" 19 November 1841, vol. 35, "R," RG 5, NSARM.

47. *Mechanic and Farmer;* 2 February 1842; and *Pictou Observer*, 25 January 1842.

48. Henry Poole, cited in George Smith, "Report on Riots at Albion Mines," 19 November 1841, vol. 35, "R," RG 5, NSARM.

49. Poole became a manager and promoter in the post-monopoly period; see Henry S. Poole, *Notes on the Coal Field of Pictou;* and Henry S. Poole and J. Campbell, *Additional Papers on the Nova Scotia Gold Fields.*

50. See the comments of George Smith and Henry Poole in George Smith, "Report on Riots at Albion Mines," 19 November 1841, vol. 35, "R," RG 5, NSARM.

51. George Smith, "Report on Riots at Albion Mines" 19 November 1841, vol. 35, "R," RG 5, NSARM; *Mechanic and Farmer*, 9 February 1842. The *Pictou Observer*, 3 February 1842, claims that the 2d cut that the men accepted was their initial position and, therefore, that they had won the strike. On the other hand, the acceptance of a cut of 2d per cubic yard instead of a 4d cut certainly sounds like "splitting the difference." . . .

52. *Mechanic and Farmer*, 2 February 1842. A petition from Egerton Township officials requesting additional poor-relief funds also noted that a number of striking men had "fled for the United States" and left their families behind; see "Petition from Egerton Township," 3 February 1842, no. 114, vol. 81, "P," RG 5, NSARM. The quotation is from "Petition from Egerton Township," no. 17, vol. 8(a), "P," RG 5, NSARM.

53. "Petition from Egerton Township," no. 17, vol. 8(a), "P," RG 5, NSARM. See also *JHA* (1844), 4 February 1843, 381.

13 Encounters with Industrial Space

Nicolas Kenny

Upon completing his nearly 20-year reign as first magistrate of Brussels, Charles Buls devoted himself to the study of urbanism and embarked on a series of trips that took him across Europe and around the world. In the late summer of 1903 he travelled to North America, first visiting New York, Toronto, and Niagara Falls. On 11 September, he described in his diary his "fantastical arrival" into Montreal. From the first moment of his encounter with the city's industrial landscape, Buls's senses were irritated and offended:

> The sun was setting and cast a red glow in the sky, the city, fully wrapped in black smoke, was definable only by the silhouette of its factory chimneys, of its elevators and of a few skyscrapers, vaguely reflected in the pallid billows
> truly infernal city—
> Dantesque city—
> electric streetcars await you, and carry you through a blackened city, poorly lit, lacking fine shops as in Toronto, and of a dirty and sinister aspect—[1]

Buls's judgment of the city was premised on his bodily appreciation of the environment: the light, the smoke, and the dirt affected his senses in displeasing ways. Seeing the glowing red sky, the city covered in a shroud of black smoke, and the outline of a few towering industrial buildings, Buls had the impression not of arriving in a place of modernity, progress, and prosperity, as many in Montreal described their city, but of descending into the pits of hell, an impression reinforced by his reference to Dante.[2] As he explored the city the following day, he noted only its uninspiring architecture, its wooden sidewalks, its neglected streets. Nor was he particularly impressed with the panoramic view from Mount Royal, mentioning once more the omnipresence of smoking chimneys. That these impressions were hastily scribbled into a private journal further attests to the intimate and visceral nature of his reaction.

It might well be argued that Buls overstated his reaction, that his known aversion to industrial landscapes skewed his observations of Montreal. Nevertheless, the sometime mayor touched upon a sensitive matter that was felt in many industrial cities. As historian Stephen Mosely has demonstrated in his study of Manchester, exposure to thick clouds of smoke was a daily reality for inhabitants of industrial towns. To arguments that industrial smoke symbolized productivity

---

Citation: Nicolas Kenny, "Encounters with Industrial Space," in *The Feel of the City: Experiences of Urban Transformation* (Toronto, ON: University of Toronto Press, 2014): 78–119. © University of Toronto Press 2014. Reprinted with permission of the publisher.

and prosperity, that it signified a steady source of employment, and even that the patterns it formed in the sky were a source of beauty, middle-class reformers and health professionals increasingly retorted that such emanations were instead signs of waste and inefficiency, whose harmful nature was compounded by the health risks it posed.[3] In both Europe and North America, smoke abatement campaigns picked up steam during these years; the dark soot covering cities raised the ire of townspeople, who increasingly resented its incompatibility with modern bourgeois notions of cleanliness.[4] Montreal's boiler inspector, Édouard Octave Champagne, frequently denounced the effect of what he called the "scourge" of industrial smoke on the city's image. Only a few years after Buls's visit, he noted that, despite smoke abatement measures for factories, the 320 trains rolling into the city each day and the numerous steamboats filling its harbour continued to sully the landscape, and suggested that until the federal government moved to regulate the nuisance, "there will remain reasons for objecting to this interference with views of the city and landscape."[5] . . .

This chapter examines the way representations of urban factories and workshops drew on both sensorial experiences and ideas about the body. Because these establishments transformed cities in such a marked fashion, we will first examine them from the outside, reflecting on the messages their architectural form etched onto the landscape, but also on the way nearby residents interpreted, indeed resented, their loud and smoky presence. Crossing the threshold of their imposing doorways and drawing on labour commission proceedings and factory inspections, we will see that the tensions between employers and labourers that marked this period found an embodied form in workers' experiences of the factory atmosphere. Finally, the paramount role of corporeal experiences in navigating industrial spaces resulted in new understandings of the body itself. Doctors, hygienists, factory inspectors, and writers mused on the meaning of the

worker's body in particular, representing it as a metaphor for industry and as the incarnation of their views about work, hygiene, and class and gender dynamics in modern urban society. From distant impressions to direct contact with the manufacturing process, the industrial activity of the turn of the century intensified bodily experiences and nourished perceptions of the body, both of which underlay the spatial stories told by inhabitants of these cities as they looked for ways to make sense of the monumental changes reshaping their working and living environments.

The Industrial Landscape

Palaces of Industry

The industrialists whose fortunes materialized in these transformations were predictably eager to present this new landscape as a welcome result of modernity. The Montreal Board of Trade, for instance, boasted that thanks to "the foresight and perseverance of the great princes and captains of trade and manufacture," the city "is rapidly, very rapidly, becoming a veritable hive of industry." The spread of industrialization propelled Montreal's metropolitan status, and the prominent smokestacks on the skyline were seen as the foundations on which entire communities were built.[6] While the overall industrial landscape exercised an undeniable sensorial and psychological impact on urban dwellers, the individual constructions that comprised it were also designed to provoke the sense of sight and to shape mentalities. Indeed, many of the new factories and workshops displayed innovative architectural qualities and frequently displayed elaborate ornamentation and aestheticism embellishing their exterior appearance. These installations were the outward and visible expression of the economic elite's sense of pride and accomplishment. As historian John Kasson has argued in reference to the American industrial landscape, "the desire to fuse beauty and use, to see technology not simply as prosaically utilitarian but a source of aesthetic satisfaction" was widespread.[7]

To be sure, industrialists did not invest in gigantic structures out of simple megalomania—they needed space in which to house the machines, materials, and workers with which they attempted to keep pace with the growing opportunities for production. New construction techniques and innovative building materials played a determining role in the look of industrial buildings.[8] This landscape emerged from the actions of investors, legislators, bankers, and industrialists whose influence rested in the amount of capital they controlled and whose motivations lay in their will to maximize profits while maintaining the social order.[9] In this light, some scholars are uncomfortable contemplating nineteenth-century manufacturing space from the point of view of its supposed beauty. To architectural historian Adriaan Linters, the decorative elements on such structures constituted only an inopportune and inappropriate form of aestheticism, one hastily applied to the facade in the hopes of "erasing the content of the building, of rubbing out the functional." The rosettes, cartouches, and engravings that decorated factories thus were merely cosmetic touches. And if they could be said to express a message, it was simply one of deceit, a false representation on the part of industrialists wishing to conceal the social realities that hid behind a seemingly unbridled rate of production.[10]

Without denying these utilitarian considerations, however, interpreting the industrial landscape as purely the result of brute economic forces fails to account for the complexity of the reigning atmosphere of modernity, and for the roles played by economic transformations and material developments in the ways individuals understood their sense of self vis-à-vis a society defined by constant change. As historian Anders Aman reminds us, the bourgeoisie of the period combined pragmatic efficiency with a keen interest in the symbolism and aesthetics of the

built environment.[11] Beyond their primordial economic and functionalist surface, what do the forms of these new and unique urban spaces express about the interiority, the ambitions, and preoccupations of those who, in conceiving them, were major players in the reconfiguration of the urban environment?

The industrial bourgeoisie desired a setting that corresponded both to its economic ambitions and to the aspirations of artistic refinement it entertained. Their buildings thus conveyed a distinctive visual imagery, one that was rooted in an idyllic vision of the past, inspired by ancient Roman or Gothic styles. The decors were designed to intimidate workers, impress clients, and display a "dramatized factory environment" that reflected the educated elite's passion for historical dramas and romantic operas.[12] Here, an important distinction arises between the imposing presence of industry in Montreal and its more discreet form in Brussels, where factories tended to be of small or medium scale, housed in correspondingly diminutive installations, or often hidden from public view behind rows of shops and houses. . . .

In Montreal, gigantic mills, refineries, breweries and shipyards had a more forceful presence, their impact compounded by the scores of elaborately decorated smaller workshops that completed a highly industrialized urban fabric. With its stone foundations, layered brick facade, metallic window frames, and enormous decorative *oeil-de-boeuf*, the Royal Electric headquarters in the heart of the Griffintown district, for example, reminds the observer more of a temple of worship to the miracle of electricity than a simple power plant.[13] Around the corner, the airy and nuanced patterns of the Arts and Crafts movement–inspired Darling Brothers Foundry contrasted starkly with the hot and heavy smelting going on inside.[14] As people moved through these neighbourhoods, their senses were stimulated not just by the loud hum of industry, but also by an aesthetic language that espoused much softer and more pleasing accents, aimed at taming the harsh physical realities of industrial work and putting a celebratory face on changes that some saw as disfiguring the city.

. . .

Stepping In

To and From

Not only did increasing industrialization change the landscapes beheld by the eye and the air ingested by the nose, it also brought new rhythms to urban life that modified the way bodies moved through the city. Crowds of workers walking to and from work at fixed hours of the day filled the streets, contributing to the atmosphere of perpetual movement that characterized these cities. In his examination of a Montreal working-class district, Herbert Ames tested the hypothesis that a high proportion of individuals employed in the area's industrial establishments came from other neighbourhoods. "The main avenues leading north, east, and south were watched for several evenings at about six o'clock," he explains. On each of the major thoroughfares observed, the number of people going each way were counted; it was found that for every person who entered Griffintown at that time of day, three to four people left, in a "constant stream pour[ing] outward."[15] Ames's scientific objective was to quantify the movement of commuters to Montreal's main industrial district in order to reflect upon strategies for facilitating workers' accessibility to their place of employment. But even through this prosaic language, as we picture his research assistants posted at busy intersections frantically counting the passersby, we can imagine the sight of these crowds, the mass of people moving in the same direction, their feet hitting the pavement, their voices buzzing together.

Others described this movement of people with more imagery and constructed this mundane, daily event as a key signifier of the bodily movement that fed the atmosphere of modernity. Typically, representations of these crowds were tinged with sadness at the fate of the workers and the conditions in which they were employed. One Montreal writer focused especially on the troubling image of children going to work in factories: "Have you seen them, on cold and foggy winter mornings, an hour before sunrise, these bands of young children, boys and girls, going, pale-faced and serious, to take up their customary tasks?"[16] . . .

These descriptions of workers' commutes focus explicitly on the atmosphere of the streets around the factories—an atmosphere that is cold, foggy, and dark, despite the streetlights. The atmosphere is made even heavier by the regular and dejected movement of workers' bodies, young and old, exhausted by gruelling work and lack of rest. The groups of labourers filling the streets before and after work were the visible embodiment of what went on behind the closed doors of the industrial establishments, these "caverns of anaemia and exhaustion," to cite the author Franz Mahutte. "They erect, like blind beacons of misery," he continues, "the annealed chimneys from which beats down the corrosive smoke. From the inside come hollow noises, of grumbling machines, of friction from conveyor belts giving rhythm to the pulsations of labour." But these are the words, like so many others we have heard thus far, of an observer standing outside, feeling the smoke and noise pouring out, able only to speculate on what is happening inside: "One imagines that hundreds of beings toil and die in there."[17]

Having looked at them from the exterior, let us now step inside these temples of industrial production and listen to what those who experienced them first-hand had to say about the atmosphere and spatial meanings they generated.

Workers' Voices

To begin, who better to consult about both the material and intangible atmosphere of urban factories and workshops than workers themselves? Records offering first-hand working-class perspectives on the city and the body at the turn of the twentieth century are sparse. Factory life, however, is one issue about which we can glean at least some thoughts of industrial labourers. To be sure, these commentaries are those of a minute handful among the thousands who laboured in these industries. To the extent that workers might have shared class-based spatial stories, are these few voices representative of them? On the question of the physical experiences of factory work and of the sensorial nuisances and corporeal risks that workers confronted regularly, the accounts we have, though limited to a few sources, are rather consistent in both Montreal and Brussels. These sources show workers' sensibilities to their working environment as well as their principal demands for improving it. They also show how the various pressures placed on workers' bodies by industrial activity during this period were central to their broader attitudes about the atmosphere and meaning of industrial spaces.

. . .

For both Brussels and Montreal we have first-person accounts of these experiences from workers who testified before nationwide investigations into the nature of industrial work in Belgium and Canada. Taking place only a few months apart in 1886, these inquiries offer a wide-ranging view of attitudes to industrial work on the part of both employers and workers. The Commission du travail, which took both written and oral testimonies in several Belgian localities, was set up by the national government as a response to the working-class riots in Walloon industrial centres earlier that year. The Royal Commission on the Relations of Labour and Capital held 11 days of public hearings in the principal manufacturing centres of central and eastern Canada at a time when the frenetic rate of production and growth brought tensions between industrialists and their employees to a head. Though more forceful legislation would not be passed until later in the twentieth century, these commissions coincided with the first timid steps toward the legislation of such workplace issues as safety, health and hygiene, and child labour.[18]

In both countries, governments feared the social unrest bubbling beneath this ever-increasing industrial productivity and deployed similar attempts to understand the nature of the relationship between employers and the labour force. These investigations were different in their methodology and results, and are not comparable on a strictly empirical basis. For instance, the number of testimonials for Montreal is much higher than those concerning Brussels.[19] Moreover, historians have pointed to structural biases in both investigations. Were the workers' voices representative, especially in Belgium where people refused to testify for fear of reprisals and where the commission lacked the power to subpoena witnesses? While testimony was given by individuals from a diversity of class backgrounds and both linguistic groups present in the two cities, the voices heard were primarily those of men. Finally, although a concern for political balance on these commissions seems to have informed both governments, these exercises were largely associated with strong conservative tendencies and, as such, were widely discredited by the left in both countries.[20] Despite these differences and lacunae, however, these parallel investigations offer a rare glimpse into the tense, corporeally constructed atmosphere within industrial establishments themselves.

Immediately evident in the workers' comments is the climate of mistrust and hostility that reigned between them and their employers. While owners and managers described the rapport as cordial and respectful, workers responded that any politeness was superficial. "The worker is forced to make a good impression, since the bosses have all the power," pointed out a Molenbeek mechanic. "Such and such a worker displeases them? Without any reason or pity for his family, they fire him, giving incapacity as an excuse, after 10 or 15 years of work."[21] Montreal workers echoed these sentiments, with accounts of beatings and physical intimidation giving corporeal form to this strained atmosphere. "There is no bond of sympathy existing between the capitalist of the large mill and his employés [sic]," notes one Royal Commission report, comparing the constables some factories hired to enforce discipline to "Oriental despot[s]."[22] The most frequently cited sources of tension between management and labourers concerned salary and working hours. Faced with pressing financial obligations, concerns over the odours and sounds of the factories seemed less urgent to workers than to the residents of luxurious neighbourhoods. When asked about the water closets at the foundry in which he worked, for instance, a Montreal moulder replied that although there was sometimes an "awful smell," he was often too busy working to notice such details.[23] . . .

Indeed, while some factory "operatives" may have been too occupied to notice the foul smells surrounding them, others complained bitterly about the physical discomforts of their workplaces. "Imagine a vast hangar covered by a glass roof where one bakes in summer and freezes in winter, and where water leaks in through one of many cracks," described a Brussels typographer of his workshop, exemplifying the sentiments of many workers in the two cities. Another layer of embodied meaning can be read in the expression of repulsion at the smells coming from the workers' deficient sanitary installations. Owen Duffy of Montreal even mentioned that he was occasionally forced to stay home because of the unbearable smell of the water closets situated next to his work station.[24] Many workers defined their workspace in terms of physical dangers, deploring the lack of security measures for machinery, materials, and chemicals, as well as the risk of fires. Also at issue was the nature of the tasks they performed and the debilitating effects on their bodies. They breathed in chemicals in small, unventilated workshops, climbed insecure scaffolds, and lost limbs to the machines they used. "I first learned my trade in an attic, then in a basement, which, nonetheless,

belong to a very rich boss," noted a shoemaker from Brussels, adding that it was there that he "lost a great deal of my eyesight."[25]

In one gruesome tale, a Montreal carpenter reported having his entire arm ripped away by a machine on which he was changing the timing belt, a job he was ordered to do even though he was not qualified. Did the company he worked for pay any compensation or medical fee, he was asked. "Not at all," he answered, "I was even upbraided for the scrap of cotton on which I had rested after the accident, and which was stained with my blood."[26] Many employers denied responsibility for such matters, insisting that their establishments were irreproachable in terms of hygiene and security. Confronted with the testimonials put forth by the workers, the employers placed the responsibility squarely on their shoulders, attributing accidents or deteriorating health to the workers' lack of attention or propensity to drink on the job. . . .

Factory Inspections

Another point of comparison in the responses to the pressures of rapid industrialization lies in the establishment of routine inspections in manufacturing establishments. In Quebec, these were mandated by the 1885 Manufactory Act, while in Belgium they stemmed from the creation of a ministry for work and industry in 1895. The inspectors' reports for the Montreal and Brussels areas confirm the dangerous and unhealthy conditions denounced by labourers. Year after year, these first-hand witnesses of industrialization condemned the excessive smoke, noise, and dust to which workers were exposed, the lack of adequate ventilation, and the absence of appropriate sanitary installations. These observations were rooted in emerging preoccupations with industrial hygiene, during a period in which the dangers of economic space were increasingly seen as superseding the threats associated with the city in general. From the mid-nineteenth century to World War I, notes Corbin, hygienists became increasingly interested in the working environment—its ventilation, lighting, and heating—and conceptualized the factory in relation to its impact on the bodies of those inside.[27]

Year in and year out, these inspectors began their reports by lauding what they perceived as major and constant improvements in matters pertaining to safety and hygiene and expressed their faith in the capacity of modern technology to ensure the health of all who toiled in industry. "The need for well-being, even of luxury, which has developed in contemporary society, has manifested itself in the domain of industry," proclaimed Émile Van de Weyer, a factory inspector in Brussels.[28] Noting that steam boilers had once been manufactured by hand in sheds "constantly filled with unbearable smoke . . . the workman chilled in winter and sweltering in summer," the Montreal inspector Louis Guyon rejoiced that the invention of the riveting machine, compressed air, and electric lightning had improved not just the productivity of this industry but also the material conditions and "comfort" in which workers operated.[29]

But behind this "cheerful and hopeful feeling,"[30] the inspectors' reports also betrayed a sense of uneasiness with the corporeal realities they witnessed on their visits to manufacturing establishments. If they frequently resorted to bureaucratically dry and repetitive language, they sometimes expressed more vivid indignation. When the inspectors denounced the "glaring neglect" in certain establishments, described them as "ugly, dingy, dirty," and accused their owners of being "without heart or intellect," they told their own spatial stories premised on sensorial encounters. In some cases, their concerns had to do with the inadequate safety measures in certain factories. If the generalized spread of modern mechanization facilitated workers' tasks, it also exposed them to greater physical risk.[31] While these risks were sometimes attributed to "inattention to duty and giddiness on the part of the operators,"[32] the inspectors nonetheless recognized a broader problem with bodily

safety. Elevator shafts were sometimes left wide open, fire measures were often nonexistent, and hydraulic motors, turbines, and other machinery were frequently positioned in out-of-reach, obscure, damp, and slippery corners, making maintenance and repair work awkward and dangerous. . . .

Relatively simple and inexpensive solutions like protective rails around machinery or closed elevator shafts could easily prevent accidents and save lives, argued Guyon. But the real problem underlying the physical relationship to the factory environment was not so outwardly visible. "In the vitiated air of the manufactory, where the worker is forced to spend half his life, there exists a danger that is far greater because it is constant," noted the inspector, for whom the true menace lay in the air entering workers' lungs, harming their bodies, and ruining their youth.[33] From this perspective, the culprits of industrialization were the acids used in the manufacture of matches, paper, or even explosives and the various types of dust ingested on a daily basis—not detectable by sight yet so highly pernicious to workers' bodies.

The inspectors also regularly decried the overall hygienic conditions of certain establishments, particularly in older workshops that operated from converted basements and dwellings, where ceilings were low, windows were small, lighting was artificial, and the evacuation of "vitiated air" and "gas and vapours" was too slow.[34] In some cases, the filth and disorder that prevailed in many workshops appeared even more harmful to workers' health than the actual tasks they performed or substances they handled. Accumulations of trash, unclean lavatories, puddles of gear grease on the floor, and closed windows preventing air circulation all contributed to what the doctor described as a dangerous accumulation of germs. Attempts at cleanliness even seemed to worsen the situation. "Sweeping stirs up the germs, the unhealthy dust, and carries them to the respiratory organs. Done during working hours, it constitutes a veritable heresy against sanitary science," professed the Montreal doctor C. I. Samson, emphasizing his faith in the hygienic principles of his times.[35]

This poor sanitation, the inspectors added, did not correspond with modern management techniques that sought to maximize the workers' physical output for greater productivity and efficiency. New installations were "clean, warm, well lighted and ventilated," noted the Montreal inspector James Mitchell, because "dirty surroundings, excessive heat or cold, poor light and bad air induce physical discomforts, which tend to the production of an inferior quality of work, as well as a decreased quantity."[36] While noting that, by the beginning of the twentieth century, basement workshops had almost disappeared from the district for which she was responsible, Louisa King observed that "this is due less to a humane feeling on the part of the employers than to the fact that artificial light injured the sight of the work-people, thereby causing the work and consequently the employers' profit to suffer."[37]

Was it up to the workers to keep their work areas clean, or were the employers responsible for providing them with adequate facilities? The inspectors did not always agree on the answer to this question, but they always discussed it in terms of the interaction between bodies and space. What is particularly revealing, however, is the tone with which hygienic problems were reported, a tone that betrayed the inspectors' own disgust at what they saw and smelled. Take, for instance, Samson's recounting of the sanitary installations he witnessed in certain factories, a theme frequently commented upon by the inspectors. Leaving no doubt as to the "repugnance" they "inspired," he describes how "lacking a seat, the visitor climbs on the rim, crouches, and the parquet almost inevitably receives a certain quantity of urine that seeps into the interjoist or that is supposed to be absorbed by a layer of sawdust that is renewed from time to time." Acknowledging the nature of the conditions they faced, Samson is also critical of workers for not improving workplace hygiene. . . .

Representing the Worker's Body

Industrial work was, by its nature, physical work; and the tenets of industrial hygiene concerned not just the spaces of production, but also the bodies of those who produced. Preoccupations about the atmosphere inside and around the factories, and the physical experiences they generated, thus extended to the body itself. Recurring images of the strong, powerful, and muscular bodies of valiant workers or, more frequently, of the suffering and deteriorated bodies of overworked labourers, reveal the terms in which doctors, hygienists, inspectors, reformers, and authors conceptualized the effects of industrialization. As Corbin reminds us, the contrasting images elites produced of workers' bodies must be treated with caution, as they are the product of observations based on specific convictions and expectations through which workers' behaviour and their place in society were defined.[38] But these representations also allow us to discern the processes that shaped these constructions and to account for the relative fear or admiration they inspired.

An Industrial Metaphor

The worker's body was frequently put forth as a metaphor for industrialization itself, and represented as a machine, a tool for production. Like the machines that required large shipments of coal and vast hydraulic resources to operate, so too the working body needed fuel. Like the machines whose output sullied the air of the city, so too did the working body pollute its own environment. Like the machines that required upkeep and maintenance, so too was the working body susceptible to overheating and malfunctioning. As historian Anson Rabinbach argues, this analogy enthused scientists and social reformers of the late nineteenth century, who saw in this equation of the body and machine a "new scientific and cultural framework" that would lead to greater productivity.

Harnessing this energy, exploiting this "human motor" more efficiently, also held the promise of objective and neutral solutions to labour-related economic and political conflicts. A new "science of work" led researchers to believe they could "resolve the 'worker question' through science" by investigating, studying, measuring, and photographing the body's movements, its rhythms and labour capacities. Maximizing the efficiency of the working body, went the reasoning, would nullify the perceived advantage in productivity of overly long shifts and convince workers of the validity of employers' claims by replacing moral exhortations to work with "experiment and reasoned argument." Like the city itself, the worker's body in this period was conceptualized in rationalized terms, as an object that could be shaped and moulded according to imperatives of progress and prosperity.[39]

. . .

Much as the machines used in factories polluted cities with the smoke, dust, smells, and sounds they emitted, the body at work also vitiated the air around it, further poisoning the atmosphere. In *Le livre du travailleur*, a guide for workers about health and safety in the factory, the hygienist Lucy Schmidt noted that, even at rest, through breathing alone, the body's emanations were harmful. With the added effects of smoking, of poor dental and corporal hygiene, of artificial lightning, of coal heating, of the various dust particles in factories, workers found themselves carrying out their physically strenuous activities in a toxic cloud formed in large part by their own bodies and bodily practices. In this economic context dictated by an impulse for sustained industrial production, these ambient threats to the body were heightened by the body's own inability to keep up with modernity's rapid pace. Indeed, Schmidt and other hygienists pointed to overwork, or *surmenage*, an excess of intense physical effort, as a major problem that faced not just individual workers, but entire industries that relied on their capacity to maintain a rhythm of production.[40] The human machine, like the mechanical one, was prone to breaking down when overtaxed; as a result, by the turn of the century, notes Rabinbach, fatigue had replaced idleness as the main challenge to productivity in the minds of the bourgeoisie. Like other forms of energy, human energy was seen as a valuable resource, one that had to be managed and conserved to avoid waste and inefficiency. This framework intensified hygienists' reliance on vivid descriptions of the body and the effects of the factory upon it.

As a result, industrial work was typically represented in terms of the painful muscle spasms, the accident-inducing fatigue, or the life-threatening infectious diseases to which workers were exposed. Those who defended workers' interests before production-driven industrialists used modern scientific discourse and drew on bodily representations to point out that there were physical limits to the amount of time a person could work; thus regular days of rest and restricted hours were also in the employer's best interests, as workers would be more productive.[41]

. . .

Women Workers

Factory inspectors and hygienists expressed a particular concern for the bodies of working women, whose presence and visibility in industry increased considerably through the nineteenth century.[42] . . . [W]omen were often subjected to violence and mistreatment within the walls of industrial establishments, and in both Brussels and Montreal pleas were made for particular attention to this issue.[43] In a long list of demands presented to the Commission du travail, a delegate of the Molenbeek workers' league called for inquiry into factories and workshops that employed women and children "to know how these beings are treated, and the precautions that are taken to protect them from the dangers of machines, with which they are in daily contact."[44] Though the recommendation was not taken up in Belgium, such investigations were carried out in Quebec as of 1896, when, after successful lobbying by the Montreal Local Council of Women, female inspectors were hired to report on industrial establishments that employed women.[45] After this date, the tone of the reports changed noticeably as gender-related issues concerning industrial work became more prominent. "The textile and other industries where children, girls and women are employed have our especial care as there is much greater cause for vigilance and close supervision there than in places where only men are employed," ensured factory inspector James Mitchell, underscoring his thoughts on women's particular vulnerability in the industrial labour force.[46]

In commentaries like these, the uneasiness was caused by the proximity in which women and men worked. The notion that members of the two sexes should physically exert themselves while positioned side by side struck many observers as indecent, and their remarks are coloured by moral undertones that determined their view of appropriate interaction between men and women. The lack of separate sanitary facilities for each sex in many factories was also considered particularly problematic. Indeed, 10 years after women began inspecting Montreal's industrial establishments, Louise Provencher noted that progress was being made to ensure women's well-being in the workshops, but wondered "does not the moral side of her nature also need to be watched and safeguarded?" For the "inspectresses," as they were called, the conversations that "working girls" could be heard having in the workshops, even the "illustrated catalogues and advertisements of at least doubtful taste" to which their eyes were daily exposed, were enough to make one blush. While many workshops placed male and female employees in separate rooms, Provencher recommended that this practice be made mandatory, that women workers be supervised only by other women, and that all conversation be banned during working hours. Furthermore, she repeatedly suggested that the very rhythm of the workday be

modified to better accommodate women workers by allowing women to arrive later in order to avoid walking to work among the crowds of men who descended into the dark streets in the early morning hours.[47]

While the inspectors expressed reservations about the propriety of women's factory work and fought to establish what they considered appropriate conditions, others were opposed to the very idea of women working. Conservative commentators in both Belgium and Quebec tapped into prevailing notions that women's social role was in the home, emphasizing in spatial and bodily terms their vision of the factory as inappropriate for women. "What! A woman in the workshop?" exclaimed the Belgian priest and educator Victor Van Tricht. Then, responding to his own disbelief, "Yes! We live in times that make us witness this lamentable spectacle!" According to his understanding of femininity, women's presence in industry exposed them to both a physical and social environment that debased and sexualized them, and robbed them of their very "nature":

> She will thus go off, far from her husband, far from her child; she, a woman, will cross the tumultuous threshold of the textile mill. Suffocated first by this atmosphere where sneers that make her red in the face fly about, trembling with fright in the middle of these workmen whose stares and smiles sear her like a hot iron, ah! she suffers in her soul and in her honour.

> But let time do its bidding, let the first blushes of her insulted modesty dissipate, let the first jolts to her menaced chastity settle, and she will get used to this world and this atmosphere. To the men's remarks, she will have answers that will make them laugh; in response to their looks and their advances, her eyes, her gestures and her demeanour will flash an insolent shamelessness that will chill us with horror.

Tricht offers a familiar critique, but his characteristically evocative style and his drawing on the material and corporeal dimensions of industry show the level of subjectivity on which opposition to women's right to paid employment was formulated. The physicality of the factory space, the tumult, the suffocating air, the burning iron all represent fears about the unhealthy moral atmosphere that was believed to corrupt women through the transformation of gendered interaction. Can such a woman still be a mother, he wonders.[48]

Though their perspectives on the merit of female labour varied, commentators frequently defined these moral considerations in terms of corporeal preoccupations, ranging, as in the examples above, from immediate issues of personal risk and security to more socially grounded questions of appropriate bodily deportment. Hygienists, for their part, brought up the issue of the body much more directly. For instance, women were considered to be at greater risk of suffering from the effects of overwork because they were seen as physically weaker than men.[49] The Montreal-area hygienist F. A. Baillairgé, who focused on both the moral and the bodily factors, argued that legislation should prevent women from working in industries that presented more serious health hazards. Citing the case of Belgium as an example to avoid, Baillairgé referred to women's factory work as an "antisocial crime." "And I would ask whether a young woman, bent forward all day, for months, over a sewing machine, will not contract some form of infirmity," he demanded, his vivid bodily imagery adding emphasis.[50] . . .

As these discourses demonstrate, questions about women's bodies had a distinct place in broader corporeal representations of industrialized society. Evolving ideas about women and their place in the workforce were part of this debate, and there was certainly no unanimity among women themselves. If the middle-class female factory inspectors sought to conciliate social norms with women's determination to join the industrial workforce, other women positioned themselves more firmly on either side of the debate. Relying on her research in industrial hygiene, Lucy Schmidt objected in no uncertain terms to the presence of women in industrial establishments. "Woman," she argued . . . "loses her strength and her health to industry; and thus, she harms not only herself, as a human being: the very soul of the race, the seed of workers' life is affected by the work of women in industries that require them to strain themselves, or to spend time in insalubrious atmospheres."

For Schmidt, the judgment was unequivocal: Women who exposed themselves to the poisons of industry risked degeneration and death, if not a miserable existence, "worse than death itself!"[51] While Schmidt's point of view was premised more on corporeal concerns than on political or moral convictions, feminists of the period refuted the argument that the physical risk of industrial work was greater for women than for men, seeing this as little more than a perpetuation of existing inequalities. The Montreal Local Council of Women and its president, Julia Drummond, for instance, had lobbied actively for the appointment of women inspectors before 1896, denouncing the fact that women were placed in the same category as children when it came to regulating the length of workdays. Men and women, they argued, should be seen as equals in the industrial workforce, and the benefits of legislation enforcing shorter hours and adequate conditions "should be secured for all." Given that women were actively seeking equal educational and professional opportunities and fighting for equal pay for equal work, it seemed inappropriate to them to request special privileges for industrial work in particular, privileges that in any case served to justify existing salary disparities.[52]

Imagining the Worker

The imprint of industry on the urban fabric in Montreal and Brussels was so prevalent that reflections on the corporeal nature of this process were by no means limited to its direct participants or to scientifically educated experts in the field. These questions also preoccupied those who commented on the city in more impressionistic, literary terms. Through these representations emerge tensions between images of the bruised and battled labourer, whose suffering was the embodiment of anti-modern critiques of industrial development, and of the powerful, muscular worker, whose strength and courage gave corporeal form to a cherished optimism in industrial expansion, prosperity, and social advancement. Examining the transformations wrought by the steel business in Pittsburgh during this period, historian Edward Slavishak has shown how urban elites constructed images of workers' bodies that corresponded to their own ideals of industrial productivity, masculinity, and racial homogeneity. The turn-of-the-century worker, he argues, "was represented by others—artists, journalists, social reformers, employers—for public consumption; through these representations his role as a worker became merely acting, his body standing in for his subjectivity."[53] Central to this process, however, were the subjectivities and corporeal experiences of those doing the representing. In defining the corporeal otherness of the worker, these commentators relied on their own felt experiences. Beneath the purported objectivity of the calculating eye lay the powerful impressions created by the conditions in which these observations were made. Through middle-class accounts of workers' bodies emerge hints of the individual authors' own haptic encounters with the unique atmosphere of industrial spaces, their bewilderment at the sights and sounds of machinery operating at breakneck speeds as well as the clouds of dust and gas and the intense heat that envelop their own bodies.

. . .

A promotional pamphlet on Montreal, released to commemorate Queen Victoria's Diamond Jubilee and to celebrate Montreal's metropolitan expansion and its place in the British Empire, used equally evocative descriptions of workers' bodies in reference to the city's industrial capacity. . . . [T]he tone here is celebratory and triumphant, almost exuberant. Though Montreal's recent history is portrayed as one of "commercial and financial matters," of "peaceful if unromantic development which builds a state of mighty ends," the author nevertheless wants to add a warmer, more human touch to the story. "Nay, commerce is not unromantic," he insists, using the atmosphere of the factory and the bodies of workers inside to support his assertion that it is only "constant life within [industry's] bounds" that has "but dulled the mind to it."

> The dilettante who peers in at the rolling mills' doors, where titans, half-nude, swing the white hot bars from infernal fires, and others shape them like children playing with putty; who passes through the sugar refineries, where, percolating through enormous filters, or boiling to grain in huge vacuum kettles, the sweet produce of the cane is prepared for market; who visits the electric engines of the Street Railway or the Royal Electric, where at headlong speed the spinning wheels furnish the energy which moves half the town by day and lights it by night; who penetrates to the mysterious precincts of the gas works, where, in their round houses the vast receivers rise and fall like balloons: such a man will see the romance not seen by others.[54]

The contrast with the description of industrial work in the commission testimonials is remarkable. Here the workers are a breed of supermen who handle their tools as children play with toys, their brute strength and virility emphasized by their near nakedness. They do not suffer from their work, but thrive on the hellish atmosphere and fiery heat. The imagery is vivid, highlighting the physical experience of the spectacle of industrialization in a glorification of the economic elite's achievements and of their pride in their city.

But against these celebratory spatial stories of titans and massive engines, others saw the state of factories and workers' bodies in a worrisome light. Here the workshop atmosphere is degenerative and harmful, while workers' bodies are weakened, damaged, and suffering. In the well-known observation of urban mores, *Montreal by Gaslight*, this atmosphere is used to "expose" the city's "sin, shame and sorrow" in an attempt to "stir up citizens to seek a remedy for each particular evil." The "hideous noises" and smoke, the "weary toil" in the factories, workshops, mills, and foundries debase workers, exposing them to the worst "social, mental, moral and physical" conditions, writes the anonymous author, making explicit references to the Royal Commission and taking readers on a tour of the city's cotton mills, boot and shoe establishments, and its notorious cigar factories. The author brings us in, "up two flights of narrow stairs," onto a work floor drowned in "the sound of machinery and the hum of voices." Continuing, the author wants to make readers feel the atmosphere for themselves: "Here, in stifling air foul with odours of tobacco, machine-oil, perspiration, and a thousand other evil-smelling substances, are seated the slaves of the leaf." Men, women, and children—no one is spared the long hours for meagre pay. "There are no toilet appliances, no fire escapes, no facilities for ventilation: there is nothing but work and a brutal foreman to enforce it."[55]

. . .

Are these workers valorous heroes of a coming age or downtrodden vassals of an oppressive regime? While these interpretations are diametrically opposed in their intentions, they tell the vivid and contrasting perspectives of middle-class observations of the worker's body. A bourgeois author contesting social norms, a crusading moral reformer, [and] an influential business association . . . all wrote in terms of specific expectations and assumptions about industrialization and workers. Whichever side they were on, their visions of the body were fundamentally representative of the interior, emotional responses elicited by the rapid industrialization of turn-of-the-century society. In contemplating the tensions between the vast, outward processes initiated by capitalist enterprise and the subjective sentiments they evoked, these authors situated their discourse in the body and its movements in space, a body through which these processes were lived, a body simultaneously defined by them.

Conclusion

"When the Roman Empire was at its highest, all the industries of the country, in fact all the labour of the country, was performed by men who had been taken prisoners in battle and converted into slaves and whose lives and comfort were considered matters of little consequence," said Thomas Duffy, Commissioner of Public Works, to the delegates of the 1899 Convention of the National Association of Factory Inspectors held in Quebec's legislature. "To-day, however, both in England and America," he continued, "our workingmen are regarded as our strength and the very foundation of the nation's greatness."[56] Celebrating the accomplishments of modern industrialization on both sides of the Atlantic and the social evolution that accompanied it, Duffy expressed pride in the physical conditions in which workers contributed to this growth. As this chapter has demonstrated, the growing intensity of industrial activity at the turn of the twentieth century, and the distinct environment it produced, made the body and senses particularly relevant in urban dwellers' relationship to the modern city, whether this was in terms of individuals' own corporeal experiences with industrialization or through representations of the bodies of the workers whose labour was the force behind these transformations. Even these representations, we have seen, were in themselves the product not only of visual observation, but also of the direct tactile and sensorial experiences of the industrial milieu.

For those who, like Duffy, felt a great sense of confidence in modern developments, the factories and workshops that sprouted on the landscapes of cities like Montreal and Brussels were visual symbols of prosperity, which, in their size, layout, and aesthetic appeal created an atmosphere that bespoke order, productivity, sophistication, and progress. The workers inside were seen as strong, muscular titans, who deftly wielded massive tools in rhythmic motions that symbolized the steady pace of forward movement. In contrast, for those whose homes were situated nearby, who laboured at the service of industrialists, or whose professional activities brought them into close contact with the realities of these factories, the corporeal referents they used evoked distinct fears about the direction in which modernity was taking them. As archival records in both cities demonstrate, many urban residents took exception to the smells, sounds, dust, and smoke which the encroachment of industry brought to the places where they lived—nuisances that affected their physical comfort and health but also threatened them with financial loss as a result of the devaluation of their property.

As for the countless men and women whose livelihoods depended on industrial work, their relationship to industrial spaces was one of constant physical exertion within the confines of damp conditions, where muscle cramps, respiratory problems, accidents, disease, and violence were commonplace. Their testimonies poignantly illustrate how this physical stress contributed to the climate of tension, mistrust, and suspicion that characterized their rapport with their employers and that reigned on many factory floors in these two cities. Finally, the doctors and hygienists whose work kept them abreast of the latest developments in the expanding field of modern medical research relied on the vivid imagery of overtaxed bodies to drive home the urgency of their message in favour of more balanced, safer, and more hygienic working conditions. Industrialization and urbanization, the very foundations of Montreal and Brussels's claim to metropolitan status, were also understood to be the causes of the diseases, death, and decay that plagued urban life.

. . .

 More online.

Notes

1. Travel diary of Charles Buls, 1903. Archives de la Ville de Bruxelles (Archives of the City of Brussels, hereafter AVB), Fonds Buls, box 95. . . .

2. As Homberger notes, social reformers commonly evoked the image of Dante's descent to hell when characterizing urban slums. Here, Buls is intensifying the critique by applying the metaphor to the entire landscape of Montreal. Eric Homberger, *Scenes from the Life of a City: Corruption and Conscience in Old New York* (New Haven, CT: Yale University Press, 1994), 11. . . .

3. Stephen Mosley, *The Chimney of the World: A History of Smoke Pollution in Victorian and Edwardian Manchester* (Cambridge, UK: White Horse Press, 2001). . . .

4. On smoke abatement campaigns, and the angry discourses that fuelled them, see Frank Uekoetter, *The Age of Smoke: Environmental Policy in Germany and the United States, 1880–1970* (Pittsburgh, PA: University of Pittsburgh Press, 2009).

5. Édouard Octave Champagne, *Annual Report of the Boiler Inspector of the City of Montreal for the Year 1908* (Montreal, QC: Perrault Printing, 1909), 4. . . .

6. Montreal Board of Trade, *The Board of Trade Illustrated Edition of Montreal: The splendour of its location, the grandeur of its scenery, the stability of its buildings, its great harbour, its stately churches, its handsome homes, its magnificent institutions, its great industries, fully illustrated and described* (Montreal, QC: Trade Review, 1909), 2.

7. John F. Kasson, *Civilizing the Machine: Technology and Republican Values in America, 1776–1900* (New York, NY: Penguin, 1977), 139–40.

8. Peter Collins, *Concrete: The Vision of a New Architecture*, 2nd ed. (Montreal, QC: McGill-Queen's University Press, 2004); Reyner Banham, *A Concrete Atlantis: US Industrial Buildings and European Modern Architecture, 1900–25* (Cambridge, MA: MIT Press, 1986); Claire Poitras, "Sûreté, salubrité et monolithisme: l'introduction du béton armé à Montréal," *Revue d'histoire urbaine* 25, no. 1 (1996).

9. Peter Scholliers, "L'archéologie industrielle: définitions et utilités," *Cahiers de la Fonderie* 8 (1990): 62.

10. Adriaan Linters, *Industria: Architecture industrielle en Belgique* (Brussels, BE: Pierre Mardaga, 1986), 42. . . .

11. Cited in Lise Grenier and Hans Wieser-Benedetti, *Les châteaux de l'industrie. Recherches sur l'architecture de la région lilloise de 1830 à 1930* (Brussels, BE and Paris, FR: Archives d'architecture moderne et Ministère de l'Environnement et du Cadre de Vie—Direction de l'Architecture, 1979).

12. Ibid., 20–1. René Leboutte, Jean Puissant, and Denis Scuto, *Un siècle d'histoire industrielle, 1873–1973: Belgique, Luxembourg, Pays-Bas: Industrialisation et sociétés* (Paris, FR: SEDES, 1998), 45.

13. On the building and its presence in the surrounding urban fabric, see Douglas Koch, *Les quartiers du centre-ville de Montréal 1: Récollets* (Montreal, QC: Sauvons Montréal, 1977), as well as Cité Multimédia Montréal et al., *Les promenades architecturales de la troisième Biennale de Montréal* (Montreal, QC, 2002), CD-ROM.

14. *Montreal Illustrated, 1894: Its growth, resources, commerce, manufacturing interests, financial institutions, educational advantages and prospects, a brief history of the city from foundation to the present time* (Montreal, QC: Consolidated Illustrating, 1894), 203. . . .

15. Herbert Brown Ames, *The City below the Hill: A Sociological Study of a Portion of the City of Montreal, Canada* (Toronto, ON: University of Toronto Press, 1972 [1897]), 21.

16. N. Legendre, "Les enfants dans les usines," *Journal d'hygiène populaire* 1, no. 21 (15 March 1885), 151.

17. Franz Mahutte, *Bruxelles vivant* (Brussels, BE: Bureaux de l'anthologie contemporaine des écrivains français et belges, 1891), 305.

18. For a comparison of the Belgian and Canadian commissions and their value as historical sources, see Eliane Gubin, "Les enquêtes sur le travail en Belgique et au Canada," in Ginette Kurgan-van Hentenryk et al., *La question sociale en Belgique et au Canada, XIXe–XXe siècles* (Brussels, BE: Éditions de l'Université de Bruxelles, 1988), 93–107.

19. Nearly half of the 649 witnesses in Quebec were from Montreal. Fernand Harvey, *Révolution industrielle et travailleurs: Une enquête sur les rapports entre le capital et le travail au Québec à la fin du 19e siècle* (Montreal, QC: Boréal Express, 1978), 83. . . .

20. Harvey, *Révolution industrielle et travailleurs*, 63. Susan Mann Trofimenkoff, "102 Muffled Voices: Canada's Industrial Women in the 1880s," *Acadiensis* 3, no. 1 (1977). . . .

21. Commission du travail instituée par arrêté royal du 15 avril 1886, *Réponses au questionnaire concernant le travail industriel*, 4 vols. (Brussels, BE: Société belge de librairie, 1887), 1: 389.

22. *Report of the Royal Commission on the Relations of Capital and Labor in Canada* (Ottawa, ON: A. Senecal, 1889), 88.

23. *Report of the Royal Commission on the Relations of Capital and Labor in Canada, Evidence, Quebec Part I* (Ottawa, ON: A. Senecal, 1889), 457.

24. Ibid., 460.

25. Commission du travail instituée par arrêté royal du 15 avril 1886, *Procèsverbaux des séances d'enquête concernant le travail industriel*, 4 vols. (Brussels: A. Lesigne, 1887), 2: 7.

26. *Report of the Royal Commission on the Relations of Capital and Labor in Canada, Evidence, Quebec Part I*, 246.

27. Alain Corbin, "Douleurs, souffrances et misère du corps," in Alain Corbin, Jean-Jacques Courtine, and Georges Vigarello, eds., *Histoire du corps*, 3 vols. (Paris: Seuil, 2005), 2: 254. . . .

28. Émile Van de Weyer in *Rapports annuels de l'inspection du travail 6e année (1900), 3e and 8e année (1902)*, 6.

29. "Report of Louis Guyon," in Province of Quebec, *Sessional Papers #7* 39, no. 1 (1906), 181.

30. "Report of James Mitchell," in Province of Quebec, *Sessional Papers #7* 35, no. 1 (1902), 147.

31. Pol de Bruycker in *Rapports annuels de l'inspection du travail 15e année (1909)*, 28–9.

32. "Report of James Mitchell," in Province of Quebec, *Sessional Papers #* 7 39, no. 1 (1906), 188.

33. "Rapport de Louis Guyon," in Province of Quebec, *Documents de la Session* 27, no. 1 (1893), 226.

34. Van Overstraeten in *Rapports annuels de l'inspection du travail 1er année (1895)*, 71.

35. "Rapport du Dr C. I. Samson," in Province of Quebec, *Documents de la Session* 27, no. 1 (1893), 252.

36. "Report of James Mitchell," in Province of Quebec, *Sessional Papers #7* 36, no. 1 (1903), 203. The Brussels inspector Émile Van de Weyer observed that improvements to sanitary conditions improved workers' productivity. *Rapports annuels de l'inspection du travail 8e année (1902)*, 7.

37. "Report of Louisa King," in Province of Quebec, *Sessional Papers #7* 35, no. 1 (1902), 171.

38. Alain Corbin, "Douleurs, souffrances et misère du corps" in Corbin, Courtine, and Vigarello, eds., *Histoire du corps*, 2: 251.

39. Anson Rabinbach, *The Human Motor: Energy, Fatigue, and the Origins of Modernity* (Berkeley, CA: University of California Press, 1992), 1–8, 208–9. On the link between body and workplace, see also Ava Baron and Eileen Boris, "'The Body' as a Useful Category for Working-Class History," *Labor: Studies in Working-Class History of the Americas* 4, no. 2 (2007): 35–42. . . .

40. Lucy Schmidt, *Le livre du travailleur: hygiène industrielle* (Frameries, BE: Dufrane-Friart, 1913), 7–9, 15–16.

41. Though Corbin cautions against the "excessive" focus on pain in such representations, Rabinbach demonstrates how the ideal of a "body without fatigue" was shared by proponents of the science of work and

workers alike. Alain Corbin, "Douleurs, souffrances et misère du corps," 251; Rabinbach, *The Human Motor*, 1–8, 208–9. . . .

42. By 1911, women represented 22 per cent of the workforce in Montreal, 40 per cent of whom were employed in the industrial sector. Marie Lavigne and Jennifer Stoddart, "Ouvrières et travailleuses montréalaises, 1900–40," in Marie Lavigne and Yolande Pinard, eds., *Travailleuses et féministes: Les femmes dans la société québecoise* (Montreal, QC: Boréal, 1983), 100–1. . . .

43. Historians have chronicled the abuses and exploitation to which working women were subjected in this period: long hours, low pay, sweating system, and dangerous working conditions, among others. On Montreal, see especially Micheline Dumont et al., *L'histoire des femmes au Québec depuis quatre siècles*, 2nd ed. (Montreal, QC: Le Jour, 1992); Bettina Bradbury, *Working Families: Age, Gender and Daily Survival in Industrializing Montreal* (Toronto, ON: McClelland & Stewart, 1993). . . .

44. Commission du travail instituée par arrêté royal du 15 avril 1886, *Procèsverbaux des séances d'enquête concernant le travail industriel*, 17.

45. Elizabeth Kirkland, "Mothering Citizens: Elite Women in Montreal, 1890–1914" (Ph.D. thesis, McGill University, 2011), 169–70.

46. "Report of James Mitchell," in Province of Quebec, *Sessional Papers #7* 35, no. 1 (1902), 147.

47. "Report of L. D. Provencher," in Province of Quebec, *Sessional Papers #7* 39, no. 1 (1906), 192; 32, no. 1 (1898), 83; 33, no. 1 (1900), 68.

48. Victor Van Tricht, *L'enfant du pauvre: Causerie* (Namur, BE: P. Godenne, 1895), 39–40.

49. Province of Quebec, *Report of the Royal Commission on Tuberculosis*, 57.

50. F. A. Baillairgé, *La nature, la race, la santé dans leurs rapports avec la productivité du travail: Applications à la province de Québec* (Joliette, QC: by the author, 1890), 59–63.

51. Schmidt, *Le livre du travailleur*, 15.

52. Local Council of Women of Montreal, *Montreal Local Council of Women: 21st anniversary, 1893–1915* (Montreal, QC: Witness, 1915), 16. . . .

53. Edward Slavishak, *Bodies of Work: Civic Display and Labor in Industrial Pittsburgh* (Durham, NC: Duke University Press, 2008), 15.

54. *The Metropolitan Jubilee Souvenir* (Montreal, QC: W. Wallach, 1897), 7.

55. *Montreal by Gaslight*, (Montreal, QC: s.n., 1889), 24–32.

56. "Speech of the Honourable Thomas Duffy, Commissioner of Public Works," *Sessional Papers #7* 33, no. 1 (1900), 44.

14

"The Best Men That Ever Worked the Lumber"
Aboriginal Longshoremen on Burrard Inlet, BC, 1863–1939

Andrew Parnaby

Aboriginal people in Canada, like Aboriginal people across the continent, have been engaged in wage labour for centuries. Yet despite a long and diverse history of paid employment, this dimension of Aboriginal life is understudied by Canadian scholars.[1] Generally, anthropologists and ethno-historians have focused on "traditional" Aboriginal cultures and Native–newcomer relations, while political scientists and legal experts continue to probe questions of treaty rights and government policy. This intellectual orientation is not surprising. To some extent, it reflects scholars' engagement with contemporary Aboriginal politics: documenting the existence and persistence of a customary way of life—the occupation and use of a certain territory or the practice of a specific ritual—has been, and continues to be, a critical dimension of the ongoing struggle for title to land and rights to resources. As a consequence, however, the significance of wage labour to Aboriginal communities—a phenomenon that suggests change, not continuity; modernity, not custom—has been neglected. It does not fit easily into scholarship aimed, to varying degrees, at bolstering Aboriginals' historical and moral claim to self-determination.[2]

. . . Of interest, now, is not whether Aboriginal people worked for wages, but why they chose to do so, what that experience meant, and how long it lasted.[3]

This cluster of questions is at the core of this essay, an examination of Aboriginal longshoremen, most of whom belonged to the Squamish First Nation, a linguistic subdivision of the Coast Salish, on Burrard Inlet, British Columbia, from 1863 to 1939. . . . Organized into four sections, this essay begins with an analysis of the Squamish's adaptation to wage labour in the mid- to late nineteenth century. It then considers the ways in which Aboriginal workers negotiated the daily demands of longshoring—an occupation characterized by hard physical labour, intense competition for work, and raw employer power. Throughout their long tenure on the waterfront, Aboriginal dockers adopted numerous strategies to bolster their collective power as workers and their particular objectives as Aboriginal people. The third and fourth sections of this essay explore these tactics, and in doing so, highlight some of the ways that Aboriginals' workplace struggles influenced, and in turn were shaped by, the Squamish's wider search for autonomy in the face of sweeping economic, political, and demographic change in British Columbia's Lower Mainland. Often mentioned in the scholarly literature, but never studied in a systematic

Citation: Andrew Parnaby, "'The Best Men That Ever Worked the Lumber': Aboriginal Longshoremen on Burrard Inlet, BC, 1863–1939," *Canadian Historical Review* 87, no. 1 (March 2006): 53–78. Reprinted with permission from University of Toronto Press (www.utpjournals.com).

way, the "Indian" waterfront provides a window into the importance of waged work to Aboriginal people on Burrard Inlet and the sophisticated ways that the Squamish responded to Canadian colonialism *and* capitalism.

***

Cheakamus Tom understood the history of Native–newcomer relations in British Columbia very well. "For many years, our people could and did gain a living suitable for our wants from the forest and the sea," he stated in a letter written to the Royal Commission on Indian Affairs, which was holding hearings in the province from 1912 to 1916. "The different tribes or bands had their own territory in which they fished and hunted, and over which they had control," he continued. "But when the White man came he was allowed to go where he pleased to hunt, trap, or fish. Then our troubles began."[4] Pithy and succinct, Tom's assessment evokes an era prior to European settlement, when his people, the Squamish, utilized a swath of land between Howe Sound and Burrard Inlet in southwestern British Columbia; seasonally harvested aquatic and terrestrial resources in groups of family or extended family members; and, with these resources in hand, periodically held potlatches—a collection of ceremonies that reaffirmed the prestige, status, and influence of particular leaders or families through feasting, dancing, and gift giving.[5] Flexible and mobile, this kin-ordered social formation, and the rituals lodged deeply within it, underwent an important adjustment after the first sawmill appeared on Burrard Inlet in 1863. Shortly after its construction, Squamish families gravitated to the area, incorporating wage labour into their seasonal migrations.[6] . . . "A great number of these Indians live and exist by the work of their hands," Indian Agent Peter Byrne observed in 1913, referring specifically to those Squamish resident on the North Shore. "They work in the sawmills, at longshoring, and . . . at other occupations of a like character."[7]

As this short list of jobs suggests, sawmills—Sewell Moody's on the North Shore, then Edward Stamp's on the south shore—were harbingers of things to come. From the mid-nineteenth century to the early years of the twentieth century, British Columbia underwent a far-reaching economic transformation, a shift illustrated well by the rise of Vancouver as an important Pacific Coast port. Spurred on by the completion of the Canadian Pacific Railway in 1886 and the opening of the Panama Canal in 1914, large piers, grain elevators, and warehouses were constructed up and down Burrard Inlet, while numerous rail lines were laid along both its north and south shores (see Figure 1).[8] Like the physical environment of the port, capital was reorganized too. Individually, shipping companies in Vancouver invested in iron hulls, steam technology, and larger vessels; collectively, shipping, railway, and stevedoring companies banded together to form the Shipping Federation in 1912 to better manage the increase in maritime traffic and the waterfront's burgeoning labour force.[9] . . . By the interwar period, the paternalism and single-staple exports of the mid- to late nineteenth century had given way to more sophisticated economic structures. As David Montgomery has remarked, "The waterfront of a great port dramatized both the organizational achievements and the social chaos of industrial capitalism."[10]

Squamish men and women were important, if unequal, actors in this new industrial context. They stacked lumber in the mills, acted as guides for recreational hunters and fishers, built fences on farms, felled trees in the coastal forests, gutted fish in the canneries, piloted small boats in the salmon fishery, and loaded and unloaded cargo on the waterfront, usually combining a range of occupations to earn a modest livelihood. That all of the occupational pursuits undertaken by Aboriginal workers were seasonal is important, hinting at the ways in which the temporal and spatial rhythms of a customary, kin-ordered way of life articulated with the logic of a burgeoning capitalist labour market.[11] The result was a mixed economy in which Squamish men and women

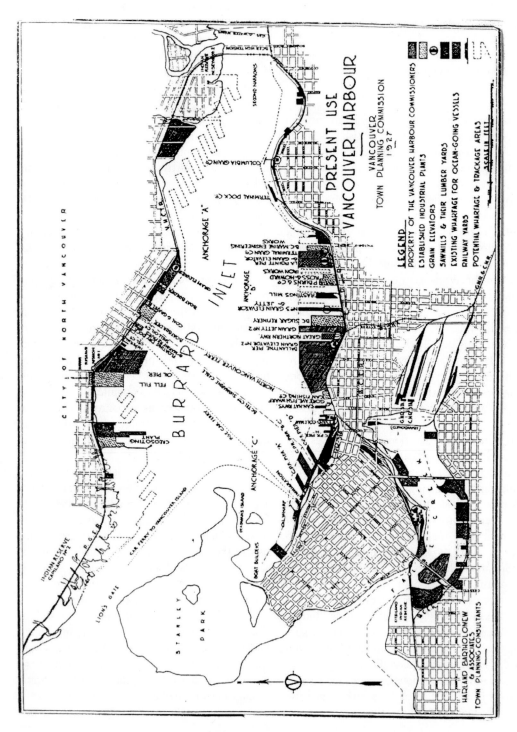

Figure 14-1. Port of Vancouver, 1927. Note the Squamish Reserves on the North Shore in North Vancouver and at the mouth of False Creek in Vancouver. *Source:* Vancouver Town Planning Commission, *A Plan for the City of Vancouver* (Vancouver, 1929).

deployed some of their labour power some of the time in a new way—working for wages—while simultaneously maintaining older methods of regulating access to resource sites and affirming links between their families and larger Aboriginal groups. There was a culturally specific logic in operation here that was internal to Coast Salish society: It is likely that Squamish men and women engaged in wage labour because their earnings could be used to purchase the goods necessary to hold a potlatch—a rationale shared by the Lekwammen and Kwakwa̱ka'wakw of Vancouver Island. Fragmentary evidence reveals that the Squamish continued to hold potlatches throughout this period of economic adjustment, although it is difficult to assess their size and frequency.[12] In short, cash and culture were connected, the persistence of the latter tied, to some degree, to the successful acquisition of the former.

Decisions about the utility of wage labour were not always made under conditions of the Squamish's own choosing, however. As an "old man" who could "remember when there was no Indian agent," Cheakamus Tom knew this: "The White man thought we ate too much fish, too much game, and passed laws to prevent our people from killing game or fishing except for a short time each year."[13] From the earliest days of the colonial project in British Columbia, the state played a critical role in setting limits on, and erecting boundaries around, the scope of Aboriginal life—a dynamic particularly obvious in the context of land. By the late 1870s, the Squamish, who, along with other Coast Salish groups bore the brunt of white encroachment, occupied a clutch of reserve sites in and around Howe Sound and on the North Shore of Burrard Inlet, an archipelago of Aboriginal territory in a sea of white pre-emptions.[14] Urban development, population growth, and economic expansion in the Lower Mainland, backed by a state that refused to recognize Aboriginal title to land, eroded this modest land base even further.[15] "A long time ago, the Indians depended upon hunting and fishing as their only means of living,"

Mathias Joseph, a Squamish leader, observed in 1913. "Now things have changed."[16] While the Squamish were drawn into the capitalist labour market by a desire to continue potlatching, they continued to work for wages because, as time went on, they possessed few other options, save for selling their labour power in the canneries or on the waterfront.

***

For waterfront workers on Burrard Inlet, as for longshoremen the world over, the experience of work was shaped by the demands of both a casual labour market and the "shape-up" method of hiring—a combination that persisted, in various guises, from the mid-nineteenth century until the 1920s. Typically, when vessels arrived in port, men swarmed the docks, and there, in a ring around a foreman, cargo hooks in hand, they jostled for position in hopes of securing a day's work.[17] In this context, work came in fits and starts, earnings fluctuated, and competition among men was often intense. Not surprisingly, then, waterfront workers tended to stress different skills and abilities in order to carve out a degree of security in an otherwise chaotic labour market. Organized into gangs, some men worked on ship, others laboured on shore, and within both categories men specialized in handling a particular cargo or operating a piece of technology. As long-time longshoreman Joe Gagnier recollected, referring specifically to the early twentieth century, "There were gangs who regularly worked the Australasian boats and those same gangs worked general cargo and practically nothing else." "You cannot get lumbermen to trim grain," echoed a waterfront employer in 1928.[18]

Socially constructed, and sometimes bitterly defended, demarcations of skill and ability intersected with cleavages of race and ethnicity on the job to produce a complex and hierarchical occupational milieu. Between 1908 and the late 1930s, the years for which solid evidence is available, white longshoremen dominated general cargo, Italian men tended to work as coal heavers, and Aboriginal workers monopolized logs and lumber.[19] . . .

Lumber handling gangs loaded cut wood into a ship's hold. On a sailing ship, lumber was transported by hand over the stern or through a porthole, each piece sliding down a series of ramps to the hold. Alternatively, the cut wood, what longshoremen sometimes called "boards," "sticks," or "timbers," was placed inside a sling, which was then fastened by a series of cables to a portable steam-powered engine called a "donkey"; the donkey engine, which was situated on a barge or on the wharf, lifted the "sling load" to the sailing ship to be stowed. Steam-powered vessels, which had all but replaced sailing ships in the lumber trade by the mid- to late 1920s, utilized deck-mounted winches, as well as derricks or cranes, to accomplish the same task, albeit at a much faster pace. Once inside a ship's hold, the load was disassembled and each "stick," which ranged widely in length, width, and weight, was carefully packed away.[20]

Each member of a lumber handling gang was assigned a specific task. The gang leader, or "hatch tender," coordinated the efforts of the men on ship, shore, and/or barge: He called for loads, sent signals to the donkey or winch driver, and dealt with personnel from the ship or stevedoring company who meddled in the work process ("Look, do this") and pushed the men to move faster ("Come on, you guys down there, move").[21] "Wire pullers" assisted the donkey driver; "slingmen" assembled loads; and "side runners" organized the men in the ship's hold—the men who, in pairs, handled each "timber." Experienced men, like "the Indian Charlie Antone," were able to work at a variety of jobs within a single gang; "[He] could run side pretty darn good," long-time waterfront worker Axel Nyman recollected. "Good man on the boom, [too]."[22] Above or below the ship's deck, lumber handling was both physically demanding and repetitious. It was not, however, without skill. On the "top side," winch drivers and slingmen

prided themselves on being able to manoeuvre long pieces of lumber through a small hatch into the ship's hold; "'tween decks," gang members valued men who understood how to stow lumber no matter what the configuration of a ship's hold. As one Squamish longshoreman observed, reflecting on his skills as a lumber handler, "When I was running side I used to watch the load coming down the hatch. There might be six or eight timbers in the load and I would size it up as soon as it landed I would know where each timber was going."[23]

The number of "Indian" gangs working on Burrard Inlet between 1863 and 1939 varied over time. Estimates by veteran longshoremen, who were thinking specifically about the early 1900s, put the number between four and six—which means that, depending on the size of the vessel, and whether or not it was being loaded or unloaded, anywhere between 40 and 90 "Indian" lumber handlers could be found on the docks on a given day. The figures available for the early 1920s, drawn from the records of a longshoremen's union and the Department of Labour, are higher, placing the number at approximately 125. Almost entirely absent from the docks in the mid- to late 1920s, for reasons that will be explored later, "Indian" longshoremen turn up in greater numbers after 1935; personnel records kept by waterfront employers indicate that between 40 and 55 men were actively handling lumber in the early 1940s.[24] In the context of the waterfront, "Indian" was an elastic category that included individuals born to Squamish parents, as well as those, Aboriginal and non-Aboriginal, who married Squamish women. An assortment of other workers, drawn from a range of national, cultural, and racial backgrounds, including other First Nations, rounded out the ranks of the "Indian"-dominated gangs. This diversity is captured well by the personnel histories of William Nahanee and Joe Jerome. Nahanee, who started on the waterfront in 1889 and remained a longshoreman for over 50 years, was of Hawaiian and Squamish ancestry, while Jerome, who, it appears, began his career on the docks sometime in the 1930s, was born to Tsimshian parents and married to a Squamish woman.[25]

The "Indians'" status on the waterfront as lumber handlers flowed, in part, from their long history of paid employment in and around Burrard Inlet. They had been handling logs and lumber, either in the sawmills or in the woods, for a long time.[26] With this employment history, it is no surprise that they emerged as adept waterfront workers: Both logging and longshoring were physically demanding jobs, and the skills acquired in one occupational context—the ability to run a donkey engine, for example—were easily transferred to another.[27] Specialization in a particular commodity helped Aboriginal longshoremen shore up their prestige as well, for it enabled them to gain greater knowledge of a specific cargo and, over time, a strong reputation for loading and unloading it. "The Indians were 'it' on the sailing ships," one old-timer recollected. "They were the greatest men that ever worked the lumber," observed another.[28]

Great, but not quite equal: While Aboriginal dockers chose to work "the lumber" because they possessed the right skills, and specialization helped to bring some predictability to casual work, they did so in an occupational context in which their options, although not closed off entirely, were constrained. Significantly, white waterfront workers tended to dominate general cargo, which was less dangerous and more lucrative than working the lumber.[29] Their position of relative privilege was girded by a sense of entitlement that all whites possessed by virtue of being white in a society in which race mattered. In British Columbia, this structure of feeling was deeply imbricated in culture, discourse, and space, formalized in law, and bound up in the province's political economy. In the specific context of the waterfront, it was reinforced by employers who benefited from competition from racially distinct gangs and who tended to hire non-Aboriginal men to handle general cargo— day-to-day decisions that, over time, helped to

create the conditions in which such divisions were naturalized and legitimated. It is not hard to see how white longshoremen's own sense of powerlessness on the job would make them more receptive to the authority derived from, to borrow from David Roediger, "the fiction that they are 'white.'"[30]

Aboriginal men negotiated the politics of waterfront work in a variety of ways—individual and collective struggles marked by the tensions associated with being both a longshoreman and being an "Indian." "[My Indian friend] George Newman, he was always full of fun. He would holler down the hatch in Indian language and then he would start to laugh," Edward Nahanee observed, the punch line being that white workers "'tween decks" did not understand George's orders: "Those Indian boys could talk behind their backs."[31] On the Vancouver waterfront, longshoremen's use of a shared language— nicknames, slang, profanity, and occupational jargon—accentuated the differences between employers and employees, and distinguished dockers from other ostensibly more respectable and skilled workers.[32] As this anecdote suggests, however, the use of the "Indian language" on the job reinforced *internal* divisions of allegiance and identification as well—a dynamic that likely subverted white workers' sense of racialized camaraderie and entitlement, if only for a moment. At times, the "Indian language" could be more physical than verbal. During his tenure on the waterfront in the late 1910s and early 1920s, Dan George, who became chief of the Squamish band in the 1950s, perfected what he called his "big dumb Indian look." Intimidating, defiant, and mocking in equal measure, it was used by George and other Squamish men to protest harsh working conditions, enforce standards of appropriate behaviour on the job, or to communicate, silently, between themselves.[33]

In other situations, Squamish men sought to neutralize white privilege in a more forceful way. "There was a one eyed [Indian] fellow running . . . side and he hated the sight of a white man. Sure enough, inside of two hours he threw a plank on [Moose] Johnson's foot and he had to go home," one docker recalled.[34] On the docks, physical strength was both an occupational requirement and a badge of working-class masculinity; as such, it played a key role in shaping longshoremen's sense of themselves as working men and, by extension, the wider dockside world that they inhabited. Yet, as the plight of Moose Johnson suggests, physical strength could be used to set boundaries around a particular type of cargo, job classification, or the composition of a work gang—dimensions of waterfront labour that were simultaneously defined in racial terms. In Vancouver, as in other port cities, a longshoreman's success or failure in the competition for work was dependent on a wide range of factors, not the least of which was the ability of racial groupings to mobilize in defence of their particular occupational niches, no matter how undesirable or difficult the work within that niche was.[35] Use of the "Indian" language and physical confrontation were part of this process; so, too, was labour recruitment. It was not uncommon for the sons and nephews of Aboriginal longshoremen to follow their fathers and uncles to the waterfront, and, in the process, learn the arts and mysteries of "working the lumber." On other occasions, experienced Aboriginal longshoremen could be found enticing "young fellows" from the Mission and other reserves to work on a specific lumber ship—a manoeuvre facilitated by the extensive familial relationships that characterized Aboriginal life on the North Shore and elsewhere.[36]

The experience of Simon Baker illustrates this final point. Born in 1911, Baker was raised on the North Shore of Burrard Inlet by his grandfather (and longshoreman), Squamish chief Joe Capilano, and his grandmother, Mary Agnes Capilano. As a young man, Baker attended a residential school, where he "organized" a "strike" to protest poor food and harsh discipline, and worked in a variety of occupations, including waterfront work. "After I got back home [from hop-picking], Dan Johnson, who is a relative of ours, asked me to go with him. I knew why he asked me, because we're good longshoremen," Baker recalled in his autobiography. "Joe Horton, the boss of the longshoremen, came to Westholme Reserve, near Duncan [on Vancouver Island], and came to Dan's house. 'Dan,' he said, 'do you want to go to work?' 'No,' said Dan, 'I'm tired but I have a young man; he's a good longshoreman.' So that was my first [job] longshoring [in 1926] at fifteen years of age." . . . "Our legend began in the 1800s during the days of the sailing ships. They had one mill at the time on the North Shore. They hired all the Indians on the North Shore who were able to work," Baker observed. "Five generations of our family have worked on the waterfront."[37]

Baker's recollections are significant for another reason: They illustrate the ways in which longshoremen, in the context of the waterfront labour market, utilized the idea of race to sort out who should have access to the docks, what gang to join, and which cargo to handle. Key to white longshoremen's monopoly on general cargo, race was deployed simultaneously by Aboriginal longshoremen to defend their status as skilled men on the lumber and to facilitate the entry of other "Indians" into waterfront work, thereby perpetuating their presence on the docks over time. In a more intimate way, working the lumber, and all the associations of race that went with it, helped Baker to further establish a dichotomy between himself as an Aboriginal person and other non-Aboriginal individuals. That understanding of difference, as his autobiography suggests, was critical to the formation of his identity as an Aboriginal man, and to his understanding of the need for political action, on the job and off. That specific idea—the ways in which working on the waterfront helped to mark off the boundaries of identity, and the political questions that flowed from that differentiation—is particularly evident in the context of political action and class conflict.

***

Labour relations on the waterfront were rarely peaceful. Between 1889 and 1935, Vancouver's waterfront workers joined a wide range of unions—from the conservative to the communist—and went on strike at least 18 times, a pattern of militancy that was matched by few other occupational groups, either provincially or nationally.[38] Aboriginal longshoremen were deeply involved in these struggles. In 1906, lumber handlers on Burrard Inlet, most of whom were Squamish, founded Local 526 of the Industrial Workers of the World (IWW), a radical organization that offered up a heady mix of revolution and reform to those workers who did not fit well into the established craft union structures: the unskilled, the migratory, and the marginal.[39] Its highly decentralized form of union organization, which was rooted in part in the itinerant lifestyle of its members, likely suited Squamish lumber handlers well, for they continued to hunt, fish, and work seasonally. Limited evidence suggests that Local 526 included approximately 50 or 60 men and held its meetings on the North Shore's Mission reserve.[40] A nasty waterfront strike in 1907, which, according to one source, was characterized by impressive levels of racial solidarity, apparently marked the local's demise.[41]

That Aboriginal workers were pioneers of industrial unionism in British Columbia is important to note, for it was this commitment to organizing the unorganized that would inform the challenge mounted by the Socialist Party of Canada and the One Big Union—radical alternatives to the Trades and Labor Congress—on the waterfront and in other workplaces in the years running up to and immediately following the Great War.[42] Equally striking is the fact that the IWW emerged at the same time that coast and interior Salish peoples were experimenting with new forms of resistance. In 1906, representatives from both communities met on Vancouver Island. There they nominated a delegation of three chiefs, including Joe Capilano, to take their demands directly to King Edward in London. Although the mission was unsuccessful—the

British government maintained that the question of title to land was strictly a Canadian issue—the unity of coastal and interior groups was, as Paul Tennant has argued, "a step in the evolution of pan-Indianism" that set the stage for future political innovations in the 1910s and 1920s.[43] Without question, the assertion of Aboriginal rights, particularly title to land, was part of a specific history of resistance among the Squamish that stretched back to the earliest days of white settlement and drew upon the cultural resources of their community. At the same time, however, it is important not to underestimate the political contribution of their participation in the industrial economy. Travelling great distances and working in a variety of occupational settings likely enhanced the Squamish's understanding of the breadth and depth of the changes wrought by white society and allowed for the wider dissemination of political ideas among different Aboriginal groups. "In my young days . . . we lived in shacks with outside toilets. . . . We didn't seem to know that we could have things, the same as the white man," Simon Baker recalled. "It wasn't until I was young and traveled to other places in BC [to work] that I realized that we could do better."[44]

The importance of migration, and the realizations it prompted, is particularly evident in the realm of waterfront work. . . . In this context, the links between the emergence of the IWW and the first pan-Salish organization comes into sharper focus. Not only were the same people involved in both movements—Joe Capilano paid for his trip to England with money earned on the waterfront—but, on a wider canvas, both were attempting to assert control over an economic and political context in which the balance of power had shifted decisively in favour of white society with the emergence of industrial capitalism and the incursion of the colonial state.[45] This dialectic of politicization is captured by the nickname adopted by Aboriginal dockers for Local 526: It was called the "Bows and Arrows," an assertion of difference and identity at a time when white society was bent on political margin-alization and cultural assimilation.

After the demise of Local 526, Squamish waterfront workers formed Local 38-57 of the International Longshoremen's Association (ILA) in 1913, about a year after white workers had established ILA Local 38-52 in Vancouver. "The Indians used to handle nothing but lumber and the whites, the general cargo. Sometimes they'd be working in the next hatch to each other and they'd get talking. That's how some Indians learned English and that kind of talk led to the formation of the ILA," one lumber handler recalled. "Things were dying out and ILA was getting bigger and bigger," remarked another.[46] Communication across divisions of race and specialization was no doubt important in this process of union building, but so too were the broader structural shifts taking place in the shipping industry, which brought larger numbers of workers together to load and unload a wider range of commodities on a single vessel. By the eve of World War I, only a handful of ships took on large volumes of lumber, while sailing vessels, once the domain of Aboriginal dockers, continued to disappear.[47]

The decision to disband the Bows and Arrows and join the ILA sparked a debate among Squamish workers. While no transcripts or minutes of this discussion survive, the memories of Ed Long, a lumber handler during these years, suggest that Aboriginal workers were politicized both as workers and as "Indians." During this debate they laid bare an agenda that linked workplace struggle to other Aboriginal concerns: "A lot of the old Indian boys didn't like it because they could go to work and quit and the boss would go and get him because he was a good lumber handler. They couldn't do without him."[48] Long's recollection highlights one dimension of casual work that many longshoremen—Aboriginal or not—valued: the ability to choose when and where to work, even if that choice meant taking one's chances on the daily shape-up.[49] More specifically, it suggests that at the

core of the "Indian boys'" critique was an abiding sense of pride in their status as skilled men "on the lumber" and a desire to protect their usual practice of merging waterfront work with other pursuits, such as waged work in the hop fields or hunting and fishing.[50] In the end, according to one source, about 90 per cent of the Bows and Arrows backed a move into their *own* ILA local—the men, evidently, opting for political separation in order to maintain control over their union affairs.[51]

. . .

From the emergence of the IWW to the creation of the ILA, Aboriginal men were involved in the political fermentation that characterized working-class life in Vancouver in the early twentieth century. Presumably they took part in the debate surrounding the amalgamation of ILA locals 38-57 and 38-52 in 1916, the new union's subsequent support for the One Big Union, and the strike wave that gripped Vancouver during and after the Great War. Edward Nahanee was among the waterfront workers barricaded inside the ILA hall on 3 August 1918 when it was attacked by returned soldiers who were protesting the dockers' unanimous support for the "Ginger Goodwin" general strike. "There were swarms of soldiers storming the doors, and on the roof of one of the warehouses, three machine guns were trained on us by the RCMP, so close I could practically see down their barrels," he recalled.[52] Woven into this wider pattern of collective action were moments when Aboriginal longshoremen's language and tactics addressed issues that were specific to them as "Indian" workers in a workplace segmented by differences ascribed to race: the desire to work the lumber, influence the composition of work gangs through labour recruitment, and take on other jobs when the need or desire arose. Significantly, the politics of work influenced, and in turn were shaped by, the emerging struggle for Aboriginal rights. . . .

That specific goal—independence—would become increasingly difficult to secure on the job after 1923 as class conflict, coupled with a plan by waterfront employers to reform the dockside labour market, threatened to marginalize "the best men that worked the lumber" from an occupation they had possessed since the mid- to late nineteenth century.

***

The 1923 longshoremen's strike was a lengthy all-or-nothing affair that marked a turning point in the organization of the waterfront workplace.[53] In that conflict, the Shipping Federation moved decisively to break the ILA, establish an open shop, and reconfigure the local labour market. For its part, the longshoremen's union, which had played an important role in fomenting "the spirit of discontent" that accompanied the Great War, was pushing for a five-cent wage increase and greater control of hiring through a union-run despatch hall.[54] Fragmentary evidence from the 1923 saw-off suggests that Aboriginal dockers were opposed to going on strike at first, but later took an active role in "holding the fort." William Nahanee, Edward's father, was a member of the union's negotiating committee, rubbing shoulders for a time with veteran radical and longshoreman William A. Pritchard.[55] An anecdote from the pages of the ILA's strike bulletin hints at involvement at the rank-and-file level as well. "It is beyond the ability of my mental apparatus to understand why those who boast of having a higher degree of intelligence and civilization than that of the Indian will be so base as to scab on their fellow workers when the Indian will not do so," an anonymous writer opined. "Were scabs able to understand the Indian language they would receive an education on an Indian's opinion of a scab."[56] After two months on the picket line, the ILA, which had mounted "one hell of a fight," was broken, its efforts undercut by the Shipping Federation's effective use of strikebreakers, limited unity among Pacific Coast waterfront workers, and the conservatism of the labour movement—locally, provincially,

and nationally—after the heady days of 1919.

Aboriginal workers paid a heavy price for their activism. After decades of class conflict, the Shipping Federation embraced a new philosophy of workplace relations: welfare capitalism. Inspired by similar innovations in other industries, it sought to secure long-term industrial peace by building institutional and social bridges across the chasm of class difference and decasualizing the local labour market. Dubbed a "good citizens policy," the latter initiative took aim at the use of the shape-up method of hiring and the overabundance of casual workers who, it was thought, were "inclined to agitation." Under the terms of the post-strike settlement, members of the ILA, if they were not blacklisted outright, were entitled to only a small portion of available work; the lion's share of employment opportunities was reserved for strikebreakers who, after the end of the strike, were enrolled in a new company-sponsored association, the Vancouver and District Waterfront Workers Association.[57] In this context of defeat, whatever unity existed between Squamish longshoremen and their white counterparts dissolved. By January 1924, former members of the Bows and Arrows, in particular Andrew Paull, were pressing the Shipping Federation to create a new lumber handlers' organization, the Independent Lumber Handlers' Association (ILHA). Not only did they want to control their own political affairs, but they objected "to being placed in [full-time] gangs because of the necessity of working whenever the gangs in which they were placed were equipped"—a practice key to the Shipping Federation's vision of decasualization.[58]

. . .

Aboriginal longshoremen were marginalized from waterfront work after the 1923 confrontation. Placed at a considerable disadvantage by the blacklisting of former ILA men and the creation of a company union, their desire for some control over when and where their gangs were "equipped" was at odds with the Shipping Federation's long-term vision of creating a permanent pool of full-time longshoremen under its direction.[59] The logic behind the ILHA's position reflected a preference among its Aboriginal members for a more migratory working life, one that combined a variety of occupations with other customary forms of support, such as hunting and fishing.[60] Not only did this attachment to mobility resonate with their specific histories as Aboriginal people, but, in the context of waged work, it provided a means to assert their independence on the job. At the same time, however, a migratory working life was born of necessity. The terms of the post-strike settlement, which reduced the earning power of the ILHA's membership, coupled with the limits placed on other Aboriginal economic practices by the colonial state, made it difficult for them to make ends meet without working on the docks, aboard a fishing vessel, or in the hop fields in a single year. "In ten days it was all over," Edward Nahanee observed, referring to the 1923 strike. "We lost our jobs and everything."[61]

Aboriginal workers' absence from the waterfront lasted until 1935, when they returned to work in the midst of a gruesome six-month confrontation between the Shipping Federation and the Vancouver and District Waterfront Workers Association, which had forged links with the Communist Party of Canada in the early 1930s and become more and more militant as the Depression wore on.[62] Leaflets identifying "scab" workers circulated by the longshoremen's strike committee contained the names of several Aboriginal men; one communist-backed newspaper, *Ship and Dock*, asserted that the Department of Indian Affairs was helping waterfront employers in recruiting replacement workers.[63] "Some would call us strikebreakers," Tim Moody recollected. "But that is a matter of opinion. The men whose jobs we took were those who broke the strike in 1923 . . . My father said my grandfather had been a longshoreman and we had to hang on to what he had started. It was all we had."[64] Hanging on in the aftermath of the 1935 strike meant being members of the North

Vancouver Longshoremen's Association (NVLA), a union created by the Shipping Federation, with the assistance of the North Vancouver Board of Trade, to both reward "Indian" workers for opposing the "forces of disruption" and act as a bulwark against bona fide unions that were active in other Pacific Coast ports.[65] The new organization was guaranteed 10 per cent of waterfront work and possessed 86 members, 40 to 55 of whom were Aboriginal.[66] In many cases, the men who belonged to this cohort worked alongside other members of their family or extended family, suggesting that the link between kin relations, labour recruitment, and working the lumber remained strong. Dan George and seven of his relatives belonged to the new North Shore union; so, too, did Simon Baker and five members of his family.[67]

Strikebreakers, not strikers, this time around, "Indian" dockers fared better in the wake of the 1935 confrontation than they did after the 1923 strike. Indeed, in the mid- to late 1930s, they dominated the union's executive and worked nearly as often as other gangs that handled similar cargo, despite the ongoing effects of the Depression on maritime traffic. After a long hiatus, the Bows and Arrows were back "on the lumber"—an occupation that they would retain during World War II and after.

* * *

Aboriginal men on Burrard Inlet figured prominently in the industrialization of British Columbia, taking up longshoring, among other occupations, almost from the moment that sawmills first came to the area in the early 1860s. On the docks, they worked in an occupational setting characterized by turbulent labour relations, strong competition for work, and sharp distinctions of specialization. The intersection of class and race was significant in this complex context, shaping the day-to-day decisions that Aboriginal longshoremen, most of whom were Squamish, made about what job they might do, whom they might work with, and what their political options were, on the waterfront and off. That waterfront unionism and organizations dedicated to Aboriginal rights emerged at the same time illustrates this point well. Men who were politically active on the "Indian" waterfront were also involved with the Salish delegation to London, the Allied Tribes of British Columbia, and the Squamish Tribal Council—a cross-pollination that persisted into the early 1940s, when Tim Moody of the NVLA joined the Native Brotherhood of British Columbia, a group created by coastal First Nations in 1931 to advance the concerns of Aboriginal commercial fishers.[68]

Skilled and knowledgeable longshoremen, Aboriginal workers' longevity on the waterfront was due to many factors, not the least of which was their ability to specialize in a particular cargo and, over the span of several decades, ensure that "Indian" men were available to work it. Family relations were vital to this process of labour recruitment; so, too, was the passage of workplace knowledge from one generation of Aboriginal waterfront workers to the next. Absent from waterfront work after the 1923 strike, the Bows and Arrows returned to the docks in 1935, and in short order, they made up about half of the NVLA's membership and dominated its executive.

By that time, the waterfront workplace had changed considerably. Decasualization was firmly in place. Within the ranks of the newly formed North Shore lumber handlers' union, however, casual sensibilities—the desire to work where and when one wanted—persisted into the late 1930s, 1940s, and 1950s, a structure of feeling evident throughout Aboriginal workers' lengthy tenure on the docks. . . . "It was murder at first [to give up fishing]," recalled one Aboriginal longshoremen after deciding to work on the waterfront full time. "But now we've got no squawks. I wanted to live here in town and it was getting too hard to make any money fishing."[69]

Inspired by Rolf Knight's pioneering *Indians at Work*, this analysis illustrates the significance of wage labour to Aboriginal life on Burrard Inlet between 1863 and 1939. Rooted in a specific location, time period, and configuration of power relations, the Bows and Arrows's history of waged work was, simultaneously, part of a more general phenomenon: the expansion of capitalism on a global scale. Indeed, Indigenous people from southeast Alaska to Puget Sound faced broadly similar challenges with the advent of paid labour from the mid-nineteenth to the early twentieth century; so, too, did waterfront workers from Seattle to London, Montreal to Mombassa, who struggled with decasualization as it took hold in other labour markets in other ports during the same time.[70] Perhaps the experiences of Tlingit cannery workers or London dockers were known to the Bows and Arrows—information, as well as commodities, circulated in port cities—and, from their vantage point on Burrard Inlet, they recognized a common pattern of conflict, resistance, and adaptation to capitalist development.

For the "best men that worked the lumber" that pattern was intimately connected to their encounter with colonialism. As a consequence, their struggle for autonomy not only embraced questions of land, resources, and self-government—as the existing literature suggests—but issues related to the day-to-day realities of life "on the hook" as well. By bringing Aboriginal history and labour history into closer contact, two disciplines that are typically conceptualized and researched separately, the very notion of Aboriginal politics expands and changes shape. Class, as a structured reality and a lived daily experience, mattered to the Squamish. To ignore or downplay this dimension of their lives is to obscure many of the key issues that they thought about often, struggled with daily, and hoped, in the end, to be free from.

 More online.

Notes

Gregory S. Kealey, Mark Leier, and Todd McCallum read drafts of this essay and provided important feedback; special thanks to anonymous "Reader B" whose close reading of this text and lengthy evaluations proved invaluable. The research upon which this essay is based was supported by the Social Sciences and Humanities Research Council.

1. A "bibliography of major writings in aboriginal history" that appeared in [the *Canadian Historical Review*] illustrates the point well. Of the 130 books published between 1990 and 1999, only six focused on "economics," and of those six, three were editions of books that originally appeared in the 1930s and 1970s. See Keith Thor Carlson, Melinda Marie Jetté, and Kenichi Matsui, "An Annotated Bibliography of Major Writings in Aboriginal History, 1990–99," *Canadian Historical Review* 82, no. 1 (March 2001): 122–71. Writing in "Top Seven Reasons to Celebrate and Ask More from *Labour/Le Travail*," *Labour/Le Travail* 50 (Fall 2002): 88–99, David Roediger argues that Aboriginal workers have fared even worse in the context of Canadian labour history where the experiences of newcomers, not natives, dominates the literature concerned with race and ethnicity.

2. For the Canadian context see Steven High, "Native Wage Labour and Independent Production during the 'Era of Irrelevance,'" *Labour/Le Travail* 37 (Spring 1996): 243–64. For the American context see Alice Littlefield and Martha C. Knack, eds., *Native Americans and Wage Labor: Ethnohistorical Perspectives* (Norman, OK: University of Oklahoma Press, 1998). . . .

3. John Lutz, "After the Fur Trade: The Aboriginal Labouring Class of British Columbia, 1849–90," *Journal of the Canadian Historical Association* (1992): 69–94; Lutz, "Gender and Work in Lekwammen Families, 1843 to 1970," in Kathryn McPherson, Cecilia Morgan, and Nancy M. Forestell, eds., *Gendered Pasts: Historical Essays on Femininity and Masculinity in Canada* (Toronto, ON: Oxford University Press, 1999); Lutz, "Making 'Indians' in British Columbia: Power, Race, and the Importance of Place," in Richard White and John M. Findlay, eds., *Power and Place in the North American West* (Seattle, WA: University of Washington Press, 1999), 61–84.

4. Chief Cheakamus (Tom) to "Honourable Gentlemen," [n.d., likely 1912 to 1916], file 520c, vol. 11021, RG 10, British Columbia Archives (hereafter cited as BCA). I consulted RG 10, the records of the Department of Indian Affairs, in both the British Columbia Archives and Library and Archives Canada (LAC); for this reason, citations for RG 10 may refer to either the BCA or the LAC.

5. Homer Barnett, *The Coast Salish of British Columbia* (Eugene, OR: University of Oregon Press, 1955); Cole Harris, *The Resettlement of British Columbia: Essays on Colonization and Geographical Change* (Vancouver, BC:

UBC Press, 1997), 68–102; and Wayne Suttles, *Coast Salish Essays* (Vancouver, BC: Talonbooks, 1987).

6. "Sproat's Report on the Squamish River Reserve, 1877," file 3756-7, vol. 3611, RG 10, BCA.

7. Testimony of Peter Byrne, 20 June 1913, Union of BC Indian Chiefs, Add. Mss 1056, BCA.

8. On the transformation of the port of Vancouver, see Alexander Gibb, *The Dominion of Canada: National Ports Survey, 1931–32* (Ottawa, ON: King's Printer, 1932); Leah Stevens, "Rise of the Port of Vancouver, British Columbia," *Economic Geography* (January 1936): 61–71.

9. Andrew Yarmie, "The Right To Manage: Vancouver Employers' Associations, 1900–1923," *BC Studies* 90 (Summer 1991): 40–74.

10. Robert A. J. McDonald, *Making Vancouver: Class, Status, and Social Boundaries, 1863–1913* (Vancouver, BC: UBC Press, 1996). The quotation is in David Montgomery, *The Fall of the House of Labor* (New York, NY: Cambridge University Press, 1987), 97.

11. This generalization is based on the annual reports of the Department of Indian Affairs published by year as part of Canada, *Sessional Papers* (1877–1930). See Andrew Parnaby, "On the Hook: Welfare Capitalism on the Vancouver Waterfront, 1919–1939" (Ph.D. thesis, Memorial University of Newfoundland, 2001), 204–7, 453, 454.

12. References to potlatches held by the Squamish can be found in Byrne to assistant deputy, 3 February 1914, vol. 1479, Letterbook, RG 10, BCA; Devlin to Vowell, 16 July 1896, file 121,698-53, vol. 3944; Charles Hill-Tout, "Notes on the Skqomic of British Columbia," in Charles Maud, ed., *The Salish People* (Vancouver, BC: Talonbooks, 1978), 49; testimony of Chief Mathias Joseph and Chief Harry, 1913, Add. Mss 1056, BCA; "Gilbert Malcolm Sproat's Summarized Report . . . 1877," file 3756-11, vol. 3611.

13. Chief Cheackmus (Tom) to "Honourable Gentlemen." . . .

14. Cole Harris, *Making Native Space: Colonialism, Resistance, and Reserves in British Columbia* (Vancouver, BC: UBC Press, 2002), maps 3.6, 5.1, and 5.2 on 67, 110, and 111 respectively.

15. The sale of the Kitsilano reserve captures this development well. See William John Zahoroff, "Success in Struggle: The Squamish People and Kitsilano Indian Reserve No. 6" (Master's thesis, Carleton University, 1978).

16. Testimony of Mathias Joseph, 1913, Add. Mss 1056, BCA.

17. The global perspective is detailed in Colin J. Davis, David de Vries, Lex Heerma van Voss, Lidewij Hesselink, and Klaus Weinhauer, *Dock Workers: International Explorations in Comparative Labour*

History, 1790–1970 (Aldershot, UK: Ashgate, 2000). For Vancouver see John Bellamy Foster, "On the Waterfront: Longshoring in Canada," in Craig Heron and Robert Storey, eds., *On the Job: Confronting the Labour Process in Canada* (Montreal, QC: McGill-Queen's University Press, 1986), 281–308; ILWU Pensioners, *Man Along the Shore! The Story of the Vancouver Waterfront as Told by the Longshoremen Themselves, 1860s–1975* (Vancouver, BC: ILWU Pensioners, 1975), 8–61; Robert McDonald and Logan Hovis, "On the Waterfront," in Working Lives Collective, ed., *Working Lives* (Vancouver, BC: New Star Books, 1985), 71–2; Parnaby, "On the Hook."

18. ILWU Pensioners, *Man Along the Shore!* 40; "Meeting . . . the Shipping Federation . . . and a Committee from North Vancouver City Council," 17 October 1928, file 10, box 5, Add. Mss 279, Shipping Federation of British Columbia records, City of Vancouver Archives (hereafter cited as CVA).

19. ILWU Pensioners, *Man Along the Shore!* 27, 29, 41, 45, 99.

20. Ibid., 16, 24–9, 36–7, 44–5, 55–6.

21. Interview with Ed Long, tape 17:35, International Longshoremen's and Warehousemen's (ILWU) records, University of British Columbia, Special Collections (hereafter cited as UBC-SC).

22. Interview with Axel Nyman, tape 17:19, ILWU records, UBC-SC.

23. ILWU Pensioners, *Man Along the Shore!* 56.

24. Ibid., 15, 33, 41, 80 (early 1900s); *Longshoremen's Strike Bulletin*, 9 November 1923 (early 1920s), vol. 37; "North Vancouver Longshoremen's Assn., membership" (post-1935), file 3, box 46, Add. Mss 279, CVA.

25. According to "Squamish Longshoreman Has Watched Vancouver Grow into Great Port," *Vancouver Daily Province*, 10 May 1941, Nahanee's father was Hawaiian and his mother was a "Capilano Indian." . . .

26. "Agricultural and Industrial Statistics, 1899–1919," vol. 1493, RG 10, BCA.

27. Hilda Mortimer with Chief Dan George, *You Call Me Chief: Impressions of the Life of Chief Dan George* (Toronto, ON: Doubleday, 1981), 113–14; ILWU Pensioners, *Man Along the Shore!* 74.

28. ILWU Pensioners, *Man Along the Shore!* 27, 29. Similar sentiments are expressed in an interview with Paddy McDonagh, tape 17:4, ILWU records, UBC-SC.

29. "Accidents for the 1st Half of 1925," file 1, box 36, Add. Mss 279, CVA.

30. David Roediger, *Towards the Abolition of Whiteness: Essays on Race, Politics, and Working-Class History* (New York, NY: Verso, 1994), 8.

31. Interview with Edward Nahanee, tape 17:9, ILWU records, UBC-SC.

32. David De Vries, "The Construction of the Image of the Dock Labourer," in Davies et al., *Dock Workers*, 695–700.

33. Mortimer and George, *You Call Me Chief*, 115.

34. ILWU Pensioners, *Man Along the Shore!* 29.

35. Bruce Nelson, "Ethnicity, Race, and the Logic of Solidarity," in Davies et al., *Dock Workers*, 655–80.

36. ILWU Pensioners, *Man Along the Shore!* 56; Dorothy Irene Kennedy, "Looking for Tribes in All the Wrong Places: An Examination of the Central Coast Salish Social Network" (Master's thesis, University of Victoria, 1995), 122–6.

37. Simon Baker, *Khot-la-cha: The Autobiography of Chief Simon Baker*, ed. Verna J. Kirkness (Vancouver, BC: Douglas and MacIntyre, 1994), 2–4, 8–11, 36–7, 53–60, 76–8.

38. Parnaby, "On the Hook," 1–15. For the national strike trends see Gregory S. Kealey and Douglas Cruikshank, "Strikes in Canada, 1891–1950," in Gregory S. Kealey, ed., *Workers and Canadian History* (Kingston, QC: McGill-Queen's University Press, 1995), 345–418. . . .

39. Mark Leier, *Where the Fraser River Flows: The Industrial Workers of the World in British Columbia* (Vancouver, BC: New Star Books, 1990).

40. Herbert Francis Dunlop, *Andrew Paull as I Knew Him and Understood His Times* (Vancouver, BC: Order of the OMI of St. Paul's Province, 1989), 80, 166; ILWU Pensioners, *Man Along the Shore!* 33, 46; interview with Axel Nyman, tape 17:19, ILWU records, UBC-SC.

41. *Industrial Union Bulletin*, 2 November 1907.

42. Allen Seager and David Roth, "British Columbia and the Mining West: A Ghost of a Chance," in Craig Heron, ed., *The Workers' Revolt in Canada, 1917–25* (Toronto, ON: University of Toronto Press, 1998), 231–67.

43. Paul Tennant, *Aboriginal People and Politics: The Indian Land Question in British Columbia, 1849–1989* (Vancouver, BC: UBC Press, 1990), 85.

44. Baker, *Khot-la-cha*, 98.

45. Knight, *Indians at Work*, 124; William John Zaharoff, "Success in Struggle: The Squamish People and Kitsilano Indian Reserve Number 6" (Master's thesis, Carleton University, 1978), 143–4.

46. ILWU Pensioners, *Man Along the Shore!* 46; Stuart Bowman Philpott, "Trade Unionism and Acculturation: A Comparative Study of Urban Indians and Immigrant Italians" (Master's thesis, University of British Columbia, 1963), 44.

47. ILWU Pensioners, *Man Along the Shore!* 46–7.

48. Ibid.

49. On this point see Klaus Weinhauer, "Power and Control on the Waterfront," in Davies et al., *Dock Labour*, 580–603.

50. Dunlop, *Andrew Paull*, 80, 163–6; interview with Axel Nyman, tape 17:19, ILWU records, UBC-SC.

51. ILWU Pensioners, *Man Along the Shore!* 46–7.

52. Mortimer and George, *You Call Me Chief*, 115–16.

53. Logan Hovis, "The 1923 Longshoremen's Strike," in Working Lives Collective, *Working Lives*, 175.

54. *Longshoremen's Strike Bulletin*, 24 October 1923, vol. 37, Add. Mss 279, CVA.

55. Ibid.

56. Ibid., 9 November 1923.

57. For an introduction to welfare capitalism see the entire issue of *International Labor and Working-Class History* 53 (Spring 1998). For the Vancouver waterfront see Parnaby, "On the Hook," 26–74.

58. McVety to Harrison, 23 February 1924, Strike 95 (vol. 2), vol. 332, RG 27, LAC.

59. Crombie to Labour Committee, 11 February 1924, file 4, box 23, Add. Mss 279, CVA.

60. On the importance of migration to other Aboriginal workers in BC see Paige Raibmon, "Theaters of Contact: The Kwakwa̱ka̱'wakw Meet Colonialism in British Columbia and at the Chicago World's Fair," *Canadian Historical Review* 81, no. 2 (June 2000): 157–90.

61. Philpott, "Trade Unionism," 45.

62. Richard McCandless, "Vancouver's 'Red Menace' of 1935: The Waterfront Situation," *BC Studies* 22 (Spring 1974): 56–70.

63. "Where are these men working?" file 10, 75-E-5, series 200, Vancouver Police Department fonds, CVA; "Indian Agency Is Used to Break Strikers' Ranks," *Ship and Dock*, 14 November 1935, Strike 87A, vol. 369, RG 27, LAC.

64. Philpott, "Trade Unionism," 47.

65. Canadian Transport to Johnson, 18 February 1938, file 2, box 46, Add. Mss 279, CVA.

66. "Agreement . . . 25 Day of March . . . 1937," file 9, vol. 25, Add. Mss 332, ILWU Local 501 records, CVA; assistant labour manager to president, 14 August 1941, file 3, box 46, Add. Mss 279, CVA. The low number is taken from "North Vancouver Longshoremen's Assn., Membership," file 3, box 46, Add. Mss 279, CVA; the high number appears in Philpott, "Trade Unionism," 46.

67. "North Vancouver Longshoremen's Assn. Membership."

68. Philpott, "Trade Unionism," 48–9; Tennant, *Aboriginal People and Politics*, 114–24.

69. . . . Philpott, "Trade Unionism," 22; the quotation appears on 52.

70. Russell Lawrence Barsh, "Puget Sound Indian Demography, 1900–1920: Migration and Economic Integration," *Ethnohistory* 43, no. 1 (Winter 1996): 65–97; Frederick Cooper, "Dockworkers and Labour History," and Klaus Weinhauer, "Power and Control on the Waterfront: Casual Labour and Decasualisation," in Davies et al., *Dock Workers*, 523–41, 580–603; Cairn Elizabeth Crockford, "Nuu-chah-Nulth Labour Relations in the Pelagic Sealing Industry, 1868–1911" (Master's thesis, University of Victoria, 1991); Victoria Wyatt, "Alaskan Indian Wage Earners in the 19th Century: Economic Choices and Ethnic Identity on Southeast Alaska's Frontier," *Pacific Northwest Quarterly* 78, no. 1–2 (January–April 1987): 43–9.

15 "Miss Remington" Goes to Work
Gender, Space, and Technology at the Dawn of the Information Age[1]

Kate Boyer

Introduction

Beginning at the end of the nineteenth century, the financial services sector began to undergo a technological "revolution" with the introduction of new information and communication technologies such as the telephone, typewriter, dictaphone, and mimeograph machine. These technologies changed social–spatial relations within the white-collar workplace, the scope and scale of the networks of branch banking, and even how people thought about city life. At the same time as this process was occurring, the gender of labour within the financial services sector was also changing, such that by the end of the first quarter of the twentieth century most of the work taking place within white-collar offices was performed by women.[2] This paper concerns how these two processes impacted one another and how together they reshaped the spaces and experiences of the early twentieth-century, white-collar workplace.

A growing body of scholarship within (and beyond) geography has begun to theorize information technology and the information economy as spatial phenomena that create and foreclose opportunities at different scales.[3] Meanwhile, feminist geographers have long been interested

in the workplace as a site for the production of identity.[4] Sharing elements with both these literatures while infusing complementary theoretical concerns and disciplinary traditions, scholars in science and technology studies and the history of technology have examined gender and the construction of socio-technical systems in the workplace.[5] In this paper, I draw on and hope to link these lines of inquiry in geography on the one hand and science and technology studies on the other through an analysis of the interplay between technology and gender within the early twentieth-century information economy in what was the centre of the Canadian financial services sector at the time: Montreal.

I argue that the early twentieth-century financial services sector created new geographies of mobility and fixity that differed by sex and by scale. Specifically, the branch-banking system created a network in which men flowed through and women functioned as fixed points. This pattern was echoed at different scales, from the level of the body and the workplace up through spatially dispersed national-level networks, and was supported through regimes of temporal and spatial surveillance as well as rhetorics about women's supposedly staid nature. After introducing the broader project from which this paper is drawn,

Citation: Kate Boyer, "'Miss Remington' Goes to Work: Gender, Space, and Technology at the Dawn of the Information Age," *The Professional Geographer* 56, 2 (2004): 201–12. Copyright © 2004 Routledge.

I will provide some background on Montreal at the time period under review. I will then turn to a consideration of social relations in the early wired workplace, and conclude by examining how women and men fit into the broader networks of branch banking that new information and communications technologies helped create.

The Study

This paper draws on research conducted for my doctoral dissertation on the feminization of clerical work in Montreal between 1900 and 1930, the central aims of which were to consider processes of identity formation in the early information technology workplace and link the feminization of clerical work to changing representations of women in the city more generally.[6] . . .

At the corporate archives under review I was able to draw upon materials such as employee files, company journals, photographs, internal correspondence relating to company policy and personnel issues, and records documenting company-sponsored extracurricular programs. The three companies, for which I had preserved information on individual employees in the time period considered, were the Bank of Montreal, Sun Life, and the Bank of Nova Scotia. At the Bank of Montreal I examined records for the 593 women employed between 1902 and 1923, gathering information on age at hiring, place of birth, and years of service. At Sun Life, I was able to chart the number of women employees between 1900 and 1930, though this company did not preserve any other data on individual employees.

The most detailed records of women employed as clerical workers in the financial service sector during this time were preserved by the Bank of Nova Scotia in files that typically included information on home address, religion, educational background, letters of reference, yearly evaluations, and salary information. Some also contained letters from managers of branch offices, personnel in head office, and employees themselves relating to employee behaviour.

However, because the head office of this bank was not located in Montreal, the number of women in my sample was smaller at this institution than at others under review. From my reading of 2,880 of the 6,216 total employee files housed at this archive, I found records for 27 women who had worked at the Montreal Branch of this bank in the first third of the century. Though smaller in number than records from other corporations, these documents were valuable because they illuminated the limits of acceptable behaviour in this workplace.

I approached print media not as a transparent window to past times and places, but rather, after Hall et al. and Tuchman, Kaplan-Daniels, and Benét, as a mediated site for reinforcing dominant social values.[7] In addition to being a fundamental part of their working lives, reading and writing were an important component of working women's leisure time. Moreover, newspapers served an important role in shaping ideas about city life. As Domosh has noted, "the metropolitan press pioneered journalistic practices that satisfied people's need for information about the bewildering place they found themselves in, the other inhabitants, and themselves."[8] Though written in reference to the nineteenth-century city, this observation holds true for the time period under review here. Based on an analysis of these sources, I argued that the feminization of clerical work created important new spaces for identity formation and heterosociability in the white-collar workplace; that this process opened up the city to women in new ways; and finally, that the early twentieth-century clerical workspace, and women clerical workers themselves, provide a useful vantage point from which to think about modern urban subjectivity.

Setting the Scene: Gender, Work, and Ethnicity in Early Twentieth-Century Montreal

As today, early twentieth-century Montreal was a rich mix of language, religion, and ethnicity, with English-Protestant, French-Catholic, and Irish-Catholic constituting the three major cultural groups. Montreal was also home to significant Jewish, Italian, and other smaller immigrant communities.[9] Most Montreallers spoke French as their first language and claimed Catholicism as their religion. Of those claiming British origins, about two-thirds were Protestant, and one-third Irish-Catholic. While the Catholic Church controlled an impressive array of social institutions, economic power was concentrated in a bourgeoisie comprised largely of Anglo-Scottish Protestants, with Irish- and French-Catholics composing the majority of the middle and working classes.[10] Montreal served as the centrepoint both for the national banking and financial services industry, as well as for the smaller French banking system. The financial services sector overall was disproportionately English-Protestant in composition, both in terms of language spoken and religious–linguistic background of the workforce, though among clerical employees Irish-Catholics were overrepresented relative to the city as a whole.

The technological revolution that began in the late nineteenth century created an explosion of paperwork that required keeping track of and a concomitant explosion of low-paid, routinized office jobs in the financial services sector.[11] For class-conscious companies attuned to their public image, it made sense for companies to hire educated, middle-class women to perform office work. In the early twentieth century middle-class femininity still evoked Victorian notions of the "cult of ideal womanhood," understood through attributes of piety and moral purity, domesticity, and submissiveness,[12] traits that companies in the financial services sector were happy to attach to their employees. And although considered morally superior to men, educated middle-class women were cheaper to employ than their male counterparts and could be paid wages equivalent to a male bricklayer. At the same time, viewed from the perspective of female job seekers, clerical work paid more than nearly any other type

of job open to women, and companies did not lack for applicants to fill out their employment rolls. . . . By 1911, clerical work had become the third most important source of employment for women in Quebec after manufacturing and domestic service.[13]

Not unlike the North American economy of the late 1990s, the 1910s saw the emergence of an employment market that sucked workers in. Labour-saving innovations in agricultural technologies meant that fewer people were needed on farms, and increasing numbers of rural inhabitants, especially women, began to look for work in cities. At the same time, Montreal served as the major Canadian destination point for overseas immigration throughout this period. As early as 1901, one-third of the women claiming employment as clerical workers, stenographers, or typists on the Montreal census were born outside the city itself. Of the 588 women employed at the head office of the Bank of Montreal between 1902 and 1923 for whom place of birth is known, more than half were born outside of Montreal, with one-quarter hailing from the United Kingdom and smaller portions from the United States and other countries.

As a group, clerical workers in the early twentieth-century city were overwhelmingly young and single. Reinforcing the findings of Dagenais and Rudin, my research found that the average age at hiring for all women employed at the Bank of Montreal between 1902 and 1923 was 20 years old.[14] . . . The average length of tenure was two years, and over 98 per cent of these young women were single. Though for a small number of women, clerical work served as a means to remain financially independent throughout adult life, for most it represented a time of independence and relative freedom between young womanhood and married life.

While Victorian-era notions of idealized middle-class femininity based in domesticity, purity, and piety continued to circulate, by the 1910s, they were joined in the popular press by depictions of the "New Woman" and independent working girl.[15] Liberated from family (who some-times remained behind in the country or even in another province), the so-called New Woman enjoyed the pleasures of the city and a greater degree of freedom than her rural (or more trad-itional) sisters. The New Woman was marked by her sophistication, explicit rejection of Victorian gender stereotypes, and urban milieu.[16] As Elizabeth Wilson argues, rejection of traditional gender ideology is key to understanding the modern woman as a distinctly urban type: "Since nature was altogether overturned in the city," she argues, "a new form [of] beauty and new form of sexuality were appropriate for its iron landscape, a form that combined masculine grandeur and strength with feminine allure."[17]

Employed in the heart of downtown, this workforce of young, mostly single, clerical work-ers and other working "girls" came to be consti-tuted as an urban "type" associated with New Womanhood and the nocturnal urban landscapes of an entertainment industry that was expanding at this time through cinemas, dance halls, and cabarets. Consider the following excerpt from a 1926 article in the *Montreal Daily Herald*:

> Eight o'clock and the entrance to each of the many theatres that open their jaws along St. Catherine Street holds its group of wait-ing ones, a stenographer waiting for her girlfriend, a saleslady keeping a tryst with her fellow. . . . [A] young sheik waits for a dance-hungry jazz baby inside the portal of the hall of the theatre just down the street.[18]

Similarly, a series of articles appearing in the national [magazine] *Maclean's* in 1931 comparing office work to marriage for young women offers a vivid example of how the freedom enjoyed by clerical workers was contrasted in popular media to the constraints of life for the young mother at home. Entitled "This Bondage" (referring to mar-ried life), the article is accompanied by an image of a young woman flanked by two young children and shackled to a ball and chain labelled "home."

From her imprisonment on one side of the text, she looks wistfully toward a busy office on the other side of the page, as if recalling a memory from an earlier time. Through advice columns, pieces with such titles as "Saturday Talks to Business Girls," and articles chronicling the need for more work-ing women's clubs in the city, newspapers of the day cast clerical workers as a recognizable urban type, characterized by their youth, freedom, and (importantly) their unmarried status. This con-trasted both the confined lives of their "married sisters," as well as notions of middle-class femin-inity that located women's worth in their identi-ties as . . . mothers and wives.[19]

Space, Technology, and Gender in the Early White-Collar Office

In contrast to the freedom by which clerical work-ers were portrayed in the popular press, women's widespread entrance to the financial services sector as employees was happening at the same time as the widespread adaptation of principles of scientific management, or Taylorism, to the white-collar workplace.[20] The goal of scientific management was to increase productivity, an activity that required devising and vigilantly employing systems for tracking progress, out-put, and employees themselves.[21] In the finan-cial services industry this meant employing punch clocks and hall passes to track workers' movements in time and space and establishing standards such as words-per-minute to meas-ure productivity.[22] At Sun Life, one of the largest employers in early twentieth-century Montreal, employees were not allowed to leave their depart-ments unless on company business, and depart-ment heads were instructed to report offenders.[23] Loitering in locker rooms, washrooms, and cor-ridors was specifically forbidden, and employees wishing to leave the building during business hours required a pass from the department head, to be presented to the hall porter in exchange for passage through the building. Though I did not find any specific evidence of this motivation on the part of management, forbidding workers to congregate away from their workstations during the business hours may have also served as a strategy to deter unionization. In addition to monitoring employees' movements within the building, workstations were arranged to be efficient and cost effective. At most of the corporations under review by the 1920s, stenography and clerical work was centralized within company headquarters and performed at desks in large, open-floored workspaces. The Bank of Nova Scotia had a typing pool by 1911,[24] and in that same year the Sun Life employee journal (then *Sunshine*) described the "army of typewriters" and typing pools filled with women.[25]

Though clerical work offered women better wages than other kinds of jobs open to them, within any individual company, women were concentrated at the bottom of the managerial hierarchy. Workers in these jobs were seen as needing more supervision and were subjected to more stringent regimes of spatial and temporal control relative to those higher up the management ladder. Workers in these jobs were also disproportionately women. In contrast to the small desks and open-floor plans in which women clerical workers laboured, management (at Sun Life and elsewhere) typically worked in large offices decorated so as to evoke middle-class domestic space.[26] Freed from the typewriter or dictaphone, these men worked at desks designed for conversing, reading, and thinking, in offices equipped with doors and secretaries to buffer and regulate contact with others. Meanwhile, at the bottom of the organizational hierarchy, clerical workers were "tied" or tethered to spatially fixed pieces of equipment such as a typewriter or dictaphone, in workspaces that more easily lent themselves to visual and auditory surveillance.[27] For such employees, location and productivity were intimately linked: For those whose work was identified most closely with a certain piece of machinery, being anywhere but at one's workstation meant not "doing one's job." Thus, in contrast to the highly *mobile* nature of women's lives

as suggested by 1901 census and birthplaces of Bank of Montreal employees noted earlier, within the space of the office, clerical workers were allowed relatively little spatial freedom. Through the close connection to the machines they worked with, clerical workers functioned as "part of the machinery" in a way that recalls nineteenth-century textile mills.

As clerical work became increasingly feminized throughout the early twentieth century, women also came to be viewed as having a certain degree of expertise regarding the technologies they used. As an illustration of this point, consider the following two advertisements for Remington typewriters, the first from 1888 and the second from 1910. The first advertisement hails from a time not long after the typewriter had been invented and before its use was widespread in offices. This was at the beginning of women's entrance into the clerical sector. As Figure 1 illustrates, the advertisement depicts a woman in shadow-tone seated at a typewriter inside a house. She is being observed through a window by a man who does not understand that she is typing, but mistakenly thinks she is playing the piano. This early ad constitutes a clear effort not only to inform consumers about a product, but also to link that product with middle-class femininity. By locating their product in the middle-class home (and thus, material comfort) and linking it to an activity already associated with respectable middle-class womanhood (and an appreciation of arts and culture), the ad sought to portray typewriting as an activity that would reinforce conceptions of middle-class femininity rather than challenge them (presumably even when the activity took place *outside* the home).

As typewriter use became more widespread and women's presence in offices became commonplace, advertisers no longer had to sell consumers on the appropriateness of women typists. In the second image (from 1910) the typist has become a respectable office worker (and product spokesperson), the idealized "Miss Remington" (Figure 2). Because Miss Remington has been

Figure 1. Advertisement, *Montreal Daily Star*, 25 October 1888.

Miss Remington

Says

that she has used the Remington Typewriter for years and always preferred it, but that the new model 10 is a revelation to her in new time and labor saving features.

It has always been so with every new Remington model. The new model 10, like all its predecessors, offers a brand new proposition to the buyer, something more and better for his money than he has ever before obtained in a writing machine.

Remington Typewriter Company (Limited)
101 Notre Dame Street West, Montreal

Figure 2. Advertisement, *Montreal Daily Herald*, 9 January 1910.

working in an office for some time (despite her young appearance), she has gained experience evaluating office machinery, and, as we are told, she is familiar not only with the new model but with its predecessors as well. From the side of the frame, Miss Remington advises us that the new model 10 is "a brand new proposition," offering the buyers "something new and better for his money than he has ever before obtained."[28] We are invited to take Miss Remington's word for it, based on her status as an expert user.

Yet this technological expertise had its limits. Arguably, the intended goal of women becoming "part of the system" was to disencumber men's minds from the prosaic end of office work, so that they could concentrate on the "real" (read, masculine) work to be done. At the same time as quotidian technologies such as the typewriter were becoming ever more closely associated with women's work, projects of city and nation-building—and the technologies that enabled both—continued to be viewed as men's domain. Indeed, at least to some, scaled, gender differences in the ability to understand and use technology were not culturally determined, but inborn. This view can be seen in a 1931 article on why women could not become managers, in which an anonymous manager at the Canadian Imperial Bank of Commerce argued in the pages of his company journal that women were unfit to manage because they had not gained (nor were capable of acquiring) the "right kind of knowledge."[29] "Boys and men," the author claimed, acquired this knowledge "by their very nature," because "from earliest boyhood," males take an interest in animals, material things, and in the working of machinery. As an illustration, the author enclosed a test comprised of questions on industry, manufacturing, trade, and agriculture that prospective managers could take.

Explaining why men could be expected to answer these questions while women could not, he argued that the young boy, in contrast to the young girl, "goes as a matter of boyish interest where these things are going on, asks questions and imitates such activities in his play."[30] Applying this point to the work of bank managing, the author stressed the importance of knowledge about broader systems of manufacturing and production to the banking business and the work of investing. Surely, he argued, this knowledge was as foreign and unknowable to women as the remote lumber camps that managers were required to visit. In this way, the author located the experiences and knowledge required for managing a bank in spaces that were off limits to "respectable" women.

Though "Miss Remington" may have known her typewriters, as gender stereotypes of the day would have it, the workings of technology, city building, forestry, and trade, together with sites where this knowledge could be procured, were beyond her grasp as a respectable, homebound, middle-class female. To summarize: in contrast to both the highly mobile nature of so many clerical workers' lives—migrating from farms and even from overseas—and media representations highlighting this group's freedom, within the workplace itself, clerical workers were spatially fixed: "tied-down" to their machines and workstations. In addition, women and men were posited as having quite different relationships to the different technologies that enabled networked branch banking. While women were free to claim authority over small, discrete pieces of office machinery, comprehending the broader socio-technical systems of which those machines were a part was still considered men's work.

Gender and Networked Branch Banking

In addition to creating new geographies of opportunity and constraint at the level of the workplace, the feminization of clerical work created new geographies of mobility and fixity that differed by gender at the broader scale of networked branch banking. Enabled by new information and communications technologies, branch banking served to reconcentrate power, in terms of people, information, and capital, in "command and control" centres in larger cities.[31] Making spectacular use of interior steel-frame construction developed in the late nineteenth century, head offices gave companies new symbolic significance on the urban landscape and introduced ideas about rationality, modernity, and in the Canadian case, empire, in physical form. Head offices represented the power of both the company itself (as a logo on stationery and company products), as well as the city in which that company was headquartered, thus contributing to a process of skyline-based urban branding.

Though situated in urban areas rich in services and amenities, the trend in the case of the companies under review was for head offices to function as much as possible as total worlds, in which employees could engage in both work and nonwork activities. For example, according to E. F. Chackfield, an engineer reporting in 1931 on the structural marvels of the Sun Life Insurance Company head office in the *Municipal Review of Canada*, the 24-storey structure amounted to no less than "a city within a city."[32] Assuring readers that the 35 acres of interior space was every bit as impressive as its exterior, the author highlighted the 38 elevators, five miles of telephone cables, and three basements housing entertainments such as archery ranges, shooting galleries, and a bowling alley, all to amuse the 10,000 to 12,000 employees in off hours.[33]

By drawing on what was then technology's cutting edge, head offices could keep employees linked to each other and the outside world, while at the same time satisfying as many employee needs as possible (including dining, sports, and other leisure activities) in-house, under watchful eyes. Descriptions such as these highlight the fact that not only were twentieth-century head offices impressive, they were impressive in a way that older examples of corporate architecture were not. They suggest a system for measuring the value and importance of commercial space based on magnitude of scale and level of technological sophistication that would endure throughout the century and beyond.

While information had to be managed in centralized head offices, early twentieth-century banking was also marked by the expansion of networks to hinterlands and overseas in order to extract profit from an ever broader territory. For the larger companies, the goal was clearly to be global. For example, Sun Life had branches in Britain, the United States, Asia, and the Caribbean by the 1920s, and as early as 1912 the Bank of Montreal had 167 branch offices nationwide, as well as branches in Great Britain, the United States, and Mexico, and affiliate branches in major cities in Asia, Europe, Australia, New Zealand, Argentina, Bolivia, Brazil, Chile, Peru, and British Guiana.[34]

In the companies under review, transferring between different branches was how one advanced up the managerial hierarchy. Transferring provided a way to familiarize management trainees with different positions within the company, standardize practices across the corporate network, and strengthen corporate allegiance. As Benedict Anderson has observed, spatially mobile employees can be thought of as human "nodes," which strengthen a sense of shared corporate identity.[35] As they moved from one place to another within the network, everywhere meeting people with whom they shared common cultural references, these mobile male employees (and their wives and children) built webs of community nationally and internationally.

Yet women were barred from transferring. Although this can be explained in part by the fact that women were not put on management tracks as a matter of policy in the time period under review, I also found evidence suggesting a reticence to transfer women on principle. For example, records from the Bank of Nova Scotia Archives suggest that requests from women seeking to transfer within the same job category during this period were routinely denied, even when applicants offered to cover their own travel and relocation expenses.[36] Although I was not able to find a corporate policy on this issue, we can gain some insight from a 1927 article in the Royal Bank employee magazine entitled "The Duties of the Country Junior":

> As regards promotion, it should be remembered that in one respect the female employees are at a disadvantage. A young man entering banking with the intention of making it his life-work is prepared to undertake service at any branch, however remote, whenever directed to do so by Head Office . . . the circumstances and inclinations of female employees, as a rule do not permit them to serve in any but the branch or branches located in their hometown or city.[37]

As this passage suggests, within the middle-class ideology that informed gender relations at this time, women were imagined to be "naturally" more immobile and "home-based" than men, even when they were at work. Thus, whereas men flowed through the networks created by early twentieth-century branched-banking systems, women were positioned as fixed points within them: echoing their spatial fixity at the level of individual offices discussed earlier.

Conclusions

Through an analysis of textual and visual print media, company journals, and employee records, I hope to have shown that the spaces and technologies that sustained the information economy in the early twentieth century were not politically neutral, but rather, that they actively helped produce asymmetries of power and opportunity. As I have argued, women in the early wired workplace were more likely to be "tethered" to specific machines in the office, and, owing to rules barring their advancement, were subject to higher levels of surveillance and corporeal constraint than their male counterparts. This stood in sharp contrast to actual levels of

mobility among this population as suggested by the census and employee records, as well as the freedom by which female clerical workers were characterized within the popular press of the day. I have also argued that the new technologies that enabled the expansion of branch banking came to have gendered associations, which also differed by scale. Whereas large-scale work of city building and infrastructural development were conceived of as . . . male activities, downstream office technologies were feminized.

Finally, I have argued that women and men were positioned differently within the broader networks that branch banking created. In addition to advancing goals of profit-making and augmenting imperial glory, networked branch banking constituted a system for career advancement that worked to constrain women at various scales, both physically and metaphorically. While men moved through the system, making human networks and moving up the career ladder, women were conceived of as fixed points, tethered to their branch and hometown as they were to their typewriter or dictaphone. In these ways, new technologies reinforced power relations of class, sex, and ethnicity, even as they opened new opportunities for both sexes. As the digital information economy continues to take shape, I hope this example from the past can serve as a reminder of the importance of interrogating the relations between space, gender, and technology in the workplace.

 More online.

Notes

1. My thanks to two anonymous reviewers for their helpful commentary and suggestions on earlier drafts of this paper.

2. See L. Fine, *Souls of the Skyscraper: Female Clerical Workers in Chicago 1870–1930* (Philadelphia, PA: Temple University Press, 1991); G. Lowe, *Women in the Administrative Revolution: The Feminization of Clerical Work* (Toronto, ON: University of Toronto Press, 1987); and A. Kwolek-Folland, *Engendering Business: Men and*

Women in the Corporate Office, 1870–1930 (Baltimore, MD: Johns Hopkins University Press, 1994).

3. See S. Graham and S. Marvin, *Splintering Urbanism: Networked Infrastructures, Technological Mobilities and the Urban Condition* (London, UK: Routledge, 2001); M.-P. Kwan, "Time, Information Technologies and the Geographies of Everyday Life," *Urban Geography* 23, no. 5 (2002): 471–82; W. Mitchell, *City of Bits: Space, Place and the Infobahn* (Boston, MA: MIT Press, 1996); and J. Wheeler, Y. Aoyama, and B. Warf, eds., *Cities in the Telecommunications Age: The Fracturing of Geographies* (New York, NY: Routledge, 2000), to name just a few.

4. See K. England, "Suburban Pink Collar Ghettos: The Spatial Entrapment of Women?" *Annals of the Association of American Geographers* 83, no. 2 (1993): 225–42; K. England, "Girls in the Office: Recruiting and Job Search in a Local Clerical Labor Market," *Environment and Planning A* 27 (1995): 1995–2018; S. Mackenzie, "Building Women, Building Cities: Toward Gender Sensitive Theory in the Environmental Disciplines," in C. Andrew and B. Milroy, eds., *Life Spaces: Gender and Household Equipment* (Vancouver, BC: UBC Press, 1998), 13–30; L. McDowell, "Social Justice, Organizational Culture and Workplace Democracy: Cultural Imperialism in the City of London," *Urban Geography* 15, 7 (1994): 661–80; and L. McDowell, *Capital Culture: Gender at Work in the City* (Malden, MA: Blackwell, 1997).

5. See C. Cockburn, *Machinery of Dominance: Women, Men, and Technical Know-How* (London, UK: Pluto Press, 1985); F. Kittler, *Gramophone, Film, Typewriter* (Stanford, CT: Stanford University Press, 1999); and C. Marvin, *When Old Technologies Were New: Thinking about Electric Communication in the Late 19th Century* (New York, NY: Oxford University Press, 1988).

6. K. Boyer, "The Feminization of Clerical Work in Early 20th-century Montreal" (Ph.D. dissertation, McGill University, 2001).

7. See S. Hall, C. Critcher, T. Jefferson, J. Clarke, and B. Roberts, *Policing the Crisis: Mugging, the State, and Law and Order* (London, UK: Macmillan Press, 1978); and G. Tuchman, A. Kaplan-Daniels, and J Benét, eds., *Hearth and Home: Images of Women in the Mass Media* (New York, NY: Oxford University Press, 1978).

8. M. Domosh, *Invented Cities: The Creation of Landscape in 19th-century New York and Boston* (New Haven, CT: Yale University Press, 1996). See also G. Barth, *City People* (New York, NY: Oxford University Press, 1980).

9. See P. Linteau, *Histoire de Montréal depuis la confederation* (Montreal, QC: Boréal Press, 1992); C. McNicholl, *Montréal: Une société multiculturelle* (Paris: Editions Belin, 1993); and S. Olson, "Ethnic Strategies in the Urban Economy," *Canadian Ethnic Studies* 33, 2 (1991): 39–64.

10. See J. Dickinson and B. Young, *A Short History of Quebec: A Socio-Economic Perspective* (Toronto, ON: Copp Clark Pitman, 1988); and A. Germain and D. Rose, *Montréal: The Quest for a Metropolis* (New York, NY: Wiley, 2000).

11. G. Lowe, *Women in the Administrative Revolution*, and G. Lowe, "Mechanization, Feminization, and Managerial Control in the Early 20th Century Canadian Office," in C. Heron and R. Storey, eds., *On the Job: The Labour Process in Canada* (Montreal, QC: McGill-Queen's University Press, 1984).

12. See R. S. Cowan, *More Work for Mother: The Ironies of Household Technology from the Open Hearth to the Microwave* (New York, NY: Basic Books, 1983); L. K. Kerber, "Separate Spheres, Female Worlds, Woman's Place: The Rhetoric of Women's History," *Journal of American History* 75 (1988): 11; M. L. Roberts, "True Womanhood Revisited," *Journal of Women's History* 14 (2002): 150–7; B. Welter, "The Cult of True Womanhood," in *Dimity Convictions: The American Woman in the 19th Century* (Athens, OH: Ohio University Press, 1976).

13. Census of Canada. 1911. Vol. 4, Table 11.

14. M. Dagenais, *Division sexuelle du travail en milieu bancaire: Montréal, 1900–1930*, memoir présenté a l'Université du Quebec à Montréal comme exigence partielle de la matrise en histoire Université du Québec à Montréal, 1987; M. Dagenais, "Itinéraires professionnels masculins et féminins en milieu bancaire: Le cas de la Banque d'Hochelaga, 1900–29," *Labour/Le Travail* 24 (1989): 45–68; and R. Rudin, "Banker's Hours: Life behind the Wicket at the Banque d'Hochelaga, 1901–21," *Labour/Le Travail* 18 (Fall 1986): 63–76.

15. See E. Freedman, "The New Woman: Changing Views of Women in the 1920s," *Journal of American History* 61 (September 1974): 372–93; C. Smith-Rosenberg, "The New Woman as Androgyne: Social Disorder and Gender Crisis, 1870–1939," in C. Smith-Rosenberg, *Disorderly Conduct: Visions of Gender in Victorian America* (New York, NY: Oxford University Press, 1985); and E. W. Todd, "Art, the 'New Woman,' and Consumer Culture," in B. Melosh, ed., *Gender and American History since 1890* (New York, NY: Routledge, 1993).

16. E. Wilson, "The Invisible Flâneur," *New Left Review* 191 (January/February 1992).

17. Ibid., 128.

18. *Montreal Daily Herald*, 7 January 1926, 3.

19. A. Douglas, *The Feminization of American Culture* (New York, NY: Knopf, 1977).

20. G. Lowe, "Mechanization, Feminization, and Managerial Control."

21. A. Pred, *Lost Words and Lost Worlds: Modernity and the Language of Everyday Life in Late 19th-century*

Stockholm (Cambridge, UK: Cambridge University Press, 1990).

22. M. Banta, *Tailored Lives: Narrative Productions in the Age of Taylor, Veblen, and Ford* (Chicago, IL: University of Chicago Press, 1993). See also Kwan, "Time, Information Technologies and the Geographies of Everyday Life."

23. *Company Rules and Regulations*, circa 1920, Box 406, Sun Life Archives.

24. G. Lowe, "Class, Job and Gender in the Canadian Office," *Labour/Le Travail* 10 (Autumn 1982): 11–37.

25. *Sunshine*, November 1911, 142. See also Florence M. Richards, "Half A Century of Girls," *The Sun Life Review*, January 1945, 23. Both: Sun Life Archives.

26. Kwolek-Folland, *Engendering Business*.

27. For more on gender, space, and power in the white-collar workplace, see R. Pringle, *Secretaries Talk: Sexuality, Power, and Work* (London, UK: Verso, 1989); D. Spain, *Gendered Spaces* (Chapel Hill, NC: University of North Carolina Press, 1992); and A. Van Slyck, "Gender and Space in American Public Libraries, 1880–1920," Working Paper No. 27 (Southwest Institute for Research on Women: University of Arizona, 1992).

28. Whether the juxtaposition of Miss Remington and the promise that the model 10 offers "a brand new proposition to the buyer" is intended as sexual innuendo is not clear. For more on the interpretation of visual sources, see G. Rose, *Visual Methodologies: An Introduction to the Interpretation of Visual Materials* (London, UK: Sage Publications, 2001).

29. Anonymous Canadian Bank of Commerce bank manager, "Women Bank Managers," *The Caduceus* 12, no. 3 (October 1931): 51–3, quoted passage, 51.

30. Ibid.

31. P. Knox, *Urbanization: An Introduction to Urban Geography* (Englewood Cliffs, NJ: Prentice Hall, 1994).

32. E. F. Chacksfield, "A City within a City," *The Municipal Review of Canada* 27, no. 3 (March 1931): 12–13.

33. Ibid.

34. *Report of Annual General Meeting 1912*, Bank of Montreal Archives.

35. B. Anderson, *Imagined Communities: Reflections on the Origin and Spread of Nationalism* (London, UK: Verso, 1983).

36. Cases 28, 31, and 50, All Bank of Nova Scotia Archives.

37. W. L. G. Cumming, "The Duties of Country Junior," *The Royal Bank Magazine* (August 1927): 8. Royal Bank Archives.

16 Even the Turnips Were Edible

Merle Massie

April 1934. In the midst of a violent early spring dust storm, tenant farmer Sargent McGowan of the east Weyburn district of southern Saskatchewan loaded a boxcar at the local siding. Stripping his farmhouse, machine shed, and barn, McGowan put everything he had into the boxcar: cows, chickens, plow, other implements, seed grain, household furniture, kitchen supplies, bedding, and provisions. He loaded his horses and wagon last, driving them up the ramp and into the boxcar. Unhitch, stow, organize, tie up, and tie down. At last, all was ready. He stepped down to hug his wife, Muriel, and two young daughters, who would take the passenger train to join him after one last visit with parents and grandparents.

McGowan climbed in to keep the animals settled, fed, and watered. As the train prepared to leave the siding, McGowan turned for one last look at the drought-stricken land that he was abandoning, wondering once again if he was making the right decision. But the landscape answered him. A brutal wind sent clouds of once-productive black soil billowing straight across the field toward the track. Dust blocked his vision. He could not see the caboose, though his settler car was just in front of it. With a face full of dirt, he withdrew, shut the door, wiped

his eyes with a handkerchief and settled in for the three-day journey.

The train headed north to the village of Paddockwood. When the train pulled into the station, McGowan slid open the boxcar door and gasped. There were still two feet of snow on the ground, and the little town was ringing with the sights, sounds, and smells of hundreds of teams and sleighs. It was more activity than he had seen for years in the broken communities around Weyburn. The contrast between the violent prairie dust storm and the snow and busy humanity was "enough to put the memory of Weyburn back behind a huge cloud of dust, and there it stayed."[1]

In Saskatchewan, an estimated 45,000 people moved north during the Great Depression.[2] The massive internal migration, known as the Great Trek, changed the face of the province: Prairie farms were abandoned or sold to neighbours, parkland regions filled to capacity, and agriculture pushed back the eaves of the forest. Great Trek refugees moved, not just away from the dried-up prairie, but also toward a place of hope, a place with water, trees, garden produce, and hay. Trekkers defined the new landscape in terms of the old, comparing what they had left behind with what they found in the

Citation: Merle Massie, "Even the Turnips Were Edible," in *Forest Prairie Edge: Place History in Saskatchewan* (Winnipeg, MB: University of Manitoba Press, 2014): 213–53.

north. The forest edge landscape was desirable because it was *not* the prairie.

The ecology and the economy were different along the forest edge. In the midst of the worst depression in living memory, forest fringe towns across Saskatchewan, including those in the north Prince Albert region, became oases in a desert landscape. "The 1930s were boom times for Paddockwood," local residents remembered.[3] Mixed farming, lumber and cordwood, freighting, commercial fishing, wild game, berries, and tourism combined to offer Depression migrants an economic as well as an ecological refuge.

For some, moving north was a temporary retreat; others found long-term resilience, drawing back full circle to traditional First Nations use of the north Prince Albert region. The ecological edge had provided a seasonal place of refuge for prairie First Nations in times of stress, such as a harsh winter or when bison were scarce. Small forest-adapted bands found long-term resilience at the ecological edge. During the Great Depression, wheat farmers—like their bison-dependent First Nations counterparts 60 years before—faced starvation and were forced to rely on government assistance. Many chose to move north to the forest edge simply to obtain the basic essentials of life: food, shelter, and warmth. There they encountered a small but temporally deep culture embraced by both First Nations and newcomers. It was a northern paradigm of resilience that drew heavily on mixed farming, occupational pluralism, and forest resources to provide a practical, self-sufficient way of life in which subsistence was the first priority.

. . .

Tempted by stories of desperation and despair, Great Trek analysts have focused on hungry and frantic families, devastated by drought and poor agricultural prices, forced north to a "place of last resort." Geographer J. David Wood in particular advocated the theory that hapless migrants occupied northern farms "in desperation after the more accessible land further south had been colonized."[4] Historians and geographers have presented the migration through government relief and resettlement policy analysis, agricultural hazards, and the shocking stories of loss, brutal conditions, and bewilderment of urban and prairie people trying to eke out a living in the bush.[5] Although there is ample evidence to support these characterizations, the story is incomplete. To assume that northern lands were taken only when the better agricultural land of the prairie had all been settled negates the experience of northern migrants who had already tried prairie farming and found it wanting. For those who abandoned the prairie, which was the more "marginal" landscape? The "place of last resort" storyline also dismisses the extensive "pull" factors that drew people north. Depression migration was not, in fact, a radical reaction to particular environmental and economic circumstances. The Great Trek was a proactive response, an injection of hope and energy to improve living conditions and open new possibilities for earning a living. Drought migration continued, and increased, internal migration practices that had been in place for a long time.

. . .

The Great Trek

Geographer Denis Patrick Fitzgerald used the term "the Great Trek" to describe the south-to-north migration of prairie settlers into the northern forested environment during the Great Depression, but he drew the words from Depression migrants and contemporary commentators.[6] As southern farmers felt the dual prongs of dust and economic disaster, northern migration escalated.[7] From 1931 to 1937, the worst year of the drought, northern migration was part of the fabric of life in Saskatchewan.[8]

Environmental devastation and economic depression slammed prairie farmers in a double whammy. Wheat prices slumped and then plummeted after the stock market crash in the fall of 1929. In addition, extreme drought conditions devastated cereal cash crops. Farmers reaped poor returns. Those who had taken mortgages, purchased equipment, or had other loans in the boom years of the mid- to late 1920s were faced with payments that they could not meet. Nor did they have enough crop to keep any for seed for the following year. Those who relied on wheat returns to meet payments or purchase basic supplies were soon in trouble.

Perhaps even more devastating, the drought burned fodder crops such as oats and hay to a crisp. Farmers faced the dilemma of owning animals that they could not feed. Relief feed and fodder—the majority from northern regions that had not been hit by the drought—eased the burden, but hundreds of animals died from malnutrition and starvation. Others were taken north or into Manitoba to graze, reinforcing the image of parkland and forest as a place of natural abundance. Animals were also shot to save feed and fodder costs.[9] "I thought of our stock trying to get feed off the sand-filled pasture," Mrs. A. W. Bailey said.[10] Moving north, where feed and water were more accessible, seemed the only humane option.

Drought conditions and sand storms shredded prairie gardens and crops, leaving sand and dust piled and covering what remained. Historian Peter Russell suggested that drought-prone farms "had a limited capacity for either subsistence or diversification," preferring to use their cash crop (wheat) to purchase all household staples, including food. Some wheat farmers neither kept animals nor grew gardens prior to the Depression, he noted.[11] The economic slump pushed many to attempt those traditional farming practices, but environmental devastation stymied those attempts. The same drought that shattered the wheat economy would not allow diversification or even simple subsistence strategies such as growing a garden, keeping some hens, or feeding a milk cow. Grass, water, and feed were scarce, and farmers began to rely on government handouts. Those who wanted to keep body and soul together moved north.

Moving was indeed a trek for many families. Although the McGowan family chose to move their possessions north in a boxcar, thousands of migrants made the move over land, using their own cars, trucks, wagons—"makeshift vehicles constructed from old implement wheels and boards torn from an empty granary"—or ubiquitous Bennett Buggies. To make a Bennett Buggy, you would remove the engine of the family car (since there was no cash for gas, oil, or repairs) and lash a wagon tongue on the front. After harnessing and hitching a team of horses to the wagon tongue, the driver carefully removed the front window and slid the reins through. Most drivers would disengage the steering mechanism, but leave the brakes intact. Cars had springs and nicer interiors, and many had a roof to keep off the rain and snow. The resulting crossover vehicle was named after R. B. Bennett, the prime minister of Canada from 1930 to 1935—a folk tribute and public commentary on his leadership during the Depression.[12]

During the Great Trek, motley vehicles, from trucks to wagons to Bennett Buggies, were loaded precariously with furniture, goods, children and grandparents, food for the journey, as well as any agricultural implements, crates of chickens, or the family cat. Larger stock, such as horses, milk cows, and the family dog, walked alongside. Migrants likened their outfits to those of gypsies or the great wagon trains that snaked across the Great Plains in an earlier time. Families, often several from one community making the move together, or several adult siblings moving as an extended unit, camped out each night, their fires dancing along the roadsides for miles. Soldier settlers commented that the exodus reminded them of war refugees in Europe.[13]

. . .

Edna Dobie (née Brook) of Prince Albert was a 12-year-old girl when her extended family made the move from a farm near Moosomin to the north Prince Albert region in late 1931. A flat tire on the first day caused the overloaded Model T to roll, smashing the windshield and top and tumbling all those inside. Edna recalled her mother screaming when she saw her children splattered in bright red in the back seat. A quart of precious strawberry jam had smashed. Her parents and uncles breathed a sigh of relief, righted the car, used barbed wire to hold things together, poured oil into the engine, and were then ready to continue. The family eventually arrived at their homestead about 15 miles north of Paddockwood, in an area bypassed by fire. Tall spruce and deep moss greeted the prairie children, who thought that they had moved to fairyland—it was green, damp, and filled with Christmas trees.[14]

The contrast between the environmental devastation of the prairies and the green northern forests resonated in family histories published in *Cordwood and Courage* and other local history books from forest fringe communities. Trekkers—even those who eventually moved away—reminisced about the transition from dust to mud (or snow) and from brown to green. "How green everything looked!" said Elsa Blumer, who moved to the Paddockwood district in 1931. "I really did not care where we moved to as long as we could get away from that windy dustbowl prairie," she declared. Esther Craig remembered that, when she arrived at their Paddockwood farm in 1930, "the clear air and the green trees were lovely after the dusty prairie."[15] The striking contrast formed a large part of Mrs. Bailey's published account of her family's move north: "We talked of moving to a place where there were green grass and shade. It would be a veritable heaven after so much dust and wind," Bailey recalled.[16] When the family arrived, Mrs. Bailey, born a prairie girl, was overcome with homesickness, but her children delighted in climbing trees, making forts in the brush, and swimming in lakes and ponds. For the parents, though, a rough bush homestead meant an enormous amount of work. Historian Jim Wright commented that "once more the log cabin with earthen floor swept by a broom made

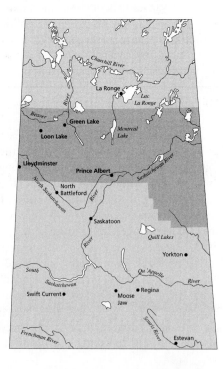

Figure 1. Great Trek Destinations in Saskatchewan. Source: Adapted from Fitzgerald, "Pioneer Settlement."

of willows became a reality in Saskatchewan. Dad ploughed the grey bush soil for a garden plot. The lads tracked and snared bushrabbits, and rabbit pie appeared with monotonous regularity on the family table."[17]

The number of acres farmed in Saskatchewan went up during the 1930s across most of the census divisions. The rising acreage reflected a threefold expansion: the surge north to develop new farms, the opening of more acres in parkland regions, and the expansion of prairie acreage to try to grow more crop. When wheat prices declined dramatically, farmers increased their acreage to grow more bushels on newly broken, fresh land—a move that signalled their recognition that the land was not able to hold its fertility.

Each family's situation or inclination dictated the decision to make the move, but economics and drought were two primary motivations. "For the past six or seven years crop failures have occurred . . . and once prosperous farmers who had fairly large bank accounts were reduced to near poverty. Seeing their savings dwindle every year, with no returns from the land or their livestock, they decided to leave," reported the *Regina Leader* in 1934.[18] G. J. Matte, minister of the Northern Settlers Re-Establishment Branch (created in 1935), explained that trekkers included farmers from every class:

All manner of people were to be found in this movement. There was the rich farmer, owner of vast acres of wheat fields turned overnight into a drifting sea of sand. There was the small landowner who made a fine living from a small farm which cost little in effort and gave large returns. There was the man who had been expanding, farming many acres in which he had a large equity. We might call this man the greatest loser because he not only lost all he owned, but was left with enormous debt which he despaired of ever paying. There were the renters, and those who had always been on the edge of poverty but found themselves now in equal circumstances. They were all completely destitute.[19]

The decision to move north was a strategy of adaptation that addressed the immediate needs of the farmer and his family: The choice was either to accept relief and stay on the prairie or move to a place where at least part of the family's needs could be met with garden produce, natural hay to feed stock, and local forest resources of fish, game, and berries. Those who moved north in the early years, 1930 or 1931, generally had more savings and established a firm hold. Others hung on in the south, breaking more prairie land and hoping each year for a crop until their savings were exhausted. By the time they trekked north, some were virtually destitute.

. . .

The social safety net that Canadians enjoy today did not exist prior to or during the Depression, when the inability to feed or clothe yourself or your family was generally a source of shame.[20] For many, the move north allowed a measure of pride and self-sufficiency in providing (at the least) food, shelter, and fuel for their families. For the first few years of the Depression, relief measures were municipal matters, handled at the local level, with considerable assistance from churches and other volunteer groups that ran soup kitchens, shelters, or organized clothing drives. As the Depression wore on, the provincial government took over and coordinated direct relief efforts with substantial loans from the federal government. Government aid in the form of agricultural loans such as seed grain or fodder relief, direct relief for families, or assistance in moving north was recorded as a loan or lien and as such was expected to be repaid by the recipient as soon as possible.[21]

. . .

The Northern Boom

The village of Paddockwood, at the end of the CNR railway line running north of Prince

Albert, experienced a significant boom during the Depression in part because of the influx of southern and urban refugees. In a risky move, the local Board of Trade issued a pamphlet in 1933 that crowed *Paddockwood: The Mixed Farming Paradise of Saskatchewan.*[22] Relief at the time was a municipal burden. Actively recruiting migrants during a major economic depression was acutely ironic. Southern municipalities were overburdened by relief requests and discouraged destitute individuals and families from relocating to nearby towns or empty farms.[23] In contrast, Paddockwood not only encouraged migrants but even enjoyed a boom:

> At this time Paddockwood had five general stores, a butcher shop, a drugstore, two harness repair shops, a lumber yard, hardware store, two blacksmith shops, one pool room, two hotels, three restaurants, a bakery, a second hand store, a barber shop, and twice weekly the ladies of the community could visit a beauty parlor operated in the hotel. The implement companies were represented by agents for International Harvester, Case, Massey Harris, Oliver and Cockshutt. A resident MD set bones and performed minor surgery (without anesthetic) for the people, at most reasonable rates. Talent abounded in other fields too. There were men who filed saws, repaired radios, practiced veterinary medicine, tanned robes, made illegal spirits and told fortunes. One individual was known as the "Pea Man." He made a living of sorts by growing and selling seed peas.[24]

Paddockwood was full of bustle and hustle, with piles of cordwood for trade and barter, garden produce and berries in abundance, easy access to resorts and water recreation, the Red Cross Outpost Hospital, and plenty of stores and services. The nearby communities of Henribourg and Albertville, and the growing resort communities at Christopher and Emma Lakes, shared the north Prince Albert boom. They were islands in an ocean of Depression despair. The boom created an economic and cultural flow, a movement of goods and services at odds with the "broken" communities of the open plains.

. . . [P]rairie families looked to the northern ecological edge to provide a landscape of diversity and resilience through the mixed-farm ideal. The McGowan family's experience was an excellent example. On their newly purchased quarter section near Paddockwood, Sargent and his wife, Muriel, concentrated on self-sufficiency, using a combination of ingenuity and exchange:

> We exchanged "clucking" hens for an orphan ewe lamb from our neighbour. This was the nucleus of a small flock kept for a few years until coyotes became a nuisance. Dairy cattle provided us with milk, meat, cream and butter for home use, as well as some cash from butter sold, or whole milk sold to a cheese factory at Henribourg, or cream sold to dairies in Prince Albert. Pigs thrived on surplus skim milk and provided meat, especially the cured pork so necessary for summer protein before refrigeration. Chickens provided meat and eggs. Turkeys, although more difficult to raise, provided meat as well as some cash when sold in the fall. Sheep gave us meat and wool. We learned how to clip the sheep, wash and card wool for quilt batts. The garden soil produced a bountiful supply of vegetables. Wild fruit and some hardy tame ones were usually available. Blueberry, Saskatoon, and raspberry picking expeditions were not only necessary but a pleasant break from our daily routine. Everyone canned food of every kind—fruit, meat, vegetables, and pickles.[25]

Muriel McGowan's description (though idyllic) of the techniques of barter and exchange, and the combination of cash and subsistence strategies, were essential components of back-to-the-land practicality. The ideal subsistence farm was a mixed farm.

The majority of those who heeded the call to move to the forest edge found their land in one of three ways. Some found a farm to rent. Others, such as the McGowans, purchased a farm through a private deal with the landowner, with a down payment and yearly payments until the debt was cleared. Farms that had been patented with only the minimum acreage cleared were cheaper than developed farms with a larger acreage. Deals between buyer and seller were often private since banks were reluctant to issue mortgages. Finally, a migrant could enter a homestead claim and build the place of residence. The primary method of farm acquisition varied from one region to another along the forest fringe: in older settlements, such as Paddockwood or the Carrot River country, 36 per cent of the farms were homesteaded, while almost half were purchased. In areas developed as new settlements, such as Pierceland in the Northwest, almost 90 per cent of the farms were new homesteads.[26]

Years of mixed-farming boosterism and advertising proclaimed a difference between wheat monoculture and a more diversified, stable, and resilient mixed farm at the forest edge.[27] Yet creating a mixed farm took time, energy, luck, and investment. Each family of southern refugees experienced better or worse conditions depending on several key factors: their previous residence and vocation (particularly farming experience); their method of acquisition of land (purchased or homesteaded); their age and composition when they went north; their net worth when they started (including implements, tools, stock, and furniture); their progress in clearing and breaking the land; and the productivity of the soil. A family with some cash, stock, and equipment who purchased a partly cleared farm with moderate to good soil generally did better than a virtually destitute family with few resources or stock who ended up on a new homestead with 160 acres of heavy bush covering grey podzolic soil.[28]

. . .

Environmental Difficulty

On each farm or homestead, agricultural progress varied. Those facing heavy scrub and trees took longer to clear less acreage. Those who rented or purchased partly developed farms, or found new homestead land with light scrub or open glades, could clear more land in less time. In five years, a homesteader on light scrub might clear 60 acres; those who faced heavy clearing and breaking would accomplish less than half that amount. As well, clearing rates quickly went down over time. A homesteader would clear the easiest areas of the farm first. Clearing and breaking became more difficult once the farmer encountered larger trees and more scrub.[29] Although mechanized methods of land clearing were available, few prairie refugees had the capital to invest in, operate, or hire tractors to do the work. Clearing trees, pulling stumps, picking stones and roots, and other duties were done by hand or with horses. It was as if "the clock of history had been turned back" to a more primitive type of agriculture.[30]

The amount of land that each family managed to clear, break, and turn to productive agriculture meant the difference between the continued need for relief help and the ability to eke out a living. Land clearing in northern areas to 1928 was completed primarily by the farmer, but just over 20 per cent of the land was cleared by hired labour. During the Depression, farmers cleared more of their land on their own, as much as 87 per cent. Hired labour rose again between 1938 and 1940, to pre-Depression levels. Stone and root picking, however, was overwhelmingly completed by the farm family, with a tiny proportion—between 1 and 3 per cent—picked by hired help, often local First Nations casual day labourers.

During the Depression, later analysts noted, a family on black or transitional soil needed at least 50 acres cleared and worked to manage a bare living; on grey podzolic soil, 88 acres would support a family without any off-farm income. Unfortunately, it took as many as 10 years—or even 15—to clear that many acres on the heavy bush land common to grey podzolic soil.[31] Even if a family moved north to a new homestead early in the trek—1930 or 1931—they might not have found economic sufficiency strictly from agricultural pursuits until the end of the decade, when farmers once more could afford mechanized land-clearing techniques. A family who moved later in the trek, with no cash reserves or resources left, faced an even more difficult battle.[32]

The amount of time and back-breaking work that it took to clear and break enough land to make a farm profitable was the single most important factor in encouraging or discouraging those who tried northern settlement. In the bush, as few as 10 acres cultivated and seeded were sometimes enough to convince the homestead inspector to approve a farm patent. Patent, however, did not make a farm profitable. Settlers had to choose between continuing clearing, breaking, and seeding activities and accessing off-farm cash labour opportunities or selling the land and moving. As with the initial choice to migrate away from the prairie, the choice to stay on or leave a northern farm varied from family to family as circumstances and inclination—and opportunity—dictated.

Although optimism and hope infused most of those who went north, the reality of trying to establish a viable mixed farm in the bush produced much adversity. Historian John McDonald suggested that "many half-truths about conditions in the north continued to be circulated, engendering an optimism . . . based on a distorted image of true environmental conditions in the forest fringe."[33] Another historian, T. J. D. Powell, suggested that people who moved north "received assurance through the media, government officials and word-of-mouth that the northern lands would certainly provide the necessities of life if not improve their standard of living. Some families, in fact, did improve their economic status, but others experienced poverty or even worse conditions."[34] The difference, later analysts declared, lay in the combination of experience, rate of land clearing, soil profile, and sheer good luck.[35]

Indeed, northern refugees "had much to learn before becoming adapted to living in bush country," wrote "Prairie Immigrant" for the Paddockwood local history book. To clear the land to create a farm, they "first had to learn to use swede saw, axe and grub-hoe without endangering life or limbs." Fire, though a useful tool for clearing scrub brush, had a dark side: "An innocent-looking fire, started in a brush pile, can smoulder all winter under feet of snow, consuming much of the good topsoil." Not just people but also prairie animals had a tough transition from prairie to bush. Prairie immigrants "watched and wondered as animals began chewing on sticks, bones, harness and sweat-pads, until realization dawned that the poor beasts were in need of salt, an ingredient that was seldom lacking in their diet on the prairie." Although the mixed-farming movement and other promoters lauded the lush northern hay crop, trekkers learned that it "proved to be more filling than nutritious and compared unfavourably with the prickly prairie wool. Brome grass and alfalfa had to be seeded to keep the animals satisfied." Stock farmers and their animals valued the northern water sources, but farmers soon learned to fence their animals "away from dangerous muskegs, after some had become mired more than once and dragged out by the neck to dry land." Unlike the open prairie, where a farmer could see for miles, stock hid in the northern bush. Farmers learned to "hang a bell around the neck of the 'boss' cow, if ever they hoped to find the herd." Other nasty surprises included "swamp fever," an infectious anemia thought to reside in wet marsh grass. Many horses died, and this placed incredible pressure on farm families. With agricultural commodity prices still at an all-time low, where would a family find the money to replace valuable horses, the main mode of transportation and motive power for the farm? Such a calamity could wipe out a sense of hope or optimism and place a family in even more desperate straits than they had been in on their prairie farm.[36]

. . .

Cold and wet conditions plagued many northern homesteads. As settlement pushed north, the growing season, or average number of frost-free days necessary for cereal grain ripening, shrank. Late spring or early fall frosts hit farmers hard. Cereal crops, particularly wheat, suffered. Just as on the prairie, expected income from wheat disappeared when environmental disaster struck. As Muriel McGowan noted, the grain grown on their northern farm was more often than not converted to animal feed. Wheat prices were abysmal throughout the Great Depression, so meagre wheat crops were rarely worth the cost of harvesting. Freight deductions were also higher for northern farms. In addition, northern grain typically graded lower. In some years, after deductions and fees, grain cost more to ship than to keep. Farmers found themselves facing a bill rather than a cheque.[37]

Flooding was a problem in some areas or on some quarters. The homestead inspector for the north Paddockwood area, James Barnett, commented on a homestead at Moose Lake in 1931: "The wetness of this country probably appeals to those from the dried out areas. This may prove the other extreme and not turn out so pleasant as it first seems."[38] In a wet season, the settler had to wait longer to get seed in the ground, further courting the risk of frost. Over time, settlers noticed that, as more land was cleared, roads built, and ditches dug, drainage and frost issues improved. As tree cover and roots were removed, the land warmed up and dried out. Soldier settlers and other older residents assured newcomers that they had also faced bush, frost, and water. Their larger acreages, somewhat more prosperous despite the ravages of the Depression, offered hope.

. . .

Forest Resources

Although northern settlement initiatives sponsored by the various levels of government focused primarily on agriculture and its successes and failures, trekkers and established settlers relied on—and expected—nonfarm income to supplement mixed farming, relief, and re-establishment measures. Although drought and depression on the open plains sent many trekkers looking for water, green grass, and trees, they were also drawn to the economic and cultural prospects offered at the forest edge.

Of all the nonagricultural resources and opportunities found at the forest edge, the most important was the forest itself. The 1933 Paddockwood Board of Trade pamphlet declared that "all through the brief history of Paddockwood there can be little doubt that the great beckoning force has been the trees—the timber." The primary farm product, more important than grain or stock, came from the trees: "Thousands of cords of wood and millions of feet of lumber, ties and fence posts are sold annually to nearby points."[39] Clearly, in the north Prince Albert region, wood was a crop to be harvested and sold for profit. The concept of mixed farming at the forest edge took on a new meaning: Not only was the mixed forest suited to stock raising and cereal grain growing, but also the forest itself could be turned into cash.

Local men Pat O'Hea and Herb Endicott wrote a history of Paddockwood for the Royal Commission on Agriculture and Rural Life in 1953. Cordwood was the bedrock of the Paddockwood economy during the Depression, they insisted:

Came the lean and hungry 30s: Up to this time the forest growth, made up principally of white poplar, was a barrier to a settler being granted title deed to his homestead. There being no mechanized method of clearing the land, it was a monotonous, ding-dong battle of chopping, clearing, and grubbing. One did well to have five acres ready for breaking in a year. Then our enemy, the poplar, became our ally when turned into cord wood, and was a big factor in our weathering or surviving the thirties. . . . We beat the 30s, also the bush, thereby winning two battles, but "'twas a tough fight."[40]

As the Depression deepened, the cordwood industry symbolized both the ecological and the economic struggle. Trees were the enemies of progress for homestead development but became the allies when converted into fuel for sale. Cordwood became the Paddockwood equivalent of the "made beaver" currency of the old fur trade; all else was measured against it.

During the Depression, the cash economy virtually disappeared, particularly in southern Saskatchewan. Communities were paralyzed. Without some form of flowing economy outside relief payments, families were unable to go to dances or the lake, pay a teacher's salary, or buy a new teapot. Bill Grohn pointed to this paralyzing effect when he claimed that the east Weyburn district was broken by the Depression. Community life, in almost all of its forms, stopped, and the community died. In contrast, the cordwood economy and healthy system of cash and barter that existed along the forest edge meant that communities could thrive, even boom. Cutting and hauling cordwood were hard and dangerous work, with sometimes pitiful cash returns, but most residents agreed that it was better than nothing, and it kept some of them off, or at least reduced, relief. If a farmer did not have adequate trees on his own farm, he could work in a cordwood or railway tie camp, leased from the provincial government. Several operated along the Montreal Lake Trail and the Mosher Trail to Candle Lake, just south and east of the original boundary of Prince Albert National Park.

The cordwood economy allowed community members to organize and build schools, invest in social and recreational clubs, take short holidays to lakes or even build cabins, support sports days and hockey clubs, and allow musicians to play for pocket change at dances held in homes, schools, and halls. The importance of the cordwood economy resonated through the years, leading the Paddockwood History Book Committee to call their local history *Cordwood and Courage* when it was published in 1982. Geographer Denis Patrick Fitzgerald commented that "the psychological role of forest resources might well have been of more significance than the material. Many pioneers . . . felt that the forest lands themselves were a type of insurance policy; they acted as a safe refuge or shelter." The trees, as well as other forest resources, acted to sustain the morale of northern homesteaders, even when life was particularly grim.[41]

The forest edge environment provided household resources, particularly food through berry picking, wild game, and fish. Indeed, the Paddockwood pamphlet expressly advertised products of the landscape as a way to supplement household diet cheaply. Local history books proudly displayed photographs of these resources, including several canners full of blueberries from 1931, wild game piled on the railway station platform, and strings of fish from successful expeditions to local lakes. Numerous family histories recount excursions to hunt, fish, and pick berries as a way of adding to and varying diet. Some, however, admitted defeat in this regard. Muriel McGowan noted that "although living in this area where fish and game are plentiful neither Sargent nor I became enthusiastic hunters or fishermen." When Sargent accompanied a neighbour on a highly successful fishing expedition, Muriel was perplexed by the sheer amount of fish. Some were eaten fresh, some canned, and the rest salted "and later buried in the bush." A hunting expedition also went awry when Sargent became hopelessly lost. He "vowed never to go again, that he would pick his own meat, on the hoof, in his own farmyard, which he did."[42] Although hunting regulations were in place throughout the Depression, game wardens were encouraged to look the other way when it came to families clearly harvesting elk, moose, and deer as food resources—unless, of course, those animals were shot within the boundaries of the national park.

In addition to mixed farming, forest-based food resources, and the cordwood economy, the forest edge landscape supported labour opportunities from freighting, fishing, lumber and railway tie camps, mining camps, tourism, and trapping. These opportunities allowed occupational pluralism that combined on-farm with off-farm income. Such pluralism was characteristic of the northern boom, particularly for those who homesteaded within the wooded grey soil zone. These farms, the majority of which were homesteaded during the 1930s, rarely exceeded a quarter section, and most had only a few acres cleared, grubbed, and broken for cultivation.[43] Off-farm cash income supplemented mixed-farming returns and relief vouchers and contributed to the general northern boom.

. . .

Homestead families in the Alingly, Spruce Home, Albertville, Paddockwood, Forest Gate, and Christopher Lake districts also engaged in the burgeoning tourism industry. Men with extensive bush experience became park wardens; others worked on park roads, cooked for the hotels (or relief camps), or opened tourist facilities such as cabin or boat rentals, bus services, or grocery and supply stores. Others loaded up their wagons with meat, eggs, milk, butter, and fresh garden produce and sold them to the camps and hotels or door to door at the cabins and on the beaches at the lakes. Earl Daley, for example, sold his milk for 10 cents a quart and had enough cows to offer 50 to 60 quarts a day to picnickers and beachgoers.[44] Mrs. Oscar Anderson of the Elk Range School District (between Northside and Paddockwood) took butter and eggs to Neis beach on Emma Lake in 1931. But George Neis, who homesteaded the land and owned the resort, had his own butter and eggs to supply the campers. When he physically removed her from his property so that she could not sell her wares, Anderson charged him with assault. Neis hired John Diefenbaker as his lawyer and succeeded in having the case dismissed since Anderson had clearly been trespassing.[45]

The Jacobsen family, who initiated much of the tourist development at Anglin Lake, moved from Frontier, Saskatchewan, in 1930. "As soon as the car stopped [after the three-day trek north] one little brother grabbed a hatchet and claimed territory by cutting down a small tree. As I look back I realize that no one minded leaving the prairie, we loved the forest and lakes."[46] For the Jacobsens and many others, the move away from the open plains reflected what geographer Robert Rees called "the Cult of the Tree." For many immigrants to western Canada, the strangeness of the prairie landscape—treeless, flat, dry, hot, and immense—caused an intensely negative reaction.[47] For prairie-born children, that landscape was home but became disfigured and alien by drought. The love of trees and a connection between forest and beauty pervaded Anglo-Canadian culture.[48] The trek north was a move, in part, from poverty to subsistence, brown to green, despair to hope, ugly to beautiful.

First Nations and Métis

As homesteaders pressed north past the Forest Gate region into the grey soil zone at Moose Lake, Hell's Gate, and east to Candle Lake, new homesteaders competed with trappers, cordwood and railway tie camps, hunters, and berry pickers for available resources. All were constrained by the boundaries of Prince Albert National Park, which disallowed homesteading, trapping, or hunting within its borders. First Nations families from Little Red River Reserve who traditionally used northern boreal territory had to share the trails and restricted resource base with an ever-increasing number of drought refugees. The results were devastating to the First Nations population. Moving farther and farther away from the reserve to access forest resources placed excessive strain on reserve families. Throughout the 1930s, increased hardship could be found.

Several Métis families, such as the Lavallées, were forcibly displaced by the creation of Prince Albert National Park. Louis Lavallée had a cabin on the shores of what is now known as Lavallée Lake, at the north end of the park.[49] He at first found a measure of fame at his home when journalists visiting the park arrived to take his picture. He was also featured in the Department of the Interior film *Modern Voyageurs* in 1931 as one of the more colourful personages living in the park. Sometime in the 1930s, though, Lavallée was pressured to leave. Other families, such as the Clares, also lived within what became the park boundaries, where they made their living fishing, trapping, and hunting. When trapping and hunting were prohibited, the Métis families found their livelihoods severely diminished. Banished from their homes, they were eventually offered land at the Green Lake Métis settlement north and west of Big River under the direction of the Northern Settlers Re-Establishment Branch.[50] Several families eventually settled at Fish Lake, a Métis settlement that grew between Little Red River Reserve and Prince Albert National Park within the Emma Lake Provincial Forest.[51]

The "road allowance" people, as many Métis were known, found themselves a people "in between." They were not allowed to reside on Little Red since they were not status Indians of either the Montreal Lake or the La Ronge band, even though many had relations on the reserve. They were entitled to land consideration through their Métis heritage. The provincial government set aside otherwise unused Crown land for these small, family-oriented communities, such as Fish Lake or the Crescent Lake settlement south of Yorkton.[52]

The nature of First Nations and Métis life at the forest edge reveals opposing and ironic twists in how the story of the forest fringe has been told. Agricultural analysts considered wheat monoculture the apex and norm of farming. As a result, occupational pluralism and off-farm income commonly found along the forest fringe—freighting, fishing, hunting, picking berries, harvesting lumber, and trapping—became indicators of a marginal environment. Within the agricultural paradigm, families were "forced" to use off-farm resources to supplement meagre farm returns. At the same time, First Nations and Métis inhabitants of the forest fringe routinely combined landscape resources with occupational pluralism. The culture embraced seasonal movement and flow. Through cultural racism, their lifestyle was often denigrated. Yet during the Depression, off-farm occupations and forest products provided the key to the northern boom and were an important drawing card for many southern refugees. Racist explanations separated Aboriginal pursuits from homesteader practices by emphasizing the role of time: white homesteaders would use the resources of the landscape only until their farms were large and profitable enough to sustain their families; First Nations bands had no intention of changing their pluralistic pursuits, in which farming provided only a portion of income or food.[53] Although each family's daily activities might be the same, racial profiling and slurs created difference.

. . .

Conclusion

. . .

The Great Trek migration, in many ways, was the end-game of the battle between wheat farms of the prairie and mixed farms of the parkland and forest fringe. Northern migrants, a *Regina Leader-Post* journalist noted in 1931, knew that the northern country "cannot afford a rapid career to a prospective wheat grower, but it will at least afford a living to a family with pioneer instincts better than that promised at present in the districts they have been forced to abandon."[54] The northern forest fringe did not offer single-cash-crop agriculture, and the vast majority of southern refugees knew it. What they searched for, and what many found, was a way of life that offered some balance: wood and water, garden produce, game and fish, and hay to feed stock. At the forest edge, migrants learned that mixed farming was more than just a mix of crops and livestock; it was culturally and economically embedded in the forest edge landscape, engaged in resource harvesting and the cordwood and barter economy. Like their First Nations neighbours, there were two kinds of people who used the forest edge: those who accessed its resources as a refuge for a short period to relieve economic or environmental stress, and those who developed a broadly mixed lifestyle that combined forest and prairie pursuits to find a measure of resilience.

Analysts who have used the government records of the Land Settlement Branch or the Northern Settlers Re-Establishment Branch found the stories of those who most needed and accessed government help. Those sources do not record the experiences of those who went north without government assistance. Local history books, and the reminiscences of drought trekkers, offer a new perspective on life at the forest edge.[55] Their stories of barter and exchange, a booming local economy, social capital and hope, short-term refuge, and long-term resilience in a mixed-farming and resource base tell a story at odds with traditional interpretations. Those who moved north considered a myriad of pull factors, primarily the contrast between the drought-ravaged open plains and the northern forested and wet landscape. They also wanted to access nonagricultural resources of fish, game, fur, and timber from the forest. The rise of tourism throughout the 1920s and 1930s culturally reinforced a divided Saskatchewan identity in which the south was flat and treeless while the north was lush, green, and forested. Weary drought refugees remembered, and celebrated, this contrast.

Today, in the north Prince Albert region, the line between farmland and Northern Provincial Forest is stark and entirely human made. Fields and pastures cut a straight edge along the quarter line. One step divides farmland from forest. Within that forest, past the agricultural edge, there remains Crown land that has either never been surveyed or was surveyed but not homesteaded. Hidden in the forest, though, are remnants of the northern push. Old sawmill sites, trappers' cabins, and Hell's Gate–type abandoned homesteads, with rotting shacks sinking into the bush, can be found. Acreages once cleared by axe or fire and cultivated have grown lush with poplar and willow in the ensuing years, to be succeeded once again by spruce, tamarack, and fir. The boreal forest stands, as always, at the ready to take over any farmland temporarily or permanently abandoned along the forest edge. But the overgrown caragana hedges, lilac bushes, and patches of rhubarb, remnants of long-forgotten garden plots, recall the Great Trek migrants who "watched in amazement as late-seeded crops and gardens grew inches, it seemed, overnight. They were thankful for the flavourful, bountiful harvest from the small garden plot, enough to last until the next harvest, and even the turnips were edible."[56]

 More online.

Notes

1. S. E. McGowan, "Gee and Haw," in *Cordwood and Courage* (Altona, MB: Friesen Printers, 1982), 634–5. For the McGowan story, see "McGowan, Sargent Hugh and Muriel," in *Cordwood and Courage*, 354–7.

2. This number was conservatively calculated in G. E. Britnell, *The Wheat Economy* (Toronto, ON: University of Toronto Press, 1939), 202–3. . . .

3. Paddockwood Museum, "Down Memory Lane," *Paddockwood Pow-Wow*, Diamond Jubilee edition, 1965.

4. See J. David, Wood, *Places of Last Resort: The Expansion of the Farm Frontier into the Boreal Forest in Canada, c. 1910–40* (Montreal, QC: McGill-Queen's University Press), end cover.

5. In particular, see Dawn Bowen, "Forward to a Farm: The Back-to-the-Land Movement as a Relief Initiative in Saskatchewan during the Great Depression" (Ph.D. dissertation, Queen's University, 1998); T. J. D. Powell, "Northern Settlement, 1929–35," *Saskatchewan History* 30, no. 3 (1977): 81–98; John McDonald, "Soldier Settlement and Depression Settlement in the Forest Fringe of Saskatchewan," *Prairie Forum* 6, no. 1 (1981): 35–55; and Wood, *Places of Last Resort*. Fitzgerald also examines some of the government schemes, but not in great detail. For a general overview of land

settlement policies across the northern fringe, see Robert England, *The Colonization of Western Canada: A Study of Contemporary Land Settlement 1896–1934* (London, UK: P. S. King and Son, 1995); and "Land Settlement in Northern Areas of Western Canada 1925–35," *Canadian Journal of Economics and Political Science* 1, no. 4 (1935): 578–87.

6. Denis Patrick Fitzgerald, "Pioneer Settlement in Northern Saskatchewan" (Ph.D. dissertation, University of Minnesota, 1966), chapters 5 and 6.

7. Interpretations vary regarding which years saw the greatest exodus. Some, like Fitzgerald, argue that the strongest migration years were 1932 and 1933; others suggest that northern migration peaked in 1934 and 1935. Britnell noted the highest population movement in 1931 and 1932. For an overview of this debate, see McDonald, "Soldier Settlement and Depression Settlement," footnote 55.

8. See Mrs. A. W. Bailey, "The Year We Moved," *Saskatchewan History* 20 (Winter 1967): 19–31. See also Harold Fenske, *Riverlore: The Headwaters of the Assiniboine Will Always Be Home* (Self-published, 2002).

9. For an example, see "Five Hundred Horses Die over Winter," *Western Producer*, 31 January 1932.

10. Bailey, "The Year We Moved."

11. Peter Russell, "Subsistence, Diversification, and Staple Orientations on Saskatchewan Farms: Parklands vs. Prairie, 1911–26," *Saskatchewan History* 57 (2005): 15–28.

12. See the recreated Bennett Buggy at the Western Development Museum, Saskatoon. Quote from Jim Wright, *Saskatchewan: The History of a Province* (Toronto, ON: McClelland & Stewart, 1955), 225.

13. Fitzgerald, "Pioneer Settlement," 314–5.

14. Interview, Edna Dobie with Merle Massie, November 2008. See also Edna Dobie, "Brook, Arthur John and Bertha," in *Cordwood and Courage*, 126–7. Dobie has written a memoir of these events with her sister, which is unpublished.

15. See "Blumer, Jack and Elsa" and "Craig, Frederick and Esther," in *Cordwood and Courage*, 100, 150.

16. Bailey, "The Year We Moved."

17. Wright, *Saskatchewan*, 226.

18. "60 Families Move North From Farms. Stoughton District Land Abandoned as Feed Situation Becomes Serious." Special Dispatch to the *Regina Leader*, 30 August 1934.

19. Saskatchewan Archives Board (SAB), MA.3.8, Local Improvement Districts Branch, Northern Settlers Re-Establishment Branch. Address given by G. J. Matte, Commissioner, Northern Settlers Re-Establishment Branch over Station CJRM on 31 January 1939.

20. W. J. Mather, "Trek to Meadow Lake," *Maclean's*, 1 April 1932.

21. Many of these loans were eventually reduced or cancelled, which did much to improve farming conditions in the 1940s and 1950s across Saskatchewan. See James Struthers, *No Fault of Their Own: Unemployment and the Canadian Welfare State 1914–1941* (Toronto: University of Toronto Press, 1983).

22. Prince Albert Historical Society, Bill Smiley Archives, "Paddockwood: The Mixed Farming Paradise of Saskatchewan," found in the Walter Whelan Scrapbook, oversize shelf. The pamphlet emphasized what dust-covered prairie citizens wanted most: trees for shelter and fuel, water, mixed farming, recreation, garden produce, and a low cost of living.

23. Some northern municipalities did express concern with northern migration. The community of Medstead, for example, raised the issue at various meetings of the Saskatchewan Association of Rural Municipalities, confronting the provincial government and asking for guarantees that northern migrants would be supported by the provincial government and their municipality of origin, should they need relief, and not their new host community. *The Western Producer*, 28 February 1935. . . .

24. "Down Memory Lane."

25. "McGowan, Sargent Hugh and Muriel," 355.

26. R. A. Stutt and H. Van Vliet, "An Economic Study of Land Settlement in Representative Pioneer Areas of Northern Saskatchewan," *Technical Bulletin* 52 (Ottawa, ON: Department of Agriculture, Marketing Service, Economics Division, 1945), 30.

27. See Catherine Mary Ulmer, "The Report on Unemployment and Relief in Western Canada in 1932: Charlotte Whitten, R. B. Bennett, and the Federal Response to Relief" (Master's thesis, University of Victoria, 2009), chapter 3, "Whitton on Tour."

28. Ibid., 36–40. . . .

29. Stutt and Van Vliet, "Economic Study of Land Settlement," 36–41.

30. Fitzgerald, "Pioneer Settlement," 318. See E. C. Hope and R. A. Stutt, "Economic Study of Land Settlement in the Albertville-Garrick Area of Northern Saskatchewan, 1941" (Dominion of Canada: Department of Agriculture Multilith Report, January 1944), 26.

31. Stutt and Van Vliet, "Economic Study of Land Settlement," 68.

32. The post-1930 settlement records showed that many quarters in the north Paddockwood district were homesteaded several times, particularly throughout the 1920s to early 1930s. Each homesteader might clear a few acres, put up buildings, build a fence, or dig a well. If they subsequently abandoned the land, they would be paid for any improvements made by the next homesteader. Sometimes, the homesteader who finally

succeeded in gaining patent was building not only on their own efforts, but on the efforts of those who preceded them on the land.

33. McDonald, "Soldier Settlement and Depression Settlement," 44.
34. Powell, "Northern Settlement," 81.
35. Stutt and Van Vliet, "Economic Study of Land Settlement," 7, 68.
36. "Rambling Thoughts by a Prairie Immigrant," in *Cordwood and Courage*, 636–7. Many loans from the Northern Settlers Re-Establishment Branch went to purchase horses.
37. See "McGowan, Sargent Hugh and Muriel."
38. SAB, S43, 2004-220, S10184, Post-1930 Settlement Records, Jas. Barnett, Inspector Dominion Lands, 4 July 1931 regarding NW ¼ 26 54 25 W 2. Eventually this quarter was successfully homesteaded and patented, but the land was taken over by the provincial government to create a community pasture in the 1960s.
39. "Paddockwood: The Mixed Farming Paradise of Saskatchewan."
40. SAB, RC 236, File C67, box 12, Royal Commission on Agriculture and Rural Life, Community Brief, Paddockwood.
41. Fitzgerald, "Pioneer Settlement," 410.
42. "McGowan, Sargent Hugh and Muriel." Interestingly, their son Sargent Ernest became a prolific and highly successful hunter, fisherman, and trapper.
43. R. A. Stutt, *Land Settlement in Northern Pioneer Areas of Saskatchewan*, reprinted from *Agricultural Institute Review* (Agricultural Institute of Canada, January 1946), 13.
44. See, for example, "Arne Jacobson and family," in *Tweedsmuir: Community and Courage* (Prince Albert, SK: Campbell Printing, 2006), 85–90; "the Merrell family," in *Cordwood and Courage*, 369–70; Bryce Dunn's memoirs, "Yesteryears Reflections: A Pictorial and Written History of Times Past Seen through the Eyes of a Boy Who Lived Those Times to the Fullest," self-publlished, n.d.; "Daley, Fred and Thelma," in *Cordwood and Courage*, 167–8.
45. *Prince Albert Daily Herald*, 7 August 1931; 14 August 1931.
46. "Arne Jacobsen and family." 85–90.
47. Ronald Rees, *New and Naked Land: Making the Prairies Home* (Saskatoon, SK: Western Producer Prairie Books, 1988), 95–6.
48. Ibid., 96–9.
49. The lake, originally called Pelican Lake for its tremendous pelican population, was not part of the park's original boundaries. When the boundaries were extended north in 1929, most of Lavallée Lake fell within the expanded park. See W. A. Waiser, *Saskatchewan's Playground: A History of Prince Albert National Park* (Saskatoon, SK: Fifth House, 1989), 104. Because the lake was so remote, and only occasional canoeists found their way to the lake, Lavallée was not, at first, pressured to move.
50. Fitzgerald, "Pioneer Settlement," 338.
51. For an overview of the settlement at Fish Lake and its people, see *Tweedsmuir*, 93–100.
52. For an overview of Métis history in Saskatchewan, see Darren Préfontaine, "Métis Communities," *Encyclopaedia of Saskatchewan* (Regina, SK: Canadian Plains Research Centre, 2005); Maria Campbell, *Stories of the Road Allowance People* (Penticton, BC: Theytus Books, 1995). Two excellent documentaries include *Jim Settee: The Way Home* and *The Story of the Crescent Lake Metis*.
53. First Nations historian John Tobias declared that drought trekkers went north to "live like the Métis." Private communication, June 2008.
54. *Regina Leader*, 17 October 1931. The journalist was probably W. J. Mather, who published a similar article, with similar phrasing, in *Maclean's* magazine, 1 April 1932.
55. See John W. Bennett and Seena B. Kohl, *Settling the Canadian and American West, 1890–1915: Pioneer Adaptation and Community Building* (Lincoln, NE: University of Nebraska Press, 1995).
56. "Rambling Thoughts by a Prairie Immigrant," 637.

17 The National Selective Service Women's Division and the Management of Women War Workers

Jennifer A. Stephen

On 26 August 1942, National Selective Service Women's Division head Fraudena Eaton reported to Labour Minister Humphrey Mitchell on the progress of the female mobilization campaign. Her report, while generally positive, struck a note of concern for the moral conditions confronted by women war workers. The situation at the Cockshutt Plow Company was particularly disturbing. Indeed, conditions at the Brantford, Ontario, plant teetered dangerously on the brink of anarchy. Eaton was especially concerned about the "lack of supervision and discipline" at the munitions plant. Women were free to wander away from their work stations whenever they felt the urge, "loitering and lounging" willy-nilly on the job, hanging about the washrooms in gossipy klatches when they ought to have been at their workstations. "The cloak rooms serve as lunch rooms and as there are no lockers or racks, clothing lies and hangs all over. These rooms and the washrooms are in bad condition and are not kept clean,"[1] Eaton declared. If the minister thought the National Selective Service Women's Division (NSSWD) was responsible only for finding and placing women in war work, he was quite mistaken. The NSSWD was entrusted to safeguard the moral status of these young women, for their own sake as well as the nation's.

There was good reason for concern. War work drew women from every province. From farms and hamlets women flocked to the major industrial districts, at this time concentrated around Toronto and Montreal, eager for the high wages promised by jobs only now open to the female wage earner. The wage and employment picture changed dramatically once women joined the war effort, with both wages and employment more than doubling in the brief span of five years. Long years of depression made particularly welcome this opportunity to add to one's own and the family purse. When Canada entered the war in 1939, more than 400,000 women and men were unemployed, according to official estimates.[2] At that time, women's average industrial earnings were just 54.1 per cent of men's, an average that had increased to 69.3 per cent by 1944. Average weekly wages, meanwhile, rose from $12.78 in 1939 to an astounding $20.89 by 1944, while for the same period women's labour force participation rate climbed from 24.4 per cent to 33.5 per cent.[3] The hourly wage gap was closing: In 1939 women earned 47.9 cents for every male dollar, a figure

Citation: Jennifer A. Stephen, "The National Selective Service Women's Division and the Management of Women War Workers," in *Pick One Intelligent Girl: Employability, Domesticity and the Gendering of Canada's Welfare State, 1939–47* (Toronto, ON: University of Toronto Press, 2007): 38–65. © University of Toronto Press 2007. Reprinted with permission of the publisher.

that rose to 71.2 cents by 1944.[4] Employment patterns shifted significantly as well. In 1939, domestic service was the largest occupational sector for women. By war's end, manufacturing was. The percentage of women working in domestic service plummeted from 18.6 per cent in 1939 to only 9.3 per cent by 1943, while for the same period, as a proportion of women in the labour force, manufacturing employment rose from 27 per cent to 37 per cent.[5] Finally, the number of women working in the formal waged economy doubled from 600,000 in 1939 to 1.2 million by 1943. Of this total, approximately 250,000 were working in essential war industries; 439,000 in the services sector; 373,000 in manufacturing; 180,000 in finance and trade; 31,000 in transportation and communications; and 4,000 in construction.[6]

The campaign to recruit women was by all accounts an outstanding success, due in no small measure to the diligent efforts of Fraudena Eaton and her colleagues at the NSSWD. Eaton pressed for clear policies to ensure the rapid movement of women from all parts of the country to the industrial manufacturing centres in Ontario and Quebec. The NSSWD oversaw the implementation of comprehensive personnel measures to integrate women into unfamiliar workplaces, to ensure appropriate training and vocational guidance on the job, and to provide some measure of supervision off the job. Women's Division staff, many of whom were policy experts in female labour force patterns, understood that the current federal initiative would be short lived. Whatever their views on the question of women's right to work, they were determined to demonstrate that female labour was as viable, productive, and reliable as that of the traditional breadwinner.

From her appointment in 1942, Eaton worked closely with the federal deputy minister of labour, Arthur MacNamara.[7] From the start, the Women's Division was guided by two key objectives: through employment policy came the national enterprise—fighting the war—and

through domestic policy, securing the peaceful withdrawal of women workers from the industrial workforce once the war was finally ended. How did the Women's Division take up the challenge of mobilizing and managing Canada's womanpower? Training and the special Industrial Welfare program worked in tandem to accommodate the "special needs" of women, if only for the duration of the war. Because the call to women was temporary, to last only as long as the war, Women's Division staff had to narrow the campaign's focus, knowing that they would soon need to redirect thousands of workers from war employment across the industrialized economy into a limited range of occupations, waged and unwaged. In this context, I approach postwar planning in much the same way as did the policy practitioners whose work is considered here; that is, as an integral part of the organizational approach to planning for the war itself.

. . .

"Keeping Workers in Their Jobs"

Eaton certainly had her hands full. Women came from as far as Newfoundland to work in war plants scattered across southern Ontario and Quebec. Getting them to the workstation was a complex task that had to be accomplished quickly. Keeping them there was a further challenge. When women objected to conditions on or off the job, they made their views known, sometimes through direct protests such as work refusals and related collective job action. Even harder to address were the individual acts of resistance as women quietly drifted away one by one, draining vital national labour resources. The obvious policy response was direct supervision through personnel programming. Thus began a concerted effort to convince the male bureaucrats that the needs of women war workers had to be taken seriously. Eaton addressed her concerns directly to the minister of labour, reporting in detail on the substandard conditions faced by the new recruits. She selected three war plants, each of which epitomized just how bad things were in these essential industries under contract with the federal government. Defence Industries Limited was contracted to supply the war effort, and thus enjoyed generous terms and a regular infusion of federal subsidies. The Pickering plant suffered a chronic labour shortage, despite the fact that the NSSWD regularly sent women there. The reasons were not hard to understand. Workers had to deal with inadequate housing and limited public transportation. These problems were serious enough, but the underlying issue was negligence. Meals provided by this and other employers were regularly described as poorly prepared and inadequate. Women had to pay for this substandard fare whether or not the meals were consumed. Eventually, the "girls" at Defence Industries took matters into their own hands, staging mass demonstrations to protest the unpalatable meals served up by an indifferent management. If ever there was a case for the introduction of progressive personnel policy, this was it. In some cases, a company might have a personnel manager, but it was evident to Eaton that the position existed in name only. For example, one offending plant had a personnel manager, "Mr. Russell," who was clearly delinquent. So great were the problems in this plant that production was all but derailed. It appeared that the hapless personnel manager had failed to take the concerns of women recruits seriously. "Mr. Russell," Eaton stated, "unfortunately adopts the attitude that 'if they don't like it, they don't have to stay.'" It appeared that they did not like it. In one month alone, of the 350 young women sent from Nova Scotia to work at the plant, 90 insisted that they be placed in jobs elsewhere.[8]

The Women's Division extended its attention to women's leisure time as well. Was it unreasonable for young women to expect steps to be taken to provide recreational facilities? The issue cut both ways. Attention to leisure activities contributed to safeguarding the young women's morality as well as their morale. NSSWD staff were concerned that young women, unaccustomed

to urban life, should be supervised during off hours, directed toward wholesome recreational activities such as bowling, roller skating, and similar innocuous pursuits. The Women's Division fielded numerous reports recounting "sordid details of events that had occurred amongst women in war industries" and was as concerned about protecting the reputation of the NSS as it was that of the woman war worker.[9] Bad publicity was to be avoided at all costs, especially in Quebec. Early in 1943, Eaton received an urgent appeal from Mme Martel, NSSWD's Quebec representative. Ottawa was grappling with wide-ranging opposition to the female mobilization campaign. In Quebec, the Catholic Confederation of Workers led the charge, arguing that industrial labour was "incompatible with the French Canadian philosophy of family life." Not only that, but the hard physical labour and indiscriminate intermingling of the sexes such work entailed posed "physical and moral dangers" to women.[10] . . .

Given the obviously delicate political situation in Quebec, reports of moral delinquency were precisely what NSS wanted to avoid. And so, whenever such a report came to the Women's Division's attention, it was immediately investigated. Such was the case in Brownsburg [Quebec]. Several hundred young women had been sent from New Brunswick to work at the plant, mingling with male workers on the job and, it seemed, off the job as well. At least some of the female workforce were said "to seek solace in alcohol" at a village beverage room during their off hours, there being "few amusements" with which they could occupy their leisure time in more appropriate (that is to say, feminine and wholesome) pursuits. Eaton called on Renee Morin, NSSWD officer and women's employment specialist, to conduct a discreet investigation, being careful not to advertise the reason for her visit. In March 1943, Morin reported back to Eaton and the chief commissioner of the UIC [Unemployment Insurance Commission], Mr. L. J. Trottier, "on the moral situation of men and women workers." There was scant evidence of the morally deleterious conditions recounted by the opponents of women's employment, she observed. "From what people have told me," Morin advised, "it seems that the conduct of the employees of the two sexes in the factory is irreproachable."[11] The mere suggestion that women were engaging in any morally delinquent behaviour in the local village was enough to arouse the ire of the local curé notwithstanding Morin's painstaking attempts at investigative "tact." "Brownsburg," she concluded, "does not present a more sombre picture than other industrial municipalities." Moral inquiries by federal officials were clearly unwelcome, having left the local curé "a little offended by the very fact that there was some suspicion about the conduct of his parishioners. Personally, he seemed very satisfied with the situation at the factory."[12] The company in question treated its employees with care, maintained a recreation room, and conducted its business appropriately. Such problems as had occurred were addressed and readily resolved. What the workers, men and women alike, did during their own time might be the business of the local church but was clearly considered off limits to NSS snoops.

. . .

Having made their way through the factory gates, women asserted their right to be accorded the freedoms traditionally enjoyed by their wage-earning fellows. If conditions were poor, some women exercised such rights by refusing NSSWD assignments. The Women's Division arranged accommodations for out-of-town workers, but such efforts were not always enough to entice young women with a newly independent turn of mind. This was the situation in the Ontario town of Belleville. Although Women's Division officers reported no shortage of female labour, the women in the small city refused work at the nearby Bata Shoe Company plant. Accommodation was available at a new "staff house," but only a few had taken up residence since it was little more than a building with beds.

The recreation room doubled as the entrance hall. Women complained that there was nothing to do in the off hours, not even "a game room where they can play even simple table games." The local moving picture theatre had been closed for more than six weeks. As though this were not enough, the plant cafeteria provided an uninspired selection of food described as "badly cooked and of inferior quality."[13] The situation was described in terms that made obvious the only solution: Women required proper health, welfare, and recreation facilities to attend to their unique needs as workers in an unfamiliar and inhospitable environment. Proper meals had to be provided, along with wholesome recreation and properly supervised accommodations. The workplace environment itself required careful organization and supervision under the expert guidance of trained women personnel specialists whose assignment was to safeguard the femininity of their charges.

In contrast, progressive managerial techniques had succeeded in solving the absenteeism problem at the John Inglis Company in Toronto and at nearby Small Arms Limited in Long Branch. The minister of labour's office publicized the commendable example set by the John Inglis Company, obviously hoping that others would follow suit and so deal with their absenteeism and turnover problems. For example, Inglis employed a female welfare supervisor plus a recreation supervisor. Women employees enjoyed access to the nearby community swimming pool and gymnasium. The neighbourhood roller-skating rink had been converted into a recreation club, reserved for the exclusive use of the women at the plant. Never before had women received such careful attention to their needs as workers, inducted into a leisurely worker-centred culture that was usually the exclusive preserve of working men. Organized recreational activities and other forms of entertainment, together with the collegiality of fellow women at the plant, must have provided a crucial camaraderie to help relieve the stress of high-paced production on the job, not to mention a world at war, when there was time to think of such matters.

Comradeship also provided an opportunity to compare notes in the articulation of grievances. For the NSSWD, supervised recreation was welcomed, but collective action was not. Eaton, along with her fellow women bureaucrats, regularly pointed out the structural causes of high turnover, and not only in lower-wage industries. In the absence of central collective bargaining strategies and in the presence of a tight labour market, workers usually voted with their feet and left in search of jobs with better wages and working conditions.[14] Even though women were but temporary sojourners in the labour market, ministry officials were well advised to heed their demands as they exercised new-found power in their wage-earning capacities. The NSSWD promoted industrial welfare as a way to deal with both concerns. Women's needs as workers had to be attended to and their leisure hours turned to useful purposes. The Industrial Welfare program had solved the problem of labour instability at Inglis and would be sure to do the same for other war plants. Expense was a poor excuse for inaction, as this case made all too clear: the community, when asked, had willingly pitched in and made available several facilities in an excellent example of local community and private industry coming together to eradicate absenteeism, the number-one threat to the war effort. Labour Minister Mitchell coined yet another pithy slogan to remind Canadians of their duty: "Absence makes the war last longer."[15]

. . .

[T]he Department of Labour took up the issue of absenteeism through an investigation of its own.[16] The internal study laid the basis for the productivity-boosting campaign of 1943, publicized through [John] Grierson's Office of War Information.[17] The campaign institutionalized the Industrial Welfare program as the solution to lagging productivity, while low production levels were blamed on absentee workers. Every plant was advised to establish fact-finding missions to root out absenteeism. Unions and labour–management committees were enjoined to take leadership in the workplace, enlisting workers' support and confidence. Day nurseries and extended store hours would considerably ease the burden on working mothers. Grierson was also keen to launch a major campaign aimed directly at improving bad plant conditions, such as poor heating, inadequate locker and washroom facilities, and slow and insufficient medical attention for accidents. At the very least, a publicity campaign would assure workers that government was keeping a watchful eye on the workplace. For its part, government would see to it that adequate housing, transportation, and recreation were provided. Management had to do a better job of convincing its employees that the company was all out for production and did not discriminate in promotion and upgrading. Safety rules and faithful use of safety devices were everybody's responsibility. Workers deserved hot, nourishing meals at reasonable prices. Employers were again encouraged to improve in-plant training, intended to facilitate workers' adjustment to new jobs and communities. And finally, perhaps the most central element in the newly enlightened approach, "Prevention and remedy are better than punishment."[18] Lest employers be put on the defensive, dangerous health and safety conditions would be "improved" but would not be subjected to penalty and/or eradicated. Finally, the principles of modern personnel planning enlisted individual identification with goals and objectives, routines, and rituals of the enterprise, the pursuit of which were held to satisfy everyone—the worker, the company, and the national interest.

Developing Women's Personnel Work

In 1942, the NSSWD convened its first Women's Personnel Conference in Montreal to plan precisely how the movement of women into war production would proceed. It was an opportunity to educate delegates on the finer points of worker assessment and job placement. Placement work was a professionalized body of knowledge, and much depended on the initial interview with the applicant. Placement efforts were challenged from all sides, not least on account of "wide discrepancies in the general field of employment." Finding potential labour recruits was hard enough. Experienced workers openly criticized the work assignments handed to them by beleaguered NSS staff. Even worse, raw recruits might be brimming with enthusiasm, but eagerness to earn did not compensate for lack of qualifications. NSSWD employment officers were beset by organizational problems that were as prosaic as they were integral to efficient labour deployment. The list was a long one: "controlling distribution of workers, bringing together the right applicant and the right job, setting up suitable offices for placement, obtaining competent staff." Employers were digging in their heels at the prospect of having women descend upon their territory. Government bureaucrats outside the Women's Division did not always appreciate the different challenges posed by the employment of women. And, of course, the women themselves held ambitions that did not always match NSSWD priorities. Where all else failed, however, authorities could at least appeal to patriotism and "the constant feeling on the part of the employee that there is first a war to be won."[19]

. . .

With MacNamara's backing, Eaton encouraged the formation of women's personnel associations, such as the Women's Personnel Group of Toronto. Personnel planning was a new professional outlet for graduates of the women's business colleges and provided a valuable contribution to the overall war effort. "I think we should give further service to industry in connection with personnel departments," Eaton argued, consolidating the presence of women's personnel work as a regulatory device—a measure supported by the considerable resources and educational expertise made available by the NSSWD.[20] Women, at least those conforming to the criteria of British origin and middle-class location, were looked upon as particularly well suited for personnel work. Women possessed a special expertise, one they might apply to the problems women workers were most likely to face. Women were best left to supervise other women, particularly in matters of moral guidance and guardianship. For instance, physical and mental examinations required greater discretionary and interventionary powers. Medical examinations were required of all women recruited by the NSSWD. Typically, employers were becoming far too lax on the subject, loosening standards in order to fill job vacancies as quickly as possible. What better evidence of the need for hands-on female supervision by trained personnel experts?

NSS regional women's division heads, the National Council of Women of Canada (NCWC), and the Toronto Welfare Council held an emergency conference in June 1943 to develop a more appropriate response. They agreed that close monitoring of all travel and accommodation was necessary, in keeping with the broader moral regulatory measures instituted through the campaign against venereal disease.[21] Employers clearly could not be relied upon to enforce mandatory medical inspections of all women employees. Moreover, it would be a difficult measure to implement with any tact or discretion, and discretion was the watchword, given the close scrutiny of morality generated in the heat of the VD panic. Eaton advised her lieutenant, Mary Eadie, to put the case to NSS Women's Division supervisors, suggesting that medical examinations be made mandatory and that they be conducted "before the girl leaves her own community," no matter how strenuously employers agitated for any general relaxation of medical examination standards. Moreover, each woman would be required to have "twenty dollars in her possession." As a further safeguard, no young woman under the age of 18 would be transferred from her home community.[22]

In this way, the NSSWD steadily built up a parallel system of women employment officers, personnel experts, and industrial welfare officers through the NSS apparatus. The YWCA, the local welfare councils, and women's personnel staff from industry and local councils of women—all were in place to oversee the activities of women war workers. Building on the sponsorship model that had worked so well in the previous decade, this matrix of women experts sought intimate contact with the female worker, monitoring, supervising, and guiding women throughout their tenure as war workers. The same network was to perform a crucial function in the post-war program of rehabilitation and demobilization. This was by no means a compensatory measure filling a perceived void in a government-run employment service. Local councils of women worked in close collaboration with community welfare agency workers as part of a web of localized governance, in concert with the centralized NSS Women's Division network of offices and regional staff. Local formations such as these were one of the many ways that state and "community" established coextensive, overlapping networks. Women personnel supervisors worked with welfare officers, and the YWCA co-operated with employment placement staff from the NSS, with each consolidating the other's position.[23]

The NSSWD soon found that its hard work was beginning to pay off. The National Association of Manufacturers might ridicule women as making poor supervisory staff—given their greater propensity to "throw their weight around"—but a trained female supervisor could accomplish a great deal with the "girl munitions workers" in her charge. *Maclean's* magazine ran a lengthy article about Canada's new womanpower in 1942, lending much-needed publicity to the Industrial Welfare program, and to the professionalization of women's personnel work. Thelma LeCocq, the author of this exegesis about the new industrial "woman power," explained how the featured personnel supervisor cheerfully lobbied for improved wages and working conditions at her plant:

> The manager of [an aircraft manufacturing] plant has women draughtsmen on his staff and says they're swell. As personnel manager he has a cheerful, competent woman who worked the floor herself for three weeks so that she knows what it's all about. It is she who got the girls a fifteen minute break both morning and afternoon and proved to the management that they work better for it. It is she who encourages girls to fit themselves for men's jobs and is going to get them men's pay for it if it's humanly possible.[24]

Like the coach of a sports team, the female supervisor cultivated group identity, obedience, and a sense of fair play—good qualities for both workers and citizens.

"She Has No Chance to Develop Poor Work Habits": Training and Personnel Management

When the minister of labour rose in Parliament to report on the success of the new War Emergency Training Programme (WETP), he drew explicitly upon the image of the "unemployable man." This figure of the Depression was not a victim of economic upheaval or the collapse of financial capital markets. The unemployable man symbolized personal failure, the family breadwinner whose masculinity was compromised by deficiency. That spectre of uncertainty and social dissolution could now, however, be remedied through a coherent program of training and vocational guidance. Training promised a measure of stability, regularity, and order. Skill would become a stabilizing force, a vector linking the individual to the market. Mitchell heaped praise on the "fine achievement" of the new wartime training apparatus: "Over 68,000 persons have been trained in industrial classes in the last year to man the thousands of machines in the factories making the tools of war."[25] . . .

Training was integral to the government's mobilization plans. Vocational training for women was deeply informed by understandings of differential skill and learning capacity, guiding principles for the "skills dilution" approach to work reorganization. Vocational or "pre-employment" training was designed to convert the female reserve into a viable and productive labour force. It was also conceived of as a second tier within the federal training and employment strategy—a second tier that would be instrumental in the post-war employment settlement.

. . .

The WETP trained workers up to the semi-skilled or skilled level to meet the demands of war production. Program content was intended to maintain employment fitness or to enable the individual "to obtain better or more suitable" employment, according to the terms approved by the labour minister.[26] As a national strategy, vocational training aimed at producing a productive labour force of war workers in the shortest amount of time possible. It was an ambitious policy, the results of which were truly impressive. In the early years of the war, at least to 1941, policy practitioners and employers alike assumed that women's training would be minimal and short term. "Up to the present time occupations for which women are being used in war industries are of a nature which require very little training and this training is being given in industry rather than in pre-employment classes established under the War Emergency Training Programme," Minister of Labour Norman McLarty explained to his cabinet colleague, Minister of Pensions and National Health Ian Mackenzie, in May 1941.[27] Similarly, the *Labour Gazette* reported that women did not require formal training for the limited tasks they would be expected to perform.[28] By 1943, this approach would change dramatically, in direct response to the deepening labour crisis.

The new push for female recruitment drove the NSS and industry into a complex campaign to reorganize production tasks on the plan recommended by the engineering experts, known as "skills dilution." In the Fordist model of industrial production, all knowledge and production technique was embedded within the technology itself, both in the physical machinery and the managerial technologies organizing the work of production: for example, through time-motion and engineering studies. Engineers designed the equipment and organized production schedules and sequential job tasks; workers executed assigned tasks. All of this work had been conducted long before the woman worker set foot in the workplace. The vocational training program also changed, in the new knowledge that women would now be channelled into jobs requiring greater skill. Plant instructors seemed flummoxed at the prospect of training the new recruits. In 1943, the Nova Scotia director of training for the Department of Labour described the scene as his department was called on to train a group of women as machine operators. His report proved a familiar narrative of problems instructors encountered as they tried to figure out how they might possibly deal with this unique group of "workers." It is worth citing at length:

The instructors who had had no previous experience with women in productive shop work were inclined to be sceptical of their capacity to learn to run machines and were loath to take on the job of teaching them. Advertisements were inserted in the daily papers asking for applicants and a ready response brought out a large number who were eager to enter the training course. They were subjected to the same psychological tests for intelligence and mechanical aptitude as had been used previously with men. It was found that the latter was of little significance when applied to female applicants probably because they had not become familiar with common tools and mechanisms as they grew up. Through critical interviewing those were selected who seemed to possess outstanding qualities of teachability and dependability.[29]

Training for men proceeded smoothly on the basis of mass testing and instruction. The limited exposure and differential capacities of women required an individuated approach, organized around the "teachability" of the female trainee in the absence of any innate propensity for the work at hand. Women simply possessed no mechanical "aptitude," or so the story went.[30] But did they have the capacity to be taught? The answer to this question cut to the core of women's identity as workers. Given their limited labour force attachment, women were observed to possess an equally limited desire to learn the whole trade. The narrative neatly complemented the managerial strategy of work reorganization through "skills dilution": Female recruits were best instructed on a task rather than a trade basis, an approach that embedded the segmentation of apprenticeable trades within the overall training strategy. The narrative from the Nova Scotia director of technical education cited above made a convincing argument for this approach. Women were deemed more timid in the use of machining tools—given their exposure to mechanical instruments no more complicated than a sewing machine. They were also characterized as less inclined to respond to skilled trades training, having no aspiration to continue working in an apprenticeable trade once the war had ended. This apparent lack of "long-term ambition" reinforced the view that women had only a transitory attachment to the labour force: "Their general attitude showed that they felt their effort was directly connected with war activity and [was] based on a keen feeling of patriotism," wrote the Nova Scotia director of technical education, describing the progress made by his department in training women as electric welders in the Nova Scotia shipyards, where they were to work installing gun mounts and related military weapons systems.[31]

Training the woman worker became a task of instilling good work habits as the new work routines were learned. As a reporter for the business press explained, "One of the big advantages of this training is that the new employee starts off on the right foot and learns how to be a good operator from the beginning. She has no chance to develop poor working habits."[32] Training was a process of orientation to routines, rules, and procedures of work. Absenteeism and turnover could be prevented from the outset in a program greatly enhanced by mental testing. *Canadian Business* reporter Mary Oliver investigated conditions at the Small Arms Limited facility in Long Branch, on the outskirts of Toronto. Management at the plant was so impressed by the results of the new program that they intended to make these methods a regular feature of all personnel work:

> When, on the third morning, Mary graduates from the school and takes her place on the production line, she doesn't feel at a loss. Nor is she left to the tender mercies of the foreman—two "patrolling instructresses" watch new operators at their work, offer suggestions, and, if more instruction is needed, give it on the spot. This supervision continues until Mary and her friends are quite able to carry on alone. Occasionally a girl can't make the grade; she goes back to school again and an attempt is made to find a job for which she is better suited. As time goes on, the management plans to branch out into job placement and aptitude tests for all their workers.[33]

A key focus of progressive managerial technique, therefore, became the capacity of the individual worker. . . .

Surveillance and inspection were the signature of modern personnel development, in stark contrast to the haphazard and unscientific practice of hiring at the plant gate. The training infrastructure built up around the war effort ushered in an entirely new approach to Canada's working classes, now cast as a national resource. The theme of surveillance was a central feature in descriptive and prescriptive narratives detailing the advantageous effects of training and personnel planning. Articles appearing in the popular media keenly promoted the government plan: The surest route to workplace order and stability was a close system of scrutiny and monitoring that began at the level of the individual worker. Such was the routine at Central Technical Collegiate in Toronto.[34] The school operated on a 24-hour schedule, turning out war workers ready to take up their positions in essential industries, all the while under the "watchful eye" of a battery of personnel planners, plant superintendents, inspectors, and instructors. The classroom was a microcosm of the developing continuum the NSS was so keen to replicate within its own regulatory infrastructure: screening, training, recruitment, employment placement, and continuous tracking. The classroom was transformed into a transparent public space of order and predictability, its internal routines open to public view, its occupants displayed as potential labour, and its techniques readily transferable to other locations, provided that the carefully developed knowledge practices around which it was organized were closely adhered to. Educational psychology had left its bold imprint. Remedial vocational instruction replaced the disciplinary ordering of workers' bodies; the interior of individual "trainees" was made available to governance in classroom, the workplace, even the community, through assessment, calibration, and regulation. The new vocational training integrated the best insights of personnel development, now techniques for the development of the "self"—the trained worker. "Personnel executives, shop foremen and plant superintendents are constantly inspecting classes sponsored by their firms, seeing for themselves the progress made by each individual—or the absence of it," explained Frederick Edwards, a feature writer for *Maclean's* magazine. In his article "Night and Day School," Edwards recounted how the trainee might "at any given moment . . . find himself under critical scrutiny by the man he expects and hopes to be working for in a few weeks' time." Sponsoring firms would get regular reports on their charges and, best of all, "slackers or misfits are eliminated ruthlessly—something that cannot happen to regular students."[35]

Mingling among the potential misfits and slackers were "baldish oldsters," "dignified white-haired matrons," and "pert misses": those groups specifically identified as the potential labour reserve. Skill capacity was a central theme in these gendered narratives. Where men might receive up to 20 weeks of instruction on "some highly technical subjects," three weeks was considered sufficient to instruct most women in machine operation or assembly-line work. But the real bonus came in the detailed work for which women appeared ideally adapted. "Meter assembly," according to one report, "requires the accurate weaving of twenty-six strands of wire, each wrapped in a different coloured covering. No men need apply here. The male sex, it seems, is affected with colour blindness to a much greater degree than are women."[36] Women's training requirements could still be characterized as minimal, given their "natural" proclivity for such mundane but precise tasks and their apparent tolerance for boredom and fatigue. The message carried through popular media, likely designed to encourage women to sign up and employers to welcome the new recruits, minimized the complexity of the work at hand: A few days' training was all that was needed, provided that the "natural qualifications of dexterity, patience and keen eyesight" were present and intact.[37]

The special aptitudes women were deemed to possess, if not monopolize, were instead described as attributes, more a function of gender than of innate intelligence to be developed as skill. Indeed, any interest in machinery at all was characterized as "queer," and queer, as everybody knew, was most certainly not feminine. *Maclean's* feature writer Thelma LeCocq implied as much. The average woman might not possess any "passion for machinery," but her "deft fingered" ways made her an ideal candidate for assembly-line work. Assembling the machinery of war was no more complicated than assembling a new housedress, even if it was a bit dirtier. Some women, however, readily took advantage of the rare opportunity afforded by war production work. LeCocq described the typical experience of this atypical female type: "Being a stenographer wasn't her idea of a career, so she got a job with a typewriter firm doing repairs. That was the best she could do in a world where a woman interested in machinery was regarded as queer. Then the gun plant called for women workers."[38] In narratives like these, femininity was unlikely to survive intact unless the closely delineated standards of normative gender identity were adhered to. It was the task of industrial welfare and pre-employment training to ensure that they were.

The "Housewife's Shift": A Case Study of Work Reorganization

As part of the mobilization campaign, Eaton and her staff at the Women's Division engineered another innovative strategy: the housewife's shift, modelled on the Victory Shifts in Britain. By 1943, part-time employment was an important focus of NSS policy in a campaign that targeted older, married women with children in order to free younger single women for regular war work. Senior officials hoped this strategy would draw workers to fill the gaps in less remunerative work such as domestic employment in hospitals.[39] As a financial incentive, women were reminded that they would only be required to pay UI contributions if they worked more than four hours per day and that they were exempt from paying income tax if annual earnings were $660 or less.[40] Employers were advised that women had to be made to "feel" that they were regular employees. It was best to defer to the expertise of personnel

supervisors (and if they did not have such staff, the implication was that they most certainly ought to) whose task would be to encourage the part-time worker to "feel welcome and a necessary part of your organization." There remained the ever-present danger that this woman might degenerate to the status of the transient worker whose interests were increasingly removed from those of her employer; that she might treat both job and employer in the "off-hand inconsiderate manner of a casual or temporary employee." A note of challenge pervaded the prescriptive policy literature on this question: The women whose aid was to be solicited were also described as far more independent and therefore more likely to resist poor treatment. For such women, the tug of patriotic duty was strong but unlikely to withstand employer indifference or exploitive working conditions. Supervision by trained, preferably female personnel was crucial to the successful deployment of this segment of the female workforce, given their stronger identity as alderwomen with home, family, independence, and responsibilities. Together, these factors made such women unused to the subordinate status of the regular employee. NSS employer advice literature explained that the part-time mature woman was "serious of purpose," and for that reason all the more likely to criticize carelessness on the job. Any sign of "bullying" or "nagging" would be "keenly resented by the older women." Unlike regular employees, these women would be more likely to quit "than to stand their ground and fight it out." The Women's Division addressed the matter head on: "As a rule, these older women know exactly why they are working and what for and their purpose is usually an unselfish and self-sacrificing one."[41] Thus, at one and the same time, the older woman as part-time worker was both driven by self-interest and compelled by her natural patriotic duty, itself a function of her role as mother, wife, and guardian of the middle-class home. She was more responsible, imbued with an agency that permitted greater freedom of movement to come and go, to enter the labour force but just as readily to leave rather than "stand her ground and fight." Identification with national purpose through patriotic spirit, an unselfish attitude of self-sacrifice, and "sound common-sense" were all pointed to as advantageous features accompanying the introduction of the older part-time woman into the workplace, where she might provide a good example for younger and more impressionable women to follow.

Conversely, the autonomy that was so important to the maintenance of a healthy household was here a hindrance to that other subject of industrial welfare policy discourse: the productive worker capable of submitting to the sterner realities of the workplace. In fact, on closer examination, the individual household was seen to be more removed than ever from the structured space of the modern workplace. The part-time worker was more likely to request time off for "trivial matters," to which supervisors had to respond with a firm but sympathetic attitude. Workers on the housewife's shift had to be taught that responsibility to employer and nation demanded unflagging personal sacrifice and commitment. All regulations, those of the employer in the workplace and of the NSS, constituted an undifferentiated, continuous field of procedure and obligation that simply had to be adhered to. "These women must be continuously reminded of their obligations," according to NSS advice literature, and this could be done by "constantly stressing the regular rather than the casual nature of their duties." Supervision was essential to ensuring punctuality and regular attendance. NSS employment officers were advised to be vigilant and firm in dealing with the older woman, recognizing that "her domestic obligations weigh heavily with her" and would likely affect work attendance and performance. "Careful and sympathetic consideration" in helping her deal with such problems went firmly in hand with a close eye to her extreme individualism. According to the policy analysts at the Women's Division, home management was a matter of individual caprice and whim, and "if

the discipline of fixed schedules and punctuality has ever been known, it is likely to have been forgotten."[42] The average household, it seemed, existed in a state of extreme individualism, as far removed from the orderly workplace as it was possible to be.

The part-time worker posed an interesting challenge because of her identity as housewife and mother and her tangential relation to the waged labour force. She was unused to the patterns of authority and standards of compliant behaviour of the conventional employment relationship. Through personnel technique, the women, who were the target of the "housewife's shift" had to become imbued with a new "worker-identity," a form of "labour as dressage."[43] NSS policy directives drew on these conceptions to emphasize the unstable identity of the part-time worker, especially when compared to the stable male worker, whose attachment to the labour force was known and therefore calculable. As would become clear, the woman at the centre of this narrative was white and married, the autonomous figure of idealized middle-class domesticity whose labours were motivated by a sense of patriotic duty, an affinity with the national purpose. Personnel guidance eased the transition from domestic household to the unfamiliar space of economic modernity signified by the modern workplace. Discipline, power, agency, and identity were the operative terms in this discursive field. Domesticity and employability intertwined in the documentary practice of the NSS advisories, underscoring the temporary, marginal, and therefore ambivalent location of women workers generally and part-time workers in particular.

Conclusion

The NSS Women's Division was responsible for overseeing all areas of labour market policies and programming involving the employment of women. NSS training and employment strategies mobilized gender-based assumptions about female employability at the same time as they constituted women workers as moral regulatory subjects. As concerns about labour shortages intensified, so too did moves to institute a comprehensive program of "industrial welfare." The presence of women in the industrial workplace was, of course, not a new phenomenon. The "manpower shortage" intensified scrutiny of workers' bodies as disciplinary subjects as well as potentially morally disordered subjects. At the same time, compulsion was to be avoided at all costs. Democracy and the fight to defend it was a central organizing precept in this total war against fascism. The Dominion government walked a very fine line on the issue of conscripted labour for either military or industrial purposes, in the case of women's employment even more than men's. Consent, compliance, and, better yet, a call and willing response to service closely informed the sentiments to which policy officials wanted to appeal as part of the fusion of individual interest and the national enterprise. On closer examination, policy practitioners would discover a disturbing rate of absenteeism and turnover in industries designated essential to the war effort.[44] Regulatory procedures had to be tightened considerably to ensure that working women, in particular, not only reported to work on time but actually stayed put in their jobs for the duration of the war. Something simply had to be done to discourage women from wandering off in pursuit of higher wages and/or more favourable working conditions elsewhere. Intensification of managerial technique became a key strategy for regulating this new-found, if somewhat unruly, labour supply. NSS officials drew on the diagnostic and prescriptive expertise of psychologists, psychiatrists, employment researchers, vocational guidance experts, industrial engineers, and management specialists to assist in the project of overseeing and adjusting the work habits of women alleged to be unused to the rigours and challenges of regular industrial employment. As a strategy of gender-based regulation, NSS officials launched a series of policy initiatives that effectively reorganized and intensified gender coding in the workplace through a program of skills dilution, a core organizing principle underpinning the pre-employment training strategy.

Employability discourses worked to organize the differential capacities of groups of women according to occupation and domestic affiliation, while conditioning women's access to what came to be constituted through these same discourses as the regular, formal, waged economy. Industrial welfare and personnel programming were drafted on the basis of the new expertise of employment researchers, psychologists, and management consultants—proponents of the new managerial techniques that would reorganize Canadian enterprise. Similarly, the public employment office gained new significance as a strategic public space for directing the flow of labour. As workers, women were constituted as capable of only partially achieving and maintaining desired productivity levels: as mothers, whether actual or potential, women needed careful scrutiny and regulation through industrial welfare programs. These policy discourses collectively articulated the boundaries of nation, of the labour market as the productive site of national strength and security, and of the differential citizenship capacities of those called upon to secure the interests of the nation on the domestic front of total war.

  More online.

Notes

1. Library and Archives Canada (LAC), RG 27, Vol. 605, File 6-23. Employment, Health, Welfare and Recreation for Workers. Eaton to Hon. Humphrey Mitchell, Minister of Labour, "Situations Existing in Certain War Industries," 26 August 1942.

2. Peter S. McInnis, "Teamwork for Harmony: Labour–Management Production Committees and the Postwar Settlement in Canada," *Canadian Historical Review* 77, no. 3 (September 1996): 319. A measure of under-employment and forced withdrawal from the formal waged economy would no doubt have yielded a higher count.

3. Ibid., 113.

4. Ruth Pierson, *"They're Still Women After All": The Second World War and Canadian Womanhood* (Toronto, ON: McClelland & Stewart, 1986), 117.

5. Ann Porter, "Women and Income Security in the Postwar Period: The Case of Unemployment Insurance, 1945–62," *Labour/Le Travail* 31 (Spring 1993): 113. Porter characterizes this as a movement from domestic service "and unskilled occupations" to "higher-paid, skilled positions" in manufacturing. See n10 at 113.

6. G. C. Brandt, "Pigeon-Holed and Forgotten: The Work of the Subcommittee on the Post-War Problems of Women, 1943," *Histoire Sociale/Social History* 14, no. 29 (May 1982): 241–2.

7. Michael D. Stevenson, "National Selective Service and the Mobilization of Human Resources in Canada during the Second World War" (Ph.D. dissertation, University of Western Ontario, 1996).

8. LAC, RG 27, Vol. 605, File 6-23. Employment. Health, Welfare and Recreation for Workers. Eaton to Hon. Humphrey Mitchell, Minister of Labour, "Situations Existing in Certain War Industries," 26 August 1942.

9. LAC, RG 27, Vol. 605, File 6-24-1, pt 1. NSS Employment of Women. Fraudena Eaton to Mme Paul Martel, 12 March 1943.

10. LAC, RG 27, Vol. 605, File 6-24-1, pt 1. NSS Employment of Women. Alfred Charpentier, "Women"s Work." Confederation of Catholic Workers, 11 May 1942.

11. LAC, RG 27, Vol. 605, File 6-24-1, pt 1. NSS Employment of Women. Renee Morin, letter marked "Confidential" to Mr. L. J. Trottier, Chief Commissioner, UIC, 15 March 1943.

12. Ibid.

13. LAC, RG 27, Vol. 605, File 6-23. Employment. Health, Welfare and Recreation for Workers. Eaton to Hon. Humphrey Mitchell, Minister of Labour, "Situations Existing in Certain War Industries," 26 August 1942.

14. LAC, RG 27, Vol. 36. Department of Labour. Report on National Selective Service Operations for Civilian Employment. Section III, "Employment of Women—Textiles." September 1943.

15. LAC, RG 27, Vol. 605, File 6-23. NSS Employment. Health and Welfare and Recreation for Workers, Department of Labour press release, Ottawa, 5 September 1942.

16. These results were compiled from a census of 18 war plants. Again, married women were found to have the highest number of absences, followed by single men, single women, and married men. "New residents of a community" were absent more frequently than "regular residents." . . .

17. LAC, RG 27, Vol. 1524, File NSS Manpower Surveys of Canadian Industry. Stevenson and Kellogg, "Proposed Procedures for Manpower Survey of a Canadian Industry."

18. LAC, RG 27, Vol. 605, File 6–18. Absenteeism. Office of War Information, "OWI Advance Release 1822 for Monday Morning Papers," 17 May 1943, 3.

19. LAC, RG 27, Vol. 605, File 6-24-1, pt 1. NSS Employment of Women—General Minutes of a Personnel Conference by the National Selective Service (Women's and Welfare Division) for Female Personnel Officers and Welfare Workers in War Industries, held at the Windsor Hotel, Montreal, 15 December 1942, 3.

20. LAC, RG 27, Vol. 605, File 6-24-1, pt 1. NSS Employment of Women—General. Fraudena Eaton to Mary Anderson, Director of U.S. Department of Labor Women's Bureau, 23 January 1943. Eaton to Laura Smith, War Department HQ Services and Supply, 26 January 1943. Smith to Eaton, 17 February 1943.

21. For an account of the VD scare during this period, see Pierson, *"They're Still Women After All."*

22. LAC, RG 27, Vol. 60S, File 6-24-1, pt 1. NSS Employment of Women—General. Eaton to Mary Eadie, Supervisor, Women's Division Employment and Selective Service Office, Toronto, 8 June 1943.

23. LAC, RG 27, Vol. 605, File 6-24-1, pt 1. NSS Employment of Women—General. B.G. Sullivan to Eaton, "Re: Women's Personnel Group of Toronto," 21 June 1943.

24. Thelma LeCocq, "Woman Power," *Maclean's*, 15 June 1942, 40.

25. LAC, RG 27, Vol. 3384, File 2. Binder, "Vocational Training and Wartime Bureau of Technical Personnel," 2.

26. LAC, RG 27, Vol. 728, File 12-2-1. Letter from McLarty, 27 November 1941. For the period 1941–2, McLarty authorized the transfer of $4.76 million to the provinces for the training of war workers.

27. LAC, RG 27, Vol. 3533, File 3-26-41, pt 1. Administration: Suggestions and Representations re: Training—General Correspondence. McLarty to Ian Mackenzie, Minister of Pensions and National Health, 2 May 1941.

28. Canada, Department of Labour, *Labour Gazette*, March 1941, 271.

29. LAC, RG 27, Vol. 605, File 6-24-1, pt 1. NSS Employment of Women—General. "Training of Women for War Industries in the War Emergency Training Program" (n.d., n.a.), 1–2; Report from Department of Education, Technical Education Branch, F. H. Sexton, Director of Technical Education, to T. D. A. Purves, Deputy Minister of Labour, Nova Scotia, 30 April 1943.

30. See Ann Phillips and Barbara Taylor, "Sex and Skill," in Feminist Review, ed., *Waged Work: A Reader* (London, UK: Virago, 1986), 54–66. See also Gillian Creese, *Constructing Masculinity: Gender, Class and Race in a White-Collar Union, 1944–94* (Toronto, ON: Oxford University Press, 1999). As Creese argues in her study,

"to define a job as technical was to define it as masculine." Creese, 113.

31.   LAC, RG 27, Vol. 605, File 6-424-1, pt 1. NSS Employment of Women—General. Report from Department of Education, Technical Education Branch, F. B. Sexton, Director of Technical Education, to T. D. A. Purves, Deputy Minister of Labour, Nova Scotia, 30 April 1943.

32.   Mary Oliver, "A Wartime Schoolroom," *Canadian Business* (January 1944): 90.

33.   Ibid.

34.   Frederick Edwards, "Night-and-Day School," *Maclean's*, 1 May 1942, 16–17, 22–4.

35.   Ibid., 17.

36.   Ibid., 22.

37.   LeCocq, "Woman Power," 11.

38.   Ibid., 10.

39.   For a discussion of the campaign to increase part-time war workers, see Pierson, *"They're Still Women After All."*

40.   LAC, RG 27, Vol. 605, File 6-24-1, pt 2. NSS Employment of Women—General. Department of Labour Employment Service and UI Branch, Ottawa, 24 August 1943. NSS Circular Number 277, "Part Time Workers," Allan Mitchell, Director of Employment Service and UI. "Planning for Part-time Workers," by Miss E. R Cornell, Regional Adviser, Montreal, 3–4.

41.   Ibid., 3–5.

42.   Ibid., 5.

43.   Dressage in this context references the third of Foucault's three functions of labour: productive, symbolic, and dressage, denoting the management of work as taming, performance, and discipline. Labour as dressage addresses the performative character of work, a normative although not necessarily productive and economically functional dimension of managerial technique. See Norman Jackson and Pippa Carter, "Labour as Dressage," in Alan McKinlay and Ken Starkey, eds., *Foucault, Management and Organization Theory: From Panopticon to Technologies of the Self* (London, UK: Sage Publications, 1998): 49–64.

44.   LAC, RG 27, Vol. 1516, File 0-14.2, pt 1. Wartime Information Board, Minutes of Meeting of Committee on Industrial Morale, Friday, 11 June 1943. . . .

18 Exploring Post-War Consumption
The Campaign to Unionize Eaton's in Toronto, 1948–52

Donica Belisle

Unionized employees have substantially increased their purchasing power. This is *your* Opportunity Day to do so by joining Local 1000.

> —Leaflet distributed by the Canadian Congress of Labour to Eaton's Toronto employees, 1950

Though it occasionally delves into the topics of fordism and leisure,[1] Canadian labour history is not usually associated with research on consumer culture. Recent work by US labour historians suggests that through their politicization of salaries, job security, living standards, commodity distribution, and mass culture, unionists have made consumption central to labour politics.[2] Exploring a campaign by the Canadian Congress of Labour (CCL) to organize 12,000 Toronto Eaton's employees between 1948 and 1952, this article offers a preliminary investigation of Canadian unionism's relationship with consumption. Led by up-and-coming members of the Co-operative Commonwealth Federation (CCF) and supported by the Congress of Industrial Organisations (CIO) and such major unions as the Steelworkers, the Amalgamated Clothing Workers (ACW), and the United Automobile Workers (UAW), the "Eaton Drive" was the largest single union campaign in Canadian history and "the closest thing to a crusade in the English-speaking union movement."[3]

At the middle of the twentieth century the T. Eaton Company was not only Canada's largest department store, it was the country's third-largest employer.[4] Its two major Toronto stores were the acknowledged jewels in the company's crown. Located at the present site of the Eaton Centre, Eaton's flagship Main Store hummed with customers daily, and Eaton's College Street Store was a haute couture shopping mecca.[5] Twelve thousand Toronto Eaton's employees were eligible for collective bargaining, more than half of whom were women. Prior to the late 1940s, Canadian organized labour had made sporadic attempts to unionize white-collar workers, but its major victories remained concentrated in male-dominated production industries. Seeking to expand its membership after World War II, the CCL decided to organize the service industries. Choosing Eaton's as its first target, the Eaton Drive was intended to be a springboard for a white-collar movement. Yet after four years of intense campaigning, Eaton's employees voted against certification. This defeat spurred unionists to retreat from white-collar initiatives, and to this

Citation: Donica Belisle, "Exploring Post-War Consumption: The Campaign to Unionize Eaton's in Toronto, 1948–52," *Canadian Historical Review* 86, no. 4 (December 2005): 641–72. Reprinted with permission from University of Toronto Press (www.utpjournals.com).

day Canadian retail employees remain almost entirely nonunionized.

As the Eaton Drive was the most sustained attempt in Canadian history to unionize a retail workforce, an investigation of its literature and events provides unique insight into how a male-dominated and production-focused labourist tradition understood a female-dominated and consumption-focused industry. Three decades of feminist work within Canadian labour historiography demonstrates that many pre–World War II labourists and leftists assumed that productive and political work outside the home was masculine.[6] Associating commodity production with muscular masculinity, some labour and left advocates even suggested that the bourgeois order was effeminate; they called on strong and heroic male workers to overthrow capitalism's chains and bring about a newly vigorous world order.[7] . . .

By analyzing the CCL's portrayals of Eaton's employees, we can determine whether this equation of femininity with consumption affected the Eaton Drive. Such investigations are intrinsically important, for they help to develop an understanding of Canadian unionists' thoughts on consumption. Yet they also have practical significances. Since World War II the presence of women within the labour force has steadily increased, particularly within the service sector.[8] Employers' sophisticated union-busting tactics are largely responsible for retail's nonunionization, as Walmart's notorious anti-unionist manoeuvres demonstrate.[9] Nonetheless, scholars must also seek to determine whether organized labour's and the left's views of women and consumption have affected attempts to unionize consumer workers.

. . .

Historians sometimes imply that unionism's post-war emphases on bargaining strategies and salary increases indicate a retreat from radicalism. Three mid-century developments—the legalization of collective bargaining, labour's belief that purchasing power would stimulate mass production and create full employment, and the

inducement to conservatism prompted by Cold War anti-Communism—caused a narrowing of unionism's goals. As Peter McInnis puts it, after World War II, "trade unions embraced exclusive contractual obligations premised on productivity bargaining and mass consumerism. Thus, broad social reforms for the working-class majority were sacrificed for the gains of the few who could claim membership in mainstream trade unions."[10] A study of the Eaton Drive illustrates how this "fordist compromise" played out at the organizational level. Increased purchasing power for Eaton's employees was a central campaign issue, but importantly, organizers perceived salary increases as part of a broader strategy for social–democratic reform. They believed that Canadian society was inequitable because working people did not have the same material opportunities as did more affluent Canadians. Unionism would increase workers' material entitlements, thus enriching workers' lives and helping them become full Canadian citizens. In this view, purchasing power was not a retreat from politics but a point of entry into civic life.

Finally, this article reveals the importance of gender to ideas about consumption, work, and citizenship in post-war Canada. In the late 1940s different groups of female activists, including the Housewives' Consumer Association (HCA), demanded that the federal government reintroduce wartime price controls on household goods, especially food, because inflation was causing a significant gap between income and necessities. Their arguments drew on a sense of what Magda Fahrni calls "economic citizenship"; they also drew on the conventional association of femininity with household labour.[11] During the Eaton Drive CCL organizers also made consumer demands. Whereas female activists called on the state to lower prices, the CCLers called on business—in this case, Eaton's—to increase wages. Like female consumer activists, the CCLers made gender central to their claims; unlike them, they appealed to masculinity. Working people deserved higher wages, they suggested, because they had to support their families. The typical worker, in this opinion, was a male breadwinner.

The CCLers' quest for the family wage underscores the importance of patriarchal domesticity in Canadian post-war life. Although the late 1940s and 1950s were not characterized by total gender conformity, they were years in which women were encouraged to leave wartime jobs and raise increasing numbers of children.[12] Many women took on full-time marriage and motherhood, but a few struggled to balance household responsibilities with paid labour. In Ontario "at the beginning of the war," notes Joan Sangster, "only one in twenty married women worked for pay; by 1951 it was one in ten."[13] Women were disproportionately represented in low-level white-collar positions, including those in department stores. In 1949 women constituted 57 per cent of Toronto Eaton's employees eligible for unionization, and they dominated all of Eaton's unskilled occupations. Fifty-three per cent were between the ages of 21 and 44, while 31 per cent were older than 44. Forty-seven per cent were single, 45 per cent were married, and 7 per cent were widowed.[14] Their presence encouraged some organizers to include women in the Eaton Drive, but the CCL's overarching commitment to male breadwinner rights overshadowed their efforts. In the literature of the Eaton Drive, female wage earners were secondary workers, secondary union members, and secondary citizens.

Reconstruction and the Eaton Drive

The desire to strengthen the male breadwinner/female homemaker family model, along with the notion that increased prosperity would foster national improvement, guided both the state's and the CCF's approaches to post-war reconstruction. The governing Liberals believed that increased production and investment would provide full employment for male breadwinners. The result would not only create social stability

but increase individual households' purchasing power, thereby fuelling the nation's productive capacity.[15] Founded during the Great Depression, the social–democratic CCF envisioned a world in which Canadians shared equally in the fruits of industrial production and modern cultural life. In their famous 197-page outline of their post-war vision, *Make This Your Canada* (1943), CCF executives David Lewis and Frank Scott argued that Canadian society was grossly inequitable: Although "workers, farmers and middle classes" comprised 99.4 per cent of the Canadian population, they faced "inadequate living standards, [a] dependent condition, [and] individual helplessness and lack of opportunity." To eradicate inequality, Canadians had to "expand" their "political democracy" to "economic and social democracy"; by voting for the CCF, which promised to nationalize industry, business, and social services, Canadians would enhance all people's standards of living and create "opportunities for full enjoyment by all of the riches of modern society."[16]

Although *Make This Your Canada* pays lip service to women's presence in political life, it portrays Canada's inhabitants as men. Not only is the masculine pronoun used to refer to all Canadians, as was common during the era, but all workers and farmers—the CCF's target voters—are represented as males. One illustration depicts a man in overalls as a "worker" and a man with a pitchfork as a "farmer." Women are not illustrated anywhere in the publication.[17] Elsewhere, the CCF did portray women as political actors. As Sangster notes, they tended to use "a representational figure" of "the suffrage era: the homemaker, with apron and broom, ready to 'tidy up' political life and anxious to have her home-centred concerns heard."[18] Such depictions reflected Canadian leftists' assumption that men's and women's political interests arose from the sexual division of labour. The CCF's central concerns in the post-war period were male workers and farmers, people whom CCF leaders believed were the nation's main economic and civic actors.[19]

. . .

In 1946 the CCL created a Department Store Organizing Committee (DSOC) to oversee the Eaton Drive. The DSOC, in turn, cultivated an impressive team of union organizers. After appointing Eileen Tallman, a talented Steelworker organizer with white-collar unionization experience, as head organizer, the DSOC hired Lynn Williams, Marjorie Gow, and Wally Ross, all Steelworker organizers; Angus Sumner, a Retail, Wholesale, and Department Store Union (RWDSU) organizer; Olive Richardson, an experienced clerical worker; Ernest Arnold, a former United Auto Workers (UAW) organizer; Alex Gilbert, a former All-Canadian Congress of Labour (ACCL) organizer; and Mae Coulston, a long-time Eaton's cafeteria employee. No one other than former CCF National Secretary and co-author of *Make This Your Canada*, David Lewis, agreed to provide legal counsel. Most of these organizers had participated in the CCF Youth Movement during the Depression, and after the Drive, Tallman and Williams became prominent advocates of social–democratic unionism. In Tallman's 1982 history of the Drive, she recalls that team members shared "the same political philosophy . . . We believed that unions had a vital role to play in the democratic achievement of social and economic change." Tallman herself felt that "a solid base of organized workers was a prerequisite to the success of a socialist political party." Like many of her CCF colleagues, she was anti-communist, and in 1943 she had worked in the Steelworkers' Vancouver office to help start "a monthly tabloid for our BC membership, to provide an alternative to the policies advocated by the Labour Progressive Party, the wartime name used by the Communists."[20]

In her 1982 book about the Eaton Drive, Tallman contends that the team did not "press [their] political views upon the [Eaton] Local or on individual members." A review of the Drive's literature, however, indicates that organizers made social–democratic unionism central to the campaign. One of the first broadsides distributed to employees was titled "For a *happier* new year—take the *union road!*" Featuring a picture of two young workers trying to decide between unionism and Eaton's paternalism, the leaflet urges Eaton's workers to unionize: "Unionization is modern—efficient. It is the up-to-date way of approaching management for increased salaries and improved working conditions. . . . Union membership makes for better workers and better citizens . . . A union is *democracy in action.*" As did the CCL executive, these CCL organizers believed that unionism would enable workers to overthrow outmoded types of labour management and become decision-making participants in the workplace and broader polity. As "F. W. Dowling of the United Packinghouse Workers" put it in another Eaton Drive leaflet, "The organized labour movement is the most articulate voice in the country for a better world. . . . We look forward with pleasure to having Eaton employees join with us in making democracy work for themselves and for others."[21]

Along with the Main Store and Eaton's College Street, Eaton's Toronto operations after World War II included a discount store called the Annex, a mail order building, a factory building, several small "workrooms," and a few delivery and dispatch locations. The Main Store boasted the largest number of employees eligible for union membership: 4,000. Eaton's mail order building had 1,900 eligible employees; Eaton's College Street had 1,350; Eaton's factory, 1,000; and Eaton's Annex, 700. Other eligible employees included 1,000 office workers, 800 delivery workers, 220 warehouse workers, and 210 maintenance workers.[22] From 1947 to 1952 organizers led a massive, multipronged campaign to convince these disparate workers to form one large union. *Unionize*, a four-page broadside that organizers delivered each Saturday morning to Eaton's employees, was central to their efforts. Edited by Marjorie Gow until 1950 and by Eileen Tallman for the remainder of the campaign, it featured written, illustrated, and photographic contributions from organizers, volunteers, Eaton's employees, and other unionists.

In her 1982 history of the Eaton Drive, Tallman pays especial attention to Eaton's female employees. Because many women had temporary and part-time status, organizers found them difficult to organize. All the same, relates Tallman, the Eaton Drive proved that "women can be quite . . . strong and committed [to unions] . . . despite their double workload . . . Dozens of . . . women made the extra effort to . . . bring the number of women members in Local 1000 to about half."[23] What Tallman's history of the Drive neglects to mention is the organizing team's own ambiguous approach to female wage earners. According to Sandra Aylward, the CCL sought to supplant Eaton's patriarchal paternalism with patriarchal unionism. While organizers supported equal pay for equal work, they also perceived women's work as less valuable than men's. In discussions of pay rates, organizers concentrated on "same-sex age and favoritism discrepancies" and "mitigat[ed] those based on sex and marital status." In 1948 *Unionize* remarked that "Girls" in the "Provision Packing" department receive "$24 weekly" and "Single men" receive "$27"; since these wages were higher than those received in the Drug Stock department, the Drug Stock wages should be increased.[24] Instead of comparing "girls'" and "men's" wages, this contribution compared pay rates across departments. Aylward views this as logical because "women, along with some boys, were simply defined [by organizers] as unskilled workers doing unskilled work."[25]

My own reading of the Drive supports Aylward's findings. Some of the CCL organizers obviously believed that unionism was a tool for enhancing male breadwinners' entitlements. In 1949 *Unionize* ran an anonymous poem called "Swan Song," dedicated to Eaton's employees:

Rockabye Baby, in the tree top,
When you grow old, you'll work in a shop,
When you get married,
your wife will work too,
So that the rich will have nothing to do.
Hushabye Baby, in the tree top,

When you grow old your wages will stop,
When you have spent the little you save,
Hushabye, Baby—off to the grave.[26]

Suggesting that it was a matter of working-class pride for men to provide for their families, this poem implies that working-class wives entered the workforce only because their husbands' wages were inadequate. It was undignified for a married woman to earn money. Not only did the working man derive his sense of manhood from his ability to provide for his family, the respectability of the working-class family hinged on the husband's ability to earn a family wage. Such sentiments were likely responsible for some organizers' holding of a union seminar entitled "Should Eaton's Employ Married Women?"[27] While this seminar may have been a vehicle for probing members' thoughts on working wives, its title does suggest that the CCLers were prepared to advocate that married women leave Eaton's if this were what members desired.

Not everyone involved with Local 1000 believed that unionism's main objective was to further male workers' entitlements. Unfortunately, most *Unionize* contributions are unsigned, so it is difficult to pinpoint particular people's perspectives. However, certain *Unionize* sketches, which were likely drawn by Marjorie Gow, portray female and male white-collar employees working together to build Local 1000. Some unsigned *Unionize* articles, likely authored by Tallman, draw attention to women's particular grievances. One article notes that female groceteria workers were angered that Eaton's conveyor belt system, requiring much heavy lifting, caused back injuries.[28] And some female union members spoke out against disparities between men's and women's wages. In 1949 Tallman hosted a radio show designed to increase support for Local 1000. She asked Local 1000 member Mrs. Mould about her opinion about "the Union objective of equal pay for equal work." Mould replied, "There should be a rate set for a job, not for the person who does the job. What difference does it make whether it is a man, woman, or boy who does the job? . . . In Eaton's, many women salesclerks have as much responsibility as men, but get much lower pay."[29]

Despite some organizers' and employees' commitments to gender equity, the belief that unionism was intended to protect male workers dominated the campaign. Following older labourist and leftist traditions, campaign broadsides depicted typical workers as men. They also personified Local 1000 by portraying it as a brawny man (Figure 1). This utilization of masculine imagery in a drive to unionize a predominantly female labour force suggests that the CCLers found it difficult to develop a labourist discourse that would encompass both female and male wage earners. It also speaks to the pervasive mid-century assumption that wage earning was a male right. On the same radio show in which Mould voiced her support for fair pay, pro-union employee Fred Tinker stated that men should support equal pay for equal work because higher pay for men's jobs imperilled men's employment rights: "We men must make it our business to see that women do not undercut our rates of pay. [I]f . . . a depression comes along, we'll find women doing our work . . . and we'll be out in the cold. I think equal pay for equal work . . . is the best job security our Union can aim to get."[30]

In December 1951 CCL organizers were devastated to learn the results of Local 1000's certification vote: 41 per cent of employees voted to certify the union, but 50 per cent voted against certification.[31] After another certification attempt failed, Local 1000 disbanded. For over 30 years former members harboured resentments. Especial hostility was directed toward female workers. In the early 1980s one male employee stated that "the married women and part-timers killed us. Then there were the old maids, Loyal Eatonians, who had been at Eaton's since they were 14. There was no way people like that were going to change."[32] While scholars have identified a range of factors causing employees to vote against certification—an unfounded belief that

Figure 1. Unionization as masculine.
Source: *Unionize*, 30 November 1948.

Local 1000 was communist, rapid turnover, loyalty to the Eaton family, fears that unionists would lose privileges, fears that unionists would be fired, and a notion that white-collar workers did not need unions[33]—the CCL's privileging of male workers may also have been influential. Former Eaton's employee Doris Anderson, who later became editor of *Chatelaine*, stated in the 1990s that while she thought Eaton's needed a union, she was alienated by Local 1000's approach to gender. "The men held forth in the union," she recalled, "while the women did the donkey work like taking notes and making coffee."[34]

Consumption and the Creation of Local 1000

Recognizing that the Eaton's principle of free entry into its stores could work to their advantage, organizers made shopping central to their campaign strategies. Although it was illegal to discuss union matters with employees while they were working, in autumn 1949 and spring 1950 organizers held "Union Shopping Days," during which volunteers from other CCL unions walked around Eaton's stores carrying bags with the phrase "Join Local 1000" printed on them. During the autumn event volunteers wore badges with the words "Union Pay Is Good Pay—I Get It!" on them. During the spring event, volunteers stood outside Eaton's doors and handed out 5,000 Join Local 1000 bags to sympathetic shoppers. They also handed out helium-filled balloons with the words "Join Local 1000" on them to customers' children. Tallman recalls that Union Shopping Days were "lots of fun" for everyone except "management": "Predictably, when a child let go of a balloon, it floated up to the ceiling. The sight of a manager in the Main Store climbing a ladder to retrieve this novel form of union propaganda caused considerable comment."[35]

Since almost half of Eaton's Toronto employees eligible for unionization occupied customer service positions, organizers made frequent references in their campaign literature to salespeople's work experiences. Disparities between affluent customers and low-income employees were especially remarked upon. Throughout Eaton's stores tensions regularly flared between customers who demanded deferential treatment and employees who behaved as though they were customers' equals.[36] Picking up this aspect of customer service, organizers occasionally poked fun at customers' assertions of superiority. One joke in *Unionize* described a female customer "holding her lapdog up for a drink at one of the fountains" in a department store. A manager spotted her doing this and rushed over. "My dear Madam," he said, "this fountain is for the use of customers." The woman apologized: "Oh, I am sorry," she replied. "I thought it was for employees."[37] Alluding to employees' shared experiences of class discrimination, this anecdote demonstrated that Local 1000 could be an alternative, dignity-affirming organization for Eaton's employees.

Early in their campaign, the CCLers recognized that many of Eaton's employees were regular Eaton's customers. Not only did they purchase fashionable goods from Eaton's, so did many buy their household staples from their employer. One early *Unionize* quoted a male caretaker who stated that his manager's practice of paying them sometimes on Wednesday and sometimes on Thursday "is an inconvenience to ourselves and to our wives who are accustomed to meeting us in the store Wednesdays to do the family shopping."[38] When the CCLers found out that some of Eaton's workers were scared to unionize because they heard that Eaton's would take away these discounts, they rebuffed this fear. Emphasizing the revenue Eaton's received from employees' purchases, *Unionize* stated that "this discount is very good business for the Eaton company. . . . Would a company give up this large group of buyers for whom they have to put out no special service or advertising? Not likely!"[39] Attempting to ease some workers' concerns about unionizing, organizers tried to demonstrate that Eaton's workers had significant financial clout.

Since Eaton's employees were also Eaton's customers, organizers suggested that Eaton's should treat them with more respect. In May 1952 *Unionize* drew readers' attention to a recent Eaton's customer service training pamphlet. After quoting the pamphlet on the importance of treating customers well, the broadside inserted more comments: "You can easily tell a customer from an employee. The employee has a number. When we dispense with an employee, his number is just handed on to the next one we hire. . . . Unlike a customer, an employee has no feelings or emotions." After concluding its revisions, *Unionize* asked, "What? You say to remember that . . . employees are customers too? That spoils everything. Now we'll have to find a new definition for 'What Is a Customer!'"[40]

Organizers also encouraged employees to view shopping as an opportunity for forging labourist solidarity. One *Unionize* article recommended that when members of Local 1000 were shopping in Eaton's departments, they should "speak to [their] fellow employees about the Union [and] *sign the non-members!*"[41] Another suggested that when employees went shopping at Eaton's they "should ask to be served by a union clerk."[42] Not only did organizers attempt to build cohesion among Eaton's employees, they also tried to create camaraderie between Eaton's workers and members of other unions. In 1950 *Unionize* urged Eaton's employees to purchase suits carrying the Amalgamated Clothing Workers' (ACW) label. "Let the [Eaton's] clerk who serves you know that it makes a difference to you that goods are made by union paid workers," it stated, continuing, "Many salesmen in Eaton's Men's Furnishings are members of Local 1000. Ask for a union clerk when you go in to buy that new union-made suit!"[43] Organizers' stress upon the ACW label was strategic. Earlier that year, the ACW had promised to donate $2,000 per month to the Eaton Drive. Asking employees to support the ACW, organizers nurtured connections between Local 1000 and the ACW and created international lines of solidarity.

When trying to politicize consumption for progressive ends, organizers spent much time on what leftist scholars sometimes call "mass culture,"[44] or the for-profit sports, entertainment, fashion, and beauty industries. In her study of the CIO in 1930s Chicago, Cohen demonstrates that unionists made dances, bowling leagues, and radio programs part of their organizational strategies. During the 1920s welfarist employers had used these activities to create loyalty; by incorporating them into unionism CIO leaders demonstrated that recreation could be part of a labour-identified culture.[45] Welfare programs had existed at Eaton's in Toronto since the early 1900s; by the 1940s they included summer camps, dances, self-improvement classes, drama and musical societies, and athletic activities.[46] Many such activities had mass cultural components, as did the large dances that required stylish clothes, the fashion and cosmetics classes that required interest in the grooming industries, and the sporting events that required commodities like badminton racquets and ice skates. Eaton's employees' working lives were even more heavily saturated by mass culture. Training literature informed employees of new products, and several employees worked in sales departments that sold fashionable clothing and accessories, radios, and in the early 1950s, television sets. They were thus deeply familiar with what in 1947 Theodor Adorno and Max Horkheimer disparagingly called the "culture industry."[47]

Although the modernist equation of mass culture with bourgeois effeminacy might have led Eaton Drive organizers to criticize workers' interests in mass culture, they instead perceived mass culture as an opportunity to convince Eaton's employees to unionize. In 1949 they established a social committee, whose members oversaw movie nights, a bowling league, Christmas parties, banquets, and, most popularly, numerous dances. Some of the smaller dances were held at union halls and were usually put on for particular occupational groups. Other, larger, dances were extravagant affairs. . . .

Unionize also utilized mass culture as an organizational tool. One . . . cartoon features a woman applying cosmetics in front of a theatre-style vanity. . . . Accompanying the sketch is the heading, "You Can't Buy '*talent*' at bargain-basement prices. And the reason you can't is because it's *unionized*"; underneath, *Unionize* states, "The big names . . . in Movies, Theatre, Television, Radio, and Music are union members" and by "joining" the union, "you're not only helping yourself to a *better life*, you will be helping to raise retail standards for hundreds of thousands of men and women across Canada."[48] Calling attention to the fact that many celebrities were unionized, *Unionize* tried to demonstrate that unionization was compatible with glamour and prestige.

. . .

While organizers knew that mass entertainment held special attractions for Eaton's employees, a few disempowering overtones did creep into the Eaton Drive's references to fashion and entertainment. In one *Unionize* cartoon, two women are imploring a man to go with them to a show and a dance. The man refuses, saying, "Sorry girls, some other time—tonight is my department meeting!" (Figure 2). Though the women in this cartoon probably are not meant to represent Eaton's female employees, the sketch does connect political agency to masculinity and frivolity to femininity. In this way it echoes the modernist vision of civic culture as a male sphere as well as reflects some leftists' attitudes toward mass culture. In 1894 Thorstein Veblen decried the irrationality at the heart of women's interests in fashion and beauty; more than 40 years later Adorno and Horkheimer suggested that those who participated in mass culture were in danger of cultural castration.[49]

. . .

A few CCLers recognized this dynamic of Eaton's female employees' experiences. Sometimes they contended that Eaton's should pay wages commensurate with Eaton's employees' clothing requirements. One 1949 leaflet stated, "Today [selling] is far below on the salary scale, yet store employees must pay much more for appearance on the job than any other type of worker."[50] They also praised working women's skills in style and appearance. A leaflet handed out early in the campaign describes a fictional saleswoman: "Sally Smith is a slick chick. From her Firm Form Foundation to her slim black gown with bustle drapery in the rear, from her

Figure 2. Masculine rationality versus feminine frivolity. Source: *Unionize*, 17 January 1950.

ankle strap slippers to her shining, sculptured hair-do, Sally is sleek perfection." The leaflet went on to discuss Sally's small salary, arguing that she had difficulties making ends meet. "*But*," the leaflet asserted, "Sally is as smart as she is beautiful. She has signed a card in the [union]."[51]

A 1950 campaign event made organizers' awareness of Eaton's employees' interests in fashion even more explicit. Between twelve and one o'clock one April day, they staged a "Fashion Parade" outside Eaton's flagship store and repeated this performance at five o'clock outside Eaton's College Street.[52] During the interwar years, fashion shows had become staple public relations events at Eaton's. Intended to demonstrate the company's fashion leadership, they featured elaborate settings, professional models, and fashions by prestigious designers.[53] Local 1000's Fashion Parade followed a decidedly different trajectory. Under a heading titled "Easter Fashion Parade" in organizers' meeting memoranda, "suggestions" for the parade included "Frayed white collars; Boss with folding money sticking out of pockets, followed by a miserable little employee with empty pockets hanging out . . . Girl in barrel with sign 'My new Easter outfit' [and another employee with a sign featuring the words] Budget Plan buying: 'In 16 months this suit will be mine.'"[54] Parodying Eaton's role as a fashion merchant, the parade constructed comedic, visual evidence of the class disparities engendered by, on the one hand, Eaton's high clothing prices, and on the other, low wages paid to workers. Recognizing that employees were interested in stylish garments, the parade appealed to employees' interests in fashion and argued that they should unionize to gain salaries that could cover their fashion needs.

A few employees responded enthusiastically to such efforts. In June 1948 a salesperson, who did not indicate her or his gender loyalty, wrote a letter to *Unionize*'s editor:

Dear People:
    Glad you are taking an interest in the Big Store. Do try and get us a weekly pay, as every other week we are half starved—no money to go shopping. It certainly is a drag to live on Eaton's meagre wage and keep up an appearance before the public with clothes and food prices the way they are. . . .
    The way the price of meals is soaring up it's no wonder the employees look as if they had TB or tapeworm.[55]

By referring to the costs of keeping up appearances, organizers sparked at least some employees' interests in taking action against their powerful employer.

Yet even while convincing fashionable female employees to unionize, the CCL team suggested that women with fashion and beauty interests were secondary union members. On the leaflet praising Sally Smith, organizers printed an illustration of a young woman holding a pennant on which the words "Union Maid" are emblazoned; she is smiling invitingly at a man standing behind her. Because she is holding a pennant, the picture suggests that women belong in the union in an auxiliary, cheerleader-like fashion. In 1951 this dynamic of praising stylish women while relegating them to secondary status again appeared. That spring the Social Committee sponsored a Miss Local 1000 Beauty Contest at the Royal York Hotel. On the night of the event 14 "beauties from Eaton's" donned fashionable party dresses and evening gowns, put on jewellery and makeup, paid special attention to their hairstyles, and stepped into high-heeled evening shoes. At half past ten they "paraded" before a "three-man jury": "Murray Cotterill, president of the Toronto Labor Council; Jim Perna, United Automobile Workers, and executive board member of Toronto Labor Council; and Eamon Park, MPP and United Steelworkers' Director of Publicity." A 19-year-old elevator operator won first prize. After the contest she phoned home to Cochrane to share the good news with her family, and later that summer she wore her "Miss Local 1000" banner while riding in a convertible in the Toronto Labour Day Parade.[56]

. . . The judging of women by prominent male leaders was an objectifying action that transformed youthful female unionists into depoliticized targets of a masculine gaze. In fact, the *Unionize* article that described the beauty pageant was titled "Line of Lovelies Judged."[57] Both the contest and *Unionize* suggested that organized labour valued women only because they were attractive.

. . .

While mass culture was integral to the Eaton Drive, organizers had a more overarching vision of consumption in post-war Canada. As we have seen, CCLers believed that social–democratic unionism would enable workers to achieve higher standards of living, thereby allowing them to become full, participating citizens in Canada's polity.[58] The CCF similarly felt that social democracy would create a more equitable distribution of goods, hence improving workers' material conditions. In keeping with their parent organizations' emphases on material disparities in Canadian society, the Eaton Drive's organizers' literature referred often to a "decent living standard."[59] Believing that everyone was entitled to a life that was enjoyable, comfortable, and fulfilling, they contended that if people were too busy earning money to cover subsistence costs, they would have no time to spend with their families and no energy to contribute as citizens. In 1950 organizers distributed an extraordinary broadside called "Opportunity Day." Spoofing Eaton's "Opportunity Day" sale flyers, the leaflet declared that "Unionized employees have substantially increased their purchasing power. This is *your* Opportunity Day to do so by joining Local 1000." It depicted a number of goods and services that would become available for purchase after unionization. Although this leaflet is indicative of organizers' belief that Eaton's employees should have increased living standards, it is also suggestive of the egalitarian assumptions underpinning this belief. Organizers did not want workers to be affluent for affluence's sake; rather, they wanted them

to share in the fruits of post-war production. As the section titled "Television Set" declared, "Working people should have access to the newest inventions."

. . .

The CCLers suggested that both male and female employees would benefit from increased purchasing power: One sketch hinted that Eaton's low wages prevented both male and female employees from buying their own homes. Most references to living standards, however, implied that working-class families should contain a male breadwinner and a female homemaker. One *Unionize* responded to reports that some employees were working two jobs to "make ends meet." "Of course if they *want* to use their leisure in these ways, the union has no objection." However, "The union's contention is that *one* full-time job should pay enough to keep a man and his family in decency."[60] Another *Unionize* cited cost-of-living statistics released by the Toronto Welfare Council and argued that Eaton's did not pay enough money to keep "a man, his wife and three children" in "good health, decent living and self respect."[61] *Unionize* cartoons also emphasized the need for Eaton's to pay a family wage. One depicts a husband handing his wife his paycheque, stating, "Well, Dear, here's my pay check—it looks pretty measly after all those deductions." The wife stirs a pot on the stove and imagines a refrigerator, washing machine, and iron flying away from her (Figure 3).

Though CCLers' abstract discussions of purchasing power did imply that male breadwinners were responsible for both earning and spending wages, direct references to household consumption suggested that women, not men, were responsible for budgeting and shopping. One of the campaign's earliest broadsides stated, "Your Wife's *Expecting* You to Bring Home the Bacon—Not Your *Beefs*."[62] Such depictions highlight the centrality of consumption to women's domestic responsibilities in the post-war years. They also subtly imply that it would have been unmanly for men to wish for household goods. Organizers

Figure 3. Consumer dreams. Source: *Unionize*, 16 November 1948.

never depicted breadwinners as desiring household commodities; rather, they portrayed them as earning money so that they could buy things for their wives and children. In 1949 *Unionize* carried an illustration in which an Eaton's manager is firing a male employee; the employee's wife and son are waiting outside. The little boy is restless, so his mother says, "Be patient, dear, Daddy will be through at one o'clock." The boy replies, "Gee, and it's payday too, mebee Daddy will buy me my bike today."[63] Organizers' disinclination to suggest that men bought commodities for themselves indicates they may have been uncomfortable with the developing association between unionization and purchasing power. Working men earned money to provide, not to consume.

Because some organizers believed that unionism was a tool for enhancing male breadwinners' authority within the family and broader polity, they had difficulties rationalizing married women's presence at Eaton's. In trying to understand married women's motivations for working for wages, some *Unionize* contributions suggested that they worked to earn extra household income. One article declares, "*If* you are only working for 'pin money' . . . or just want to work long enough to get that new rug or refrigerator paid for . . . then maybe you don't feel the need for collective bargaining." While this piece seems sympathetic toward working wives, it does not suggest that unionism would strengthen working women's entitlements. Instead it implores working wives to join Local 1000 and help facilitate working men's quests for high salaries: "*In the community* as a whole, the standard of living of your fellow employees affects *you*. If your husband is working in an organized industry and enjoying union standards, so long as Eaton's . . . remain unorganised, it is a constant threat to the gains his Union has won."[64] Just as organizers asked youthful, fashionable women to support their male co-workers' goals, this article asks married women to sign union cards so they could bolster their husbands' efforts.

As long as married women remained full-time homemakers, organizers had no difficulties with their desires for household goods. When wives obtained jobs to pay for their own domestic purchases, however, they became unsettled. The presence of married women at Eaton's challenged the CCL's and the CCF's assumptions that wage earning and citizenship were masculine. It also called into question the foundation of working men's identities: If married women earned their own wages, then working men could no longer define their manhoods through their abilities to provide for their families. In 1951 *Unionize* ran an illustration that demonstrated the depth of organizers' apprehensions. A matronly woman gets a job as a salesclerk so that she can purchase a new stove. A slender, youthful unionist asks her to join Local 1000, but she refuses, stating, "What's the use?—I'll only be here till I get my new stove." According to the cartoon's artist, this woman's refusal to join harms the "majority" of Eaton's workers. "Don't be a 'gimme pig,'" it instructs. The figure of the gimme pig surfaced again in *Unionize* in a description of a nonunion male employee, so the porcine imagery is not intentionally misogynist.[65] Nonetheless it does illustrate some organizers' distrust of wage-earning wives. Neither docile feminine unionists nor dutiful housewives, they existed outside certain organizers' understandings of acceptable feminine behaviour.

Gender, Unionism, and Consumer Culture

Between 1948 and 1952 in downtown Toronto, the CCL made consumption central to the Eaton Drive. References to shopping and mass culture arose from a recognition that Eaton's employees were involved with these aspects of consumption, and references to purchasing power and living standards arose from a commitment to a "decent living standard" for all working people. Particular assumptions governed the Drive's consumer references, including a minority of unionists' belief that women deserved unionism's benefits, the CCL's belief that the civic sphere was masculine, and the CCL's belief in the family wage. Some unionists portrayed working

women's consumer interests sympathetically, while others depicted female worker–consumers as secondary union members. And certain unionists' support for the family wage spurred them to depict wage earning and breadwinning as masculine, and homemaking and consumption as feminine.

In 1947 CCL Vice-President Pat Conroy declared in a speech to the Canadian Club, "Security is labour's chief objective. Our [democratic capitalist] system is capable of providing the material wealth necessary for happiness, and the worker wants to secure *his* share."[66] This statement neatly captures the CCL's developing vision of social–democratic unionism. More socialist than the TLC [Trades and Labor Congress] but more conservative than the Labour Progressive Party, the CCL supported liberal industrial capitalism on the condition that it could provide job security and purchasing power for all-male labourers. When compared to other mid-twentieth-century perspectives, this vision is hardly revolutionary. The female-dominated HCA lobbied for state control of production, distribution, and pricing,[67] but the CCL believed that unionization was the best way to level material wealth. Pro-woman unionists, including some of the Eaton Drive's own organizers, challenged Canadian unionism's masculinity,[68] but the CCL sought to strengthen the patriarchal nuclear family. When compared with Marxist and environmentalist perspectives, the CCL's postwar platform also appears conformist. Since the nineteenth century Marxists have condemned individual property ownership,[69] but the CCL believed that workers should own their own commodities. Since the 1960s environmentalists have disparaged the modernist link between industrial development and social progress,[70] but the CCL felt that industrial development could create greater opportunities for all.

It is hardly surprising, then, that some scholars interpret the CCL's post-war trajectory as conservative. This article supports this assessment, but it also shows that a few CCLers challenged patriarchal and modernist conventions. Going against masculinist labourist traditions, some organizers suggested that unions could be spaces in which men and women could participate equally and argued that unions should expand both men's and women's entitlements. Believing that workers' interests in mass entertainment, fashion, and beauty did not necessarily indicate *embourgeoisement*, they proved that mass culture was not inimical to labour-identified collective action. In an historical moment when most retail workers remain unorganized, these actions remain significant. Since World War II, consumption has become important not only to workers' leisure and domestic activities but also to their workplace experiences. If we are to adequately understand this historical development we must continue inquiring into unionism's and working people's relationships with consumer culture.

 More online.

Notes

1. Peter S. McInnis, *Harnessing Labour Confrontation: Shaping the Postwar Settlement in Canada, 1943–50* (Toronto, ON: University of Toronto Press, 2002); Bryan D. Palmer, *Working-Class Experience: Rethinking the History of Canadian Labour, 1800–1991* (Toronto, ON: McClelland & Stewart, 1991), 229–36, 336–9. Labour scholars use the term *fordism* to refer to the postwar industrial regime characterized by high employment, high wages, and high levels of consumption.

2. Lizabeth Cohen, *A Consumer's Republic: The Politics of Mass Consumption in Postwar America* (New York, NY: Knopf, 2003), 152–5; Nan Enstad, *Ladies of Labor, Girls of Adventure: Working Women, Popular Culture, and Labor Politics at the Turn of the Twentieth Century* (New York, NY: Columbia University Press, 1999). . . .

3. Desmond Morton with Terry Copp, *Working People: An Illustrated History of the Canadian Labour Movement*, rev. ed. (Toronto, ON: Deneau, 1984), 215.

4. *Eaton's of Canada* (Toronto, ON: T. Eaton, 1952), 2; Eileen Sufrin, *The Eaton Drive: The Campaign to Organize Canada's Largest Department Store* (Toronto, ON: Fitzhenry and Whiteside, 1982), 33–6.

5. Cynthia Wright, "'The Most Prominent Rendezvous of the Feminine Toronto': Eaton's College Street and the

6. Nancy Christie, "By Necessity or By Right: The Language and Experience of Gender at Work," *Labour/Le Travail* (Fall 2002): 117–48.

7. Todd McCallum, "'Not a Sex Question'? The One Big Union and the Politics of Radical Manhood," *Labour/Le Travail* (Fall 1998): 15–54.

8. Peter S. Li, *The Making of Post-War Canada* (Toronto, ON: Oxford University Press, 1996), 36–58.

9. Bill Quinn, *How Wal-Mart Is Destroying America and What You Can Do About It* (Berkeley, CA: Ten Speed, 1998).

10. McInnis, *Harnessing Labour Confrontation*, 8.

11. Magda Fahrni, "Counting the Costs of Living: Gender, Citizenship, and a Politics of Prices in 1940s Montreal," *Canadian Historical Review* (December 2002): 483–504. . . .

12. Ruth Roach Pierson, *"They're Still Women After All": The Second World War and Canadian Womanhood* (Toronto, ON: McClelland & Stewart, 1986), 215.

13. Joan Sangster, "Doing Two Jobs: The Wage-Earning Mother, 1956–70," in Joy Parr, ed., *A Diversity of Women: Ontario, 1945–80* (Toronto, ON: University of Toronto Press, 1995), 98.

14. T. Eaton Papers (hereafter cited as TEP), series 181, box 1, Statistics Notebook, Archives of Ontario (hereafter cited as AO).

15. Robert Malcolm Campbell, *Grand Illusions: The Politics of the Keynesian Experience in Canada* (Peterborough, ON: Broadview, 1987), 19–54; Peter Neary, "Introduction," in Peter Neary and J. L. Granatstein, eds., *The Veterans Charter and Post–World War II Canada* (Montreal, QC: McGill-Queen's University Press, 1998), 9–12.

16. David Lewis and Frank Scott, *Make This Your Canada: A Review of C.C.F. History and Policy* (Toronto, ON: Central Canada, 1943), 22, 96, 190, 147, 195.

17. Ibid., 197, 98.

18. Joan Sangster, "Consuming Issues: Women on the Left, Political Protest, and the Organization of Homemakers, 1920–60," in Sharon Anne Cook, Lorna R. McLean, and Kate O'Rourke, eds., *Framing Our Past: Canadian Women's History in the Twentieth Century* (Montreal, QC: McGill-Queen's University Press, 2001), 245–6.

19. Dan Azouley, "Winning Women for Socialism: The Ontario CCF and Women, 1947–61," *Labour/Le Travail* 36 (1995): 59–90.

20. Sufrin, *The Eaton Drive*, 44, 38–9.

21. Ibid., 123–4; "For a HAPPIER new year," leaflet, January 1948; Sufrin, *The Eaton Drive*, 86. All Eaton Drive campaign literature mentioned herein is in vol. 1, MG 31 B 31, Library and Archives Canada.

22. Sufrin, *The Eaton Drive*, 47–8.

23. Ibid., 152.

Organization of Shopping in Toronto, 1920–50" (Ph.D. dissertation, University of Toronto, 1992).

24. As quoted in Sandra Aylward, "Experiencing Patriarchy: Women, Work, and Trade Unionism at Eaton's" (Ph.D. dissertation, McMaster University, 1991), 218.

25. Aylward, "Experiencing Patriarchy," 210, 218, 222.

26. "Swan Song," *Unionize*, 12 July 1949. Emphasis added.

27. "Local 1000 Membership Meeting," *Unionize*, 1 February 1949.

28. "Pyramids or Groceries," *Unionize*, 5 October 1958.

29. As quoted in Aylward, "Experiencing Patriarchy," 225–6.

30. Ibid., 226.

31. Sufrin, *The Eaton Drive*, 186.

32. As quoted in Sufrin, *The Eaton Drive*, 189.

33. Sufrin, *The Eaton Drive*, 69–70; Patricia Phenix, *Eatonians: The Story of the Family behind the Family* (Toronto, ON: McClelland & Stewart, 2002), 245.

34. Doris Anderson, as quoted in Phenix, *Eatonians*, 246; also Aylward, "Experiencing Patriarchy," 210–1.

35. "Union Shopping Day," *Unionize*, 27 September 1949; Sufrin, *The Eaton Drive*, 106, 120.

36. Donica Belisle, "Consuming Producers: Retail Workers and Commodity Culture at Eaton's in Mid-Twentieth-Century Toronto" (Master's thesis, Queen's University, 2001), 97–102.

37. "For Women Only," *Unionize*, 30 November 1948.

38. "Shop News," *Unionize*, ca. 1948.

39. "Employee Discount," *Unionize*, 13 December 1949.

40. "What Is an Employee?" *Unionize*, 8 May 1952.

41. "Shopping?" *Unionize*, 16 May 1950.

42. "Be Union, Buy Union," *Unionize*, 23 October 1951.

43. "Men," *Unionize*, 25 April 1950.

44. Fredric Jameson, "Reification and Utopia in Mass Culture," in Michael Hardt and Kathi Weeks, eds., *The Jameson Reader* (New York, NY: Blackwell, 2000), 123–48.

45. Lizabeth Cohen, *Making a New Deal: Industrial Workers in Chicago, 1919–39* (New York, NY: Cambridge University Press, 1990), 340–2.

46. Susan Forbes, "Gendering Corporate Welfare Practices: Female Sports and Recreation at Eaton's during the Depression," *Rethinking History* 5 (2001): 59–74.

47. Theodor Adorno and Max Horkheimer, *Dialectic of Enlightenment*, trans. John Cumming (New York, NY: Continuum, 1976), 120–67.

48. "You can't buy 'TALENT,'" *Unionize*, 13 August 1951.

49. William Leach, *Land of Desire: Merchants, Power, and the Rise of a New American Culture* (New York, NY: Pantheon Books, 1993), 92; Donica Belisle, "Toward a Canadian Consumer History," *Labour/Le Travail* (Fall 2003), 186; Andreas Huyssen, *After the Great Divide: Modernism, Mass Culture, Postmodernism* (Bloomington, IN: Indiana University Press, 1986), 48.

50. "Organise Main Store," 12 September 1949.

51   "Union Maid," February 1948.

52. "Watch for the 'Fashion Parade,'" *Unionize*, 3 April 1950.

53. The Scribe, *Golden Jubilee: 1869–1919* (Toronto, ON: T. Eaton Company, 1919), 212–8; "Fashion Shows," file 1027, box 48, series 162, TEP, AO.

54. "Final Drive," 4 March 1950.

55. "Letters," *Unionize*, 7 June 1948.

56. "Miss Local 1000," *Unionize*, May 1951; "Substantial Raise," *Unionize*, 15 May 1951; "Line of Lovelies Judged," *Unionize*, 15 May 1951.

57. "Line of Lovelies Judged," *Unionize*, 15 May 1951.

58. Don Taylor and Bradley Dow, *The Rise of Industrial Unionism in Canada* (Toronto, ON: University of Toronto Press, 2000), 19, 22, 51.

59. "Time To Wake Up!" leaflet, January 1948.

60. "More Than 5 1/2 Days?" *Unionize*, 20 September 1949.

61. "Time To Wake Up!" broadside, January 1948; "Too Close to the Danger Line," *Unionize*, 27 April 1948; quote from "Time To Wake Up!"

62. "Your Wife's Expecting . . ." Winter 1948.

63. "Without Warning," *Unionize*, 1 March 1949.

64. "Are You a Part-Timer?" *Unionize*, 5 October 1948.

65. "Thanks Folks!" *Unionize*, 17 April 1951.

66. As quoted in McInnis, *Harnessing Labour Confrontation*, 183; emphasis added.

67. Sangster, "Consuming Issues," 240–7; Julie Guard, "Women Worth Watching: Radical Housewives in Cold War Canada," in Gary Kinsman, Dieter K. Buse, and Mercedes Steedman, eds., *Whose National Security? Canadian State Surveillance and the Creation of Enemies* (Toronto, ON: Between the Lines, 2000), 73–88.

68. Julie Guard, "Fair Play or Fair Pay? Gender Relations, Class Consciousness, and Union Solidarity in the Canadian UE," *Labour/Le Travail* (Spring 1996): 149–50; Meg Luxton, "Feminism as a Class Act: Working-Class Feminism and the Women's Movement in Canada," *Labour/Le Travail* (Fall 2001): 63–88.

69. C. B. MacPherson, *The Political Theory of Possessive Individualism* (New York, NY: Oxford University Press, 1962).

70. Veronika Bennholdt-Thomsen and Maria Mies, *The Subsistence Perspective: Beyond the Globalized Economy* (New York, NY: Zed Books, 1999).

Special thanks to the United Steelworkers for allowing reproduction of Eaton Drive campaign material. Bryan Palmer, Karen Dubinsky, Karyn Taylor, Brian Thorn, participants at the 2002 Carleton Graduate History Colloquium and the 2002 CHA Conference, and the *Canadian Historical Review*'s editors and reviewers offered valuable criticisms of earlier versions of this article. Financial assistance from the Symons Trust Fund at Trent University and the SSHRC Doctoral Fellowship program is gratefully acknowledged.

19 When Ghosts Hovered
Community and Crisis in the Company Town of Britannia Beach, British Columbia, Canada, 1957–65

Katharine Rollwagen

Britannia Beach is not a ghost town today, but between 1957 and 1965 residents and employees of the former company-owned copper mining town, located 48 kilometres north of Vancouver, British Columbia, had good reasons to believe it would become one.[1] The town faced two major crises in less than a decade, triggering mine shutdowns that threw the future of the town into question. Plummeting copper prices led to a 10-month closure in 1958 that divided the town and left many employees and residents feeling helpless. Ultimately, workers were unable to resist the shutdown, and many left to find work elsewhere. The second shutdown, triggered by a labour dispute in 1964, escalated when the company threatened to close the mine. This time, workers came together to fight for their jobs.

How did two shutdowns within a decade and affecting the same company town prompt such different reactions? This article explores the extent to which employees' notions of community were, in historian Steven High's words, a "sufficiently empowering myth," capable of mobilizing Britannia's workforce to resist the mine closures when ghosts hovered over the town.[2] While economic conditions were certainly a factor, dampening already low spirits

in 1958 and encouraging optimism in 1964, employees' sense of community contributed significantly to these events. In 1958, employee loyalty to the company and divisive notions of community based primarily on marital status helped prevent opposition to the closure. In 1964, social interaction and rhetorical appeals to local and national communities fostered solidarity and garnered support to sustain the workers' campaign against the company.

Britannia in Context: Company Towns in Canada

The 1958 shutdown ended a period of relative stability at the formerly prosperous mine, altering the company-owned town irrevocably. The Britannia Mining & Smelting Company, Limited (hereafter BM&S) began mining on the property in 1904. Initially it was a small operation, made up of several isolated mining camps scattered high in the mountains. Britannia was a low-grade copper mine, meaning that large amounts of ore had to be taken from the ground, and the copper carefully extracted from the rock using mechanical and chemical processes. By 1905 the company had built a mill on the shores of Howe

Citation: Katharine Rollwagen, "When Ghosts Hovered: Community and Crisis in the Company Town of Britannia Beach, British Columbia, Canada, 1957–65," in Marcelo J. Borges and Susana B. Torres, eds., *Company Towns: Labor, Space, and Power Relations across Time and Continents* (New York, NY: Palgrave Macmillan, 2012): 151–80.

Sound, which crushed mined rock into powder and then separated copper ore from the powder using a froth floatation process.[3] The separated copper ore was then shipped to smelters around the world. As production increased, the company's workforce grew. Between 1910 and 1920 the company built two town sites for its several hundred employees.[4] Britannia Beach itself, in the shadow of the mill, housed primarily company officials and mill workers. Many of the underground workers lived near the mine in the mountains above, in an area known both as the Townsite and Mount Sheer.

These were quintessential company towns, completely owned and operated by one employer, and—until the late 1950s—accessible from Vancouver only by boat. For more than 30 years, Britannia's employees and their families lived in company housing, shopped at the company stores, and participated in recreation programs organized with the company's blessing. Despite the efforts of several unions, the workforce remained unorganized until 1943. Even after BM&S closed the Townsite and declared bankruptcy in 1958, and the mine was sold to the Anaconda Company in 1962, Britannia Beach remained an unincorporated entity under corporate control. Although critics, particularly in the labour movement, protested the company's continuous and extensive control of daily life in its town sites, journalists and industry supporters often portrayed Britannia as a picturesque, close-knit, and well-serviced community.[5] Similar to other communities . . . such as Catumbela, Angola, company town planning created the appearance of order and unity. Many observers admired the uniformity of Britannia's white clapboard houses against the dramatic mountain backdrop of Howe Sound. Some reacted to news of the possible closures in 1958 and 1964 with shock and concern, fearing that this "ideal community . . . far from the rush and congestion of the big city" would become another ghost town in British Columbia, a province vulnerable to the boom-and-bust nature of the resource industries

that dominated—and continue to shape—its economy.[6]

Britannia's development mirrored that of scores of other mining towns in Canada between World Wars I and II. In the early decades of the twentieth century, many mining companies were realizing that it was in their interest to build communities for their workforces. The Klondike Gold Rush in 1898, in which thousands of prospectors and their followers—including "the promoters, drifters, lawyers, gamblers, and prostitutes"—rushed to the Yukon Territory of northern Canada and erected Dawson City practically overnight, demonstrated how unmanageable resource development could be. The Klondike was not an isolated case. Sandon, British Columbia, and Cobalt, Ontario, were only two of many other examples of instant, unplanned, and unruly mining camps characterized by hard-drinking miners, prostitution, and ramshackle accommodation.[7] Communities built by employees were open to anyone, democratically operated, and subject to Canadian laws. However, communities built on land owned by a private company were not subject to the same regulations. Mining companies saw the benefits of being able to control who lived close to their operations. For example, visitors to Britannia had to request permission before their arrival. In the 1920s and 1930s the property's general manager promptly fired anyone caught violating the company's alcohol prohibition, or showing pro-union sentiments. In Canada's undeveloped hinterland, company towns were usually isolated and closed communities, where mining companies exerted a great degree of control over their employees.

However, even if mining companies built stable communities for their employees, they had little control over the resource they mined; once a mineral was depleted, or prices dropped below the price of extraction, many mines closed and company towns were left deserted. Mine closures happened regularly throughout the twentieth century. When Britannia was shut down in 1958, some residents could likely recall the experiences of Phoenix and Anyox, British Columbia. These copper mining towns had been bustling one week and abandoned the next—Phoenix stopped mining in 1919; Anyox closed in 1935. The sorry fate of these and other mining towns in British Columbia made it seem likely that Britannia was destined to disappear.

. . .

Defining Community

While historians have often assumed that readers know what community means, or limited its scope to "the ideas of a shared place and a static, self-contained entity,"[8] this study defines community in two, interconnecting ways. Community is seen as both a continuous process of constructing and sustaining social bonds, as well as a rhetorical tool that joins people imaginatively. Britannia's workers and residents developed their sense of community working and playing together, and also by emphasizing the common identities—such as miner, or housewife—that they believed they shared. As historian Thomas Bender argues, "community is defined better as an experience than as a place"; it is something understood through relationships with others.[9] As relationships and power relations shift, so do a community's boundaries. This results in the inclusion of some people while necessarily excluding others. In Britannia's case, employees in 1958 were more likely to include the company in their definition of community than those in 1964, when most viewed the company as an outsider. During the earlier shutdown, workers' notions of community impeded worker solidarity, while in the latter, they facilitated it. This approach recognizes that community is never solely a positive force; it simultaneously divides and unites.

Community is also a cultural construct. Benedict Anderson's notion of "imagined communities" has demonstrated that language can create feelings of commonality among people who will never meet, cultivating regional and national identities.[10] Britannia's managers often tried to conjure this type of community in their publicity, and the union similarly appealed to imagined local and national solidarities. In this study, community is examined as both a discursive construct and a social process, which was continuously formed and imagined in Britannia's mines, homes, and social clubs. Britannia's workers and residents challenged and appealed to these varied notions of community during times of crisis.

This chapter builds on the work of recent deindustrialization scholars, many of whom no longer assume that plant closures are inevitable or uniformly destructive occurrences. As Jefferson Cowie and Joseph Heathcott have argued, deindustrialization is better conceived of as a nonlinear process that changes—for good or ill—the social fabric of the affected community.[11] Indeed, when ghosts hovered over Britannia, the copper mine's fate was anything but sealed. The shutdowns did not destroy an ideal community, but refashioned it (traumatically, for many) in the eyes of its workers and residents. While the 1958 shutdown divided the workforce and scattered a Britannia community that had catered to married workers and encouraged loyalty to the company, it did not prevent new expressions of community from emerging later on. By 1964, Britannia's physical and social geographies had changed; many workers commuted, and the 1958 shutdown had curtailed many of the social and institutional structures that had previously fostered interaction and common identity. Nevertheless, a strike against their new employer brought workers together in solidarity and spawned rhetorical appeals to local and national community that bolstered their campaign.

. . .

One Town, Two Crises

Rumblings of the first shutdown began in early 1957, when declining world copper prices created a "serious economic situation" for the mine's owner, BM&S.[12] In 1958, the North American economy was in recession. The London price of copper had fallen more than 50 per cent since 1956, from 435 pounds sterling to 160 pounds sterling.[13] In July, general manager George Lipsey announced the mine would close unless employees were willing to accept a 15 per cent pay cut.[14] The company told newspapers it was losing $65,000 per month.[15] The workers, represented by local 663 of the International Union of Mine, Mill and Smelter Workers (hereafter Mine Mill), refused to take a reduction in wages, but offered to work longer hours and sacrifice other benefits to keep the mine operating. The company accepted, and operations continued on a regular basis for several months.

In October, the situation became "more precarious" and company President E. C. Roper told Lipsey that "efforts to maintain some semblance of an operation are in jeopardy."[16] In early December, the federal and provincial governments agreed to provide a subsidy to help keep the mine open. Despite the financial assistance, on 17 December the company announced it would limit operations and reduce staff to remain afloat. By the end of the month, 40 per cent of underground workers, 59 per cent of mill workers, and 12 per cent of salaried employees had lost their jobs.[17] There were more layoffs in subsequent months, as mining continued on a more limited basis. Now-vacant houses at the Townsite were boarded up, and the local branch of the only national bank in town closed its doors.[18]

On 27 February, the company announced that economic conditions had made it "impractical to prolong operations even with the assistance which has been received."[19] The mine was shut down completely. Six months later, BM&S was placed in "voluntary liquidation," and its parent, Howe Sound Company, took charge of the Britannia property.[20] By December 1958 copper prices had risen, and the new managers resumed limited operations in the mine and mill in 1959. To save money, the company moved all

operations to the Beach and closed the Townsite, burning many of its buildings.[21] The shutdown, which many had believed permanent, lasted 10 months.[22]

While world commodity prices were the main cause of the 1958 shutdown, employer–employee relations played a prominent role in the 1964 crisis. It began as a dispute between the Mine Mill union and the mine's new owner, the Anaconda Company, over annual contract negotiations. The union's demands included a 40-hour workweek with no loss in take-home pay, extra pay for weekend work, a 20-cent per hour raise, and more control of job classification.[23] Talks were lengthy, and the company called on a conciliation board to help the two sides reach an agreement. However, in July, Britannia's 350 workers rejected the conciliation board's report, and voted 97.3 per cent in favour of a strike. The strike began 11 August 1964.

The company hinted almost immediately that it would close the mine if the strike persisted. Negotiations continued sporadically through August and September. The company tabled an offer on 21 September, but three days later, before union members had voted on the proposal, the company announced it was closing the mine. Union president Ken Smith believed the announcement was intended to frighten workers into accepting the company's offer, but Anaconda manager Barney Greenlee claimed the expense of the strike had precipitated the closure announcement. Strikers at Britannia immediately mounted a picket line to prevent the company from removing mine equipment, and over the following months, held rallies and petitioned government officials to oppose Anaconda's closure efforts. When Anaconda claimed ownership of the union hall, located on company property, union members staged a sit-in and took the company to court to regain their right to use the hall. After a court injunction prevented strikers from blocking entrances or picketing in the industrial areas of the property, company managers began dismantling and removing equipment themselves, and the *Province* newspaper reported that Britannia "would be a ghost mine in every sense of the word by mid-February."[24]

Despite these predictions, British Columbia's Minister of Mines, Donald Brothers, was able to coax both parties back to the bargaining table in early March 1965. The company and the union reached an agreement, accepted by 92 per cent of the striking workers, and the strike ended on 5 March. Four days later, 25 employees were restoring equipment to the mine, while others anticipated their return to work. It took several months for the mine to resume full operations.[25]

Given the different economic and labour relations climate during the two shutdowns, the differing responses of workers may at first seem unsurprising. It makes sense that employees would be resigned to losing their jobs during an economic recession such as in 1958 and angry with a company that would rather close the mine than bargain with them in 1964. However, when we consider workers' differing notions of community, their responses to the shutdowns appear contradictory. In 1958, one might expect employees who had lived in Britannia for many years, raised their families, and formed social bonds in the community to fiercely resist the closure of their workplace and town. Yet, during the 1958 shutdown there was little collective action to protest the company's decision. Social divisions between married and single employees, coupled with feelings of loyalty toward the company, meant that no coherent opposition to the shutdown emerged. Community hindered militancy. Ironically, in 1964, workers mounted an effective campaign against their employer despite the fact that many of the social structures that had promoted cohesion had disappeared and many employees now commuted to the mine from nearby towns. The strike fostered an animosity toward Anaconda that helped workers present a more united front to preserve their jobs. Community became both a rallying cry for strikers and a rhetorical strategy to garner wider support for Britannia based on economic

nationalism. In both cases, workers' reactions to the mine closures do not immediately square with their shifting notions of community.

1958—A Workforce Divided

In 1958, social divisions among workers help explain residents' failure to resist the shutdown. These divisions, based primarily on marital status, played a central role in defining community membership in Britannia in the years following World War II. While married employees considered themselves respectable, stable community members, they characterized many of the single workers as rough transients, and often treated them as outsiders. Single employees came to Britannia from across the province and country looking for work. At the mine, they lived in bunkhouses, separated by a creek at both the Beach and Townsite from the houses inhabited by married residents. The creeks served as physical barriers between rough and respectable activity.[26] Socially, single men were largely excluded from local organizations. BM&S sought to attract stable family men to its mine, and made families and children a priority when planning recreational events, creating playgrounds, and sponsoring picnics and sporting events. These events held little appeal for most bunkhouse dwellers.[27] Evidence also shows single men were more likely than their married counterparts to be employed intermittently or seasonally, and were thus less able to commit to local organizations. A study of Britannia workers and residents mentioned in the town newspaper, the *Townsite Reporter*, between 1949 and 1955, reveals that married employees and their families were much more involved in local activities; bunkhouse dwellers were rarely mentioned in the newspaper because few attended social club meetings or held leadership positions in local organizations.[28] Since single workers were less likely to participate in events or volunteer for committees, few married residents considered them equal community members. Although married workers constituted a minority of Britannia employees, they enforced a code of respectability that largely excluded the more numerous and transient bunkhouse inhabitants.[29]

The social divisions between workers helped prevent the emergence of a collective opposition to the 1958 mine closure. Because of their exclusion, few single employees developed the same kind of devotion to Britannia as their married co-workers, many of whom had made the Beach or Townsite their permanent homes. When the mine closed, they had few reasons to stay in Britannia and saw little point in opposing the shutdown. While they may have felt sadness at the closing or frustration at losing their jobs, they would likely not have considered allying in opposition to the shutdown with the married residents who had persistently, if subtly, excluded them. As the *Province* reported, "Single miners had no illusions. They began packing at once and headed for the PGE trains."[30] The day after the company announced the shutdown, recalled miner Al McNair, bunkhouse occupants began "leaving like a bunch of flies."[31] With a large portion of workers gone, it would have been difficult for the remaining employees and their families to muster the critical mass needed to mount an effective opposition campaign. Ultimately, married residents' close-knit sense of community speeded the town sites' dissolution.

However, even married residents failed to maintain a sense of unity or cohesion during the long shutdown process. The many months of uncertainty that preceded the mine closure did not bring residents closer together. Indeed, as *Province* columnist Jean Howarth observed two months before the shutdown, Britannia was "a town torn by internal strife, totally without security, disturbed by a steady stream of rumors."[32] The December layoffs created further instability for residents. No one knew whose job would be cut, or when. National unemployment figures were approaching those last seen during the 1930s, and few Britannia residents could have been enthusiastic about the idea of finding a new job during a recession.[33] Furthermore, because the town sites were small and many married residents formed a close-knit community, friendships were unavoidably severed when supervisors and managers had to fire their neighbours.[34] Some families moved away, and the busy routine of meetings and events was disrupted. Resentment grew when the company transferred employees from the Townsite to replace terminated workers at the Beach, and vice versa. Miner's son Jim Walton claimed "the uncertainty of the mine closing caused a lot of heartache, a lot of tragedy in terms of personal suffering." His parents relied on their creditors' kindness to stretch their limited income, and several other families were in similarly stressful financial situations.[35] Columnist Jean Howarth wrote that shortly after the layoffs, people were "withdrawing into themselves, avoiding even their friends." Residents were "caught in the frightening wave of fear and insecurity" that made them less likely to trust their co-workers.[36] This attitude made any cohesive reaction to the mine's closure difficult.

. . . Only a handful of families remained during the shutdown, either because they were hopeful the mine would eventually reopen, or because they saw few job prospects elsewhere.[37] The apparent "death" of the town evoked mostly sadness, blunting any attempts at organized opposition to the mine's closure.

1964—Crisis as Catalyst

Between 1958 and 1964 the town's physical and social shape altered considerably. Physically, the community was smaller; with the Townsite in the mountains closed, all residents lived at the Beach. Anaconda also employed fewer workers than BM&S.[38] Thanks to the recently completed highway linking Britannia Beach to the growing city of Vancouver, workers did not need to live at the mine site. Several employees now commuted to work from nearby communities such as Squamish, Horseshoe Bay, and North

Vancouver.[39] While Britannia Beach was still a company-owned property, it was no longer a closed community. These changes affected the way remaining residents and new employees defined themselves as a community. Britannia was no longer a remote town where residents believed people had to "make their own entertainment and fun." While organizations such as the church and Ladies' Auxiliary remained active, and the Britannia Beach Community Club continued to hold dances and baseball games, residents could now easily drive to Squamish or Vancouver for an evening's entertainment. After the road went through, "the people went their own way," remembered miner's wife Betty Manson: "the closeness wasn't there."[40] Cohesiveness, stability, and active local participation—characteristics that had shaped married residents' understanding of community before the 1958 shutdown—were less evident in the early 1960s. Residents who had previously relied on these characteristics to identify themselves as community members were left feeling that Britannia Beach was no longer a community.

Even though some residents believed Britannia's community spirit had waned after the 1958 shutdown, the 1964 strike and shutdown fostered a renewed sense of unity in the face of instability. The strike acted as a catalyst, exposing employees' shared vulnerability at the hands of a large company, and providing some of Britannia's workers with a renewed sense of community that motivated them to act collectively. "The solidarity of the working people is tremendous," miner's wife and *Squamish Times* correspondent Betty McNair reported in the second month of the strike.[41] While the strike's duration caused financial hardship and uncertainty about the future, the sense of fear and weariness that plagued residents during 1957 and 1958 was not as evident in 1964. . . . Mine Mill leaders held frequent meetings with strikers, and formed committees to organize social events and fundraisers, and to publish strike bulletins.[42] This kind of assistance brought employees, some

of whom lived in different towns, in close and regular contact with each other. It also helped striking workers focus on walking picket lines and opposing the company's threatened closure, keeping feelings of uncertainty partially at bay.

The union also provided a common program around which employees could rally. Workers and residents were working toward a common goal, and assisting each other. The result was a noted "return of community interest which had not been in evidence for some years," as one woman told a *Squamish Times* reporter: "It's almost as if the strike has brought us all closer together."[43] Betty McNair believed the picket lines and the efforts of the strike committees had prompted "more visiting and togetherness" than "since before the road opened."[44] The strike provided a rallying point for many employees, creating a level of social interaction not seen since before 1958. While exclusive notions of community divided residents in 1958, the sense of community precipitated by the 1964 strike helped to unite and sustain workers during the period of uncertainty.

Loyalty and Hostility: Including and Excluding the Company from the Community

The union's ability to foster a renewed sense of community at Britannia was particularly significant given the circumstances the International Union of Mine, Mill and Smelter Workers faced as a known "Red" union during the Cold War. Since the late 1940s, the union had been subjected to continuous red baiting, and resisted attempts—both from inside and outside the labour movement—to purge its leadership of Communist Party members and sympathizers.[45] As a "centre of communist strength," Mine Mill was particularly susceptible; its members were harassed and its delegates prevented from attending union conventions in the United States.[46] Between 1949 and 1965 the union also faced a series of certification challenges from the competing Steelworkers' Union. The tense atmosphere may account for the union's seemingly quiescent reaction to the 1958 shutdown. In 1955, Mine Mill's international leadership granted autonomy to its Canadian locals, but the red baiting continued.[47] During the 1964 strike, several journalists accused Mine Mill of making Britannia "an issue they can sink their pink teeth into." Britannia was a "fertile field for reds," according to the *Province*'s editor, who claimed the workers' protest was a futile "red-led furor."[48] Despite the attacks, union leadership was able to rally Britannia's workers and residents against their employer.

The union solidarity that fed opposition to the company in 1964 contrasted sharply with the company loyalty prevalent six years earlier. How residents viewed the company within or without the community influenced their divergent reactions to the shutdown and strike. Loyalty to the company among married employees, especially, helped to inhibit collective opposition to the mine's closure in 1958. . . . Married workers were more likely to benefit from employee incentives—such as life insurance and company store dividends—because they stayed at the mine longer on average than their unmarried co-workers, and because the company favoured benefit schemes tied to employee loyalty and stability.[49] They also benefited from the company's low-rent housing, recreation facilities, hospitals, and schools. They were encouraged to raise their children at Britannia and make it their home. Several long-time residents remembered how the company tried to help employees during the lean 1930s, extending store credit, stockpiling copper, and retaining as many married workers as possible on a reduced work schedule.[50] The goodwill generated by the company's acts made it more difficult for residents to blame BM&S for the shutdown. Since the 1920s, BM&S had engaged in a form of civic capitalism that, while it did not avert employer–employee conflict, in Philip Scranton's words, "bounded and channeled it, humanized it, and obstructed that abstraction

and generalization from experience that could constitute class consciousness."[51] Thus, although residents remembered the shutdown as "devastating," and "quite a shock," they believed the company had always been, in the words of one resident, "on guard for the welfare of the community," and hesitated to blame BM&S for the mine's closure.[52] Some residents appeared unable to imagine Britannia without the company.

Conversely, in 1964 many employees believed the company was treating them unfairly. This belief was due in part to the high price of copper at the time the company was pleading poverty. During the strike the price per tonne continued to rise, from 209 pounds sterling in March 1964 to 245 pounds sterling six months later.[53] In this favourable economic climate, strike supporters saw the company's threat to close the mine as a mere "bargaining weapon," a way to force the workers to accept the company's contract offer. Union president and former Britannia employee Ken Smith called it an empty threat: "All along they have said they'd close if we didn't accept their proposals," he told reporters. "I won't believe it 'till they move out the track and hoisting equipment."[54] . . .

Employees also did not have the same sense of loyalty to the Anaconda Company that previous employees had shown BM&S. While BM&S had tried to foster loyalty and unity through welfare schemes, the Anaconda Company did little to establish such a social contract with its employees.[55] By the 1960s, the tenets of civic capitalism that BM&S had sustained since the 1920s were being replaced by ideas of global capitalism, in which shareholders' interests were paramount.[56] Although BM&S was owned by an American parent company that operated three other mines, Britannia was always managed locally. The managers' longevity, autonomy, and paternalistic approach gave the mine a family-owned feel.[57] Anaconda, on the other hand, was an American corporate "empire" of mining, transportation, lumber, and real estate companies. It owned subsidiaries in four countries, and had a reputation for using "coercion and persuasion to maintain control" over its employees.[58] Anaconda showed less consideration for Britannia's workers and residents than did BM&S. Miner's wife and long-time resident Olive Baxter noticed the difference between the companies' approaches. Under BM&S management, she remembered, "it was more like a big family. But when the Anaconda come [sic], they were more into industry . . . and it was more business."[59] . . . The strike helped workers to redefine community in opposition to the company.

Death and Murder: Rhetoric of Local and National Community

Residents' loyalty, coupled with the sustained co-operation of union and company officials to prevent the closure, helps to explain why there was little public opposition when BM&S announced in February 1958 that it would have to close Britannia until base metal prices improved.[60] Because of the union and company's extended efforts to keep the mine open, many residents believed that "everything possible had been done," and the closure was unavoidable.[61] "You can't do anything once the copper prices are down," former resident Will Trythall claimed.[62] Miner John Dickinson did not blame the company either; business was bad, and BM&S "just couldn't make a go of it, that's all."[63] . . .

This sense of helplessness and pessimism is evident in the language residents and observers used to describe the mine's closure. Their words often evoked images of death. Resident Elsie Hamelin called the drop in copper prices Britannia's "death knell," while Mrs. Robinson, the postmaster's wife, claimed that watching the mine close was like "sitting by the deathbed of an old friend." Vancouver's newspapers announced the town's unfortunate fate; "Britannia Dies," one headline read, while another article claimed, "the life-blood is draining from Britannia." Reporters claimed there was an "eerie silence" in the quickly emptying town, and described

the shutdown as a "tragedy."[64] These images reinforced the presumed finality of the closure, and underlined the futility of disputing the company's actions. Death, it seemed, was inevitable. Britannia's ghost town status was all but assured.

While the 1958 shutdown was portrayed as the slow death of a town, Anaconda's actions in 1964 were seen as the unprovoked "murder of a community." Union leaders, strikers, and supporters were not despondent, but positive, insisting after several weeks on the picket line that the strike "remains solid" and "morale is high."[65] Their rhetoric, instead of embracing death, evoked images of local and national community to garner wider support for their cause.

On one hand, strikers and supporters described Britannia as a close-knit community threatened by a heartless corporation. Union bulletins and newspaper reports employed what anthropologist Elizabeth Furniss has called the "politics of victimization." This does not imply that the union's claims about the company were unfounded or fabricated, but they were worded to emphasize Britannia's small size and the hard-working nature of its residents in order to highlight the "discrepancies of power" between the company and the community. The technique transformed Britannia's seeming powerlessness into a moral authority that could be used to justify the union's actions.[66] This was a David versus Goliath struggle. Union bulletins often described the strikers as "little local 663," while the company was termed "the Anaconda giant" or the "giant metal monopoly." Union leaders reminded strikers and supporters that the company was a "billion dollar" enterprise, the "world's largest copper producer." By reinforcing the disparities of resources and power between Anaconda and its employees, the strikers were trying to demonstrate the integrity of their cause. The company was a bully, they claimed, whose "every Scrooge tactic . . . only serves to stiffen the resistance of the workers." The workers were the "good and faithful long-service employees," the "miners and their families who over the years have produced [the mine's] wealth."[67] The union's rhetoric described Britannia's workers as united small-town folks, an image that excluded the approximately 20 per cent of employees who did not participate in the strike.[68] Britannia's embodiment of small-town values made it worth saving, supporters argued, even if, in reality, many of the mine's employees now lived in other towns and commuted to work. Those opposed to the mine's closure appealed to the image of a close-knit community standing up to a corporate giant to help convince the general public that theirs was a just cause.

. . . [B]y 1964 feelings of economic nationalism had become more prevalent in Canada. Historian Steven High argues that "by the mid-1960s, a growing number of English-speaking Canadians believed that their country was in imminent danger of becoming an American colony."[69] While some lamented the invasion of American culture in magazines and television programs, others pointed to high levels of foreign investment as proof of the United States's imperialist intentions. Indeed, by 1960, 47.4 per cent of capital invested in Canada came from the United States.[70] Canada faced a choice, according to former federal Minister of Finance Walter L. Gordon, between independence and colonial status. This new nationalism became, in Steven High's words, "a powerful rhetorical weapon in the hands of working people to be used against companies that closed plants."[71] . . . In 1964, the union was able to play more successfully on nationalist fears, placing Anaconda's threat to close the mine within an emerging discourse criticizing American influence in the Canadian economy. In an effort to save their jobs and town, residents and employees began imagining community on a larger scale than they had in 1958.

. . .

Union leaders and strike supporters . . . claimed all Canadians had an interest in keeping the mine in operation, and implored their fellow citizens not to "let the Yanks rule Britannia." In a letter to the *Northern Miner*, Mine Mill president

Ken Smith argued that Canadian taxpayers, who had been willing to provide a subsidy to keep the mine operating in 1958, should expect the company to "reciprocate when times are good for them." A petition circulated at a union rally in October 1964 asserted that the decision to close the mine was made "without regard for the welfare of the Canadian people," and accused Anaconda of trying to destroy "millions of tons of valuable ore" that could have been contributing to the Canadian economy.[72] This ore, union leaders insisted, was "an asset belonging to the people and should not be abandoned." In this context, the strike became more than a struggle to keep the mine open and secure improved working conditions for employees. It was, according to the union, a struggle to "re-establish the rights of the people of this Province and our sovereign government" against foreign resource extraction companies. To this end, Mine Mill asked the provincial government to enact legislation to ensure that mining properties, claims, grants, and leases abandoned by corporate interests became the property of the Crown.[73] The union wanted the mine "put to use for the benefit of Canadians," not, as one Mine Mill bulletin put it, left in the hands of an "arrogant American monopoly."[74]

Unlike in 1958, many people responded favourably to the strikers' nationalist appeals. They agreed that, as Canadians, they were part of a community that needed to rally to help their fellow citizens. . . . In a letter to the *Vancouver Times*, Arthur Turner, an elected member of British Columbia's legislative assembly and a member of the left-leaning New Democratic Party, said Anaconda's attempt to close the mine should "shock and startle Canadians into action." Turner claimed he was not as concerned about the dispute between the company and the union as he was about "the fact that Canadian wealth—known and potential—can be willfully destroyed" by "a large corporation with headquarters in the United States." . . . Private citizens also used nationalist sentiments to voice their dismay at the mine closure. "The obvious solution," one writer to the *Province* suggested, "is expropriation and operation of the mine by the B.C. government."[75] The union's nationalist rhetoric clearly struck a chord, emphasizing all Canadians' vulnerability at the hands of American corporations.

As these examples illustrate, other unions, politicians, and private citizens shared the union's fears about increasing American control of Canadian industries. Many believed the union's assertions that, as members of the same country, they belonged to the same community of interest as the Britannia strikers, and therefore should send the miners assistance and support. Although neither the federal nor provincial government introduced legislation or took steps to nationalize the mine, many people saw the strike in Britannia as an attempt to stand up to foreign companies. This was a community, whether imagined locally or nationally, defending its interests. The financial and moral support strikers received as a result of their nationalist appeals sustained their campaign for eight months— long enough to convince both union and company officials to return to the bargaining table. Whereas in 1958 many observers had only pity for Britannia's "tragic" and scattered residents, in 1964 observers were invited to become part of the strikers' community. This ensured at least some opposition to the shutdown came from across the country, not only from local residents.

Company Town: Shack Town, New Town, Hometown

During both crises, workers' diverse notions of community played an influential role in their response. The rapid changes affecting Britannia during these years did not destroy the community, but forced employees to re-examine their understandings of what connected them to each other. In 1958, notions of community obstructed collective action, dividing workers and diffusing blame. Residents who had used marital status

to define community membership were unwilling or unable to express any effective or united opposition when the mine suddenly closed. However, in 1964 understandings of community motivated many workers to act collectively. Striking employees believed the shutdown gave them a common purpose and a common opponent in the company. They were able to embrace notions of local and national community that broadened their struggle and garnered support from outside Britannia's boundaries.

Employees' experiences during these crises underline the often sporadic and inconsistent nature of deindustrialization. They remind us that resource town closures cannot be characterized as inevitable or tragic; these are dynamic periods of intense change, shaped by both material realities, such as income and commodity prices, and discursive factors, such as loyalty and community, that deserve more focused historical attention. Other town sites and abandoned industrial relics likely hold similarly complex stories, most still awaiting scholarly exploration. Not only do Britannia's shutdowns reveal how community identity shaped workers' responses to deindustrialization in unexpected ways, they also help debunk the notion that the post-war era in Canada was a time of labour stability and worker prosperity. Shutdowns that occurred in this period reinforce the idea that, historically, deindustrialization has been a process, in Cowie and Heathcott's words, "pockmarked with explosions, relocations, desertions, and competitive struggles."[76] People in Britannia characterized deindustrialization both as a drawn-out, traumatic, and dislocating experience, as well as a renewing, unifying, and strengthening one for their community. No one metaphor suffices to explain the diverse reactions of residents when ghosts hovered over the future of the town.

. . .

Today, Britannia Beach lives off the memory of its mining days. When Anaconda ceased operations for good in 1974, residents were ready with a museum plan that saw the copper

concentrator and other historic buildings preserved as part of the British Columbia Mining
Museum. In the face of mounting pressure from
developers to take advantage of the site's breath-
taking mountain views and convenient proximity to Vancouver, residents and former employees
again united to assert their town's mining identity. Today, as commuters and tourists drive by
on the Sea-to-Sky highway, the giant copper mill
stands in quiet testament, one of the few remaining material reminders that this was a place
where people worked hard, raised families, and
endured repeated crises that threatened their
livelihood and refashioned their community—
while always keeping the ghosts at bay.

 More online.

Notes

1. This article appeared in *Urban History Review* under the
    title "When Ghosts Hovered: Community and Crisis
    in a Company Town: Britannia Beach, B.C. 1957–65,"
    Urban History Review 35, no. 2 (March 2007): 25–36.
    . . . This research was conducted with support from the
    Social Sciences and Humanities Research Council and
    the University of Victoria.

2. Steven High, *Industrial Sunset: The Making of North
    America's Rust Belt, 1969–84* (Toronto, ON: University
    of Toronto Press, 2003), 9.

3. For further details about the mill (also known as the
    concentrator), see the online exhibit at the British
    Columbia Museum of Mining, which is located in
    Britannia Beach. www.theconcentrator.ca.

4. The exact number employed at Britannia varied con-
    tinuously, but averaged 600 to 800 workers during the
    1950s. In the 1960s, the workforce was much reduced,
    averaging closer to 350 employees at the mine.

5. Politicians sympathetic to labour repeatedly called for
    company towns to be "opened up," and claimed com-
    pany authority violated workers' rights. For examples
    see *Victoria Daily Times*, 11 March 1919, 4; *Vancouver
    Sun*, 13 February 1934, 16; *Victoria Daily Times*, 13
    February 1943, 2; *Victoria Daily Times*, 29 February
    1944, 8; *Victoria Daily Times*, 26 February 1944, 5.

6. "Shutdown Threatens Britannia," *Vancouver Sun*,
    11 July 1957, 1; "$15,000 Homes to Make B.C.'s New
    Ghost Town," *Vancouver Sun*, 22 July 1957, 3.

7. Gilbert Stelter and Alan Artibise, "Canadian Resource
    Towns in Historical Perspective," in Roy Bowles, ed.,

*Little Communities and Big Industries: Studies in the Social
Impact of Canadian Resource Extraction* (Toronto, ON:
Butterworths, 1982), 50.

8. John C. Walsh and Steven High, "Rethinking the
    Concept of Community," *Histoire Sociale/Social History*
    32, no. 64 (1999): 255. Thomas Bender similarly criti-
    cized American historians for their stilted approach
    to community in his monograph, *Community and
    Social Change in America* (New Brunswick, NJ: Rutgers
    University Press, 1978).

9. Bender, *Community and Social Change in America*, 6.

10. "Imagined communities" does not imply that com-
    munity does not exist; the interesting question asks
    not about a community's authenticity, but inquires
    as to how and why it was imagined in a certain way.
    Benedict Anderson, *Imagined Communities: Reflections
    on the Origin and Spread of Nationalism* (London, UK:
    Verso Editions, 1983), 15.

11. Jefferson Cowie and Joseph Heathcott, "The Meanings
    of De-industrialization," in Jefferson Cowie and Joseph
    Heathcott, eds., *Beyond the Ruins: The Meanings of
    De-industrialization* (Ithaca, NY: Cornell University
    Press, 2003), 5–6.

12. "Progress Report—November 1st to 15th, Inclusive."
    Howe Sound Company (Britannia Division) Records,
    Box 83b, File 24, UBC Special Collections (hereafter
    UBC SpColl), Vancouver, BC.

13. Bryan D. Palmer, *Working-Class Experience: Rethinking
    the History of Canadian Labour, 1800–1991* (Toronto,
    ON: McClelland & Stewart, 1992), 338; Ferdinand E.
    Banks, *The World Copper Market: An Economic Analysis*
    (Cambridge, MA: Ballinger Publishing Company,
    1974), 10.

14. "Shutdown Threatens Britannia," *Vancouver Sun*, 11
    July 1957, 1. Given that the average weekly metal
    mining wage in 1957 was $81.68, this amounted to a
    net loss of approximately $12.25 per week. "Averages
    of weekly wages of hourly rated wage earners, select
    industry groups, Canada, 1945–70," E78-85, F. H.
    Leacy, ed., *Historical Statistics of Canada, Electronic edi-
    tion* (2003), http://www.statcan.ca/english/freepub/
    11-516-XIE/sectiona/toc.htm, 21 April 2006.

15. This is approximately $485,000 in 2006 dollars. By
    November 1957, the price of copper had dropped fur-
    ther, and the company stated it was losing $80,000 per
    month ($623,500 in 2010 dollars). "Inflation Calculator,"
    http://banqueducanada.ca/en/rates/inflation_calc
    .html (accessed 1 November 2010). International
    Union of Mine, Mill and Smelter Workers (Western
    District), "Submission to Select Standing Committee
    on Labour of the B.C. Government, Re: Closing of
    Britannia Mine," 11 March 1958, 4–5, IUMMSW Fonds,
    box 115, file 11, UBC SpColl, Vancouver BC.

16. E. C. Roper, Letter to G. C. Lipsey, 16 October 1957,

Howe Sounds Company (Britannia Division) Records, Box 54, File 34, UBC SpColl, Vancouver, BC.

17. The total workforce was reduced by 32 per cent. "Analysis of Labor at November 20, 1957," and "Summary of Labor at December 31, 1957," Howe Sound Company (Britannia Division) Records, Box 63, File 14, UBC SpColl, Vancouver, BC.

18. Royal Bank of Canada, Letter to J. E. Nelson, 31 January 1958, Britannia Mining and Smelting Company, Limited, MS1221, Box 57, File 55, British Columbia Archives (hereafter BCARS), Victoria, BC.

19. E. C. Roper, Telegram to J. S. Roper, 27 February 1958, MS1221, Box 74, File 1, BCARS, Victoria, BC.

20. Minister of Mines, Province of British Columbia, *Annual Report 1958* (Victoria, BC: Don McDiarmid, Printer to the Queen's Most Excellent Majesty, 1959), 56.

21. Interview with Al McNair, 22 September 2004.

22. Interview with Kay Pickard, 24 September 2004.

23. "Bargaining Demands," *Mine-Mill Herald*, February/March 1964, Greenlee Papers (hereafter GP), UBC SpColl, Vancouver, BC.

24. "Britannia Miners Spurn Wage Report," *Vancouver Sun*, 24 July 1964; "Britannia Faces 'Indefinite Shutdown,'" *Squamish Times*, 13 August 1964, GP, UBC SpColl, Vancouver, BC; "Britannia Wage Talks to Start Again Today," *Province*, 11 September 1964, GP, UBC SpColl, Vancouver, BC; "Britannia Strikers Lose Jobs as Mine Company Pulls Out," *Sunday Sun*, 26 September 1964, GP, UBC SpColl, Vancouver, BC; "Women Join Line at Britannia Gate," *Vancouver Sun*, 29 September 1964, 1; "200 Autos Join Miners' Motorcade," *Vancouver Sun*, 31 October 1964, 29; "Union Men Stay in 'Padlocked' Hall," *Vancouver Sun*, 3 November 1964, 23; "'Border' Maps Ready for Britannia Pickets," *Province*, 3 October 1964, 29; "Ghost Mine Spectre Looms at Britannia," *Province*, 26 November 1964, 20.

25. "Talks Bring New Hope in Britannia Mine Strike," *Province*, 2 March 1965, 9; "Long Strike Ends," *Vancouver Sun*, 5 March 1965, 1; "Britannia Bustles Again," *Vancouver Sun*, 9 March 1965, 13.

26. Katharine Rollwagen, "Bunkhouse and Home: Company, Community, and Crisis in Britannia Beach, British Columbia" (Master's thesis, University of Victoria, 2005), 58–60.

27. These men were not necessarily all unmarried; a housing shortage in the 1950s made it necessary for some married men to live in the bunkhouses and house their families in Vancouver. Ibid., 39–42.

28. Approximately 75 per cent of those named in the *Reporter* were married employees or family members. *Townsite Reporter* 1:1– 9:8, LS856-536 and LS856-474, BCARS, Victoria, BC. . . .

29. The company did not keep exact population statistics; however, in 1957 Coast-Capilano MP James Sinclair told the House of Commons the mine employed approximately 800 people, and the town housed 312 families. Since all families contained at least one employee (only employees could live in Britannia), we can estimate there were no more than 325 married employees, and the remainder were bunkhouse inhabitants. Debates, House of Commons, Canada. Session 1957–1958, vol. 2, 1114.

30. "For Mr. Gaglardi—A Message: You Still Can Save Britannia's Life," *Province*, 3 March 1958, 17; "Britannia Folk Wait and Wonder," *Vancouver Sun*, 3 March 1958, 2.

31. Interview with Al McNair, Britannia Mines Oral History Project (hereafter BMOHP), 1878-29, University of British Columbia Archives (hereafter UBCAR), Vancouver, BC.

32. Jean Howarth, "Britannia Very Unhappy Town," *Province*, 7 January 1958.

33. Unemployment levels varied between 2.5 and 5 per cent in the early 1950s, but rose as high as 10 per cent between 1956 and 1959. Between 500,000 and 750,000 people were unemployed across Canada at this time. Palmer, *Working-Class Experience*, 271.

34. Jean Howarth, "Britannia Very Unhappy Town," *Province*, 7 January 1958.

35. Interview with Jim Walton, BMOHP, 1878-43, UBCAR, Vancouver, BC.

36. Jean Howarth, "Britannia a Divided Town," *Province*, 9 January 1958, 20.

37. The exact number is unknown; however in 1964, only 5 per cent of the then-striking employees had been working at Britannia prior to the 1958 shutdown, suggesting few remained or returned when the mine reopened.

38. BM&S employed approximately 800 people before the layoffs of December 1957 and the 1958 shutdown. Anaconda employed 350 people at the time of the 1964 strike. See House of Commons Debates, 14 November 1957, 1117; "Miners Strike At Britannia," *Vancouver Sun*, 11 August 1964, 7.

39. Employee addresses noted on strike registration forms. See Strike registration forms, IUMMSW Fonds, Box 120, File 14, UBC SpColl, Vancouver, BC.

40. Interview with Kay Pickard, 24 September 2004; Interviews with Mary Smith and Muriel Green, BMOHP, 1878-40 and 1878-20 (respectively), UBCAR, Vancouver, BC.; Transcript from interview with Betty Manson, BMOHP, Box 3, File 11, UBCAR, Vancouver, BC.

41. Betty McNair, "Britannia a Troubled Town," *Squamish Times*, 8 October 1964.

42. "Local 663—Strike Bulletin," 1:5 (2 September 1964), GP, UBC SpColl, Vancouver, BC.

43. "Britannia People Hope Mine Will Re-open Soon," *Squamish Times*, 26 November 1964, GP, UBC SpColl, Vancouver, BC.

44. "Betty McNair, "Strikes and Pickets," *Squamish Times*, 8 October 1964.

45. The American Taft-Hartley Act of 1947 limited unions' right to strike and required union officials to sign anti-communist affidavits. Although it was American law, it was also applied to the leadership of international unions active in Canada. For more on Taft-Hartley, see Robert H. Z. Zieger and Gilbert Gall, *American Workers, American Unions* (Baltimore, MD: Johns Hopkins University Press, 2002), 152–3.

46. Ken Smith, Britannia employee and union delegate, was turned back at the border in 1948 and arrested in Seattle during a later attempt. See Mike Solski and John Smaller, *Mine Mill: The History of the International Union of Mine, Mill and Smelter Workers in Canada since 1895* (Ottawa, ON: Steel Rail Publishing, 1984), 52–3. Quote is from Palmer, *Working-Class Experience*, 248.

47. Solski and Smaller, *Mine Mill,* 130.

48. Ormond Turner, "Around Town," *Province*, 2 November 1964, 25; "Britannia: Fertile Field for Reds," *Province*, 4 November 1964, 4.

49. Residents' varied reactions to company paternalism are detailed in Rollwagen, "Bunkhouse and Home," 49–53.

50. Interview with Lucille Gillingham, BMOHP, 1878-18, UBCAR, Vancouver, BC.

51. Philip Scranton, *Proprietary Capitalism: The Textile Manufacturer at Philadelphia, 1800–85* (Cambridge, UK: Cambridge University Press, 1983), 418, quoted in High, *Industrial Sunset*, 89.

52. Interview with Elsie Anderson, 23 September 2004; Report on interview with Reg Eades, Jr., BMOHP, Box 2, File 15 and Report on interview with Mrs. Betty Manson, BMOHP, Box 3 File 11, UBCAR, Vancouver, BC.

53. The company's actual financial situation is of little relevance here; the residents' belief that they were being cheated affected their actions regardless of whether these beliefs can be substantiated. In dollars, the price of copper increased from $580 to $680 per tonne. "The Truth about Britannia Mine," *Vancouver Sun*, 9 September 1964, 9.

54. Doug Collins, "Bob's Ghost," *Vancouver Times*, 3 October 1964; "Mine Will Close," *Province*, 26 September 1964; "Britannia to Shut but Vote Goes On," *Province*, 28 September 1964, GP, UBC SpColl, Vancouver, BC.

55. The term *social contract* is used to describe a relationship between employees and employers in which employers recognize the way their business affects individual workers, their families, and communities.

See Steve May and Laura Morrison, "Making Sense of Restructuring," in Cowie and Heathcott, eds., *Beyond the Ruins*, 260.

56. High, *Industrial Sunset*, 89.

57. From 1922 until its bankruptcy, BM&S employed three general managers. One, C. P. Browning, held the position for 25 years. Each had worked for the company in various capacities before becoming general manager.

58. Norman Girvan, *Copper in Chile: A Study in Conflict between Corporate and National Economy* (Mona: Institute of Social and Economic Research, University of the West Indies, 1972), 37; Laurie Mercier, *Anaconda: Labor, Community, and Culture in Montana's Smelter City* (Urbana, IL: University of Illinois Press, 2001), 20.

59. Interview with Olive Baxter, BMOHP, 1878-3, UBCAR, Vancouver, BC.

60. "For Mr. Gaglardi—A Message: You Still Can Save Britannia's Life," *Province*, 3 March 1958, 17.

61. Doug Collins, "My MP," *Vancouver Times*, 7 November 1964, GP, UBC SpColl, Vancouver, BC.

62. Interview with Will Trythall, 23 September 2004.

63. Interview with Elsie Hamelin, BMOHP, 1878-14, UBCAR, Vancouver, BC.

64. Report from interview with Elsie Hamelin, BMOHP, Box 3, File 4, UBCAR, Vancouver, BC.; "$15,000 Homes to Make B.C.'s New Ghost Town," *Vancouver Sun*, 22 July 1957, 3; "Death of a Whole Town at Least Deserves an Inquest," *Vancouver Sun*, 11 March 1958, 4; "For Mr. Gaglardi—A Message: You Still Can Save Britannia's Life" *Province*, 3 March 1958, 17; Jack Scott, "Our Town: Man with Ghost," *Vancouver Sun*, 26 May 1958, 21.

65. "We Can't Allow Town's Murder," *Victoria Colonist*, 18 November 1964, 27; "Local 663 Strike Bulletin" No. 5, Vol. 1, September 2, 1964, GP, UBC SpColl, Vancouver, BC.

66. The term is often used to explore how rural settler communities oppose intrusion by urban governments and/or expanding resource industries. Elizabeth Furniss, *The Burden of History: Colonialism and the Frontier Myth in a Rural Canadian Community* (Vancouver, BC: UBC Press, 1999), 88–9.

67. "Local 663—Strike Bulletin," No. 1, Vol. 2, February 12, 1965, IUMMSW Fonds, Box 120, File 12, UBC SpColl, Vancouver, BC; "Historic Victory of Mine Miller's at Britannia"—bulletin dated 11 March 1965, GP, UBC SpColl, Vancouver, BC; Ken Smith, Letter to "All Trade Unionists," 17 September 1964, GP, UBC SpColl, Vancouver, BC; "Britannia," *Western Miner*, October 1964; "Save Britannia: Cavalcade Sunday," *Pacific Tribune*, 30 October 1964, GP, UBC SpColl, Vancouver, BC.

68. Although 97.3 per cent of the unionized employees voted in favour of the strike, only 268 out of the

approximately 350 workers (77 per cent) completed strike registration forms, which allowed them to volunteer for picket duty and receive strike pay. Of the remaining employees, it is possible they did not want to participate in the strike, or left Britannia for jobs elsewhere. See Strike registration forms, IUMMSW Fonds, Box 120, File 14, UBC SpColl, Vancouver, BC.

69. High, *Industrial Sunset*, 168.

70. Herb Gray, *Foreign Direct Investment in Canada* (Ottawa, ON: Information Canada, 1972), 15.

71. High, *Industrial Sunset*.

72. "Britannia Miners Stage Big Rally on Sunday," *Squamish Times*, 5 November 1964, GP, UBC SpColl, Vancouver, BC; "Union Takes Exception to Britannia Editorial," *Northern Miner*, 5 November 1964, GP, UBC SpColl,

Vancouver, BC; Petition from rally, IUMMSW Fonds, Box 118, File 3, UBC SpColl, Vancouver, BC.

73. Paper presented to the members of the Legislative Assembly of British Columbia, 26 January 1965, 3–4, IUMMSW Fonds, Box 118, File 3, UBC SpColl, Vancouver, BC.

74. "Save Britannia: Cavalcade Sunday," *Pacific Tribune*, 30 October 1964, GP, UBC SpColl, Vancouver, BC; "Historic Victory of Mine Miller's at Britannia," 11 March 1965, IUMMSW Fonds, Box 120, File 11, UBC SpColl, Vancouver, BC.

75. "Take Over Mine," *Province*, 17 November 1964, GP, UBC SpColl, Vancouver, BC. . . .

76. Cowie and Heathcott, "The Meanings of De-industrialization," 14.

20 Spectacular Striptease
Performing the Sexual and Racial Other in Vancouver, BC, 1945–75

Becki Ross and Kim Greenwell

In the late 1940s, in the words of *Vancouver Sun* night-beat reporter Jack Wasserman, "Vancouver erupted as the vaudeville capital of Canada, rivalling and finally outstripping Montreal in the East and San Francisco in the south as one of the few places where the brightest stars of the night-club era could be glimpsed from behind a post, through a smoke-filled room, over the heads of $20 tippers at ringside. Only in Las Vegas and Miami Beach, in season, were more superstars available in nightclubs."[1] Fellow Vancouver journalist Patrick Nagle recalled a "show business railway" that moved largely American performers, including showgirls and striptease headliners, up and down the Pacific coast from San Francisco to Las Vegas to Seattle and on to the lush, mountain-ringed port city of Vancouver, British Columbia.[2] The city's geographical proximity to the western United States meant that talent flowed steadily south to north across the US/Canada border much more than it flowed east to west beyond the physical and symbolic barrier of the perilous Rocky Mountains. American entertainers rehearsed new material in Vancouver, often at discounted rates for discerning fans; at the same time, the burgeoning nighttime entertainment scene supplied opportunities for aspiring local talent. Professionally staged female striptease began to prosper inside the maturing city's nightspots and it contributed greatly to Vancouver's growing reputation as "home to the hottest nightclubs north of San Francisco."[3]

Despite the city's history as a key node in entertainment circuits, commercial striptease remains an unexplored contribution to Vancouver's social and economic heritage. We explore one aspect of the staging and status of striptease in post-war Vancouver. From a rich store of archival documents and 40 interviews conducted from 1999 to 2003 with retired dancers, club owners, booking agents, and musicians, we unsettle the hegemonic notion of "stripteaser" as a homogeneous category of identity and occupation. Specifically, we examine how processes of racialization shaped the production and perception of striptease in Vancouver, differentiating the ways in which white dancers and dancers of colour negotiated strategies of success and survival in this highly competitive industry. Our single city focus provides a window onto both transnational, circuit-wide trends and the specificities that made Vancouver stagings unique. We employ the racialized (and classed) geography of the city as an analytical frame, focusing on striptease in two spaces—the supper clubs of the predominantly white and affluent uptown West

Citation: Becki Ross and Kim Greenwell, "Spectacular Striptease: Performing the Sexual and Racial Other in Vancouver, B.C., 1945–75," *Journal of Women's History* 17, no. 1 (2005): 137–64.

End and the "ethnic" working-class nightclubs within and around Vancouver's Chinatown in the downtown East End. . . .

We begin our inquiry after 1945, in the context of the demise of classic burlesque and the crystallization of professional female striptease as a financially rewarding, though risky, career choice. Nineteen seventy-five marks the endpoint of both an era and our study, with the mid-1970s heralding radical transitions: the shift in the stripping business to full nudity; the replacement of live musical accompaniment with tapes and disc jockeys; the relocation of the industry from independent, free-standing nightclubs to an ever-proliferating number of hotel "peeler pubs"; the restaging of performances to include pole, table, and lap dancing, spreading or "split beavers," and showers on stage; and the cross-national movement of migrant dancers from Japan, Eastern Europe, the former Soviet Union, and Latin America in the 1980s and 1990s.[4] Revisiting the three-decade span from 1945 to 1975—a time of considerably more continuity than change in the business—we focus on what Canadian former dancer Lindalee Tracey has described as a golden era, "before striptease fell from grace because the world stopped dreaming."[5] Our findings suggest that the "gold" of this golden era was unevenly distributed among dancers. White striptease dancers dominated the "A-List" headliner category in ways that exposed the racial grammar of post-war "glamour" and "sexiness"—a grammar that simultaneously encoded dancers of colour as "novelties" with limited marketability. Further, inequalities embedded in racialized discourses of desirability had material effects: Dancers of colour earned less money, were relegated to "B-List" East End and Chinatown clubs, and were unable to invest in the same fancy costumes and props or to enjoy the same lighting, stages, and dressing rooms associated with West End marquee status. We argue that stripteasers of colour negotiated different discursive fields—both literally and figuratively—experiencing and resisting the exhibition of their bodies differently than white dancers. At the same time, we examine how some white dancers performed "exotic" racial Otherness in ways that avoided the indelible stigma of nonwhiteness in a city dominated by Anglo-Canadians until the mid-1970s, at which point waves of Asian and other non-European immigration propelled significant demographic changes.[6]

Post-War Vancouver Heats Up

The post-war business of bump and grind in Vancouver stirred opposition as it had decades earlier before the rough-edged frontier town donned a mid-century patina of sophistication. Always teetering on the edge of legality and never granted the same respect afforded "legitimate" small business operators, nightclub owners faced persistent pressure from anti-vice factions to clean up the acts. Police raids, arrests, and nightclub closures engineered to stamp out immorality and revitalize law and order discourse were commonplace in Vancouver and elsewhere throughout this period.[7] The State Burlesque Theatre was raided by the Vancouver Police Department's Morality Squad in 1946 and again in 1950, 1951, and 1952; each time its licence was revoked due to an "indecent strip act."[8] Twenty years later, the Café Kobenhavn pushed the erotic envelope to include full nudity in 1971, and two dancers were charged with obscenity under the Canadian Criminal Code. Far from succumbing to the concerted proliferation of speech and acts intended to repress and prohibit it, striptease flourished in the city's entertainment venues. Vancouver's economy thrived upon the employment options that erotic spectacle guaranteed while moral reformers protested that the "lewd and obscene" public performances destroyed communities, family values, and the nation. Undaunted by criticism and police incursions, nightclub owners began to bill female striptease as enticing adult entertainment for locals and tourists alike in the late

1940s and early 1950s. The profitability of the industry revealed the hypocrisy beneath the hysteria and helped cement the prevailing image of an increasingly cosmopolitan Vancouver at once culturally and sexually permissive. By the early 1950s, the fast-growing city of 400,000 inhabitants not only had drive-in movie theatres, 19,000 neon signs, the refurbished Orpheum Theatre, and the newly built Empire Stadium (site of the 1954 British Empire and Commonwealth Games), but also a range of nightclubs to choose from and a bevy of striptease artists to behold.

As a number of studies have shown, striptease dancers—members of the "second-oldest profession"—were, and largely still are, perceived as sex deviants.[9] Striptease has long conjured negative stereotypes of female dancers as prostitutes; nymphomaniacs; survivors of broken homes and sexual abuse; degraded victims of men's immoral lust; home wreckers; drug users; and dangers to the social order, the family, and the nation. Notwithstanding the fame and fortune garnered by a handful of striptease queens—Americans Sally Rand, Ann Corio, Margie Hart, Georgia Southern, and Gypsy Rose Lee—in the 1930s, 1940s, and 1950s, erotic dancers across North America laboured under the shame attached to the stigma of being of a "stripper."[10] And yet stripteasers negotiated the male-dominated business with courage and savvy, balancing moral condemnation of their overtly sexual behaviour with their love of dance, music, applause, and (varying degrees of) notoriety. To Canadian ex-dancer Margaret Dragu, striptease performers played the role of conscientious objector by bravely testing and defying society's sexual limits, and they experienced outsider status as "sexual offenders."[11] In effect, the business of striptease, like the city of Vancouver itself, was a jumble of contradictions: It promised women more lucrative dividends than any other service work in the "pink ghetto" at the same time that it produced them as sexual others whose acts triggered competing meanings of adulation and contempt. Attention to the social

and geographical distribution of the "heat" referenced in Vancouver's risqué reputation reveals an industry as structured by inequalities as it was solidified by stigma.

The Racialized Spaces of East versus West

After World War II, the production and consumption of female striptease in Vancouver was split along racialized lines of perceived prestige and class. All erotic dancers were measured against the idealized contours of slim, white, young, glamorous, and heterosexy femininity defined and upheld by men in the homosocial game of buying and selling erotic fantasy to other men. White "features" or "A-dancers" with their elaborate costumes, props, and sets were featured at high-end Vancouver nightclubs— the Cave Supper Club (1937–81), the Palomar Supper Club (1937–51), the Penthouse Cabaret (1947–present), and Isy's Supper Club (later Isy's Strip City) (1958–76) in Vancouver's affluent and predominantly white West End. Beginning in the late 1940s, the Italian- and Jewish-Canadian men who owned these clubs—Joe Philiponi, Isy Walters, and Sandy De Santis, among others— took their cue from the magnetic influence of Las Vegas and began to book big-name striptease dancers. Most sought after were "classy" American headliners. . . . Until the mid-1970s, all of the most famous erotic dancers who performed in Vancouver were white, American-born women who milked Canadians' fascination with talent imported from south of the 49th parallel. Scantily clad, plumed, and spangled, they worked a circuit that moved south to north across the Canada/US border; a select few worked an international circuit that included bookings in Europe. These extraordinary headliners were professionally managed, commanded celebrity status, and invested a considerable percentage of their substantial earnings back into their careers, including expensive gowns, choreography, props, music, and makeup. Salaries were as high as

$2,000 to $4,000 per week, and until the arrival of recorded music and disc jockeys in the mid-1970s, they were accompanied on stage by the top-ranked (male) jazz musicians in the city.[12]

As city residents demonstrated a hearty appetite for bump and grind, a localized industry of dancers, choreographers, makeup artists, and costume designers sprang up to supplement imported acts with regional talent. Vancouver choreographer Jack Card attained widespread renown for the elaborate Ziegfeld-inspired production numbers he staged at the Cave and Isy's (Figure 1). With striptease increasingly showcased on a nightly basis, white women from the city and surrounding area could secure regular gigs in the West End clubs. But the West End clubs were not the only places where striptease was staged. Card admitted that women of colour were overrepresented in the "B-list" and "novelty act" categories and routinely limited to employment in a tightly knit circuit of less "respectable"

East End clubs.[13] These nightclubs were owned by men of colour—Chinese, South Asian, and African-Canadian—marginalized in similar (but not identical) ways as the women of colour they employed.[14] Throughout the 1950s, 1960s, and 1970s, small nightclubs such as Lachman Das Jir's Smilin' Buddha (1953–89), Leo Bagry's New Delhi (1956–73), Ernie King's Harlem Nocturne (1957–66), and Jimmy Yuen's Kublai Khan (1960–80) in the East End's working-class Chinatown and Main Street neighbourhoods played up the "ethnic status" of their performers—not only stripteasers but also masters of ceremonies, singers, musicians, and comics—in a bid to net prospective patrons' entertainment dollars. Here, in the 1950s, striptease dancers earned an average of $50 to $100 for six nights a week which increased to $600 to $800 per week by the mid-1970s, although dancers of colour we interviewed noted that they were paid less than their white counterparts and the quality of their

Figure 1. The Jack Card Dancers, Isy's Supper Club, c. 1965. Photographer unknown.

working conditions was poor compared to the white-owned West End clubs. Card explained that performers at the East End clubs simply had to make do without the elaborate stage lights, collapsible stairways, velvet curtains, big orchestras, professional choreography, and handsome paycheques that the almost exclusively white dancers at the Cave and Isy's enjoyed. Moreover, denied liquor licences until the late 1960s (more than a decade longer than their West End rivals), East End clubs were subjected to much more intense police surveillance and raiding even as they were able to use the "forbidden" aura of the unlicensed bottle club to promote themselves as an illicit alternative. African-Canadian club owner of the Harlem Nocturne, Ernie King, harbours bitter memories of this disproportionate attention: "No one was harassed more than me. No one. It got to the point the cops would harass me two or three times a night. Because I was the only man that owned a black nightclub!"[15]

In 1967, an article in the Vancouver *Province* noted: "As a tourist attraction, Chinatown probably ranks second only to Stanley Park, and so contributes greatly to Vancouver's fame abroad. With its restaurants, stores and nightclubs, it adds entertainment spice for resident and visitor alike. . . . Few Vancouverites are unfamiliar with the color and romance of Chinatown."[16] . . . In competition with their more prestigious West End counterparts, East End clubs were both tainted and made titillating by their location in the Chinatown area. Their tendency to trade in the allure of sexual and racial Otherness indeed may have bolstered racial stereotypes, but likely served as a shrewd strategy in a city rife with (often enforced) "ethnic enclaves." For many people of colour in Vancouver, the cheaper, more accessible, and less formal East End nightclubs were considered "the place to be." Indeed, the very names of the clubs—Kublai Khan, New Delhi, Smilin' Buddha, and Harlem Nocturne— belie the myth of Chinatown's homogeneity and suggest that in the area's nightclub scene, a diverse group of communities of colour

converged, carving for themselves a social and economic space that was unavailable in other parts of the city.

At the same time, these venues also marked a popular destination for middle-class white Vancouverites and tourists who crossed the city after seeing the "big stars" at the Cave and Isy's, much as white New Yorkers travelled to such Harlem nightspots as the Hot Feet, the Clambake, and the Cotton Club, and white San Franciscans sought entertainment in the city's Chinatown clubs.[17] For some white residents, voyaging from Vancouver's West End to East End nightclubs was entangled with racialized and classed notions of "slumming it" because the East End clubs were located not only in Chinatown, but also adjacent to the area's historic skid road, Vancouver's first so-called slum district. Inhabited by waves of immigrants, unemployed poor, and mobile male labourers— loggers, sailors, fishers, mill workers, cannery workers, and miners—the East End's skid road was dotted with cheap, single-room occupancy hotels and lodging houses dating to the early twentieth century.[18] By the 1950s, the area was widely perceived as a dangerous and disorderly home to male addicts, criminals, alcoholics, and sex deviates who frequented nearby nightclubs and engaged in other morally suspect activities. The historic separation of Vancouver's East End from the West End along class lines was simultaneously rooted in racial segregation: Small communities of Chinese- and African-Canadians had residential and commercial interests in the eastern working-class districts of Chinatown, Strathcona, and Hogan's Alley, and they both owned and supported nightclubs, restaurants, groceries, and laundries after World War II. Coincidentally, the city's police station was located on the edge of Chinatown, affording the overwhelmingly white police force easy access to what they deemed the "trouble zone" of the East End.[19] Intersecting notions of gender, sexuality, race, and class thus fused the "pathological masculinity" of skid road with the resilient imagery of Chinatown as a "vice town," and ensured the quasi-illicit reputation of East End clubs, enhanced by nightclub owners' tendency to publicize promises of more skin and raunchier acts than could be found "uptown."[20] While dancers of colour had few options outside performance in these venues, white dancers regarded East End clubs as shady destinations that they generally sought to avoid. In the business from the early to mid-1970s, April Paris recalled that the East End clubs failed to eschew "that opium-tinged" connotation and seemed like "dark and strange places" to her and other white performers.[21]

"Racy" Acts: Black Stripteasers and the White Imagination

Although East End nightclubs may have seemed off limits to such white dancers as April Paris, these were the venues where stripteasers of colour, particularly Black women, were most likely to find employment. Jack Card stated that most of the city's Black striptease performers danced at the Main Street and Chinatown clubs, sometimes finding extra work at the carnival "girlie shows" of the Pacific National Exhibition.[22] . . . This is not to say that Black women never appeared at Vancouver's West End clubs. Josephine Baker, famous burlesque dancer and American expatriate, performed at the Cave in 1955, more overdressed than underdressed. At 49, her status as an international vedette still assured her top billing in the nightclub's advertisement—a status earned through earlier acts in which she catered to the fantasy of the jungle animal, dancing in banana skirt and feathers to feed white audiences' appetite for the spectacle of "savage" sexuality.[23] At the same time, however, it is likely that Baker's performance in Vancouver stirred anti-Black sentiment, coming only a few years after singer Lena Horne was denied a room by racist proprietors at the Hotel Vancouver, the George Hotel, and the Devonshire Hotel. This and other anecdotes of racism in Vancouver's more affluent clubs suggest that the East End's ethnically diverse venues may have offered a safer, less hostile environment in which Black performers could work. At the same time, club owners in this area readily exploited certain racialized stereotypes when it proved to be profitable. In contrast to the white-owned West End clubs, the East End clubs openly promoted dancers of colour, especially Black women, as "Harlem cuties," "ebony sexologists," and "Afro-Cuban specialists."[24]

While not international stars, stripteasers such as Coffee, Zoulouse, Sugar, Coco Fontaine, Lottie the Body, Choo Choo Williams, Miss Wiggles, Lawanda the Bronze Goddess, Mitzi Duprée, and Miss Lovie were among the Black women (both American and Canadian) who danced in Vancouver. Born in 1929, Choo Choo Williams grew up in the Black community of Amber Valley, Alberta. Her father was from Texas, her mother was from Oklahoma, and they were part of the migration of African-Americans who were promised free land for homesteading in Canada in the 1910s and 1920s.[25] After moving to Vancouver to marry band leader and trombonist Ernie King, Choo Choo began a 12-year dancing career (1954–66) as a professional showgirl, first at the New Delhi and the Smilin' Buddha nightclubs, and later, at the Harlem Nocturne, which she co-owned with King from 1957 to 1966. Williams was initially inspired to launch her striptease career after witnessing other Black dancers "shimmy and shake" at Vancouver's Pacific National Exhibition in the early 1950s: "I went to the 'Harlem and Havana' show at the PNE and I seen these girls up there wearing these costumes and dancing and shaking. I thought to myself, 'Gee, do they make money doing that?' I thought, 'Well, jeez, I can do that!' I seen this girl named August May Walker and she was cute. So I went and got myself some work."[26]

With little money to spend on training or fancy costumes and accoutrements, Choo Choo Williams sewed her own lavish "Carmen Miranda" outfit and did the limbo to a Latin beat: "I had a sewing machine, so I made a turban, sewed a bunch of fruit on top. I had a chiffon skirt with hooks on the front, I'd take it off and dance. I had a leopard costume, I had bras and panties with sequins and fringes, fishnets. . . . I was pretty good for a country girl who had no training. As I got older, I got bolder (laughs)." . . . Not only was Choo Choo a contributing partner to the success of "The Harlem" nightclub, but she also reaped other benefits from striptease dancing: "I could be home with my kid in the daytime and then go out and dance at night. . . . I like music, I've always liked music, and I like dancing."[27] Running the Harlem Nocturne, Vancouver's only Black nightclub, was truly a family affair and Ernie King was Choo Choo's biggest fan: "I used to like to watch the show. I got a kick out of looking at her. She could shake it up! She had some shake-up costumes! I wasn't jealous. She was being paid to dance, and I was being paid to play the trombone, and I'm playing the trombone on the stage above her and I'm keeping her in line!"[28] When she finished her floor show, Choo Choo changed her clothes and either worked as the cashier or waitressed at the club. Her religious parents in Edmonton, Alberta, disapproved of the Harlem Nocturne, and although they never said anything about their daughter's dancing "with no clothes on," Choo Choo speculated that they viewed the entertainment business as Satan's work.

At the same time that King and Williams enjoyed a measure of fame in East End entertainment circles, each noted that the doors to the West End's Cave Supper Club and the Palomar Supper Club "were pretty much closed to them."[29] King had his own band, The Harlem Kings, and he recalled the barriers to better-paying and more esteemed gigs in the West End supper clubs: "I was qualified enough to play in the Cave, but they didn't want a guy like me. They knew our Black musicians had as much talent or more than anybody else. But the owners wanted an all-white band, not a colored band with me sitting in there. It was like two different worlds."[30] Dancing at East End nightclubs, Choo

Choo remembered that she was paid about $50 a week, sometimes $100 if it was a special gig. She stated that "the white women probably made more money, but I didn't work with any. The only white women I worked with were singers, like Judy Hope and Eleanor Powell."[31]

Miss Lovie was arguably Vancouver's most successful Black dancer. She worked for 10 years (1965–75), first in the "B-List" East End clubs and in the early 1970s in the West End's Penthouse Cabaret. She eventually shifted her career from stripteaser to master of ceremonies to singer, and, at one point in the early 1970s, to nightclub owner in Powell River on the province's Sunshine Coast. Born in Texas and raised in Chicago by a working-class single mother, Miss Lovie was a pediatric nurse in Seattle when she discovered she could earn her weekly salary of $100 in three days as a striptease dancer. Miss Lovie recalled her start in the business: "I met another dancer, Tequila. She was the one that told me, 'Girl, you don't need to be at that. Get out of there, you dance too good!' So, I started dancing in a little club in Seattle, the Black and Tan with Big Mama Thornton on the bill."[32] By the time Miss Lovie moved permanently to Vancouver in 1964, she had developed an act for the New Delhi Cabaret in which she sat on the floor, bikini-clad, facing away from her audience and rhythmically twitching the muscles in her legs and buttocks to the beat of numerous Conga drums. She explained her signature act: "I made things happen with my body. I'd sit on the floor, I'd stick my legs up high, up above my head, and I'd make my butt pop. I made my buttocks work like drums through muscle control. I could move around the floor like a clock, in a circle. I did the splits. I used to do a lot of black light dancing, and I used to wear a lot of glitter all over my body. That use to be my thing: I glittered."[33]

Miss Lovie quickly became a regular feature at East End nightclubs New Delhi, Kublai Khan, Harlem Nocturne, and the Smilin' Buddha, where she was advertised as "the world's foremost exponent of Afro-Cuban dancing" and an "Artist of Rhythm." An advertisement for the New Delhi Cabaret appeared in the *Vancouver Sun* newspaper throughout the late 1960s (Figure 2).[34] Here, Miss Lovie poses on the ground, wearing a zebra-striped bikini top, fur anklets, bracelets, and ears. Another photograph of Miss Lovie in leopard-skin bikini remained on display in the window of the New Delhi long after she had retired from dancing. Like Choo Choo Williams, she was expected to embody an animal-like primitivism, and like other Black dancers, she found steady work in the East End nightclubs.

Other Black women were carefully contained and marginalized within the racialized category of "novelty act." Miss Wiggles stripped to pasties and g-string upside down with her head on a chair. Lottie the Body was an American dancer who, like Miss Lovie, invented a repertoire based in Afro-Cuban music and movement. She was also known to have balanced a chair in her teeth while nearly naked. A "fierce performer" with a "truck driver's mouth on her," Lottie danced at a range of East End nightclubs.[35]

In the 2002 documentary film *Standing in the Shadows of Motown*, she described herself as "one of the greatest exotic dancers in the world." Uriel Jones, a Motown jazz musician and member of the legendary Funk Brothers, reminisced about Lottie: "If she moved one cheek, there was a certain drum she wanted you to hit; if she moved her left foot you had to catch all of that stuff, plus keep in rhythm with the band."[36]

Vancouver-based jazz drummer Dave Davies developed a special relationship with African-American dancer Lawanda Page in the 1960s: "She was a big black woman. She and I were tight, tight friends for years. She used to be a stripper in the New Delhi Cabaret amongst other places. She had an incredible figure in those days and she called herself Lawanda the Bronze Goddess and she did a fire act. She'd light her finger and go around lighting guys' cigarettes in the club. Then the lights would go off and she'd light up the tassels on her pasties and spin them like propellers, in opposite directions. It was wonderful. After the gig, Lawanda and I would go back to the Regent

Figure 2. Miss Lovie at the New Delhi nightclub, advertisement in the *Vancouver Sun* (14 March 1969), 40.

Hotel, which was a sleazy place on Hastings Street. We'd sit up all night and talk while she sewed costumes. She was a real free spirit."[37]

Perhaps most notoriously, African-American Mitzi Duprée, originally from Los Angeles, was a crowd favourite in Vancouver, across the province of British Columbia, and throughout Alberta. Beginning in the late 1970s, Mitzi dexterously sprayed ping pong balls and played "Mary Had a Little Lamb" and "Frère Jacques" on the flute with her vagina. Wildly popular, she was arrested for performing an "indecent act" in Kamloops, British Columbia, in 1981, acquitted in 1982, and finally deported to the United States from Vancouver in 1984 after a conviction in Calgary, Alberta, for participating in an "immoral, indecent or obscene theatrical performance."[38] White women and women of colour alike recognized the wisdom of advice immortalized in song in the 1962 Hollywood film *Gypsy*: "You've got to have a gimmick, if you want to get ahead."[39] White female striptasers borrowed from a rich reservoir of symbols of white glamour, pageantry, and feminine sophistication from performers at the Moulin Rouge, the Lido, the Folies Bergère, various nightclubs on the Las Vegas strip, and on Hollywood's silver screen. By contrast, dancers of colour did not and could not invent their gimmicks and stage personas from the same set of possibilities or expectations as did white dancers who exercised a near monopoly on glamour.[40] Sometimes subtly, sometimes blatantly, club owners, booking agents, promoters, and patrons pressured Black dancers to incorporate props, costumes, music, and makeup that fit racialized and sexualized colonial tropes of African primitivism and hypersexuality.[41] Racist imagery and expectations routinely cast Black women as tragic mulattas, comic maids or mammies, or oversexed jezebels. These narrowly defined roles constricted Black women's power to perform unencumbered by white racist fantasies.[42]

Interviews with Black dancers themselves, however, shatter any illusions of a uniform, shared Black experience, and invite analysis attentive to contradictions. Miss Lovie argued that being an African-Canadian in Vancouver in the 1960s accorded her, and other Black entertainers such as singer Ron Small and MC Teddy Felton, special status as a novelty. She reminisced: "We were spoiled. Everybody wanted to be around you." Far from making her feel tokenized, Miss Lovie said that the attention made her feel "wonderful," and through her dancing, Miss Lovie may well have mined an otherwise rare opportunity to celebrate Afro-Cuban traditions of dance and music. At the same time, she shouldered a stigma that no striptease dancer completely eluded: "I upset my family, that's why I did it in Canada. And my stepdad's a minister! Women were not supposed to go out and be assertive—you were a hussy! Strippers were the low side of the totem pole, though we didn't feel that way. We felt wonderful and we made good money."[43]

Yet other Black dancers have less rosy recollections about their experiences of a still predominantly white Vancouver. Coco Fontaine began dancing in Calgary, Alberta, in 1968, and she moved to work full time in Vancouver in 1973. She described Miss Lovie as an important mentor who stood up for women of colour in the business. In the late 1970s, Miss Lovie helped Sugar, another Black dancer from Montreal, lodge a human rights complaint against the discriminatory practices of a West End club, revealing that she was far from oblivious to issues of racism. Coco recalled feeling "lots of really strong discrimination" and described Vancouver as "quite racist."[44] Painfully aware that "there were only certain jobs Black women were allowed to get into," she related a pivotal conversation with her mother, who had also worked as a burlesque dancer with the Royal American carnival shows: "'Mom, I can be a chambermaid all my life. Or I can dance.' And my Mom just laughed and said, 'Okay, if you're going to be one, be a damn good one!' And she gave me hints on how to dance."[45] Club owner Isy Walters put Coco on the road for $350 a week "to prove herself" in Kamloops, Fort St. John, Prince Rupert, Nanaimo, and Granisle, British Columbia. "In some places," she remembered, "we changed in the beer coolers."[46] Walters invented her stage name, Coco Fontaine, and her birthplace, Chicago, in order to manufacture a more exotic mystique. For years, she performed four shows a night, six nights a week, largely on the road where she made a maximum of $800 per week before retiring from the industry in 1983. She noted that white feature dancers tended to work less—only three shows a night. At an average of $1,500 to $2,000 per week and up to $4,000 for Lili St. Cyr, they were paid more and had first choice of music and colour of costumes in the mid- to late 1970s.

Former booking agent Jeannie Runnells admitted that "a lot of nightclubs didn't want Black girls, and it was harder for Black dancers to get booked in the 'A'-rooms."[47] White dancer Tarren Rae added that Black dancers "weren't as marketable." She continued: "Club owners were like, 'drop one in there amongst the mix, but don't give me a whole line up. Don't give me two Black girls, or two Chinese girls.'" Jazz pianist Gerry Palken added that "Black dancers were expected to be more erotic, more loose, do more things that supposedly would turn men on."[48] When asked whether she felt pressure to perform a primal, jungle bunny routine, Coco Fontaine laughed and said she did not need to be told. She "danced primitive" on advice from her father to "do what they expect you to do, but beat them at their own game." As a born-in-Alberta girl dancing to the beat of the supposed jungle, she remembered laughing to herself and thinking, "Oh god, you stupid fools." With satirical parody disguised within their performances, Black dancers resisted racialized, sexualized expectations internally at the same time that they staged them outwardly.[49] Still, none of the Black striptease dancers who worked Vancouver venues achieved the stardom enjoyed by some of their white peers, although as Choo Choo Williams commented, light-skinned or "high yellow" dancers

were more likely to reach higher heights in the business than darker-skinned women. Working-class Black dancers had more difficulty purchasing expensive costumes, dance lessons, props, and promotional photographs. Even if they possessed the material resources necessary to attain a career as a headliner, the colour line persisted, sutured into place by stubborn, racist beliefs about the "nature" of Black dancers and where they did and did not belong. Yet first-person accounts of Choo Choo, Miss Lovie, and Coco, among others, reveal resilient subjectivities that both accommodated and exceeded the terms of white voyeurism.

Beyond Black and White: Others Absent from the Spotlight

Despite the fact that so many nightclubs were located in and around Chinatown, none of our narrators have been able to recall more than a handful of Asian dancers. In fact, when Asian dancers were seen in Vancouver, it was most likely not in any of the Chinatown clubs, but rather as part of a "song-and-dance" show playing at the Cave or Isy's such as the China Girls or the China Doll Revue, both of which advertised Asian women "direct from New York." In spite of Vancouver's growing Asian-Canadian population, few Asian women became professional strip-teasers. Like dancer Sen Lee Fu, memorialized as "The Most Exotic Dancer of Them All" in burlesque memorabilia, and Tokyo and Japan who appeared in 1950s trade magazines, the handful of local Asian-Canadian women who found work in the business highlighted their exotic ethnicity in order to capitalize on their "novel," albeit limited, marketability.[50] Interviewees tell of local Asian dancer Suzie Wong, who wore traditional Chinese dresses and used makeup to emphasize the shape of her eyes, and Damien, who incorporated fans and jade ornaments into her act.

Other women of colour were neither exoticized nor misrepresented on Vancouver's stages: They were simply absent, unrepresented as spectacles of even the most graphically racialized sexuality. Interviews suggest that only one or two First Nations women danced in Vancouver, and they were able to do so only because they were "part-Native" and light skinned enough to pass as white, or in the case of Tia Maria, to pass as Asian. The representation of Native women, or rather the lack thereof, in striptease performance suggests that while colonial discourse cast Native women as thoroughly sexualized, as historian Jean Barman has shown, it rarely cast them as "sexy" in the idealized, ultra-feminine sense of the term.[51] The fact that a biracial First Nations dancer's best chance of success lay in passing herself off as anything other than Native reveals the uniquely denigrated status of Native women's sexuality in a province long steeped in anti-Indian discourse and practice.

Since we were able to interview only four women of colour about their experiences, we asked white participants in the business of striptease to speculate about the relatively small numbers of nonwhite dancers.[52] In the case of Black women, for example, white narrators normalized the sparse representation by referring to the general absence of blacks in Vancouver. Yet this assumption that few Black women were in the business because Black people simply did not live in Vancouver is propped up by widespread ignorance of the history and existence of the Black neighbourhood, Hogan's Alley,[53] and the larger African-Canadian community in Vancouver. For white narrators, it was likely easier to reference a "nonexistent" Black community in the 1950s, 1960s, and 1970s rather than to reflect critically on how the super-idealization of white, sexy female bodies (even those that staged "exotic" Otherness only to discard it at night's end) operated both to shape the appetites and desires of Vancouver audiences, and to shrink opportunities for nonwhite dancers in the city.

In the case of South Asian and Asian women, white narrators cited the "conservative" nature of "those" cultures, and argued that these women's families would have objected to them working

as erotic dancers. This argument fails to recognize that white Euro-Canadian women chose to dance for a living despite the fact that they too came from cultures that stigmatized their profession, and a hegemonic "white Canadian" culture which still desires to exclude them from the "national" historical memory. Indeed, whether or not Asian and South Asian women faced harsher prohibitions against careers in professional striptease than white women, the well-documented anti-Asian history of Vancouver suggests that the "exoticized" ethnicity of all Asian dancers would have had limited purchase before an audience beset with warnings of immigrant, unassimilable "hordes" from the east and the resilient imagery of "yellow peril."[54]

Impersonating the Exotic Other

Nightclub and carnival displays of Otherness also drew on the rich discursive tradition of Orientalism. In his analysis of this discourse, Edward Said used a theatrical metaphor to describe understandings of the Orient in the European imagination. Representative figures or tropes such as the Sphinx, Cleopatra, Eden, Babylon, the harem, and others, he argued, are to the Orient "as stylized costumes are to characters in a play."[55] But throughout the history of carnivals, circuses, and sideshows in both Europe and North America, these stylized costumes were literally put on and the metaphor was performed before audiences hungry for the mysteries of the Orient. From the turn of the twentieth century onwards, dancing girls at Canadian and American carnivals were regularly described simply, but sufficiently, as "Oriental dancers," and shows with such names as "Persian Palace," "Turkish Village," "Little Egypt," "A Trip to Babylon," "Mecca," and "A Street in Cairo" flourished. Here, the tourist discourse of escape used to lure white travellers to exotic destinations, especially robust after World War II, was materialized in Vancouver, where nightclub owners and Exhibition programmers marketed "naked girls" from "faraway villages" and "palaces" as cheap alternatives to vacation sites and sights beyond provincial borders. In particular, the treatment of colonized India in shows worked implicitly to sanction British imperial rule and to promote the superiority of *British* Columbian spectators.[56] An intriguing facet of such shows is that Oriental dancers were often white women, participating in yet another long-established carnival tradition—the impersonation of the Other by white performers. . . .

In 1945 Vancouver, white headliner Yvette Dare, whose trained parrot helped her to disrobe on stage, was billed as presenting a "Balinese dance to the bird god." In an interview in the *Vancouver Sun*, Dare admitted using brown makeup all over her body and revealed that Jeta, her parrot, was not actually from the "exotic isle of Bali" as advertised, but rather was "a New York

department store bargain" who had "never been nearer to Bali than Macy's basement."[57] Such a confession reveals the complex character of white performances of racial Otherness. To deploy such "exotic" trappings and then proceed to call your own bluff publicly suggests a uniquely situated form of "passing" intended to deceive no one. Recalling her "exotic" repertoire at the State Burlesque Theatre in 1951, chorus line dancer Nena Marlene noted the industry demands for Otherness, while she self-reflexively gestured to her own duplicity: "Our line filled in between the comedians, the accordion player, and the magician, and before the headlining strippers. We'd do Hawai'ian dances, and Indian tom-tom dances because we had to keep changing themes, but we weren't authentic one bit"[58] (Figure 3). . . . Even in the mid-1970s, it was commonplace for dancers—including local, Vancouver-based

Figure 3. Nena Marlene strikes a "Hawaiian" pose at the State Burlesque Theatre, Vancouver, British Columbia, c. 1951. Photographer: Jack Uter.

women—to be billed as imports from the United States and abroad in order to ratchet up the "exotica quotient" and restabilize the racialized norm that all-Canadian (white) girls were somehow innocent and immune from what was believed to be the sordid, commodified behaviour of (non-white) foreigners.

The Respectability Sweepstakes: Stubborn Legacies

As much as lines separating "good girls" from "bad girls" were drawn and redrawn between 1945 and 1975, one taboo endured: The proper, self-respecting, morally upstanding, white Canadian woman did not undress in public with the explicit goal of sexually arousing men for a living. Ironically, after World War II, professional female figure skaters with the Ice Capades and Canadian Ice Fantasy,[59] fashion models, beauty pageant contestants, magicians' assistants, female trapeze artists, and baton-twirling majorettes also wore very skimpy costumes and traded on their (hetero)sexual allure.[60] According to jazz historian Sherrie Tucker, even female big-band jazz and swing instrumentalists in the 1940s and 1950s were promoted to "look like strippers" with "gowns revealing plenty of bosoms."[61] However, the respectability of good girls (that is, nonstrippers) who performed in beauty contests, parades, magic acts, fashion shows, musical combos, circuses, and figure skating spectacles was virtually guaranteed by the legitimizing stamp of their participation in "family-oriented" entertainment in reputable venues. Of necessity, these mainstream female entertainers developed a keen sense of how to position themselves on the safe side of the (ever-shifting) class-specific, gendered, and racialized line dividing the tasteful from the vulgar.

From the late 1940s through the 1970s, television and Hollywood film popularized and glorified white female entertainers who knew all too well that their success hinged on adherence to strict norms of conventional (yet nonthreatening) beauty and conservative gender roles.[62] Mass-market, post-war ideals of white, middle-class, full-time, suburbanized wifedom and motherhood were symbolized by Betty Crocker, June Cleaver, and Donna Reed, and propagandized in women's lifestyle magazines. In actuality, the domestic stereotype was displaced by female anti-war and union activists, *Playboy* models, munitions workers, and other nonconformists.[63] Striptease dancers, both white and nonwhite in Vancouver, British Columbia, were denied association with bourgeois feminine respectability, especially after "bottomless" performance was decriminalized in the early 1970s. Even in the context of women's liberation, the sexual revolution, and the relaxation of some gender and sexual mores, erotic dancers continued to provoke shock, anxiety, and moralizing judgment among feminists and nonfeminists. No erotic dancer raising children, especially if she was nonwhite, was ever honoured for her role as mother and moral guardian of "the race." Perceived by many as no better than disgraced whores, dancers were positioned outside of discourses that elaborated what it meant to be a normal, moral, and patriotic Canadian citizen. At the same time, none of the 17 retired dancers we have interviewed ever considered herself a powerless dupe of patriarchal control, in spite of difficult, sometimes demoralizing working conditions, and a steady climate of moral opprobrium.[64] In the mid-1970s, a cross-racial union drive brought Coco Fontaine, Tia Maria, and Miss Lovie together with white dancers Lee, Tarren Rae, and Silver Fox. They fought for decent pay, decent dressing rooms with showers, and better treatment, recalled Coco Fontaine, "because we were worth it"—although race-specific complaints were never publicly aired and a first contract was never secured.[65] Stymied by booking agents and club owners threatened by the labour unrest, the dancers nonetheless took pride in their rebellious campaign for justice.

In Vancouver, whether they drew audiences to posh, upscale, West End supper clubs or grittier, downscale, East End nightclubs, strip-tease dancers and their promoters capitalized on the cultural fascination with heterosexy female bodies. What made the "naughty" art of strip-tease unique was the dancers' self-conscious, premeditated, and primary purpose to sell sexual thrills to voyeurs in the already excessively sex-saturated spaces of burlesque halls, stripclubs, and summer carnivals. White striptease dancers, including those who donned blackface or manipulated other nonwhite tropes, could take on the symbols and signifiers of the racial Other as erotic spectacle or play up the pageantry of white glamour. Indeed, they were not indelibly stigmatized by their skin colour as Black dancers and Asian dancers were. However, even the most successful white dancers courted disapproval (and criminal sanctions) for disrupting defin-itions of white femininity and respectability. Yet, ironically, the stigmatization of stripteasers as deviant, abject subjects served to stabilize the colonial myth of white female sexual civility.[66] Those men (and women) who attended spec-tacular striptease at Vancouver nightclubs could rationalize their consumption of wayward sexu-ality by assuring themselves that good (that is, domesticized, genteel) white ladies would never perform commercial striptease unless coerced and/or drugged by pimps or mobsters, as popu-lar lore would have it. And spectators could con-firm racial and sexual stereotypes that "coloured girls" on stage embodied a primordial foreign-ness appropriate to their licentious "nature" in a city visibly governed by Anglo-Canadian elites. Patrons desired and disavowed stripteasers of colour whose bodies carried the weight of white cultural projections and preoccupations with dif-ference and deviance. And yet African and Asian dancers in Vancouver from 1945 to 1975 negoti-ated racist and sexist expectations with humour, anger, courage, and irony; like other workers of colour in colonial contexts, they made difficult choices and concessions all along the way.

Inquiry into the post-war history of pro-fessional female striptease is enriched through attention to the complexity of memories narrated by retired dancers, club owners, choreograph-ers, and booking agents. In Vancouver, British Columbia, all erotic dancers navigated the thorny business of male-controlled and racially segre-gated erotic entertainment. It was not until the mid-1970s that the racialized and class-specific stratification of commercial striptease was some-what flattened out as hotel beer parlours prolifer-ated across the Lower Mainland and independent nightclubs spiralled into oblivion. With more hotel stages than dancers to fill them, white dan-cers and dancers of colour were booked into many of the same hotels, although white dancers were first offered the esteemed, local gig of "house fea-ture" and dancers of colour had to "prove them-selves" on the road. Before the explosion of hotel bars, dancers of colour were largely confined to the city's East End and Chinatown stages where prospects to attain marquee status, top salaries, and adequate working conditions were notably constrained. Our case study affords a window onto the post-war social organization of hierarch-ies of beauty, glamour, and sexiness: Elite white club owners booked "classy," Eurocentrically attractive and predominantly white striptease headliners for white, middle-class patrons. In so doing, they reproduced the classed and racial-ized divide that split the affluent West End from the impoverished East End. In a city scarred by more than a century of class and racial conflicts, some white Vancouverites were comforted by the association of working-class Chinatown with vice and immorality, and the physical and psychic distance of the East End from their tony neigh-bourhoods on the West side. Dancers of colour and white dancers were differently ensnared in these complex relations, and they resisted differ-ently. The broad category of "stripteaser" meant that all dancers shared many experiences, and our study invites us to reconsider received, racialized assumptions about the post-war "golden era" of bump and grind.

   *More online.*

Notes

We would like to thank the Social Sciences and Humanities Research Council of Canada (SSHRCC) for financial support, and Michelle Swann for research assistance. We would also like to acknowledge the trenchant, stimulating, and insightful feedback from anonymous reviewers, as well as the patient, talented editorial staff at the *Journal of Women's History*.

1. Jack Wasserman, "Saloon Crawler's Notebook," *Vancouver Sun*, 19 October 1971, A5.
2. Patrick Nagle, interview with Becki Ross, Victoria, British Columbia, 28 July 2000.
3. Wasserman, "Saloon Crawler's Notebook," A5.
4. See Estanislao Oziewicz, "Canada's Bare Essentials," *Globe and Mail*, 19 February 2000, A15.
5. Lindalee Tracey, *Growing Up Naked: My Years in Bump and Grind* (Vancouver, BC: Douglas & McIntyre, 1997), 210.
6. In 1951, the total population of British, French, and other Europeans in British Columbia was 93.2 per cent, the Asian population was 2.4 per cent, and the Aboriginal population was 2.2 per cent (other: 2.2 per cent); in 1961, British/French/other European was 93.4 per cent, Asian was 2.5 per cent, Aboriginal was 2.4 per cent (other: 1.7 per cent); in 1971, British/French/other European was 92.4 per cent, Asian was 3.5 per cent, Aboriginal was 2.4 per cent (other: 1.7 per cent). Cited in Veronica Strong-Boag, "Society in the Twentieth Century," in Hugh Johnston, ed., *The Pacific Province: A History of British Columbia* (Vancouver, BC: Douglas & McIntyre, 1996), 276.
7. Robert Campbell, *Sit Down and Drink Your Beer: Regulating Vancouver's Beer Parlours, 1925–54* (Toronto, ON: University of Toronto Press, 2001), 107–26. . . .
8. Arthur Moore to Chairman and Members of the Licenses and Claims Committee, City Hall, 5 September 1946, 28–D, File 20, City Clerk fonds, Series 27, Vancouver City Archives; "5 Convicted of Indecent Stage Show," *Vancouver Sun*, 18 January 1952, 25; and "Burlesque Show Closed; Appeal Next," *Vancouver Sun*, 19 January 1952, 6.
9. On striptease as the second-oldest profession, see Margaret Dragu and A. S. A. Harrison, *Revelations: Essays on Striptease and Sexuality* (London, UK: Nightwood Editions, 1998), 23. On the construction of the stripper as sex deviant, see James Skipper and Charles McCaghy, "Stripteasers: The Anatomy and Career Contingencies of a Deviant Occupation," *Social Problems* 17, no. 3 (1970): 391–405; and David Scott, *Behind the G-String* (Jefferson, MD: McFarland & Company Inc. Publishers, 1996), 37–8, 132–3.
10. On the pernicious imposition of shame, see Angela Latham, *Posing a Threat: Flappers, Chorus Girls, and Other Brazen Performers of the American 1920s* (Hanover, NH: University Press of New England, 2000), 113–18. . . .
11. Dragu and Harrison, *Revelations*, 53–7.
12. All examples of salaries are in Canadian dollars.
13. Jack Card, interview with Becki Ross, Kim Greenwell, and Michelle Swann, Vancouver, British Columbia, 28 January 2000.
14. Jack Card, interview with Becki Ross, Kim Greenwell, and Michelle Swann, Vancouver, British Columbia, 14 March 2000.
15. Ernie King, interview with Becki Ross, Vancouver, British Columbia, 4 February 2002.
16. Cited in Kay Anderson, *Vancouver's Chinatown: Racial Discourse in Canada, 1875–1980* (Montreal, QC: McGill-Queen's University Press, 1991), 206.
17. On racialized entertainment in post-war Montreal, Quebec, see Meilan Lam, *Show Girls: Celebrating Montréal's Legendary Black Jazz Scene* (National Film Board of Canada, 1998), filmstrip. On slumming, see George Chauncey, *Gay New York: Gender, Urban Culture and the Making of the Gay Male World, 1890–1940* (New York, NY: Basic Books, 1994), esp. 246–7. . . .
18. See Jeff Sommers, "Men at the Margin: Masculinity and Space in Downtown Vancouver, 1950–1986," *Urban Geography* 19, no. 4 (1998): 292.
19. See Greg Marquis, "Vancouver Vice: The Police and the Negotiation of Morality, 1904–35," in David Flaherty, ed., *Essays in the History of Canadian Law*, vol. 6 (Toronto, ON: University of Toronto Press, 1995), 242–73.
20. On "pathological masculinity," see Sommers, "Men at the Margin," 292.
21. April Paris, interview with Becki Ross, Vancouver, British Columbia, 30 Aug. 2000.
22. Card, interview 28 January 2000. On twentieth-century "girl shows" at carnivals, circuses, and exhibitions, see A. W. Stencell, *Girl Show: Into the Canvas World of Bump and Grind* (Toronto, ON: ECW Press, 1999).
23. See Phyllis Rose, *Jazz Cleopatra: Josephine Baker in Her Time* (New York, NY: Doubleday, 1989), 12; and Andrea Stuart, "Josephine Baker: Looking at Josephine," in *Showgirls* (London, UK: Jonathan Cape, 1999), 75–110.
24. Advertisement, *Vancouver Sun*, 21 February 1964.
25. See Bruce Shepard, *Deemed Unsuitable: Blacks from Oklahoma Move to the Canadian Prairies in Search of Equality Only to Find Racism in Their New Home* (Toronto, ON: Umbrella Press, 1997).
26. Choo Choo Williams, interview with Becki Ross, Vancouver, British Columbia, 4 February 2002.
27. Ibid.

28. Ernie King, interview with Becki Ross, Vancouver, British Columbia, 4 February 2002.

29. Ernie King and Choo Choo Williams, interview with Becki Ross, Vancouver, British Columbia, 4 February 2002. On Black histories in Vancouver, see Wayde Compton, ed., *Bluesprint: Black British Columbian Literature and Orature* (Vancouver, BC: Arsenal Pulp Press, 2001), 95–120.

30. King, interview, 4 February 2002.

31. Williams, interview, 4 February 2002.

32. Miss Lovie, interview with Becki Ross and Kim Greenwell, Vancouver, British Columbia, 22 September 2000.

33. Miss Lovie, interview, 22 September 2000.

34. Advertisement in *Vancouver Sun*, 14 March 1969, 40.

35. King, interview, 4 February 2002.

36. See Paul Justman, *Standing in the Shadows of Motown* (Vancouver, BC: Lions Gate Films, 2002), documentary film.

37. Dave Davies, interview with Kim Greenwell and Michelle Swann, Vancouver, British Columbia, 27 June 2000.

38. For press coverage, see "Ingenious Mitzi Stirs Up Strippers," Vancouver *Province*, 4 October 1981; and "Stripper Bounced to the U.S.," *Vancouver Sun*, 28 July 1984.

39. Jules Styne and Stephen Sondheim, "You Gotta Have a Gimmick," in *Gypsy*, DVD, directed by Arthur Laurents (1962; Burbank, CA: Warner Home Video, 2000).

40. See Peter Bailey, "Para-Sexuality and Glamour," *Gender and History* 2, no. 2 (1990): 148–72.

41. On the imperialist exhibition of Sara Bartmann, an African woman captured by Dutch colonizers in the early nineteenth century, see Yvette Abrahams, "Images of Sara Bartman: Sexuality, Race, and Gender in Early Nineteenth Century Britain," in Ruth Roach Pierson and Naupur Chaudhuri, eds., with assistance from Beth McCauley, *Nation, Empire, Colony: Historicizing Gender and Race* (Bloomington, IN: Indiana University Press, 1998), 227. . . .

42. Patricia Hill Collins, *Black Feminist Thought: Knowledge, Consciousness and the Politics of Empowerment* (New York, NY: Routledge, 1990), 67.

43. Miss Lovie, interview, 22 September 2000.

44. Coco Fontaine, interview with Becki Ross, Vancouver, British Columbia, 20 September 2000.

45. Ibid.

46. Ibid.

47. Jeannie Runnalls, interview with Becki Ross and Michelle Swann, Coquitlam, British Columbia, 21 June 2000.

48. Gerry Palken, interview with Becki Ross, Delta, British Columbia, 18 February 2002.

49. Paige Raibmon makes a similar point in "Theatres of Contact: The Kwakwa̱ka̱'wakw Meet Colonialism in British Columbia and at the Chicago World's Fair," *Canadian Historical Review* 81, no. 2 (2000): 186–90.

50. See Len Rothe, *The Queens of Burlesque: Vintage Photographs from the 1940s and 1950s* (Atglen, PA: Schiffer Publishing Ltd., 1997), 35.

51. See Jean Barman, "Taming Aboriginal Sexuality: Gender, Power, and Race in British Columbia, 1850–1900," *BC Studies* 115/116 (Autumn–Winter 1997/98): 237–66. . . .

52. Richie Walters, interview with Becki Ross and Kim Greenwell, Vancouver, British Columbia, 8 July 2000; Ross Filippone, interview with Becki Ross, Kim Greenwell, and Michelle Swann, Vancouver, British Columbia, 15 June 2000; Runnalls, interview, 21 June 2000; and Card, interview, 14 June 2000.

53. See Cornelia Wyngarden and Andrea Fatona, *Hogan's Alley*, 1994, documentary film, available from Video-In, 1965 Main St., Vancouver, British Columbia, Canada.

54. On the racist, anti-Asian discourse of "yellow peril," see Patricia Roy, "The 'Oriental Menace' in British Columbia," in John Friesen and Harry K. Ralston, eds., *Historical Essays on British Columbia* (Toronto, ON: Gage, 1980), 243–55. . . .

55. Edward Said, *Orientalism* (New York, NY: Vintage Books, 1979), 71.

56. On how circus spectacles featuring "Indian subjects" glorified British imperialism, see Janet Davis, "Spectacles of South Asia at the American Circus, 1890–1940," *Visual Anthropology* 6 (September 1993): 125.

57. Advertisement in *Vancouver Sun*, 12 May 1945, 6; Ray Gardner, "After Dark," *Vancouver Sun*, 12 May 1945, 6.

58. Nena Marlene, interview with Becki Ross, Vancouver, British Columbia, 27 February 2002.

59. On the careers of the Canadian Ice Fantasy skaters from 1952 to 1954, see Michael Scott, "The Original Blade Runners," *Vancouver Sun*, 2 February 2002, 18.

60. On the image of glamour constructed by and for white elite figure skaters Sonja Henie, Barbara Ann Scott, and Janet Lynn, see Michelle Kaufman, "Gaining an Edge," in Lissa Smith, ed., *Nike Is a Goddess: The History of Women in Sport* (New York, NY: Atlantic Monthly Press, 1998), 159–68.

61. See comments made in the late 1940s by trumpeter and bandleader Joy Cayler about how she was promoted in the "glossies," cited in Sherry Tucker, *Swing Shift: "All Girl" Bands of the 1940s* (Durham, NC: Duke University Press, 2000), 58–9.

62. See Susan J. Douglas, *Where the Girls Are: Growing Up Female with the Mass Media* (New York, NY: Random House, 1994), 17–20.

63. Contributors to Joanne Meyerowitz's excellent

collection, *Not June Cleaver: Women and Gender in Postwar America, 1945–60* (Philadelphia, PA: Temple University Press, 1994) acknowledge the conservatism of the post–World War II years, but argue persuasively for new, otherwise excluded histories of women in a complicated era. . . .

64. For stories of former dancers before 1980, see Ann Corio with Joseph DiMona, *This Was Burlesque* (New York, NY: Madison Square Press, 1968); Misty, *Strip!* (Toronto, ON: New Press, 1973); Annie Ample, *Bare Facts: My Life as a Stripper* (Toronto, ON: Key Porter Books, 1988); Tracey, *Growing Up Naked*; Lucinda

Jarrett, *Stripping in Time: A History of Erotic Dancing* (London, UK: HarperCollins, 1997); and Dragu and Harrison, *Revelations*.

65. Coco Fontaine, interview, 20 September 2000.

66. Anne McClintock, borrowing from Julia Kristeva, wisely theorizes the paradox of abjection: "Abject peoples are those whom industrial imperialism rejects but cannot do without: slaves, prostitutes, the colonized, domestic workers, the insane, the unemployed, and so on." *Imperial Leather: Race, Gender and Sexuality in the Colonial Context* (New York, NY: Routledge, 1995), 72.

21 Visualizing Work

From the late nineteenth century to the present day, employers have used photographs and other visual materials for a wide variety of purposes. Public relations departments employed such images not only to sell products or services, but also to project their own workers and work spaces as healthy, happy, and inviting. Since the vast majority of historical images of waged work are handed down to us from company archives or originated as commissioned material by employers, historians need to be aware that such representations of labour are inherently problematic. The materials in this section are ideal projections of working bodies and work spaces that tell us a great deal about the social expectations of workers and the spatial organization of industry and service settings. Photographs and floor plans make claims to represent the real, but when the company is commissioning the material, it is the company's point of view that is represented and circulated in advertisements, magazines, and other public venues.

In addition to the specific questions below, it is worthwhile considering some of the broader issues of absence in these images. What kinds of work were not typically photographed or advertised? How might workers themselves have represented their own work differently? Where does unwaged labour fit into our visual understanding of work?

Series 1: Rural Landscapes

The conditions of rural life underwent significant changes in the late 1800s and early 1900s. While there were variations across the country, especially as new areas were being colonized by agricultural settlement, farmers increasingly moved toward a global market economy, spurred by increased mechanization and what contemporaries called "scientific agriculture." At the same time, older forms of barter and exchange continued well into the twentieth century, as Merle Massie's chapter shows. Manufacturers encouraged the shift to capital-intensive operations at the turn of the twentieth century, and their advertisements marketed farm implements in such a way as to balance the appeal of modern labour-saving machines with nostalgic understandings of the farm as an anchor of stability even in times of economic upheaval. They had to promote the betterment of the rural ideal while also celebrating the modern industrial know-how that made their products possible to produce and, in turn, useful to the farmer. They also had to acknowledge the realities of community-based work while also celebrating the independent yeoman farmer.

Advertisements such as those in Figures 1, 2, and 3 were used in periodicals, distributed at fairs and exhibitions, appeared on broadsheets, and were featured in an ever-expanding range of ephemera given to farmers by salesmen such as postcards, greeting cards, and pocket calendars. Such a small selection of images does not teach us very much about how technology actually changed farm life, but it does provide insight into the ways in which workers and the sites of rural work were invested with deep socio-cultural meanings.

1. How are these technologies framed by gender, race, and class ideals? Why would advertisers do this?
2. How does each advertisement present the rural landscape as progressive and modern? How are work and workers represented within this landscape?
3. What elements of rural work are missing or are deliberately marginalized by these advertisements?

Series 2: Industrial Spaces

The process of industrialization transformed the Canadian economy in the late nineteenth century, but industrial work spaces continued to evolve well into the twentieth century. The scale of industrial production expanded dramatically as industries consolidated, built increasingly larger factories, and turned to scientific management techniques that "rationalized" the workforce. Rather than being dispersed across many different sites, work was centralized by industrial architects who designed large-scale workplaces that brought together power plants, machine shops, manufacturing, and transportation facilities.

The E. B. Eddy Company, located in Hull (now Gatineau), Quebec, reflected this consolidation. Established in 1854, this sprawling pulp and paper mill, located directly across the Ottawa River from Parliament Hill, expanded its production in the twentieth century to include matches, wrappings, tissue, and specialty papers. In 1919, the company boasted that its machinery and "a small army of very efficient girls" could produce 1,200 rolls of toilet paper per hour. The images in Figures 4–7 were all taken inside the E. B. Eddy facilities, roughly from the 1940s to the 1950s, and they show the different stages of production for various products.

1. These photographs clearly demonstrate a gendered division of labour within the plant. Examine how the spaces are organized. How does gender play a role in relation to the different stages of production?
2. Industrial photographers were often hired to take "heroic" pictures of both machines and workers. How are the bodies of the workers arranged in these images, and what role does gender play in positioning the bodies and machinery? How has the photographer arranged the scenes to demonstrate an aesthetic or artistic representation of the factory floor?
3. Although difficult to see, in Figure 7 there is a "pinup girl" calendar posted on a pillar in the middle of the room. What does this suggest about space, power, and the ability to enact a "gaze" (a way of looking, or having the power to look) on the factory floor?

Series 3: Selling Service

With the introduction of Pullman sleeping cars in the late nineteenth century, Canadian railway companies started to employ Black porters to offer service to first-class passengers. While some were recruited from the United States and the Caribbean, many Black Canadians also found employment in this position. Porters were responsible for cleaning, stocking, and heating or cooling the cars, as well as taking care of passengers' needs. Their duties could range from polishing shoes to mixing drinks to caring for those suffering motion sickness. Although Black railwaymen performed a wide variety of jobs for Canadian railway companies, their most public role was as porters, a position that was racially defined by the turn of the century.[1] Black porters remained a significant presence on railways even after World War II, as demonstrated by the four photographs in Figures 8–11 taken in the late 1940s or 1950s as publicity material for Canadian National Railways (CN).

1. How can you tell that these photographs are staged and not simply snapshots of everyday life?
2. Examine the sequence of the four photographs. What is the narrative or story that the company is trying to portray? Why would CN want to link the porter's home life with his work?
3. In these photographs, how are the spaces of home and work gendered? How are assumptions of class and race a part of viewing these images from the perspective of a CN customer?
4. What was the audience for such images? How might people have read these photographs differently in the 1950s from how we might interpret them today?

Series 4: Business at Work

In the first decades of the twentieth century, a revolution in corporate management and administration led to a dramatic expansion of paperwork, from general records and bookkeeping to marketing and investment management. In this period, clerical workers as a profession grew by more than 80 per cent and numbered over 100,000. As Kate Boyer's chapter reflects, such a rapid growth was only possible by allowing large numbers of women into what had formerly been a male work space. As the feminization of clerical work proceeded, men found themselves struggling to define new codes of masculinity that stressed the "rationality" of business.

Women did not, however, enter on equal terms. Employed for less pay and blocked from career advancement, women clerical workers were often viewed as transitory, entering the workforce as young adults but expected to withdraw once they were married. As Boyer explains, women also found themselves "tethered" to work stations by technologies and routines, while men exercised much greater mobility in and around the office. Similarly, the public visibility of office workers also raised questions regarding sexuality, dress, and outward appearance.

Figures 12 and 13 offer contrasting images of two Montreal offices, one from 1924 and one from the late 1950s or early 1960s. The changing technologies of the workplace are evident in both photographs and are the subject of Figure 14, an advertisement for Gestetner.

1. Comparing Figures 12 and 13, what similarities and differences do you find in the physical layout of office space?
2. From Figures 12 and 13, how is the physical space within the office gendered? How does the spatial ordering of the office reflect the hierarchical relations between those who work within it?
3. In its advertisement (Figure 14), how does Gestetner use body language and positioning to sell copy machines? How are the roles of office workers and managers gendered, both in the image and in the text?

Series 5: Servicing the Suburbs

Between 1945 and 1964, motor vehicle registrations grew by 400 per cent, and this was accompanied by a transformation in the commercial landscape. As part of the post-war growth in auto mobility, service stations became ubiquitous in Canadian cities and towns. Figures 15 and 16 represent a classic "oblong box" service station design. While companies provided franchise owners some variety to choose the best layout for their local conditions, the oblong box design was the dominant form of service station until the 1970s, and one still finds traces of them today. Using strong, visible signage, these stations offered lots of glass to allow observers to see products and services for sale; customers were encouraged to look whether or not the station was open. While service stations were thus in high demand and usage, and competition among them was stiff, they were also perceived by some to be part of the problem of urban modernity.

It was in this context that in 1962 *Imperial Oil Review*, an internal company magazine, ran a story about Joan Crowhurst's service station in Vancouver. "It's Utopia, men . . . the ladies wait on you!" A veteran of World War II, Crowhurst hired an all-female staff to work in the station. Such profiles were intended to help guide Esso station dealers and employees on the importance of good customer service, keeping facilities clean, and how to market automobile accessories. In Crowhurst's case, the magazine focused both on the uniqueness of her staff as well as her success in managing the business and winning service awards. At the same time, the discourse of gender was deeply ingrained in the text and the accompanying photographs that were commissioned to support the story. Figures 17, 18, and 19 are staged images that show women working at the service station.

1. Figures 15 and 16 show a typical service station layout. What do you notice about how the washrooms are positioned? What does this difference say about the gendering of this type of service space in the 1930s and 1940s? What might the inclusion of display racks in the mechanical bays indicate? Who is being targeted as the consumer in these spatial decisions?

2. How are the representations of traditional gender roles transgressed and reinforced in the photographs of Crowhurst Motors?

3. How are the women's bodies in these photographs put "on display" in a way that would be different from representations of men's bodies? How do these forms of display compare and contrast to the women's bodies on display in Ross and Greenwell's chapter?

4. Why might the story of Crowhurst Motors and images such as Figures 17 and 18 be so compelling for other station operators and company employees?

Note

1. Sarah-Jane (Saje) Mathieu, "North of the Colour Line: Sleeping Car Porters and the Battle against Jim Crow on Canadian Rails, 1880–1920," *Labour/Le Travail* 47 (Spring 2001): 9–41.

Figure 1. "National Cream Separator Manufactured by the Raymond Mfg. Co. of Guelph Limited," 1908. Baldwin Room Broadsides and Printed Ephemera Collection, Toronto Public Library.

THE ASPINWALL POTATO PLANTER

MARKS, FURROWS, DROPS, COVERS.   ALL AT ONE OPERATION.

Saves the work of five men and two horses in planting potatoes.   Will plant five acres a day.

FERTILIZER AND CORN-PLANTER ATTACHMENTS can be added, and by their use
Artificial Manures, Corn, Peas, Beans, &c., may be planted as desired.

THE MODERN WAY.   THE ASPINWALL POTATO PLANTER IN THE FIELD.

LE SEMOIR À PATATE ASPINWALL

Trace le Sillon, Sème et Couvre la Patate tout en même temps.

Sauve l'ouvrage de cinq hommes et de 2 chevaux en semant des patates.   Semera cinq arpents par jour.

L'APPAREIL POUR L'ENGRAIS ET LE SEMOIR A BLÉ-D'INDE peuvent être ajoutés
et par leur usage, l'on peut semer l'engrais artificiel, le Blé-d'Inde, les Pois, les Fèves, tel que désiré.

Figure 2. "The Aspinwall Potato Planter," 1885. Archival and Special Collections, University of Guelph Library. XA1 RHC A0389, MM 15 (Massey Manufacturing Co. 1891 catalogue).

Figure 3. "The Monarch of the Meadow: The Toronto Mower and the Massey-Toronto Binder: The Mighty Monarch of the Harvest Field," 1891. Massey-Harris-Ferguson, Archival & Special Collections, University of Guelph Library. XA1 RHC A0389, MM 13.

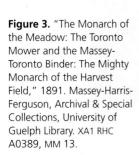

Figure 4. "Hull Upper Mill. Workmen load pulpwood logs into the grinder to produce groundwood pulp." 1951 (photo by Malak). Domtar Eddy Booth Collection, Pho-399, Canada Science and Technology Museum/Musée des sciences et de la technologie du Canada.

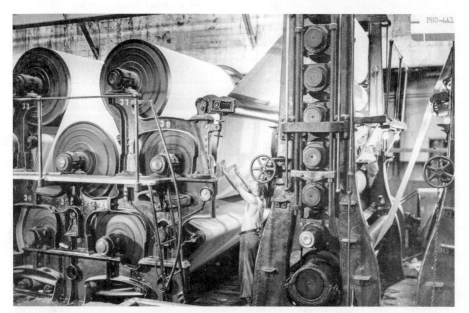

Figure 5. "Hull Upper Mill. Man checks the paper as it leaves the dryer section of Paper Machine No. 1." c. 1950 (photographer unknown). Domtar Eddy Booth Collection, Pho-441, Canada Science and Technology Museum/Musée des sciences et de la technologie du Canada.

Figure 6. "Hull Upper Mill, Tissue Converting Department. A different shot of wrapping the rolls of White Swan toilet paper." c. 1951 (photographer unknown, but probably Malak). Domtar Eddy Booth Collection, Pho-553, Canada Science and Technology Museum/Musée des sciences et de la technologie du Canada.

Figure 7. "Hull Upper Mill, Finishing Department. Female employees sorting and counting sheets of paper." c. 1951 (photo by Malak). Domtar Eddy Booth Collection, Pho-374, Canada Science and Technology Museum/Musée des sciences et de la technologie du Canada.

Figure 8. CN porter and family at table. Canada Science and Technology Museum, CSTM/CN collection/Musée des sciences et de la technologie du Canada, MSTC/CN collection, image 49315-2.

Figure 9. CN porter and family at doorstep. Canada Science and Technology Museum, CSTM/CN collection/Musée des sciences et de la technologie du Canada, MSTC/CN collection, image 49315.

Figure 10. CN porter on train. Canada Science and Technology Museum, CSTM/CN collection/Musée des sciences et de la technologie du Canada, MSTC/CN collection, image 49315-8.

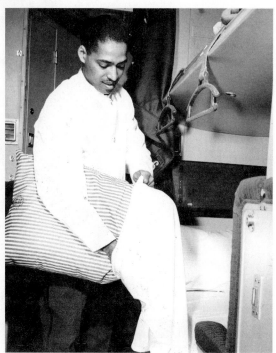

Figure 11. CN porter at work. Canada Science and Technology Museum, CSTM/CN collection/Musée des sciences et de la technologie du Canada, MSTC/CN collection, image 39403.

Figure 12. An office in Montreal, 1924. Photo by Wm. Notman & Son. McCord Museum, Montreal, view–21089. © McCord Museum.

Figure 13. Office, c. 1950s– 1960s. Canada Science and Technology Museum, CSTM/CN collection/Musée des sciences et de la technologie du Canada, MSTC/CN collection, image 55246.

Clean, Clear Copies?

Spotless. Clean Fingers, too!

Boss and Girl-Friday <u>both</u> like Gestetner—and that's <u>important</u>! He likes its clear, "printlike" reproduction. She likes running it without getting ink on hands or dress.

<u>Anyone</u> can get good results with Gestetner. Setting up the job—from a one-page letter to a price list illustrated in colours—is easy and clean. Operation is so automatic that <u>she</u> can "set it and forget it". But don't <u>you</u> forget to use our coupon!

Gestetner

1924 · *Forty Proud Years in Canada* · 1964

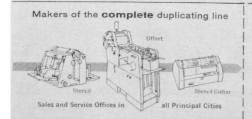

Makers of the **complete** duplicating line

Offset

Stencil

Stencil Cutter

Sales and Service Offices in   all Principal Cities

Figure 14. Gestetner, "Clean, Clear Copies?" *Maclean's*, 8 November 1964.

Figure 15. Artist rendering of Esso service station Type BT3 from the 1930s. *Imperial Esso Dealer Service Station Construction Manual*, n.d. Imperial Oil Limited Vertical Files, Box 33b, Series 33, Service Stations— Design, construction, location, Glenbow Archives.

TYPE B DESIGN PROVIDES SERVICE BAYS OF EQUAL SIZE TO TYPE A BUT LOWERS CONSTRUCTION COSTS BY REDUCING THE SIZE OF SALES ROOM AND DISPLAY FACILITIES. TYPE BT3 PROVIDES 3 SERVICE BAYS AND WILL ACCOMMODATE PASSENGER CARS AND THE LARGEST TRUCKS.

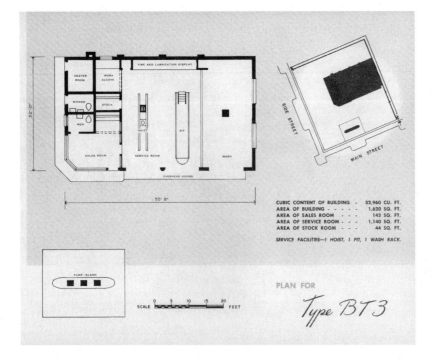

Figure 16. Floor plans for Esso service station Type BT3 from the 1930s. *Imperial Esso Dealer Service Station Construction Manual*, n.d. Imperial Oil Limited Vertical Files, Box 33b, Series 33, Service Stations—Design, construction, location, Glenbow Archives.

Figure 17. Publicity photograph showing Barbara von Schleinitz checking the oil for a male customer. IP-13m-6, Imperial Oil Limited Photographs, Glenbow Archives. Used to illustrate Bob Metcalfe, "And Check the Oil, Please, Baroness," *Imperial Oil Review*, April 1962, 14–18.

Figure 18. Publicity photograph showing Dorothy Halvorson, an employee at Crowhurst Motors. IP-13m-6, Imperial Oil Limited Photographs, Glenbow Archives. Used to illustrate Bob Metcalfe, "And Check the Oil, Please, Baroness," *Imperial Oil Review*, April 1962, 14–18.

Figure 19. Publicity photograph showing Joan Crowhurst and Pat Elworthy changing a tire. In the final article for Imperial Oil Review, the caption read "An incredulous male watches Joan and Pat get truck chains ready." IP-13m-6, Imperial Oil Limited Photographs, Glenbow Archives. Used to illustrate Bob Metcalfe, "And Check the Oil, Please, Baroness," *Imperial Oil Review* (April 1962): 14–18.

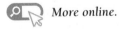 *More online.*

PART III

At Play

While the social history of home and work emerged as serious fields of research in the 1970s, the social history of play did not move into the mainstream of scholarly study until the late 1980s and early 1990s. Historians of home and work had certainly mentioned leisure activities, such as sport and tavern life, but these were often considered to be extensions of other, more significant, histories, rather than subjects to be studied in their own context. Cultural acts, such as parades, were usually framed as expressions of class consciousness, ethnic identity, or religious affiliation. Some scholars, inspired by cultural anthropology, started to view acts of play as symbolic expressions of social status, gender, or other identities. For other sites of play, especially sports history, it was university kinesiology and physical education programs rather than history departments that took the lead. Here, gender conflicts, the tension between amateurism and professionalism, and the social organization of sport were the central strands of research. Despite many calls at the time to embrace cultural history as a bridge between intellectual, social, and political history, the fields of play remained at the margins of historians' narratives.

In the 1990s, however, the line between social and cultural history blurred considerably. Inspired by new fields of study, particularly cultural studies and the postmodern rethinking of cultural representations, sites of play moved into the foreground of historical analyses. New books on exhibitions, roller rinks, tourism, and parks started to reshape what "culture" meant for historians. These works did not ignore the social or political implications of cultural acts; rather, cultural spaces became sites for asking new questions about regulation, surveillance, and resistance. This line of investigation was enhanced and extended by scholars studying sexuality, who mapped out new geographies of sexuality, traced sexual encounters in urban spaces and, in turn, questioned how heterosexuality was imposed as the normative ideal for defining spaces of courtship and leisure. As a result of these cross-currents of scholarship, historians started to question the very categories of play and how they had been socially constructed, from the expression of sexual identities to the racialized and gendered grounding of sports to the "wildness" of nature.

In the twenty-first century, two notable trends have reshaped our approach to spaces of play, building upon these earlier interpretive stances. The recent "spatial turn" in cultural geography and humanities scholarship has drawn our gaze not only to the players, but also to the playing fields and even into the stands. While the moral geographies of certain leisure spaces, such as taverns, have long been part of social history, the spatial construction and regulation of different landscapes of leisure offer new avenues for understanding discourses of power, identity, and competing claims to place. From donut shops to hockey arenas, historians are exploring how such spaces were designed, how they were imagined, and how they were used.

The second development is the conceptualization of cultural acts as bodily expressions of performance. It is not simply the space that matters, but how bodies move and behave within the space, where multiple identities can be at play. From snowshoeing on Mount Royal to "Playing Indian" at summer camp to cruising for sex in Winnipeg, spaces of play are made meaningful by the performative acts of bodies on display. Such acts also take place at the level of representation, as films, photographs, and advertisements can also perform as expressions of bodily and spatial imaginings.

These historiographical developments allow us to ask, "What has it meant, historically, for Canadians to play?" In the articles that follow, the social history of play refers to the social history of leisure, of recreation, of having fun. But the meanings of play are far more complex than the pure joy of fun. For example, dance halls, gaming houses, taverns, and even donut shops were all spaces subjected to the anxious watching of those who worried about what these spaces were doing to the moral, spiritual, and physical health of both individual bodies and the nation. Entertainment industries transformed and professionalized spaces of play, focusing less on individual acts and more on the experience of spectatorship. Over the twentieth century, advertising has shifted the moral geographies of play and behaviour, whether from the selling of toy guns to the selling of the wilderness. What scholars have shown is that we cannot artificially separate "play" from the politics, the discourses, and the social experiences of everyday life.

The concept of play as a social space is complicated by the fact that it overlaps many of the areas of study we have already examined. What functioned as leisure for some people served as work for others, while some forms of recreation were framed as proper pursuits within the home. These essays, therefore, offer an opportunity for readers to question the very division of these worlds and to examine how play was constituted by the shifting relations between home and work. They also afford the chance to think about how the imaginings of a moral geography sought to structure experiences and identities while also being contested and negotiated by a whole range of actors and organizations. How did leisure and recreational activities create boundaries of community that included but also excluded at the same time? What did contemporaries think about these communities of play, especially those that featured people of different ethnic or racial identities, from different classes, and from both sexes? How did these boundaries extend to regional or national imaginings, as the articles by Gillian Poulter and Colin D. Howell point to? How can we think of such markers and boundaries as nodes in a wider network of spaces and places within the moral geography of Canada?

These questions help make clear that having fun in Canada has been fundamental to the experience of social history, but such encounters also offered platforms for performing identities—identities of gender, race, class, sexuality, and indeed the self—while also making visible the power relations that could affirm or challenge broader structures of social organization. To separate cultural performances from the political or social realm is to create an artificial separation that depoliticizes acts and activities that were deeply political. "Playing Indian" at summer camp is not just an act of cultural appropriation, it is also an act of erasure that speaks to wider ongoing processes of colonialism.

In the course of reworking multiple editions of *Home, Work, and Play*, the section on play is the one that has changed the most over the past decade. This speaks to how rapidly the field is evolving as historians come to terms with space, performance, and the production of bodies at play. Earlier generations of social historians saw play as an extension of more established fields; in the twenty-first century, histories of leisure, recreation, and spaces of play no longer require such buttressing. As zones of interaction, of contact, of watching and being watched, spaces of play speak to the same central discourses, concerns, and social relationships that historians have long recognized in spaces of home and work.

Further Readings

Adams, Mary Louise. *Artistic Impressions: Figure Skating, Masculinity, and the Limits of Sport*. Toronto, ON: University of Toronto Press, 2011.

Barbour, Dale. *Winnipeg Beach: Leisure and Courtship in a Resort Town, 1900–67*. Winnipeg, MB: University of Manitoba Press, 2011.

Bouchier, Nancy B. *For the Love of the Game: Amateur Sport in Small-Town Ontario, 1838–95*. Montreal, QC: McGill-Queen's University Press, 2003.

Cook, Sharon. *Sex, Lies, and Cigarettes: Canadian Women, Smoking, and Visual Culture, 1880–2000*. Montreal, QC: McGill-Queen's University Press, 2012.

Dawson, Michael. *Selling British Columbia: Tourism and Consumer Culture, 1890–1970*. Vancouver, BC: UBC Press, 2004.

Dubinsky, Karen. *The Second Greatest Disappointment: Honeymooners, Heterosexuality, and the Tourist Industry at Niagara Falls*. Toronto, ON: Between the Lines, 1999.

Heron, Craig. *Booze: A Distilled History*. Toronto, ON: Between the Lines, 2003.

Howell, Colin D. *Northern Sandlots: A Social History of Maritime Baseball*. Toronto, ON: University of Toronto Press, 1995.

Kelm, Mary-Ellen. *A Wilder West: Rodeo in Western Canada*. Vancouver, BC: UBC Press, 2011.

Marks, Lynne. *Revivals and Roller Rinks: Religion, Leisure, and Identity in Late Nineteenth-Century Small-Town Ontario*. Toronto, ON: University of Toronto Press, 1996.

Moore, Paul S. *Now Playing: Early Moviegoing and the Regulation of Fun*. Albany, NY: SUNY Press, 2008.

Morton, Suzanne. *At Odds: Gambling and Canadians, 1919–69*. Toronto, ON: University of Toronto Press, 2003.

Roberts, Julia. *In Mixed Company: Taverns and Public Life in Upper Canada*. Vancouver, BC: UBC Press, 2009.

Ross, Becki. *Burlesque West: Showgirls, Sex, and Sin in Postwar Vancouver*. Toronto, ON: University of Toronto Press, 2009.

Rudy, Jarrett. *The Freedom to Smoke: Tobacco Consumption and Identity*. Montreal, QC: McGill-Queen's University Press, 2005.

Walden, Keith. *Becoming Modern in Toronto: The Industrial Exhibition and the Shaping of a Late Victorian Culture*. Toronto, ON: University of Toronto Press, 1997.

Wong, John Chi-Kit, ed. *Coast to Coast: Hockey in Canada to the Second World War*. Toronto, ON: University of Toronto Press, 2009.

Vertinsky, Patricia and Sherry McKay, eds. *Disciplining Bodies in the Gymnasium: Memory, Monument, Modernism*. London, UK: Routledge, 2004.

Wall, Sharon. *The Nurture of Nature: Childhood, Antimodernism, and Ontario Summer Camps, 1920–55*. Vancouver, BC: UBC Press, 2009.

22 "Brave North Western Voyageurs"
Snowshoeing in Montreal

Gillian Poulter

Human lives are shaped not only . . . by the ideas we have in our minds, but even more by the actions we perform with our bodies . . . we constitute ourselves through our action.
— Tom F. Driver, *The Magic of Ritual*

Cheers, applause, and a rousing rendition of "God Save the Queen" filled the air in November 1878 as the royal carriage passed under the ceremonial arch erected and manned by dozens of men dressed in the uniform of the Montreal Snow Shoe Club in honour of the arrival of the newly appointed governor general of Canada, His Excellency the Marquis of Larne, and his wife, Her Royal Highness Princess Louise. To be sure, triumphal or commemorative arches were not a new feature of public celebrations in nineteenth-century Canadian cities. In Montreal they were erected at significant sites along the route of the annual Saint-Jean-Baptiste Day parade, and elsewhere they were potent political symbols for groups such as the Orange Order. Elaborate arches decorated with evergreen boughs, flags, royal emblems, and crests had been positioned at significant sites along routes taken by both the Prince of Wales and Prince Arthur during their visits in 1860 and 1870, but this was the first

one built specifically by snowshoers. Moreover, it was not just a flimsy little structure but a tripartite triumphal arch covered with green boughs, with a circular arch in the centre and a tower on either side. "A Hearty Welcome" was emblazoned across the top around a rosette of snowshoes, dozens more snowshoes and lacrosse sticks decorated the surface, and the Union Jack and Red Ensign flew overhead. The novel aspect of the design was that members of the Montreal Lacrosse Club and members of the Montreal Snow Shoe Club, all dressed in their snowshoe costumes, had climbed up onto the structure and were waving heartily, creating a "living arch."[1]

In subsequent years, snowshoe arches became a regular feature of major Montreal civic celebrations because they were a satisfying solution to the problem of displaying Canadian identity. In 1840 Lord Durham had sought to impose English character on the French-speaking inhabitants of the United Province of Canada and to swamp them politically and demographically in a sea of British settlers. This presented the new British colonists with a challenge: how to become "Canadian" and how to show French Canadians how to be British Canadians. In the political realm, this embroiled provincial politicians in a struggle against the

Citation: Gillian Poulter, "'Brave North Western Voyageurs': Snowshoeing in Montreal," in *Becoming Native in a Foreign Land: Sport, Visual Culture, and Identity in Montreal, 1840–85* (Vancouver, BC: UBC Press, 2009): 21–64. Reprinted with permission of the Publisher. © University of British Columbia Press 2009. All rights reserved by the Publisher.

British Colonial Office for the right to responsible government—a struggle that was, nevertheless, in line with British beliefs in the principles of parliamentary democracy. In asserting the right of provincial legislatures to self-determination and rule by elected representatives, British colonists were asserting their identity as a special type of Briton and, in contrast to the United States, as a special type of North American.

But national identity is not just a political construct; to be realized (made real), it must be imagined and envisioned, embodied and performed by national subjects. Further, this performance has to be witnessed, accepted, and emulated by an audience in order to achieve widespread recognition that it constitutes a distinctive national identity. Therefore, to find out how people came to feel and know themselves to be "Canadian," we need to look beyond the political to the cultural realm and to sources that indicate how people *represented* themselves as Canadian. For anglophone immigrants and the new Canadian state, creating a national identity was problematic. Internationally, it had to distinguish Canadians from the British and Americans, with whom they shared a language and cultural and political traditions. It is certainly true that "British liberties" were highly prized and seen as a point of difference from the United States. But a British-style parliament and shared monarch gave rise to the problem of how to assert Canadian autonomy and independence and how to distinguish the nation from its imperial parent. . . . Domestically, the foreseen national identity had to unify English, Scottish, and Irish immigrants, both Protestant and Roman Catholic, as well as incorporate French Canadians and Aboriginal peoples, all of whom were proving difficult to assimilate. Montreal was the place where the cultural and political tensions between colonizer and colonized were most directly felt, and this relationship was made more complex by the fact that French Canadians were not only colonized subjects but also had themselves been the original colonizers of New France.

By the time of the British Conquest in 1760, the long history of settlement in New France meant that French Canadians felt themselves to be as much native "sons of the soil" as the Native peoples they had colonized. Nevertheless, by 1885 Canadian-born descendants of immigrants from the British Isles also felt they had a legitimate claim to call themselves "native Canadians."[2] The snowshoe arches provide clues to the ways that Montrealers grappled with the problem of distinguishing themselves from Britons and Americans to forge the "new nationality" called for by Thomas D'Arcy McGee and Robert Grant Haliburton. Mingled together on these structures were decorative elements chosen by the clubs as suitable symbols characteristic of both Canada and Britain. The evergreen boughs, snowshoes, and lacrosse sticks referred to the environment and Indigenous peoples; the snowshoes and blanket coat uniform referred to the fur trade and French Canadian culture; and the flags, royal emblems, and national anthem proclaimed loyalty to the queen and empire. As they stood waving from atop the arch, the club members were displaying the constituents of their new hybrid identity, central to which was the appropriation and transformation of the Indigenous activities of lacrosse and snowshoeing.

The Montreal Snowshoe Clubs

Snowshoeing was the first Indigenous activity to be taken up by British colonists. . . .

In 1843 the Montreal Snow Shoe Club (MSSC) was officially organized and began to hold annual competitive races. During the next two decades, 10 more clubs were started, although some, like the Beaver, Aurora, and Dominion clubs, had a fleeting existence of only a few seasons.[3] During the winter season a group of MSSC members would muster every Wednesday evening at their club rooms on Mansfield Street for a tramp to an inn or hotel, and on Saturday afternoons they might go for a longer tramp outside the city. Until the first snow, they walked to their destination via the Côte-des-Neiges road, but once snow had fallen members donned their snowshoes and began their regular weekly tramp over the mountain. At their destination they enjoyed a meal followed by some merrymaking before their return home. Enthusiasm for the sport increased over time, and by the 1880s snowshoeing was at the peak of its popularity in Montreal and other major Canadian towns and cities. In the mid-1880s there were approximately 25 clubs in Montreal, of which the MSSC alone had 1,100 active members.[4] The possibility of enjoying this activity was limited, however, to a privileged sector of society, for membership in the nineteenth-century snowshoe clubs was contingent upon social class, race, and gender.

Between 1840 and 1860 Montreal was emerging as an industrialized city, and her citizens were regrouping to form new alliances along ethnic and class lines in order to fit changing working and living conditions. . . . Professional men—lawyers, doctors, engineers, and architects—who had once served and identified with the aristocracy, now saw their interests shared more closely by the new entrepreneurial classes and formulated their own ideal of service as justification for working for a living. Small-scale entrepreneurs—merchants, storekeepers, contractors, and businessmen—as well as salaried managers, journalists, accountants, and clerks, shared the liberal leanings of the professional men and saw themselves as distinct from both the landed elite and the working poor. It was this middling group, which I describe as the professional and commercial middle classes, that made up the bulk of sports club membership in the second half of the nineteenth century. Club membership was a way for these men to publicly claim and display their status. Inspired by liberal individualism and evangelical zeal, the members jealously guarded their reputations as respectable, hardworking citizens. This distinguished them from the ultra-rich, members of what Brian Young calls "the patrician elite,"[5] namely the wealthiest, most powerful, and most well-connected

families, such as the McCords, the Molsons, the Redpaths, and the Allans. These families were a colonial aristocracy, and their interests and allegiances were often oriented toward Britain rather than Canada. They belonged to exclusive sports clubs such as the Montreal Hunt Club or the Montreal Curling Club that promoted British rather than Indigenous sports, and they were much less interested in asserting their Canadian identity than they were in maintaining their ties and allegiances to England.[6] As a commentator in the Toronto Globe so aptly put it, "Though living among the other settlers they were not of them."[7] In contrast, the vast majority of members of the snowshoe clubs were either new immigrants from the British Isles or Canadian-born, English-speaking Montrealers who felt strong ties of loyalty to the empire while still desiring to make for themselves an identity as Canadians, as demonstrated by the public debate over the participation and identity of "native Canadians."[8]

French Canadians made up only a small percentage of club members, even though they constituted almost half of the population of Montreal at mid-century. They were not actively discouraged from joining, but the need to be sponsored by two existing members mitigated against their membership, as did the fact that there were far fewer francophones than anglophones in the professional and commercial middle classes, which accounted for the bulk of snowshoe club memberships. Sports facilities were concentrated in the anglophone West End of Montreal, and clubs often appealed to specific constituencies (the St. George's, St. Andrew's, and Emerald clubs would hardly have appealed to French Canadians), so this too mitigated against francophone participation. Exclusively French Canadian clubs such as Le Trappeur and L'Union Commerciale were not formed until the end of the 1870s and gained greater popularity in connection with the Winter Carnivals in the 1880s. Admittedly, the Canadian Snow Shoe Club was founded in 1870 "in the hope that it might encourage the practice of the sport among young French Canadians," and by 1873 half of its 50 members were French speaking. However, it is apparent from a newspaper account of the annual dinner of that year that the leadership and conduct of the club were dominated by English-speaking members.[9] It was re-formed in 1878 as Le Canadien, a French Canadian club.[10] In general, before 1880 French Canadians were either uninterested in participating in snowshoeing, rejected it because it was dominated by anglophones, or were respectful of the Catholic Church's disapproval of organized sports as being a morally dubious and subversive force.[11]

. . .

Native people initially participated in the annual races that were a feature of the Montreal snowshoeing season but were increasingly excluded when the number of snowshoe clubs grew dramatically after 1868. Whereas in the early years Native people competed with whites in all the events, over time they were restricted to entering a few specific "Indian Races," retained largely because they were a crowd-drawing spectacle. Native people had little power to resist their exclusion but took whatever opportunities they could to turn the situation to their advantage. For instance, at the 1873 Maple Leaf Snow Shoe Club races, the white contestants protested when a race was won by Peter Thomas, a Native snowshoer. The protest was decided in favour of Thomas since the race had been advertised as "open," although the race organizers had intended this to mean open to members of other clubs. Thomas had challenged this by entering the race, and the principle of fair play overrode racism in this case.[12] It was probably not a coincidence that shortly afterward the Montreal Pedestrian Club became the first Canadian sports club to adopt a definition of amateur status. This excluded anybody who had ever competed for money, or had ever been paid for any reason in connection with athletics, or "is a labourer or Indian." This effectively disqualified all the celebrated Indian runners, snowshoers, and lacrosse players.[13] There was further controversy at the 1875 Caledonia Snow Shoe Club races over the running of the "Indian race" owing to a rumour that the first and second contestants had shared the prize money. White members were "outraged," mostly through fear that this would have a deleterious effect on the viability of the races because the "Indian races form one of the attractions of a snowshoe race, and should be contested fairly and honestly." Even more blatantly contrary to white intentions was the running of the Indian race at the 1875 Grand Military races, when the leading snowshoer fell and the next runner waited for him and let himself be overtaken, thus losing the race. Although the protestations made by white commentators in these cases were probably the result of concern over fair *gambling*, they were couched in terms of the need for fair *play*. At other times, for instance when Native snowshoers entered the "open" race or when players did not "dress up" as the white man's Indian, Native people refused to be complicit in their own oppression. This, for instance, led white commentators to complain that the war costume worn by Natives in the Ottawa Snow Shoe races of 1873 "was not calculated to strike awe into the hearts of strangers."[14]

Women were generally excluded from participation in the snowshoe clubs and team sports because they were considered unsuited to women's supposed physical and mental frailty. Members of "the fair sex" were mostly associated with snowshoeing as desired spectators, especially at the annual club races, when efforts were made to make them more comfortable by spreading the stand with tarpaulin.[15] . . .

It is unclear when women began actively snowshoeing with the clubs. . . . [B]y the 1880s some women were active snowshoers, albeit not as club members. In 1889 an illustration from the *Dominion Illustrated Monthly* depicted women snowshoers mustering at the McGill Gates, and in 1903 N. M. Hinshelwood reported: "the ladies are as enthusiastic as the men."[16] At times women were included for the rhetorical purpose of proving the vigorous nature of Canadians as a race. A cartoon of 6 April 1872 in the *Canadian Illustrated*

News showed Canadian women as proficient snowshoers, while a male visitor failed miserably, which indicates that nationality could transcend gender when a patriotic comparison was desired.

To be sure, there was also an element of sexual titillation involved in women participating in the manly sports of snowshoeing and, later, tobogganing. In fact, by the 1880s sports activities had become an opportunity for young people to mix socially. Writing in 1928, W. S. Humphreys claimed that private couples' clubs had existed 50 years earlier, thus affording the opportunity for courting.[17] This was also the purpose of the skating parties initiated by Lady Dufferin at Rideau Hall in the 1870s, and [Dr. W. George] Beers commented that the skating rink "has become a sociable club for both sexes, where they may meet and enjoy a chat, etc, as well as skate."[18] A snowshoe club was even formed to facilitate social intercourse for young Montrealers—the policy of the Mary Bawn Club was apparently to enrol brothers and sisters jointly so that every girl would have an escort on the weekly tramp, but this did not always turn out to be her brother.[19] . . . The writer of *Bishop's Winter Carnival Illustrated* positively revelled in the titillating possibilities snowshoeing presented for publicly touching female flesh: "the foot of feminine gender looks its prettiest in a well-fitting moccasin. It is more attractive, and tying on the snowshoe the thongs pass over the arched instep and around the neat ankle; and the strings get loose so often, and the shoe comes off at the fences. Thus the gallantry of the stern escort is called forth very often. In this kind of snowshoe tramp, needless to say, they do not walk in Indian file, they saunter along two by two, and very often continue to do so through their after life."[20]

Men, of course, never needed help with their laces!

The Snowshoe Costume

Just as snowshoeing was appropriated because it was considered a characteristically Canadian activity, the uniform adopted became a characteristically Canadian "look." The snowshoe clubs adopted a uniform that consisted of a white blanket coat tied with a long sash around the waist, worn with leggings, moccasins, and tasselled tuque. By the mid-1870s each club had its own distinguishing colour scheme for the epaulettes and trim on the coats and for the matching tuque and stockings. Dr. Beers, for instance, was photographed in the William Notman Photographic Studio wearing the uniform of the St. George's Snow Shoe Club: white coat with distinctive membership badge, purple epaulettes, and purple and white tuque (Figure 1). Since the snowshoe clubs from time to time made rules regulating the colour, style, and detailing of their respective uniforms and stipulated when they should be worn, it is clear that these clothes were not just everyday winter wear but actually a special set of clothing that one wore when snowshoeing.[21] In putting on this uniform, the snowshoe club members were dressing up as "composite natives": the moccasins and leggings were Aboriginal, the woven sash was a French Canadian *ceinture fléchée*, the tuque was a French liberty cap, and the blanket coat resembled typical habitant winter clothing cut from the blanket cloth associated with the North West fur trade.[22]

The existence of cross-cultural exchange between Native and European is well recognized, but emphasis is usually placed on the impact of European tools and technology on traditional Native culture. Similarly, attempts to assimilate Indigenous people to white culture have been discussed in many different contexts,[23] whereas the cultural appropriations made by Europeans of Indigenous cultural activities and the assimilation to Native culture by the colonizer have "not been made much of," according to Olive Dickason.[24] In snowshoeing, we can see the ways that the culture of the colonized determined national culture. As the British were not the first colonists of North America, in appropriating Native culture they were also appropriating aspects of French Canadian culture. For if

Figure 1. "Dr. W. George Beers, St. George's Snowshoe Club, Montreal, 1881." Source: Notman Photographic Archives, McCord Museum, Montreal, II-60469.1. © McCord Museum.

we look back in the history of snowshoeing in Canada, we find a succession of erasures. Early explorers who arrived in the New World were at first startled by the strange "gutted shoes" worn by Native peoples but quickly realized what an efficient method of transportation they had devised. During the French Regime, the military, habitant farmers, *engagées* in the fur trade, and unlicensed *coureurs de bois* all used snowshoes as a matter of course. So when British merchants and settlers arrived after the Conquest, snowshoes in their eyes were as much an attribute of French Canadian culture as they were of Native peoples, and they considered both groups to be "native." . . .

. . . [T]he snowshoe tramps were cultural performances in which members envisioned themselves as Nor'Western voyageurs. The Nor'Westers were members of the North West Company, which had originated as a loose association of Scottish, English, and French fur traders based in Montreal. They were in competition with the British-run Hudson's Bay Company until the two outfits merged in 1821. Imagining themselves as members of a fur brigade linked snowshoers to the history of the fur trade, in which Native peoples and French Canadians had a shared history. Thus snowshoers were enacting a cultural fiction, and their clothing invented memories of Canada's "olden days," linking British colonists to the Aboriginal and French Canadian past of the continent. Snowshoers positioned themselves within an invented mythological national past and appropriated the visual attributes of both the Aboriginal and French "real" Canadian Natives in order to do so. Organized club snowshoeing functioned to usurp and erase the Aboriginal and French Canadian histories of snowshoeing, rendering them instead as part of the British history of Canada. Organized club snowshoeing therefore allowed colonists to link themselves with selected aspects of the history of the continent, and since the activity itself was Indigenous, performing it naturalized them as "native Canadians," whether they were Canadian-born or not.

The Tramps

. . . During the 1870s and 1880s, when a plethora of snowshoe clubs were in existence, their members mustered on different week nights to make the trek "over the mountain." This regular route and routine made the presence of snowshoers a common occurrence on the streets of Montreal. They were considered a novel and picturesque sight and constituted a distinctively Canadian "look" that was photographed extensively. "Picturesque," a term associated with painting and drawing, was popularized by William Gilpin in the late eighteenth century and persisted throughout the nineteenth century.[25] It referred to a system of composition by which a landscape was made "pleasing" through a careful combination of "rough" and "smooth" elements. Rustic figures were positioned in specific areas of the composition to provide interest and indicate scale. . . . When nineteenth-century newspaper writers recorded the "picturesque sight" created by snowshoers, it implied that the figure of the snowshoer evoked rustic connotations, namely that these were figures reminiscent of a rural idyll from days gone by, nostalgic reminders of "Old Quebec." Thus, if the snowshoers were considered picturesque and rustic, it meant that they were seen, and saw themselves, as engaged in re-enacting historical activities closely linked to the rural landscape.[26]

. . .

Harkening back to the days of the fur trade, when it was the custom for traders to meet at posts in the North West, sociability was always a principal feature of MSSC routine. The destination of every tramp was an inn or restaurant. Once arrived, the snowshoers would enjoy a meal

punctuated by toasts, then someone would start up a tune on a piano or other musical instrument, and the members would join in with songs and dancing. To convey a sense of their activities at the club rooms for the concert audience, several members performed a series of musical entertainments, including piano and violin solos, duets and choruses, and a comedy turn called "The Governor-General's Body Guard." Similar stories of sociability are told about the voyageurs in their winter camps and about the Beaver Club, whose meetings were held in Montreal in the winter season, beginning at four o'clock on Wednesday afternoons and often going on into the small hours of the morning.[27] The Beaver Club was founded by elite members of the North West Company in 1785 and lasted until the early 1820s as a dining club whose membership was restricted to active and retired fur traders who had wintered in the *pays d'en haut*. Those members who were not wintering in the north met at various hotels or taverns in Montreal for "winter bacchanalian feasts" at which they would sing voyageur songs and reminisce about their adventures in the trade. As Carolyn Podruchny has demonstrated, those occasions celebrated the masculinity and fraternal ties of the trade.[28] The snowshoe club socials played a remarkably similar role: After a meal some songs would be sung, the men might dance (a red armband being used to denote the "female" partner), or they might tell tales of club exploits from "long ago." But unlike the notoriously riotous Beaver Club meals, this was decorous and temperate carousing, as befitted the respectable image cultivated by middle-class men of their time.[29]

. . .

The National Landscape

. . .

Although at 759 feet Mount Royal is in reality not much more than a large hill, in the popular imagination "the mountain" is a key feature of the city and its history. Situated one and a half miles outside of the old city walls, Mount Royal was originally regarded as being out in the country. In the 1850s urban development reached the southern slopes, where the first large mansions were built, and by the 1870s commerce and housing were well developed along Sherbrooke Street at the base of the eastern slope of the mountain and along St. Laurent Boulevard to the north.[30] Until the twentieth century, Mount Royal was believed to be an extinct volcano, and Dr. Beers, who was never averse to a little hyperbole when it suited his purposes, likened the snowshoers to "Basque Mountaineers" as they "scale the mountain and descend the farther side," a distance he reckoned at two and three-quarter miles.[31] A composite photograph produced by the Notman Studio portrayed the club's destination in 1872 as an isolated country outpost, when in fact it was situated on the well-travelled Côte-des-Neiges toll road, only a short sleigh ride from the club rendez-vous at the McGill Gates. . . . This tendency to exaggerate the size and ruggedness of Mount Royal is evident in reports of the Torchlight Snowshoe Parade held in honour of Lord and Lady Dufferin in 1873: "The route lay along the mountain slope, over hill and dale, fence and wall, occasionally through the bush, here a gully had to be jumped, there a steep descent made, requiring all one's agility to avert a tumble. On, on went the line of fire, the irregularities of the ground adding to the effect as the procession now meandered through the trees and again broke into a jog trot across the plain."[32] This litany of geographic features—slope, hill, dale, bush, gully, steep descent, meander, plain—has the effect of moving Mount Royal far outside the city, expanding the size and scale of the landscape, and increasing the apparent difficulty and isolation of the tramp. In fact, in very successful years, such as 1878–9, when there was snow from the end of December right through to the beginning of April, the weekly tramps of the numerous clubs would have taken only 30 or 40 minutes on an easily followed, well-beaten track

over the mountain to the well-established and growing rural communities on the other side.[33]

. . .

These representations of the landscape of Mount Royal imagined it as more than just a large, treed hill and portrayed it instead as a wilderness space apart from the city: wild terrain in which men experienced the harsh and unforgiving Canadian climate. Symbolically, surviving and triumphing in this environment were part of a cathartic indigenizing experience through which the snowshoers proved themselves worthy successors of the Nor'Westers. That the route over the mountain began with an ascent of the steepest face, which was also the route of frequent steeplechases, was not coincidental. The vigour of the performance trained and transformed the body. The snowshoers' ability to reach the top demonstrated their "bush masculinity."[34] They had the qualities of endurance, stamina, and skill admired in the *hommes du nord*, the most experienced and skilled of the voyageurs.[35] It proved they had the manly "pluck" and Native ability required to overcome Canada's natural obstacles and could claim to be Haliburton's "Men of the North" themselves.[36] Furthermore, when members arrived at "The Pines," they had reached the summit. They had physically conquered the mountain and were in a commanding position, being visually and strategically in possession of the city and its environs. . . .

The terms in which these tramps are described indicate that the snowshoers saw themselves as latter-day pioneer explorers, facing down obstacles of terrain and climate to reach their destination. The ability to survive and navigate in the wilderness was a skill lauded by snowshoers, and mapping was an important modern skill in Victorian Canada, but there is no mention of the use of maps in the records or reports of the MSSC. Instead, club tales commemorated feats of instinctive navigation, as for instance in March 1879 when President Angus Grant "made an exact beeline" from the eastern promontory of Mount Royal to the church spires of St. Vincent de Paul. "It was one of the best calculated 'lines' in the history of the Montreal [club]."[37] This was considered all the more remarkable since the spires would have been out of view for most of the tramp and he did not use a compass, just his "natural" or "Native" sense of direction. Not needing navigation aids demonstrated the degree to which the snowshoers were "at home" in the environment—only a "native Canadian" could show such ability. Times when the troop got lost—such as on another visit by the MSSC to the village of St. Vincent de Paul when they "went 15 miles astray" and on the famous race to St. Hyacinthe when one group made three miles in 25 minutes, while another "found themselves, after half an hour's hard running, further from the 'Mountain House' than at the start"—were also memorable because they illustrated the difficulty of navigating in "the wilds" and demonstrated the pluckiness and stamina of the snowshoers who survived the difficulties.[38] In one of his articles, Beers conjured the image of intrepid snowshoers finding their way through uncharted territory in bitter winter weather while refusing all assistance:

> A real Canadian winter day, my friend! How the nipping wind whistles . . . snow blows a blinding storm, like a shower of needles in your face, obliterating any track if there was one. But stiffening your lip you never think of once giving in . . . you have to cross country, taking fences and brush on the way, directly due north . . . The snow has filled the roads, and in many places tracks are made for sleighs . . . but the snow-shoers turn up their noses at beaten tracks and keep on due north. As you cross a highway some habitant . . . offers . . . a drive in his sleigh, but to drive now would be dishonour . . . The lay of the land is indistinct in the sweeping storm. The wind whistles as at sea. But for your snow-shoes you might resign yourself to an untimely cold end.[39]

Beers emphasizes that in potentially fatal cold the snowshoers were travelling across country, eschewing tracks or roads, cutting across lines of settlement in a northerly direction. In doing this, they were enacting a pioneering expedition, going where no white men had gone before, or . . . re-enacting the cross-country treks of the Nor'Westers by leaving Montreal, the home base of the fur trade, and making their way across country to the rural hotel, which stood in for the fur trading post.

. . .

The snowshoe tramps can, therefore, be read on several levels as what Richard Gruneau has termed "a meaningful dramatization" of the Canadian past.[40] The city was the modern metropolis from which snowshoers set out to colonize the surrounding wilderness. At the same time, they were acting out symbolic treks from modernity into the historical past. The repeated penetration of the wilderness and return to the city simulated life in the North West fur trade and thus linked snowshoers to the French Canadian and Aboriginal histories of the nation. The indigenizing experience of the tramps further transformed foreigners into Natives; these middle-class merchants and professionals were substituting themselves as the new "native Canadians" and writing themselves into the history of the colony.

. . .

Snowshoeing was a cultural performance that worked to construct national identity because it was an Indigenous and indigenizing activity that brought members into contact (and sometimes conflict) with the landscape. The *performance* of snowshoeing was vital to members because it was a romanticized re-enactment of the historical past of the nation and thus a way to become and to feel oneself native in a foreign land. Snowshoeing and the imaginative re-creation of the landscape allowed the snowshoers to imagine the nation as a space and themselves as a people. The reports of their activities and the publicity their concerts received in the local press allowed this identity to be recognized by others. Hence, just as the exaggeration of geographic features extended and generalized the landscape around Montreal and represented it as a national space, so too did the physical performance of the tramp and the landscape in which it was enacted become characteristic of the nation and its citizens.

The significance of the active performance of snowshoeing should not be underestimated. To be sure, social relationships and power hierarchies are constituted and made explicit through bodily practices; but there is more to such practices than this. Paul Connerton has persuasively argued that physical performance plays an essential role in the construction of social memory. As an activity that became habitual through repetition and clearly observed rules of decorum, snowshoeing constituted what he calls a "mnemonics of the body."[41] The physical act of performance constructed cognitive knowledge and memory of the "proper" characteristics of the white, male Canadian body. Moreover, acting out these myths of origin caused the performer to feel himself part of that history on a conscious, cognitive level, and through bodily knowledge this feeling became a matter of fundamental belief, a sensation of physical rootedness in the land. . . .

Snowshoeing as an "Organized" Sport

. . . [M]odern organized sports are differentiated from premodern folk games and children's play by the way that a hierarchy of clubs, teams, and leagues is established with shared rules and regulations that govern the game as well as apparel, equipment, site, behaviour, and so on. Snowshoeing straddled the divide between premodern and modern sport. Sport historians Don Morrow and Kevin B. Wamsley call snowshoe clubs "the pivotal and transitional activity through which Montreal sport was ushered into the modern era of commercial organized

sport."[42] It was not a team sport, but once snowshoe clubs were founded, it was transformed into an organized sport with increased emphasis on competition. Regular races were organized, and clubs competed with each other on an inter- and intracity basis. The snowshoe clubs were run in a modern, businesslike fashion. There was a written constitution, membership was carefully controlled through a voting system, and a group of executives was in charge of scheduling tramps, arranging banquets, renting rooms, formulating regulations, accounting, recordkeeping, and so on. Furthermore, technical "improvements" such as lighter, narrower shoes were adopted to make the sport a more "modern," "civilized," and "scientific" activity. Club members favoured these new shoes because they facilitated competitive racing, but they were inadequate for the needs of hunters or lumberers, thus completing the transformation of snowshoeing from utilitarian to leisure activity, from historical to modern.

The clubs were formed not just to promote physical exercise, for that was not their only cultural function. They were also instrumental in promoting and inculcating desired behaviours and values. The "English character" that Lord Durham sought to impose on French-speaking Canadians combined manliness and a desire for order and hierarchy with admiration for modern progress and science. Manliness was an ideology that combined physical prowess, stamina, and "pluck" with mental discipline, loyalty, and moral virtue. Although industrialization did not get fully underway in Montreal until the 1860s, even by the 1840s ideas about class, gender, and race had created a masculine, white, colonial, bourgeois identity based on the belief that hard work was its own reward, and moral conduct rather than material wealth was a measure of success and usefulness in society. As recent scholarship shows, this was a profoundly gendered identity, one in which the male was the measure of all things and women were considered the subordinate repositories of moral virtue.[43] Similarly, the manliness of the strenuous outdoor activities of the snow-shoe clubs was emphasized by the exclusion of women from active participation. Whereas women's virtue was located in the home, middle-class men demonstrated their virtue in the fraternal associations and networks that gave their lives meaning and conferred status. Sports clubs, and associational life in general, were a place outside the home in which this code of middle-class, respectable, manly behaviour was formulated and inculcated.

As early as 1842 snowshoeing was referred to as "manly exercise," a term that would be reiterated countless times over the next five decades as its status became increasingly elevated and linked to the nation. In 1868 snowshoeing was called "the manliest and best of all sports." In 1872 it was "a healthful and manly exercise, besides being a purely national pastime." And in 1870 a commentator in the Toronto *Globe* opined that national greatness was not just dependent on commerce or intellectual and moral training but also required "*the development of the physical energy of the people.* Let Canada . . . learn that health-giving and sport-elevating recreations tend to dispel effeminacy from any people."[44] Hence strenuous sport and the homosocial character of club activities were considered antidotes to feminized society.

Manliness had several connotations. The ideal snowshoer was "plucky" with a "never-say-die" attitude; he had tremendous stamina and a healthy constitution, and he was loyal to his nation and the empire and ready to fight when called. These were essential components of what sport historian Don Morrow has so aptly called "the snowshoe ethos," and they were encouraged and imbued by vigorous outdoor exercise and the exclusive company of men.[45] This code of manliness assumed its members would also be models of moral virtue. Thus when an article appeared in the *Montreal Daily Witness* on 6 February 1873 that condemned the presence of "an unlimited supply of champagne" at the dinner given for the governor general by the

snowshoe clubs, which purportedly had disastrous effects on the young boys present, it was considered a serious black mark. An editorial a few days later informed readers that the "presidents of two of the snowshoe clubs" denied there was any "uproariousness as the result of the use of champagne," but the criticisms were apparently deemed so damaging that a libel suit was filed against the *Witness*. A subsequent letter from "an old snow-shoer" published in the *Montreal Gazette* of 27 February 1873 indicated that the suit had been decided against the *Witness*. The writer claimed that most of the snowshoers at the tramp were married men, not "lads." He affirmed that "snow-shoers are proverbially small drinkers, and do not look to intoxicating drinks for that strength of wind and limb so necessary to carry them over our tough mountain track, our weekly tramp to Lachine, or elsewhere."[46]

This incident illustrates the gravity with which the snowshoe clubs viewed accusations impugning their moral propriety. The temperance movement was strongly supported in Canada East, where half the population were teetotallers in 1850. The MSSC was particularly jealous of its reputation, and its executive asserted that the club was not an excuse for intemperate drinking. This was not the first time snowshoeing had been linked to drinking, for a newspaper report of the annual steeplechase held a month earlier had defensively averred that "a tramp across the mountains is not, as some think, an excuse for liquor drinking, a cup of good hot coffee being all that the boys desire."[47] In March, after another steeplechase up Mount Royal, a reporter noted "the frugal meal snowshoers affect."[48] In fact, liquor and wine were always forbidden from MSSC meetings, and even malt beer was prohibited in the mid-1870s. The St. George's Snow Shoe Club's rules also prohibited "card playing and the use of spiritous liquors in the Club room."[49] However, complaints continued to plague the clubs from time to time, and Beers came to their defence again in an 1877 article. He claimed that at the weekly club suppers, there was "never a breath of vulgarity, perhaps too much smoking, but never any drinking; always the restraint of gentlemen with the *élan* of healthy athletes."[50] Notwithstanding these avowals of temperance, there were again complaints about drinking and misconduct, notably the firing of guns on the streets after an annual MSSC dinner held at the Windsor Hotel in February 1878, at which drinks were again allegedly available to youths.[51]

. . . [The snowshoe clubs] facilitated indigenizing forays into the countryside, as well as being a space in which the newly emerging professional and commercial middle classes could construct and rehearse their class and gender identities. However, they were also a place where members could safely transgress these identities. James Scott argues that the powerful have a vital interest in keeping up the appearances appropriate to their form of domination within their own social circle. They demand a performance of deference and loyalty by subordinates, and in public they show themselves as they want to be seen in order to affirm their power and euphemize their misdeeds. He calls this the "public transcript." What they keep hidden from subordinates in order to maintain their claim to power—their "dirty linen"—he calls the "hidden transcript."[52] Since middle-class values eschewed drinking and excess, the public transcript proclaimed by the snowshoe clubs officially proscribed such behaviour; thus the struggle these men had with sobriety could be concealed in the safe space of the club. The clubs may have been a refuge in which they could from time to time indulge in alcohol privately, without compromising their respectability by being seen drinking by subordinate "others."[53] The whole range of practices that the snowshoe clubs invented were ways that the public transcript instilled, proclaimed, and maintained their social status—although not always with total success.

. . .

Performing Identity

. . .

The rules and regulations of the snowshoe clubs promoted particular characteristics and values that provided the basis of a shared group identity—how "an 'I' became a 'we,' a 'me' became an 'us.'"[54] Through club membership and the interaction between clubs, men were able to recognize a consciousness of kind that was middle class, masculine, and predominantly Protestant. In a time when the Roman Catholic proportion of the population in Montreal was growing due to the influx of Catholic Irish immigrants and rural French Canadians, Indigenous sports clubs may have been a way to forge a Protestant/Scots/British identity, but they also established a new Canadian stereotype—the physically vigorous, outdoor-loving "Canuck" who was at home in the iconic northern landscape and rigorous winter climate. By demonstrating their ability to survive and navigate in the Canadian environment, the snowshoers justified their claim to be a new type of autochthon.

Historians have paid some attention to the idea that class is "presented," "demonstrated," "exhibited," and "displayed" (i.e., made visible), but few take it seriously as an enactment—a performative act that is constitutive.[55] On the tramp, identity, time, and space intersected and blended together;[56] by emulating the heroic past as signified by the exploits of the Nor'Westers and Beaver Club members, the snowshoers wrote over the history and contributions of both French Canadian and Native peoples and constructed myths of origin that constituted the foundation of a new British history. This was a highly restricted, middle-class notion of citizenship that did not include women, Native peoples, the labouring classes, or even the majority of French Canadians. However, for the middle-class, male, mostly anglophone snowshoers and for the members of the public who saw them on the streets, attended their concerts, or read about their exploits in the local press, the regular repetition of snowshoe activities on a weekly, seasonal, and yearly basis constantly reinforced this Canadian identity. Club stories, carefully compiled and repeatedly retold through reminiscences and songs, confirmed for participants a sense of their own identity and history while constituting what I will call, with thanks to Homi Bhabha, a narrative of nation.[57] Postcolonial scholarship has recognized that cultural power is as important as political, economic, or military policy in maintaining colonial rule and gaining the consent of the ruled. Stories and narratives are a "method colonized people use to assert their own identity and the existence of their own history," but in white-settler colonies like Canada, the colonizers can use the same strategy to assert their domination and make their own claims for autonomy from the metropole.[58]

To be sure, it is unlikely that the significance of snowshoeing as a cultural practice was consciously understood in this way. For one thing, snowshoers did not always take themselves completely seriously. Their club songs and tales are often humorous, poking fun at themselves and the mishaps they suffered on the trail . . . They valued snowshoeing as a physical rather than social pursuit, as was illustrated by the active members' disapproval of "driving members," those who joined the club for its social benefits but did not actually participate in the weekly tramps, and by their disdain for "hippodroming"—parading the streets in snowshoe costume rather than engaging in "bona fide" snowshoeing.[59] This was why some disgruntled veteran snowshoers formed Our Club in 1874 and organized a 45-mile tramp to St. Andrews, which was recalled as an epic journey for years to come. Evidently, snowshoeing had been getting too soft in "these days of light shoes and well-beaten tracks." One reporter commended the participants "for their pluck" and trusted "that the example they set will be worthily followed, and that before long we may return to the days of legitimate snow-shoeing."[60] Hence we can infer that it was crucial that the snowshoers actually

performed the activity, and it was equally important that this performance took place outside the city in open countryside, preferably on fresh snow. Otherwise, the performance (and hence the identity constructed) would not be authentic. . . .

 More online.

Notes

1. *Montreal Gazette*, 27–29 November 1878.
2. I use "native" as an adjective synonymous with "indigenous" or "autochthon" (i.e., "born here" or "sprung from the land"). I use the noun "Native" as synonymous with First Peoples or Aboriginal peoples. By using the term "native Canadian," I mean to imply that anglophone Montrealers wanted to claim that they were indigenous Canadians (i.e., the equivalent to born here). This is discussed more fully in the Introduction [to Poulter's book].
3. Between 1867 and 1885, 63 snowshoe clubs were in existence, although many lasted only a few seasons; see Alan Metcalfe, "Organised Sport and Social Stratification in Montreal: 1840–1901," in Richard S. Gruneau and John G. Albinson, eds., *Canadian Sport: Sociological Perspectives* (Toronto, ON: Addison Wesley, 1976), 85. . . .
4. Don Morrow, "The Knights of the Snowshoe: A Study of the Evolution of Sport in Nineteenth-Century Montreal," *Journal of Sport History* 15, no. 1 (1988): 5, 37; and Alan Metcalfe, "The Evolution of Organized Physical Recreation in Montreal, 1840–95," *Histoire Sociale/Social History* 11 (May 1978): 149.
5. Brian Young, "Death, Burial, and Protestant Identity in an Elite Family: The Montreal McCords," in Bettina Bradbury and Tamara Myers, eds., *Negotiating Identities in 19th- and 20th-Century Montreal* (Vancouver, BC: UBC Press, 2005), 104.
6. This was also true of Toronto sports clubs. See R. Wayne Simpson, "Toronto's Early Sporting Clubs: A 'Compact' History," in *Proceedings of the Fifth Canadian Symposium on the History of Sport and Physical Education* (Toronto, ON: University of Toronto Press, 1982), 199–204. . . .
7. *Globe* (Toronto), 24 May 1878, quoted by Nancy B. Bouchier, *For the Love of the Game: Amateur Sport in Small-Town Ontario, 1838–95* (Montreal, QC: McGill-Queen's University Press, 2003), 90.
8. Many of these middle-class men were Scottish or English, but using the term "British" as a short form has some legitimacy since the term was popularized

quite successfully by the early decades of the nineteenth century; see Linda Colley, *Britons: Forging the Nation, 1707–1837* (New Haven, CT: Yale University Press, 1992).

9.   Montreal Amateur Athletic Association (MAAA) Scrapbook 1, 33. The records of the MSSC are contained in the MAAA archives deposited at Library and Archives Canada, MG 28 1-351. . . .

10. Leon Trepanier, "Le Trappeur, le premier club de raquetteurs," *La Patrie*, 12 December 1954, in City of Montreal, Records Management and Archives, VM 15/4-33.

11. Donald Guay, *La Conquête du sport: Le sport et la société québecoise au XIXè siècle* (Montreal, QC: Lanctot, 1997), ch. 5.

12. MAAA Scrapbook 1, 33.

13. Frank Cosentino, *Afros, Aboriginals and Amateur Sport in Pre-World War One Canada*, Canada's Ethnic Group Series, Booklet No. 16 (Ottawa, ON: Canadian Historical Association, 1998), 18.

14. "Caledonia Club," 5 March 1875, in MAAA Scrapbook 1, 292; MAAA Scrapbook 1, 33.

15. Newspaper clipping, February 1873, in MAAA Scrapbook 1, 4.

16. N. M. Hinshelwood, *Montreal and Vicinity, being a history of the old town, a pictorial record of the modern city, its sports and pastimes, and an illustrated description of many charming summer resorts around* (Montreal, QC: Desbarrats, 1903), 90.

17. W. S. Humphreys, "Tales of Old Montreal," *Montreal Standard*, 4 February 1928, in City of Montreal, Records Management and Archives, VM 15/3-41.

18. W. George Beers, *Over the Snow, or The Montreal Carnival* (Montreal, QC: W. Drysdale and J. Tho. Robinson, 1883), 40.

19. John C. Martin, "A Montreal Winter Glimpse," *Outing* 9 (1886–87): 358.

20. *The Winter Carnival Illustrated, or Bishop's Winter Carnival Illustrated* (Montreal, QC: George Bishop, February 1884), 10.

21. The significance of uniforms and clothing is discussed by Paul Connerton, *How Societies Remember* (Cambridge, UK: Cambridge University Press, 1989), 7–11; and by Nathan Joseph, *Uniforms and Nonuniforms: Communication through Clothing* (New York, NY: Greenwood, 1986).

22. The blanket coat was a version of the French *capote*, a mid-length, hooded coat made from wool-blanket cloth; see Eileen Stack, "The Significance of the Blanket Coat to Anglo-Canadian Identity," paper presented at the 25th Annual Symposium of the Costume Society of America, Sante Fe, New Mexico, 22–25 May 1999, 1. . . .

23. See, for instance, J. R. Miller, *Skyscrapers Hide the Heavens: A History of Indian-White Relations in Canada*,

rev. ed. (Toronto, ON: University of Toronto Press, 1991); and Sarah Carter, *Lost Harvests: Prairie Indian Reserve Farms and Government Policy* (Montreal, QC: McGill-Queen's University Press, 1990). . . .

24. Olive Dickason, "When Europeans and Indians Met in Canada," *Ontario History* 96, no. 2 (November 2004): 107. There are a few exceptions. The most recent is a collection of essays by David Newhouse, Cora Voyageur, and Daniel Beavon, eds., *Hidden in Plain Sight: Contributions of Aboriginal Peoples to Canadian Identity and Culture* (Toronto, ON: University of Toronto Press, 2005), although few of the entries pertain to the issue of national identity. . . .

25. William Gilpin, *Three Essays: On Picturesque Beauty; on Picturesque Travel; and on Sketching Landscape; to which is added a poem, on Landscape Painting* (1792; reprint, Westmead, UK; Gregg, 1972).

26. Snowshoe costumes were considered to be a nostalgic reminder of "Old Quebec" by commentators in the 1890s; see Frank Abbott, "Cold Cash and Ice Palaces: The Quebec Winter Carnival of 1894," *Canadian Historical Review* 69, no. 2 (1988): 167–202.

27. Colonel Landmann describes a dinner that included 120 bottles of wine and dancing on tables; see his *Adventures and Recollections* (London, UK: Colburn, 1852), quoted by Lawrence J. Burpee, "The Beaver Club," *The Canadian Historical Association Annual Report* (1924), 86.

28. Carolyn Podruchny, "Festivals, Fortitude, and Fraternalism: Fur Trade Masculinity and the Beaver Club, 1785–1827," in Jo-Anne Fiske, Susan Sleeper-Smith, and William Wicken, eds., *New Faces of the Fur Trade: Selected Papers of the Seventh North American Fur Trade Conference, Halifax, Nova Scotia, 1995* (East Lansing, MI: Michigan State University Press, 1998).

29. Some ways that middle-class men cultivated a particular image of respectability are examined by Andrew C. Holman, *Sense of Their Duty: Middle-Class Formation in Victorian Ontario Towns* (Montreal, QC: McGill-Queen's University Press, 2000).

30. Lawrence Peter Kredl, "The Origin and Development of Mount Royal Park, Montreal, 1874–1900: Ideal vs. Reality" (Master's thesis, York University, 1983), 12, 27. . . .

31. Newspaper clipping, March 1873, in MAAA Scrapbook 1, 35. This clipping is a reprint of Beers, "Canada in Winter."

32. "The Torchlight Procession," January 1873, in MAAA Scrapbook 1, 4.

33. *MSSC Annual Report, 1878–79*, 4.

34. Kevin B. Wamsley contrasts the "bush masculinity" of voyageurs, coureurs de bois, and First Nations with "gentry masculinity," which valued personal honour, class, duty, and sportsmanship; see his "The Public

Importance of Men and the Importance of Public Men: Sport and Masculinities in Nineteenth-Century Canada," in Philip White and Kevin Young, eds., *Sport and Gender in Canada* (New York, NY: Oxford University Press, 1999), 26.

35. The *hommes du nord*, or Northmen, were voyageurs who travelled beyond Grand Portage and spent the winter in the northwest interior. They prided themselves on their "strength, skill, and endurance on the job and mocked the manhood of those who could not meet these standards"; see Carolyn Podruchny, "Baptizing Novices: Ritual Moments among French Canadian Voyageurs in the Montreal Fur Trade, 1780–1821," *Canadian Historical Review* 83, no. 2 (June 2002): 178. . . .

36. Robert Grant Haliburton, *The Men of the North and Their Place in History: A Lecture Delivered before the Montreal Literary Club, March 31st, 1869* (Montreal, QC: John Lovell, 1869), 1. . . .

37. MAAA, MSSC Minute Book, March 1879, 470.

38. *MSSC Annual Report*, 1878–79, 9; and MAAA, MSSC Minute Book, 15 February 1868, 93. . . .

39. W. George Beers, "Canadian Sports," in MAAA Scrapbook 2 (1878), 128.

40. Richard S. Gruneau, "Power and Play in Canadian Society," in Richard J. Ossenberg, ed., *Power and Change in Canada* (Toronto, ON: University of Toronto Press, 1980), 158.

41. Connerton, *How Societies Remember*, 74.

42. Don Morrow and Kevin B. Wamsley, *Sport in Canada: A History* (Toronto, ON: Oxford University Press, 2005), 55.

43. Cecilia Morgan, *Public Men and Virtuous Women: The Gendered Languages of Religion and Politics in Upper Canada, 1791–1850* (Toronto, ON: University of Toronto Press, 1996), 162.

44. *Montreal Gazette*, 8 January 1842; Report on Annual Races, 15 February 1868, in MAAA, MSSC Minute Book, 1861–69, 93; MAAA Scrapbook 1, 4; *Toronto Globe*, 1870, quoted by Mary Fallis Jones, *The Confederation Generation* (Toronto, ON: Royal Ontario Museum, 1978), 87.

45. Morrow, "Knights," 16, 29.

46. MAAA Scrapbook 1, 7. . . .

47. MAAA, MSSC Minute Book, 19 January 1862, 551, in LAC; MAAA Scrapbook 1, 3.

48. MAAA Scrapbook 1, 6. The same phrase was used in a report dated 29 January 1874, in MAAA Scrapbook 1, 132.

49. Records of the St. George's Snow Shoe Club, 1874–90, Article 9, 3, in LAC, MG 28 1421.

50. Clipping from Beers, "Canadian Sports," in MAAA Scrapbook 2 (1878), 127. . . .

51. MAAA Scrapbook 2, 93.

52. James C. Scott, *Domination and the Arts of Resistance: Hidden Transcripts* (New Haven, CT: Yale University Press, 1990), 17–18. . . .

53. Taverns provided a similar service for working-class men; see Peter DeLottinville, "Joe Beef of Montreal: Working-Class Culture and the Tavern, 1869–89," *Labour/Le Travail* 8, no. 9 (Autumn–Spring 1981–82): 9–40. . . .

54. Walt Whitman, *Leaves of Grass*, quoted in Alan Trachtenberg, "The Group Portrait," in Leslie Tonkonow and Alan Trachtenberg, eds., *Multiple Exposures: The Group Portrait in Photography*, exhibition catalogue (New York, NY: Independent Curators, 1995), 23.

55. This is not the approach taken by H. V. Nelles, *The Art of Nation-Building: Pageantry and Spectacle at Quebec's Tercentenary* (Toronto, ON: University of Toronto Press, 1999). Even in a collection of essays promisingly entitled *The Theatre of Sport*, the authors fail to consider the performative aspect of sport, concentrating instead on "topophilia"—the sport site; see Karl B. Raitz, ed., *The Theatre of Sport* (Baltimore, MD: Johns Hopkins University Press, 1995).

56. Brian S. Osborne, "The Place of Memory and Identity," *Diversité Canadienne* 1, no. 1 (Summer 2002): 10.

57. Judith Butler emphasizes that performativity "is always a reiteration"—it is "that discursive practice that enacts or produces that which it names"; see her *Bodies That Matter: On the Discursive Limits of "Sex"* (New York, NY: Routledge, 1993), 13. Homi K. Bhabha's term is "narrating the nation"; "Introduction: Narrating the Nation," in Homi K. Bhabha, ed., *Nation and Narration* (London, UK: Routledge, 1990), 1–7.

58. Edward W. Said, *Culture and Imperialism* (New York, NY: Knopf, 1993), quoted by Catherine Hall, "Introduction: Thinking the Postcolonial, Thinking the Empire," in Catherine Hall, ed., *Cultures of Empire: Colonizers in Britain and the Empire in the Nineteenth and Twentieth Centuries: A Reader* (New York, NY: Routledge, 2000), 15.

59. "The Snowshoe Parade," *Montreal Gazette*, 24 January 1885, 5. . . .

60. Newspaper clippings, in MAAA Scrapbook 1, 145.

23

"Every Boy Ought to Learn to Shoot and to Obey Orders"
Guns, Boys, and the Law in English Canada from the Late Nineteenth Century to the Great War

R. Blake Brown

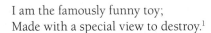

I am the famously funny toy;
Made with a special view to destroy.[1]

In 1899, Stephen Leacock poked fun at the lies parents told (and tell) children at Christmas. He described a young boy, Hoodoo McFiggin, bursting with excitement prior to opening each gift delivered from Santa Claus, and who, oddly, remained excessively cheerful as each present turned out to contain a practical item, such as a toothbrush or a Bible. Leacock's story included a wish list of what young McFiggin, and presumably other Canadian boys at the time, dreamed of acquiring. The boy "prayed every night for weeks that Santa Claus would bring him a pair of skates and a puppy-dog and an air-gun and a bicycle and a Noah's ark and a sleigh and a drum."[2] To modern eyes, this list may seem unremarkable. However, the assumption that an "air gun" was a suitable gift for a boy was relatively new. In the late nineteenth century, Canadians encouraged young people to develop familiarity and skill with weapons.[3] The after-effects of inculcating a gun culture in young people remains with us, as anyone who has surveyed the armoury of toy guns at every Toys 'R' Us well knows.

From the late nineteenth century to the Great War, firearms became a key part of boy and male youth culture in English Canada.[4] While firearms had long been useful tools for rural Canadians to hunt, kill pests, protect property, and sometimes commit crimes, in the late nineteenth century guns became more than practical implements—they became desired consumer items. Two factors contributed to the growing nexus between guns and young people before the Great War. The first was an interwoven set of cultural assumptions concerning manhood and imperialism. By the 1890s, imperialist sentiments had infused the growing interest in hunting, advocates of which celebrated the value of rifle shooting on the ground that it made boys into ideal British men. Worries about both the alleged feminization of urban youth and boys' lack of discipline also motivated proponents of military drill and rifle training. The perceived value of rifle shooting thus led governments to encourage training for school-age children in shooting. The second factor was economic. Businesses heavily marketed cheap, mass-produced arms in this period. Gun manufacturers and retailers employed several aggressive sales techniques, such as emphasizing that using firearms could inculcate manly virtues, and redefining some weapons as toys to make them into acceptable and desirable consumer items.

Citation: R. Blake Brown, "'Every Boy Ought to Learn to Shoot and to Obey Orders': Guns, Boys, and the Law in English Canada from the Late Nineteenth Century to the Great War," *Canadian Historical Review* 93, no. 2 (June 2012): 196–226. Reprinted with permission from University of Toronto Press (www.utpjournals.com).

The use of weapons by boys and youth led to a number of apprehended social ills. Critics complained of accidental shootings. Some people also expressed environmental concerns, including the belief that young people armed with small rifles decimated animal populations. In addition, a few Canadians worried about the long-term effects of militarizing a generation of youth. Given the state's interest in encouraging gun use by boys and youth, however, legislative efforts to limit access to firearms were minimal. In 1892 and 1913, the Canadian government passed Criminal Code provisions that placed modest limitations on to whom certain weapons could be sold, but the widespread assumption that some kinds of arms were acceptable for most boys and youth helped ensure that these measures frequently went unenforced.

. . . . A full examination of firearms, gun control, and young people requires drawing from, and contributing to, a diverse set of historiographical literatures relating to hunting, environmentalism, militarism, consumer culture, imperialism, gender, state formation, legal change, social reform, and youth culture. The analysis is divided into four parts: a survey of the arms available to Canadian youth by the early twentieth century; a consideration of the cultural attitudes expressed regarding boys, youth, and guns; a discussion of the perceived dangers of these weapons; and, finally, an examination of governments' responses to the apprehended dangers of arming a generation of young people.

Firearms for Boys

The appearance, functionality, and cost of arms available to boys and youth changed dramatically by the early twentieth century. Technological advances, for example, revolutionized pistols. The most important innovation was the creation of multishot "revolvers." Such arms declined markedly in price through the 1870s and 1880s, in part because of the excess manufacturing capability developed in the United States during the American Civil War. By the early 1880s, Toronto and Winnipeg retailers sold various kinds of revolvers, some for $1.50 or less.[5]

"Toy pistols" also became available in Canada. These pistols took several forms. Some were small calibre (.22 calibre) guns that fired blank cartridges. Others exploded a detonating wafer charged with a fulminating compound.[6] These extremely cheap "toys" were sold in the 1880s in the United States, often to celebrate the Fourth of July. Many Canadian retailers also offered such toy guns. For example, as early as 1869 one Halifax merchant advertised a "patent revolver for boys" as "quite a new and ingenious Toy, which can be fired fives [sic] times in succession."[7] By the end of the nineteenth century, many other retailers carried toy pistols. The Consolidated Stationery Company of Winnipeg, for example, advertised toy pistols in 1900 and 1901 as a means of celebrating Victoria Day, while Simpson's included a cap gun in its Christmas 1906 catalogue.[8]

Air rifles also appeared in Canada. The air gun was long deemed an "assassin's weapon" because of its ability to fire almost silently. American companies, however, reshaped public opinion about such guns when they began to mass produce and market inexpensive air rifles. In 1888, the Plymouth Iron Windmill Company manufactured the first all-metal air gun. The company subsequently changed its name to the Daisy Manufacturing Company, began developing new models, including repeating air rifles, and slowly consolidated its market position. At first, businesses did not usually target children; instead, they often advertised air guns as suitable for adult entertainment. For example, in 1896 the Griffiths Corporation appealed to middle-class men and women, suggesting that air guns "furnish excellent amusement for lawn or parlor." The company's air guns sold for $1.00 and up.[9] This low price was not unusual. A new Daisy air rifle could be purchased for just 99 cents in Saint John in 1896, while in 1913 one Edmonton retailer offered several models ranging in price from \$1.10 to \$1.98.[10] Youth could graduate from air rifles to more powerful arms, especially .22 calibre rifles. A number of companies produced such rifles, the small size of which often created the sense that they could be safely handled by young people. Like air rifles, such guns were inexpensive. Eaton's, for example, offered .22 calibre rifles for as little as \$2.00 in 1899.[11]

A Fertile Field for Boys and Guns

An interconnected set of cultural attitudes concerning masculinity, modernity, imperialism, militarism, and hunting led many English Canadians to accept and even encourage the use of arms by young people. For example, imperialist sentiment was perceptible in Canadians' growing interest in hunting with firearms. As John MacKenzie notes, hunting was "a mark of the fitness of the dominant race, a route to health, strength, and wealth, an emblem of imperial rule, and an allegory of human affairs."[12] Imperialists saw hunting as having the added benefit of improving the martial skills of Canadians. Men learned to track prey, subsist in natural settings, and, most importantly, shoot at moving targets. Deer, moose, bears, or rabbits would, in wartime, be replaced by enemy soldiers. Sport, especially hunting, was thus "ideal training for the manly game of war."[13] This assumption encouraged efforts to give boys access to firearms.

A number of Canadians also believed too many urban boys led sedentary lives that provided little opportunity for differentiation between the sexes. The sense of uncertainty created by the social adjustments of the late nineteenth century seemed to require a return to "core" cultural values, which, for many, meant socializing young people in how to be manly men. The growth of hunting as a pastime reflected this concern. Middle-class, urban Canadian men took cues from British gentlemen in advocating sport hunting as a respectable, manly activity. British sport hunters (and their Canadian counterparts) were part of a movement for outdoor middle-class recreation at a time when reformers decried cities as unsanitary and rife with poverty. Urban residents thus sought out "pure" outdoor recreation. As the size of the middle class grew, so did the pool of potential recreational hunters responding to a desire to demonstrate their manliness in the face of the modern industrial, urban world.[14] This interest in hunting had important ramifications for the regulation of firearms, as most men encouraged young people to shoot as well.

Imperialist sentiment also resulted in renewed interest in the militia and military affairs throughout English Canada—a trend that led to efforts to make arms available to youth. By the 1890s, various journalists, politicians, and militia leaders argued that Canada could support Britain effectively in future wars only if Canadian men developed acumen in rifle shooting. As well, those worried over a possible attack by the United States believed that marksmanship using modern magazine-loading rifles was key to defending Canada. Canadians' limited experience with armed conflict strengthened the desire to create an armed citizenry. A key lesson taken from the Anglo-Boer War of 1899–1902, for example, was that future conflicts would be won by armies of amateur citizen-soldiers trained to be crack rifle shots. According to the magazine *Rod and Gun in Canada*, for example, the "great lesson of the South African war" was that "every Briton must know how to shoot."[15] This emphasis on shooting skill led to efforts to train boys and youth to practise with rifles. The idea of instructing boys in military drill was not an entirely new idea, but more calls to train young people in rifle shooting found expression as imperialist sentiments intensified in the 1890s.[16]

Military drill and rifle shooting, like hunting, were also responses to concerns that modern urban life threatened the masculinity of men and youth. Exercise and participation in martial activities could stem moral and physical decay and encourage good character. Military drill, for instance, was believed to combat youth delinquency. Many urban residents expressed concern that boys loitered in the streets, made lewd remarks, spit tobacco, and violated middle-class ideals of proper behaviour. Such commentators called for lessons in good posture, healthy living, and obedience to authority. Training in the mass use of particular kinds of violence would create order by inculcating morality, manliness, and an ability to resist the evil temptations of the city.[17]

These attitudes led to efforts to train boys in the art of war. Boys' brigades represented an early effort to uplift youth in poor areas by blending recreation with military training. In Montreal, Major Fred Lydons enlisted into a boys' brigade young people who pledged abstinence and accepted military obedience. The group purchased rifles and drilled. Two other organizations proved even more important. First, the scouting movement begun by Robert Baden-Powell came to include rifle training. Baden-Powell's *Scouting for Boys* appeared in Canada in 1908, and by 1910 Canada had approximately 5,000 Scouts, a figure which climbed to 13,565 by September 1914. As several historians have noted, scouting was an imperialist organization influenced by muscular Christianity, antimodernist sentiments, and middle-class ideas of hunting. Generally catering to boys between the ages of 11 and 14, scouting sought to turn boys into good citizens and good soldiers by inculcating patriotism and imperialism.[18] Baden-Powell, in fact, suggested that scouting was good training for war. He encouraged boys to shoot, writing in *Scouting for Boys* that "every boy ought to learn to shoot and to obey orders, else he is no more good when war breaks out than an old woman."[19] Some Scouts practised target shooting in Montreal before the Great War. Following the outbreak of war, Baden-Powell published *Marksmanship for Boys*, in which he outlined how boys could receive the Red Feather award if they proved they could drill and shoot. The Canadian scouting movement awarded hundreds of marksmanship badges during the war.[20]

Even more important than Scouts in inculcating the importance of shooting was the cadet movement, which grew quickly with the support of Canadian governments. In 1898, Ontario promised to grant $50 to any school board that had a cadet corps of at least 25 boys. Ottawa integrated the cadets into the militia system with the 1904 Militia Act, which allowed Ottawa to provide cadet corps with arms. Minister of Militia Frederick Borden entered negotiations with the provinces to incorporate military training in schools as part of a national system so that every boy would learn to use a rifle. Borden's efforts received a boost with the establishment of the Lord Strathcona Trust designed to encourage drilling, physical training, and shooting in public schools. The cadet movement picked up even more steam after Sam Hughes became minister of militia following the 1911 election. Hughes increased the federal budget for cadets from $93,000 in 1912 to $400,000 in 1913, and ordered several thousand .22 calibre Ross rifles for cadets. By 1914 the number of cadets had reached almost 45,000.[21]

Gun retailers and manufacturers buttressed state efforts encouraging young people to shoot. . . . While retailers deemed pistols too dangerous for young people, businesses aggressively marketed other types of arms to children and youth, especially air guns. Retailers often described or portrayed such guns as toys. Eaton's employed this approach for a time, including air guns in the toy section of its 1892–3 Fall–Winter catalogue, while a Victoria retailer sold a variety of "military toys" in 1897, including Daisy air rifles. Eaton's shifted air guns to the firearm section of its catalogue in 1902, although the primary market for the air guns remained boys, as evidenced, for instance, when Eaton's called the King Air Rifle "a splendid rifle for boys" in 1910.[22] Many other retailers continued to advertise air rifles as toys. Simpson's included air rifles in the toy section of its 1906 Christmas catalogue, while a Red Deer, Alberta, retailer in 1914 advertised an air rifle as a "good toy for boys 7 to 15 years old."[23] Other

Figure 1. Boy dressed in miniature replica of uniform worn by the 2nd Canadian Mounted Rifles in South African War, Quebec (ca. 1900). Source: Glenbow Archives NA-3034-27.

retailers did not overtly claim that air rifles were for boys, but advertised them beside toys, thus implicitly suggesting the suitability of air rifles for young people.

A number of businesses suggested that young people could safely handle air rifles by offering them as compensation for selling products. This practice, according to Gary Cross, stemmed from toy-makers' realization that "children had limited financial autonomy," but "unlimited desires."[24] In Ontario, for example, boys could receive a free air rifle for selling 12 boxes of Dr. Groves's Famous Stomach, Kidney, and Liver Pills. Businesses advertised similar offers in almost all parts of Canada, including in small-town newspapers, thus ensuring the availability of air rifles to boys and youth in smaller communities and rural areas. For example, a Toronto company offered a Daisy air rifle to boys in Wetaskiwin, Alberta, who sold 40 sets of greeting cards.[25]

. . .

Companies sought to make firearms attractive consumer items for young people by emphasizing the beauty of their guns. C. Flood & Sons of Saint John described its air rifle as "the handsomest air rifle in the world,"[26] while the Western Specialty Company of Winnipeg offered a "genuine Steel, Black Walnut Air Rifle, handsomely nickelled and polished" to anyone who sold 12 Japanese silk fans.[27] Retailers also employed the ultimate symbol of the new consumerist mentality, Christmas, to sell air guns and .22 calibre rifles. Toronto's Charles Stark & Co., for instance, suggested in 1904 that as a Christmas present nothing was "nicer for a boy than a small 22 caliber rifle,"[28] while in 1910 Eaton's listed air guns and small game rifles as desirable "Gifts for Lively Boys" at Christmas.[29] Gun manufacturers enticed parents to purchase weapons for their children using Christmas. The Stevens Arms Company showed Santa Claus carrying a rifle and told parents that Santa would be speeding over rooftops "loaded down with Stevens Firearms for the youths of the land."[30]

In employing the holiday season to market guns, retailers and manufacturers thus sought to take advantage of the burgeoning Canadian consumer culture.

Retailers also emphasized that owning or using a gun could transform boys into men. Given the cultural context in which many Canadians both celebrated imperialism and saw hunting and rifle shooting as antidotes to the deleterious effects of modern urban life, retailers advertised guns to boys with images and language that suggested using arms signified manliness and/or love of empire. The Stevens Arms Company emphasized the role of firearms in turning boys into men in blunt terms: "Make a man of your boy by giving him a 'Stevens'; he will surely appreciate it, and you will add to the education of your son."[31] Businesses promoted the role of guns in bringing together father and son, thus allowing for invaluable bonding and the transfer of wisdom regarding how to be a man. A common suggestion was that arming your son would instill in him manly qualities, such as independence, self-sufficiency, and an ability to protect personal property, all of which were desirable characteristics in a liberal nation.[32]

. . .

The Dangers of Boys and Guns

Willie had a new toy pistol,
Loaded it, and felt no doubt;
But the doctor, with a twist'll
Probe most of the fragments out.[33]

By the early twentieth century, Canadian boys and youth had available to them a veritable arsenal of weapons. Mass produced and cheap, revolvers, toy pistols, air guns, and .22 calibre rifles found their way into the hands of young people from coast to coast. The accessibility of these weapons, however, led to various concerns, including fears of gun accidents, worries over environmental destruction, and apprehension about creating a generation of violent youth.

Figure 2. Many retailers and gun manufacturers, including the J. Stevens Arms & Tool Company, employed the Christmas season to sell their firearms. Source: *Rod and Gun in Canada* 5, no. 7 (December 1903).

Accidents were the biggest concern. Although it is impossible to quantify the problem, it is apparent that weapons of all sorts caused injuries and deaths. For example, cheap revolvers sometimes found their way into the hands of children, often with disastrous results. In the nineteenth century, there was no legislation dictating that revolvers be stored safely or be unloaded when not in use, nor was there any age restriction (prior to 1892) regarding who could be sold a pistol. Not surprisingly, children got their hands on guns, and, beginning in the late 1870s, newspapers contained numerous stories of tragic pistol accidents.[34] In reflecting on one accidental shooting, a coroner's jury in 1901 thus called attention "to the careless way in which the revolver and cartridges were left lying around where children could get access to them."[35] Charles Allan Stuart of the Supreme Court of Alberta also heavily criticized the availability of handguns. "It is beyond my understanding why a revolver is allowed to be sold," he mused.[36] The *Globe* expressed concern as well, suggesting that "the unguarded revolver has more victims to its discredit than smallpox or any other infectious diseases." It thus made an appeal: "Let moral and social reformers consider the revolver."[37] The reference to moral and social reformers was telling, indicating that some people believed that the regulation of pistols should become part of the broader effort to more closely regulate society.[38]

. . .

Twenty-two calibre rifles and air guns were also deemed dangerous. Air rifles resulted in a spate of accidents. One example can illustrate the problem. In 1907, two boys in Toronto went down Dufferin Street with an air rifle. They came across a 6-year-old boy and told him to raise his hands. The air rifle went off, striking the child in the eye.[39] Such accidents led to warnings, such as when the *Manitoba Morning Free Press* suggested that air guns were "exceedingly dangerous weapons in the hands of careless boys."[40] There were also many accidents involving .22 calibre rifles. For example, in 1910 a 13-year-old Montreal boy stumbled, causing the discharge of the .22 calibre rifle he carried, and the bullet lodged in the hip of his 14-year-old companion.[41] Such accidents led the *Cayley Hustler* of Alberta to complain about the frequency of accidents and to suggest that many men and boys were unaware of the dangers of guns, and "should be forbidden to handle a rifle at all for generally some one else is the victim of their ignorance."[42]

While accidents were the major concern, some Canadians also expressed worries that toy pistols encouraged boys to become too attached to real guns. The *Globe*, for example, believed that toy pistols contributed to the tendency of young men to arm themselves. The manufacturers and vendors of toy pistols had to accept blame because these "suggestive playthings breed in children a desire to handle the genuine article, and are thus directly answerable for many lamentable happenings."[43] A writer in Edmonton made a similar complaint in 1906. A young man described being surprised by a boy pretending to rob him with a toy pistol. The writer condemned the use of realistic toy arms: "Does it not seem altogether beyond belief that any man in his right senses, after all the warnings we have had in the shape of murders and accidents, should allow his son the possession of even a supposedly harmless air gun, knowing how one thing leads to another?" "Firearms," he concluded, "and small boys have, or should have, no thing in common."[44]

Another complaint was that boys from cities used small rifles in suburban areas to shoot indiscriminately at animals and property. A newspaper from rural Ontario, the Temiskaming *Speaker*, discussed this problem in 1909 when it described an accident in which a man had been shot by a .22 rifle, presumably fired by a youth, while waiting on a railway platform. "Better to cut out the 'twenty two' and the 'air gun' entirely than have these accidents continue," concluded the *Speaker.*[45] A particular worry was that armed boys might destroy animal populations. In the first decade of the twentieth century, many

Canadians expressed concern with the destruction of wildlife, and they deemed thoughtless boys to be part of the problem.[46] In Victoria, for instance, the Society for the Prevention of Cruelty to Animals discouraged boys and youth from slaughtering birds.[47] Complaints from the suburban areas of Toronto led the *Toronto Star* to suggest in October 1911 that the "annual invasion of the suburban districts by the city lad with his 22-calibre rifle has begun." The boy "goes out into the country bordering on the city limits and shoots squirrels, chipmonks [sic], birds, and anything that comes before his eyes," lamented the *Star*.[48] Thus, while Canadians generally encouraged boys to shoot, many believed there were reasonable limits to this activity that required enforcement.

Guns, Boys, and the Law

Canadians worried about the use of firearms by boys and youth at a time of growing concern with child safety. Social reformers in the prewar period believed that the autonomy of young people had to be constrained in a rapidly changing social, cultural, and economic context. The result was, according to Cynthia Comacchio, the "expanded regulation of adolescence" with the purpose of "training the ideal, responsible, conscientious adult citizen."[49] As noted earlier, the goal of creating ideal citizens led to efforts to train young people to use firearms. Several provincial governments also enacted child protection legislation, established family courts, created evening curfews, and extended the period of compulsory schooling. In addition, the federal government passed the Juvenile Delinquents Act of 1908, which created the category of "juvenile" crime and empowered the state to deal aggressively with those deemed delinquent.[50] The concern that some boys had access to arms but lacked sufficient training or mental maturity, and the belief that young people might use guns for nefarious ends, led to efforts to regulate the availability of *some* weapons to *some* youth. The

choices legislators made in framing these laws illuminates how they determined when youth had sufficient capacity to be entrusted safely with weapons, and how legislation sought to delineate boundaries between the problematic categories of "safe" and "unsafe" weapons and between "toys" and "firearms."

. . .

Pressure for limiting young people's access to pistols emerged in the Senate by the late 1880s, and in 1892 the first Canadian Criminal Code prohibited the sale or gift of pistols (and ammunition for such arms) to anyone under the age of 16. This was the first time that Ottawa placed an age restriction on who could purchase guns. The government's decision to impose an age restriction was a typical response to perceived social problems in this period, a time when legislators imposed or altered the minimum age at which youth were allowed to leave school to enter the workforce, or to engage in sexual relations. An age restriction on to whom guns could be sold fits within this approach; it created a demarcation line between youth and adulthood that sought to prevent the use of pistols by reckless young people. The 1892 Criminal Code also prohibited the sale or gift of air guns to anyone under the age of 16.[51] This reflected the traditional sense that air guns were sneaky, unmanly, and potentially dangerous arms. In 1892, air rifles were not yet widely accepted as toys. As air rifles became defined as toys, however, the law would be frequently disregarded, as many people saw little potential harm in young people owning an air gun.

The 1892 legislation contained important loopholes that reflected attitudes toward other weapons and the ability of adults to successfully supervise armed boys and youth. One important loophole was that Ottawa did not ban the *possession* of air guns or pistols by those under 16. Parliament therefore allowed parents or organizations to place such guns in the hands of young people. Nor did the law ban the sale of rifles to youth. The widespread support for efforts to train boys and youth in rifle shooting and the mesh of ideas concerning imperialism, hunting, and manliness meant that the state would not completely disarm young people. Parliament thus made no effort to regulate weapons deemed beneficial, and boys and youth continued to have free access to rifles until 1913.

. . .

Given the widespread encouragement of shooting by boys and youth, [calls for new laws] often went unheeded, and debates over the wisdom of allowing young people to have access to rifles were largely one-sided. This can be seen in a parliamentary debate stemming from rural objections to the policy of encouraging boys to shoot. There were concerns that military drill was so attractive to youth that it was drawing farm boys into cities. As well, a few parliamentarians suggested that boys need not be inculcated with militarism at too early an age. Ontario MPP Thomas Simpson Sproule expressed all of these concerns in 1903, and he asserted that there was "a possibility of carrying this military spirit a little too far."[52]

Advocates of teaching boys to shoot dismissed such claims by arguing that rifle practice created manly character and by drawing upon the rhetoric of imperialism. Sam Hughes asserted that wherever "you have a strong military spirit, you have more manhood in the youth of the country."[53] Frederick Borden also defended the policy of teaching boys to shoot. He quoted from literature suggesting that the discipline and exercise of rifle training would improve boys' "health, strengthen their moral fibre and add to their professional, industrial or labour value when they are attained to manhood and entered on the serious business of their lives."[54] Advocates of teaching youth to shoot thus saw nothing wrong with boys arming themselves with rifles, hunting small animals, practising target shooting, and pretending to be soldiers for the Crown. While accidents were a real concern, the perceived solution was to give boys *more* training in the use of arms, not less.

For example, in a column devoted to women's issues, the *Victoria Daily Colonist* advised mothers to have their children trained to use firearms. While guns were dangerous, "a well-trained youngster will soon learn to be proud of the fact that he is trusted with a real gun."[55] Given the dominance of these attitudes, Ottawa took little action to prevent boys and youth from acquiring most weapons.

. . .

A general desire to pass new gun control measures grew in the early 1910s. This had much to do with the fact that the 1910 to 1913 period saw especially heavy rates of immigration, peaking at over 400,000 in 1913.[56] Many Canadians believed that the new immigrants who came from southern and Eastern Europe were inherently violent and "un-British." In Manitoba, for example, Justice James Prendergast of the Manitoba Court of King's Bench deemed foreigners too quick to use revolvers, and he implored a grand jury to make a presentment asking for tougher gun laws. New immigrants were "introducing a custom from which we have been free in the past," for they were "indulging in the foolish practice of carrying firearms."[57] The grand jury agreed with Justice Prendergast, recommending stronger laws to regulate sales and to stop recreational shooting along the Red River and Assiniboine River.

Several provinces passed legislation designed to disarm immigrants in the early 1910s. Ontario acted first, enacting the Offensive Weapons Act in 1911, which stipulated that persons who sold a pistol or air gun to someone lacking a certificate issued under section 118 of the Criminal Code (which under the Criminal Code was needed to carry a handgun) or a permit from the superintendent of the Ontario Provincial Police or from a chief constable of a city or town were liable to fines, or to imprisonment for up to six months. Sellers also had to keep detailed records of handguns and air guns sold. The desire to target immigrants carrying guns was evidenced by the act's requirement that police make a report to the minister of the interior when they found foreigners with illegal weapons "with the view towards deporting such person under the Immigration Act."[58] Other provinces soon passed similar legislation, including Manitoba and Saskatchewan in 1912, and British Columbia in 1913.[59] Requiring a permit to purchase an air rifle caused some consternation. Toronto Deputy Chief William Stark, however, lauded the measure because the "supply of guns and air rifles to boys will be stopped." In his view, there were "altogether too many air rifles in the hands of careless boys. They are very dangerous, and very mischievous. No living thing, bird or squirrel, or anything else, is safe within the city limits, or the suburbs."[60]

The federal government eventually passed Criminal Code amendments in 1913 that largely copied these provincial acts. Ottawa made it an offence for anyone to sell any kind of firearm to a minor under 16, or to sell or give a pistol or air rifle to anyone under 16. Once again, there were important loopholes. Ottawa did not ban the possession of weapons by boys under 16— just the sale and/or gift of weapons—and thus allowed for parents or organizations to provide rifles to young people to hunt or to target shoot as part of an organized group.[61]

Conclusion

The period of the late nineteenth and early twentieth centuries was a key time in the formation of a relationship between young people and firearms. Imperialist sentiments led to efforts to encourage boys and youth to use rifles. Antimodernist concerns also helped promote the use of guns, as many Canadians believed firearms could instill masculinity in a generation whose urban environment risked making them effeminate. The mass production and skilled marketing of inexpensive firearms further cemented the connections between guns and boys and youth. Businesses redefined some arms, in particular air rifles, as toys. Other guns, such as small

calibre rifles, were clearly marketed to youth, but Canadians debated whether they were guns or toys. Despite widespread support for encouraging the use of firearms by boys and youth, the perceived spike in accidents caused by pistols, toy guns, air guns, and small rifles, and worries over the use of arms by immigrants eventually led to modest action. Ironically, the very factors that led Canadians to train young people to use guns, such as industrialization and urbanization, made it necessary to regulate weapons through state mechanisms and organizations like the Scouts and the cadet movement.

In the interwar period, Canadians would continue to struggle with this issue. There were many more complaints about gun accidents, property damage, and the possibility that using firearms or playing with toy guns risked creating a generation of violent youth. The same period, however, saw Ottawa exert less effort in encouraging young people to shoot. This decreased government involvement reflected many of the lessons taken from the Great War that undermined the rationales for strengthening the relationship between boys and guns. The war destroyed the belief that conflicts could be won by citizen-soldiers trained as expert rifle shots. Instead, it demonstrated the importance of massed artillery, tanks, aircraft, and machine guns. The war also sapped imperialism of much of its allure. As a result, efforts slackened to create a new generation of citizen-soldiers.[62]

This is not to say that the connection between young people and guns was broken. The marketing of toy arms, air guns, and small calibre rifles to boys and youth continued, and, in some respects, increased in intensity. Hollywood films, critics charged, encouraged a celebration of gun-toting gangsters. By the 1930s, retailers marketed air rifles and toy guns with advertisements influenced by the "cowboy craze" that swept North America. Millions of toy pistols allowed American (and Canadian) boys to celebrate alleged cowboy values, such as rugged manly individualism. After World War II, guns remained a staple part of Canadian toy catalogues and were often portrayed in popular culture as implements of humour (on shows like Bugs Bunny) or tools of valour (think G. I. Joe).[63]

The history of weapons laws and young people in the late nineteenth and early twentieth centuries also hinted at the challenges that advocates of gun control have long had to deal with: Gun regulation is very difficult to enforce. Historians of social and moral reform note that police often shied away from implementing statute law to the letter. Limitations on police resources and the attitudes of individual officers toward the particular offence often meant that criminal activity, even when detected, went unprosecuted.[64] The regulation of guns and boys thus highlights what Sharon Myers has recently described as the "fractured, conflicted, confused, and apocryphal character of state regulation and response."[65] This is discernible in the implementation of the 1892 and 1913 laws. Authorities often failed to enforce the 1892 Criminal Code provision, and 20 years after the passage of the 1913 legislation several members of Parliament expressed surprise that the Criminal Code included a law limiting the availability of guns to boys and youth. Of the parliamentarians who knew about the provision, many stated that the ban was widely disregarded.[66] Preventing the use of guns by young people would thus prove challenging, perhaps because of the strong link between masculinity and firearms created earlier in the century.

 More online.

Notes

1.   "The Toy Pistol," *True Witness and Catholic Chronicle*, 9 August 1882, 1.
2.   Stephen Leacock, "Hoodoo McFiggin's Christmas," *Canadian Magazine*, January 1899, 285.
3.   Historians have made conceptual distinctions between *boy* and *youth*. As Cynthia Comacchio, among others, has shown, the term *youth* (and *juvenile*) came to refer to the transitional life stage between boyhood and male adulthood. This article considers the connection between weapons and both boys and youth, focusing on young people 16 years of age and under. Cynthia R. Comacchio, *The Dominion of Youth: Adolescence and the Making of a Modern Canada, 1920–50* (Waterloo, ON: Wilfrid Laurier University Press, 2006), 2–3.

4.   Analyzing the changing attitude to firearms and young people in all of English Canada is of course a challenging exercise. The research plan employed for the present article entailed an examination of a range of sources, including provincial and federal legislation, parliamentary debates, reported judicial decisions, department store catalogues, hunting and police periodicals, archival records of the scouting movement, and an array of digitized Canadian and American newspapers and journals. Unfortunately, these materials capture public discourse by adults over the use of arms by young people, but shed less light on how boys and youth thought about firearms. . . .

5.   David A. Hounshell, *From the American System to Mass Production, 1800–1932: The Development of Manufacturing Technology in the United States* (Baltimore, MD: Johns Hopkins University Press, 1984), 46–50; Lee Kennett and James LaVerne Anderson, *The Gun in America: The Origins of a National Dilemma* (Westport, CT: Greenwood, 1975), 83–107; *Globe*, 26 August 1882, 5; *Winnipeg Daily Sun*, 16 April 1883, 6; [Winnipeg] *Morning Telegram*, 26 July 1900, 2.

6.   Firearms are frequently designated by the internal diameter of their barrel. A ".22 calibre" thus has a barrel with an internal diameter of .22 inches.

7.   "Toys for the Million," *Halifax Citizen*, 2 November 1869, 3.

8.   "Celebrate!" *Commercial*, 12 May 1900, 1128; "Fire Works and Flags," *Commercial*, 11 May 1901, 864; *Simpson's Christmas Catalogue*, 1906, 92, Library and Archives Canada (LAC). . . .

9.   "Air Guns," *Globe*, 22 September 1896, 8. On the sale of air guns as parlour games in the United States, see Gary Cross, *Kids' Stuff: Toys and the Changing World of American Childhood* (Cambridge, MA: Harvard University Press, 1997), 24, 66. On Daisy, see Michael Landry, "It's a Daisy!" *Michigan History* 90, no. 1 (2006): 28–38.

10. *Saint John Daily Sun*, 20 May 1896, 7; *Edmonton Capital*, 5 September 1913, 9. For other examples of inexpensive air guns, see *Cycling*, 10 June 1891, 155; *Toronto Star*, 17 December 1901, 8; *Red Deer News*, 16 December 1914, 4.

11. T. Eaton Co., *Spring and Summer 1899 Catalogue*, F229-1-0-17, Archives of Ontario (AO). Also see [Winnipeg] *Morning Telegram*, 26 July 1900, 2; *Red Deer News*, 21 August 1912, 9; T. Eaton Co., *Fall and Winter 1913–1914 Catalogue*, F229-1-0-47, AO; *Red Deer News*, 20 August 1913, 7.

12. John M. MacKenzie, "Hunting and the Natural World in Juvenile Literature," in Jeffrey Richards, ed., *Imperialism and Juvenile Literature* (Manchester, UK: Manchester University Press, 1989), 170. Also see George Colpitts, *Game in the Garden: A Human History of Wildlife in Western Canada to 1940* (Vancouver, BC: UBC Press, 2002), 63–102; Greg Gillespie, "The Empire's Eden: British Hunters, Travel Writing, and Imperialism in Nineteenth-Century Canada," in Jean L. Manore and Dale G. Miner, eds., *The Culture of Hunting in Canada* (Vancouver, BC: UBC Press, 2007), 42–55. . . .

13. R. G. Moyles and Doug Owram, *Imperial Dreams and Colonial Realities: British Views of Canada, 1880–1914* (Toronto, ON: University of Toronto Press, 1988), 62.

14. Cynthia Comacchio, "Lost in Modernity: 'Maladjustment' and the 'Modern Youth Problem,' English Canada, 1920–50," in Mona Gleason, Tamara Myers, Leslie Paris, and Veronica Strong-Boag, eds., *Lost Kids: Vulnerable Children and Youth in Twentieth-Century Canada and the United States* (Vancouver, BC: UBC Press, 2010), 53–71; Greg Gillespie, *Hunting for Empire: Narratives of Sport in Rupert's Land, 1840–70* (Vancouver, BC: UBC Press, 2007), 35–59; Tina Loo, "Of Moose and Men: Hunting for Masculinities in British Columbia, 1880–1939," *Western Historical Quarterly* 32, no. 3 (2001): 296–319; Sharon Wall, *The Nurture of Nature: Childhood, Antimodernism, and Ontario Summer Camps, 1920–55* (Vancouver, BC: UBC Press, 2009).

15. "Learn to Shoot," *Rod and Gun in Canada*, March 1900, 194. . . .

16. Mark Moss, *Manliness and Militarism: Educating Young Boys in Ontario for War* (Toronto, ON: Oxford University Press, 2001); K. B. Wamsley, "Cultural Signification and National Ideologies: Rifle-Shooting in Late Nineteenth-Century Canada," *Social History* 20, no. 1 (1995): 63–72.

17. Susan E. Houston, "The 'Waifs and Strays' of a Late Victorian City: Juvenile Delinquents in Toronto," in Joy Parr, ed., *Childhood and Family in Canadian History* (Toronto, ON: McClelland & Stewart, 1982), 129–42; Lynne Marks, *Revivals and Roller Rinks: Religion, Leisure, and Identity in Late-Nineteenth-Century Small-Town Ontario* (Toronto, ON: University of Toronto Press, 1996), 81–6; Steven Maynard, "'Horrible Temptations': Sex, Men, and Working-Class Male Youth in Urban Ontario, 1890–1935," *Canadian Historical Review* 78, no. 2 (1997): 191–235; Moss, *Manliness and Militarism*, 112.

18. R. S. S. Baden-Powell, "The Boy Scout Movement," *Empire Club Speeches*, vol. 8 (1910–11), http://speeches.empireclub.org/62214/data?n=1; . . . Desmond Morton, "The Cadet Movement in the Moment of Canadian Militarism," *Journal of Canadian Studies* 13, no. 2 (1978): 59. . . .

19. Quoted in Moss, *Manliness and Militarism*, 118.

20. Minutes of Executive Committee Meeting of Dominion Council, Canadian Boy Scouts, 16 May 1914, MG28-I73, LAC; Canadian General Council of the Boy Scouts Association, Report of the Third Annual Meeting held in Ottawa, 21 April 1917, MG28-I73, LAC; Annual Report of the Canadian General Council of the Boys Scouts Association, March 1919 (Ottawa: n.p., 1919), 8, MG28-I73, LAC.

21. Ronald G. Haycock, *Sam Hughes: The Public Career of a Controversial Canadian, 1885–1916* (Waterloo, ON: Wilfrid Laurier University Press, 1986), 140–1; The Militia Act, SC 1904, c.23, s.67; Morton, "Cadet Movement," 56–68; James Wood, *Militia Myths: Ideas of the Canadian Citizen Soldier, 1896–1921* (Vancouver, BC: UBC Press, 2010), 150–61, 279.

22. T. Eaton Co., *Fall/Winter 1892–93 Catalogue*, F229-1-0-6, AO; "Spencer's Arcade," *Victoria Daily Colonist*, 10 December 1897, 4; T. Eaton Co., *Fall/Winter 1902–03 Catalogue*, F229-1-0-24, AO; T. Eaton Co., *Spring/Summer 1910 Catalogue*, F229-1-0-40, AO.

23. *Red Deer News*, 16 December 1914, 4; *Simpson's Christmas Catalogue, 1906*, 93, LAC. . . .

24. Cross, *Kids' Stuff*, 50–1.

25. *Calgary Weekly Herald*, 22 March 1900, 7; *Globe*, 21 April 1900, 3; *Calgary Weekly Herald*, 11 May 1900, 8; *Globe*, 23 March 1901, 4; *Toronto Star*, 22 February 1902, 3; *Globe*, 1 November 1902, 4; "Free Rifle," *Globe*, 31 January 1903, 4; *Globe*, 24 February 1905, 11; *Twillingate Sun*, 30 October 1909, 3; *St John's Evening Telegram*, 19 November 1909, 3; *Twillingate Sun*, 27 November 1909, 3; *Waterford Star*, 9 December 1909, 6; *Toronto Star*, 22 January 1910, 7; "Free to Boys," *Wetaskiwin Times*, 28 March 1912, 3; *Rod and Gun in Canada* 16, no. 9 (February 1914): 1001.

26. *Saint John Daily Sun*, 23 May 1896, 7.

27. *Grain Growers' Guide*, 15 June 1910, 2.

28. *Toronto Star*, 17 December 1904, 9.

29. *Grain Growers' Guide*, 23 November 1910, 15.

30. *Rod and Gun in Canada* 5, no. 7 (December 1903). For other examples of retailers advertising guns as Christmas gifts, see "Xmas," *Globe*, 21 December 1896, 10; *Red Deer News*, 9 December 1908, 1; *Victoria Daily Colonist*, 20 December 1908, 9; *Edmonton Capital*, 14 December 1911, 11; "Xmas Gifts," *Red Deer News*, 16 December 1914, 5; "Christmas Suggestions," *Globe*, 2 December 1916, 8; *Bassano Mail*, 18 December 1919, 10.

31. *Rod and Gun in Canada* 5, no. 7 (December 1903).

32. Cross, *Kids' Stuff*, 111–12; Steven Mintz, *Huck's Raft: A History of American Childhood* (Cambridge, MA: Belknap, 2004), 217. After 1900, publishers (and advertisers) became more interested in

targeting particular markets determined by gender. Russell Johnston, *Selling Themselves: The Emergence of Canadian Advertising* (Toronto, ON: University of Toronto Press, 2001), 192–6. On liberalism and the connection between liberalism and consumption, see Donica Belisle, "Toward a Canadian Consumer History," *Labour/Le Travail* 52 (2003): 191–4; Ian McKay, "The Liberal Order Framework: A Prospectus for a Reconnaissance of Canadian History," *Canadian Historical Review* 81, no. 4 (2000): 616–78.

33. "Echoes of the Fourth," *Toronto Star*, 11 July 1905, 6.

34. For a small sample of such accidents, see "Fatal Firearms Accident," *Globe*, 30 April 1877, 4; *Globe*, 5 April 1879, 8; "Notes from the Capital," *Globe*, 8 July 1879, 1; "A Revolver Accident," *Globe*, 22 April 1885, 6; "Accidentally Shot," *Globe*, 2 April 1887, 16; "The Fatal Revolver," *Globe*, 3 August 1888, 1; "Shot by a Boy," *Manitoba Daily Free Press*, 30 November 1892, 1; "Boy Shoots His Sister," *Toronto Star*, 27 May 1901, 1.

35. "Thomas Ryan Was Careless," *Toronto Star*, 28 May 1901, 3.

36. "Judge Scores the Sale of Revolvers," *Manitoba Morning Free Press*, 17 October 1912, 16.

37. *Globe*, 28 May 1901, 6.

38. On social and moral reform in the period, see Craig Heron, *Booze: A Distilled History* (Toronto, ON: Between the Lines, 2003); Carolyn Strange and Tina Loo, *Making Good: Law and Moral Regulation in Canada, 1867–1939* (Toronto, ON: University of Toronto Press, 1997); Mariana Valverde, *The Age of Light, Soap, and Water: Moral Reform in English Canada, 1885–1925* (Toronto, ON: McClelland & Stewart, 1991).

39. "Played Wild West," *Globe*, 26 October 1907, 1. For a sample of accidents involving air rifles, see "Police Court," *Saint John Daily Sun*, 14 June 1906, 2; "Boy Shot in the Eye," *Montreal Gazette*, 20 January 1910, 6.

40. "The Law on Air Guns," *Manitoba Morning Free Press*, 12 November 1898, 12.

41. "City and District," *Montreal Gazette*, 12 May 1913. For a sample of other incidents, see "Shot in the Eye," *Globe*, 5 November 1895, 10; "Shooting Accident at London," *Globe*, 14 April 1900, 20; "Another Shooting Accident," *Globe*, 30 May 1901, 12; "Hamilton Boy Killed," *Globe*, 7 September 1903, 1; "Boy Sportsman Killed," *Globe*, 20 July 1904, 9; "Hamilton Boy Shot," *Globe*, 20 March 1905, 1; "Shot through the Brain," *Globe*, 11 July 1905, 1; "Another Gun Victim," *Montreal Gazette*, 17 December 1908, 11; "Youth with Rifle Kills Companion," *Globe*, 27 October 1913, 8.

42. "Accidentally Shot," *Victoria Daily Colonist*, 23 September 1896, 5; "Shot through the Head," *Victoria Daily Colonist*, 29 October 1897, 2; "Gun License," *Victoria Daily Colonist*, 11 January 1901, 7; *Cayley Hustler*, 20 September 1911, 5.

43. *Globe*, 23 May 1885, 9.

44. "Bad Boys at the Bijou," *Manitoba Morning Free Press*, 24 March 1896, 6; *Globe*, 6 August 1887, 4; "Influence the Imagination," *Educational Journal* 5, no. 16 (January 1892): 604; "The Mirror," *Saturday News*, 13 January 1906, 4.

45. "Boys Handling Fire Arms," *Temiskaming Speaker*, 29 October 1909, 1. Also see "The Boy and the Gun," *Temiskaming Speaker*, 8 November 1912, 1.

46. The history of wildlife protection has been studied by J. Alexander Burnett, *A Passion for Wildlife: The History of the Canadian Wildlife Service* (Vancouver, BC: UBC Press, 2003); Colpitts, *Game in the Garden*; Janet Foster, *Working for Wildlife: The Beginning of Preservation in Canada* (Toronto, ON: University of Toronto Press, 1978); Tina Loo, *States of Nature: Conserving Canada's Wildlife in the Twentieth Century* (Vancouver, BC: UBC Press, 2006).

47. "Engaged in a Noble Work," *Victoria Daily Colonist*, 4 November 1903, 6. . . .

48. "Small Boys with Rifles a Menace in the Country," *Toronto Star*, 26 October 1911, 17; "The Killing of Birds," *Toronto Star*, 7 May 1904, 6; "The Boy and the Gun," *Toronto Star*, 6 November 1911, 6; "Firearms in Suburbs," *Toronto Star*, 24 October 1913, 1.

49. Comacchio, *Dominion of Youth*, 28.

50. Dorothy E. Chunn, "Boys Will Be Men, Girls Will Be Mothers: The Legal Regulation of Childhood in Toronto and Vancouver," in Nancy Janovicek and Joy Parr, eds., *Histories of Canadian Children and Youth* (Toronto, ON: Oxford University Press, 2003), 188–206; Dorothy E. Chunn, *From Punishment to Doing Good: Family Courts and Socialized Justice in Ontario, 1880–1940* (Toronto, ON: University of Toronto Press, 1992); Comacchio, *Dominion of Youth*, 29; Tamara Myers, *Caught: Montreal's Modern Girls and the Law, 1869–1945* (Toronto, ON: University of Toronto Press, 2006); Tamara Myers, "Nocturnal Disorder and the Curfew Solution: A History of Juvenile Sundown Regulations in Canada," in Gleason et al., *Lost Kids*, 95–113.

51. Canada, *Senate Debates* (4 April 1889), pp. 427–9; (9 April 1889), pp. 449–50; The Criminal Code, S.C. 1892, c.29, s.106(1); Chunn, "Boys Will Be Men," 194. In 1890, British Columbia banned most boys under 14 from carrying a gun without the accompaniment of his father or guardian. An Act to Prevent Minors from Carrying Fire-arms, S.B.C. 1890, c.18. This was increased to those under 16 in 1913. Firearms Act Amendment Act, 1913, S.B.C. 1913, c.23.

52. Canada, *House of Commons Debates* (29 May 1903), p. 3773 (Thomas Simpson Sproule, MP). Also see "The Mail Bag," *Grain Growers' Guide*, 27 May 1914, 23.

53. Canada, *House of Commons Debates* (29 May 1903), p. 3777 (Sam Hughes, MP).

54. Canada, *House of Commons Debates* (10 July 1905), p. 9120 (Frederick Borden, MP). Also see "Let the Boys Shoot," *Victoria Daily Colonist*, 26 May 1890, 3.

55. "Let the Boys Shoot," 3. See also "Feminine Fancies and the Home Circle Chat," *Victoria Daily Colonist*, 8 March 1908, 22; "Young Sportsmen," *Strathmore Standard*, 6 May 1914, 3; "Young Sportsmen," *Gleichen Call*, 14 May 1914, 7.

56. John Herd Thompson, *Ethnic Minorities during Two World Wars* (Ottawa, ON: Canadian Historical Association 1991), 3.

57. "Grand Jury against Weapon Carrying," *Manitoba Morning Free Press*, 8 July 1911, 17. See also Canada, *House of Commons Debates* (27 January 1911), pp. 2557–59 (Hon. E. N. Lewis, MP).

58. The Offensive Weapons Act, S.O. 1911, c.66, s.5.

59. The Offensive Weapons Act, S.M. 1912, c.57; The Offensive Weapons Act, S.S 1912, c.24; Offensive Weapons Act, S.B.C. 1913, c.83.

60. "Permit Is Now Necessary for Keeping an Air Rifle," *Toronto Star*, 21 April 1911, 1.

61. The Criminal Code Amendment Act, 1913, S.C. 1913, c.13, s.5.

62. Comacchio, *Dominion of Youth*, 114. There were, however, efforts to encourage cadets in World War II. Tamara Myers and Mary Anne Poutanen, "Cadets, Curfews, and Compulsory Schooling: Mobilizing Anglophone Children in WWII Montreal," *Histoire Sociale/Social History* 76 (2005): 367–98.

63. Angela F. Keaton, "Backyard Desperadoes: American Attitudes Concerning Toy Guns in the Early Cold War Era," *Journal of American Culture* 33, no. 3 (2010): 183–96.

64. Greg Marquis, "Vancouver Vice: The Police and the Negotiation of Morality, 1904–1935," in *British Columbia and the Yukon*, vol. 6 of *Essays in the History of Canadian Law*, ed. Hamar Foster and John McLaren (Toronto, ON: University of Toronto Press and the Osgoode Society, 1995), 242–73.

65. Sharon Myers, "The Apocrypha of Minnie McGee: The Murderous Mother and Multivocal State in 20th-Century Prince Edward Island," *Acadiensis* 38, no. 2 (2009): 27.

66. Canada, *House of Commons Debates* (29 March 1933), pp. 3526–31; Chief Constables' Association of Canada, *Forty-Third Annual Conference, Vancouver, B.C., September 22nd, 23rd, 24th and 25th, 1948* (n.p.: n.d.), 167–8.

24 Borderlands, Baselines, and Big Game
Conceptualizing the Northeast as a Sporting Region

Colin D. Howell

Borderlands, baseball, and big game! Bluenose sailors, Boston Marathoners, Bobby Gimby, and the Bangor Mall! Other than alliteration, what unites these diffuse examples of northeastern popular culture, from sport to song to shopping expeditions? What might discussion of their interconnectedness offer us beyond a foray into postmodernist eccentricity or unfettered speculation? This study, part of an ongoing project on sporting culture along the Mexican– and Canadian–American borders over the past century, places borderland sporting life, in all its quirkiness, ambiguity, *and* significance, at the centre of historical inquiry rather than at the periphery.

Interest in borderlands studies as a way of inquiring into questions of power, conflict, identity, and cultural formation has grown significantly over the past decade. Along with the process of globalization, the growth of ethnic nationalisms, the seeming fragility and impermanence of existing nation states, and the increasing mobility of peoples, ideas, and capital—the new interest in border relationships reveals a growing fascination with questions of cultural identity (or identities) and issues of national integrity.[1] Nations themselves, we are now told, are invented, imagined communities[2] that have the possibility of being reconceptualized quite differently from the way they are now perceived.

The very meaning of borders in both the past and the present is now an issue of considerable controversy. According to W. H. New in *Borderlands: How We Talk About Canada*, borders are metaphorical constructions, and borderlands are "symptomatic of the contemporary condition, a condition of 'interstititality,' *in-betweenness*, an experiential territory of intervention and revision."[3] But borders nonetheless distinguish one community from another. One need only think of the recent discourse over the treatment of suspected terrorists to know that borders carry powerful images of identity and differentiation. Borders, then, unite and divide—often at the very same moment.

In a recent article entitled "How Canadian Historians Stopped Worrying and Learned to Love the Americans!" Phil Buckner has warned against accepting a notion that borders are "artificial" impediments to closer and more "natural" relations with friendly neighbours.[4] Buckner's argument is a useful counterweight to the attitude of those who would ignore differences in

Citation: Colin D. Howell, "Borderlands, Baselines, and Big Game: Conceptualizing the Northeast as a Sporting Region," in Stephen J. Hornsby and John G. Reid, eds., *New England and the Maritime Provinces: Connections and Comparisons* (Montreal, QC: McGill-Queen's University Press, 2005): 264–79.

institutional arrangements, social and economic policies, and cultural values that derived from the experience of border making, but his blanket critique of borderlands historiography nonetheless obscures the complex and often ambiguous history of transnational interactions between America and her neighbours to both the north and south. This is especially the case with respect to social and cultural production. In fact, as becomes apparent with respect to sporting life, it is possible to write the history of borderlands interactions and yet maintain one's distance from the contemporary continentalist or global capitalist agenda.

A useful starting point for any discussion of sport in hinterland or borderland regions is the recent literature that has developed around the process of ludic diffusion, or the diffusion of sport. Several sport historians and sociologists have suggested that sporting culture radiates from the more developed nations outward to the rest of the world, and enters host cultures at the elite level, before descending through the social order and eventually reaching the working class and common people.[5] But a top-down approach to the development of popular culture often overlooks the complexity of the process of cultural formation and the lived social, cultural, and economic experience of local communities or hinterland regions, where history is made "on the ground." Of course, these contrasting orientations need not be mutually exclusive. The significance of the history of peoples on the margins and their cultural creativity—their agency, if you like—is that they can be seen as neither dependent upon nor independent of their relationship to the nation or the metropolis. This is particularly evident from a study of the barnstorming baseballists, big-game hunters, Bluenose sailors, and Boston Marathoners of the interwar years. Baseball, hunting, competitive international schooner races, and Maritime involvement with the Boston Marathon were essential components of the interwar conceptualization of the northeast as a transnational sporting region.

Of course, this imagined sporting community was not the only manifestation of the metropolitan influence over the Maritime provinces that Boston had exerted prior to this period—and would continue to exert more than 60 years after Confederation. Nor did it displace the presence and expression of other allegiances, particularly to Canada, in the sporting culture of the Maritimes. It does appear, however, that the assumption about a transnational northeastern sporting region was the *dominant* construction of the interwar years. The later emergence of nationalist discourses in the 1960s, including Bobby Gimby's musical testimony to Canadian Confederation and the patterns of consumption that encouraged the development of the Bangor Mall, however, undermined such earlier configurations of sporting life in the northeastern borderlands and created new forms of cultural interaction between the Maritimes and New England.

Barnstormers

In 1936, just a year after his retirement from baseball, Babe Ruth climbed aboard the SS *Atlantic* in Portland, Maine, for a vacation trip to Nova Scotia. After arriving in Yarmouth, Ruth spent a few days in the southwestern part of the province in the company of friends and playing golf at the Digby Pines golf course. He then drove through the Annapolis Valley to Halifax before travelling to Westville in Pictou County to give a hitting exhibition. Although many Nova Scotians still recall this visit—and a second one in 1942 when Ruth helped open the new Navy recreation centre in Halifax—Ruth's connection to the Maritimes was more than simply incidental.

Born in Baltimore in 1895, Ruth had grown up along the city's rough-and-tumble waterfront where his parents ran a saloon catering to longshoremen, merchant sailors, roustabouts, and waterfront drifters. Considered an "incorrigible youth," Ruth was consigned for most of his childhood after the age of seven to the Saint Mary's

Industrial School for boys, a reform school run by the Xaverian Brothers religious order. The brothers had a lasting influence on Ruth. "It was at St. Mary's," Ruth wrote in his autobiography, "that I met and learned to love the greatest man I've ever known . . . Brother Matthias of the Xaverian order." Brother Matthias was born Martin Leo Boutilier in Lingan, Cape Breton, the son of a mining engineer with extensive family connections around the Bras d'Or Lakes. He and his older brother had both grown up playing pickup baseball before entering the Xaverian brotherhood and following many of their Maritime compatriots before World War I down the road to the "Boston States." Indeed, a number of Ruth's major league colleagues had family in the Maritimes, among them two future Hall-of-Famers: Harry Hooper, whose father was a Prince Edward Island ship's captain, and Harold "Pie" Traynor, whose father, Jimmy, had lived in Halifax before moving to Framingham, Massachusetts. Then, too, there was John Phalen "Stuffy" MacInnes of Gloucester, a member of the Philadelphia Athletics's famed "hundred-thousand-dollar infield," whose family had roots in Cape Breton, and who, after his playing days were over, returned briefly to coach semi-pro baseball in Nova Scotia. And finally, Ruth's first wife, Helen Woodford, whom he met in South Boston, had grown up in Nova Scotia and joined her family in the southward exodus from the Maritimes to Boston.[6]

Of course, given the demands of travel associated with a major league schedule, Ruth had little opportunity for summer visits to the province—in fact for summer vacations of any sort—during his 20-year career as a major league player. Had he not retired from baseball early in the 1935 season after a disappointing 28-game stint with the Boston Braves, however, he would no doubt have come to Nova Scotia with the Braves when they visited the province later that summer to play the Maritime champion, Yarmouth Gateways. A midseason junket to the Maritimes by a major league team would

be incomprehensible today, but in the interwar years this was part of a broad tradition of itinerant baseball barnstorming that drew the northeast together as a sporting region, a tradition that endured until the 1950s. Both of Boston's major league clubs, the Braves and the Red Sox, regarded northern New England and the Maritimes as their hinterland and asserted that claim through numerous tours of the region and in their promotional materials. Most of these visits took place at season's end, but in 1935 the Braves came north to St. Stephen, New Brunswick, in the middle of their summer schedule with the express purpose of challenging the Maritime champion, and they followed up with a visit to Yarmouth to play the new champions the following summer.

Baseball connections between the Maritimes and New England were nothing new, however. As early as the 1870s, teams and players from the northeast were regular summer visitors to the Maritimes, and by the end of that decade imported professionals were beginning to show up in semi-pro lineups in Halifax, Moncton, Saint John, and Fredericton. Before 1900, travelling teams from Boston and nearby towns such as Haverford, Dorchester, and Lowell, as well as from Portland, Augusta, and Bangor in Maine, had helped create a shared baseball culture within which the border played a rather insignificant role. Various semi-professional leagues such as the Maine–New Brunswick League also spanned the border. In 1912, for example, the Saint John Marathons (winners of the Maine–New Brunswick league pennant) played a three-game series against the champion Lowell club of the New England League in what amounted to the minor league baseball championship of the Maritimes and New England.

After the war, New England teams flooded the region. In addition to the Braves and Red Sox, Eddie Carr's Auburn Club from Cambridge, Massachusetts, which the *Boston Post* dubbed the "fastest amateur team around Boston," Bob Bigney's South Boston All-Stars, Dick Casey's Neponsett All-Stars, the James A. Roche team of

Everett, Massachusetts, Frank Silva's Connecticut Yankees, and touring teams from Arlington, Dorchester, Quincy, Newburyport, Somerville, Malden, Salem, Taunton, and Attleboro would turn Maritime ball diamonds into "burned over districts" of New England baseball barnstorming. They were joined, moreover, by various assemblages of African-American ballplayers from the so-called Negro leagues. As Chappie Johnson's Travelling All-Stars, the Philadelphia Colored Giants, the New York Black Yankees, the Ethiopian Clowns, and the Zulu Cannibal Giants barnstormed the province, they gave Maritime fans the opportunity to see leading stars of the Negro leagues, such as Bill Jackman and others, playing against their own clubs. Without question the most popular of these teams was Burlin White's Boston Royal Giants, who mixed straight baseball with clownish routines. These routines, or reams as they were called, demonstrated their baseball skills and dramatized their "otherness" as a way of attracting fans to the park. The Giants returned to the Maritimes year after year during the thirties, playing over 300 games against predominantly white local teams. Despite the carnivalesque nature of these tours, which often involved the Giants mocking their white opponents, baseball fans in the Maritimes responded warmly to the Giants, and in the process contributed to an idealized image of the northeast as a region with a shared sporting identity that transcended both the border and the racial divide.[7]

This romanticized transnationalism, of course, stood in contrast to the discourses of betrayal and regional neglect that surrounded the place of the Maritimes within Confederation, and which had been given political expression in the Maritime Rights movement.[8] Indeed, the language of regionalism within Canada and linkages with New England resonated throughout the interwar years in the sporting pages of Maritime newspapers. In addition to the constant coverage of the baseball connection with New England, what is particularly striking is the absence of teams from the rest of Canada from Maritime baseball diamonds in these years. Indeed, the 1935 visit of the Montreal Dow team for two games marks the only instance of a team from elsewhere in Canada playing in the Maritimes and being reported in the region's newspapers during the entire period from the turn of the century to World War II.

Big-Game Hunters

Another component of the interwar imagining of the northeastern borderlands as a sporting region is connected to baseball but not restricted to it. To illustrate, let me return to Babe Ruth. Most Nova Scotians regarded Ruth's visits and those of the touring ball clubs from the United States as an indication of the region's modernity. To get to the Maritimes, these visitors took advantage of improved rail and highway systems. At the same time, the hotly contested matches seemed to demonstrate that Nova Scotians could play on a par with some of the best ballplayers in North America. The need to compete effectively with barnstorming clubs was thus something Nova Scotians took seriously. It is hardly surprising, therefore, that Claude "Dingie" McLeod, the young pitcher who would serve up Ruth's plate offerings in Westville, would take the opportunity to show the crowd that he could strike out baseball's demigod. After a mixture of fastballs on the inside of the plate and curveballs away, Ruth had had enough. He walked out to the mound and told McLeod that he seemed to be missing the point. The crowd was there not to see him strike out, but to watch him hit home runs. "So just give me some of those big drug store fastballs down the middle like you're supposed to do."[9]

Of course one can find multiple meanings in incidents of this sort. For one thing, Maritimers' perceptions of the significance of these baseball interactions seem to have differed from those of the visitors. The fans in Westville may well have been delighted, even if a little embarrassed, to see one of their own reduce the Babe to the status of a mere mortal. Ruth, on the other hand, had come to the region not because of its modernity or the level of competition that ballplayers in the Maritimes could provide, but rather because it represented to him a natural sporting paradise where he could golf, fish, and hunt to his heart's content and at the same time bask in public adulation. Romantic images of northern New England and the Maritimes as a sportsman's paradise were commonplace in the interwar years, and local newspapers delighted in reporting on hunting trips involving American sporting celebrities. The *Sydney Record* of 13 November 1925, for example, reported on a moose-hunting expedition "40 miles into the wilds of Canada," more specifically into New Brunswick, involving Ruth and three of his baseball buddies. Apparently Ruth did not impress his guide, because he could only walk the first 15 miles into the bush and needed a horse to complete the other 25. He did, however, bag his moose, and later regaled the press with his triumph. "As soon as I can get a freight train to carry the head back and get it stuffed, I'll show it to you," Ruth gloated. "The Yankee Stadium is the only place big enough to hold it."[10]

Two years later the press reported on another postseason moosehunting trip by a group of players from the World Series champion Yankees and some of their former teammates. The players were accompanied by newspaperman William Slocum of the New York *Evening Telegram* and Dr. J. Wolford, a big-game hunter and baseball devotee from Philadelphia. Wolford had led a group of baseball stars on a hunting trip to New Brunswick in 1924, an expedition that had brought down four bull moose and five deer. On this trip, Jack Doran, a catcher for the Fredericton Tartars, guided the hunters into the woods at Clarendon on the main line of the CPR. This was reported to be the same territory that heavyweight boxer Jack Dempsey had stalked a few years before and where "the fistic star knocked out his first moose."[11] There are a number of similar reports of baseball

big-game hunters and other celebrities such as Zane Grey stalking the woods of Maine and the Maritimes.[12] Furthermore, the Boston Red Sox star Ted Williams purchased a summer camp on the Miramichi River in order to pursue his avocation as a fly fisherman after his retirement from baseball.

These stories of celebrity hunting trips reinforced musings about the region as a haven for American capitalists who, in seeking out the recuperative benefits of a natural paradise, might in turn come to recognize the potential for future resource development.[13] As Ian McKay has pointed out, the interwar period had witnessed a reconceptualization of the Maritimes as an idyllic paradise, a more authentic and simple place with a population living closer to nature than inhabitants of bustling North American cities. In the wake of deindustrialization and the consequent economic distress of the 1920s and 1930s, the language of industrial progress and modernity that had predominated before the war had given way to anti-modernist fantasies about the virtue and innocence of the Maritime folk.[14] Yet the romanticization of rural innocence often carried with it the thirst for commercial advantage. According to Beatrice Hay Shaw's *Nova Scotia: For Beauty and Business*, a 1923 publication promoting the province and its untapped resources, for example, the province offered American businessmen a respite from their hectic lives as well as a resource base ready to be exploited and developed. Shaw's imagery, in fact, bordered on the salacious. She depicted Nova Scotia as the innocent blue-nosed lady-in-waiting sitting patiently for "the man of rod and gun. At this moment [she] holds her arms outspread, and bares her rich bosom to the world, calling to it to come and receive nourishment and life from her ripe breasts."[15]

Indeed, in conceptualizing the northeast as a sporting region, Maritimers created a discourse that married anti-modernist assumptions about regional simplicity and a "natural" lifestyle to a cautious hope of a future transformed by modern technology. Anti-modernism might have offered some consolation to a region that was already experiencing the destructive implications of industrial capitalist consolidation and the dismantling of its secondary manufacturing, but this nostalgia did not necessarily imply a rejection of all things modern.

Boston Marathoners

For most Maritimers, the city of Boston symbolized modernity and opportunity and acted as a safety valve for those unable to make a living in hardscrabble communities throughout the provinces. Centuries of economic interaction beginning in the seventeenth century and a history of widespread out-migration from the Maritimes to the northeastern United States in the decades following Confederation reinforced New England's metropolitan connection to its Maritime hinterland. Moreover, for many Maritimers in the interwar period, Boston seemed to exert a stronger and seemingly more benign influence than either Montreal or Toronto. While Toronto and Montreal were often criticized for their predatory behaviour in an age of deindustrialization, and while the rhetoric of Maritime Rights attributed the shortcomings of Confederation to central Canada's broken promises, Boston was for many Maritimers literally their second home.

The seemingly benign nature of Boston's metropolitan authority explains in part both the fascination and the considerable involvement that Maritimers had with the Boston Marathon during the interwar years. Interest in marathon running at the turn of the century grew out of the sportive nationalism of the day and the inauguration of the modern Olympic Games in 1896. The brainchild of a French nobleman, Baron Pierre de Coubertin, the modern Olympics were associated with the classical symbols of Greek antiquity, not the least of which was the marathon run. At the 1896 games in Athens, the marathon distance was set at 24.8 miles, the distance a legendary Greek foot-soldier was supposed to have run across the plains of Marathon to carry to Athenians the news of the Greek army's victory over a mighty Persian invasion force. John Graham, manager of the American track and field team at the Athens Games and a member of the Boston Athletic Association (BAA) founded a decade earlier, was so impressed with the majestic spectacle that on his return he set about organizing the first Boston marathon, to be hosted by the BAA in 1897. It has been held annually without interruption ever since.

Boston's significant presence in the turn-of the-century world of track and field was hardly surprising. The first US Olympic team had been an aggregation of students and "gentlemanly amateurs" drawn largely from American northeastern universities, including Princeton, Harvard, Yale, Boston College, and the Massachusetts Institute of Technology. Graham had taken with him a six-man delegation from the Boston Athletic Association, and they were accompanied by James Connolly of Boston's Suffolk Athletic Club. In the 12 track and field events at Athens in 1896, members of the BAA won seven gold medals, and Americans attending the games delivered the club cheer, "B.A.A.-Rah-Rah-Rah," to an approving audience.[16]

Although the first Boston Marathon was won by New Yorker John J. McDermott, Canadians were prominent competitors in the years before World War I. Canadian Ronald MacDonald, a student at Boston College, won the 1898 race, and two years later a Canadian contingent led by John Caffery of Hamilton took first, second, and third places. Caffery won again in 1901. In 1907 Hamilton-based Onondaga runner Tom Longboat captured the crown. Three years later Fred Cameron of Amherst, Nova Scotia, became the first Boston Marathon champion to hail from the Maritime provinces, leading the race from beginning to end.[17]

Nova Scotia's interest in the Boston race intensified during the 1920s, spurred on by the remarkable success of homebred marathoners Victor MacAulay of Windsor, Silas McLellan from nearby Noel in Hants County, and Billy Taylor and Johnny Miles from Sydney Mines. Of the four, Miles was the most accomplished, winning the event in 1926 and again in 1929 and becoming, in the words of local sportswriter Gee Ahearne, "the long distance champion runner of the world." Although the victories of Miles overshadowed the careers of MacAulay, McLellan, and Taylor, it is nonetheless worth remembering that Maritimers in the 1920s and 1930s applauded the accomplishments of all these fine runners. MacAulay's top five finish in the 1924 Boston Marathon catapulted him to a spot on the Canadian Olympic team that year. In 1925 he returned to Boston and finished a respectable seventh. Just two weeks after Miles's victory in the 1926 Boston Marathon, McLellan won the annual Italian Athletic Association 10-mile marathon in Lynn, Massachusetts, over Clarence DeMar, a multiyear champion of the Boston race. Billy Taylor finished second to Miles and ahead of DeMar in a race in Halifax in 1927 and joined the others on Nova Scotia's provincial team at Boston the following year. The province's 1928 team wore shirts emblazoned with a red maple leaf surrounded with "Nova Scotia" in large black letters, dramatizing the tension that surrounded the relationship of the Maritimes to the nation itself.[18]

Maritime involvement in the Boston Marathon contributed to the imagining of the northeast as a coherent transnational sporting region. It also gave vent to the ambivalent allegiances and deep frustrations that accompanied post-war economic decline. Both the marathoners themselves and the newspapermen who reported upon them constructed stories that reinforced contemporary discourses about regional identity, national betrayal, and Maritime Rights. In many ways, Maritime sporting heroes and officials of the Maritime Provinces Amateur Athletic Association (MPAAA) became stalking horses of post-war Maritime regionalism. In the summer of 1924, for example, Victor MacAulay charged that Maritime athletes on the Canadian

Olympic team had been discriminated against by head coach J. R. Cornelius. MacAulay complained that he had had to wear running shoes that were two sizes too large for him, and that Maritimers had received poor lodgings in comparison with athletes from central Canada and the west.[19] Charges of this sort led J. G. Quigley of the MPAAA to attend a meeting of the Canadian Amateur Athletic Union in 1925 where he called for "Maritime Rights" for the region's athletes.[20] Silas McLellan lodged a similar complaint to that of Victor MacAulay during the 1928 Olympics. The third Canadian to finish in the Olympic marathon that year, McLellan complained that officials of the Canadian Olympic Committee had woken him up at 11 o'clock at night to give him a rub-down, and made him sleep in a room with five others. His complaint prompted A. C. Pettipas, Maritime representative on the Canadian Olympic Committee, to protest McLellan's shabby treatment.[21]

Issues of regional alienation and allegiance— not to mention the difficulties involved in making a living in a chronically depressed region where the British Empire Steel Corporation, the main employer in industrial Cape Breton, teetered on financial ruin—were equally evident in the career of Nova Scotia's premiere marathoner of the interwar period. When Johnny Miles, a 19-year-old delivery boy from Sydney Mines, won the Boston Marathon in 1926 in his first marathon competition, he became an immediate hero in his native province. For young working-class men such as Miles, running offered an inexpensive means of exercise since it required only a pair of shoes and the time and space to train, and victory in a big event could lead to a steady job. At the same time, the more accomplished a runner became, the heavier the financial costs associated with training. Unlike team sports such as hockey, football, baseball, and lacrosse, track and field offered few opportunities to make money from competition, and amateur athletes like Miles found themselves dependent on financial support from the community in order to defray travel and accommodation cost. In 1926, for example, Miles received financial assistance from his hometown and from the Cape Breton Club of Boston, before rewarding his supporters with a victory in the big race.[22]

When Miles and his parents returned from Boston, they were thrown into a dizzying whirl of local functions throughout Sydney Mines, North Sydney, Glace Bay, and Sydney. They also were inundated with invitations to compete in races across the Maritimes and New England. While he could not compete in them all, he did contest 19 major races in the northeast, until winter brought the 1926 racing season to a merciful close. The price of success was high. In return for financial support and media coverage, Miles and his family were expected to participate in the maintenance of their communities, local, provincial, or regional. The strain of this implied social contract, when combined with Johnny's hunger for success, took its inevitable toll. On 12 June, less than two months after his victory in Boston, Johnny collapsed just 220 yards from the finish line in a 10-mile race in Melrose, Massachusetts. According to the *Halifax Herald*, he suffered from heat exhaustion. Miles's biographer, Floyd Williston, suggested that Johnny had gorged himself on rich pastries at a reception earlier on the day of the race. Neither considered the likelihood that the public appearances associated with Johnny's "social contract" were a factor contributing to his exhaustion.[23]

Just days after Miles's collapse in Melrose, press reports surfaced that he had received offers of financial support from track and field clubs in Boston and Hamilton, Ontario. Johnny's father expressed to the media his concern about the possibility of leaving Sydney Mines, but made it clear that the family would stay in Cape Breton only if he and his son were provided with steady jobs. "There is absolutely no beating about the bush on this score," he told the *Halifax Herald*. "We either get jobs which will not have us tied down hard and fast in order to make a comfortable living or we change our place of residence.

Hundreds who found themselves in exactly the same position as we are now have done just this, and why shouldn't we? I have received many promises in order that we might remain in Nova Scotia, but to date they have just been promises."[24] Throughout the summer of 1926, negotiations continued between the Miles family and prospective clubs, and on 13 August the *Halifax Herald* reported that Miles had accepted an offer from the BAA. This report was premature, however. The family eventually declined that offer and returned to Cape Breton.[25]

Over the winter and into the spring of 1927, Johnny trained for the defence of his Boston Marathon title, supported by the Johnny Miles Training Fund set up by the *Halifax Herald*. The candid "Gee" Ahem wrote that the family was in need of "tangible" support and that all well-wishers should "say it with cash." Donations for the fund poured in from all over Nova Scotia and from Johnny's supporters in Boston. The publisher of the *Herald*, William Dennis, believed that support for Miles was warranted because he was both an "asset and advertiser" to a province interested in attracting tourists.[26] An investment in Miles was thus an investment in one's self and one's country. The material circumstances that faced the Miles family were difficult to endure. Even when combined, Miles's father's mining pay and his pay as a clerk could not meet the costs of competing on a regular basis. Nor was it easy to raise money from Cape Breton miners, who faced wage cuts in their struggles with BESCO and themselves relied upon relief from across the country to battle chronic poverty. Still, over $1,500 was collected for the Miles family before their departure to Boston to train for the 1927 event.[27]

The 1927 marathon was run in what was unusually hot weather for Boston in April. Miles quickly succumbed, as steaming tar from the hot pavement seeped through the thin base of his shoes. Apparently his father had shaved the bottoms of his sneakers with a straight razor, hoping that thinner soles would translate into a faster time. Before he called it quits at the seventh mile Miles's feet were burned, blistered, and bloodied. He was not alone. More than a hundred runners dropped out because of the heat, including 35 before the second mile.[28] Nevertheless, his supporters were quick to criticize. Bill Cunningham, a *Boston Post* sportswriter and friend to Miles, suggested that "Miles should have finished the race if he had to crawl across the line on his hands and knees after the hour of midnight with his bleeding feet wrapped in newspaper."[29] There was initial underlying resentment in the Maritimes as well. It was as if Johnny had reneged on his obligation to those who supported him. Their disappointment quickly healed upon his return to Cape Breton, however. Ten thousand fans turned out to see him defeat Jimmy Henigan, United States 10-mile champion, and Clarence DeMar, eight-time winner of the Boston Marathon (including 1927), in a five-mile race at the Black Diamond track in Glace Bay. On Dominion Day another 10,000 people turned out in Sydney to witness his third-place finish behind Albert Michelson and Jimmy Henigan, and ahead of Clarence DeMar, who finished fourth.[30]

The race in Sydney was one of Miles's last in the Maritimes. In September he left for Hamilton to attend the Olympic trials. After a disappointing ninth-place finish in Hamilton, the Canadian Olympic Committee suggested that he was in poor physical condition and requested that he remain there to train. His father also wanted him to stay in Hamilton, where he would work with top-notch trainers in first-class facilities and be given a job at International Harvester inspecting twine.[31] The Hamilton Olympic Club had been trying to recruit him for over a year. Although Miles did not make a formal public announcement that he would be leaving the Maritimes and taking up permanent residence, the invitation from Hamilton and the pressure applied by the Olympic committee made the decision to leave irresistible. His family soon followed him to Ontario, and they purchased a house adjacent to Hamilton Stadium where Miles frequently trained. He finished sixteenth at the Amsterdam Olympics in 1928.

Interestingly, after his departure, Nova Scotians began to cheer instead for runner Billy Taylor. Had Miles gone to Boston he would likely still have been regarded as a Maritimer in the Boston States; but for some, forsaking Nova Scotia for Ontario was tantamount to betrayal. Like Miles, Taylor was also a British immigrant, an ex-miner and ex-grocery clerk from Sydney Mines. After finishing second to Miles and ahead of DeMar in Halifax in 1927, it seemed that Taylor might well be the next Marathon Champion. In 1928 Taylor dominated Maritime races while Miles was winning his share in central Canada. For Maritimers the 1929 Boston Marathon was Billy Taylor versus Johnny Miles. Miles won the race and set a course record, while Taylor finished sixth.[32] In June the two appeared at the Black Diamond track in Glace Bay. Residents of the colliery districts cheered lustily as Taylor lapped Miles on the seventh mile of a 10-mile race that Taylor went on to win.[33]

While back in Cape Breton for the race Miles finally explained his decision: "I never would have left the Maritime Provinces if there had been anything here for me or any prospects at all for my future . . . Every place I went to look for something in my line the answer was we have nothing for you just now."[34] He raced for a few more years and finished fourteenth at the 1932 Olympics before retiring at 26. Miles went on to receive an MBA degree and was employed for 43 years with International Harvester.[35] Ironically, Taylor also left the region to further his career, moving to Montreal in 1930 to join the distinguished Campbell Park Athletic Club. After several victories, however, he died suddenly from complications after suffering sunstroke at a race in Montreal in June 1931.[36] That both Miles and Taylor finished out their athletic careers in other parts of Canada attests both to their national sensibilities and the limited employment opportunities available to them in Cape

Breton. Nevertheless, for most of the interwar period, Maritime sporting connections with New England were more visible than those with the rest of the country.

Bluenose Sailors

In the post-Confederation years,[37] many Maritimers from ports such as Lunenburg, Yarmouth, and Gloucester, Massachusetts, who made their livelihood fishing or sailing the waters of Georges Bank and the Gulf of Maine, or carried on coastal commerce between Nova Scotia and New England, were also tempted down the road to the "Boston States." Not surprisingly, it was their pride in nautical skills or shipbuilding and the sense of competitiveness that accompanied the exploitation of marine resources that provided the impetus for sporting competition across the international border. In 1905 a 360-nautical-mile sailboat race from Marblehead, Massachusetts, to Halifax was contested for the first time. The Marblehead race was held on a sporadic basis before and after World War I until the Boston Yacht Club and the Royal Nova Scotia Yacht Squadron agreed in 1939 to organize and sponsor the event. The race continues to be run even today on a biennial basis, and in recent years has featured over 100 boats in five divisions.

The connections between the Maritimes and New England were further consolidated after World War I when the schooner *Bluenose*, under the direction of Captain Angus Walters, made her reputation for speed on the open sea. Built in Lunenburg in 1921, the *Bluenose* won every racing competition she entered but one, and over the years established a secure place in regional folklore. The *Bluenose*'s reputation was founded largely upon her successes in the International Fisherman's Trophy Race, a contest first proposed by Colin McKay, one of the region's most influential socialist leaders, as a way of kick-starting the region's struggling post-war economy.[38] Dennis, publisher of the *Halifax*

Herald and notable defender of regional causes, whether they involved Maritime Rights or the promotion of Johnny Miles, immediately saw the value of a series of races pitting Canadian fishing schooners against American vessels, in order to settle the claims of fishermen in Lunenburg and Gloucester as to who had the faster fleet. After the American vessel *Esperanto* won the first two races in the fall of 1920, work began on the construction of the *Bluenose* in Lunenburg's Smith and Rhuland shipbuilding yards, and she was launched in time for the 1921 fishing season. Once she met the requirement of a full season in the bank fishery, the *Bluenose* was ready to contest the International Fisherman's Trophy. She won the trophy for the first time in 1921, and never relinquished it until the series was brought to a close by the outbreak of war in 1939.

Dennis's promotion of a race involving fishing schooners at the very time that the fishery was being transformed by the introduction of the gas-powered fishing trawlers was just one manifestation of a broader construction of fishermen and life at sea as the embodiment of Maritime folk identity. According to Ian McKay, as Nova Scotia's post-war culture producers constructed anti-modernist images of a sturdy and virile folk, they offered a culture of consolation to a region suffering from deindustrialization and the failed promises of capitalist modernity.[39] It was not only Maritimers who found these romantic images appealing, however. Reporting on the 1922 series involving the *Bluenose* and the American vessel the *Henry Ford*, the Toronto *Globe* described rival captains Angus Walters and Clayton Morrissey as "hard fisted, rollicking sailormen, whose vocation necessitates almost constant defiance of death, [and who] display a brand of sportsmanship that might well be emulated by certain others . . . in the sporting eye."[40]

In the first few years of the competition, disputes arose concerning eligibility requirements for the race between those who celebrated the fishermen's skills at sea and members of the yachting fraternity who, in the tradition of the America's Cup competition, were more interested in improvements in racing technology. Dennis agreed that there had to be practical rules for the governing of competition, but insisted: "They should be interpreted and carried out by men who know every phase of the fishing and shipping industry." No yachtsmen, Dennis argued, should "be connected with the competition in any capacity."[41] Earlier, Halifax trustees of the international trophy had barred the Boston schooner *Mayflower* from the race because it had not abided by the rules requiring that vessels be working fishing schooners, and this decision was upheld by the United States Racing Committee, which barred the *Mayflower* from the American elimination finals.

Over the next 15 years, as the races continued without interruption and disputes over eligibility were held in check, the *Bluenose* came to symbolize the close association of Nova Scotia and New England. Since 1937 the ship's image has been reproduced on the Canadian dime, and the *Bluenose II* was constructed in 1963 in the same shipyards as her predecessor. Although the replica never races, she continues to evoke romantic memories of an earlier age of sail and of past sporting glories.[42] As Cheryl Sullivan has written, "People from all walks of life and from ports all over the world still respond to the romantic past which *Bluenose II* suggests. Millions of people have boarded her, sailed on her, or simply looked at her; and when the time comes for an extensive and expensive refit, it is to these people who feel an emotional connection to the *Bluenose* that the government turns."[43]

Conclusion: Bobby Gimby and the Bangor Mall

In the interwar period Maritimers and New Englanders developed a sense of a shared sporting culture through connections on sporting diamonds, in hunting grounds, on the ocean, and along long-distance race courses. With the exception of ice hockey, which helped link Canada together through nationwide competition and weekly Hockey Night in Canada radio broadcasts beginning in the 1930s, the emerging national sport culture of the interwar period garnered little support in the Maritimes. Of course, sporting connections between the Maritimes and Canada can be found, especially in regard to Olympic competitions; yet interwar Maritime sporting allegiances were likely to be regional and transnational, rather than pan-Canadian. Only with World War II would the dominant assumption of the northeast as a coherent transnational sporting region begin to give way to alternative constructions. New patterns of consumption—and the growing influence of television—would lead to the perception that the Maritimes truly shared in a Canadian sporting culture. The post-war years also witnessed new patterns of migration that weakened transnational linkages. Instead of making the traditional exodus to New England, Maritimers increasingly left the region in search of jobs in Toronto, and eventually in cities further west.[44] In the 1960s, moreover, amid the heightened nationalism of the day (evident in the flag debate, and the Expo 67 celebrations) the Canadian state took a more active role in the development of a national sporting culture. Canada Games competitions, the coming of two major league baseball franchises, coast-to-coast television diffusion of hockey and Canadian football, and the marginalization of hunting as a sporting pursuit prompted a reimagining of the Maritime sporting universe. And so, as Maritimers followed Bobby Gimby in singing about their love of Canada at the "hundredth anniversary of Confederation," or were "goin' down the road" in new directions in search of work and well-being, their once intimate connections with northern New England were displaced by the occasional holiday shopping trip to the Bangor Mall.

 More online.

Notes

1. See, for example, Jeremy Adelman and Stephen Aron, "From Borderlands to Borders: Empires, Nation States, and Peoples in Between in North America," *American Historical Review* 104, 3 (June 1999): 814–41; and the articles by David Thelen, Bruno Ramirez, Ian Tyrrell, Robin Kelley, and Mauricio Tenorio Trillo in "The Nation and Beyond: International Perspectives on United States History. A Special Issue," *Journal of American History* 86, no. 3 (December 1999): 965–1187. . . .

2. Benedict Anderson, *Imagined Communities: Reflections on the Origin and Spread of Nationalism*, rev. ed. (London, UK: Verson, 1991: orig. pub. 1983). For a similar discussion in a Canadian context, see Daniel Francis, *National Dreams: Myth, Memory, and Canadian History* (Vancouver, BC: Arsenal Pulp Press, 1997).

3. William New, *Borderlands: How We Talk About Canada* (Vancouver, BC: UBC Press, 1998), 27.

4. Phillip Buckner, "How Canadian Historians Stopped Worrying and Learned to Love the Americans," *Acadiensis* 25: 2 (Spring 1996): 117–40.

5. Allen Guttmann, *Games and Empires: Modern Sports and Cultural Imperialism* (New York, NY: Columbia University Press, 1994).

6. Ruth's upbringing and his connection to the Maritimes are chronicled in Robert Creamer, *Babe: The Legend Comes to Life* (New York, NY: Simon and Schuster, 1974); Robert Ashe, *Even the Babe Came to Play: Small-Town Baseball in the Dirty 30s* (Halifax, NS: Nimbus, 1991); William Humber, "Babe Ruth Comes to Canada in Search of ??" *Saskatchewan Historical Baseball Review* (1996): 24–35; and Colin Howell, "The Man Who Taught the Bambino: The Mystery of Brother Matthias," in William Humber and John St James, eds., *All I Thought About Was Baseball: Writings on a Canadian Pastime* (Toronto, ON: University of Toronto Press, 1996), 149–52.

7. The baseball connection between New England and the Maritimes is addressed in fuller detail in Colin Howell, *Northern Sandlots: A Social History of Maritime Baseball* (Toronto, ON: University of Toronto Press, 1995).

8. Ernest R. Forbes, *The Maritime Rights Movement, 1919–27: A Study in Canadian Regionalism* (Montreal, QC: McGill-Queen's University Press, 1979).

9. Ashe, *Even the Babe Came to Play*, 102–3; Howell, *Northern Sandlots*.

10. *Sydney Record*, 13 November 1925.

11. Ibid., 21 October 1927; *Halifax Herald*, 1 November 1924.

12. See, for example, the lengthy article entitled "Where Gun, Canoe and Fishing Rod Are the Tourist's Joy," in a special tourist edition of the *Halifax Herald*, 24 March 1925.

13. James Morrison, "American Tourism in Nova Scotia, 1871–1940," *Nova Scotia Historical Review* 2, no. 2 (December 1982): 40–51.

14. Ian McKay, *The Quest of the Folk: Antimodernism and Cultural Selection in Twentieth-Century Nova Scotia* (Montreal, QC: McGill-Queen's University Press, 1994).

15. Beatrice M. Hay Shaw, *Nova Scotia: For Beauty and Business* (Halifax, NS: Royal Print and Litho Ltd., 1923), vii.

16. Mark Dyreson, *Making the American Team: Sport Culture, and the Olympic Experience* (Urbana, IL: University of Illinois Press, 1998), 40–6.

17. A brief history of the Boston Marathon and the results of each race can be found at the official Boston Marathon website, www.bostonmarathon.org/history. htm. I am also indebted to my student research assistant Daniel Macdonald for collecting material relating to the career of Johnny Miles used in this essay.

18. *Halifax Herald*, 5 April 1928.

19. Ibid., 29 July 1924.

20. Ibid., 19 September 1925.

21. Ibid., 3 September 1928.

22. Ibid., 13, 17 April 1926; Floyd Williston, *Johnny Miles: Nova Scotia's Marathon King* (Halifax, NS: Nimbus, 1990), 2.

23. *Halifax Herald*, 14 June 1926; Williston, *Johnny Miles*, 35.

24. *Halifax Herald*, 29 June 1926.

25. Ibid., 13 August 1926.

26. Ibid., 7, 9, 19, 25 March 1927.

27. Ibid, 7 April 1927.

28. Williston, *Johnny Miles*, 44–5; Tom Derderian, *Boston Marathon: The History of the World's Premier Running Event* (Urbana, IL: Human Kinetics Publishers, 1990), 112–14; *Halifax Herald*, 20, 21 April 1927.

29. Derderian, *Boston Marathon*, 114.

30. *Halifax Herald*, 2 July 1927.

31. Ibid., 10, 19, 24 September 1927.

32. Ibid., 15, 18, 19, 20 April 1929.

33. Ibid., 13 June 1929.

34. Ibid., 10 June 1929.

35. Derderian, *Boston Marathon*, 133.

36. Williston, *Johnny Miles*, 75–6.

37. Alan Alexander Brooks, "The Exodus: Migration from the Maritimes to Boston During the Second Half of the Nineteenth Century" (Ph.D. dissertation, University of New Brunswick, 1977); Patricia Thornton, "The Problem of Out-migration from Atlantic Canada, 1871–1921: A New Look," *Acadiensis* 15, no. 1 (Autumn 1985): 3–34; Betsy Beattie, "'Going up to Lynn': Single, Maritime-Born Women in Lynn, Massachusetts,

1879–1930," *Acadiensis* 22, no. 1 (Autumn 1992): 65–86.

38. Ian McKay, "Of Karl Marx and the Bluenose: Colin Campbell McKay and the Legacy of Maritime Socialism," *Acadiensis* 27, no. 2 (Spring 1998): 3–25.

39. McKay, *Quest of the Folk*.

40. Toronto *Globe*, 24 October 1922.

41. Ibid., 27 October 1922.

42. James Marsh, "The Bluenose."

43. Cheryl Sullivan, "The Paradox of *Bluenose II*: Antimodernism, Capitalism and the Legacy of the Schooner *Bluenose* in Nova Scotia," *Nova Scotia Historical Review* (1997): 2–22.

44. Gary Burrill, *Away: Maritimers in Massachusetts, Ontario and Alberta: An Oral History of Leaving Home* (Montreal, QC: McGill-Queen's University Press, 1992).

25 Totem Poles, Teepees, and Token Traditions
"Playing Indian" at Ontario Summer Camps, 1920–55

Sharon Wall

In 1899 Pauline Johnson, famous "Mohawk princess" and Aboriginal performer, paid a visit to the small northern Ontario town of Sundridge. As Johnson served up her fare of dramatic poems and recitations, one 10-year-old girl was particularly enthralled. Recounting the incident later in life, Mary S. Edgar, the young white girl in question, recalled, "I was fascinated and wished I were related to her," a longing only heightened by Johnson's later visit to the Edgar family home. Some 20 years later, little Mary's wish was, in one sense, granted. The summer of 1922 found the 33-year-old Edgar the director of a newly established summer camp for girls. There she presided over the camp's Indian council ring, crafted her own Indian legends, and entertained campers in her wigwam-style cabin. On a visit to the camp sometime in the interwar years, Chief Mudjeekwis of the Rice Lake Ojibway extended the hand of friendship and bestowed on Edgar the honour of an "Indian" name. Over the years, in her role as "Ogimaqua," Edgar, the white woman, would imaginatively weave herself and her campers into the family of "Indians."[1]

In her fascination with all things Indian, Edgar was not alone. At least as early as the 1890s white audiences throughout Canada, the United States, and Britain thronged local halls and auditoriums to see and hear celebrities like Johnson, whose appearances fanned the flames of interest in the performing Indian. In the same period, North Americans crowded into the rodeos and Buffalo Bill shows that prominently featured Aboriginal performers. If, as with Edgar, this outsider fascination slipped into the desire for insider status, what most of these "wannabee" Indians did with the impulse to "go Native" is not well known. The story of Grey Owl's faux-Indian fame points in one direction, but it is unlikely that many took their enthusiasm to such extremes. For many who were not seeking wholesale changes of identity, playing Indian part time would suffice.[2] Summer camp was one site in which this impulse could be readily indulged, a place where, it was understood, children learned to "live like Indians during the camping season."[3]

This article attempts to make sense of this curious cultural phenomenon, to place this cultural appropriation in a broad historical context. By exploring camps' Indian programming and representations of Native people in camp literature, it takes a critical look at the fascination with playing Indian. What becomes apparent is that the incorporation of so-called Indian traditions was part [of] a broader anti-modernist impulse

Citation: Sharon Wall, "Totem Poles, Teepees, and Token Traditions: 'Playing Indian' at Ontario Summer Camps, 1920–55," *Canadian Historical Review* 86, no. 3 (2005): 513–44. Reprinted with permission from University of Toronto Press (www.utpjournals.com).

in twentieth-century Ontario. Like the summer camp phenomenon as a whole, it reflected middle-class unease with the pace and direction of cultural change, with a world that appeared to be irrevocably industrial, decidedly urban, and increasingly secular. As historian Leslie Paris has concluded in the American context, racial play acting at summer camp was not a matter of respecting the experiences of racial minorities.[4] So also at Ontario camps, "going Native" had little to do with honouring (or even accurately portraying) Aboriginal tradition, but much to do with seeking a balm for the non-Native experience of modernity. Above all, at summer camp playing Indian reflected modern desire to create a sense of belonging, community, and spiritual experience by modelling anti-modern images of Aboriginal life. These impulses point to a racialized expression of twentieth-century anti-modernism—one springing from adult experience, but articulating itself on the landscape of childhood. . . .

The first camps in Ontario, founded by charitable organizations, private individuals, and the YMCA, appeared at the turn of the century, but before World War I they served a limited clientele composed mainly of older boys. In the 1920s there were significant developments, including the appearance of girls' camps, camps for a broader age range of children, and the establishment of several private camps whose directors would become important leaders in the field of camping. By the 1930s, the impulse to take children of all sorts "back to nature" spawned something of a camping movement, with the newly established Ontario Camping Association playing a prominent role. Its efforts to educate the public about the benefits of camp and its attempts to raise standards of the camps themselves seem to have paid off. In the early 1950s *Saturday Night* magazine claimed that "between 5 and 7 per cent of all Canadian children attend a summer camp," while a *Financial Post* article quantified this at 150,000 children. If one considers that a majority of Canadian camping took

place in Ontario—one journalist estimating roughly 70 per cent by 1960—it would seem that the camp certainly had come of age by the end of this period.[5]

. . .

Playing Indian has most often been understood as a form of cultural appropriation, a practice that has been the source of intense debate among scholars, literary critics, journalists, and others. Hartmut Lutz, a German literary scholar, provides a useful explanation of the concept: "What is at issue . . . is the kind of appropriation which happens within a colonial structure, where one culture is dominant politically and economically over the other, and rules and exploits it. . . . It is a kind of appropriation that is selective . . . and that is ahistorical in that it excludes from its discourse the historical context, especially, here, the history of Native–non-Native relations."[6] This is clear enough from other histories of "playing Indian"—studies by Phillip Deloria and Shari Huhndorf among others—which show the phenomenon was clearly rooted in desires to fill the personal, social, and national aspirations of whites. . . . Other scholars argue that the appeal of playing Indian was heightened as time went on by the marginalization, displacement, even death of real Aboriginal peoples. With the latter posing a decreasing threat to white society, negative images of Indians could now, more often, give way to positive ones.[7]

Though much useful analysis emerged from such studies, more explicit connection can yet be made between the phenomenon of "playing Indian" and the broader context of twentieth-century modernity and anti-modernity. In the guiding work on the subject, Jackson Lears pinpointed anti-modernism's North American origins in the late nineteenth century. As a result of broad social changes wrought by industrialization, turn-of-the-century intellectuals, literati, and other members of the urban bourgeoisie suffered feelings of "weightlessness" and "overcivilization." Their efforts to compensate, to replace "weightlessness" with "intense experience," took many forms, from renewed fascination with "the simple life," to the arts and crafts movement, the revival of martial ideals, and explorations of medieval and eastern mysticism. Scholars since Lears confirm that such responses were not a strictly American, nor Victorian, phenomenon. In early twentieth-century Nova Scotia similar quests for identity and meaning spawned what historian Ian McKay has termed a "quest of The Folk"—a premodern incarnation of Nova Scotians, one that folklorists and cultural producers would claim as the region's true cultural core. Like the camp industry, this image had important economic implications, serving as the cultural myth that fuelled modern tourism in that province.[8]

. . .

The backdrop for the emergence of this strain of anti-modernist sentiment was a province that had seen rapid cultural change. Though the notion of "modernity" is a notoriously slippery concept, suffice it to say that Ontario was very much a modern entity by the interwar years. To a greater degree than any other Canadian province, it was capitalist, industrial, and distinctly urban. In 1921, when 47 per cent of all Canadians were urban dwellers, the number in Ontario was at almost 60. By 1951, when the national average reached 62 per cent, in Ontario the figure was already 10 per cent higher.[9] Possibly more significant than the physical consequences of modernity was the shift in cultural consciousness that underlay them. At the broadest level, this entailed the unadulterated exaltation of reason and commitment to the rationalization of not only production, but ever-expanding realms of social life. In the realm of child psychology, professional experts preached the wonders of "habit training" by which children, no less than the tools of industry, could become efficient working machines. Interwar child-rearing experts agreed that what children needed was unbending and factory-like routine, not the emotional inconsistencies that marked traditional child-rearing. By rigid scheduling of the child's day, restrained

shows of affection, and a reasoned rather than punitive approach, children would develop along healthy and predictable paths and grow into the reasonable, well-behaved citizens modern living demanded.[10]

. . . If modern expertise and professional advice promised to turn out well-adjusted children, other cultural developments seemed to threaten healthy child development. In camp literature, concern was expressed about the fact that, already in childhood, Canadians were becoming soft, habituated to technological comforts, and alienated from "real" experience. "Children today, especially in large cities, have little opportunity for really creative living," one camp director lamented. "Lights go on at a switch, heat comes when a knob is turned . . . [and] drama means sitting in the movies."[11] Given twentieth-century understandings of child development—and of the lasting import of early experiences—the impact of these modern conditions was felt to be especially worrying. With few countervailing influences, many feared children would grow into adults incapable of enjoying life's simpler pleasures or of appreciating the importance of physical exertion and hard work. If the notion of childhood had always implied a degree of protection for the young, under conditions of twentieth-century modernity, the notion that children needed protecting from the very culture that surrounded them would deepen. To be a modern North American parent would be to contemplate no end of worries about the possible negative influences of modern culture.

Primary among these worries was children's presumed vulnerability to the lure of consumer culture. Paradoxically, having put an end to the most extreme forms of child labour, middle-class observers now worried about the uses to which children's expanding leisure time would be put. Crime comics and pulp novels, movie theatres and youth dance halls all worried bourgeois onlookers, some of whom worked to prohibit or restrict access to such attractions. On the other hand, proponents of "rational recreation"—another modern innovation—took a positive approach, offering wholesome entertainment alternatives at local YMCAs, community centres, and post-war teen canteens.[12]

Founders of summer camps took this critique one step further, suggesting that what children needed was a complete break with city life and experience with more natural living. In this way of thinking, they were heavily influenced by Ernest Thompson Seton and, to a lesser extent, G. Stanley Hall. The widely sought-after Seton was popular as a naturalist, artist, master storyteller, and founder of the League of Woodcraft Indians. Seton's critique of modernity was inseparable from a marked romanticization of Aboriginal culture, one instrumental in fuelling youthful interest in "going Native." "Our civilization is a failure," he commented on one occasion, while his writings on Indian lore conversely idealized "Indian life" and encouraged Euro-North Americans—especially children—in its emulation. His instructional manuals like *The Red Book: Or, How To Play Indian* were widely read at camp (and elsewhere), while in the case of at least one camp, he was brought on as temporary staff. Less directly, camps were likely also influenced by theories of "race capitulation" popularized by Victorian psychologist G. Stanley Hall. In Hall's view, boys in particular needed to indulge their savage tendencies in childhood so that they might, as the human race itself had ostensibly done, progress beyond them to civilized adulthood.[13]

Emerging from a culture of increasingly secular proportions, with anti-modern concerns over childhood and a penchant for "playing Indian," the camp offered itself as not only a physical escape from the city, but also—in its use of Indian programming—metaphoric release from the emotional confines of modern childhood. Here was a world, geographically removed from home and city, where the combination of newness and isolation offered the perfect backdrop for the construction of alternate identities. Indeed, as children first heard of these camps—Temagami, Keewaydin, Ahmek, and so on—the foreign nature of the experience was announced. Arrival at camp quickly confirmed that it was one designed to usher youth out of the modern world and into the realm of the Indian past. As they first passed though gates that demarcated the boundary between the two worlds, campers frequently encountered camp names constructed from purportedly "Indian" languages. One camp director's son recalled, "All the popular camps of the day had Indian names."[14] Campers themselves were sometimes "renamed," with Ojibwa, Algonquin, Cree, and Blackfoot commonly marking their cabins or sections. Gazing about the grounds, children would quickly have noticed that not only names, but the material culture of camp—its teepees, totem poles, and sometimes whole "Indian villages"—confirmed the Indian connection. At camps of all sorts, arts and crafts period saw children variously carving, painting, and constructing their own totem poles, teepees, and "Indian heads." As they went about their activities, children were reminded that the very earth on which they walked had once been "Indian land." This point was brought home in a special way to campers who thrilled at the chance to observe, listen, and learn from the Aboriginal staff employed at certain camps. Finally, campers would also have discovered the Indian council ring, set off geographically from the rest of camp. In this woodsy, chapel-like setting, "young braves" would "sit in solemn pageant" on their rough-hewn benches, awaiting the words of "the chief" delivered from his sacred "council rock." Having been duly blanketed and face-painted, and sometimes in "breech clouts," these make-believe Indians would make use of everything from tom-toms and rattles to shields and headdresses.[15]

While camps offered surprisingly similar renditions of Indian programming, boys and girls also encountered distinct aspects of "Indianness" at their respective camps. At boys' camps the Indian was frequently represented as bearing a kind of violent hypermasculinity, a model deemed particularly fitting for male campers. In keeping with theories of "race capitulation," boys were encouraged to indulge their "savage" impulses in games of "scalping" and "pioneers and Indians," which, in one case, was happily reported to include "blood-curdling yells" from "fierce-visaged boys of ten."[16] Girl campers, on the other hand, were encouraged to emulate a very different sort of Indian. At their camps the emphasis on Native activities was on the development of artistic abilities, not on primitivist catharsis, with weaving and painting of "Indian themes" being popular. Although sometimes providing campers with more independent models of girlhood, the tone of other Indian programming was also more appropriately feminine. For instance, a description of "Indian day" at Camp Tanamakoon had no savage or primitivist overtones: "[The girls] had been in another world," it was recounted, "a world of quiet feet, gliding canoes and spirited dances."[17]

Broadly speaking, and whatever its gendered components, the summer camp experience was understood as a re-creation of the Indian way of life. "The Native Canadians . . . were campers," educator Mary Northway put it. "In their small groups they lived a simple, outdoor life, striving against the elements and using natural resources to furnish their existence."[18] In this way of thinking, Indians were campers and campers were Indians. Nothing, it seemed, could be more "Indian" than camping.

Meanings behind the Masks

Indian programming was straightforwardly explained by administrators as having educational value. . . .

. . . [S]trict attention to historical accuracy was, unfortunately, not the rule. Ironically, since praise of Indians had as its premise the presumably "primitive," even ageless, nature of their practices, so-called Indian culture at camp was sometimes quite literally made up. Perhaps the most familiar example is the use of simulated Indian names. If certain camps were careful to choose names that had real meanings in Indigenous languages, many others were happy enough if the overall effect was an Indian tone. Thus were born institutions like the New Frenda Youth camp and Camp Wanna-com-bak. . . .

Invention could also take more inadvertent forms, sometimes through careless blending of one Aboriginal tradition with another. All too often objects of Native material cultures were presented in utterly jumbled fashion. The desire to create an Indian atmosphere at Bolton, for instance, meant that the totem pole (a uniquely West Coast tradition) and the teepee (used only by Plains groups) could be displayed unproblematically side by side, with an Omaha "tribal prayer" thrown in for good measure. . . . In such cases, camps were not penetrating the intricacies of Native history or culture; rather, like those of a long line of explorers, settlers, and academics before them, their images of Native people were based on a fantastical amalgam of Aboriginal traditions projected onto one mythic Indian Other, another version of the white man's Indian.[19]

In all of these cases, the child's experience of this culture—and not its realistic depiction— was clearly the central concern, a point underscored in the following advice:

If you have no serious objection to a little subterfuge, it is possible to enliven your Indian program . . . by "discovering an Indian Burial Ground." It can either just happen or you can make it known that this camp was once the home of such and such a tribe and that arrow heads, bits of pottery and other evidence has [sic] been found. . . . Please yourself how far you want to go with this kind of thing. Once started, the ball will continue to roll. Bones and all kinds of things will be brought to your attention for there's nothing excites a camper more than discovery.[20]

If discovery excited children, if Indian ceremonies awed them, and if games of scalping allowed them to let off steam, Indian programming was a success. In contrast to the regimentation recommended by child-rearing experts, campers were sometimes (though by no means always) encouraged to be excitable and to indulge in imaginative and often passionate play.

Clearly, Indian programming was not really about honouring Aboriginal traditions, but it was not without purpose or meaning in the life of the camp. Like anti-modernists of earlier periods, camp enthusiasts were on the trail of intense experience, which Indian programming offered in abundance. Council ring, for instance, could function not merely as Saturday night entertainment, but also as the symbolic centre of camp. It was here that important visitors were introduced, here that opening and closing ceremonies were held, here that directorships sometimes formally changed hands. In effect, council ring offered the ritual, solemnity, and spirit of communalism that such events demanded and seemed to be lacking in modern life.

. . . Indeed, part of the essential meaning of camp was that it was more than a collection of unconnected individuals; above all, it was a community. A common spiritual striving, broadly defined, was deemed invaluable in nurturing this sense of community, even at camps without a primarily religious focus. We see this at Ahmek where references to "the value of persons," the search for "higher values," and the indescribable "camp spirit" suggested incorporation of a liberal, humanistic spirituality. Despite its distancing from institutional religion, this camp still ultimately claimed, "To many counsellors and campers, Ahmek has been their one outstanding religious experience." They were careful to add, however, that religion was a concept "as flexible, changing and real as life itself."[21]

. . .

At many summer camps the council ring ceremony was the central vehicle for channelling experience of this "pure religion" to urban campers. Through it, campers could immerse themselves in ritual that contained no reference to Christian theology, but rather offered an air of novel freshness. The ceremony was often a weekly or biweekly event, held after dark, and involving the entire camp. "It has been used as a vehicle through which much sound teaching can be given without effusive moralizing," a short history of Bolton Camp explained.[22] At the Statten camps the ceremonies were treated with equal seriousness. Only those who had actively participated, it was claimed, could "know the deep meaning of such an hour."[23] Discussions of council ring's physical layout point out similar understandings of its import. The area itself was treated as semi-sacred space, and the rituals it facilitated, as quasi-religious. "The choice of a site for the Council Ring is important," one handbook advised. "Select an area reasonably remote from any buildings. . . . A flat space . . . surrounded by trees will lend enchantment. Atmosphere is very important. . . . Find another site for the ordinary camp fires and wiener roasts."[24] Without question, the backdrop of nature was deemed essential in creating the desired atmosphere. At Bolton, this was achieved by situating the ceremonies "in a most appropriate forest setting," while at Glen Bernard, Mary Edgar rejoiced in her discovery of "the glen, a perfect amphitheatre for a Council Ring."[25] According to this way of thinking, trees became markers of the borders of intimacy, rocks became symbolic altars to be used by presiding chiefs, and the wide open sky suggested the loftiness of the entire enterprise.

Organization of council ring proceedings points to further parallels with religious ritual, as well as that blend of catharsis and control, freedom and order that characterized the rest of the camp experience. The usual roster of activities included a dramatic fire-lighting ceremony followed by prayers to "the gods," some form of camper recitations or reports (often of nature sightings), "Indian challenges" or contests, and a sombre closing ceremony. All was to be guided by a strict "order of procedure," in keeping with the belief that "everything that is done at the council ring is deliberate," or as it was put at Bark Lake Camp, "everything on the programme is planned ahead."[26] Creating the desired atmosphere also depended on knowing when to keep quiet and when to join in the noise making. At certain points "absolute silence" was considered something of an iron law, while at other times input from the "braves" (like lay participation) was essential. As council ring's central organizing feature, the fire itself cannot be overlooked. Fire, which often holds a sacred place in religious ritual, here held pride of place, providing a circular and thus communal ordering to the ritual.

Before gaining entry to this sacred space, campers were expected to undergo transformation on several levels. If, broadly speaking, all of camp life reflected the desire to "go Native," it was at council ring ceremonies that campers were, in essence, "born again" as Indians. The first step in this process was external change. Here nature itself helped, eliciting positive reference to the Indian appearance of sun-browned campers. Suntans were assumed to be one of the healthy by-products of a summer at camp, providing not only physical benefits, but also the psychospiritual advantages of "going Native," as both Deloria and Paris have shown. In the Ontario context, one mother and her children who returned from fresh-air camp were described as "mortals from another world. The mother is browned by the kiss of summer winds. . . . And the children? They look like four little nut-brown papooses— as tough as nails—sparkling and effervescent."[27] To compliment their Indian "skins," campers anticipating council ring were expected to take on Indian dress. At Bark Lake Camp it was stated, "Campers dress up in blankets, towels, feathers and war paint," while photo evidence suggests that "dressing up Indian" was also the routine at other private, fresh-air, and agency camps.[28]

Other aspects of transformation were less visible, if no less real. Fundamentally, one was to be open to a new way of feeling and of experiencing the self. . . . More than anything, however, it required a willingness to be transported metaphorically to another time and place, to enter into a new state of mind, and to open oneself up to mystical experience. Directors . . . were also told that this required not only "dress[ing] for the part," but also that the chief himself "become enchanted" and open to "the emotional appeal of the Red man."[29] Judging from a description of council ring proceedings at Ahmek, director Taylor Statten apparently played his part well. "Each week at camp seemed to await the Council Ring," it was recalled.

> One gathered a blanket and a flashlight and marched off to the Council Ring as an actor in a well-rehearsed play . . . somehow, the austere and [pervasive] presence of the Chief transformed the play into a realistic re-enactment of all Indian ceremonies of all time. The twentieth century slipped away in the darkness and all evidences of modern civilization were . . . somehow forgotten. . . . It was a shock returning from this other world in which we had all been participants . . . and the validity of the experience was owing to the magnificent skill of the Chief. He was really THE CHIEF.[30]

In this atmosphere, members of the camp community could find themselves emotionally stirred, personally connected, and perhaps even spiritually moved. . . . Here, without explicit reference to religion, one could taste the beauty of ritual, embrace feelings of awe, and experience the power of the communal event. In this context, Aboriginal people were far from mind and one's own experience, the focal centrepiece.

. . .

Playing Indian could engender experience; it could also inform identity at all manner of camps. As in the world of art, literature, and sport, proving one's connection to Indians was a surefire way to found a "Canadian tradition" and to establish one's "Canadian" roots.[31] To achieve this feat at camp, outdoor enthusiasts ignored their immigrant roots and constructed themselves—as those who chose to "live like Indians"—as the figurative "heirs" of Native tradition. . . . Director Mary Hamilton's account of Algonquin Park history is illustrative:

> To the uninitiated the name of Algonquin spells Indian. One thinks of wise men of the forest who knew this country well and trapped and fished here in the days when all the wilderness of forest and stream belonged to them. These associations are true, but Algonquin Park is much more than an Indian hunting ground. It is an expanse of twenty-seven hundred square miles of forest. . . . It is a land that finds a place in history associated with the records of Champlain, it was the happy hunting ground of the Algonquin Indians. . . . In the days of Tom Thomson it became the gathering place for members of the Group of Seven.[32]

Clearly, there was tension here between giving the Aboriginal peoples their due and the construction of a narrative that assumed their eventual irrelevance. The same tone marked Mary Edgar's prompting to past campers: "We need often to remind ourselves that this country which we proudly call 'this land of ours' once belonged to the Indians," that, "it was the smoke from their camp-fires which first ascended to the sky."[33] Clearly, camps had much in common with the salvage anthropologist who lamented, but also assumed the inevitability of, the Indian's cultural demise.[34] From this perspective, Indians were those of strictly pre-contact innocence. Any cultural change or adaptation on their part was read simply as decay. "Real Indians," so it was understood, were no longer a people who "lived among us" or who had a place in the modern world.

Having rendered contemporary Aboriginal peoples virtually invisible, white campers could now step in to fill the void as their remaining heirs. In doing so, they distinguished between themselves—true lovers of nature—and less-enlightened elements of their society. In a 1931 article, parallels were drawn between campers and early Aboriginal peoples. The author suggests that, like "the redmen" of the past, it is now "the new dwellers of the out-of-doors" who are being "pushed further and further afield." The enemies now are not from the east, but annoying cottagers from the south who "bring with them their city habits and customs." These philistines are described as "inane bands of jazz-makers [who] violate the silence of the night," who bring "hot dog stands and shabby food 'joints'" to the wilderness, and ultimately, as "idolaters in the temple of the Great Spirit."[35] By contrast, camps painted themselves as respectful followers of Indian ways, inheritors of Native traditions and practices. In their use of the Aboriginal tumpline—a heavy leather strap that was tied around goods, then around the forehead of the hiker—Camp Keewaydin considered itself to be "the custodian of ancient practices and devices long since discarded elsewhere."[36] At Bolton, campers who fished, tented, and chopped wood were depicted as receiving "instruction in skills of the historic past," while CGIT [Canadian Girls in Training] campers were said to be learning to live "as did their Indian brothers and sisters."[37] Ultimately, if campers were the children of these earlier Aboriginal siblings, their role as inhabitants of Indian land—the entire country, of course—could be regarded as only natural. They were legitimate "Canadians," and this was their home.

Such retellings, borrowings, and inventions were the base elements of camps' Indian programming. They suggest that the history of playing Indian is not only one of longing, but also of privilege. Clearly, dramatic reinventions of campers as Indians merely emphasized the shared whiteness of the actors under the paint, to their freedom in taking "Indianness" on and off at will. Indeed, it was precisely because they felt so deeply assured of their status as "white" that they could play at being, and long to be, Indian. Camp enthusiasts were not seeking a true change of status, but a revised, more pleasing image of their own racial character. Through their role as summer campers, lovers of the outdoors claimed an identity that was vaguely countercultural but, at the same time, still clearly white. One would be hard pressed to argue, for instance, that playing Indian was a truly progressive form of "transgression"—that it inverted and thus challenged the social status quo—even if it contained some carnivalesque features. As most scholars of American minstrel performances agree, when whites put on other racial faces, they were not making attempts at accurate representations of the Other or at honouring the experience of subaltern cultures. On the other hand, neither should their acts be read as simple denigration, since they also revealed a certain ambivalence toward racial Others. This included a privileged longing to experience racialized ways of being and acting normally deemed unacceptable within the dominant culture. . . .

Playing Indian at camp, like "blacking up," represented a similar white, middle-class, and privileged longing to identify with the socially marginal, the "low-Other" of Canadian society. Like the Setons and the Grey Owls they resembled, camp enthusiasts sought from Aboriginal peoples a connection to a time of premodern simplicity, a golden age of social harmony and calm. . . . In the context of the summer camp, Aboriginal peoples were seen as living the enviable simple life, and whites as those impoverished by modernity's flow. Indeed, at camp, antimodernist tendencies were frequently expressed in racialized terms, with a simple, if unarticulated, equation undergirding common thinking on the question. Quite simply, white equalled "modern," and "Indian," "premodern" or "primitive." Rearticulating much older primitivist tendencies in western culture, twentieth-century camps in this way also fuelled their own unique version of primitivism.[38] From this perspective Indians were regarded as the quintessential primitives, identification with them as a way of distancing campers from distasteful elements of mainstream society. Note this description of the Aboriginal worker at Camp Keewaydin: "The guide's values were different from those of a white middle- or upper-class young man," it was explained. "[He] had no schooling but had been educated by Nature and life."[39]

Admiration for this proximity to nature was coupled with romanticization of the Indian's presumed distance from modernity. The *Toronto Star*'s reading of the camp project at Bolton explained, "City children . . . will learn there were no department stores, super-markets or Saturday matinees for the Indians."[40] Where Aboriginal guides were employed, they were similarly praised for their total lack of implication in the culture of consumption. Keewaydin's camp historian claimed of their Native workers, "The early guide never owned an automobile. He owned a canoe. With it, he earned his livelihood, hunted . . . and engaged in any leisure activity."[41] The Indian, then, was one who did not rely on the comforts of mass culture, but who instead accepted the challenge of real physical work. . . .

Paralleling camps' praise for the idealized Indian was a mock derision and scorn for "the white man." In keeping with earlier primitivist tendencies, those who glorified the Indian also offered a social critique of their own society, however limited. In the case of playing Indian, this manifested as a semi-serious attack on "whiteness," otherwise understood as [a] symbol for implication in modernity. . . . At Bolton Camp, boys participated in dramatic re-enactments of historic Native–white conflicts, with one description noting "the treachery of a band of marauding whites."[42] Use of the derogatory *pale-face*—"pale-faced campers" or white visitors as "chiefs in the pale-faced world"—also reveals attempts to look through Aboriginal eyes and to decentre whiteness as the assumed vantage point.[43] Looking back on the dominant culture from this new perspective, campers could join in the performance of the fire-lighting ceremony, which bid them to declare, "Light we now the council fire, built after the manner of the forest children. Not big like the whiteman's where you must stand away off so front all roast and back all gooseflesh; but small like the Indian's, so we may sit close and feel the warmth of fire and friendship."[44] Here, whiteness was represented as not only synonymous with ostentation, but also with a cold, impersonal culture, lacking in true intimacy. By superficially critiquing whiteness, members of the camping community could distance themselves from the hollowness of modern alienation and excess, essentially allowing them to reconceptualize their relationship to modernity. Through the summer camp experience, white urban Ontarians could think of themselves as existing outside the limits of the dominant culture. Clearly, the critique was a shallow one that lasted only so long as one's stay in the woods. What made "going Native" at camp such an act of privilege was that campers could comfortably go home to whiteness once returned to their urban environments, settings where the benefits or "wages of whiteness" were generally irresistible.

. . .

Assessing Impact

. . . [I]f Indian programming was of clearly adult origin, it also had its impact on children. That certain families patronized the same camps over several generations suggests that powerful loyalties engendered in childhood sometimes endured into adult years. Many children, it seems, were strongly affected by their stays at camp, and it is likely that lessons learned there—Indian programming included—followed campers into later life. Fitting as it did with the rough-and-tumble aspects of boy culture sanctioned in other social contexts, Indian programming was particularly popular with boys. At Bolton Camp, one observer remarked, "The Indian Ceremonial has been of never-failing interest to the boys," while participation in one "Indian pageant" of 1938 was said to have given its male campers "a thrilling experience, so thrilling indeed that many of them insisted on wearing paint,

feathers and tomahawks for the rest of their stay at camp."[45] Where Native guides were employed at more northerly, private camps, boys' fascination with the Indian could be intensified. In such cases, Aboriginal workers modelled an alluring masculinity based on their mastery of wilderness skills. At Camp Ahmek, Ojibwa canoeing instructor Bill Stoqua was described as "a perfectionist." Staff recalled, "He had the style and the physique and the appearance. . . . [A]ll the campers thought if they could paddle like [him] they would have achieved something important."[46]

When it came to council ring, boys and girls alike appear to have been moved by the ceremony, which some, looking back on it, place "in the realm of the holy."[47] Indeed, Taylor Statten claimed that "no single activity contributes more to the camp sense of unity than the weekly Council Ring," while YMCA Camp Pine Crest counted council ring "among the most attractive all-camp activities."[48] One Wapomeo camper, later director, recalls that this was no casual event. It was "always done very precisely, very organised and well planned," she explained, "Some of us were in fear and trembling that somebody would do the wrong thing and spoil the atmosphere."[49] Other former campers agreed. According to one, "We all behaved as if . . . in a church service,"[50] remaining quiet except when called on to sing or recite. Mary Northway recalls of council ring at Glen Bernard Camp, that it was "awe-inspiring. At dusk in blankets the Big Chief (little Miss Edgar [the camp director]) turned us into Indians of a long ago time."[51] In a lighter spirit, Jim Buchanan remembers council ring as "a fun event and certainly . . . one of the highlights of camp." He now admits he couldn't help indulging the idea of Taylor Statten as truly Aboriginal, even though he knew otherwise. "In many respects he struck you as stoical [sic]," he now explains, ". . . that he actually had an Indian background . . . which he sure as hell didn't. But he seemed like he did."[52]

Beyond the reaches of campers' childish psyches, playing Indian at camp had other repercussions. As we have seen, camp programming conveyed the same negative images and limiting stereotypes of Aboriginal peoples as those circulating in the wider society. In so doing, camps did more than shape attitudes of individual campers; at a broader level, they contributed to the ongoing rationalization of colonialism. Negative images of violence and savagery rationalized it from the humanitarian perspective, while positive stereotypes, by freezing Aboriginal peoples in time, suggested that such noble, premodern creatures couldn't hope to survive in a modern civilized society. Either way, the colonial project was naturalized; that is, it was simply the way things had to be. On the other hand, as with the colonial project in general, silences and omissions regarding the tragic history of Native–white relations did as much harm as these articulated messages. Indeed, perhaps more damaging than what camps had to say about the Indian was what they did not. Nothing, it seems, was ever said about the fact that, as white campers played at being Indian, contemporary Native children were the target of aggressive campaigns aimed to rid them of their "Indianness." Did campers have any idea, one wonders, that as directors donned Native headdresses, state laws attempted to bar Aboriginal peoples from appearing publicly in traditional dress? Were they ever aware that as they enthusiastically participated in Indian rituals, Native bands in western provinces were prohibited from holding their own sundance and potlatch ceremonies?[53]

Whether campers knew it or not, as they seasonally put on Indian skins, Aboriginals could not escape the taint of their Indian status. Even while scholars conclude that racial categories in general are "shifting and unstable," and even "appallingly empty,"[54] for those racialized Others, the biological "unreality" of race conflicted with its pressing social reality in their day-to-day lives. Take only the example of the Bear Island band of Temagami. By the time of this study, they faced an unenviable set of social and economic conditions. As the result of a long-outstanding land claim, the band had never been formally assigned reserve land. Despite this fact, they adapted gradually to the fact of white encroachment on their land, surviving on a combination of trapping and guiding, including even some employment at the area's summer camps. However, without clear hunting and fishing rights, the Temagami band faced continual harassment by local game wardens. Worse still, resource development in the area and the infiltration of white trappers in the 1930s put the supply of fur into serious decline, leaving many to survive increasingly on relief funds. Post-war years saw little improvement in these conditions. The province continued to equivocate on the issue of establishing a reserve, and problems of alcohol and family breakdown increased.[55]

During this time, the small but influential recreation-based community of Temagami did little to ameliorate and, in some ways, exacerbated the problems of the Bear Islanders. With their own eyes firmly on preserving the area as wilderness escape and/or tourist mecca, white cottagers and resort operators complained variously about Native health problems, their destruction of the visible shoreline, and abuses of alcohol in the Aboriginal community, calling for increased police and medical surveillance as solutions. Camp Keewaydin's employment of Bear Islanders gives some indication of how camp communities fit into this picture. At the camp's founding in the first years of the century, the administration considered Ojibwa men from Bear Island knowledgeable, experienced, and close at hand; in short, the ideal tripping guides. Primarily trappers, they spent the winter on their lines but were available and often looking for summer work. Over the years, however, Keewaydin's preference shifted away from the Bear Island band so that by the 1920s the camp no longer sought workers from within the local community. Although the camp historian is silent on the issue, it is quite possible that, given the situation already noted, the Bear Islanders were increasingly regarded as the undesirable sort of Indians, hardly the noble self-sustaining survivalists that camp life sought to glorify. As far as other questions are concerned—for instance, the Bear Islanders' outstanding land claim—there is no indication that the white community—camps included— had anything to say on the issue, much less that they played any role as advocates for Aboriginal rights. Reminding children that they walked on what had been "Indian land" was portrayed not as a matter of controversy, as the basis for a critique of colonialism, or social redress, but rather as a mildly interesting (if unchangeable) anthropological fact. Were camp administrators aware of, or concerned about, the Bear Islanders' long-outstanding land claim? Certainly, by the 1970s and 1980s some involved themselves in this struggle.[56] For this earlier period, however, decades still marked by a broad cultural confidence in the colonial project, nothing could be found to indicate camp concern about the social and economic predicament of their Aboriginal neighbours in Temagami.

In other contexts, the early post-war years saw the first indications that parts of the camping community were developing new sensibilities toward the design of their Indian programming. As early as 1946, educator Mary Northway attacked the "distortion" of Native culture that she observed in camp programs. "Isn't it too bad," she observed, "that the only conception some of our campers, living in haunts so recently inhabited by Indians, have is that Indians were a people who met on Saturday nights dressed in blankets from . . . the Hudson Bay store and engaged in marshmallow eating contests?"[57] Presumably in response to the shift in public consciousness, some camps moved to eliminate certain features of their Indian programming. In 1958 Mary Hamilton described the decision to do away with Indian council ring at Tanamakoon: "The familiar 'How! How!,' the tribal set-up and the Indian names still exist," she explained. "As for the Indian council fire, it was shortlived. We decided not to be Indians

any longer and proceeded to be our own natural selves."[58] Other camps could be slower to initiate change. At the prestigious Taylor Statten camps, it was an Aboriginal youth who apparently articulated the first critique of council ring. In the early 1970s this counsellor-in-training, also daughter of the chief of the Ontarian Curve Lake band, complained to the camp administration: "I was so shock [sic] to go to council ring last night . . . having to watch you people make fun of my people."[59] Initially, the camp administration attempted to pacify the youth by removing the "dress-up" element from the ceremony, but when this prompted others to complain that "something was lost," the ritual was reinstated in its original form.[60] By the 1980s and 1990s, some camps—like Bolton—were more self-critical. There, council ring was not eliminated but modified; the use of broken English was forbidden, and campfires were instituted, following non-Indian themes. . . . In the hot political context of late twentieth-century Native–white relations, clearly playing Indian was not always seen as harmless child's play. On the other hand, the issue is still contested, if silently; these traditions continue in many ways at different camps, with Aboriginal names and practices still in evidence. As late as 1994, Indian council ring was still going strong at Camp Ahmek, with staff carefully following Statten's original order of proceedings, and campers continuing to dress up in "blankets, feathers, and paint."[61]

Conclusion

The history of camps' Indian programming tells us something about the shifting nature of Native–white relations, but ultimately the history of "playing Indian" is the history of whites and of white middle-class culture. One aspect was a recurring anti-modernist sentiment that presented itself as a strong, if subcultural, tendency throughout this period. The fact that camps did not disappear, but indeed proliferated in the 1950s and beyond, is just one indication that anti-modernism still figured in the post-war cultural landscape. Granted, infatuation with modernity in many forms was everywhere to be seen, but anti-modernism also percolated beneath the surface, raising questions and dampening the cultural optimism of the day.

In the interwar years this ambivalence revealed itself by the fact that while child-care manuals counselled rigid and controlled approaches to rearing children, many also considered the temporary outlet of experiences like camp—its Indian programming included—as necessary antidotes. It is revealing to note that the diminishing importance of Indian programming coincided with not only a changing climate of racial politics, but also with the rise of more permissive, emotional approaches to child-rearing in the post-war period. Perhaps as children were treated less as machines and more regularly encouraged to be "their own natural selves," the catharsis of playing Indian was deemed a more dispensable frill.

. . .

The common thread connecting this and other North American incarnations of anti-modernism was its ultimate social impact. . . . Through the camp, modern ways of thinking, feeling, and imagining the self and racial Others were reinforced. Preoccupation with intense experience and with identity, and the belief that both were to be sought on the terrain of leisure, were all typical of the modern condition. That camp administrators were not above marketing this experience was also indicative of their times. Born of anti-modernism, the summer camp was a modern animal. Playing Indian in this setting was just one way it allowed for simultaneous expression of these competing cultural impulses.

 More online.

Notes

My sincere thanks to the anonymous reviewers for their comments on an earlier version of this article. Thanks also to Cecilia Morgan and Gillian Poulter for their helpful comments and collegial support.

1. Mary S. Edgar, "Our Indebtedness to Our Indian Friends," 72-007/5/16, Ontario Camping Association Papers (hereafter cited as OCA), Trent University Archives (hereafter cited as TUA). Hereafter, the quotation marks around the term "Indian" will be implied.

2. Bobby Bridger, *Buffalo Bill and Sitting Bull: Inventing the Wild West* (Austin, TX: University of Texas Press, 2002); Daniel Francis, *The Imaginary Indian: The Image of the Indian in Canadian Culture* (Vancouver, BC: Arsenal Pulp, 1992), 115–23, 142–3 . . .

3. C. A. M. Edwards, *Taylor Statten* (Toronto, ON: Ryerson, 1960), 88.

4. Independently, Paris and I have come to the similar conclusion that camps were shaped by simple life nostalgia, but also inextricably linked to the urban social worlds they claimed to be escaping. In addition to exploring racial play acting in its Indian forms, Paris also traces the fascinating history of blackface minstrelsy at summer camp. Leslie Paris, "Children's Nature: Summer Camps in New York State, 1919–1941" (Ph.D. dissertation, University of Michigan, 2000). . . .

5. On camp statistics, see Nancy Cleaver, "An Old Canadian Custom: Sending the Kids to Camp," *Saturday Night*, 19 April 1952, 16; Peter Newman, "Junior's $10 Million Adventure in the Pines," *Financial Post*, 5 June 1954, 5; "Canada's Summer Indians Hit the Trail," *Star Weekly Magazine*, 11 June, 1960, 3. On the early camp movement, see essays in Bruce W. Hodgins and Bernadine Dodge, eds., *Using Wilderness: Essays on the Evolution of Youth Camping in Ontario* (Peterborough, ON: Frost Centre for Canadian Heritage and Development Studies, 1992); and Ontario Camping Association, *Blue Lake and Rocky Shore: A History of Children's Camping in Ontario* (Toronto, ON: Natural Heritage/Natural History, 1984).

6. Hartmut Lutz, "Cultural Appropriation as a Process of Displacing Peoples and History," *Canadian Journal of Native Studies* 10 (1990): 167–82. . . .

7. Philip Deloria, *Playing Indian* (New Haven, CT: Yale University Press, 1998); Shari Huhndorf, *Going Native: Indians in the American Cultural Imagination* (Ithaca, NY: Cornell University Press, 2001). . . .

8. T. J. Jackson Lears, *No Place of Grace: Antimodernism and the Transformation of American Culture, 1880–1920* (Chicago, IL: University of Chicago Press, 1981); Ian McKay, *Quest of the Folk: Antimodernism and Cultural Selection in Twentieth-Century Nova Scotia* (Montreal, QC: McGill-Queen's University Press, 1994).

9. "Urbanization," *Canadian Encyclopedia* (Edmonton, AB: Hurtig Press, 1988), 2235.

10. Katherine Arnup, *Education for Motherhood: Advice for Mothers in Twentieth-Century Canada* (Toronto, ON: University of Toronto Press, 1994), 84–116; Katherine Arnup, "Raising the Dionne Quintuplets: Lessons for Modern Mothers," *Journal of Canadian Studies* 29 (Winter 1994–95): 65–84; Cynthia Comacchio, *Nations Are Built of Babies: Saving Ontario's Mothers and Children* (Montreal, QC: McGill-Queen's University Press, 1993). . . .

11. Mary L. Northway, "Tools for the Job," *Parent Education Bulletin* 13 (1941): 6.

12. Cynthia Comacchio, "Dancing to Perdition: Adolescence and Leisure in Interwar English Canada" *Journal of Canadian Studies* 32 (1997): 5–35; David MacLeod, "A Live Vaccine: The YMCA and Male Adolescence in the United States and Canada, 1870–1920," *Histoire Sociale/Social History* 11 (May 1978): 5–25; Margaret Prang, "The Girl God Would Have Me Be: The Canadian Girls in Training, 1915–39," *Canadian Historical Review* 66 (1985): 154–83. . . .

13. H. Allen Anderson, *The Chief: Ernest Thompson Seton and the Changing West* (College Station, TX: Texas A&M University Press, 1986); Gail Bederman, "'Teaching Our Sons To Do What We Have Been Teaching the Savages To Avoid': G. Stanley Hall, Racial Recapitulation, and the Neurasthenic Paradox," in *Manliness and Civilization: A Cultural History of Gender and Race in the United States, 1880–1917* (Chicago, IL: University of Chicago Press, 1999); Deloria, *Playing Indian*, 95–110; Adele Ebbs, interview by Jack Pearse, 22 May 1986, 83-002/10/9, OCA Sound/Tape Collection, TUA; Edwards, *Taylor Statten*, 88. . . .

14. Bert Danson, "The History of Camp Winnebagoe" (unpublished paper, 2000).

15. Neighbourhood Workers' Association (hereafter cited as NWA), "The Story of Bolton Camp," in *After Twenty Years: A Short History of the Neighbourhood Workers Association* (Toronto, ON: Family Services Association, 1938), 43, Family Services Association of Toronto Archival Collection (hereafter cited as FSATA); Hedley S. Dimock and Charles E. Hendry, *Camping and Character: A Camp Experiment in Character Education* (New York, NY: Association, 1929), 74; W. J. Eastaugh, *Indian Council Ring* (Camp Ahmek: Taylor Statten Camps, 1938); Camp Pine Crest, "Report of Craft Activities," 1951, 78-009/2/1, Camp Pine Crest Fonds, TUA.

16. NWA, *Annual Report: New Interests at Bolton Camp in 1935* (Toronto: NWA), 15, FSATA. On games of "scalping," references to "scalps" (made of hemp rope) on display in council ring, and to Native "tribes" as "mortal enemies," see Eastaugh, *Indian Council Ring*, 26, 31.

17. Mary G. Hamilton, *The Call of Algonquin: Biography of a Summer Camp* (Toronto, ON: Ryerson, 1958), 149. . . .

18. Mary L. Northway, "Canadian Camping: Its Foundation and Its Future" (paper presented to the Manitoba Camping Association Annual Meeting, May 1946), 1, 98-019/13/6, series E, Adele Ebbs Papers, TUA.

19. . . . On Bolton's Indian programming, see NWA, *Annual Report: Bolton Camp, Report of Operation, 1937* (Toronto: NWA), FSATA. On Ahmek, see Dimock and Hendry, *Camping and Character*, 73–5; "The War Whoop," *Canoe Lake Camp Echoes* 4 (June 1931): 53, Ronald H. Perry Fonds, TUA.

20. Eastaugh, *Indian Council Ring*, 30.

21. Dimock and Hendry, *Camping and Character*, 141–2.

22. NWA, *After Twenty Years*, 43.

23. Dimock and Hendry, *Camping and Character*, 141.

24. Eastaugh, *Indian Council Ring*, 1.

25. NWA, *Annual Report: New Interests*, 8; Edgar, "Our Indebtedness," 2.

26. Eastaugh, *Indian Council Ring*, 7; "Notes on Programme: Bark Lake," 1948, 98-012/1/1, Ontario Camp Leadership Centre, Bark Lake Fonds, TUA.

27. "Five Years of Drudgery Bring Proud, Brave Family to End of Their Resources," *Toronto Daily Star*, 30 August 1927, 21. Deloria and Paris also note the symbolic importance of tans in connecting campers with a "premodern time zone." Deloria, *Playing Indian*, 106; Paris, "Children's Nature," 243.

28. "Notes on Programme: Bark Lake," 1948; Dimock and Hendry, *Camping and Character*, photo, 74; Bolton Camp photo albums, 1920s–1950s, FSATA. Camp Pine Crest, *Camp Pine Crest*, 1945, 78-009/2/4, Camp Pine Crest Fonds, TUA.

29. Eastaugh, *Indian Council Ring*, 1.

30. Eustace Haydon, "Memorial Talk Delivered to Camp Ahmek: Founders' Day," 12 July 1959, in Donald Burry, "A History of the Taylor Statten Camps" (Master's thesis, University of Saskatchewan, 1985), 27. Emphasis in original.

31. Douglas Cole, "The Invented Indian/The Imagined Emily," *BC Studies* 125/126 (Spring/Summer 2000): 147–62; Francis, *Imaginary Indian*, 190; Terry Goldie, *Fear and Temptation: The Image of the Indigene in Canadian, Australian, and New Zealand Literatures* (Montreal, QC: McGill-Queen's University Press, 1989). . . .

32. Hamilton, *Call of Algonquin*, 4.

33. Edgar, "Our Indebtedness," 2.

34. For examples, see Peter Kulchyski, "Anthropology in the Service of the State: Diamond Jenness and Canadian Indian Policy," *Journal of Canadian Studies* 28 (Summer 1993): 21–50; Andrew Nurse, "'But Now Things Have Changed': Marius Barbeau and the Politics of Amerindian Identity," *Ethnohistory* 48 (2001): 433–72.

35. "Change," *Canoe Lake Camp Echoes* 4 (June 1931): 18, 82-016/2/8, Ronald H. Perry Fonds, TUA.

36. Brian Back, *The Keewaydin Way: A Portrait, 1893–1983* (Temagami, ON: Keewaydin Camp, 1983), 37.

37. "Pale-Faced City Tikes Taught Indian Lore by Expert Woodsmen," *Toronto Daily Star*, 7 June 1950, 25; "Calling All Campers," *Canadian Girls in Training Newsletter*, 1952, file 4, box 39, 85.095C, UCA/VUA.

38. On western primitivism, see Bederman "Teaching Our Sons," 112–17; Helen Carr, *Inventing the American Primitive: Politics, Gender and the Representation of Native American Literary Traditions, 1789–1936* (New York, NY: New York University Press, 1996). . . .

39. Back, *Keewaydin Way*, 142.

40. "Pale-Faced City Tikes Taught Indian Lore," 25.

41. Back, *Keewaydin Way*, 141.

42. NWA, *Annual Report, 1937*, 8, FSATA.

43. "Pale-Faced City Tikes Taught Indian Lore," 25.

44. Eastaugh, *Indian Council Ring*, 7.

45. NWA, *After Twenty Years*, 43; NWA, *Annual Report, 1938*, 11, FSATA.

46. Ron Perry, interview by Bruce Harris, 2 December 1981, 83-002/5/1, OCA Sound Tape Collection, TUA.

47. Shirley Ford, interview by author, 20 June 2000, Toronto.

48. Dimock and Hendry, *Camping and Character*, 321; Camp Pine Crest, "Director's Report," 1950, 78-009/2/1, Camp Pine Crest Fonds, TUA.

49. Ebbs, interview by Pearse.

50. Jane Hughes, interview by author, 26 June 2000.

51. "Northway Recollection of Glen Bernard Camp."

52. James Buchanan, interview by author, 26 July 2000, Toronto.

53. Douglas Cole and Ira Chaikin, *An Iron Hand upon the People: The Law against the Potlatch on the Northwest Coast* (Vancouver, BC: Douglas and McIntyre, 1990); Keith Regular, "On Public Display," *Alberta History* 34, no. 1 (Winter 1986): 1–10; Glen Mikkelsen, "Indians and Rodeo," *Alberta History* 34 (Winter 1986): 13–19.

54. Anne McClintock, *Imperial Leather: Race, Gender, and Sexuality in the Colonial Contest* (New York, NY: Routledge, 1995), 52; Constance Backhouse, *Colour-Coded: A Legal History of Racism in Canada, 1900–50* (Toronto, ON: University of Toronto Press, 1999), 8.

55. Bruce W. Hodgins and Jamie Benidickson, *The Temagami Experience: Recreation, Resources, and Aboriginal Rights in the Northern Ontario Wilderness* (Toronto, ON: University of Toronto Press, 1989), 210–28.

56. In the 1970s camp director and scholar Bruce Hodgins began researching his *Temagami Experience*, which took a sympathetic view of Aboriginal rights in Temagami. . . .

57. Northway, "Canadian Camping."

58. Hamilton, *Call of Algonquin*, 22.

59. "Margo," quoted in Ebbs, interview by Pearse.

60. Ebbs, Interview, 20.

61. Liz Lundell, *Summer Camp: Great Camps of Algonquin Park* (Toronto, ON: Stoddart Publishing, 1994), 104–6; Fred Okada, conversation with author, 15 December 1998; Dale Callendar, *History of Bolton Camp* [1997], 11, FSATA.

26 Constructing the Preferred Spectator
Arena Design and Operation and the Consumption of Hockey in 1930s Toronto

Russell Field

The Gardens was built for people who wanted to watch what was happening on the ice (or the floor below), people who didn't expect a level of comfort equivalent to their arm chair at home, who didn't expect a range of gourmet options beyond hot dogs and popcorn, who didn't have a million other leisure options to lure them away.[1]

On the occasion of the closing of Toronto's Maple Leaf Gardens, a considerable amount of ink was used by local and Canadian press memorializing the 67-year-old arena. The dominant theme of this media coverage was that Toronto was losing (although the building was not scheduled for demolition) a significant civic landmark, a place around which the city's social life had circulated since the Depression. As the building's primary tenants, the Maple Leafs, a National Hockey League (NHL) franchise, prepared to move into their modern, new arena, Air Canada Centre, another theme emerged. Captured in the above quotation is the nostalgic sentiment that Maple Leaf Gardens represented an earlier, less commercial era, when spectators expected fewer in the way of creature comforts.

But how accurate is this sentimental hindsight? Maple Leaf Gardens was certainly "built for people who wanted to watch what was happening on the ice," but just what were their expectations as they entered the then-new arena in 1931? Elsewhere in the same 13 February 1999 issue of the national newspaper, the *Globe and Mail*, as the above quotation, another columnist remembers the Gardens not as a hallmark of a simpler age, but as its own state-of-the-art facility where "Spectators no longer had to worry about spit raining down on them from the balconies, an ever-present hazard at the old arena. They were warm for the first time."[2] This too seems its own form of nostalgia—given that the "old arena," Arena Gardens, did not have balconies from which spit could rain down—but it is certainly closer to the rhetoric that accompanied the opening of Maple Leaf Gardens in 1931.[3]

Two opening-night paeans to the arena underscore the original vision of Maple Leaf Gardens. The first is from Conn Smythe, the Maple Leafs's managing partner from 1927 to 1961 and a central figure in what follows. Smythe proclaimed that "Regardless of how enticing an attraction may be, it is ever so much more pleasant to spend an evening in comfortable surroundings where the architectural design and interior decorations are in harmony with the tastes of the clientele of the arena."[4] The second, entitled "President's Address to Sports Followers of the Queen City," was written by J. P. Bickell, then president of Maple Leaf Gardens, and is found in the *Official Programme* of the opening night at Maple Leaf Gardens, 12 November 1931:

The enthusiastic support of our patrons during the past few years encouraged and warranted us in providing enlarged, better-planned and more comfortable quarters. The citizens of Toronto and the country surrounding have always given generous support to clean, well-organized athletic activities, and we are confident in the hope that our management will continue to merit a patronage commensurate with our expanded effort.[5]

These two quotations, contemporary with the building's opening, get at the heart of the rhetoric surrounding the design and construction of Maple Leaf Gardens. More precisely, they explicitly link the architecture and design of the building with the spectators it was presumed would occupy it as well as the notions of gentility and civility it was hoped would prevail. These links reveal fundamental assumptions surrounding ice hockey spectatorship in Toronto in the interwar years. Similar observations connecting the physical nature of sporting spaces and their presumed inhabitants have been made by historians on both sides of the Atlantic Ocean. As late nineteenth- and early twentieth-century sport entrepreneurs sought to maximize the profits of their enterprises—in part by maintaining respectable behaviour both on and off the field—they began, as the historian Allen Guttmann notes "to construct stadiums and arenas to which access was strictly controlled and within which social classes tended to be separated by different ticket prices."[6] . . . Similar distinctions were made in American baseball stadiums at the turn of the twentieth century, where the covered grandstand was more frequently home to middle-class spectators, both male and female, while the bleachers featured "rowdy, lower-class fans" who, the American sport historian Steven Riess notes, "comprised the majority of spectators in the low-priced sections."[7]

These different spaces engendered a variety of spectator experiences. As the Welsh historian Martin Johnes observes, spectators standing on the uncovered bank at soccer grounds in Wales during the interwar years had to cope with rain, mud, the odours emanating from the refuse on which banks were often built and one another.[8] However, before the lived experiences of sport spectators in the 1930s can be fully understood, it is necessary to interrogate the spaces within which they practised their spectatorship. Maple Leaf Gardens is an excellent case study for just such an examination. Smythe's efforts to build his new facility took place at a time when commercial ice hockey in Canada had expanded into northern US markets such as New York, Chicago, and Boston. The investment in new facilities such as New York's Madison Square Garden is an example of what Canadian historian Bruce Kidd calls the growing interpenetration of Canadian and US capital in a continental economy as well as a reflection of the increasing importance of leisure and entertainment consumption in the late 1920s.[9] These buildings dramatically changed the nature of the spaces within which ice hockey was consumed, leaving historians to ask: How were these spaces designed? With whom in mind? And to accommodate what nature of spectator practices and behaviours? In essence, was there a "preferred" spectator?

To address these questions requires an exploration of the ways in which the construction of the spectator/audience has been considered in other public performance spaces in the late nineteenth and early twentieth centuries—for example, museums, theatres, department stores, and fairs and exhibitions. As a foundation, this literature touches on important concepts such as philosopher Michel Foucault's notions of disciplinary institutions and social theorist Henri Lefebvre's conceptualization of space.[10]

The notion of a preferred ice hockey spectator was formed around "civilized" respectability at a particular intersection of class, gender, and race. The construction of preferred spectators at Maple Leaf Gardens occurred in three "spaces": the exterior of the arena and its situation within 1930s Toronto; the architectural design of the interior; and finally the ways, both formal and informal, in which Maple Leaf Gardens was operated. However, it is important to acknowledge that efforts to build and operate an arena that expected and promoted respectable spectatorship were fully implicated within the desire for profit accumulation that had motivated Maple Leaf Gardens's construction in the first place.[11]

Cultural Institutions and the Respectable Civilized Subject

In his history of nineteenth-century museums, cultural studies scholar Tony Bennett proposes that the museum be considered alongside other cultural institutions that also attracted the attention of middle-class reformers, such as libraries, public parks, and department stores. These reformers were interested in using public spaces to communicate and inculcate the values of respectable, Christian, middle-class society. Sport and physical activity fell well within the rubric of social reform, as movements such as muscular Christianity and institutions such as the YMCA, YWCA, and the Boy Scouts make clear. It is not a stretch to suggest that physical spaces of sport were also put to the same reforming ends. And while the social reform movements reached their apogee in the late nineteenth century, as theatres and movie houses competed for consumers in the post–World War I era, so too did commercial sport spaces such as Maple Leaf Gardens.

Bennett goes beyond an examination of reformers' intentions and programs to explore the ways in which physical and social spaces were mobilized in these efforts. Thus he notes that the "reorganization of the social space of the museum occurred alongside the emerging role of museums in the formation of the bourgeois public sphere."[12] He introduces the notion of the "exhibitionary complex," which sought to use the museum as a space where preferred notions of the order of the world could be displayed both within the artifact cases and among the spectators themselves, who would be educated in Victorian notions of respectable society, would act these out, and would model them for others, all in the same moment.

. . .

Notions of visibility and performance are central to the ways in which Maple Leaf Gardens worked to construct a preferred spectator. An element of this was contained within the building's design but, as Bennett argues of the museum, "this was not an achievement of architecture alone."[13] The museum was a "performative environment in which new forms of conduct and behaviour could be shaped and practised."[14]

Public spaces—as the historian Patricia Vertinsky observes of sport spaces—are never neutral. Power relations, "which construct the rules, define the boundaries and create spaces with certain meanings in which some relationships are facilitated, others discouraged," mark out who is included and excluded from such spaces.[15] The spaces of cultural institutions such as nineteenth-century museums and exhibitions communicated and reproduced classed, gendered, and racialized notions of respectability. These spaces were designed and operated in such a way as to create settings for the acting out (and replication) of respectable bourgeois culture. As Bennett notes, "the space of the museum was also an emulative one; it was envisaged as a place in which the working classes would acquire more civilized habits by imitating their betters."[16] Similarly, [E. A.] Heaman argues that "The most important exhibit at the fair was the audience."[17]

. . .

One consequence of these new sites of middle-class respectability was that they created spaces for the public consumption of entertainment by women. Turn-of-the-century department stores combined "gracious appoint-ments," "lavishly displayed merchandise," and a "range of services designed to make consump-tion more than just a process of procuring goods."[18] [Cynthia] Wright argues these amen-ities were designed to "equate purchasing with a genteel style of life, to make the department store the women's equivalent of a men's down-town club."[19] Similar process of reform also took place in the theatre, where, as a substitute for racier entertainments, for example burlesque, "vaudeville houses provided a space for hetero-social attendance."[20] Despite this, thanks in part to residual Victorian morals, women, especially unescorted women, remained in the minority among spectators.

Nevertheless, this notion of "hetero-social attendance" points to the other interests at stake in the creation of spaces respectable enough for women. While Wright argues that the depart-ment store was a "feminine" space, other cultural institutions promoted middle-class respectabil-ity and "safe" environments for women not solely to encourage female consumption of entertain-ment. As Bennett argues, "the primary target of the museum's reforming intent was the work-ing-class man."[21] Ladies' departments were also incorporated by exhibition organizers in the hope that female fair-goers would be accompan-ied by men. "Women," Heaman argues, "were a hook to lure in the men."[22] Middle-class reform attempts to lure men away from corrupting influences such as the tavern and into "cleansed" public spaces co-opted women to these efforts. From the museum to the public park to the pub-lic library, "women were held to exert a civil-izing influence through their mere presence in both embodying and enjoining a gentleness of manners."[23] Individually, notes Heaman, women "were expected to elevate the men in their lives" yet "as a social force were to elevate society by exercising domestic virtues."[24]

. . .

An examination of the intended space of Maple Leaf Gardens requires the analysis of three different perspectives, or frames. To uncover the preferred spectator, it is necessary to look at the architectural design and realization of the arena, as well as the ways in which the build-ing was operated during the Maple Leafs's NHL hockey games. The excavation begins, however, with a consideration of the exterior frame and the building's situation within the downtown Toronto consumer economy of the 1930s.

Exterior: "A Splendid Architectural Treatment"

As Wright observes in her study of Eaton's College Street department store in Toronto, "The spatial organization of the department store can be understood at a number of levels. One approach is to examine the relationship between the department store and the city."[25] This is a valuable entrée to a study of Maple Leaf Gardens on a general level, but also in the specific as well. Any examination of the location of Maple Leaf Gardens, as well as the ways in which the arena was envisioned, needs to begin one block to the west with another major commercial Toronto landmark built in the 1930s, Eaton's College Street store. Department stores and hockey arenas can be considered within the rubric of cultural institutions that sought to influence tastes by invoking notions of respectability. Both Eaton's College Street store and Maple Leaf Gardens shared this project in interwar Toronto. Yet, even more importantly, the land on which Maple Leaf Gardens was built was controlled by Eaton's and had to be purchased from the retailer by the hockey club. An examination of Eaton's reaction to and influence over the hockey arena being built in its backyard is one way to understand the exterior "frame" of Maple Leaf Gardens.

Eaton's opened its new College Street store in Toronto, at the southwest corner of Yonge and College Streets, in October 1930. The vision for Eaton's new store included "an explicit link . . . made between the modernity of the College

Street building and the transformation or "modernization" of shopping itself."[26] This reform project, directed as it was at the female "carriage trade," included "the architecture of the College Street premises [which] was planned with a view to 'the transformation of the store's image.'"[27] Maple Leaf Gardens was opened in 1931, one block east, at the northwest corner of Carlton and Church Streets.[28] For Smythe's arena project to go ahead on this site, he and his partners needed to convince Eaton's executives that the building would alter their perceptions of the clientele that hockey arenas attracted and would not compromise Eaton's own efforts to create and attract the civilized bourgeois consumer.

. . . [T]o try and negotiate the purchase of the desired corner lot, the Maple Leafs argued that their operation would bring not only potential customers, but [also] the right calibre of customer to the College Street vicinity. Moreover, they assured Eaton's that the architectural design of the exterior of the arena would make it the valuable addition to the commercial neighbourhood that the retailer desired. As J. A. Gibson, the agent acting for Eaton's in this matter, relayed back to his client:

> The intention is to have a building of handsome appearance with first class modern store fronts to produce the maximum amount of rental and give the best possible appearance.
> It would appear to us that such a project would bring a great many additional people to this section thus having a beneficial effect on property in this district.[29]

. . . Eaton's was concerned more about the use to which the land would be put rather than the sales price they would receive. Their board members wanted the land to be used in a way that complemented their intention to make the College Street store an "arbiter of distinctness and correctness."[30] The department store was not afraid of commercial competition, having tried unsuccessfully to induce its most prominent competitor in the Toronto market, Simpson's (which was located directly across the street from Eaton's main Toronto store on Queen Street), to join in the move north to College Street.[31] The concern was not competing shops, but the right kind of shops, as Elliott worried "that there would not be any stores of any importance on any property the Arena people may purchase but rather a lot of small shops."[32]

Even after an agreement had been reached to sell the northwest corner lot to the Maple Leafs, Eaton's approval was so important that the lead architect on the Gardens shared the working drawings and specifications for the new arena—in which another corporation had majority interest—with the department store so that "the T. Eaton Company should have the privilege of reviewing the plans and specifications so that we might endeavour to make any modifications that they might suggest."[33] The modifications that interested Eaton's on a philosophical and financial level, the idea of reaping the profits of respectable middle-class consumption, interested the Maple Leafs as well. These concerns were reflected in the exterior of the new arena, which dominated the Toronto landscape, as well as in its interior design.

Interior: From Box Seats to Benches

While Eaton's vice-president, Harry McGee—who would eventually become a member of the Maple Leaf Gardens board—was reviewing Ross and Macdonald's designs for Toronto's new arena he would have learned of the architects' vision for the interior of what was to become the city's largest indoor gathering place. Early drawings of the building indicate that the arena had been thought of in part as an amusement palace, including as they did a bowling alley and billiards room.[34] Eventually, however, the Gardens became primarily a spectator venue, with the emphasis firmly placed on facilitating the movement of people through the building to their seats within the arena.

Wright has argued that the interior of Eaton's College Street store was designed as a "feminine" space, where "the very spatial organization of the store's interior was 'feminized.'"[35] There were men's departments, but these were invariably found on the ground floor, assuming that men who felt the necessity to consume would be unlikely to be interested in browsing through the store's upper floors in the way that it was presumed woman would want to do. By this measure, Toronto's new hockey arena was a predominantly masculine space. Indeed, the architecture historian Sherry McKay notes that physical spaces, both private and public, historically have been designed to anticipate the male body.[36] "Sports landscapes can, therefore," Vertinsky also argues, "be appropriately read as masculine landscapes."[37] So while Maple Leaf Gardens's design, on the exterior and interior, marked it as a building different both in kind and degree from anything that had previously dotted Toronto's sporting landscape, it was still a building that catered to tastes that McKay, Vertinsky, Wright, and others label as masculine. While there was social space within the building where people could linger and, in the 1930s, smoke, the primary focus of the arena's interior design was to move people through the building to their seats.

. . .

There are other markers that indicate this space was intended, primarily, for men. On the most mundane but necessary level, the arena was designed with considerably more washrooms for men than women. . . . 87.1 per cent of the available washroom spaces were found in the men's toilets, and this ratio was consistent on every level of the building. Despite this, there were attempts to cater to women's comfort. Every women's toilet, though offering limited "seating," included (as was the custom) an anteroom. If as Wright suggests, feminine spaces are marked in one way by allowing for leisurely strolling (browsing, in the department store context), each level within Maple Leaf Gardens did include "lounge space." These were spaces where people could congregate between periods of the game to socialize and smoke, a practice which was prohibited—if not by law, then by custom—within the arena itself. And these spaces, at least on the building's opening night, were occupied by women. As the *Telegram*'s women's sports columnist Phyllis Griffiths noted, "The wide promenades at the Maple Leaf Gardens gave the women a chance to enjoy a walk and a cigarette between periods, although many preferred to do their puffing in privacy in the rooms provided on each floor."[38]

Griffiths's observation of smokers highlights shifts that were occurring in the ways in which public space in Toronto was gendered. Female spectators who chose to enjoy "a walk and a cigarette" during intermissions at Maple Leaf Gardens reflected the changing perceptions of public smoking. Whereas at the turn of the twentieth century "respectable smoking was only possible for men," the historian Jarret Rudy notes that "By the twenties and thirties, the idea that women might smoke was more acceptable yet still contentious."[39] Despite this, especially in a socially conservative city such as Toronto, Davis and Lorenzkowski argue that until "the 1940s smoking was still considered a gendered habit."[40] This may account for those female hockey spectators who "preferred to do their puffing in privacy." While smoking "gave odour and visible shape to spaces socially constructed as male," as noted of Toronto's streetcar patrons, Rudy argues that deference and self-control were equally important male smoking behaviours.[41] "Not smoking while with a woman in public," he contends, "was nothing less than a performance of masculine respectability."[42] The operating practices of Maple Leaf Gardens, which prohibited smoking in the arena's main seating areas, required this performance of respectability of all the building's male customers.

Maple Leaf Gardens's design not only marked out gendered space, it also mapped out the social hierarchies of Toronto's entertainment consumers. The nature of the seating changed dramatically the further one moved up from the floor of the arena. The box seats were opera seating with red leather padded chairs, each with their own arms, while the middle sections of the arena featured wooden seats with wooden backs and arms, and the uppermost sections offered fans long wooden benches.[43] Male patrons with the most expensive seats were also well treated when heeding nature's call. While on the upper floors the urinals in the men's washrooms were stainless steel troughs, on the main floor they were porcelain.[44]

There were not just static distinctions between the arena's individual sections. Barriers to movement were also found. The building's design precluded movement between each tier of seats. Box and rail seat customers entered on the ground level, while ticketholders in each of the upper three tiers or in the end seats had to ascend staircases. These took them to the top of their section, where they descended to their seats. The location of standing-room areas at the back of each tier, with a substantial rise to the front row of the above section, meant that there was no easy way to move between sections.

Despite the assessment that the space was largely designed to move patrons toward their seats, the interior appointments of Maple Leaf Gardens were considerably grander than those at its forerunner, Arena Gardens. This space was to be home to the respectable middle-class spectator, whose spectating experience and behaviours were ultimately influenced by how the arena was operated, both formally and informally, during games.

Operations: "Enforce a Proper Sporting Spirit"

The preferred spectator was produced not only by the design of Maple Leaf Gardens, but also through the ways in which the arena was operated. While no detailed operating plans survive,

if they ever existed, there are ways in which this theme can be explored. Media accounts not only reported on fans and spectators but also offered commentary on what was appropriate and what, in the minds of columnists, went beyond the bounds. An examination of these accounts, along with archival and oral history sources, reveals that Maple Leaf Gardens operated during the 1930s in such a way as to produce a spectator who inhabited an ideal intersection of class, gender, and racial expectations. At this nexus existed the preferred spectator, one who was both respectable and respectful. She or he was valuable not only in maintaining respectability but in modelling the correct behaviours for others.

Respectability and behavioural expectations were intertwined with spectators' attendance at hockey games. This was an issue from the very first game at Maple Leaf Gardens. During the lengthy opening ceremonies that night, 12 November 1931, arena president J. P. Bickell and others made speeches that "marked the longest stretch that some of the Chi-Hawks [Chicago Blackhawks, the Maple Leafs's opposition that night] have been on the ice in three years."[45] An impatient crowd began voicing its displeasure at the delayed start to the game. The ensuing booing and barracking was cause for rebuke in the popular press in the days after the arena's inauguration. The *Telegram* noted that "it is certainly deplorable that prominent men like the Premier and the mayor should be subjected to the howls of the impatient rabble."[46] The *Mail and Empire*'s sports columnist, Edwin Allan, remarked that Bickell and the other dignitaries were "entitled to a better reception." He went on to chastise an audience who were tiring of speeches: "but that's no excuse for the poor reception they gave some of the speakers."[47] Meanwhile, the *Mail and Empire*'s editorial page blamed the incident on "younger elements in the crowd," who needed to learn how to act in a "sportsmanlike" fashion.[48]

Alternatively, praise was bestowed on spectators who supported the home side through rapt attention and "respectable" cheering. The *Globe* noted in 1936 that "support from the crowd . . . [was] given . . . in a manner that showed what Toronto fans . . . think of their team in the final analysis."[49] In advance of praise, however, came education. A 1934 Maple Leaf Gardens program included "The President's Message to Maple Leaf Fans." There Bickell outlined the manner in which spectators could best demonstrate their support for the Maple Leafs: "To the patrons may I suggest that they match the players' skill and energy with their cheers, so that when the game starts, dull care departs, and entertainment such as no other game provides, will be our lot."[50]

The well-behaved crowd who provided these "cheers" attended hockey games within an environment where the expectations of behaviour, if not posted at the entrances, were at least understood to be significantly different from the working-class roots of early commercial sports crowds.[51] One way that the expectation of public behaviour associated with middle-class respectability could be maintained was by charging appropriate entrance fees. In the first season at Maple Leaf Gardens, 1931–2, ticket prices ranged from $1.00 to $3.00.[52] They were raised the following year, to a top price of $3.30, before being decreased part way through the season. For the rest of the 1930s, the top ticket price was $2.50. On one hand, the cost of tickets made it challenging during the Depression to attend hockey games, especially in the seats closest to the action. High prices for the best seats ensured that the latter would be filled with preferable customers. But Smythe and the Maple Leafs were still in the business of selling tickets, at a variety of price ranges. So, on the other hand, multiple ticket prices worked to establish expectations yet not preclude the working classes from attending, usually in the upper reaches of the arena, provided they behaved themselves.

It has been noted elsewhere how Smythe, in recalling the design and operation of Maple Leaf Gardens, wanted to create an environment that rivalled the finest evenings out in Toronto, where people could attend hockey games in their

evening wear.[53] This presumed environment, whether it accurately reflected who actually attended games at the Gardens and how they dressed and behaved, became wrapped up with expectations of how the entire crowd should act and behave. Fifty years later, the writer and former NHL goaltender Ken Dryden could recall that "a jacket and tie was considered compulsory attire for season-ticket holders of red (now gold) seats."[54] Even at the time of the building's opening, *Star* columnist Lou Marsh remarked, tongue-in-cheek, on "the fiendish rumor that things are so high hat around the new Gardens that the peanut men only be allowed to sell salted almonds!"[55]

. . .

While ticket prices and attire created spaces associated with very specific class expectations and the distribution of men's and women's washrooms gendered the ice hockey arena masculine, racial and ethnic identities were not so clearly delineated. Nevertheless, Maple Leaf Gardens was also a racialized space, one that was both colonized and colonizing.[56] At the time of the building's inauguration, 81 per cent of Toronto's population were of British ancestry and two-thirds of non-native Torontonians hailed from the United Kingdom.[57] In part because of Smythe's well-publicized support of Canada's place in the British Empire—evidenced by his service in the Canadian Forces in both World Wars I and II, with the latter beginning at age 45—the new arena fit within the cultural landscape of Protestant British Toronto in the 1930s.[58] From the opening of Maple Leaf Gardens, the imperial project went unchallenged. If, as Vertinsky suggests, the inclusions and exclusions that revealed the power relations inherent in physical spaces marked sporting sites as masculine places, these same processes also operated at Maple Leaf Gardens to exclude—or at least render less visible—non-Anglo bodies. The 48th Highlanders regiment playing "God Save the King" and the Union Jack prominently hung at one end of the arena reminded spectators of Toronto's Anglo majority and the nation's ties to Great Britain.[59]

Despite this, the city was home to an increasingly diverse populace. In the decade prior to Maple Leaf Gardens's construction, the proportion of Toronto's non-British residents had grown from 5 to 19 per cent of the city's population. Jews, primarily immigrants from Central and Eastern Europe, at 7 per cent of the city's 1931 population, and Italians, at 2 per cent, were the city's largest non-Anglo immigrant groups.[60] Immigrants resided primarily in ethnic neighbourhoods and faced considerable racism, of which historical geographer James Lemon notes "Jews bore the greatest burden."[61] Physical separation and racist stereotypes combined to render non-Anglo minorities invisible within public spaces such as Maple Leaf Gardens. As a result, this space actively colonized all who entered it and marginalized non-Anglo spectators. One spectator from the 1930s recalls—true or not—Jewish spectators solely as gamblers and bookies.[62] The spectator continued: "They weren't all [gamblers], naturally, but an awful lot of them were." Jews "were the smart ones to make money," as during the Depression, "everybody else was starving and they were piling it in." It is unlikely that the majority of Jewish Torontonians were "piling it in," but this remembrance suggests that some members of this community had the financial resources to buy tickets to hockey games. Despite their presence within the crowd—albeit likely as a distinct minority—non-British Torontonians spectated within a white space. Another spectator from the interwar years, when asked specifically about Toronto's Italian immigrant population, noted, "I just classify them as white."[63] Diversity may have existed in interwar Toronto both within and beyond Maple Leaf Gardens, but it went largely unacknowledged.

Similarly, [the tabloid newspaper] *Hush* questioned why "Maple Leaf Gardens . . . officials are discriminating against the employment of Jews in the face of the fact that a great portion of their support comes from this sport-loving race."[64] The criticism by *Hush* of Maple Leaf Gardens's hiring practices highlights another important element in the arena's operation: the staff. Ushers, concessionaries and others should not be ignored for the role they played in creating the preferred spectator. The staff set the tone—from demeanour to dress—and enforced the preferred behaviours. . . . The staff also reflected the ways in which Maple Leaf Gardens was a gendered space. Women provided the comfort and respectability that Smythe sought in the more expensive box and rail seats. Not surprisingly, then, one spectator from the 1930s recalls that the ushers in the least expensive seats were all male—and, it was thought, better able to deal with the potentially rowdier elements who would find their way up into the less expensive seats—while "usherettes" serviced the plusher box seats.[65] Given women's naturalized domestic roles, they too were most often used to staff the arena's concession stands.[66]

. . . Within the walls of the Gardens, as well, there were social norms that spectators believed needed to be reinforced. In response to a playful newspaper report of a 1937 incident where Lionel Conacher hit a Gardens rinkside spectator over the head with his stick, an earnest John McGinnis, a local office manager and Conacher's victim, wrote to the *Globe and Mail* to remind the sports editor that such incidents should be taken more seriously. "All I can say," Mr. McGinnis wrote, "is that as an example to the juniors every effort should be made to enforce a proper sporting spirit, instead of rank cowardice."[67]

It was not only in the events that took place at Maple Leaf Gardens that this "proper sporting spirit" could be evidenced, but in the press accounts of such events as well. McGinnis points toward the ways in which local newspapers and the radio contributed to the construction of the preferred hockey spectator. At the time, Toronto had four daily newspapers: the *Globe* and *Mail and Empire*, published in the morning, and the evening editions of the *Star* and *Telegram*. The *Globe* was Toronto's most established paper and historically a Liberal party organ, while the *Mail and Empire* was the Conservative paper. The

Telegram also took conservative, pro-Empire stances, usually in sensationalist fashion, while the *Star* offered a more liberal populism and enjoyed the largest circulation in the city. The *Star* and the *Telegram*, as Lemon has contended, "framed much of the debate of the 1920s, certainly outdoing their more respectable morning rivals."[68] Over the airwaves, program listings in the *Globe* in the late 1920s identify five Toronto radio stations, including CFCA, which was launched by the *Star* and was the city's first radio station.[69]

. . . In encouraging spectators to behave and support the Maple Leafs in particularly respectable ways, the media were complicit in the construction of the Gardens's preferred spectator. The pervasiveness of well-known Canadian radio pioneer Foster Hewitt's national hockey broadcasts from Maple Leaf Gardens allowed the medium of radio to influence spectator attitudes and behaviours, as people arrived at the Gardens having received a spectator primer. On Saturday nights in Toronto in the 1930s it was difficult to avoid Hewitt's *Hockey Night in Canada* broadcasts. Hewitt himself notes that a national "1937 survey indicated that over six million fans heard one Toronto-Detroit hockey game" on radio.[70] This became, briefly, another injustice for *Hush*: "Last Saturday, CFCA, CKCL, and CFRB, were all on a hook-up from the Maple Leaf Gardens, when one station carrying that feature would have been ample."[71]

The hockey team offered the media ample assistance in promoting events at Maple Leaf Gardens. Stories of Smythe's influence over the local media—going so far as to threaten to pull advertising from the *Star* if the newspaper did not begin running stories more favourable to the team—are part of the popular mythology of the team.[72] In two January 1944 letters to Smythe, who was serving in the 30th Battery, Canadian Army Overseas, at the time, his hockey lieutenant, Frank Selke, recalled the ways in which Smythe in the 1930s had manipulated the media to generate fan interest in upcoming games at Maple Leaf Gardens.[73] . . .

Conclusion: Subverting Respectability

Despite Smythe's attempts to create a space where middle-class respectability was acted out, he was often the very reason such efforts were undermined. In a 1937 game at Maple Leaf Gardens, Smythe transgressed the boundaries he had worked so hard to impose and "added to the entertainment in the third period when he dashed out on the ice and joined in the argument over Davidson's disallowed goal."[74] This was not an isolated incident.

Off the ice, Smythe regularly used the media to generate rivalries with other clubs in the hopes that fans would flock to see how this "hatred" played out on the ice. Smythe's most famous rivalry was with the Boston Bruins and his counterpart there, Art Ross. Their mutual antipathy was well documented and widely known. The *Mail and Empire* noted that "There has always been quite a feeling between the two clubs," while *Hush* observed that "Conny Smythe and Art Ross are not going to harmonize that popular ballad 'Just Friends.'"[75] Smythe and Selke acknowledged the value of this as a ticket sales tactic. While Smythe was overseas in 1944 and Selke was left running the club, the latter wrote to the former: "Ross made some wild charges against me having in mind the way you used to stir them up in Boston."[76] This rivalry was often blamed for inciting violence on the ice between the Maple Leafs and the Bruins—most famously in a December 1933 incident where a swing of Eddie Shore's stick ended the playing career of Ace Bailey of the Maple Leafs—but it also created an atmosphere that led to incidents among the fans and between fans, players, and officials.

The Bailey–Shore incident, though it took place in Boston, generated substantial press coverage, as Bailey remained seriously ill in a Boston hospital for several days. It gave *Telegram* sports editor J. P. Fitzgerald an opportunity to rail against hockey promoters and their "press ballyhoo . . . appealing to the public as a rowdy roughhouse affair." Hockey, Fitzgerald continued, "can add nothing in its attractiveness as an entertainment by an appeal to the lower instincts of players or spectators."[77] Nevertheless, his colleague at the *Telegram*, Ted Reeve, noted that the possibility of violence on the ice and the excitement it provided the crowd ensured that "Business at the turnstiles was better than ever." Reeve noted, lyrically, the economic benefit of stirring up the crowd in the ways that Smythe, Selke, and Ross did:

When hockey gets gentle it goes dead,
As no one is crushed through the ribs or the head,
And when it grows gentle the crowds they grow small,
So where would be shinny with no brawls at all?
What? No brawls at all?
No, no brawls at all!
Oh, where would be hockey (hold it),
With no brawls at all? (at all, at all).[78]

Reeve's poem . . . gets at an important contradiction. Maple Leaf Gardens may have been built with the preferred respectable spectator in mind, one whose behaviour would be emulated by others within the arena, but as an entertainment business in the Depression it needed more than anything to sell tickets. And this meant relying on the very customer the Maple Leafs sought to reform. In the department store context, Wright notes that Eaton's College Street, even in its attempts to attract the carriage trade, could not ignore the working-class shopper—though the creation of "bargain basements" certainly marginalized her.[79] At Maple Leaf Gardens, all manner of fans—the respectable, those labelled unrespectable, and those who enjoyed transgressing that boundary—were all welcome as paying customers.

Having set the boundaries of respectability in the stands, Smythe and others would do what

they could to present a spectacle on the ice (fast, physical, and often violent) that was appealing because it offered the tantalizing possibility of transcending these very same boundaries.[80] This points to the ways in which an analysis of space that seeks the intended audience only tells half the story. . . .

Architects and building operators could intend their spaces to be used by spectators in particular ways, but there were ample opportunities for people in the crowd to resist these strictures and spectate as they chose. Throughout the 1930s, incidents of spectators becoming involved in altercations with players, officials, or each other received comment in the popular press. The spectacle was rarely to blame for such events; rather, spectators would have to be better behaved. Following an altercation between Maple Leafs players and fans at New York's Madison Square Garden in 1931, the *Telegram* was moved to remind potential spectators in Toronto that "Whatever justification there may be for players to take the odd crack at each other in the heat of play there is none for spectators to butt into the argument and much less than that to start any fracas with players."[81] After Boston's Babe Siebert got into a fight with a spectator while in the penalty box at Maple Leaf Gardens in 1935, the *Mail and Empire* noted: "We believe it is the first time that spectators have ever interfered with the players in the penalty box at the gardens [sic], and it should be the last."[82] The frequency of these observations suggests that this was likely not the last incident of this nature.

As Lefebvre suggests, regardless of how a space is conceived, the people who inhabit the space define its existence as lived space. He argues that "the social relations of production have a social existence to the extent that they have a spatial existence," but he goes on to contend that the social relations of production "project themselves into a space, becoming inscribed there, and in the process producing the space itself."[83] Within such a perspective, the spectator within Maple Leaf Gardens did as much to define the nature of the space as Maple Leaf Gardens did to shape the spectator. The respectability project of late nineteenth- and early twentieth-century stadiums was intended to reduce undesirable elements such as rowdyism and gambling. Nevertheless, in 1937, the *Toronto Telegram* remarked on "the boys in the wagering ring—on the east side behind the blue section," while a former spectator remembers "big, burly men . . . passing the money back and forth" in the lobby of Maple Leaf Gardens.[84] Ticket scalpers, another potentially undesirable element, also graced the neighbourhood of Maple Leaf Gardens and shaped the experience of spectators entering the arena. One former spectator remembers "outside they're all these people milling around" at his first game as a nine-year-old. "These guys were definitely conducting some sort of business."[85] The *Telegram* noted of another game that "scalpers were in the lobby trying to get rid of blue tickets."[86]

The popularity of Hewitt's national radio broadcasts of hockey games from Maple Leaf Gardens has already been noted. But even the famed announcer was unprepared for the effect his play-by-play accounts would have on spectating within the arena. "I was rather startled by the increasing number of spectators who took their radios with them right into the Maple Leaf Gardens," he recalls. "One night ushers counted no fewer than eighty-nine persons carrying their receiving sets."[87] Indeed, spaces within the arena were defined as much by how people occupied them as by their design and operation. A former spectator, in recalling his first game at Maple Leaf Gardens, spent in the standing-room section behind one of the goals, noted that this space was occupied by "mostly men" who had to get to the arena early and line up to buy tickets, whereupon the most dedicated fans ran up the stairs to get the best spots—"people that knew where they were going there wanted to get up to the ends"—and remained waiting up to an hour for the game to start, not even moving during intermissions for fear of losing

a hard-earned vantage point.[88] Such practices affirm that the space of Maple Leaf Gardens was defined in a significant way by the spectators who used it.

Similarly, while Maple Leafs's president J. P. Bickell may have urged "enthusiastic" but respectable "support" from his patrons, spectators cheered in a variety of ways, at times loud, boisterous, and demonstrative. In the event of a referee's decision or physical altercation going against the home team, frustration was often vented by tossing onto the ice the very programs within which Bickell's request had been written.[89] But as one fan writing to the sports editor at the *Globe and Mail* noted of the "hollering fun": "It is all a matter of excitement, and the big crowd enjoy [*sic*] the show . . . its [*sic*] good for the lungs and helps the merry-go-round to get merrier."[90] While understanding the construction of the preferred spectator is a valuable first step, it is still only one step toward appreciating the transition from the preferred spectator to the lived experience—the "merry-go-round"—of the actual spectator. Nevertheless, the history of the commercialization of North American ice hockey in the interwar years is enhanced by understanding the ways in which new sport spaces were designed and operated to anticipate and produce respectable spectators at a particular intersection of class, gender, and ethnic expectations.

 More online.

Notes

1. Stephen Brunt, "Building on Maple Leaf Memories," *Globe and Mail*, 13 February 1999.
2. John Barber, "Ghosts of the Gardens Tell Tales of Glory and Disgrace," *Globe and Mail*, 13 February 1999.
3. Interior photo of Arena Gardens, *c.* 1921–2, Item 36, Fonds 1646, City of Toronto Archives, Toronto, Ontario.
4. Conn Smythe, cited in Barber, "Ghosts of the Gardens."
5. *Maple Leaf Gardens Official Programme*, 12 November 1931 (vs. Chicago Blackhawks), Resource Centre, Hockey Hall of Fame, Toronto, Ontario, 28.

6. A. Guttmann, *Sports Spectators* (New York, NY: Columbia University Press), 121.
7. S. Riess, *Touching Base: Professional Baseball and American Culture in the Progressive Era* (Westport, CT: Greenwood Press, 1980), 28, 33.
8. M. Johnes, *Soccer and Society: South Wales, 1900–39* (Cardiff, UK: University of Wales Press, 2002), 122–3.
9. B. Kidd, *The Struggle for Canadian Sport* (Toronto, ON: University of Toronto Press, 1996), 225; see also R. Field, "Passive Participation: The Selling of Spectacle and the Construction of Maple Leaf Gardens, 1931," *Sport History Review* 33, no. 1 (2002).
10. M. Foucault, *Discipline and Punish: The Birth of the Prison* (New York, NY: Vintage Books, 1995); H. Lefebvre, *The Production of Space*, trans. Donald Nicholson-Smith (Oxford, UK: Blackwell, 1991).
11. Field, "Passive Participation."
12. T. Bennett, *The Birth of the Museum: History, Theory, Politics* (London, UK: Routledge, 1995).
13. Ibid., 69.
14. Ibid., 55.
15. P. Vertinsky, "'Power Geometries': Disciplining the Gendered Body in the Spaces of the War Memorial Gymnasium," in P. Vertinsky and S. McKay, eds., *Disciplining Bodies in the Gymnasium: Memory, Monument, Modernism* (New York, NY: Routledge, 2004), 50.
16. Bennett, *The Birth of the Museum*, 47.
17. E. A. Heaman, *The Inglorious Arts of Peace: Exhibitions in Canadian Society during the Nineteenth Century* (Toronto, ON: University of Toronto Press, 1999), 135.
18. C. Wright, "'The Most Prominent Rendezvous of the Feminine Toronto': Eaton's College Street and the Organization of Shopping in Toronto, 1920–50" (Ph.D. dissertation, University of Toronto, 1992), 203, 205.
19. Ibid., 205.
20. S. Weathers Smith, "Spectators in Public: Theater Audiences in New York City, 1882–1929," (Ph.D. dissertation, University of California, Berkeley, 2001), 26.
21. Bennett, *The Birth of the Museum*, 31.
22. Heaman, *The Inglorious Arts of Peace*, 119.
23. Bennett, *The Birth of the Museum*, 32.
24. Heaman, *The Inglorious Arts of Peace*, 263.
25. Wright, "'The Most Prominent Rendezvous of the Feminine Toronto,'" 147.
26. Ibid., 130.
27. Ibid., 123. She cites W. Dendy, *Lost Toronto* (Toronto, ON: Oxford University Press, 1978), 157.
28. In conjunction with the opening of Eaton's new store in 1930, the city rerouted Carlton Street so that it met College Street at Yonge Street, creating a continuous east–west road.
29. J. A. Gibson to James Elliott, 29 April 1930, General Files of James Elliott, File M-103: "Maple Leaf Gardens: General Matters," F229–282, T. Eaton Co. Fonds, Archives of Ontario, Toronto.
30. C. Wright, "'Feminine Trifles of Vast Importance': Writing Gender into the History of Consumption," in F. Iacovetta and M. Valverde, eds., *Gender Conflicts: New Essays in Women's History* (Toronto, ON: University of Toronto Press, 1992), 230.
31. Wright, "'The Most Prominent Rendezvous of the Feminine Toronto,'" 121.
32. Memorandum, James Elliott, 3 May 1930, General Files of James Elliott, File M-103: "Maple Leaf Gardens: General Matters," F229–282, T. Eaton Co. Fonds, Archives of Ontario, Toronto.
33. Geo. A. Ross to Harry McGee, 21 May 1931, General Files of James Elliott, File M-103: "Maple Leaf Gardens: General Matters," F229–282, T. Eaton Co. Fonds, Archives of Ontario, Toronto.
34. "Main Floor Plan," 20 February 1931, Maple Leaf Gardens, 13-164-02M, Ross and Macdonald Archive, Canadian Centre for Architecture, Montreal, Quebec.
35. Wright, "'The Most Prominent Rendezvous of the Feminine Toronto,'" 135.
36. S. McKay, "Designing Discipline: The Architecture of a Gymnasium," in P. Vertinsky and S. McKay, eds., *Disciplining Bodies in the Gymnasium: Memory, Monument, Modernism* (New York, NY: Routledge, 2004), 133.
37. P. Vertinsky, "Designing the Million Dollar Gym: Modernism and Masculinity," in P. Vertinsky and S. McKay, eds., *Disciplining Bodies in the Gymnasium: Memory, Monument, Modernism* (New York, NY: Routledge, 2004), 47.
38. Phyllis Griffiths, "The Girl and the Game," *Toronto Telegram*, 13 November 1931.
39. J. Rudy, *The Freedom to Smoke: Tobacco Consumption and Identity* (Montreal, QC: McGill-Queen's University Press, 2005), 20, 164.
40. D. Davis and B. Lorenzkowski, "A Platform for Gender Tensions: Women Working and Riding on Canadian Urban Public Transit in the 1940s," *Canadian Historical Review* 79, no. 3 (1998): 443.
41. Rudy, *The Freedom to Smoke*, 6.
42. Ibid., 39.
43. "Diagrams Showing Types of Seats," 6 July 1931, Maple Leaf Gardens, 13-164-03M, Ross and Macdonald Archive, Canadian Centre for Architecture, Montreal; Bernie Fourier, personal communication, 17 August 2000.
44. Drawing No. 3.01 B: First Floor Plan, Maple Leaf Gardens (2), RG 56-10 D-330, Theatre Plans, Archives of Ontario, Toronto.
45. Ted Reeve, "Sporting Extras," *Toronto Telegram*, 13 November 1931.
46. J. P. Fitzgerald, "Maple Leaf Gardens Formally Opened," *Toronto Telegram*, 13 November 1931.

47. Edwin Allan, "Sporting Gossip," *Toronto Mail and Empire*, 14 November 1931.

48. "That Question of Manners at the Arena Opening," *Toronto Mail and Empire*, 13 November 1931.

49. Tommy Munns, "Scanning the Sport Field," *Toronto Globe*, 27 March 1936.

50. *Maple Leaf Gardens Official Programme*, 23 January 1934 (vs. Montreal Maroons), 2, Hockey Hall of Fame Resource Centre, Toronto.

51. Guttmann, *Sports Spectators*.

52. "Toronto Maple Leaf Ticket Prices," Toronto Maple Leafs corporate files.

53. Field, "Passive Participation."

54. K. Dryden, *The Game: A Reflective and Thought-Provoking Look at Life in Hockey* (Toronto, ON: Macmillan, 1983), 61, 81.

55. Lou Marsh, "With Pick and Shovel," *Toronto Star*, 12 November 1931.

56. S. Razack, "When Place Becomes Race," in S. Razack, ed., *Race, Space, and the Law: Unmapping a White Settler Society* (Toronto, ON: Between the Lines, 2002).

57. J. Lemon, *Toronto since 1918* (Toronto, ON: James Lorimer, 1985), Tables VII–IX, 196–7.

58. C. Smythe with S. Young, *If You Can't Beat 'Em in the Alley* (Toronto, ON: McClelland & Stewart, 1981).

59. The tradition of the 48th Highlanders playing at the Maple Leafs's first home game of each NHL season continues to this day.

60. Lemon, *Toronto since 1918*, 50.

61. Ibid., 53.

62. Interview with Colin D. (pseudonym), 9 November 2005.

63. Interview with Harry N. (pseudonym), 24 July 2005.

64. "Is It True," *Hush*, 26 November 1931.

65. Interview with Colin D. (pseudonym), 9 November 2005; Phyllis M. Griffiths, "The Girl and the Game," *Toronto Telegram*, 13 November 1931.

66. Interview with Claudia M. (pseudonym), 23 May 2005.

67. "Places Blame on Conacher," *Globe and Mail*, 2 March 1937.

68. Lemon, *Toronto since 1918*, 33; see also R. White, *Too Good to Be True: Toronto in the 1920s* (Toronto, ON: Dundurn Press, 1993), 72–5. The *Globe* and *Mail and Empire* merged to become the *Globe and Mail* in 1936.

69. White, *Too Good to Be True*, 177; Lemon, *Toronto since 1918*, 31.

70. F. Hewitt, *Foster Hewitt: His Own Story* (Toronto, ON: Ryerson Press, 1967), 56, The 1941 *Eighth Census of Canada* listed the Canadian population as 11,506,655.

71. "Weekly Whoopee by Rounder," *Hush*, 26 November 1932.

72. Smythe, *If You Can't Beat 'Em in the Alley*, 115–16.

73. Frank Selke to Conn Smythe, 13 January 1944; Frank Selke to Conn Smythe, 14 January 1944, F223-3-1-102: Hockey—Miscellaneous, 1925–1947, Conn Smythe Fonds, Archives of Ontario, Toronto.

74. Don Cowie, "Leafs Trim Hawks in Stormy Battle," *Globe and Mail*, 18 January 1937.

75. C. W. MacQueen, "Leafs' Loose Defensive Play Helps Bruins to 7–4 Victory," *Toronto Mail and Empire*, 11 March 1935; "Weekly Whoopee by Rounder," *Hush*, 31 March 1932.

76. Frank Selke to Conn Smythe, 14 January 1944, F223-3-1-102: Hockey—Miscellaneous, 1925–1947, Conn Smythe Fonds, Archives of Ontario, Toronto.

77. J. P. Fitzgerald, "Hockey Gains Nothing From Rough Appeal," *Toronto Telegram*, 14 December 1933.

78. Ted Reeve, "Sporting Extras," *Toronto Telegram*, 1 March 1937.

79. Wright, "'The Most Prominent Rendezvous of the Feminine Toronto,'" 140. See also S. Porter Benson, "Palace of Consumption and Machine for Selling: The American Department Store, 1880–1940," *Radical History Review* 21 (1979): 207.

80. I'm grateful to Ted Norman for highlighting this nuance for me.

81. J. P. Fitzgerald, "Public Has No Right to Enter Sport Fights," *Toronto Telegram*, 17 December 1931.

82. Edwin Allan, "Sporting Gossip," *Toronto Mail and Empire*, 11 March 1935.

83. Lefebvre, *The Production of Space*, 129.

84. Bobby Hewitson, "Inside the Blue Line," *Toronto Telegram*, 18 January 1937; interview with Ernest N. (pseudonym), 13 July 2005.

85. Interview with Howard T. (pseudonym), 10 August 2006.

86. Bobby Hewitson, "Inside the Blue Line," *Toronto Telegram*, 24 March 1937.

87. Hewitt, *Foster Hewitt*, 43.

88. Interview with Frank N. (pseudonym), 11 July 2005.

89. See, for example, Andy Lytle, "Leafs Obliged to Knock Karakas Out to Get Win," *Toronto Star*, 18 January 1937; Don Cowie, "Rangers Blank Leafs, 3 to 0, in Series Opener," *Globe and Mail*, 24 March 1937.

90. "The Fan's Corner," *Globe and Mail*, 19 January 1937.

27 Try to Control Yourself
The Regulation of Public Drinking in Post-Prohibition Ontario, 1927–44

Dan Malleck

Restructuring Recreation in the Drinking Space

. . .

Studying the history of the public drinking spaces of nineteenth-century North America, be they called taverns, inns, saloons, public houses, or pubs, historians have uncovered a variety of social activities accompanying drinking.[1] Some of these activities were what reformers would consider socially destructive, such as prostitution or gambling, which undermined the integrity of the family. Many other pastimes were parts of the texture of social, political, and economic life, making the drinking space often a community centre: Political gatherings, sports events, social support, job hunting, meals, and shelter might be found in the numerous and varied public drinking places. When he fell ill in 1855 from, apparently, drinking a glass of cold water, labourer John Blackie found a bed in a local tavern in Toronto.[2] Julia Roberts has demonstrated the essential position of the country tavern within the social life of the community, and Peter DeLottinville's excavation of the place of Joe Beef's Tavern in working-class Montreal suggests a similar role for the urban tavern.[3] The drinking space was not only a part of leisure activity; it was a fundamental part of life.

Nevertheless, the activities within the drinking space were increasingly the focus of scrutiny and control. By the end of the nineteenth century, the movement toward "rational recreation" sought to structure leisure time in a way that ensured this time was productive, moral, and shaped by middle-class values. As advocates of what amounts to a radical social change, rational-recreation reformers saw many of the stereotypical activities within the saloon as anathema to social progress. The ubiquitous images of the saloon, presented in bestsellers such as T. S. Arthur's *Ten Nights in a Bar-Room and What I Saw There* as well as in everyday temperance rhetoric, depicted the public drinking place as a cesspool of degradation, not to mention a place where energies, both vital and physical, along with money, were wasted. Rational recreation sought to redirect these energies, encouraging conformity through the guise of self-improvement.[4]

Although rational-recreation rhetoric was generally on the wane by the 1930s, its ideas lingered in the activities of government regulators. Robert Campbell has shown how provincial regulators in British Columbia seriously curtailed what could and could not be done in the

Citation: Dan Malleck, *Try to Control Yourself: The Regulation of Public Drinking in Post-Prohibition Ontario, 1927–44* (Vancouver, BC: UBC Press, 2012): 136–85. Reprinted with permission of the Publisher. © University of British Columbia Press 2012. All rights reserved by the Publisher.

beer parlours of Vancouver, seeing games, dancing, and music as likely to "encourage a *saloon-like* atmosphere."[5] Similarly, the Liquor Control Board of Ontario (LCBO) sought to separate the consumption of alcohol from other forms of leisure pursuit. Notably, it tried to eliminate the association between drinking and the other stars in the constellation of vices. Drinking was to be done in a staid, controlled environment, music was not allowed, most card games were forbidden, spontaneous singalongs were stopped by a visiting inspector, and single women were not supposed to mingle with single men. In effect, public drinking, as a touchstone for other forms of irrational recreation characterized by wasteful energies, was contained and sanitized. . . .

Yet these efforts presented the board with a bit of a quandary: If people wanted to socialize and indulge in various legal pastimes like singing, dancing, and playing games when they drank, being too restrictive would undermine the board's mission to facilitate public drinking so that people would forsake illegal drinking establishments in favour of the licensed beverage room. For this work to succeed, the board needed to strike a balance between a completely sanitized drinking space and the morally degraded and socially disordered stereotypical pre-Prohibition saloon. This was necessary for two main reasons. First, it was intended to keep the drinkers going to licensed establishments rather than to illegal (and therefore uncontrolled) "blind pigs" or "speakeasies." Second, more pragmatically but less often clearly stated, the board recognized the need to permit the hotels to remain solvent. No matter how preferable legal drinking might be, if the local authorized hotel went out of business, the only resort for the socializing citizen drinker was to patronize the illegal establishments. Consequently, the creation and enforcement of rules about what could take place in the drinking space did not just involve the LCBO dictating and the drinkers or establishment owners concurring. Rather, the process entailed a series of multidimensional discussions, debates,

pressures, and evaluations in which ideas of local context and social order were paramount. These elements involved various configurations of binary pairings—proper and improper, legal and illegal, permissible and impermissible—but also more nuanced discourses of control and the exercise and reiteration of biopower. In the efforts to shape the activities within the beverage room, the LCBO and other interested parties re-evaluated the relationship between alcohol consumers and the proper behaviour that made them respectable citizen-drinkers.

. . .

The 1934 Liquor Control Act's (LCA) public-drinking provisions were designed clearly (yet not blatantly) to eradicate specific unsavoury practices relating to pre-Prohibition saloon operations, and they touched directly on more egregious forms of entertainment. Section 79(2) forbade authority holders from permitting "any gambling, drunkenness or any riotous, quarrelsome, violent or disorderly conduct [to occur,] . . . any slot machine or gambling device to be placed, kept or maintained," or "any person of notoriously bad character to remain."[6] The latter provision likely referred subtly to prostitution, although it also permitted inspectors to keep an eye on any "bad elements" who frequented the beverage room. These limited proscriptions empowered the board to enact a variety of rules, often in direct response to activities taking place in various hotels. The regulations would be created by the LCBO's central administration and passed by the governor-in-council, a process that circumvented the need to go back to the provincial Legislative Assembly each time a new rule was made but also one that, according to the LCA, would imbue the regulations with legal force.[7]

Almost immediately, the board created a variety of regulations, which it modified as circumstances and experience necessitated. Consolidated annually in a *Digest of Rules, Orders, Regulations and Legislation* and distributed to hotel proprietors, these regulations outlined in some depth the expectations of proper comportment within hotel beverage and dining rooms. The first post-LCA (1934) version of the *Digest* expanded the list of activities that would not be tolerated in the beverage room. Literally at the top of the list of suspect activities to be prohibited were "music, singing, dancing, disorder, quarrelling, profane or obscene language or misbehaviour." The list that was included in Section 79 of the LCA was expanded to include "any person who is suspected of being on the premises for some improper purpose." All beverage rooms were to be closed by 11 p.m., but dining rooms would be allowed to remain open until midnight.[8] The potential for beverage room customers to move from the beverage room to the dining room at 11 p.m. for a last call was specifically addressed in the rules governing dining rooms, which forbade hotels to sell beer and wine without a suitably large food order, or "guest check" (originally 25 cents, not including the cost of beer), or to reopen their dining rooms from 11 p.m. to midnight "for the sole purpose of selling Beer and Wine with meals."[9] In its first written regulations affecting the activities of people within the public drinking space, then, the LCBO reiterated a discourse of social order that connected disorderly drinking to a broad array, or "constellation," of troublesome activities.

This decision to isolate drinking from other forms of socialization, except dining, was soon found to be inadequate. The imaginary sterile drinking place, in which patrons did nothing more than, to paraphrase Campbell, sit down and drink their beer, did not suit the expectations of drinkers and proprietors.[10] In the first few years of the LCA's operation, the LCBO's inspectors spent considerable time and effort policing the attempts by proprietors to introduce a variety of types of entertainment into their establishments. Singing, music, dancing, cards, and gambling—indeed, virtually all of the activities prohibited in the 1935 *Digest*—were some of the forms of recreation that proprietors, either wittingly or (less likely) unwittingly, permitted in their establishments.

Innovative attempts to inject some entertainment while also encouraging people to stay in the hotel were not viewed kindly by the LCBO. When the inspector learned that the Hotel Howard in Fort Erie let patrons roll dice for "ducks, geese and turkeys as prizes," he put an end to the practice immediately.[11] The Golden Hotel in Tecumseh attempted to draw customers with door prizes and was similarly reprimanded.[12] Some proprietors were persistent. In April 1939 Toronto's Ridley Arms Hotel had a "tea cup reader" in its dining room and was told not to do it again. A week later, they featured a crystal-ball reader in "an Egyptian costume."[13] The proprietor of the Bon Villa Hotel in Niagara Falls tried a variety of entertainment ventures to lure customers. One week, the hotel featured "Madame Vendus [who] purports to foretell the fortunes of patrons." The next week it brought in tap dancers.[14] Even something as seemingly innocent as playing a radio in the beverage room so that the customers could listen to baseball's World Series was refused in the case of the Station Hotel, near Welland.[15] The board looked askance at blatant attempts to encourage people to stay in order to drink.

One of the main types of leisure activities that the board's inspectors or police discovered in beverage rooms was gambling in a variety of forms. Gambling was a persistent target of the rational recreationists, who saw it as an unfortunate accompaniment to drinking. Some research has confirmed that gambling was indeed a common element within the drinking environment.[16] Gambling played many roles in working-class culture, from providing a pleasurable pastime to offering the hope of relief from financial desperation. The board received many stories from police, inspectors, and the general public about gambling activities taking place in beverage rooms. In 1937 the Ontario Provincial Police reported on a proposed hotel in Sandwich, near Windsor, arguing that the place "was no doubt a dive operated not only for the illegal use of liquor but perhaps also for gaming."[17] The same year, the

Belmont Hotel in Port Colborne was suspected of harbouring "a person of no visible means of support and of whom it was said was using the rooms for the purpose of gambling." On further discussion, Arnold Smith learned that the man "conducts poker games." He was asked to vacate his rooms, although three months later he was reportedly still there.[18] In 1934 the inspector in Welland crawled through a window in the basement of the Roma Hotel to find evidence that gambling had taken place.[19] Even "friendly" games of cards were not only forbidden but actually illegal. When the police "paid a visit" to two Ottawa clubs, the Bridge Club and the Association Athletique Montagnard, they found "a friendly game of poker . . . where very little money was involved."[20] Both clubs were charged with being in violation of the Liquor Control Act and had their beer authorities suspended. The suspensions were lifted after the management of the clubs, insisting they had not realized that they were violating any laws, promised not to let it happen again, although in the next few years both clubs committed repeat offences.

. . .

Any mention of gambling would usually receive immediate attention from the board. In any report or letter sent to the board that contained the word "gambling," it would likely be circled or underlined in the central administration's ubiquitous red pencil, and a letter of some sort would be sent out immediately. In letters of complaint, gambling became a sort of trope for more general immoral activity. In an anonymous letter that was later determined to be baseless, the proprietor of Ottawa's Palace Hotel was accused of "running a Game of Quits at the rear of the building the loser paying the drinks."[21] . . .

Most letters with accusations such as those above were found to be untrue, but of importance here is the meaning behind the repetition of this imagery. Anonymous correspondents who wrote to the board complaining of activities in local, licensed establishments were suspected of being either temperance advocates or, more often, local competition, either other hotels or illegal drinking establishments that may have been finding that the legitimate establishments were cutting into their profits. Yet significantly, all appear to have believed that using images of illicit gambling in association with drinking would damage the reputation of the beverage room. And they were right. By creating suspicion of gambling, they drew on the very constellation of vices that informed the dominant cultural metaphors of problem drinking. What they may not have counted on was that the board looked at most anonymous letters, or letters whose author could not be found, as suspicious and unlikely to be credible. So the opponents of authorized beverage rooms, be they temperance advocates or competing "blind pigs," deployed traditional imagery in their drive to discredit legitimate public drinking spaces. They put pressure on legal drinking spaces by exploiting the board's need to create respectable space. Yet this same guiding principle, the need for respectable space, in combination with the board's attempts to enforce its rules judiciously, meant that it investigated with rigour but some skepticism complaints of blatant rule transgression.

Although most gaming activities were censured by the board as clear instances of gambling, this was not to say all gaming was forbidden. Of importance was the connection between gaming and drinking; the two activities needed to be kept separate. When the proprietor of Ottawa's LaSalle Hotel renovated his basement "such as to provide room for patrons to participate in a game called 'sand bag throwing,'" the board permitted the activity, although Smith rejected inspector Alfred Larocque's rather bizarre suggestion that the room be turned into a beverage room so that patrons could drink while playing. Since games were being played, no beer could be served.[22]

Another notable form of gambling, and far less easy to conceal than card games or dice, was the use of mechanical gambling devices, especially slot machines. Just as new technology permitted gambling in the American saloons, so too did this technology appear in Ontario's hotels.[23] According to some authorities, slot machines were invented in the 1890s but became increasingly popular in the 1930s.[24] This popularity has been attributed to the invention of much lighter and quieter machines, but likely the desperation of the Depression drove people to see gambling as a possible route to some financial relief.[25] Slot machines appeared especially popular in Essex County and Niagara, border communities that were susceptible to the influence and expectations of American visitors.[26]

The term "slot machine" was given to any device that required the user to place coins or slugs in a slot, so it could apply to machines such as vending machines and other games that gave no prizes, like early pinball games. Slot machines were licensed in many municipalities across the province, mostly as simple amusements, and were legal so long as they either were games of skill or did not pay off in actual money or prizes. Yet even if the slot machine paid off with nothing more than slugs, the machines were part of a subculture of gambling. Toronto's Police Court often heard stories of patrons or undercover police officers who played the games and could exchange a certain number of slugs for gum, cigarettes, or money. This practice was illegal. In one of many slot machine cases tried by the Toronto Police Court, P. C. Deans, the officer working the slot machine beat, reported how, after winning slugs in a restaurant's slot machine, he asked the waitress to exchange his slugs for cigarettes. She said she was not allowed to do that. But after Deans continued to play for a bit, she looked at him and said, "I guess you're all right" and made the exchange.[27] In many of these trials, the defendants might attempt to argue that the games were not games of chance (which were illegal) but rather games of skill. By 1935 authorities across the province had begun to crack down on slot machines, and critics argued that the devices were a drain on the financial and moral resources of the poor. As Suzanne Morton has explained, in the 1930s slot machines and other games with minimal payoffs were an especially attractive form of recreation and gambling for poor people and were lucrative for the vendor.[28]

. . .

The clever hotel proprietor would tap into social trends to draw in customers, so although . . . innovative social activities could appeal to a broad range of people, the golden egg was laid by dancing and music. With music and dancing, the board confronted an activity whose moral status was not as clearly delineated as was gambling and gaming in a drinking space. Here, we find a considerable amount of debate and negotiation over what sort of entertainment could happen in hotels. Although the pre-Prohibition saloon was a place where music might have been played, the idea of heterosocial dancing did not fit easily into the conceptualization of this mythic space and therefore was not necessarily anathema to orderly drinking behaviour. The issues relating to the combination of drinking and music or dancing were complex. Drinking as a single social activity had to be isolated from other potentially dangerous activities, but music and dancing could fit within a bourgeois conception of a respectable night on the town. Since the LCA did permit beer and wine to be consumed with meals and since many restaurants and other establishments also held "dinner dances," the LCBO had to wrestle with repeated requests for permission to have music in the dining room, with or without dancing. The negotiation of these new connections between music, dancing, and drinking was informed by the need to avoid pre-Prohibition saloon immorality but was driven by modern ideas of leisure and recreation. Indeed, rational recreation itself embraced the value of dancing within a controlled and strictly supervised environment, and the LCBO's "Standard Hotels" supposedly epitomized such a public space. So when developing its rules on dancing and music in public drinking spaces, the LCBO opened the door to a broader place for drinking within the context of a specific form of recreation, one ostensibly controlled and under strict surveillance but not always conducted in an ideal manner.

Although many studies have looked at the dance crazes of the jazz age, often through the lens of the sensationalized speakeasy culture of Prohibition, there has been much less attention to the development of dance hall cultures in Canada during Prohibition. And few have considered . . . the link between dancing and drinking in this time. Dancing was often condemned by rational recreationists as immoral or a precursor to immorality. Many religious groups, such as the Baptists, roundly condemned dancing, but as Catherine Gidney has shown, young Baptists in the 1930s found dance pavilions (like the ones in the Niagara region's Port Dalhousie) to be an ideal location for respectable courtship.[29] . . . This youth culture was a major source of concern for middle-class, middle-aged Canadians, and many worried about the "youth dance craze," which would lead to "debauchery and degrading circumstances."[30]

. . .

Soon after the LCA (1934) became law, the board was faced with increased demands to allow dancing in hotels. If it chose to forbid outright this popular activity, it risked driving people to patronize illegal drinking establishments or to drink illegally in legal dancing establishments. But if rules were not established for the practice, the board would lose control (not an ideal situation for a "Control Board"). So it established parameters. Music and dancing in beverage rooms were strictly forbidden, but they were allowed under certain conditions in dining rooms. Many proprietors attempted to introduce some kind of musical entertainment in the beverage room and were always censured for doing so. Visiting during the day, inspector Wylie found a piano in the ladies and escorts' beverage room of the Trennick Hotel in Niagara Falls. The manager explained that the piano "was placed in this room to provide necessary music to a tap dancing class or school," but Wylie ordered the piano to be removed.[31] The Hotel Grimsby, in the town up the highway from Wylie's home in Jordan, had employed a tap dancer accompanied by "a three piece orchestra discoursing third rate jazz music . . . in the front window of [the] Hotel . . . The obvious reason for the innovation would be to direct all and sundry that there was in the village a real live tavern."[32] He worried that such a display would provide temperance forces with evidence of the terrible impact of the LCA on a small town, and his use of the term *tavern* suggests the distasteful and morally questionable (but socially alluring) connection between music, dancing, and drink. Moreover, his characterization of the band's music as "third rate" suggests that a first-rate band might have been acceptable and that the proprietor's interest was not to draw in patrons of the musical arts but patrons of the zymurgistic. In Waterloo County inspector Norman Ratz reported that the Embassy Hotel in St. Agatha was using the dining room as a ladies and escorts' beverage room. Although this practice could be acceptable, the dining room also had a music box and piano, which would "encourage the odd party to dancing."[33] Unlike Wylie's concerns about the Hotel Grimsby, Ratz explained that he had received little criticism about this hotel's operation, although within the month the board received a number of complaints about drinking and dancing parties at this hotel and wrote to the manager to remind him to behave.[34]

. . . [T]he lack of specific guidelines for hotels was not unnoticed in the central office. . . . [In 1935] Arnold Smith travelled to Essex County to deal with the persistent demands for dancing privileges in area hotels. Essex County's hotel proprietors felt considerable pressure from the many roadhouses across the Detroit River. On 8 July 1935 Smith met with Essex County hotel owners at the elite Norton Palmer Hotel in Windsor to explain the new rules. These rules, an expansion of the rules in the *Digest*, were designed to ensure that the dances would be the privilege only of diners. Each patron would have to have a seat at a table and buy a meal of at least 25 cents. The order would have to be written on a "duplicate, serially numbered food check," which the patron would have to keep as "proof that he is entitled to utilize the privileges of the Dining Room, and to dance." These rules were encapsulated in a form letter that was sent to each proprietor whose hotel was granted the privilege of having dancing in its dining room. The letter concluded with the emphatic reminder that "it is to be distinctly understood that under no circumstances is a patron to be served or allowed to purchase Beer or Wine unless seated at his proper table, and that none other than bona-fide Dining Room patrons be allowed the privilege of dancing on the premises."[35] Just as drinking in beverage rooms was to be strictly controlled, so too would dancing in dining rooms, which, although permissible, would require constant vigilance on the part of the proprietor.

. . .

It does not take a genius to figure out many ways to attempt to circumvent these rules, and the proprietors made innovative attempts to adapt the rules to suit their clientele and build their business. . . .

[One] strategy was to appear to serve meals while simply not doing so. The stipulation that the guest check had to amount to at least 25 cents could be considered a mandate for a form of cover charge, except that the board required food to be served. So in several hotels, food was available, but it was cheap and generally went uneaten. In 1938 the Mather Arms Hotel in Fort Erie asked to have a dance in its dining room "with sandwiches laid out on tables around the dance floor." Inspector Wylie discouraged the dance but learned afterward that it had gone ahead. At least this hotel's management admitted that it would be serving only sandwiches, which the board did not consider a full meal according to the spirit of the regulations. When police visited Ottawa's Victoria Hotel in April 1943, they found "sandwiches, which were not being consumed, spread all over the tables . . . [in the

kitchen] we saw a pile of sandwiches all of one kind made up of bread and pressed ham." Such sandwiches would be available at a restaurant, the inspector argued, for at most 10 cents each.[36]

To the LCBO, the ideal situation was one in which dinner and dancing were the primary attractions, with alcoholic beverages being simply a casual addition to the entertainment. The profit motive was acceptable so long as the proprietor was not attempting to make drinking the focus. After all, the LCA itself was designed to permit drinking as an adjunct to staying in a hotel, where the dining room and beverage room were but two of the conveniences of the visit. Yet it became almost immediately clear that this ideal was rarely achieved. Alcohol was simply too lucrative to be a secondary enterprise. Hotel managers were unapologetic about this fact; they needed to stay afloat, and alcohol helped them to do so. This perspective was fundamental to the LCBO's regulatory strategy. In the Depression, the threat to withdraw a hotel's authority was a threat to the hotelier's livelihood. Yet the lucrative nature of the authority was also important for maintaining order of another kind. Social order was predicated on establishing controlled and somewhat modest public drinking. So although the board asserted that it did not accept the financial need for an authority as justification for granting one, the board simultaneously saw the importance of nurturing, or at least accommodating, hotels in areas where, otherwise, thirsty locals would visit an unregulated liquor dealer or, worse still, bring their own liquor to public events, such as dances.

. . .

Building the Ladies' Beverage Room

The decision to mandate separate men's and women's beverage rooms, thereby establishing a "ladies'" beverage room (officially, it was the "ladies and escorts'" beverage room, but both terms were used interchangeably), presented many headaches for the board and for hotel management. Most of the hotels that received beer authorities on the passing of the LCA (1934) had been hotels for years, if not decades, and it often took considerable architectural innovation and expense to create another beverage room space. A number of hotels began to accommodate the provision for a ladies' beverage room by opening a room upstairs in which women and their escorts could be served beer.[37] Such a reconfiguration had practical and moral problems. First, the room was often small and noisy as well as close to sleeping quarters, presenting the possibility that patrons could move the party into more intimate quarters, opening the danger of prostitution or at least sexual impropriety.[38] Second, the room was not always near a washroom or was near the washrooms that were to be used by bedroom customers.[39] And third, beer had to be carried by waiters from the taproom on the main floor to the ladies' beverage room, which meant having beer carried through public corridors, an arrangement that was unacceptable because the LCBO sought to remove drinking from public view. So although the board's own rules permitted individuals to rent a room and drink there, when proprietors freed up some bedrooms for the use of drinking parties, the implications caused the board considerable concern.[40]

The upstairs ladies' beverage room was one problem; "overflow rooms" were another.[41] Often proprietors sought to augment space in the ladies' beverage room by allowing it to "overflow" into the dining room. Although in some communities (such as rural parts of northwestern Ontario) and specific hotels the ladies' beverage room was barely used, in other places a ladies and escorts' beverage room might become the main location for drinking and thus full to capacity. The board recognized that to forbid such overflow was to place both an unnecessary hardship on the proprietor's business and to open up the possibility that people would choose illegal drinking activities, including heading to a local "blind pig,"

drinking harder liquor in unlicensed parts of the hotel, or even just taking bottles on the road. At least in a beverage room, there was the possibility of surveillance and control.

Indeed, the very public nature of the ladies' beverage room may have been the reason for its success. This room was both a space for women to drink, alone or with male companions, and a controlled, monitored, and most importantly, separate environment. The board criticized proprietors when inspectors found that a ladies' beverage room was accessible only by passing through another room, like the men's beverage room or the dining room, or alternatively, that other rooms were accessible only via the ladies' beverage room, thus creating an opportunity for unescorted men to linger while passing through. Similarly, Arnold Smith told the manager of the Log Cabin Hotel in rural Essex County that "strict supervision must be kept at all times to see that dining-room guests stay with their own parties and that no 'picking up' of girls is permitted by male guests."[42] In Port Arthur's Kimberly Hotel, the doors to the two beverage rooms faced each other, "permitting unobstructed view and allowing for easy contact between patrons."[43] The hotel was reconfigured to meet the approval of the board, with the new layout giving "better supervision and [it] will have [a] service room between the Beverage rooms."[44] This panoptic notion of the hotel layout may have appealed to women as well. By separating the beverage rooms, making them accessible through a common hotel entrance, and keeping an eye on the individual entrances of each room, the board attempted to ensure that the ladies' beverage room in an authorized hotel premises facilitated a safe night out.

We cannot, however, assume that every woman was looking for an orderly, chaperoned evening. To do so would be to embrace rather than scrutinize the paternalistic discourse of the time. Rev. Dr. Little's prediction of "the degrading spectacle of women leading other women home who are more drunken than themselves" suggests that women drinking was a problem, but it also indicates a homosocial dimension of women's drinking.[45] Moreover, some women liked to party as much as some men. During police raids at hotels, usually when searching for after-hours drinking, police usually found men and women drinking together. Additionally, LCBO inspectors would enter hotels after midnight and often find the places lousy with men and women. Inspectors also commented at times on women who were found drunk and incoherent. For example, when Hamilton's inspector Joseph Cheeseman paid a visit to the Belmont Hotel in Port Colborne in 1939, he reported seeing an "elderly lady who was wandering about the street in front of Hotel," and while he was watching her, "she collapsed [sic]. I helped her to her feet again and started her down the street . . . It was pitiful to see her staggering and collapsing [sic]."[46] In the lobby of the Ohio Hotel in Fort Erie, inspector Wylie found "a young woman considerably under the influence." The proprietor insisted the woman had come into the hotel in this condition and had not been served.[47]

While women and their escorts were filling the ladies' beverage rooms, single men were also hoping to get in. Many times inspectors, correspondents, or the police reported on cases of single men trying to mingle with women in the ladies' beverage room.[48] Visiting the Tusco Hotel in Toronto in December 1936, inspectors Pitt, O. M. Rombough, and Reaume observed 22 men and five ladies in one of the four ladies' beverage rooms, which were simply small converted bedrooms.[49] When inspector George Skuce asked the bartender of the Avenue Hotel in Fort William why he was serving unaccompanied men in the ladies' beverage room, the man replied that he did not want any trouble. Skuce reported, "I told him he was getting into it."[50] Inspector M. C. MacDonald despaired of the condition of the Kimberly Hotel in Port Arthur, noting that "the ladies' beverage room is used pretty much as a 'hang out' for dissolute characters. Men frequent this portion of the hotel, without escorting

ladies, almost as freely as they enter the men's beverage room, in spite of the fact that I warned the proprietor's wife to put a stop to this practice."[51] The American Hotel in Sandwich, Essex County, had a "low partition" between the two beverage rooms, which the inspector noted had to be changed because there was "no privacy whatsoever."[52]

. . .

Phony Women and Competing Discourses of Respectability

Uncovering the social respectability of the woman drinker is difficult since we rarely have an opportunity to hear the voices of the drinkers themselves, unfiltered by the self-imposed constraints one might place on oneself when communicating with a regulatory agency such as the LCBO and certainly unsanitized by the bureaucratic rhetoric of inspectors. Yet it is possible to disentangle some ideas about respectability in the contrived representations of drinking spaces. Here, we look to the tool of discourse analysis to uncover some aspects of the ideas behind women's public drinking that may otherwise remain hidden. Let us consider, then, the competing discourses presented in the complaints to the board made by supposedly respectable women.

The first of these discourses is the familiar family-centred rhetoric of the temperance movement, which was transposed into complaints about the activities in certain hotels. The progressive bias toward women as agents of social advancement had its pedigree in the temperance movement and its emphasis on women as the centre of the family and the moral compass for the civilized world. This was the language of the post-Prohibition temperance movement's leadership, who were fighting a rearguard action in a battle that had turned against them. These erstwhile reformers drew their rhetorical weapons from the armoury of the pre-Prohibition movement. Here, the beverage room was just the saloon in a different form and drew in unsuspecting innocent men and women, who were subsequently debased and whose families suffered. In letters to the LCBO, this discourse was persistent. One writer complained that the Rex Hotel in Port Arthur sold "all the liquor wide open . . . my husband hauls wood with a truck and we have six children and as soon as he makes some money he goes to the Rex Hotel and spends it all."[53] The Commercial Hotel in Port Colborne had its detractors, one of whom ("Mrs. A. Jones") wrote, "I was in the Commercial at one time a certain woman came in for her husband and who had not been home for 3 days and he was sitting drinking with our so called known woman that hang out at these hotels."[54] Prostitution, drinking, and family decline went hand in hand in such letters.

Most notable is that . . . many of the letters of this kind were found to be fakes. The one from "Mrs. A. Jones" was determined not to have been written by anyone of this name. It is immaterial whether they were written by temperance agitators or, more likely, by local bootleggers who found that legitimate beverage room sales were cutting into their profits. The point is that this metaphor—the poor harried wife whose husband spends all of his money in the beverage room to the detriment of the innocent wife and children—spanned generations. Indeed, that bootleggers were using such metaphors suggests that the bootleggers thought the story of a family destroyed by liquor would grab the attention of the board more than something less sensational. In such letters, paternalism is implied in the gaze of liquor control authorities.

Yet this fictitious trope of the harried wife and mother competed with another trope: the respectable drinking woman who was troubled by the behaviour of her local hotel. Indeed, "Mrs. A. Jones" was patronizing the hotel when she saw the mythical, pathetic wife of the whoring male drinker. She was not alone. Consider a not-atypical letter written to the LCBO in 1937 regarding the activities in the two licensed hotels in Dunnville. The letter was likely written by a bootlegger or "blind pig" operator and followed the common pattern of positioning the author as a respectable drinker who was not opposed to public drinking but was offended by the activities of specific drinking places. Of note here is that the author signed the name "Mrs. Wilson." Here was an image of the respectable woman drinker, challenging the idea that all drinking women were disrespectful. "Mrs. Wilson" argued that, although she and her husband "enjoy a bottle of beer just as well as anyone," what she saw happening at these hotels was disgraceful: "You will see men walk in the ladies beverage room with no ladies and sit down also girls are served that I know are only 18 and under and people are served even when they are rolling about on the tables surely that is against the law." "She" reiterated that, unlike the members of the Woman's Christian Temperance Union, she was not against the beverage room but insisted that such behaviour was disruptive: "We are entitled to a little [quiet] drink without seeing such conditions as that."[55]

That this letter was likely written by a competitor of the hotels is significant. Instead of representing "herself" as a teetotalling moral guardian of the community, this author chose the image of a woman drinker. If the image of a woman drinker had functioned only as a metaphor for debauchery, the author likely would not have chosen a drinking woman as his fictitious correspondent. The reference to a woman who enjoyed going out for a drink, then, suggests that the woman who drank was not necessarily a problem. Women's drinking was normalized; and the woman drinker could then act as an improving influence on the men. The progressive bias of the pub reformers in Britain, who viewed women's very maternal nature as a positive influence in the drinking space, appears in the LCBO records as well.

So now we see two competing discourses: the classic temperance argument about drink debasing the family and the woman being a victim of this debasement; and the emergence of a respectable woman drinker, such as "Mrs. Wilson" or "Mrs. A. Jones," who observed and reported on problems in the beverage rooms. Both were likely the creation of competitors of the legal drinking space; and both manifested simultaneously conflicting and complementary discourses. When we peel away the differences, what remains is a dominant discourse of respectability. The respectable lady drinker and the respectable lady abstainer both wrote about disrespectable behaviour in the beverage room. The correspondents saw disorder as the feature that would motivate the LCBO to act against a hotel, and often this disorder was also connected to women behaving badly in the beverage room. Yet at the same time, the very existence of the "Mrs. Wilson" and "Mrs. A. Jones" characters meant that it was possible for a woman to drink in a hotel beverage room and still remain both respectable and a capable critic of disrespectful behaviour. To the individuals who wrote these letters, this was a viable and potent image. Since they were writing to the LCBO in an attempt to undermine the board's own legalized drinking space, they would have been careful to write in a way that appealed to the board. So in the perception of the bootlegger, who was channelling dominant values of respectability, a woman could be simultaneously a drinker and a moral guardian of the home.

. . .

One key difference between women in Ontario's hotels and those in Britain's reformed pubs was that the former were forbidden by the board to work in the men's beverage room. Even when the woman owned the hotel, she was not allowed to enter the men's beverage rooms at all. This was exclusively a male environment. The bad impression created by a woman sitting with three men in the men's beverage room, even a "very fine woman," suggests that the association between a male drinking space and women in that space was one of sexual impropriety. Yet the rule was

also tremendously impractical. The board forbade women even to act as cashiers in the beverage room, which would have just involved handling money, not beer. The reason for this decision is unclear but seems to have rested on traditional associations regarding women in men's drinking spaces; it may also have been a result of men's expectation of a homosocial environment in the men's beverage room. . . .

To this paternalistic rhetoric, we should add one more image: the struggling woman hoping to support her family by running a hotel. It was this image that female hotel proprietors and their male supporters often used as grounds for special consideration when applying for an authority or when explaining their deviation from the rules. . . . When an officer of the Ontario Provincial Police found liquor being sold in the Prince of Wales Hotel in St. Agatha, he observed that since "this woman is a widow and is having a hard time to make ends meet . . . I believe a warning should be sufficient for her this time."[56] The paternalistic approach to granting licences to women could become a liability for applicants when they were found to be violating the rules, because paternalism hinged on a power relationship in which the patriarchy looked out for the well-being of the weak, innocent, and disempowered woman.

The paternalistic view of women, in which their proper role as a moral example and positive influence coexisted with the image of women as sexually dangerous, constructed a discourse in which the latter reinforced the need for the former. So despite admitting the pragmatic necessity of allowing women to drink in hotel beverage rooms, the LCBO reiterated a paternalistic, bourgeois discourse that placed the married, middle-class woman (or at least a woman who articulated middle-class respectability) in the role of moral helpmeet and leavening influence on the male beast. This is the sort of role that Mrs. Horton saw as suiting women in a hotel:

Women managers of the smaller hotels become the "mothers" of those who abide with them and are often addressed as such. A tired traveling man is certain of a quick smile of sympathy from this understanding "mother" of the public. She deals with this stream of human souls with a finesse and sympathy that no man understands. Her life is a busy routine, but she finds the happiness of usefulness mingled with the cares. Men in a way have a broader outlook on life and expect greater returns from the business world.[57]

The LCBO based its evaluations of an individual's suitability as a hotel proprietor on such paternalistic assumptions, as did the progressives in Britain who sought to reform the drinking establishments by creating a homier environment in which drinking was not the only, or even the main, attraction in a pub.[58]

In the end, when evaluating the relationship between women, the LCBO, and the hotel drinking environment, only one thing is clear: The real and metaphorical connections between women and public drinking were as complex and diverse as the women who frequented these places. Single women, married women, and respectable and disrespectable women drank in public. Certainly, women in beverage rooms could be immoral prostitutes, or they could be moral, upstanding women keeping an eye on things. But these were not the only two roles they could fill. Accepting the "woman as whore or woman as angel" dyad ignores the very complexity that I am trying to emphasize. Although the discourses represented by these two female stereotypes helped to shape ideas of how women should fit within the authorized hotel, they were challenged not only by the apparent fact that respectable women wanted to drink but also by the fact that drinking in public did not necessarily debase them. So women in beverage rooms might be wives out for a

drink with their husbands, or single women looking for good, clean, if slightly inebriated, fun, or women looking for a male-free environment, or even women looking for a complete, sexually experimental bender.[59] This diversity likely explains why the LCBO would not ban women from beverage rooms. Just as creating entirely unfriendly beverage rooms would have driven drinkers back to bootleggers, removing women would have done the same—because, as we have seen, where women went to drink, men were sure to follow.

 *More online.*

Notes

1. Julia Roberts, *In Mixed Company: Taverns and Public Life in Upper Canada* (Vancouver, BC: UBC Press, 2009); Roy Rosenzweig, *Eight Hours for What We Will: Workers and Leisure in an Industrial City, 1870–1920* (London, UK: Cambridge University Press, 1983); Perry R. Duis, *The Saloon: Public Drinking in Chicago and Boston, 1880–1920* (1983; reprint, Urbana, IL: University of Illinois Press, 1999); Madelon Powers, *Faces along the Bar: Lore and Order in the Workingmen's Saloon, 1870–1920* (Chicago, IL: University of Chicago Press, 1998). . . .

2. See Jacalyn Duffin, "In View of the Body of Job Broom: A Glimpse of the Medical Knowledge and Practice of John Rolph," *Canadian Bulletin of Medical History* 7 (1990): 9–30.

3. Roberts, *In Mixed Company*; Peter DeLottinville, "Joe Beef of Montreal: Working-Class Culture and the Tavern, 1869–89," *Labour/Le Travailleur* 8–9 (1981–82): 9–40.

4. T. S. Arthur, *Ten Nights in a Bar-Room and What I Saw There* (London, UK: Houlston and Stoneman/ W. Tweedie, 1854). For a summary of this work, see http://www.encyclopedia.com/doc/l0123_TenNightsinBrrmndWhtSwThr.html.

5. Robert Campbell, *Sit Down and Drink Your Beer: Regulating Vancouver's Beer Parlors, 1925–54* (Toronto, ON: University of Toronto Press, 2001), 36.

6. "Liquor Control Act," *Revised Statutes of Ontario* (1937), ch. 294, sec. 79(2).

7. Ibid., ch. 294, sec. 11(1).

8. Liquor Control Board of Ontario, *Digest of Rules, Orders, Regulations and Legislation Affecting Standard*

and Other Hotels (January 1935), 14–15, Archives of Ontario (AO), RG 36-5-0-2.2.

9.   Ibid., 8.

10. Campbell, *Sit Down.*

11. Authority Holder's Conduct Report (AHCR), 14 October 1937, AO, RG 36-8 Ohio Hotel (Fort Erie).

12. Hanrahan to Smith, 20 December 1935, AO, RG 36-8 Golden Hotel (Tecumseh).

13. AHCR, 4 May 1939, AO, RG 36-1-0-1339.

14. AHCR, 21 October 1936, and Mair to Mrs. Hattie McNaughton, 29 October 1936, AO, RG 36-8 Bon Villa Hotel (Niagara Falls).

15. AHCR, 1 September 1936, AO, RG 36-8 Station Hotel (Crowland).

16. Duis, *Saloon*, 238-49; Powers, *Faces along the Bar*, 137–62; Suzanne Morton, *At Odds: Gambling and Canadians, 1919-1969* (Toronto, ON: University of Toronto Press, 2003).

17. OPP Report, 28 December 1937, AO, RG 36-1-0-256.

18. Smith to Adams, 4 November 1937, and AHCR, 21 February 1938, AO, RG 36-8 Belmont Hotel (Port Colborne).

19. Inspector's Report, 27 September 1934, AO, RG 36-8 Niagara Hotel (Welland).

20. Inspector's Report, 27 February 1937, AO, RG 36-8 Bridge Club of Ottawa (Ottawa); Larocque to Smith, 11 February 1937, AO, RG 36-8 Association Athletique Montagnard (Ottawa).

21. Anonymous to LCBO, 29 August 1937, AO, RG 36-8 Palace Hotel (Ottawa).

22. AHCR, 15 November 1938, and Smith to Larocque, 17 November 1938, AO, RG 36-8 LaSalle Hotel (Ottawa).

23. Morton, *At Odds*, 50.

24. Ken Durham, "History of Slot Machines," Game Room Antiques, 1996, http://www.gameroomantiques.com/HistorySlot.htm.

25. On gambling and financial desperation, see Powers, *Faces along the Bar*, 143–5; and Morton, *At Odds*, 23–39.

26. Dan Malleck, "An Innovation from Across the Line: The American Drinker and Liquor Regulation in Two Ontario Border Communities, 1927–44," *Journal of Canadian Studies/Revue d'etudes canadiennes* 41, no. 1 (Winter 2007): 161.

27. "No 1. Police Court," *Toronto Star*, 19 October 1936.

28. Morton, *At Odds*, 49–62.

29. Catherine Gidney, "'The Dredger's Daughter': Courtship and Marriage in the Baptist Community of Welland, Ontario, 1934–44," *Labour/Le Travail* 54 (2004): 121–50.

30. Cynthia Comacchio, "Dancing to Perdition: Adolescence and Leisure in Interwar English Canada," *Journal of Canadian Studies* 32 (Fall 1997): 5.

31. AHCR, 26 April 1938, AO, RG 36-8 Metropole Hotel (Niagara Falls).

32. AHCR, 10 November 1937, AO, RG 36-8 Grand Trunk Hotel (Fort Erie); AHCR, 21 December 1935, AO, RG 36-8 Hotel Grimsby (Grimsby).

33. Ratz to Smith, 21 January 1938, AO, RG 36-8 Embassy Hotel (St. Agatha).

34. LCBO to Bruder, 8 February 1938, AO, RG 36-8 Embassy Hotel (St. Agatha).

35. This was printed in a form letter sent to all hotels that were granted permission to have dinner dances. See, for example, the copy of Mair to Williams, 11 July 1935, AO, RG 36-8, St. Clair Hotel (Riverside).

36. Police Report, 10 April 1943, AO, RG 36-8 Victoria Hotel (Ottawa).

37. Inspector's Report, 27 December 1934, AO, RG 36-8 Imperial Hotel (Niagara Falls); AHCR, [c. 2 May 1935], AO, RG 36-8 Empire Hotel (Niagara Falls); George Hanrahan to LCBO, 30 July 1937, AO, RG 36-8 Rex Hotel (Port Arthur).

38. Unsigned Report, May 1935, AO, RG 36-8 Ritz Hotel (Port Colborne).

39. AHCR, 8 October 1934, AO, RG 36-1-0-719.

40. AHCR, 13 June 1936, AO, RG-8 Ritz Hotel (Port Colborne).

41. [A]lthough music and even dancing might be permitted in the dining room, these activities had to stop if the dining room was used as an overflow beverage room.

42. Smith to Brophy, 19 December 1939, AO, RG 36-8-0-288.

43. Hanrahan to LCBO, 30 July 1937, AO, RG 36-8 Kimberly Hotel (Port Arthur); Mrs. Wilson to LCBO, [rec'd 13 January 1937], AO, RG 36-8 Savoy Hotel (Dunnville).

44. AHCR, 26 November 1937, AO, RG 36-8 Kimberly Hotel (Port Arthur).

45. "Temptation for Girls Seen with Wine in Restaurants," *Toronto Star*, 17 April 1934.

46. Cheeseman to Smith, 3 November 1939, AO, RG 36-8 Belmont Hotel (Port Colborne).

47. AHCR, 18 March 1937, AO, RG 36-8 Ohio Hotel (Fort Erie).

48. MacDonald, Memo, [c. 3 July 1940], AO, RG 36-8 Kimberly Hotel (Port Arthur); Smith to G. Dan, 14 August 1939, AO, RG 36-8 Erie Hotel (Windsor); OPP Report, 8 April 1935, AO, RG 36-8 Embassy Hotel (St. Agatha); AHCR, 29 October 1937, AO, RG 36-8-0-1112. . . .

49. Pitt, Rombough, and Reaume to Smith, 7 December 1936, AO, RG 36-8 Tusco hotel (Toronto).

50. AHCR, 29 October 1937, AO, RG 36-1-0-1112.

51. MacDonald, Memo, [c. 3 July 1940], AO, RG 36-8 Kimberly Hotel (Port Arthur).

52. H. E. Edgecombe, Inspector's Report, 4 May 1937, AO, RG 36-8 American Hotel (Sandwich).

53. Mrs. M. D. to Coulthard, 29 December 1932, AO, RG

36-8 Rex Hotel (Port Arthur).

54. Mrs. A. Jones to LCBO, 30 May 1940, AO, RG 36-8 Belmont Hotel (Port Colborne).

55. Mrs. Wilson to LCBO, [rec'd 13 January 1937], AO, RG 36-8 Savoy Hotel (Dunnville).

56. OPP Report, 16 May 1930, AO, RG 36-8 Prince of Wales Hotel (St. Agatha).

57. Horton, "Men or Women," 26, 48.

58. David Gutzke, *Pubs and Progressives: Reinventing the Public House in England, 1896–1960* (DeKalb, IL: Northern Illinois University Press, 2006).

59. The LCBO records are entirely silent on the possibility that women in these spaces were looking to pick up other women, but it is likely to have also been the case. . . .

28 "We're the Girls of the Pansy Parade"
Historicizing Winnipeg's Queer Subcultures, 1930s–1970

Valerie J. Korinek

One time these friends of ours, and this other queen, Bobby Turner, well we used to go every week to this place in St. Boniface to play cards—a straight place. We went by streetcar in our drag and we walked in there and they just about fell over. But they enjoyed it. I don't know how wise they were to us, but they thought it was terrific, and many of the men asked me to dance. We did some silly things.[1] (George Smith, Winnipeg, 1990)

We used to gather under that [steel canopy at the Alexander Dock] and do our little routine of . . . chorus girl kicking of We Are the Girls of the Pansy Parade. They still sing that, don't they? [At this point Bert sang the interviewer the whole lyric:] "Our sucking will please, our fucking will tease. We're the Girls of the Pansy Parade!" [interviewer laughs]. . . . I can remember about 25 gays down there on a warm summer night. Just like up at the Legislative Building.[2] (Bert Sigurdson, Winnipeg, 1990)

The geography of queer Winnipeg made possible by Smith's and Sigurdson's oral histories of cruising and drag during the 1930s offers portraits of a vibrant world, largely outside the purview of heterosexual Winnipeggers, where the camaraderie of queer culture and expert knowledge of the city's sexual geographies marked one as a worldly sophisticate in a relatively staid prairie city.[3] Men discovered this world because they were alert to opportunities and difference— a code word, flamboyant clothes, makeup, or teenagers and young men engaged in "swishy" or "fairy-like" gender-transgressive behaviours. Most queer social spaces in Winnipeg were located in the downtown core.[4] Near the train depot, men patronized certain working-class beer parlours (often housed in downtown hotels), Chinese-run cafés, diners, and restaurants, the steam baths, the docks, public and commercial toilets (tearooms in gay parlance), the extensive river trails and paths along the Red and Assiniboine Rivers, and, famously, "the hill" behind the Legislature. On "the hill" they were provocatively watched over by Winnipeg's Golden Boy, one of Manitoba's most recognizable symbols and the focal point of the Legislature's domed roof.[5] By day the classically designed statue of a winged male god with his torch held aloft symbolized western civilization and enterprise. At night, subversively, Golden Boy served as signpost to a nocturnal world of male same-sex experiences.

Citation: Valerie J. Korinek, "'We're the Girls of the Pansy Parade': Historicizing Winnipeg's Queer Subcultures, 1930s–1970," *Histoire Sociale/Social History* 45, no. 89 (May 2012): 117–55.

While Golden Boy and "the hill" remained a constant from 1930 to 1970, other significant changes occurred over this time. First, the subculture became larger and increasingly visible as more men found queer venues and as the lesbian presence became visible in the 1950s. Secondly, this era would witness a transformation as queer subcultural practices receded into the background and gay and lesbian communities emerged. No longer content merely to participate in a range of queer activities, increasing numbers of Winnipeg residents began to identify themselves, personally and to others, as gay men and lesbians. The adoption and use of those labels, as well as the later establishment of organizations and social venues explicitly for gay and lesbian Winnipeggers, politically transformed social and gender relations. Conversely, as the subculture and later the communities became more visible, the dangers posed by the law, the police, and psychiatrists increased as did the risk of alienation from family, friends, and colleagues. To manage those risks, men and women utilized a variety of strategies—evasion, deception, role-playing, compartmentalization of their so-called public and private lives, and sometimes ultra-respectability—to live lives of their own choosing and design. They were also aided by a live-and-let-live ethos shared by mainstream residents of the city, who, provided certain codes were observed, remained wilfully naive and ignored "queer" moments occurring at the margins of urban life. For owners of small businesses such as cafés, bathhouses, or restaurants, this tacit support or tolerance could be financially lucrative.

This research asks provocative questions about how the nature of place (Winnipeg, a major Canadian prairie city) and space (commercial venues, public parks, and private homes) permitted, constructed, and constrained queer activity. Recapturing and analyzing Winnipeg's queer past complicates and enriches the city's history. It reminds us that the experiences and contributions of queer, gay, lesbian, bisexual, transgendered, and two-spirited people deserve to be featured in prairie histories. Queer peoples' struggles to take lovers and carve out lives and social spaces are important because they offer insights into active resistance, accommodation, tolerance, and acceptance in the prairies. The stereotype of the region as a bleak, persistently homophobic place scarred by violence and police persecution has some basis in fact, but queer women and men were not merely victims in a region noted for valorizing nuclear families, faith, and farming. Larger prairie cities like Winnipeg provided refuge. . . .

A number of the men and women whose histories are enumerated here later chose to identify themselves as lesbians and gay men, taking the now familiar journey "from desire to identity to community to political consciousness."[6] Not all did or could, however. By employing a queer perspective, as opposed to writing a gay history, I resist affixing historical identity labels and attempt "to understand the conceptual categories and ways of knowing actually used by actors in the past."[7] In so doing, this study captures individuals who would not have fit into present-day categories of sexual orientation and affords a more nuanced, accurate portrait of queer life in Winnipeg. It also permits analysis of how and why a cohort of queer participants resisted identification as gay well into the 1960s. Such resistance reminds us that the emergence of visible communities of lesbians and gays was not a linear, uniform progression. Unless the individuals specifically used the word "gay" in their interviews, I have categorized most activity prior to the mid-sixties as either homosexual or queer. By the late sixties, Winnipeggers were beginning to utilize the terms gay and lesbian, and my terminology changes to reflect this shift.

. . . [A]s the provincial capital and the largest city within the region, which encompasses Manitoba and Northwestern Ontario, Winnipeg became a destination for queer migrants. Stereotypes suggest that queer people fled Winnipeg; rather, queer youth growing up in small towns and rural areas often gravitated to the city, where one could fashion a queer life.

It was possible to meet other women and men, to frequent networks of commercial and public spaces where queer socializing or sex might be feasible. Many individuals initially came to the city to study at the University of Manitoba. Others relocated to Winnipeg for work and sometimes, as in the case of dancers with the Royal Winnipeg Ballet, that meant securing employment in a queer-defined workplace. While it was neither a "wide-open town" nor internationally recognized for homosexual opportunities or tourism, as were San Francisco, New York, and London, Winnipeg figured as a site of possibility in provincial and regional knowledge networks.[8] Once individuals found social spaces and a cohort of queer friends, the city took on a different hue. At the same time, they were under no illusions about the limited scope of urban queer activities by comparison with other North American queer tourist destinations. A determined cohort made a decision to stay in Winnipeg, and those who stayed were clear about their attachments to the city and the region. The prairies were home. . . .

Methodological Notes and Challenges

One of the primary reasons why queer westerners have not been extensively featured in prairie histories has its roots in methodological challenges and the difficulties of finding sufficient documentation. Recognizing the political importance of knowing their histories, a small group of concerned individuals initiated the Manitoba Gay and Lesbian Oral History Project in 1990. This far-sighted decision has provided an invaluable primary source without which this research would not be possible. The archive, called Lesbians and Gays in Manitoba: The Development of a Minority, is preserved at the University of Manitoba Special Collections.[9] Supplemented and enriched by existing print and cultural documents, including Jerry Walsh's self-published memoir *Backward Glances at a By-Gone Era*, these texts permit the reconstruction of a cultural history of male same-sex desire, in Walsh's words, before "homosexuals were called gays."[10] Until now, only a handful of graduate students and scholars have had the privilege of utilizing these documents.[11]

As with all oral histories, these interviews need to be approached with care, as they tell us as much about the early same-sex experiences in Winnipeg as they do about the era in which they were collected. There are obvious silences, omissions, and absences.

. . . Initially 200 people volunteered for interviews, and "75 individuals were selected as suitable for actual interviews according to the time frame of their recollections or the singularity of their recollections."[12] Ultimately 22 interviews were completed: 17 men and five women. Ethnically, the vast majority were Euro-Canadians. Only four self-declared First Nations individuals were interviewed. With respect to race and ethnicity, the organizers offered a sample that mirrored (broadly) the contours of Winnipeg's ethnic and racial composition in the post-war era. However, they were keenly aware that the small sample of lesbian interviews would be rightly criticized as unrepresentative. . . . Ultimately, the nature of the original project and its failure to recruit a more representative sampling of narrators shape the histories that can be produced. My research is sensitive to silences and strives to offer complex analytical assessments of the narrators' histories, but there are hurdles that cannot be cleared. Male voices predominate because of the source limitations, not because I intended to exclude women or because lesbians were necessarily rare in Winnipeg.[13] Future work needs to be done to recapture these missing voices.[14]

. . .

The Interwar and War Era: Pansies, Fruits, and Dirt

In the late 1930s, according to Bert Sigurdson and others, Winnipeg had a covert circuit of queer spaces in "Chinese cafés on and near Main St, such as the New Moon on Henry Avenue, and a cruising area that stretched along the west bank of the Red River from Union Station north to the Alexander Dock"[15] (see Figure 1). Bert's experiences allow us a glimpse into the lives of Winnipeg homosexuals. Born in 1922, Bert was raised by his Icelandic-Canadian parents in a house on Olivia Street in the west end of Winnipeg.[16] The youngest of six children, Bert characterized his household as one where "women had the power," both economically and practically, since his mother was the family breadwinner. His father, a former Icelandic newspaper editor, was employed sporadically. Bert attended Principal Sparling elementary school and Daniel McIntrye United College, played sports, and was interested in music and dancing. Bert's first memories of homosexuality and sexual and gender difference dated from 1933, when he met a "precocious homosexual" by the name of Ginger with whom he "experimented" sexually. Ultimately, Ginger decided that he wanted to find "real men" since, as Bert recalled, it was atypical for two "gays" to have sex together in light of the then-common practice that effeminate queer men had sex with masculine or straight-appearing men. Naturally, we cannot ultimately know how many times this "rule" was broken by Bert, Ginger, and others! Such structural practices were similar to contemporary homosexual experiences in New York and London, England.[17] This search for "real men" took Ginger and Bert down to Main Street, where they met Myrtle, Colin, and Walter at the restaurant of the Brunswick Hotel. Another group of queer men, Percy, Jack, and Mitzi (nicknamed the "society belles") hung out on Portage Avenue. Employing women's names, or camp names as they were known, and gender-transgressive behaviour, particularly ultra-femininity, were popular practices for younger men. They featured repeatedly in the interviews collected and were well-known queer signs that denoted homosexuality.[18] In fact, in some of the sources, camp names were the only ones utilized, and

men's actual names were unknown or forgotten. Because they were preteens and teenagers, they were too young to enter beer parlours lawfully. Instead, they hung out in a cluster of Chinese cafés on or near Main Street—the Modern Café, the New Main Café, and the Moon Café—where, as long as they behaved and did not "camp it up too much," the management tolerated their adolescent behaviour. As he grew older, Bert no longer participated in such gender-transgressive activities; while the interviews are largely silent about how age differences or life stage affected sexual and gender roles, it seems clear that age, and likely permanent employment, caused some men to alter their behaviour.

Bert reported that, although his group wore a bit of makeup (mascara and a little Max Factor foundation), their clothes and gaits were what really identified them as homosexuals. Myrtle's mother would create fancy shirts in eye-catching colour combinations with green fronts and salmon backs. To afford such clothes during the Depression, he recalled, they "boosted" (stole) the material from The Bay and Eaton's. While they never wore such attire to school, they routinely sported these outfits on Main Street, often attracting verbal harassment. Bert recalled that later they cruised an area along the riverbank at the foot of Alexander Street and on the docks. Because the practice of cruising can be misunderstood, I employ Mark W. Turner's expansive definition of cruising as "a process of walking, gazing, and engaging another (or others), and it is not necessarily about sexual contact."[19]

Not all of Bert's recollections were so rose-hued. Verbal and violent assault was not unknown in Depression-era Winnipeg, and Bert vividly remembered harassment on the streets. "We used to be so bloody scared of the dirt. And, thinking back, that could be realistic. There were a lot of transients looking for money," Bert recalled. These attacks were also motivated by gender and sexual difference. "'Dirt' was what we called the gay bashers," he said. "They would be looking out to bash you, trying to take your

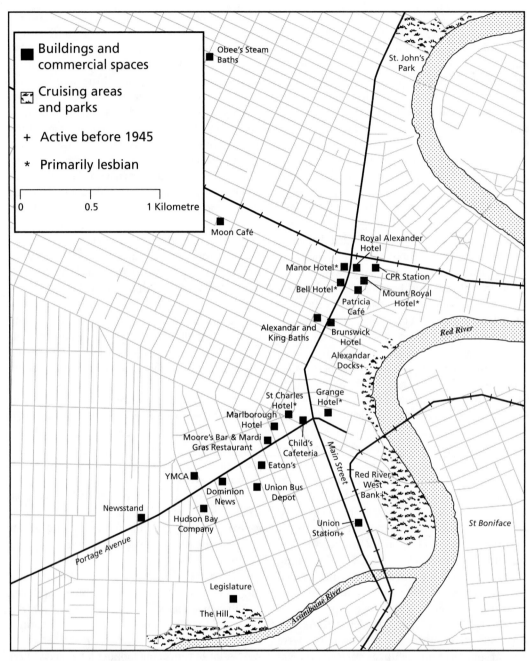

Figure 1. Map of Winnipeg Queer Spaces. Based on a map created by Geoff Cunfer, Historical GIS Laboratory, University of Saskatchewan, 2012.
Note: Information about places used for queer cruising and socializing comes from an undated document entitled "History of the G/L Community" created by the Winnipeg Gay/Lesbian Resource Centre in the University of Manitoba Archives and Special Collections. Please refer to the text for more details.

money. We also called dirt anybody who chased us. When we walked home after our night on the beach . . . they would call out 'tutti fruitti' and we'd have to take off." Drawing parallels with a later era (by employing the term gay bashers), Bert was unequivocal that some identifiable queer youth and men drew negative attention on the streets of Winnipeg. Another category of persecution came from those men Bert called "dirt bitches," whom he described as other homosexuals, though not "noticeably so," who "would pick on other gays and beat the shit out of them, to prove their masculinity." Those beaten were the more effeminate younger males, like Bert, who were derogatorily classified as "wimps, swishy, fairies."[20]

. . .

Bruce M.'s interview effectively bridged the prewar and war years and offers a more ambivalent recollection about this world. Born and raised in Winnipeg, he spent a portion of the summer of 1933 at the farm of a family friend. There, at the age of 12, he was initiated into having queer sex with an individual he referred to as "Old Uncle John." Nearly 60 years later Bruce recollected that he felt "guilty about the experience" and that his friends back in the city ostracized him when he told them what had transpired.[21] Recollections of intergenerational sexual experiences with older family friends, cousins, or siblings were routinely reported in the interviews from this era.[22] However, there were few explicit expressions of anger or victimization in either the transcripts or the recorded interviews. In this case, Bruce's guilt and the reported ostracism by his friends are the only clues to indicate these events were not representative of the average experiences of teenage males in Winnipeg.

By coincidence, while swimming near the Norwood Bridge later that summer, Bruce met "some gay guys" and then "didn't feel like the only one."[23] He left school and signed up for the Canadian Army, but this did not prove to be a positive experience. While stationed in Kingston, Ontario, he was involved in a fight after another soldier called him "queer." After this incident, he was determined to pass as heterosexual and married while overseas. Despite this attempt at conventionality, marriage was not enough to provide him with the respectability he sought. While in the army, he was called a "fairy" and a "pansy" despite his capabilities as a soldier. With anger he recalled that he "may have been passed over for promotion in the army and later at work because he was 'rumored' to be queer."[24]

Most of the male informants who were old enough to have served in World War II did so. Interestingly, though, their recollection of the war's impact on Winnipeg's queer activity was not a focal point of their interviews. The information they chose to share points to much continuity with queer social and sexual practices of the interwar period. War meant being shipped out of Winnipeg, initially east to central Canada for military training, and then usually being deployed overseas into the theatre of war. Interviewees who shared their memories of those years often identified their experiences in Toronto, Montreal, New York City, and London as highlights of their lives. What transpired in Winnipeg receded into the background until the war's conclusion. . . .

Remembering North Main Street in the late Forties and Fifties

After World War II, Jerry Walsh settled in Winnipeg. He immersed himself in queer life in the downtown core and, in the excerpt below, recalled those days evocatively:

> Unlike today, back then Main St. was a safe place to cruise day or night. The street's crowning jewel was the Royal Alexander Hotel at the corner of Higgins and Main. It was elegance at its greatest and attracted many queens who hoped that some of its glitter would rub off on them. . . . East of the hotel was the CP Station. . . . It was a bustling place both day and night as train travel was

at its peak. . . . Across Higgins was and still is the Mount Royal Hotel, which was where the gay girls hung out, but it also had its share of sleazy drag queens. No other males went there unless in the company of the girls. It was a lively and noisy place with frequent bouts of dikes duking it out. . . . It was the first place that I ever saw two guys dancing together; no one seemed to mind, so next time I brought my patent leather pumps. Between Henry and Higgins on the east side was the Moon Café, a lot of young guys hung out there and were ready to welcome you after the pubs closed. Myrtle an older queen appointed herself den mother and kept all the chicks in check. She demanded respect and if you didn't give it to her, you were told to leave and never come back. It wasn't sex she wanted just control. For a quarter you could get a piece of pie, a coke and a ten-cent package of cigarettes, and spend as much time as it took to make contact. The Chinese owners never bugged you.[25]

Bert Sigurdson also remembered that the Chinese owners were very protective of their cafés. "Chinese fellows were not bad about protecting, they didn't want anything to happen, and they'd shoo everybody out," he said. "You felt more trust with the Chinese fellows that ran the restaurant—they never said anything negative."[26] Whether this was because the owners were averse to trouble, which might bring an unwanted police presence, or a calculated business decision to protect their loyal customers is unknown. The preponderance of queer socializing in Chinese-run cafés in Winnipeg demonstrates an important symbiotic relationship that worked for owners and patrons alike.[27]

. . .

While differences of opinion were expressed in the interviews about the degree to which one could be increasingly overt about queer activities as the city shed its economically depressed prewar malaise, the opportunities for queer

socializing increased significantly. Gordon Clark noted that, in the post-war era, Winnipeg bars such as the Marlborough Hotel were wide open, and on any given night you could find a mixed crowd of "army men and screaming queens." Amendments to the liquor laws, not the war, were frequently cited as an important lever of change in Winnipeg. In 1957, the law was revised to include mixed-gender public drinking establishments, ushering in the era of the cocktail lounge.[28]

Interestingly, all of those interviewed from this post-war cohort reported a loosening of social mores, an observation that contradicts the dominant characterization of the late forties and fifties in North America as an era of conformity and family values. In part, this was clearly tied to better economic times in Winnipeg generally, resulting in more restaurants and bars and expanded opportunities for commercial leisure. It also reflected the prewar teenagers' transition into adulthood, with its commensurate economic and social freedoms. All informants noted increased opportunities for queer male sexual activity and socializing after the war, but stressed that particular codes of behaviour were observed. Newcomers were taught the "rules" by those in the know, including where to sit, what bars to frequent, and how to conduct oneself in the baths or on the trails. The paramount rule was never to identify or disclose the men whom one had met in queer cruising areas if one spotted them elsewhere in the city. Unlike their younger selves who had challenged gender norms with transgendered clothes and makeup, in the forties and fifties these interviewees largely followed middle-class conventions: They dressed appropriately to go out for the evening in suits, ties, and often hats; they obeyed the drinking rules of the day (patrons had to sit at tables, drinking their beer, instead of circulating around the room); and they avoided "camping it up" too much in public establishments. Ironically, the strict nature of the liquor laws encouraged much cruising of the men's tearooms.

. . . By comparison with the 1990s, the cruising spots in the forties and fifties were remembered as being relatively safe. Walsh recalled that the cafés and parks were safe during both day and night and bashing was seldom heard of, even on Main Street and "the hill," two spots that would become increasingly more dangerous in the seventies. Walsh was particularly proud of the savvy use queer men made of city parks, which "weren't as manicured as they are today" and provided ample "underbrush, tall grass and clumps of bush" for trysts. "Banana Park" was the campy, queer nickname for St. John's Park. "It was a family park but all the people had to leave by 10 p.m. The park officers would clear the park and then leave. There were no gates in the fences so at 10:30 the park would start filling up again with those looking for brotherly love."[29] This mixed use of a public park, in which park staff were unwittingly complicit, is one example of how multiple communities used the same spaces at varying hours for completely different purposes. The park's landscaping and the nightly clearance of people from the grounds enabled queer residents to pursue their activities without harassment or detection.

Similar outcomes but different strategies governed other mixed usage of steam baths in the city. Walsh's testimony offered detailed recollections of the Alexander and King Bath (the city's oldest), which had a primarily queer clientele.[30] Obees, the other bathhouse, was a north end institution. Located at Mountain and McGregor Streets, Obees first opened in 1914, initially providing access to baths and showers for the local immigrant population. By the early 1940s, its mission had changed from a purely utilitarian and functional space to a social one. In a recent popular history, writer Russ Gourluck suggests that "Obees remained a popular destination for men to socialize and play cards, conduct business, perhaps have a few drinks, and enjoy a relaxing steam bath."[31] By contrast, Walsh remembered how this "family" bathhouse attracted a mixed group of older men as well as a newer crowd of queer men who managed to coexist:

The elderly straight men came mainly for the steam, they spent hours steaming and hitting themselves with the oak leaf switches. They also brought food, beer or wine and made a night of it. The gays at first tried to out stay them, but it was a losing battle, so they didn't flaunt it, but went about doing what they had come for. The old timers went about their thing and didn't seem to notice or care what else went on. There were never any problems, mainly because the owner was an ex boxer and no-one wanted to spar with him. . . .

In the end, the queer men "took a tip from the straights and brought food" and "for three bucks you could buy a mickey of rye to sip on between sessions."[32] Such descriptions show how the traditions and businesses originally intended to serve Winnipeg's immigrant populations were co-opted into homosocial spaces by other men for their own purposes. For the owners of the baths, like the Chinese café owners, such queer activity was financially advantageous as it provided an essential new source of revenue. This exemplifies the live-and-let-live ethos in action. It is doubtful that the older immigrant men were unaware of the presence of so many younger, queer men in their midst, but the accommodation between the two groups (one wilfully pretending not to see while the other group did not "flaunt" their business) worked to everyone's advantage. The infusion of new customers allowed the steam bath to stay open, which provided both straight and queer men a private, male-only space away from the prying eyes of wives and families.

. . .

For middle-class lesbians in Winnipeg, . . . house parties were important social venues.[33] One informant, Ruth B. Sells, who was born in 1927 in northwestern Ontario and moved to Winnipeg at age five, remembered a profound sense of isolation during her youth. A tomboy as a child and later a rather solitary teen, she vividly recalled reading Radclyffe Hall's melodramatic lesbian novel *The Well of Loneliness*. Sells worked as a teacher for five years and subsequently chose to work in a variety of piano and retail music stores in Winnipeg. In those stores she met queer customers and slowly began to build a circle of homosexual male friends. In 1950, a male friend who lived in the same rooming house as Sells introduced her to an older lesbian couple. Sells and 40-year-old Joy Boyd clicked instantly, resulting in Boyd leaving her girlfriend and moving in with Sells. With the exception of one brief hiatus apart, Sells and Boyd were together until Joy's death in 1984 at the age of 74. A frequent traveller to American cities—Minneapolis, San Francisco, and Chicago—Sells remembered that, even though all of them were more vibrant than Winnipeg, Winnipeg was home. Sells and Boyd owned a cottage in the Whiteshell area and, looking back on their lives together, Sells reflected that they had been happy to lead quiet, discreet lives.[34] Sells and her partner were the embodiment of respectable middle-class lesbians and homosexuals.[35] Her personal good fortune did not translate into complacency about the challenges of living as a lesbian during this era. She was forthright about the hardships of compartmentalization and living "a lie to survive." This discrimination motivated her participation in two American homophile organizations, the Daughters of Bilitis and the Mattachine Society.[36]

. . .

While the 1950s witnessed changes in queer socializing and an increase in venues and opportunities, there were also important continuities. Chief among them was cruising "the hill" and the city's tearooms. Informants provided an extensive list of tearooms that included some of Winnipeg's commercial and public landmarks. Naturally, this use of commercial space was never noted in the commemorative books about Winnipeg. For instance, informants recalled popular tearooms on the third floor of Eaton's and the fifth floor of The Bay, as well as the second floor of the Rialto Theatre, the Hargrave Bus Depot and the attached Salisbury House restaurant, and the William Street Library. Such use of public space was not unique to Winnipeg: "many men, gay identified or not, engaged in public sexual encounters in parks, sauna baths, cheap movie houses, locker rooms, public toilets, highway rest stops and other such places in and around major cities."[37] For some men this activity was merely a sexual outlet, but for others "it could and did lead to self-identification as part of a community bonded by queer male desires."[38] Despite the evident bravado expressed in the interviews about these multiple sites, many men also voiced their apprehensions. Jerry declared that he was always afraid of public ridicule, the risk of losing his job, and police harassment or being arrested, particularly at "the hill." Ultimately, he said, "I lived two lives; I did not want my straight friends to spot me with my gay friends at gay spots."[39]

While many gay men stated that they feared public ridicule and the police, the lesbians interviewed from this time indicated that what women feared most was psychiatric intervention. Pat, who was born in 1931 and raised in the north end of Winnipeg, reported that in 1946 she "slept away the summer, afraid that if she told someone she was a homosexual she would be sent to the Mental Hospital in Selkirk."[40] As an adult Pat feared being fired if her work colleagues discovered her lesbianism, so she habitually hid her private life. While Pat's middle-class instincts to remain silent about her lesbianism left her isolated and apprehensive as a teen, as an adult she fared better than working-class or Aboriginal lesbians. One Aboriginal women interviewed ("Kate") disclosed that she had spent considerable time in her teens incarcerated in unnamed institutions (one can infer that these were psychiatric institutions or reform schools) where she discovered her lesbianism.[41] She recalled particularly difficult memories of former girlfriends who had committed suicide and her own suicide attempt, which earned her an admission to the psychiatric hospital. In 1965, at the age of 18, Kate participated in the Selkirk Mental Hospital Aversion Therapy program.[42] Such programs to "cure" deviant sexual expressions were part of a roster of psychiatric treatments meted out to homosexuals in the era before the American Psychiatric Association removed homosexuality from its list of mental illnesses in 1973.[43]

"The Torch of Golden Boy Burns Bright": The Sixties

By the 1960s, Winnipeg's queer culture had entered a transitional phase. Initially the shifts were subtle, as the post-war expansion of mixed social spaces in cocktail lounges continued to benefit women and men who sought commercial establishments for socialization. By the end of the decade, queer and increasingly "gay" culture was no longer invisible to the mainstream of Winnipeg residents. Equally important were the numbers of Winnipeggers now openly referring to themselves as gay or lesbian. The queer subcultural model was beginning to recede into the background (if never entirely disappearing) as an openly gay or lesbian community model began to emerge.

One of those popular cocktail lounges in the sixties was Moore's Bar on Portage Avenue. This "elegant" lounge was located above a main-floor family-style restaurant and coffee shop. Teenagers and those under the legal drinking age of 21 who wanted to cruise the traffic in the lounge sat in the fountain area of the coffee shop where they could observe the stairs.[44] Moore's queer clientele was so critical to the commercial viability of the lounge that, when it closed, the owners held a party for their gay customers. After the demise of Moore's, the Mardi Gras, located next door, began to attract a queer crowd. The Mardi Gras was profiled in journalist Peter Carlyle-Gordge's melodramatic, two-part magazine article in the *Winnipeg World* entitled "The Hill is Favorite Spot."[45] This voyeuristic article provided a glimpse into Winnipeg's homosexual

men and their haunts (the hill, private parties, and the bar). Although Carlyle-Gordge clearly identified himself as married, he eschewed the common approach of speaking primarily with psychiatrists and other "experts" but "decided to talk exclusively with homosexuals themselves and let them explain why they are as they are."[46] Part of his investigation included socializing at "the Madras" (his nickname for the Mardi Gras).

According to Carlyle-Gordge, the Madras was the "main centre to meet and socialize," although reportedly "some homosexuals abhor it because such a large proportion of its clientele is made up of exhibitionistic, 'nelly' pretty boy homosexuals."[47] On the night he visited, Carlyle-Gordge found "forty men sitting around the lounge and perhaps four women" in a room that was "brightly painted with dancing scenes."[48] The patrons were "resplendent in silk shirts, sunglasses, bright bell-bottom trousers and whatever else is the latest fashion. Some look like ordinary sober-suited businessmen and probably are. They are the 'respectable' homosexuals, either there with a friend or to eye the younger talent. . . ." In his article, Carlyle-Gordge utilized the terms gay and homosexual interchangeably, evidence that by now they were in common usage in Winnipeg. "The police know the Madras is gay and make periodic checks, though there is usually no trouble," he wrote.[49] Similar to Moore's, it had a coffee shop at street level, with the lounge upstairs. Young men waited in the coffee shop until the bar closed, when "a drag line forms outside" composed of those from upstairs and downstairs, and "within ten minutes the line has disappeared, everyone having found a suitable partner. Sometimes a whole group will troop off to a party if someone suggests one."[50] The unsuccessful often left for "the hill."

The second part of Carlyle-Gordge's series offered a detailed guide to cruising the hill. Beautifully rendered (if dramatic), it is worth excerpting here because it captures the lived reality of this nightly activity and offers a rare observation of how disparate groups of young and old, working-class and elite queers met and negotiated sex and sociability at this famous local cruising spot:

> The Hill is a strange place. Walking there at night—the whole area around the Legislative Buildings in general and in particular that area that slopes down to the river from Assiniboine Avenue—is an odd, unsettling experience. It is even odder if you are a stranger and don't know why the Hill is so famous. Or is it infamous?
>
> The torch of Golden Boy burns brightly in the night, attracting not moths as some lights do, but another kind of night creature, the homosexual. Single men go there. Lonely men. Men looking for other men. . . . They wait patiently and walk endlessly up and down Assiniboine Avenue, through the grounds of the Legislature, down the slope, down to the river, down to the bridge. That's a very favorite spot. . . . On Fridays business on the Hill begins at about 10:30 p.m. and goes on till 4 a.m. or even later, there being a noticeable increase in business soon after the bars close. . . . A man may go there, walk around for a while ("cruise" is the correct term) and see someone he likes. . . . At a reasonable distance, one will turn around and start walking in the other man's direction, slowly pursuing him at a short distance. After a while, the pursued, if he's interested may walk across to the slope and go down to the riverbank to wait. There the two will meet, talk and arrange whatever they want to arrange. . . .
>
> For every man on foot there are perhaps two or three in cars, cars that cruise round and round, picking up the pedestrians in their headlights. The Hill wouldn't be the Hill without cars. . . . If a headlight blinks and a car slows down to a snail's pace as it passes someone, the driver is very much interested in that someone. . . . This may seem a strange form of "courting," but to

> hundreds it's quite normal and it goes on every night. . . .
>
> As a rule, those driving cars tend to be older, in their 30's or 40's. Youth almost always walks. Occasionally another kind of car creeps around the grounds by the Hill. It contains not a homosexual in search of a mate, but a policeman or two policemen. The police may scare off a few people, temporarily at least, but they don't interfere too much with the homosexuals, their concern being more with hippies and other "undesirables."[51]

It is intriguing that, in assessing the risks to Winnipeg residents, Carlyle-Gordge observed that the city's police force considered hippies and unspecified "undesirables" (we can infer drug users, transients, and the indigent) as posing more of a risk to citizens than homosexuals.[52] The men themselves remained apprehensive of the police and their powers because homosexuality was still illegal, and "the police could pick you up just for being," as Jerry Walsh recalled.[53] After the 1969 Criminal Code amendments, private homosexual acts were no longer criminalized, but "public" sex, whether on "the hill" or in bathhouses, remained a criminal activity. Murray W., a self-declared working-class male and infrequent hill hustler, reported "many straight, married men cruised the Hill" in the evenings.[54] For queer men cruising who were married or living "double" lives, police harassment or criminal charges of gross indecency had the potential to shatter lives. . . .

Press coverage of cruising spots and gay practices made them far more visible than previously, and this development brought an attendant increase in anti-gay violence and police surveillance. Queer men recalled that, whenever possible, they exercised agency in resisting these attacks. Walsh cited the heroic actions of Corina, a man known only by her camp name, who fought back against such attacks: "One night a few of us were at the hill, all of a sudden we heard a great yell, and four guys came a running, being chased by Corina. She chased them all the way across the bridge [Osborne Street], then calmly came back and said 'That will teach those bastards they can't fuck around with us.'"[55] In the 1970s and 1980s, anti-gay violence became so widespread that the activist group Gays For Equality created a public education campaign to warn men about the dangers and strongly encouraged them to refrain from cruising on the hill. For the middle-class activists, this was logical and valuable work, much like anti-smoking campaigns appear logical to nonsmokers. However, reversing decades of queer geographical imprinting that marked the hill as a social and sexual space for a varied group of working- and middle-class youth and adults, some of whom identified as gay and others who were there just for the sex, was virtually impossible.

. . .

The *Winnipeg World* articles, like the oral history collection, provided little commentary about the city's lesbians, citing space limitations as the rationale. Readers were thus left with only the most fleeting of impressions of lesbian existence. Yet Winnipeg lesbians were staking claims to social spaces, though these were differentiated from those of gay men. The Mount Royal remained the venue of choice for working-class lesbians. This Main Street bar was derided for both its clientele and its location on Winnipeg's "skid row." Kate, a regular patron of the Mount Royal, recalled that, despite its reputation as "grubby and sleazy," there was a sense of protectiveness among gays in the bar.[56] Possibly this was due to the fact that police routinely surveilled and arrested patrons of the Mount Royal. During such raids it was not uncommon for gay people to flee out the back door, cross the parking lot, and enter the Patricia Café, another popular working-class lesbian and gay hangout. Kate recalled that the Mount Royal attracted gay factory workers, hairdressers, cooks, and a number of lesbians, some of whom initially attended the Mount Royal with their husbands. First Nations

lesbians were regarded as "rougher and tougher" according to Kate, and she remembered that they socialized most often at the Patricia, the Bell, and the Manor hotels. According to the abbreviated informal community history, "it was only in the 1960's that lesbians first began to appear at some of the taverns and restaurants that had become popular with gay men. The Grange Hotel and the St. Charles Hotel became two of the choicer meeting places at this time. Women also met through less visible friendship networks, softball teams, and acquaintances at work."[57]

Kate's interview corroborates the class divide among Winnipeg homosexuals that mirrored the spatial divides in the city between "north enders" and "downtowners." She reported that the downtown crowd, who patronized Moore's and the Mardi Gras, were more affluent than the Main Street, north end crowd. Not surprisingly, Main Streeters were often mistrustful of the more affluent lesbians and gays. When community or city-wide festivities, balls, or socials occurred, those special events managed to transcend class and geographical boundaries, drawing people from across the city. Race differences were not so easily shed, and few oral informants recalled Aboriginal people at such events. These histories either confirm the marginalization of First Nations people within the queer subcultures or indicate Euro-Canadian ethnocentric views that ignored First Nations participants. These conclusions are very tentative, and additional research needs to be done to analyze more fully First Nations's participation in queer, gay, and lesbian activities in Winnipeg. A more inclusive history that included their experiences would better document demographic changes in both the queer communities and Winnipeg during the 1970s, when large numbers of Aboriginal people moved into the city.[58]

. . .

Conclusion

While the history sketched here may appear linear and progressive, this was not in fact the case. During the interwar and war years, Winnipeg's queer subculture was relatively small and comprised largely of working-class and middle-class men. These men discovered and forged the queer geography of the city's core—the public and commercial cruising sites as well as the cafés, beer parlours, hotels, and transportation infrastructure where men who sought other men congregated. They marvelled at how wonderful it was to see 25 men on the docks or on "the hill" behind the Legislature in the evening. Prior to discovering these spaces, they had believed that their experiences were singular. Finding a cohort of other men was a profound experience that ended their isolation. Yet, if their recollections were accurate, the queer subculture was both vibrant and quite small until after World War II. Mainstream Winnipeggers were largely oblivious to this secretive world. However, Winnipeg's urban design, the importance of railways, and the constant ebb and flow of settlers, workers, transients, and travellers in and through the city meant that well-known modes of queer sociability were recognizable and available.

. . .

Examining Winnipeg's queer subculture from the 1930s to the late 1960s illustrates how western men and women remade commercial and public spaces to suit their needs. Beginning in the 1930s, they creatively fashioned a queer circuit within Winnipeg's downtown. These spaces evolved and expanded considerably throughout the twentieth century, although the clearest acceleration was after World War II. Western Canadian sensibilities governed how people made sense of such activities. The live-and-let-live ethos that enabled a range of businesses to profit from their queer clients while providing urban queers and lesbians with much-needed space and services was not unique to Winnipeg, and others have claimed a similar ethos in American western and midwestern cities. Unique to mid-twentieth-century Winnipeg were the city's economic and ethnic demographics and the regional characteristics that emphasized resilience, endurance, and community-mindedness at the expense, often, of individual gain or a so-called "softer" life available elsewhere. Not only did people purposefully "choose" to stay in Winnipeg over other more congenial cities, they also migrated there from elsewhere in Manitoba and Northwestern Ontario so that they could lead queer lives. Contrary to our impressions that queers fled Winnipeg, it was, for many rural, small town, and northern residents, a regional queer destination city.

Ultimately, the sense of community created within various social networks within the queer subculture during the post-war era led to the emergence of a visible gay and lesbian community by 1970. Not all members of the "pansy parade" joined the gay activist parade four decades later. Geographically, the journey from cruising "the hill" to lobbying for rights in front of the Legislature was a short one. Conceptually, however, to step over that line meant rupturing the tacit tolerance and wilful ignorance of mainstream residents. Politically, conceptually, and practically, the change was profound, both within gay and lesbian circles and outside them. Some residents would, over time, accept Carlyle-Gordge's argument that gays and lesbians in the city required acceptance and equitable treatment. Gay politics came to Winnipeg in the seventies but was not uniformly embraced by all. Other residents completely disagreed with such notions. The history sketched here resists closure and, in contrast to the goals of the oral history project, it avoids a linear narrative of emancipation and emergence. Instead, it offers a unique perspective on a "bygone era" when queer social spaces, camaraderie, and expert, insider knowledge of the city provided queer men and lesbians with remarkable latitude in remaking the city's landmarks, commercial, and social spaces to suit their own purposes.

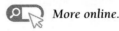 *More online.*

Notes

1. Provincial Archives of Manitoba [hereafter PAM], Manitoba Gay/Lesbian Archives Committee, C1861-1903, 1990, copies of 33 cassette tapes (25 hours)—C1869-70, tapes 9 & 10, George M. Smith interviewed by David Theodore, 25 June 1990. Copies of these interviews and transcripts are available in PAM. Originals are in the possession of the Winnipeg Gay and Lesbian Archives Collection. In 2002, I was granted access to these tapes by the archivists at PAM and by the Rainbow Resource Centre [hereafter RRC], 1-222 Osborne Street, Winnipeg, Manitoba, which held the originals. I am grateful to Donna Huen, then manager at RRC, for providing unrestricted access to these materials. According to the PAM finding aid, the "purpose of the project was to record the experiences of gay men and lesbian women in Manitoba to 1970, and to examine public attitudes about homosexuals and interactions with families and social institutions."

2. RRC, Manitoba Gay/Lesbian Oral History Project, Bert Sigurdson interview with David Theodore, 29 June 1990. My thanks to Scott de Groot who reminded me of the raunchiness of the Sigurdson lyrics!

3. A queer theoretical approach resists the binary of gay/straight and instead seeks to understand a range of gendered and sexual behaviour. See Nan Alamilla Boyd, "Who Is the Subject? Queer Theory Meets Oral History," *Journal of the History of Sexuality* 17, no. 2 (May 2008), and *Wide Open Town: A History of Queer San Francisco to 1965* (Berkeley, CA: University of California Press, 2003); John Howard, *Men Like That: A Southern Queer History* (Chicago, IL: University of Chicago Press, 1999); David Halperin, *One Hundred Years of Homosexuality: And Other Essays on Greek Love* (New York, NY: Routledge, 1989).

4. Although Peter Boag's work covers the pre–World War I era, there are some parallels between Portland and Winnipeg. See Peter Boag, *Same Sex Affairs: Constructing and Controlling Homosexuality in the Pacific Northwest* (Berkeley, CA: University of California Press, 2003).

5. "The Golden Boy, a magnificently gilded 5.25m (17.2-foot) figure, is probably Manitoba's best-known symbol. Embodying the spirit of enterprise and eternal youth, he is poised atop the dome of the building. He faces the north, with its mineral resources, fish, forest, furs, hydroelectric power and seaport, where his province's future lies" (Province of Manitoba Legislature Tour, http://www.gov.mb.ca/legtour/ golden.html).

6. Robert Mills, "History at Large: Queer Is Here? Lesbian, Gay, Bisexual and Transgender Histories and Public Culture," *History Workshop Journal* 62 (2006): 255.

7. Steven Maynard, "'Respect Your Elders, Know Your Past': History and the Queer Theorists," *Radical History Review* 75 (1999): 71.

8. Boyd, *Wide Open Town.*

9. RRC, "Lesbians and Gays in Manitoba: The Development of a Minority. Project Summary" (Manitoba Gay/ Lesbian Archives Committee, 1990).

10. Jerry Walsh, *Backward Glances: A Compilation of His Remembrances of a By-Gone Era in the Gay Community of Winnipeg,* 27 pages, undated. . . .

11. David Churchill, director of the University of Manitoba Institute for the Humanities, has worked to preserve the community histories in Winnipeg. The University of Manitoba Lesbian, Gay, Bisexual, Transgender, and Two-Spirited (LGBTT) Archival and Oral History Initiative has preserved the original 1990 and 1992 interviews and added a contemporary oral history collection. The value of having these interviews in a secure, easily accessible location for scholars is tremendous.

12. RRC, "Lesbians and Gays in Manitoba: The Development of a Minority. Project Summary" (Manitoba Gay/Lesbian Archives Committee, 1990).

13. The 1992 collection of oral interviews with Winnipeg lesbian and gay activists has a much better representation of women's voices. Similarly, in the interviews I conducted in each prairie city, I made a point of collecting equal numbers of women's and men's histories. In virtually all cases, the women were more challenging to locate.

14. In the larger study from which this paper emerges, significant coverage is given to the gay and lesbian organizational phase of Winnipeg (1971–85) and the prevalence of lesbian voices and activism is stressed.

15. *1971 Census of Canada,* Population, Volume I (Ottawa, ON: Statistics Canada, August 1974, 8-4.

16. RRC, Manitoba Gay/Lesbian Oral History Project, Bert Sigurdson interview with David Theodore, 29 June 1990.

17. See George Chauncey Jr., *Gay New York: Gender, Urban Culture and the Making of the Gay Male World, 1890–1940* (New York, NY: Basic Books, 1994), 65–97; Matt Houlbrook, *Queer London: Perils and Pleasures in the Sexual Metropolis, 1918–57* (Chicago, IL: University of Chicago Press, 2005).

18. Chauncey, *Gay New York,* 54–5.

19. Mark Turner, *Backward Glances: Cruising the Queer Streets of New York and London* (London, UK: Reaktion Books, 2003), 60.

20. RRC, Manitoba Gay/Lesbian Oral History Project, Bert Sigurdson interview, 29 June 1990.

21. RRC, Manitoba Gay/Lesbian Oral History Project, Bruce Mitchell interview with David Theodore, Winnipeg, 28 May 1990.

22. My own collection of oral interviews with gay men from Saskatoon, Regina, and Moose Jaw also reported

such activity, offering important contextual information for the Winnipeg interviews. These were clearly not isolated incidents.

23. RRC, Manitoba Gay/Lesbian Oral History Project, Bruce Mitchell interview with David Theodore, Winnipeg, 28 May 1990.

24. Bruce Mitchell's recollections are similar to those reported in Paul Jackson's work, which explores the range of experiences of queer servicemen in the Canadian Forces during World War II. See Paul Jackson, *One of the Boys: Homosexuality in the Military during World War II* (Montreal, QC: McGill-Queen's University Press, 2004).

25. Walsh, *Backward Glances*, 17–18.

26. PAM C 1874, Manitoba Gay/Lesbian Archives Committee, Bert Sigurdson interview with David Theodore, 29 June 1990, Tape 1, Side B.

27. Elise Chenier has also noted the use of Chinese-run restaurants in post-war Toronto in "Rethinking Class in Lesbian Bar Culture: Living 'The Gay Life' in Toronto, 1955–65," *Left History* 9, no. 2 (Spring/Summer 2004): 85–117.

28. See Dale Barbour, "Drinking Together: The Role of Gender in Changing Manitoba's Liquor Laws in the 1950s," in Esyllt W. Jones and Gerald Friesen, eds., *Prairie Metropolis: New Essays on Winnipeg Social History* (Winnipeg, MB: University of Manitoba Press, 2009), 187–99.

29. Ibid., 4–5.

30. Ibid., 8.

31. Russ Gourluck, *The Mosaic Village: An Illustrated History of Winnipeg's North End* (Winnipeg, MB: Great Plains Publications, 2010), 168.

32. Walsh, *Backward Glances*.

33. American historians, most notably Elizabeth Lapovsky Kennedy and Madeline D. Davis in *Boots of Leather, Slippers of Gold: The History of a Lesbian Community* (New York, NY: Rutledge, 1993), have offered considerable evidence of the importance of house parties within lesbian social networks in the city of Buffalo, New York. . . .

34. Cameron Duder, *Awfully Devoted Women: Lesbian Lives in Canada, 1900–50* (Vancouver, BC: UBC Press, 2010).

35. Duder (*Awfully Devoted Women*) focuses specifically on the strategies employed by middle-class women to be "discreet" and thus protect their lesbian relationships. . . .

36. RRC, Manitoba Gay/Lesbian Oral History Project, Ruth B. Sells interview with David Theodore, Winnipeg, 16 August 1990. . . .

37. Ross Higgins, "Baths, Bushes, and Belonging: Public Sex and Gay Community in Pre-Stonewall Montreal," in William L. Leap, ed., *Public Sex/Gay Space* (New York, NY: Columbia University Press, 1999), 9.

38. Ibid.

39. PAM 1990-233 C 1883, Manitoba Gay/Lesbian Archives Committee, Gerry interview, 2/2 [26 July 1990].

40. RRC, Manitoba Gay/Lesbian Oral History Project, "Joe" and "Pat" [both names are pseudonyms; Joe is male, Pat female] interviews with David Theodore, Winnipeg, 25 July 1990.

41. RRC, Manitoba Gay/Lesbian Oral History Project, "KC and Audrey" interviews with David Theodore, Winnipeg, 15 August 1990.

42. RRC, Manitoba Gay/Lesbian Oral History Project, "Kate" [this individual requested anonymity, so "Kate" is a pseudonym] interview with David Theodore, 9 August 1990.

43. Elise Chenier, *Strangers in our Midst: Sexual Deviancy in Postwar Ontario* (Toronto, ON: University of Toronto Press, 2008).

44. PAM C 1868, Manitoba Gay/Lesbian Archives Committee, T. Frost interview with David Theodore, 19 June 1990.

45. Peter Carlyle-Gordge, "The Hill Is a Favorite Spot: Part I," *Winnipeg World*, Summer 1969, 36–41, and "The Hill Is a Favorite Spot: Part II," *Winnipeg World*, Winter 1969/Spring 1970, 36–41. . . .

46. Carlyle-Gordge, "The Hill Is a Favorite Spot: Part I," 37.

47. Ibid., 38.

48. Ibid., 37–8.

49. Ibid., 39.

50. Ibid., 40.

51. Carlyle-Gordge, "The Hill Is a Favorite Spot: Part II," 38.

52. In this respect, Winnipeg police officers were following similar policies and procedures as their counterparts in Toronto. See Marcel Martel, "'They Smell Bad, Have Diseases, and Are Lazy': RCMP Officers Reporting on Hippies in the Late Sixties," *Canadian Historical Review* 90, no. 2 (June 2009): 215–45; Stuart Henderson, *Making the Scene: Yorkville and Hip Toronto in the 1960s* (Toronto, ON: University of Toronto Press, 2011).

53. Walsh, *Backward Glances*, 22.

54. PAM C 1892, Manitoba Gay/Lesbian Archives Committee, Murray W. interview with David Theodore, 22 August 1990, Tape 1, Side B.

55. Walsh, *Backward Glances*, 25.

56. RRC, Manitoba Gay/Lesbian Oral History Project, "Kate" interview with David Theodore, 9 August 1990.

57. "History of the G/L Community," Winnipeg Gay/Lesbian Resource Centre, author unknown, undated, 2.

58. Evelyn Peters, *Native Households in Winnipeg: Strategies of Co-Residence and Financial Support* (Winnipeg, MB: Institute of Urban Studies, University of Winnipeg, 1994), and "'Our City Indians': Negotiating the Meaning of First Nations Urbanization in Canada, 1945–75," *Journal of Historical Geography* 30 (1992): 75–92.

29

"Our New Palace of Donut Pleasure"
The Donut Shop and Consumer Culture, 1961–76

Steve Penfold

In January 1966, Country Style Donuts invited consumers to its "new palace of donut pleasure" in Oakville, Ontario, an affluent suburb 30 miles west of Toronto, by placing a half-page advertisement in the local newspaper. At this time, Country Style was an upstart chain with a handful of outlets in Ontario, and the company was no advertising innovator. In both idea and image, the ad was busy, addressing an astonishingly wide variety of potential donut eaters by delivering a 200-word pastiche of messages both practical and spectacular. At base, the ad simply announced the core features of a 1960s donut shop. It celebrated, for example, the tremendous variety and outstanding quality of the outlet's offerings, bragging loudly of "over 56 varieties" (plus fancies) and repeatedly marshalling adjectives like "mouth-watering" (twice) and "fresh" (eight times). It suggested buying donuts for special occasions (like church socials) and for everyday routines (inviting regular customers to join the "Coffee and Counter Club"). Short customer testimonials (presumably apocryphal) highlighted the many virtues of a Country Style shop declaring "everything is so fresh and clean," "there's lots of parking space," "the best coffee I've ever tasted," and "so many varieties to choose from."

The last one summed the message up: "Oakville needs something like this."[1]

. . .

This chapter examines the early years of the donut shop in Canada, focusing on how it structured the consumer experience by offering a combination of convenience, pleasure, and sociability and tried to ameliorate—only half consciously—many of the cleavages and tensions of post-war consumer culture. . . . Throughout, I argue that the donut shop offered a consumer experience that, while in part new, was at the same time built on continuities with earlier forms of popular culture. As such, it exposed some of the tensions inherent in consumer culture; it also expressed the complex social dynamics that arose as various groups—businesses, but also families, youth, police, and government officials—struggled to make (and make sense of) the post-war geography of consumption.

"Markets Today Have a New Dimension"

When Country Style arrived in Oakville, the donut shop idea was not common in Canada, though neither was it entirely new. Before the 1960s, donut retailing had many levels: small

Citation: Steve Penfold, "'Our New Palace of Donut Pleasure': The Donut Shop and Consumer Culture, 1961–76," in *The Donut: A Canadian History* (Toronto, ON: University of Toronto Press, 2008): 51–97. Reprinted with permission of the publisher.

bakers, variety stores, street vendors, grocery stores, and others. But except for donut outlets like Downyflake Donuts and Faymakers in Toronto and a few others scattered across big-city Canada, few entrepreneurs were drawn to the idea or the name "donut shop." With the advent of shopping malls in the 1950s, a few donut specialty shops began to appear in growing suburban areas. Charles Downyflake Donuts, for example, opened in the Hamilton Shopping Centre in 1956 as an extension of a local coffee shop business, using a DCA machine to grab the attention of mall patrons. The name was eventually changed to Sally's Donuts, and the outlet passed through several owners.[2]

. . .

Tim Hortons and Country Style, Canada's "indigenous" companies, began in 1962 and 1963, and initially borrowed heavily from existing American chains. Jim Charade came to the donut business as salesman and donut plant manager for Vachon, the iconic Quebec snack food company. . . . After meeting hockey star Tim Horton . . . Charade began to think that celebrity might be an effective marketing tool. The two men formed a partnership, renamed the donut shop Tim Horton Donuts, and opened a handful of Tim Horton hamburger restaurants around greater Toronto. The hamburger outlets soon failed, and the donut business expanded slowly, finally opening its first franchise on Ottawa Street in Hamilton in 1964. Tim Hortons' main Canadian competitor, Country Style Donuts, began when its Canadian founder, Alan Lowe, spotted a small American chain that he figured he could franchise for the Canadian market. Over the next decade, a few independent shops joined these early franchisors, although independents seem to have been comparatively rare until the 1970s.[3]

Donut chains aimed to feed (and to feed off) Canada's burgeoning automobile culture. Motor vehicle registrations in Canada more than doubled between 1945 and 1952, and had doubled again by 1964, far outpacing population growth.[4] Car ownership continued to vary widely by region, type of municipality (urban, surburban, or rural), and income, but the automobile's triumph in everyday life was undeniable. What was particularly notable about car ownership after the war was how deeply it penetrated the populace. Rates of ownership relative to population recorded rapid and steady increases: in 1953, no province averaged one car per household; by 1966, only Newfoundland and Quebec did not. Car ownership was especially common in metropolitan southern Ontario, where donut chains initially thrived.[5]

. . .

The car was much more than a convenient way to get to work. In Hamilton, Ontario, for example, traffic planners discovered in 1961 that the "typical" family averaged more than six car trips a day, hinting at a transformation of social patterns that went beyond the daily commute.[6] Most exciting to retailers, of course, was the stretching out of shopping patterns. "Since before the last World War, our market potentials are no longer . . . confined within city and town limits," L. R. Atwater told the Toronto chapter of the American Marketing Association. "Markets today have a new dimension. . . . The new dimension is travel time by automobile." For Atwater, speaking in 1955, the main feature of this new style of commerce was the ability of traditional downtowns to reach out to their fringes, drawing in retail dollars from suburban and exurban areas still underserviced by commercial institutions.[7] But as the 1960s approached, the new dynamics of automobile commerce changed: Consumers continued to stretch out their shopping, but increasingly bypassed traditional commercial areas for newer institutions. The shopping mall grew to rival the downtown retail district, keeping more dollars and more consumers in fringe areas, and haphazard auto-oriented commercial strips mushroomed on the outskirts of existing communities as retailers targeted booming residential populations.[8]

Donut chains positioned themselves at the heart of this burgeoning automobile culture. Dunkin' Donuts chose sites on streets where at least 15,000 cars passed by each day at no more than 40 miles per hour, figuring that anyone going faster would be unlikely to stop.[9] On its arrival in Canada from the United States in 1961, Mister Donut built free-standing outlets along busy suburban arterials or, less often, at the ends of strip malls on high-traffic roads. Aiming for such locations meant sharing space with other types of drive-in commerce. An A&W hamburger stand, a Midas Muffler outlet, two gas stations, and a strip mall flanked the Mister Donut on Eglinton Avenue East in Scarborough.[10] . . . In Scarborough, the outlet at Kennedy Road and Progress (opened 1967) had all the features of a successful donut shop: on a high-traffic strip, just off Highway 401, and at an access point to a large industrial park.[11] . . . Many independent operators chose locations based on their own knowledge of the local community and their intuitive sense of changing geography, or by informally inspecting traffic flows near a potential location. Even into the mid-1970s, Tim Hortons found many of its locations by flying over a community for a bird's-eye view of busy streets.[12]

Besides establishing free-standing outlets on suburban strips, some donut companies opened outlets in new, enclosed shopping malls. Mister Donut's outlet in St. Catharines—the first chain donut shop in the city—found a welcome home in the Pen Centre, a regional mall built on the site of an old peach orchard. In 1971, Tim Hortons located its twenty-fourth outlet in Sherway Gardens, a mammoth regional shopping mall 10 kilometres west of downtown Toronto. These indoor outlets were comparatively rare in Ontario; for the most part the chains targeted commercial strips and small plazas, where they opened free-standing outlets or storefront shops.[13]

. . .

The Geography of Convenience

Car culture, then, had many expressions. Whether a donut shop appeared on a suburban strip in a burgeoning metropolis or on the fringes of a smaller city, automobile convenience remained the key criterion for success. These donut outlets were small, typically between 1,200 and 1,400 square feet, including the production area. Their interior seating was relatively limited—often only 12 stools at the counter and a few tables. Building designs facilitated fast-in, fast-out traffic rather than comfortable surroundings: the take-out area and display cases were directly in front of the door, while the tables and eat-in counter were placed off to the side. But if buildings were small, the parking lots were not, since even a good location was useless without adequate parking. Parking could be a particular problem on traditional strips, no matter how much they had adapted to serve the automobile. John Fitzsimmons, a regular at the first Tim Hortons franchise on Hamilton's Ottawa Street in the 1960s, remembered that the parking lot at the outlet was so small that cars often lined up into the street, especially during shift change at the Dofasco plant.[14]

Losing cars to lineups in the street signalled a broader problem. Donuts were an impulse purchase—marketing studies backed up the common-sense view that most customers were attracted by the location rather than advertising or brand name[15]—so visibility and access from the street were crucial ingredients for a successful outlet. Donut shop design was a classic example of what Chester Liebs called "architecture for speed reading."[16] Pylon signs were designed for maximum efficiency in attracting motoring customers. They were tall and brightly lit and displayed a minimum number of words. Many of them spun, or were surrounded by flashing lights. Finally, the signs were placed out at the roadway rather than close to the shop.[17] Big, bright signs were useless, however, if the outlet itself was obscured. Alongside raw data from traffic counts, then, the Dunkin' Donuts real estate team considered the visibility of the outlet from either direction at a good distance down the road, since customers needed time to see the shop and slow down. In strip plazas, a location near the entrance was an absolute necessity. The Mister Donut at Kipling Plaza in suburban Toronto was sited right next to the parking lot entrance. At nearby Jane and Wilson, the same chain built a free-standing outlet at the edge of a strip plaza parking lot, positioned to capture drivers off Jane Street as well as shoppers as they came and went.[18]

Donut chains were merely one part of a new trend in the geography of convenience. Between the 1920s and the mid-1950s, roadside food service emerged haphazardly in Canada. Individual entrepreneurs dominated the trade, joined after World War II by a few small chains that spanned local markets.[19] Beginning around the mid- to late 1950s, however, existing American chains and new Canadian equivalents began to establish a real presence in Canada, altering the geographic dynamics of roadside commerce. . . . Companies like Red Barn Hamburgers, A&W Root Beer, Country Style Donuts, and Mister Donut reached out beyond a single city almost as soon as they began Canadian operations. American donut chains already had impressive reach in the United States, comprising dozens of outlets by the time they expanded into Canada in 1961, and they quickly formed nationwide aspirations north of the border. "We aim to make Mister Donut a coast to coast franchise chain with units reaching from the Maritimes through Vancouver," Canadian supervisor Joe Lugossy commented in 1965.[20] Smaller Canadian chains quickly reached out across space as well. In 1966, Country Style was only three years old, but it already had outlets in Toronto, London, and Sudbury.[21]

. . .

The Political Economy of Convenience

The geography of convenience . . . did not evolve through some inevitable process—it was *made* through conscious acts and choices. Entrepreneurial and business strategies relating to location, signage, access, and parking helped construct the geography of convenience, and the donut shop's place in it. These decisions, though, were reinforced by the actions and inactions of other groups and institutions.

In their practical daily decisions, for example, consumers helped reinforce the strategies of entrepreneurs. Albert DeBaeremaker was a construction worker in the 1960s, working many sites around Scarborough, Ontario. He remembered the way the Country Style at Progress and Kennedy—just south of Highway 401, right beside a large industrial park—served the car better than existing restaurants. "In Scarborough, where you had a small restaurant, there was generally no parking," he recalled. "[There was] maybe parking for one or two cars, [but at] a donut shop you could generally park 10 or 20 cars no problem. . . . The ones I went to generally had sufficient parking, because they were mainly built as a donut shop. . . . They were the only one in the area there where anyone could go close by and get a coffee."[22] . . .

Choosing convenience reflected a kind of consumer agency, although not the form we have been trained to expect. When cultural studies scholars began to emphasize "agency" as a theme in the 1980s, they argued that speaking to, for, and about consumers would reveal more interesting mass culture scripts, showing the reappropriation of commodities and the ironic play and transgression that shaped meaning in consumer societies. Their agenda was partly successful. While some academics now hope to swing the pendulum back toward the power of cultural producers, even scholars who are critical of cultural studies take pains to avoid dismissing consumer intelligence.[23] An additional problem was that cultural studies scholars tended to find agency in the behaviours they found most interesting, reporting the more transgressive and romantic examples and largely ignoring the mundane and routine ones.

But quite often, taking consumers seriously reveals much more pedestrian concerns:

Consumers might remember their first visit to a donut shop as dramatic, but their ongoing pattern was tied to convenience and routine. In 1969, Al Stortz of Welland, Ontario, owned an auto body shop on Niagara Street with his brothers. When Tim Horton himself came to Welland for the grand opening of outlet number 12 just up the street, Stortz went over, excited more by the great defenceman than by his donuts. "I got his autograph, which I still have to this day," Stortz told me, brandishing a letter from the Tim Hortons corporate headquarters to prove the point. He eventually became a regular—an ongoing pattern of consumption tied less to celebrity than to convenience and familiarity. He built few enduring friendships inside the shop but took salesmen there to talk business and became a familiar figure to the workers there. "I was a regular at that shop back then," Stortz remembered. "I never knew the names of the girls, but they got to the point where they'd say 'Hi Al' and have my coffee waiting when I came in." A surprising number of early customers I spoke to remembered precise details about locations and parking lots but couldn't offer even the first name of another customer or staff member. . . .[24]

But to recognize that consumer choices helped shape the geography of convenience is not the same as saying that consumers produced it. Consumer choices were structured by other forces and institutions. A native of east Toronto, DeBaeremaker moved to Scarborough for cheap housing: as a construction worker, buying a house was a challenge, and he felt he could get the best deal by heading to the fringes. Once there, his consumer preferences became structured by a landscape that he did not make nor entirely choose, and his daily decisions about travelling and stopping were reinforced by public policies that opened roads to drivers and that allowed and even encouraged drive-in commercial development. . . .[25]

. . . Across Canada, provinces and municipalities were spending millions of dollars on both new roads and highways and on widening existing ones, often based on newly minted "traffic plans" that assumed the automobile was the norm. The consulting firm Damas and Smith alone reshaped the geography of several cities and towns in southern Ontario, using the ostensibly objective tools of traffic counts and destination surveys to set the agenda for change. Based on this approach, consultants normally produced impressively detailed maps of drivers' desires, with arrows and travel lines projected over the existing road grid (symbolically relegated to the background), less often asking questions about how to build communities to make other transportation options viable or to privilege, say, aesthetic considerations over the movement of automobiles.[26]

Commercial zoning policies reinforced these trends. . . . Scarborough placed few controls on commercial growth until well after the war; then, when borough zoning regulations became more systematic, they set minimum parking standards, defined rules for proper access, and downplayed calls by some residents for controls on signage and roadside advertising. By the 1970s, many municipal officials and some residents agreed that the borough's commercial policies had helped produce a landscape dominated by fast food, car dealerships, and parking lots. Yet there had been nothing conspiratorial about these decisions. Borough officials had often merely heeded what they believed was a widespread public consensus about the benefits of convenience in car culture. Indeed, when officials began to question this form of development, they discovered that public apathy was often the biggest barrier to change.[27] "The commercial structure of Scarboro is one of the most visually assertive aspects of the Borough," noted one planning study in 1976. "[T]he commercial fabric . . . appears as a sprawling mass of car lots, fast-food eateries, grocery facilities, and department stores. . . . Parking lots, garish colours, plastic facades, shout and cajole at the passers by. It is only within the inner confines of a few residential neighborhoods that one can seemingly escape the tentacles of this 'commercial carnival.'" Planners recognized that their evocative language was not likely to produce dramatic results: "The majority of residents appear to be fairly neutral regarding the appearance of facilities such as . . . car lots, take-outs, and service stations."[28] The tentacles weren't just reaching out. For many of the people in the "inner confines" of those residential neighbourhoods, the "commercial carnival" had its attractions.

"Give Ma a Treat!"

Donut shops arrived along auto-oriented commercial strips at a time of change in the consumption of their two core products, coffee and donuts. Traditionally, Canadians had been a nation of tea drinkers, perhaps because of British cultural influence. Even so, coffee's popularity increased steadily over the first half of the twentieth century . . . finally surpassing that of tea after the war. Per capita consumption of coffee increased by over 40 per cent between 1953 and 1962, while tea drinking actually declined by 25 per cent.[29] By the end of that period, coffee had matched tea as a popular beverage, both in raw numbers and as cultural metaphor. The widespread standardization of between-meal breaks in workplaces, designated by the distinctly American term "coffee break" rather than the more British "tea time," perfectly captured the spirit of this new consumer preference. The distinction was more than semantic. By 1956, three-quarters of Canadian workers enjoyed coffee-break privileges and coffee made up half the beverages they consumed, five times as much as tea.[30] "The coffee break is the greatest single cause for both the relative swing away from coffee in the home and for the increased consumption across the country," one trade magazine reported of this development. "More and more employers, realizing the value of the break period, have included them in the working schedule."[31] . . .

Donut shops appeared, therefore, just as coffee was overtaking tea as the standard hot beverage for many Canadians. Tim Hortons' donut boxes urged customers to "take your next coffee break at Tim Hortons," and even if the Ottawa Street outlet in Hamilton was too far from large factories like Dofasco to attract workers during the day, it became a regular haunt for the merchants and retail workers along the commercial strip. No matter how busy the store got, someone from Canadian Tire managed to make a trip across the street to pick up drinks and donuts for all the workers. . . .

Today, it is only a slight exaggeration to say that donut shops are, in essence, efficient caffeine-delivery systems: donuts, bagels, muffins, and other offerings largely serve as marketing tools to sell coffee. But in the early days, although coffee was the most profitable item, selling donuts was still a core part of the business. Chains like Tim Hortons and Country Style came into a thriving donut market, riding the post-war crest of increasing sales first cultivated by industrial producers like Margaret's.[32] In addition to mere volume, donut shops had the advantages of freshness and variety. Indeed, if coffee signals the localization of vast networks of distribution, the donut . . . shows another powerful tendency in twentieth-century consumption: the multiplication of superficial choice. For the most part, donut wholesalers specialized in large volumes of limited lines—Val's in Edmonton, for example, sold only glazed cake donuts, while Margaret's produced just four varieties. Donut drive-ins, however, offered what seemed to consumers an astonishing array of choice, with toppings, dips, nuts, fillings, jams, powders, and sprinkles added and combined to transform a few basic shells into dozens of varieties.

Indeed, donut drive-ins seemed a perfect metaphor for the two contradictory impulses of consumer culture: They multiplied the variety and choice of goods even while homogenizing taste and fashion. From houses to cars to toasters, post-war mass producers offered a basic commodity with an increasing number of options and colours to give the appearance of maximum choice and varied design.[33] However mundane the particular example, the Country Style sign in front of each store—"Country Style Donuts, 56 Varieties, Superb Coffee"—announced three key pillars of mass consumption: brand name, near limitless variety, and the promise of consistent quality. That underneath 56 icings and glazes lay the same DCA or Jo-Lo mix used at Val's or Margaret's seemed less important to consumers than the almost revolutionary choice of flavours. For Tim Lambert of St. Catharines, who grew up on Homestead Bakery's honey-dipped donuts, the spinning donut case at the Mister Donut at the Pen Centre was a minor consumer spectacle, highlighting the tremendous variety and choice available.[34]

. . .

Many promotional activities aimed to create a carnival atmosphere in the shops. Mister Donut advised its franchisees to mount such public relations stunts as "Donut a Go Go" (complete with an "attractive teenager" to impress the crowds), donut-eating contests to draw children and reward maximum consumption, and tie-ins with holidays, movies, and television shows. To spruce up its core product, the chain developed a heart-shaped donut. None of these suggested much utility in buying donuts.[35] Indeed, eating a donut was a classic consumerist activity, since it involved spending on a product with little intrinsic value.

But the question of consumer behaviour was never so simple. It may have been that desire had triumphed over need, and spending over thrift, but many donut eaters were in no position to throw their money around. For many families, eating out at a restaurant continued to be a special occasion, but since the donut was cheap (at about 10 or 15 cents in the mid-1960s, compared to 40 or more cents for a fast-food meal), a trip to the donut shop could be routine. The daughter of a truck driver and veterinarian's assistant, Jenny Bryce remembered eating out being an extremely

rare and formal occasion—at the nice restaurants "up along Parkdale Avenue" in Hamilton—but donut shops were not so out of reach.[36] In this sense, the petty consumption of the donut shop reflected the practical balancing of income and pleasure within working-class family economies in a consumer age.

Moreover, even treats had a certain utility, allowing customers to exchange small purchases for time. Surviving on volume, donut shops needed to discourage excessive lingering. Counters and stools and hardback chairs subtly encouraged turnover, and by 1970, "No Loitering" signs had formalized the encouragement to eat and go, but the question of time remained complex. In Don Mills, youth worker Jesse Dean discovered servers and customers at the Donut Hole practising a kind of moral economy of lingering: "The regulars had a system worked out," he reported. "One cold drink was good for an hour of seating privilege. Then, the waitress would ask them to leave. Five minutes later, the youths returned and there was a repetition of the game one hour later. One of the most interesting things was the way the waitresses and youths managed to get along, always on a friendly basis, even when the youths had been expelled a number of times the same day."[37] Of course, the power of consumer culture was that it offered both pleasure and utility in spending and buying. Going to a donut shop offered more than products to buy—it offered a social space to experience, one that drew together several broad social developments in post-war North America.

"Neither Very Rich Nor Poor"

. . .

Then as now, consumer culture was a fascinating riddle. Anyone driving past the plazas, supermarkets, and restaurants that lined commercial streets like Scarborough's Eglinton Avenue, Oakville's Lakeshore Road, or Welland's Niagara Boulevard could see that the mass market was a real thing, an economic formation that had been carved into the landscape by countless public and private decisions. Yet at the same time, words like "mass" and "consumer" were little more than rhetorical inventions, part of a convenient shorthand to draw together people with different incomes, tastes, and backgrounds, and thus constantly dissolved into more specific identities like gender, class, age, and ethnicity. . . . Donut shops were not a single social space and never served one homogenous taste.

. . . Despite the middle-market aspirations, the owners, servers, and customers I interviewed often portrayed the donut shop as a working-class institution. "I just thought that we had to open one in Hamilton," recalled Jim Charade of his decision to open the Ottawa Street Tim Hortons. "It's a worker, blue collar kind of worker, and they come out of there at two-three o'clock in the morning and they have no place to go for a cup of coffee." Such descriptions spoke of practical and unspectacular connections based on mundane daily rituals and conveniences rather than social status, cultural image, or grand claims about working-class families joining the post-war middle market. Workers also appreciated the informality of the shops, which, unlike restaurants popping up in plazas, had no pretensions about offering full meals. The first Ideal Donut in Winnipeg drew in a lot of workers from the nearby sugar plant: "They would come in with boots and overalls and the place would clean up easily. . . . They felt comfortable, almost like a small town diner atmosphere . . . they wanted to know all the girls' names and they would joke around with each other." Workers on the road congregated at donut shops: salesmen, hydro workers, cabbies, and truck drivers came up as the core business quite often in interviews and newspaper stories. "The bulk of the business in the early days were truck drivers," recalled Linda Lalonde of her Cornwall Tim Hortons outlet. "I can remember taking calls for them in the early days. I felt like a dispatcher for Williams Transport, because all those guys came in and I'd say, 'Call the shop, somebody's looking for you.'"[38]

In interviews, almost everyone used the term "working class" to mean "working men."[39] "There were a lot of men in there," remembered Sandy Willard of a Tim Hortons outlet in east Hamilton. "When I went in, I was usually with my father or brother." Smoking reinforced the male character of the shops—a characteristic not necessarily appreciated by people who had to spend long hours in the shops. "Ninety-nine percent of the people who came in smoked, no question about it," recalled one Tim Hortons owner. "In the store, the donuts were tasting like smoke . . . it was just awful." Smoking had two effects. First, it made the place dingy and dark, no matter how much daily cleaning was performed. Costas Kiriakopoulos remembered "ashtrays all over the counter" of his family's Country Style outlet at Lawrence and Weston in Toronto. The smoke got so thick that they had to periodically wash down the walls, which had become brown with nicotine. Second, smoking also reinforced the general maleness of the place, at least for some customers. "Men smoked. It was the manly thing to do," Ed Mahaj recalled of the Ottawa Street Tim Hortons in the early 1970s. "You'd go in there if you had some time to kill. You'd order a coffee and light up a cigarette. . . . Everyone would be smoking . . . The one on Ottawa Street was always men."[40]

The sit-down counter was the hub of male culture in the outlets, carrying considerable symbolic weight in memories of donut shop socializing. More than any other feature, the counter made the shop a social space, linking the donut shop with lunch counters and coffee shops even while distinguishing it from other drive-in restaurants. At Red Barn and McDonald's, customers were handed their food by an efficient male worker behind a cash register; at the donut shop, you could get service at the counter. "It was a coffee shop, not a restaurant," remembered Lori Broadfoot, a server at Winnipeg's Ideal Donut in the early 1970s. "You would serve a person and then you could stand and talk to them." Even the shortest conversations across the counter, or seemingly trivial events like a server remembering a daily order, enhanced the donut shop's role as a social space. When repeated as part of a daily routine of working, commuting, or travelling, such cross-counter rituals allowed consumers to graduate from the status of customer to that of regular. . . .

The employment policies of donut shops cemented the male character of the sit-down counter. Fast-food companies like Red Barn and McDonald's deliberately avoided hiring female cashiers, fearing they would attract unruly teenage boys. Servers at donut shops, on the other hand, were exclusively female in the early days. Brief, informal conversations across the counter occasionally passed into longer flirtations. Jenny Bryce made it clear that there were many attractions to being a high school student working the counter at Tim Hortons #7 on Queenston Road in Hamilton. She remembered young men "who came crawling out of those holes after Friday night's adventures. Actually, I went out with a

couple of them that I'd met there—a couple of them at the same time . . . I didn't know they knew each other." One day, she needed a ride home from work, so she asked "one of those guys in the leather jackets. He used to just ride for pleasure and drink Coca-Cola and eat ice cream cones—he wasn't your real hood . . . I guess I vaguely knew who he was, but I knew [my friend] didn't think much of him. So I got a ride home from him one afternoon and the next thing you know, four months later [we got] engaged and a year later married. That was twenty-six years ago."[41] No doubt for many servers, flirting across the counter was an annoying (and perhaps, at times, disturbing) part of the job, but Bryce obviously thrived on it.[42]

Flirting between servers and customers was a stereotype of the earlier lunch counters. Though donut shops were a novelty in the 1960s, many of their key features were familiar to customers. Continuities between lunch counters, diners, and donut shops were mentioned in

Figure 1. Interior of Tim Horton Donuts, Kitchener, February 1969. With counters, stools, and simple menu boards, early donut shops borrowed designs from lunch counters and coffee shops. *Kitchener-Waterloo Record* Photographic Negative Collection, University of Waterloo Library.

interviews almost as often as references to novelty. Sometimes, the connection was direct. Tom Busnarda, who grew up on Ottawa Street in Hamilton, described the way the first Tim Hortons picked up on but also reformulated the social function of existing neighbourhood restaurants:

Around the corner and up a couple of blocks was a restaurant called the Bright Spot. The Bright Spot was a twenty-four-hour restaurant that predates Tim Hortons. It was a hangout for all this element . . . that was . . . associated with the east end . . . of Hamilton, which of course is working-class poor. And slowly, Tim Hortons started to take that element from the Bright Spot and you could see a movement to Tim Hortons. . . . The Bright Spot was probably a better place to be, because there was a full menu, but Tim Hortons was more accommodating in some ways of having people sit and not do much of a purchase, and having some place to go.[43]

. . .

A sense of place reinforced these associations. The staples of early donut shop design—small, utilitarian interiors with stainless steel and arborite fixtures, menu boards over the cash register, a straight or U-shaped counter with stools, and a few small tables in the corner—were also the mainstays of the coffee shops and lunch counters that had been common in urban neighbourhoods and fringe areas since before the war. There were quite practical reasons for adopting these layouts. Restaurateurs had known for years that stools encouraged a quick turnover of customers—as much as four times the rate of tables.[44] Moreover, it was economical for equipment companies to build to standard designs, and their prices and advice structured the decision making of both chain and independent restaurant owners. Indeed, designing a low-priced, fast-service restaurant in this period was as much a mass phenomenon as making donuts: Companies like Ontario Store Fixtures manufactured the same basic stools, counters, and fittings in varied colours, types, and sizes.[45] Most lunch counters, diners, and donut shops, then, developed a distinctive look not through dramatic innovations in layout or design, but by choosing blue instead of green, vinyl instead of plastic, straight instead of rounded counters, or booths instead of tables and chairs. But from these practical and economic decisions grew a sense of cultural familiarity and social similarity, one that connected donut shops with lunch counters and diners in a seamless architecture of informal eating out.

Yet from a consumer's perspective, features like menu boards and sit-down counters were more than simple design decisions; they were also cultural cues, as much a part of the donut shop's commercial speech as advertisements and promotions. Indeed, in many ways the appearance of an outlet was *the* key element of its commercial speech, since few donut chains advertised heavily in the early days. Ron Joyce, for example, was quite explicit about viewing the outlet itself as the primary promotional vehicle for Tim Hortons.[46] From this perspective, the design and atmosphere of donut shops expressed the complex cultural dynamics of the post-war mass market. . . .

By the 1960s . . . two trajectories of mass marketing made for a confusing and complex mix of donut shop patrons. On the one hand, the shops often acquired a reputation as male, working-class institutions; on the other, by adding tables to the lunch counter design, enforcing standards of cleanliness, serving the roadside market, pitching their advertising at baby boom families, and seeking out locations in shopping plazas and middle-income neighbourhoods, they aimed for a broader clientele. The surviving evidence suggests that overall, the early market was only slightly tilted toward men and that the social use of the shop could depend on time and location.[47] Donut shop owners and workers often spoke of a basic rhythm to the day: truck drivers in early morning, salesmen later, housewives doing shopping in the afternoon, youth in the evening, bar patrons after midnight, cabbies after that. These memories may be too neat, but they do speak to the way that time could alter the basic character of the shop. Space mattered as well: Despite being organized on a chain basis, one donut shop was not necessarily like another. One Mister Donut marketing study found that men comprised almost 70 per cent of customers at a typical free-standing outlet on a busy commercial strip, while a shopping centre location had the highest proportion of female customers. Location also affected the class character of the shops. Chris Pappas owned a number of Country Style Donut shops around Toronto in the 1960s and 1970s, and found that no matter how much they targeted the transient, car-driving market with big parking lots and easy access, the social composition of the neighbourhood affected the customer base. "It depended on the area where you were, of course," he explained. "If you are in a blue-collar area, then you get that type of people. . . . But over here at Dundas and Islington, we had a better clientele. . . . So it depends where you were." This point reinforces the importance of local residents to the shop's profitability.[48]

What Pappas described was less a grand blending of different social groups into a broad middle class than the strategy of selling to what might be called a "middle market in aggregate": Different locations might attract different sorts of customers; cabbies and truckers might sit at the counter while families stuck to the tables; the morning might be given over to salesmen and the afternoon to female shoppers. Across the chain and through the day, customers spanned the middle market. How else to make sense of Country Style locations beside an industrial park in Scarborough and in the heart of Canada's most affluent community in Oakville? Two different places, same commercial institution. . . . For donut entrepreneurs, however, changing residential dynamics were less important than convincing everyone in the area to drive in and

buy donuts. . . . But in the 1960s, class rarely arose as the key marketing problem. Their biggest challenges lay elsewhere.

"They Were Selling Drugs out of the Washrooms"

In early July 1970, during a confrontation in front of the Country Style on Lakeshore Road in Oakville, 19-year-old Peter Simpson was arrested by Constable Roy Bonham and charged with obstructing a police officer. The next day, no doubt to his horror, Simpson found his late-night confrontation on page one of both local newspapers, on the Metro page of the *Toronto Star*, and even on the TV news. All the commotion wasn't really about Simpson, however. It was the place, not the person, that attracted the attention. Judging by media reports around the time of Simpson's arrest, the Country Style at Brock Street and Lakeshore Road was a veritable snack food Sodom and Gomorrah. "Violence, Sex on Oakville Street," screamed an *Oakville Beaver* headline on 2 July. "A 'circus' that includes amusements like stomping heads until bloody, sexual intercourse on lawns, and urinating on sidewalks came up before council last night," the *Daily Journal Record* reported of the goings on around the Country Style outlet.[49] Clearly, the shop had become the site of one slice of nighttime youth culture, but there was more going on than bad behaviour. As the events around the outlet took on the trappings of a moral panic and spun into a broader discussion about civility and rights, matters soon became explicitly political. At their root, however, the problems were commercial, growing from the inherent tensions of the early donut shop form.

Donut shops attracted young people like magnets. "The Donut Hole . . . has become an informal drop-in for a cross-section of youths between the ages of 15 and 21," reported Don Mills youth worker Jesse Dean in 1971, noting that the shops filled a gap in local recreational space. Oakville youth largely agreed, complaining of restricted movies, conservative parents, and few other leisure options than donut shops and fast-food outlets. If the typical outlet became a sort of commercialized drop-in centre, the parking lot became a kind of park. The horseplay at the Lakeshore Road Country Style was matched at the Tim Hortons across town. "A group of eight boys were tossing a Frisbee around the parking lot of Tim Horton's donut shop until the cops came to break it up," the *Journal Record* commented. "What Oakville needs is some kids' space. . . . Just unstructured, open space to gather."[50] Informal styles of leisure and complaints about alternative options had been staples of youth culture for much of the post-war period.[51] As they proliferated through the late 1960s, donut shops also served as sites of the emerging underground economy. "We did have a problem with teenagers," Anita Halaiko, who owned a Mister Donut with her husband in St. Catharines, recalled. "There was a drug problem there. They were selling drugs out of the washrooms, and they were very disruptive." Drug culture in donut shops seemed to vary: during his summer in Don Mills in 1970, Jesse Dean found many stoned teenagers—"speeders" especially—in the Donut Hole, but relatively little actual drug selling (in contrast, "deals were made openly" at Edward Gardens park up the street).[52]

Youthful behaviours like horseplay, rowdiness, and drug selling were products of the age, but they were triply encouraged by the donut shop form. As informal institutions of petty consumption entailing all-night hours, small purchases, a minimum of supervision, and an informal setting, donut shops naturally attracted young people looking to socialize. In building outlets that emphasized automobile convenience, moreover, donut chains built large parking lots that became spaces in their own right, facilitating all kinds of alternative activities. Finally, because of their locational strategies, donut shop neighbourhoods were teeming with teens. By 1970 the baby boom had subsided, but the peak of its demographic bulge was aging into and out

of their teenage spending years. Young people were a lucrative market of their own, with abundant leisure time and—at least in the minds of marketers—considerable amounts of discretionary income, which they were more than willing to spend on fast food, especially if it bought them a period of socializing with friends. At the chain level, Mister Donut recognized the value of pitching advertising to the "youth component" because donut eating was inversely related to age. At the outlet level, owners knew they needed youth spending. Chris Pappas, who took over the Oakville outlet amid the troubles, knew that most local youth had cash in their pockets and were heavy spenders at the outlet.[53]

In a broad sense, these demographic, social, and economic forces brought Simpson to the front of the Country Style that evening in early July, but his confrontation with Constable Bonham flowed from the difficulties of regulating the geography of youth culture, a complex tangle of public and private jurisdictions. A donut shop parking lot was an open and accessible public space in appearance, but in law it was private property with a fairly simple regulatory regime: Misbehaving youth could simply be banned from the lot by the owner. . . .

. . . Back in Oakville, Tim Horton dealt with news of the goings on around the Country Style by making a special trip to his nearby outlet to set a firm rule: "no hippies". . . . On 7 July 1970 . . . the Oakville council passed the only bylaw in history known to be aimed specifically at a donut shop, although naturally the language was much broader. "No person," the bylaw declared, "shall by himself or with another or others, loiter on any sidewalk . . . so as to occupy more than one-half of the width thereof . . . [or] so as to interfere with any person's access to or from any private premises." The bylaw further empowered the police, after delivering suitable warnings, to arrest "any person apparently loitering" in contravention of the regulation, making that person liable for a fine of up to $300.[54] That evening, Simpson was arrested when he joined 35 youths hanging out on the sidewalk in front of the shop.[55]

Though not so surprising in a town that one academic called the "last outpost of WASP society" and a "place where observable reactions are almost sure to be at the maximum possible," the bylaw could easily be read as an extension of broader adult attacks on youth leisure, running from legal regulation through "no hippie" policies to informal harassment by police. As such, it expressed the links between generational discord, consumer culture, and the most powerful political discourses of the day. Indeed, once Brock Street residents arrived at council, the debate quickly moved to first principles, playing on notions of freedom, rights, and order. Specific complaints from small to large—from squealing tires, horn honking, and shouting to swearing, sex, violence, and "immodesty"—ran together. . . . Angry adults lamented the breakdown of authority and decorum. Councillor Michael Boyle blamed "permissiveness" for Country Style's problems. . . . Youth responded to such attacks on their leisure habits with their own dramatic rhetoric. One youth reporter condemned Tim Horton's "no hippies" policy by appropriating the language of civil rights: "In the early 60's," he reminded the great defenceman, "many restaurants in the southern states had similar policies dealing with black people."[56]

. . .

Two weeks into the troubles at the Oakville Country Style, Pappas took over the outlet at the behest of the chain's head office and proceeded to assure local residents that he would not tolerate rowdy behaviour. . . . For donut shop owners, questions of civility were refracted through their own economic interests. Everyone wanted youth to behave, since rowdiness caused trouble for neighbours and drove good customers away, but notwithstanding the occasional "no hippie" policy, few owners were willing to ban them outright. Young people had money, and donut shops were almost perfectly suited to the patterns of youthful pleasure. In this sense, Peter Simpson

stood at the margin between attempts to exploit the consumer power of youth and efforts to control and reform their behaviour. . . . In the end, these tensions were almost inevitable, built into the donut shop form, its market, its atmosphere, and its parking lots.

"Oakville Needs Something Like This"

Four years before Oakville's infamous bylaw, Country Style Donuts built its new "palace of donut pleasure" at Brock Street and Lakeshore Road with asphalt, mortar, bricks, and arborite, but the *place* it assembled was constructed from the building blocks of post-war consumer culture. Donut shops were one attempt to capitalize on the growing middle market of consumers. This market was not just the dream of the sophisticated retail expert: less erudite entrepreneurs understood that tapping car culture meant reaching consumers with money to spend, and their decisions about locations carved the dream of reaching the middle-market consumer into Canada's commercial landscape. Yet in offering customers a counter, some tables, and large parking lots, donut shops became social spaces, assembled out of broad changes in space and time, architectural informality, cheap products, and the cultural categories of customers, who fit these new places into their daily routines and into their mental maps of informal eating out. In doing so, entrepreneurs and consumers created places that attracted many working men, but that also served a broader market of families—women, children, and teens, who found their own uses for these mass commercial institutions.

. . .

 More online.

Notes

1. *Oakville Daily Journal Record* (ODJR), 15 January 1966, 5.
2. Mike Filey, *I Remember Sunnyside: The Rise and Fall of a Magical Era* (Toronto, ON: Dundurn Press, 1996); Lynn

Korbyn, co-owner, Sally's Donuts, early 1960s, interviewed by author, Hamilton, Ontario, 21 February 2002.

3. On Charade and Horton, see Douglas Hunter, *Open Ice: The Tim Horton Story* (Toronto, ON: Viking Press, 1994), 306–48. Information on Country Style's origins is from Kevin Watson, interviewed by author, 22 October 1999. (Watson is the son of one of the early directors of the company, and worked in various positions in the Country Style headquarters until the late 1990s.)

4. F. H. Leacy, *Historical Statistics of Canada*, 2nd ed. (Ottawa, ON: Statistics Canada, 1983), series T147-194.

5. In 1953, Ontario had the highest penetration of automobiles, averaging 0.9 cars per family. In 1971, British Columbia led the provinces with 1.6 cars per family (at the time, the Ontario figure was 1.44). . . .

6. *Hamilton Spectator* (*HS*), 19 August 1961, in "Streets in Hamilton" Scrapbook, vol. 4, 1960–9, 69, Special Collections, Hamilton Public Library.

7. Atwater quotation from *Financial Post* (*FP*), 5 November 1955, 30. Despite their status as emblematic of postwar commercial development, shopping malls were still few in number into the mid- to late 1950s. . . .

8. For an example of the evolution of auto-oriented strips, which often grew haphazardly to serve growing local populations that lacked sufficient commercial choices, see Adams Farrow Associates, *Yonge Street, Town of Richmond Hill, a Report* (Richmond Hill Planning Board, 1959), available in the Urban Affairs Branch, Toronto Public Library. . . .

9. Robert Rosenberg with Madelon Bedell, *Profits from Franchising* (New York, NY: McGraw Hill, 1969), 149.

10. *Might's Toronto Directory* (Toronto, ON: Might's Directories Limited), 1963.

11. *Vernon's London City Directory* (Hamilton, ON: Vernon Directories), 1965. Gerald Bloomfield, "Lodging at the Interchange in London, Ontario," *Canadian Geographer* 40, no. 2 (1996): 173–80 discusses the development of Wellington Street.

12. Allan Asmussen, co-founder of Donut Queen (Kitchener–Waterloo), 1968, interviewed by author, Waterloo, 10 September 2001; Calvin LeDrew, owner, Donut Queen, Sydney, Nova Scotia, 1964–70, telephone interview by author, 8 August 2001; *HS*, 17 April 1977; Ron Joyce with Robert Thompson, *Always Fresh: The Untold Story of Tim Hortons by the Man Who Created a Canadian Empire* (Toronto, ON: HarperCollins, 2006), 149.

13. On the Pen Centre, see John Jackson, *St. Catharines: Canada's Canal City* (St. Catharines, ON: St. Catharines Standard Ltd., 1992), 54.

14. John Fitzsimmons, interviewed by author, Hamilton, 25 January 1998.

15. Mister Donut, *Highlights from a Market Analysis of Mister Donut Stores* (Fall 1966), 2, from private collection.

16. Chester Liebs, *Main Street to Miracle Mile: American Roadside Architecture* (Boston, MA: Little Brown, 1985), 39.

17. In the early days, Tim Hortons' signs spun around.

18. No specific measurements were provided for Dunkin' Donuts' visibility. Rosenberg, *Profits from Franchising*, 137. . . . The Kipling Plaza outlet and the Jane and Wilson outlet both still exist, as do the plazas, although the former is now a Dunkin' Donuts and the latter is a Vietnamese restaurant. That an old Mister Donut would be transformed into an ethnic restaurant is symbolic of the social changes in Toronto's suburbs.

19. Hi-Ho Drive-Ins around Windsor and White Spot Restaurants in Vancouver would be two examples of these local chains. For a discussion of roadside commerce in Canada, see Steve Penfold, "Selling by the Carload: The Early Years of Fast Food in Canada," in Madga Fahrni and Robert Rutherdale, eds., *Creating Postwar Canada: Community, Diversity and Dissent* (Vancouver: UBC Press, 2007).

20. *TS*, 30 April 1965, 10.

21. *Canadian Hotel Review and Restaurant* (*CHRR*), 15 August 1961, 36–40; 15 May 1964, 42–7; 15 May 1966, 38–44; *CHRR*, 15 May 1968, 44–51; 15 March 1970, 43–9; 15 March 1971, 20–3. . . .

22. Albert DeBaeremaker, telephone interview by author, 18 March 2000.

23. Mike Dawson's excellent study of tourism in British Columbia, which emphasizes the power of cultural producers, is one recent example. Michael Dawson, *Selling British Columbia: Tourism and Consumer Culture* (Vancouver, BC: UBC Press, 2004), especially 13.

24. Al Stortz, interviewed by author, Welland, Ontario, 17 April 1998; DeBaeremaker interview.

25. On general issues of road planning in Metropolitan Toronto, see Timothy Colton, *Big Daddy: Frederick G. Gardiner and the Building of Metropolitan Toronto* (Toronto, ON: University of Toronto Press, 1980); Christopher Leo, *The Politics of Urban Development: Canadian Expressway Disputes* (Toronto, ON: Institute of Public Administration of Canada, 1977).

26. In the mid-1960s, Damas and Smith undertook traffic surveys and planning studies for several Ontario municipalities, including Sarnia, Cornwall, Oakville, Burlington, Brantford, Pembroke, Timmins, Georgetown, Renfrew, Port Colborne, Galt, Preston, and Smiths Falls. . . .

27. I discuss some issues of anti-drive-in sentiments in Steve Penfold, "Are We to Go Literally to the Hot Dogs? Drive-Ins, Parking Lots, and the Critique of Progress in Toronto's Suburbs, 1965–75," *Urban History Review* 33, no. 1 (2004): 8–23.

28. Scarboro Official Plan Review, *Commercial Policy Study*, October 1976, prepared by James F. MacLaren Ltd. for the Scarboro Planning Board, 2–9, 4–17.

29. *CHRR*, 15 December 1964, 8, citing a Bank of Montreal survey. . . .

30. *CHRR*, 15 November 1965, 68; *Restaurants and Institutions* (*RI*), February 1959, 11. . . .

31. *CHRR*, 15 November 1956, 68. The Pan American Coffee Bureau, an organization of major coffee producers, apparently coined the term "coffee break" in the early 1950s as a marketing effort. . . .

32. See Steve Penfold, *The Donut: A Canadian History* (Toronto, ON: University of Toronto Press, 2008), ch. 1.

33. On the increasing use of options within a standard format, see Joy Parr, *Domestic Goods* (Toronto, ON: University of Toronto Press, 1999); James Flink, *The Automobile Age* (Cambridge, MA: MIT Press, 1998), ch. 12; and Gary Cross, *An All-Consuming Century: Why Commercialism Won in Modern America* (New York, NY: Columbia University Press, 2000), 88–103.

34. Tim Lambert, interviewed by author, St Catharines, 19 May 1998.

35. Mister Donut, *Advertising and Promotions Manual*, 1967, from private collection.

36. Jenny Bryce, Tim Hortons server, early 1970s, interviewed by author, Selkirk, Ontario, 9 January 1998.

37. North York Public Library, North York History Collection, Jesse Dean, "Streetwork Report: Don Mills Youth Scene" (1971), 18.

38. Charade interview; Lori Broadfoot, server, Ideal Donuts, early 1970s, interviewed by author, Winnipeg, 19 October 2001; Lalonde interview.

39. Diners had typically been male spaces. See Andrew Hurley, "The Transformation of the American Diner," 1, 286–8.

40. Sandy Willard, interviewed by author, Binbrook, Ontario, 21 February 2002; anonymous former Tim Hortons franchisee, interviewed by author, 11 August 2001; Kiriakopoulos interview; Ed Mahaj, interviewed by author, Oakville, Ontario, 6 January 1998. In fact, women's smoking had achieved a certain respectability by this time, although it was not without ambiguities. See Jarrett Rudy, *The Freedom to Smoke: Tobacco Consumption and Identity* (Montreal, QC: McGill-Queen's University Press, 2005), 148–70.

41. Jenny Bryce interview. Note: For a short time in the early 1970s, Tim Hortons outlets served ice cream cones. . . .

42. Certainly the work was dangerous, especially travelling to and from late-night shifts. In 1965, one Mister Donut server was murdered on her way to a night shift in suburban Toronto. Her husband lamented that he normally drove her right to the outlet, but that he had to work a night shift that day.

43. Tom Busnarda, interviewed by author, Welland, 15 January 1998 . . .

44. *CHRR*, 15 November 1945, 30.

45. Ontario Store Fixtures had a "package plan," which it installed in restaurants across the country. *CHRR*, 15 June 1962, 44. See *CHRR*, 15 January 1965, 2–23, for discussion of the various types of counters and stools.

46. Joyce, *Always Fresh*, 49–50, 107–8.

47. Ron Buist reports that the early customer base of Tim Hortons was 55 per cent men and 45 per cent women. Buist, *Tales from under the Rim* (Fredericton, NB: Goose Lane, 2003), 203.

48. Mister Donut, *Highlights from a Market Analysis*, 4; Chris Pappas, interviewed by author, Etobicoke, Ontario, 7 December 2000.

49. *Oakville Beaver* (*OB*), 2 July 1970; *ODJR*, 30 June 1970. Peter Simpson is a pseudonym. . . . [S]ince there is no analytic value in using his real name, I have changed it to avoid dredging up old embarrassments.

50. Jesse Dean, "Don Mills Youth Scene" (North York, 1970), 10; *ODJR*, 29 December 1970, 4; 7 January 1971, 4; 15 May 1971, 4.

51. On the history of youth and leisure, see Tamara Myers, *Caught: Montreal's Modern Girls and the Law* (Toronto, ON: University of Toronto Press, 2006); Michael Gauvreau, "The Protracted Birth of the Canadian Teenager: Work, Citizenship, and the Canadian Youth Commission, 1943–55," in Gauvreau and Christie, eds., *Cultures of Citizenship in Postwar Canada* (Montreal, QC: McGill-Queen's University Press, 2003), 201–38; Shirley Tillotson, *The Public at Play: Gender and the Politics of Recreation in Post-War Ontario* (Toronto, ON: University of Toronto Press, 2000). . . .

52. Dean, "Don Mills Youth Scene," 11. On St. Catharines, see Halaiko interview.

53. *Mister Donut Market Analysis*; Pappas interview. On the timing of the baby boom, see Douglas Owram, *Born at the Right Time: A History of the Baby Boom Generation* (Toronto, ON: University of Toronto Press, 1996), 4–5. . . .

54. Town of Oakville, Bylaw 1970-98, "A Bylaw to Prohibit Loitering and Nuisances on Public Highways," passed 7 July 1970.

55. *TS*, 8 July 1970, 13. . . .

56. *OB*, 29 October 1970, A28. On the power of civil rights language in Canada, see Owram, *Born at the Right Time*, 166–7.

30 Films, Tourists, and Bears in the National Parks
Managing Park Use and the Problematic "Highway Bum" Bear in the 1970s

George Colpitts[1]

In the 1960s and 1970s, Canada's national parks system was the closest it had ever been to fulfilling its earlier promoters' wildest dreams, and their nightmares. North American automobile culture joined with a popularized wilderness movement to expand park use to unprecedented levels. Every year, Canadians and Americans by the tens of thousands drove over improved highway systems, taking advantage of a federally managed network of camp and picnic grounds within the parks. Roads offered "drive-in" convenience in nature. Camping, barely contained within crowded, centralized sites with biffies, water pumps, and standardized outdoor film screens and auditoriums, now replicated the very suburbs from which parks visitors had hoped to escape.[2] All the while, parks were more effectively colonized by tourists using a variety of newfangled "leave-no-trace" consumer tent and hiking products that could support mass back-to-nature tourism and even greater visitor numbers.[3] To say the least, meeting the needs and expectations of car-driving urbanites presented enormous challenges for Canada's National Parks Branch dealing with what Turner has termed "the paradoxes of popular wilderness."[4]

. . . Often overlooked, but indicative of the growing pressures on park managers in this period, was one of the most innovative wildlife films in Canada's government film history. Funded by Parks Canada and produced by the National Film Board, the 25-minute *Bears and Man* was filmed as [the] debate around use-versus-preservation grew in national parks across Canada, and indeed, North America.[5] This chapter, examining *Bears and Man* and other films of the era, suggests that their significance can be better understood in a longer history of visual representations of parks landscapes and of the animals and humans within them. After World War I, infrastructure and road-building projects had done more than engineer parks space to better exploit its tourist potential. Rather, these roads and automobile technology began influencing animal–human relationships whereby humans and wildlife in these "wilderness" settings evinced a host of mutualistic and rewarding behaviours. One involved the long-standing and enormously popular pastime of tourists feeding bears along roadsides and photographing themselves doing so.[6]

When *Bears and Man* appeared in 1978, it reached expanded audiences through movie

Citation: George Colpitts, "Films, Tourists, and Bears in the National Parks: Managing Park Use and the Problematic 'Highway Bum' Bear in the 1970s," in Claire Elizabeth Campbell, ed., *A Century of Parks Canada, 1911–2011* (Calgary, AB: University of Calgary Press, 2011): 153–78.

theatres and television and presented a radically different portrait of human–animal relationships in the parks system.[7] Cinematographer Bill Schmalz, with parks officials and other individuals working in the context of their times,[8] used the film to rearrange elements of North American popular culture according to the growing ethic of wilderness preservation and the emerging science of bear ecology. The final product was far more comprehensive than the original project first discussed by the Parks Branch in 1967, which had been to create a "training film" for visitors encountering bears in the parks.[9] The 1978 film offers insights into how independent filmmaking, bear behavioural science, and the wilderness movement were coalescing in new ideas about nature itself. *Bears and Man* redefined space between wild animals and park visitors in a new "hybrid landscape," and in an ideal that, arguably, remains influential to the present day.[10]

Almost from the moments of their technological birth, moving and still photo cameras complemented conservation efforts in North America.[11] American conservationists such as Henry Fairfield Osborn had long understood how wildlife films, in particular, could spread and shape conservation messages to wide audiences and gather public support for the further establishment of American parks.[12] Given the malleability of images in film and photographic media, filmmakers could blur reality and re-create Nature itself by depicting wild animals in a variety of ways.[13] In one popular medium, that of very cheap and mass-produced postcards, the wild in Canada's mountain parks—what Keri Cronin termed "National Park Nature"—was profoundly shaped by the depiction of its animal life, especially of black bears.[14] Bears eating at hotel tables, wandering around on Banff's golf course, chained to poles, sniffing for food along park roadways, or sitting behind steering wheels of automobiles were not only popular in the interwar years, they were important in defining through "photographic clichés" park wilderness for larger numbers of tourists using roads and automobiles.[15]

These postcards were made locally for the mountain parks and sold en masse in tourist shops. A "Black Bears" postcard taken in the 1940s, one of many based on a photograph by Byron Harmon, suggests how autotourism and bears joined in a wilderness ideal: It shows a mother and her cubs crossing a highway in Banff, undoubtedly looking for handouts. In turn, the postcard was purchased by an autotourist from Minburn, Alberta, and posted home with the note: "Here is a picture of the bears we keep watching for but haven't seen yet. We'll be at Banff tonight so I'm sure we'll see some there. We've had a fine time. Love, Auntie."[16] As tourists chugged through mountain parks in their new technological monstrosities—as some at first had viewed automobiles within parks—their visits were necessarily mediated in the landscape through graded roadways, roadside stops, and scenic loops and views cut through forest screens to best facilitate sightseeing, often at a rapid pace.[17] Meanwhile, wildlife finding reward by frequenting roadways and auto stops to mooch for food were quickly conditioned to tourist traffic. Both parties seem to have enjoyed their encounters. The love-at-first-sight between wildlife and automobilists was romanticized further in tourist promotion. Habituated wildlife was featured feeding along the roadsides of some of the earliest automobile road films to thrill theatre audiences in the 1920s.[18] . . . The promotion-savvy parks commissioner James B. Harkin knew how to please automobilists by suggesting that salt licks be put out beside the newly built Banff highway system in 1922.[19] Mabel B. Williams's own promotions of the new "auto parks" in western Canada celebrated the ways that wild animals seemed "tamed" along roadways, in effect sharing the road with drivers. Park drivers, she promised, would encounter animals that innately understood that "within these boundaries" humans had "laid aside" their "ancient enmity." Animals, in return, were "quick to offer in return the gift of equal friendship."[20] She did not mention that, really, most of the animals were there for the free lunch. The pandering elk, mooching squirrels, and cheeky bears in park picnic areas and driveways had conditioned themselves to the handouts and very quickly confirmed expectations of drivers and auto passengers around ideas of wilderness itself: part of a larger intellectual complex that David Louter has termed "windshield wilderness."[21]

Bear ecology and behaviour reinforced its central presence in that conceptualization. Camera-toting visitors could snap photos of many compliant park animals, from the reintroduced elk species to deer. But it was the black bear (*Ursus americanus*) that became something of a "keystone" species in road landscapes. It adapted quickly to the rising numbers of tourists and the habitat changes within park areas in Canada and parts of the United States by the mid-twentieth century. Its remarkable adaptation in turn contributed to the growing popularity in bear feeding. Research in the United States at Yellowstone and Great Smoky Mountains and in Canada's mountain parks would later show that bears displayed a manifestly "tolerant" behaviour. Once rolling in their vehicles into the confines of park boundaries, tourists could usually find a bear that had learned to "beg" along roadsides in order to elicit handouts. Many showed remarkable talent in "dancing," performing or aping gestures to please drivers and passengers. Some learned to aggress without inflicting injury in order to bully picnic tourists to share their food. Stephen Herrero found that, although the black bear did aggress tourists, it (unlike the grizzly, *Ursus arctos*) did so in much lower numbers in proportion to the numbers of encounters, and inflicted comparatively minor injuries. Animal behaviour, then, contributed to a cultured space between animal and human, with bears learning strategies that, for the most part, rewarded them.[22] Before the truly dangerous congestion of the 1960s—a decade also fraught with debate about the corruption of the wilderness by overdevelopment and tourist use—bears

and humans complemented each others' behaviours and bears themselves gained prominence in tourist–animal landscapes.

. . .

All the same, for parks staff the convergence of roads, automobilists, and bears was inviting a head-on collision of unintended outcomes, to say the least. In the United States, the bear problem loomed with increasing urgency, accelerated by greater numbers of tourists and, by the 1960s, ecologists suggesting a variety of controversial remedies.[23] Canada, of course, saw its own rapid increase in vehicular traffic in the post-war period. Vehicle passenger numbers at Banff's east gate rose from around 300,000 in 1947 to 800,000 in 1957, and to almost 2.4 million by 1970.[24] Despite increased efforts to discourage highway liaisons, National Parks Branch officials were dismayed to find bear-feeding postcards still selling in Banff town site tourist shops in 1959, the very year when the first conviction for the practice occurred.[25] Many of the maulings, as reported to wardens, often occurred at roadside lookouts, suggesting drive-in tourists had unrolled windows, much like they would have in a hamburger joint, to bear moochers in return for a photograph. Such exchanges, always loaded with misunderstandings, sometimes went very badly.[26] As J. R. B. Coleman, a senior Branch official, pointed out in one memorandum in 1965, "postcards depicting bears in the driver's seat of cars are on sale in various U.S. and Canadian National Park tourist shops and they encourage some foolish people in the belief that such a photographic set-up is easy and safe to arrange." He referred to the case of one Banff visitor who was observed *pushing* a "large black bear behind the steering wheel of his car so that he could take an unusual photograph."[27] The problem was that tourists simply saw the interaction as an integral element of a parks experience. Even the *Kingston Whig Standard* could find the Parks Branch's pamphlets that year reminding tourists "of the dangers of feeding and molesting bears" worthy of a comical editorial cartoon.[28]

With tourist expectations so dependent on such practices, it is interesting to see the somewhat mixed messages arising in a film produced in 1959 by the Branch entitled *Wildlife of the Rockies* (tellingly, originally titled "Zoo of the Mountains"). This film represented an effort by the Branch to both promote the parks system and remedy a problematic scarcity of Canadian national parks films available in the post-war period. What films it did have were perhaps informative but had all of the interest of high school biology lectures. Canadian and American audiences demanding films of Canadian mountain parks for Rotary Club dinners and bridge nights found the official selection of 16-mm films wanting, to say the least. By the late 1950s, documentary selections produced earlier by the federal government's film bureau were hopelessly bogged down in natural history detail, out of date, or simply too tattered from repetitive viewings for continued use.[29] After assessing the comparatively more exciting films promoting US national parks, the Canadian Parks Branch liaised with the National Film Board to produce something, in the parlance of the times, hipper, and used wildlife to do so.

. . .

Perhaps planning the production had left little room for innovation, but the end product worked within the expectations of tourists of the time. *Wildlife of the Rockies* introduces a hypothetical "mammalogist resident" who encouraged autotourists to stop their cars and take a moment to look at park wildlife. The film opens with a family pausing impatiently on the side of the road, having vacated their car, and, "seeing nothing," as narrator Budd Knapp tells the audience, "piling into their car, this family concludes that the woods and mountains are deserted."[30] He goes on to say, however, that the mammalogist knew better. As the family returns to its prominent 1950s American vehicle and roars off down the road, the narrator explains that had they known better or been willing to look beyond the roadside, there would be plenty of animals to view. Even when the family stops again to chat with a park warden—through a rolled-down window—they are evidently in too much of a hurry to listen to his advice. And leaving him and the viewer in the dust of their vehicle, the film then turns to the warden who scans through alpine, sub-alpine, and valley complexes where communities of animals awaited, very apparent to the eye but invisible to autotourists moving too quickly to pause and take a careful, studious glance at their surroundings.

Whatever the original intent of the production, the drafts of commentary, shortened and synced to film, ended up reinforcing tourist behaviour along park roadsides. Given that many of the shots were taken from roadside vantage points, this is not surprising. About 230 seconds into the film, the narrator says, "Finding most of the wildlife in Banff and Jasper requires some careful searching. But even the road home can bring its surprises. You don't need binoculars to spot a black bear. He moves where he wants, and the presence of a few human beings doesn't bother him at all."[31] The key objective of the film, [that is], to have tourists "spend a bit more time in the parks, instead of speeding through them in their cars,"[32] was then obscured in the very infrastructure and road amenities tourists were using. The framing of the film around autotourists, in the end, reinforced current expectations and affirmed Steve Jones's idea that "cinematic and touristic ways of seeing" complemented each other quite naturally in the post-war period.[33]

Wildlife of the Rockies was added to the roster of films being shown to audiences in campground amphitheatres across the Canadian parks system.[34] The Branch developed two more films by 1969 to encourage tourism—each, however, revealing the growing problem facing park managers who were tasked with promoting parks as much as preserving them. *Away from It All* (1961), featuring Terra Nova National Park, was a 15-minute short that juxtaposed urban life and its many "daily urban struggles" with that of wilderness parks and sanctuaries, "natural retreats for the worried man," as the outline narration read.[35] A more explicit celebration of wilderness—as opposed to tourist promotion— appeared in the Branch's award-winning *The Enduring Wilderness* (1963), directed by nature cinematographer Christopher Chapman. The film provided a montage of scenes from park spaces across Canada. It too reinforced a message of the need for parks in a society increasingly "feeling the impact of civilization" beyond roadways, the din of traffic, and technological amenities supplied for auto-driving tourists. But the film was organized around "the whole idea to provide the experience of natural beauty and the feeling for it,"[36] quite innovatively seeking to provide a "philosophy film on National Parks," one of the reasons why its initial title was planned as "The Meaning of Wilderness."[37]

In Chapman's case, however, the film's original purpose was at odds with the promotional mandate still being managed by the federal ministry overseeing the project—and paying its production costs. An initial script read by the Education and Interpretation Section and the deputy minister of the Department of Northern Affairs and National Resources—of which the Parks Branch was only a part—felt that Chapman had scripted a film that did not encourage the use of parks by visitors. "Nowhere in the script is there any direct identification of the wilderness with people," Chapman was told. "Could not some people be shown . . .? I feel rather strongly that all parks, National or otherwise, are, and should be for people—for their recreation, their education, their appreciation of nature . . . it is an obligation on the trustees [of a park] to allow it to be used appropriately by people."[38] Closer to the events unfolding around them and the pressures on the ground, parks officials backing these new films were already anxious to support such efforts and even present to the public the "use and preservation dilemma" confronting them. Winston W. Mair, the new director of the Branch, developed the extraordinary idea of a film relating "the use–conserve

dilemma as experienced system-wide—perhaps putting across the idea of public understanding as the only real solution." Mair perhaps was voicing the concerns of his own officials in a parks system grappling with logistic issues of garbage, road widening, ski hill development, and other uses. His idea of telling "the story of the wild lands, without too much concentration on the spectacular,"[39] however, was quashed at the ministerial level. The Parks Branch's most recent film, *The Enduring Wilderness*, had already gone far enough in giving "the 'soft sell' type" to the public. The minister felt that "it was *not* what he wanted. What we need is something more aggressive and spectacular to ensure his continued support for more films in the future."[40] Whatever "philosophy" of wilderness Chapman had wanted to explore in his film, the times were not best for expressing them. Chapman's original film title, indeed, had gone through its own considerable modification. From the proposed "The Meaning of Wilderness," expressing a philosophy of wilderness, the film's title was changed to the "Vanishing Wilderness." However, the Parks Branch understood even that term's problematic semantics and tweaked it to a more reassuring title: "The Enduring Wilderness." At least on film, the Parks Branch was still attempting to balance tourism and increased use with its mandate to preserve Canada's great wild lands.

Against this backdrop of massive development and increased tourism in the parks, a series of bear culls and highly publicized mauling incidents brought into stark view a number of now unsustainable traditions in parks tourism. As early as the 1940s, and certainly by 1959, western parks wardens were shooting bears in greater numbers in an effort to reduce animal–human conflicts. Superintendents explored numerous remedies to address the problems posed by these omnivore "highway bums,"[41] but, given the costs of bear-proof garbage disposal, the largely unsuccessful educational campaigns to tourists, and complicity among concession and tour bus operators who were still escorting tourists to roadside bear photo ops, parks managers believed that only large-scale culling and even complete eradication were solutions for areas frequented by visitors.[42] By the early 1960s, with some 100,000 people camping in Jasper National Park alone,[43] it was evident that there was not enough room for habituated "campground" bears in the Canadian parks system. In 1962, for example, wardens trapped 146 black bears and destroyed 112 (compared to 75 and 38 respectively a year before).[44] The superintendent of Kootenay National Park, K. B. Mitchell, voiced concern over the "highly accelerated control of the bear population." But he had also seen, as had the superintendent at Jasper, habituation increase with these expanding visitor numbers. By then, bears along the highways had "availed themselves of the supply of food offered by the increased numbers of tourists using the roadways and picnic grounds."[45] In turn, heavy culling led to noticeable declines in bear numbers by the late 1960s and early 1970s, at least in terms of animals seen by visitors. Wardens doing most of the culling, and grimly clearing out roadsides with control methods, were telling tourists wanting to see bears that the animals had simply "gone off" into the backcountry.

There was certainly more urgency in the issue now. The case brought successfully by a bear maul victim in the United States against the US Parks Service raised the worrisome possibility of legal liability arising from mauling incidents. In 1967, an Alberta man brought to the courts his own, ultimately unsuccessful, case, which had occurred in Jasper.[46] The Parks Branch now broached the possibility of having "a short film produced as a public service message in which we would attempt to explain to tourists the procedures they should follow to avoid being confronted by a wild animal or what to do in the case they are."[47] Branch director, J. R. B. Coleman, supported the idea, hoping that such could provide "a training film on bear behaviour and the results of human carelessness and lack of judgment in dealing with bears." An "invaluable

aid to such a training program," he imagined the film being shown to "general park visitors and the public-at-large as well."[48]

However, a broader change was occurring in wildlife filmmaking beyond the Parks Branch. In 1971, broadcaster and public commentator Warner Troye completed *Where Has Sanctuary Gone?*, a 23-minute film that showed, not only the rising tensions of "modern" urban life, but the contrived element of park management whereby autotourists lined up for hours to gain entrance into the national parks. The scene of traffic jams outside Banff's east gates reinforced Troye's larger message of the disappearing wilderness areas in Canada, even within the national parks. The film identified a problem of too many automobiles, too many roads, and too many campgrounds, which offered too little "wilderness" beyond that which could be found in a suburban backyard. Troye captured some of the unreasonable extremes of "use" in Canadian parks, especially that accessible by roadways and filled with family station wagons.

Even as the wilderness movement affected filmmakers and parks promoters, bear studies launched in the 1960s in Yellowstone, Alaska, Great Smoky Mountains, and Glacier National Parks were beginning to elucidate the nature and meaning of bear behaviour, migration, and habituation. These explored bear movement in park areas, surveyed bear-feeding tourists in American parks, studied habituation, and analyzed footpath encounters. Before 1970, very little scientific study of the kind on bears and their habituation had been undertaken, and parks officials had little means of understanding the behaviour or even of guessing the ratio of "campground" and "wilderness" bears in the parks system.[49] The science of bear feeding, however, changed rapidly in the early 1970s, when international conferences for bear biologists consistently featured sessions on human–animal interaction and the problematic outcomes of habituation.[50] This research led to new social and ecological understandings of animal behaviour and psychology. In Canada, sensibilities were shaped by Stephen Herrero, whose work on animal behaviour focused on Canadian bears and followed up John and Frank Craighead's research in Yellowstone.

. . .

Such streams of influence informed Parks Canada's decision to support a clearly different kind of bear film. In the early 1970s, wildlife cinematographer Bill Schmalz was returning to western Canada from a stint of work with the National Film Board when he proposed a bear documentary to the agency's prairie regional office in Calgary. Schmalz had begun his career filming a fisheries research project in the Gulf of Alaska before studying biology at UBC for a year. He then went on to spend several years filming bighorn sheep and other wildlife in the mountain parks. While with the NFB, he finished shooting and directing *Bighorn*, a theatrical short that, like Chapman's wilderness film, had no narration and instead provided a montage of images of areas "still untouched by man."[51] His knowledge that bears were "systematically being shot and killed" along roadsides, including what he believed had been the unnecessary killing of two grizzly cubs by parks wardens, prompted Schmalz to propose *Bears and Man*.[52] His idea of a bear film found evident support in the NFB organization. For the next three years, Schmalz worked with wardens at Kootenay, Banff, Jasper, and Waterton. *Bears and Man* (in French titled *L'Ours mon Frère*) can be viewed as an emerging compilation of environmentalist concerns and scientific understanding of bear behaviour. In terms of the latter, Schmalz was well aware of current science through bear conferences. He consulted with Herrero on the project, and, indeed, Herrero provided advice to Parks Canada as the film took shape.

Schmalz's proposal moved beyond a merely informational production and employed state-of-the-art film editing, music, and narration that emotively disassembled the bear–automobile landscape that had been idealized and preserved in popular photography. His first report, dated December 1974, describes the film's planning process. Its major points were developed thematically on storyboard in consultation with Parks officials. Schmalz had already collected footage of bears in parks from previous work; during his first filming on contract, he witnessed a horrific mauling when the translocation of a drugged grizzly went wrong, and the bear attacked and killed Canadian Wildlife Service biologist Wilf Etherington.[53] Deeply traumatized, but encouraged to continue the project, Schmalz spent the 1974 season capturing sequences for the "Bears in Nature" section of the film, which included shots taken in the summer of two grizzly families (counting a sow with three yearling cubs) and of two lone cubs. During the filming, the warden service helped Schmalz find locations and provided carcasses of road-killed elk and moose to attract bears to open areas "suitable for filming."[54] Eventually, the film moved from "Bears in Nature" to "Bear–People Interaction"—which included the film's most dramatic moment, "bear–people highway feeding"—to "Bear Immobilizing and Translocation." The film adhered tightly to the eventual script storyboard, although Schmalz's initial hope to include shots showing the warden service shooting problem bears in the "Bear Confrontation Conduct" section were dashed when they were "deleted from scene" by parks officials despite his protests.[55]

Blocked in five sections, the final film went far beyond "instructional" fare; its overarching message promoted a negotiated space between humans and the national parks' now-declining black and grizzly bear populations. The editor eventually working on the project, Kalle Lasn, who had returned from a filming project in Japan with "avant-guard" editing techniques, changed the first editions of the film to be more effective in that respect. Chief Dan George was chosen as narrator for the opening sequences, using narration written by Schmalz and the film editor so that the famous Salish chief could very directly plead viewers to "respect the bear."[56] The original script called for "Old Indian" to say: "The ways of the city are lost in the wilderness. Here the spirit of the great bear fills the land. He was wilder and stronger than we are, we must learn to respect its ways."[57] Considering its long exclusion from national parks, the First Nations voice was effective but also logical given the popularity of the idea of the "ecological Indian" in the North American environmental movement at the time.[58] The narrator in effect reconceptualized Aboriginal history in saying that "at the time of my great grandfather the spirit of the bear filled our land." The native voice then drew bear behaviour around tourists in critical terms. Their feeding was not idealized but criticized as "spoiling" the animal:

DAN GEORGE – Man, once he is given power over the wilderness and its creatures, but he does not have the power to make a spoiled bear natural once more.

Here, the film's characterization of bear behaviour reflected current scientific behavioural research, effectively branded in the native voice. The leading narrator, Patricia Best, went on to further define the "spoiled" bear, the animal habituated around garbage cans and roadside feeds, killed by traffic, tranquillized, transported or destroyed by parks officials. In one scene, a mother black bear and two cubs converge upon a garbage dumpster in Jasper. Adroitly lifting the lid, the mother, then a cub, nose around and disappear into the receptacle. The mother bear's sudden charge from the dumpster suggests the violence and danger of such habituated animals. It provides the transition to footage of a vehicle completely destroyed by a bear attack, its side ripped out and interior plundered for food.

NARRATOR – They call them "spoiled" bears. They have given up their natural feeding habits and learned to survive on human garbage.

The film goes on to explicitly undermine linkages between complementary automobile culture and tourist bear feeding and negotiated space for both in park recreation. In sequences played by actors, "Russ and Jenny" hike through a park to camp in the wild. They happen upon bear tracks along a stream:

RUSS – "Grizzly tracks."

JENNY – "Is it still around?"

RUSS – "Could be. We're not going to stick around to find out though. I know a better spot about a mile down the trail."

Russ and Jenny eventually locate their camp out of bear's way. They start a fire for cooking distanced at least a hundred yards from their tents. Russ pulverizes burnt cans and then elevates them and other food leftovers by a rope to a high tree limb beyond a bear's reach.

The film's most dramatic scene further defines animal–human parks space in a bear-feeding scene shot between Jasper and the Mile 45 warden station. Bear jams often formed there in a stretch of highway. The scene shows droves of camera-toting tourists converging on a mother with two cubs, which have appeared along the shoulder. Unlike earlier films showing tourists and bears sharing the photographic space, the camera trains attention mostly on the humans who appear as habituated to the bears as the animals to them. In the scene, one brazen youth is seen handing cherries to the mother, which nearly bites his hand.[59] A family passes a brown paper bag to the bears through a rolled-down window. The mother is later seen climbing atop of a vehicle, its delighted owners laughing at the bear's pandering. Perhaps the most effective shot comes at the scene's conclusion, when one of the cubs traversing the highway is nearly killed by a motorist who drags it a few metres before its screeching tires; the cub runs to safety, apparently unharmed. Film editing and another acted sequence shows a park warden arriving, radioing in a "244" bear-on-road call, and confronting the occupants of a car who had just fed the bears in question.

Bears and Man disassembled a terrifically popular, but problematic, photographic ideal that had linked humans and wildlife in North American national parks. This happened at an important moment in parks history, when the growing and increasingly heavy tourist use of national parks was animating anew the "use-versus-preservation" dilemma. It was not, however, a statist imposition into popular culture, or simply the tourist instruction film originally talked about by the Parks Branch. Herrero, indeed, remembered the film "was a celebration of the wild with suggestions on how to keep it that way."[60] Indeed, Parks Canada gave its blessing for the film project at a time when managers themselves were at something of a crossroads in solving the almost century-old "bear problem." In the context of mauling incidents, heavy culling, and the possibility that victims of bear attacks might sue the government for "mismanaging" the bear problem, this type of popular tourist recreation was no longer tenable in the parks system. Challenges raised by mass tourism had gone beyond the mere question of distinguishing between and managing differently "campground" versus "wilderness" bears. The Parks Branch itself, contemplating a complete eradication of bears in tourist areas, was likely aware of at least a minority of scientific experts who advocated the ridding of the animals in parks in order to protect visitors. The film represented, then, its endorsement of a management compromise, that of providing new scientific advice and more effective re-education to the public aimed to modify tourism and maintain space in parks for humans, black, and even grizzly bears.[61]

In reorganizing aspects of tourism, however, *Bears and Man* did as much to propose a new bear psychology as it did to delineate an ideal space between humans and these animals. Throughout Schmalz's production, viewers were asked to "respect the bear" as Chief Dan George stated in the film's opening and ending sequences, an admonition suggesting both the unknowable and frightening aspect of a bear's makeup, whatever it truly is. This did not mean that bears lost their keystone status in tourist landscapes. Hardly. If *Bears and Man* enjoyed any success in reshaping tourist behaviours, it was likely because it reassembled, rather than threw away, pieces of older, popular understandings of parks wilderness. The film reinforced the importance of bears in a wild space now understood as "bear country"; catching a larger shift, identified by Tina Loo, in wildlife conservation in Canada by the 1970s, whereby government acted to conserve wild areas and not merely wild animals within them.[62] In the new assemblage, hikers, drivers and sightseers could continue to find recreation in parks, but they did so upon a backdrop of a wilderness idealized by the bear's invisible presence, his "spirit," in Dan George's narration. The bear and its wilderness habitat is of such importance that the roadway is almost completely erased. Once used by visitors to experience and define nature in national parks, it now figured only as a backdrop element, but one now looming as another problem in parks' management of humans and wildlife.

 More online.

Notes

1.   The author wishes to thank Alan MacEachern and Jim Taylor for references to parks bear files, films, and photographs, André D'Ulisse and François Houle, National Film Board Archive, for documents; and Ted Hart and Stephen Herrero for reading and commenting on an early version of this paper. Thanks, too, must go to Pamela Banting for her initial suggestions. I am indebted, in particular, to Bill Schmalz for taking much time in recounting his experiences filming *Bears and Man*. The article is dedicated to my "little bear," Gabriel.

2.   Richard Harris, *Creeping Conformity: How Canada became Suburban, 1900–60* (Toronto, ON: University of Toronto Press, 2004), 11–12, 130–32; Doug Owram,

Born at the Right Time: A History of the Baby Boom Generation (Toronto, ON: University of Toronto Press, 1999); . . . in Ontario, see Steve Penfold, "'Are We to Go Literally to the Hot Dogs?' Parking Lots, Drive-Ins, and the Critique of Progress in Toronto's Suburbs, 1965–75," *Urban History Review* 33, no. 1 (2004): 8–23; James Morton Turner, "From Woodcraft to 'Leave no Trace': Wilderness, Consumerism, and Environmentalism in Twentieth-Century America," *Environmental History* 7, no. 3 (2002): 475–76; Alan MacEachern, *Natural Selections: National Parks in Atlantic Canada 1935–70* (Montreal, QC: McGill-Queen's University Press, 2001), 162–63, 224, 220–22; Gregg Mitman, *Reel Nature: America's Romance with Wildlife in Film* (Cambridge, MA: Harvard University Press, 1999), 105.

3. James Morton Turner, "From Woodcraft to 'Leave no Trace,'" 467–68; Victor B. Scheffer, *The Shaping of Environmentalism in America* (Seattle, WA: University of Washington Press, 1999), 41–42.

4. Turner, "From Woodcraft to 'Leave no Trace,'" 468–9; see also Mitman, *Reel Nature*, 91; PearlAnn Reichwein, "Holiday at the Banff School of Fine Arts: The Cinematic Production of Culture, Nature, and Nation in the Canadian Rockies, 1945–52," *Journal of Canadian Studies* 39, no. 1 (2005): 56. . . .

5. See "Of preservation and Use," in Alan MacEachern, *Natural Selections*, 14–19. . . .

6. Paul Schullery, *Searching for Yellowstone: Ecology and Wonder in the Last Wilderness* (Boston, MA: Houghton Mifflin, 1997), 195–98.

7. National Film Board Archives, Montreal (hereafter NFBA). See overview of the film's potential television and theatrical audiences in Hélène Dennie to Ken Preston, 4 May 1978, "Bears and Man" correspondence file.

8. From his present home in Langley, BC, Schmalz acknowledged the important contribution of parks naturalist Larry Halverson, Jasper warden Gordon Anderson, and glaciologist Dr. Ronald Goodman. He singled out Mike Porter, then information officer, later a prominent director in national parks, as key to shepherding the earlier stages of the production and seeing it approved by government. He also acknowledged the invaluable contributions of Kalle Lasn and Barbara Baxendale. Telephone interview, Schmalz to author, 2 July 2010.

9. Library and Archives Canada, Ottawa [hereafter LAC] AC. J. R. B. Coleman used the term to describe the possible film project, 21 August 1967, RG 84, A-2-a, vol. 2130, file U212, pt. 5.

10. Richard White, "From Wilderness to Hybrid Landscapes: The Cultural Turn in Environmental History," *The Historian* 66 (2004): 558. . . .

11. See Mitman, *Reel Nature*, 85–87; D. B. Jones, *Movies and Memoranda: An Interpretive History of the National Film Board* (Toronto, ON: Canadian Film Institute, 1981); Ted Magder, *Canada's Hollywood: The Canadian State and Feature Films* (Toronto, ON: University of Toronto Press, 1993).

12. Mitman, *Reel Nature*, 90–91; on Henry Fairfield Osborn and films, see 101–2.

13. Cynthia Chris, *Watching Wildlife* (Minneapolis, MN: University of Minnesota Press, 2006), x, 28–34; Ralph H. Lutts, "The Trouble with Bambi: Disney's 'Bambi' and the American Vision of Nature," *Forest and Conservation History* 36, no. 4 (1992): 160–71. In Canada, currents of post-war ideals in film are explored by Reichwein, "Holiday at the Banff School of Fine Arts," 37. . . .

14. Keri Cronin, "'The Bears Are Plentiful and Frequently Good Camera Subjects': Postcards and the Framing of Interspecies Encounters in the Canadian Rockies," *Mosaic* 39, no. 4 (2006): 77–92. On the culturing of wilderness, see I. S. MacLaren, "Cultured Wilderness in Jasper National Park," *Journal of Canadian Studies* 34, no. 3 (1999): 7–58.

15. Almost with the very official opening of some park areas to autos—in Banff by 1910—bear feeding followed. By 1921 the *Edmonton Journal* could report that "Feeding Bears Is Popular Past Time in Jasper." The 1921 article is cited (n.d.) in "Evolution of Bear Management in the Mountain National Parks" (Parks Canada, 2003).

16. Tourists were warned of the potential danger of feeding bears from the very first decades of the century; signs discouraged the practice and the parks superintendent proposed formal educational campaigns as early as 1939; the National Park Game Act explicitly prohibited feeding bears by 1951. "Evolution of Bear Management in the Mountain National Parks" (Parks Canada, 2003). . . .

17. David Louter, *Windshield Wilderness: Cars, Roads, and Nature in Washington's National Parks* (Seattle, WA: University of Washington Press, 2006), 59–60.

18. Mitman, *Reel Nature*, 97. The tamed wild animal figures centrally in the 1919 film, *Back to God's Country*, where a pet bear protects the heroine from villains. For analysis of the film, see Christopher E. Gittings, in *Canadian National Cinema: Ideology, Difference and Representation* (London, UK: Routledge, 2002), 21–5. Also, Pierre Berton, *Hollywood's Canada: The Americanization of our National Image* (Toronto, ON: McClelland & Stewart, 1975), 27.

19. See . . . John Sandlos, "Nature's Playgrounds: The Parks Branch and Tourism Promotion in the National Parks, 1911–1929," [in Claire Elizabeth Campbell, ed., *A Century of Parks Canada, 1911–2011* (Calgary, AB: University of Calgary Press, 2011).]

20. Mabel B. Williams, *Kootenay National Park and the Banff–Windermere Highway* (Ottawa, ON: Department of the Interior, 1928), 32, quoted in George Colpitts, *Game in the Garden: A Human History of Wildlife in Western Canada to 1940* (Vancouver, BC: UBC Press, 2002), 160–63.

21. Louter, *Windshield Wilderness*, 3–4, 12–13, 37–9; the individualism of autotourism is suggested in Hall K. Rothman, *Devil's Bargains: Tourism in the Twentieth-Century American West* (Lawrence, KS: University of Kansas Press, 1998), 146–47.

22. See Stephen Herrero's documentation of bear habituation along roadsides in *Bear Attacks: Their Causes and Avoidance* (Piscataway, NJ: Winchester Press, 1985), 52; and on the "tolerant black bear," 92–94.

23. In the US, parks officials were facing a similar problem on a much larger scale. Alice Wondrak Biel, *Do (Not) Feed the Bears: The Fitful History of Wildlife and Tourists in Yellowstone* (Lawrence, KS: University of Kansas Press, 2006), 14–15, 21–23.

24. R. C. Scace, "Man and Grizzly Bear in Banff National Park, Alberta" (Master's thesis, University of Calgary, 1972), 86.

25. LAC. The postcards were "detrimental" to "any campaign we carry out against the feeding of bears," Superintendent of Banff National Park, D. B. Coombs, 15 May 1959, RG 84 A-2-a, vol. 229 K212, pt. 2.

26. LAC. "[D]rivers of sightseeing buses and taxis are among the worst offenders, in that on sighting a bear they frequently stop and permit their passengers to alight from the vehicle for the purpose of taking pictures and feeding the bears." H. A. deVeber, 3 November 1951; RG 84, A-2-a, vol. 2129, file U212, pt. 2. . . .

27. LAC. J. R. B. Coleman to Johnson, 4 January 1965, RG 84, A-2-a, vol. 2130, file U212, pt. 5.

28. *Kingston Whig Standard*, 15 July 1959. The cartoon was sent on to the parks director. RG 84, A-2-a, vol. 2130, file U212, pt. 4.

29. LAC. "Catalogue of Motion Picture Films Distributed by the National Parks Bureau," appearing in National Parks files in 1964, RG 84, A-2-a, vol. 2063, file U1117-56, pt. 5.

30. NFBA "Commentary," Wildlife in the Rockies, National Film Board Archives, 54-411.

31. The narrator added a cautionary note: "Visitors should avoid the temptation to make friends, or to feed the bears. They are unpredictable, and sometimes dangerous. Their diet ranges from ant eggs to small deer." NFBA, "Commentary" Short Version, Wildlife in the Rockies, 54-411.

32. NFBA, "Mammals of the Mountain Parks" objective and description, 54-411.

33. As quoted in Reichwein, "Holiday at the Banff School of Fine Arts," 57.

34. LAC. Robinson to Greenlee, 17 January 1961, NAC, RG 84, A-2-a, vol. 2062, file U117, pt. 46.

35. LAC. 4 July 1960, Outline, "Away from it all," RG 84, A-2-a, vol. 2063, file U117-56-19, pt. 1.

36. LAC. Marsha Porte, Review, "The Enduring Wilderness," *Film News*, October 1964, in RG 84, A-2-a, vol. 2064, file U117-56-20.

37. LAC. RG 84, A-2-a, vol. 2062, reel T-16023; See RG 84, A-2-a, vol. 2063 U117-56-20 for George Stirett to Coleman, 22 October 1962.

38. LAC. S. L. Roberts to Chapman, 28 June 1962; ibid.

39. LAC. Mair to Reeve, 24 December 1964. RG 84, A-2-a, vol. 2063, file U117-56, pt. 5.

40. LAC. Alex Keen memo, same date, ibid.

41. LAC. The expression was made on 10 September 1958 by the superintendent of Kootenay National Park, RG 84, A-2-a, vol. 2130, file U212, pt. 3.

42. LAC. Coleman admitted that culling was "one of our most effective measures of control" in a memorandum 22 October 1958, ibid., Supt. G. H. W. Ashley, at Prince Albert, 12 September 1958, was pessimistic: "If we must accept that bears are undesirable in areas of the Park frequented by visitors, it is my belief that the solution to the problem will depend on the application of all of the practical aspects of the suggestions mentioned, including the trapping and destruction of all bears entering such used areas. . . ."

43. LAC. RG 84, A-2-a, vol. 229, T-12954, J 36, Jasper National Park Campground Report, 1963–64.

44. LAC. Western national parks: Cumulative totals for season as at end of October 1962, RG 84, A-2-a, vol. 2130, file U212, pt. IV.

45. LAC. Mitchell memorandum, 6 September 1962, in RG 84, A-2-a, vol. 229. K. B. Mitchell, in Jasper, stated that "up until 1957 it was a rare occurrence to see a bear [in town] but last year for some unknown reason the bear population suddenly increased and the townsite was invaded by about a dozen bears at one time." 9 September 1958, RG 84, A-2-a, vol. 2130, file U212, pt. 3.

46. LAC. R. T. Flanagan, 14 September 1967, RG 84, A-2-a, vol. 2130, file U212, pt. V. It involved a parks worker, Frederick Sturdy, who was mauled at night near the Maligne Lake garbage dump in Jasper in 1965. See Sid Marty, *The Black Grizzly of Whiskey Creek* (Toronto, ON: McClelland & Stewart, 2008), 30.

47. LAC. R. T. Flanagan, 14 September 1967, RG 84, A-2-a, vol. 2130, file U212, pt. V.

48. LAC. Coleman Letter, 21 August 1967, ibid.

49. LAC. "I am afraid there is no information on the ratio of 'wilderness' bears to 'campground' bears on which I can base a statement. Certainly there are sizeable wilderness areas in all the National Parks of the mountains but I do not know if bears living in these areas would not, on occasion, wander into visitor-use areas."

J. R. B. Coleman to Johnson, 4 January 1965, RG 84, A-2-a, vol. 2130, file U212, pt. 5.

50. Stephen Herrero, "Introduction to the Biology and Management of Bears," in *Bears: Their Biology and Management* (Papers of the International Conference on Bear Research and Management, Calgary, Canada, November 1970), (Morges: International Union, 1972), 11–12.

51. "Bighorn" Theatrical Release Publicity, NFB, 1970. National Film Board of Canada website, http://www. onf-nfb.gc.ca.

52. In a note to the author, Schmalz recounted that it "was the avoidable mishandling" of a situation involving a female grizzly and her two cubs by parks wardens that prompted him to propose the film. . . . Personal communication, Schmalz to author, 7 July 2010.

53. Herrero described Wilf Ethrington's mauling in *Bear Attacks*, 45–47. . . .

54. NFBA, Schmalz, "Bears and Man Film Report, December 1974," *Bears and Man* correspondence file.

55. Telephone Interview with Bill Schmalz, 18 August

2008; in the rough cuts, Schmalz had included the shot because it showed what happened when tourists fed bears, "the consequences of their actions. But the park service did not want that in the film."

56. Schmalz interview, 18 August 2008. . . .

57. NFBA *Bears and Man* script, undated.

58. Shepard Kretch III, *The Ecological Indian: Myth and History* (New York, NY: W.W. Norton, 1999), 20–4.

59. Schmalz remembered that teenagers on the scene had initially feared the bears, but, after a half hour of watching other tourists feeding them, they gained their bravado to join in.

60. Communicated to the author, 15 June 2010.

61. Herrero disagreed with the view of those advocating eradication and supported the need for public education, "to be carried out by parks personnel, scientists and wildlife appreciators." Herrero, "Introduction to the Biology and Management of Bears," 13.

62. Tina Loo, "From Wildlife to Wild Places," in *States of Nature: Conserving Canada's Wildlife in the Twentieth Century* (Vancouver, BC: UBC Press, 2006), 183–209.

31 Visualizing Play

Since the late nineteenth century, images of play have made their way into a variety of media. Among these are print advertisements, sports and soft news photography for print media and, of course, television, where entire networks are devoted to the broadcasting of play. Some photographs of play and recreation are taken for family reasons, to memorialize vacations or particular events. Much imagery of play, however, has been produced by industries with an interest either in promoting leisure or using the idea of leisure time to sell consumer products and services. Despite this commodification of play (or perhaps because of it), Canadians experienced an expansion of leisure as a component of everyday life, especially among the working and middle classes. As the selections in this section make clear, however, play has historically been an ambiguous site, where power was exercised and social meanings were deeply contested.

The images presented here come from a wide variety of sources. It is worthwhile asking how advertisements, postcards, and press photographs all constituted different perspectives on the many sites of play that emerged in the twentieth century.

Series 1: Bodies in Motion

The development of the bicycle in the late nineteenth century was seen as a technological triumph of Victorian progress. Although largely regarded as a masculine activity in its early form, the introduction of the safety bicycle in the late 1880s led manufacturers to focus on the "lady cyclist" as an expanding market. Such technology was deeply gendered; unlike the preceding, difficult-to-master "high wheeler" and "bone-shaker" models that had appealed to men, these new bicycles were easier to ride and their frame was dropped to allow women to wear skirts without breeching propriety. Despite facing criticism that women's presence on bicycles was unseemly, unhealthy, and immoral, manufacturers were eager to marry the modernity of bicycling with the image of respectable femininity. Critics, and some proponents, saw women bicyclists as the public embodiment of an emerging New Woman ideal, which challenged Victorian notions of female dependency by embracing women's suffrage, education, and dress reform. Whether women themselves found bicycling and the increased mobility it offered to be liberating or a form of regulation remains the subject of scholarly debate.

1. Examine the wide range of riders depicted in the Massey-Harris advertisement (Figure 1).

How is the act of riding linked to the individual identities and vocations of those depicted? How are these relationships gendered?

2. How does the Dunlop tire advertisement (Figure 2) reflect the tensions between the emerging New Woman and a reinforcement of Victorian codes of femininity?

3. What do these advertisements suggest about the bicycle as a "modern" technology?

Series 2: Battling over the Bottle

In colonial Canada, taverns and public houses were places of sociability and spaces where women and men of different classes and races could mix, within certain boundaries. As a place to eat, drink, discuss politics, gossip, or stop over on a journey, tavern life was woven deeply into the fabric of colonial society. However, as the processes of industrialization accelerated in the nineteenth century, advocates for various forms of alcohol prohibition recast the act of drinking alcohol, and the taverns themselves, as morally dangerous spaces. Middle-class Protestant social reformers, and especially groups like the Woman's Christian Temperance Union, waged a long campaign for restricting alcohol, often alongside demands for increasing women's political rights to vote. Taverns and bars, which were increasingly associated with male working-class culture, were a prime target for those who sought to blame liquor vendors for destroying the domestic lives of the poor, rather than questioning the wage structures of industrialization itself.

Between 1916 and 1919, provinces in Canada adopted various forms of prohibition, although the rules varied and the private consumption of alcohol within the home remained legal. Figures 3 and 4 show two different sides of the battle for the bottle in the Prohibition era, as temperance advocates and breweries appealed for public support with competing messages. Over the course of the 1920s, the restrictions were loosened in most parts of the country as governments shifted to enforcing moderation rather than banning alcohol. Government liquor boards, government-run stores, and strict licensing regulations for barrooms and taverns were imposed. As Dan Malleck's chapter demonstrates, government control extended to gendering the bar space, mandating what activities could take place within them, and defining what a "respectable" establishment should be. The beer ads in Figures 5–8 were all published in the 1930s in the *Hotel News*, and yet none of the breweries in the magazine showed the hotel barroom in its advertisements. As you view these illustrations, reflect on why the spaces for consuming beer are implied, rather than shown, in the era of government regulation.

1. In the Prohibition cartoon (Figure 3), how are the spaces of work and play drawn upon to produce the tavern as a morally dangerous space? How does Figure 4, published the same year as the Prohibition cartoon, reframe beer drinking as respectable? How are class and gender constructed in these two images?

2. What kinds of recreational activities are displayed in the 1930s beer advertisements (Figures 5–7)? How do they present different landscapes of "play" in their presentation? How are they linking the experience of play with the consumption of beer, without showing anyone drinking?

3. Figures 7 and 8 demonstrate the common use and appropriation of Indigenous imagery to sell products, even naming one of the beers "Big Chief." How does this parallel the summer camp experience of "playing Indian" as discussed in Sharon Wall's chapter? How are narratives of progress associated with race in these ads? How do the representations of technology, space, and landscape speak to racial assumptions of what is modern or forward looking and what belongs to the "past"?

4. In all of the beer ads, gender plays a prominent role. How are masculine identities

framed in these ads? What does this say about the imagined consumer of beer over time? How do race and class shape the depictions of masculinity? How does masculinity relate to the social spaces of play being illustrated?

Series 3: Postcard Wilderness

George Colpitts's chapter discusses the efforts of park officials and filmmakers to reshape the image of the "Highway Bum" bear in the 1970s. The postcards reprinted in this series (Figures 9–12) speak to earlier sensibilities about bears, wildlife, and the role of nature in Canadian society. These photographs remind us that despite the seemingly naturalness of wilderness spaces, park spaces are historically constructed and reconstructed in ways that promote certain kinds of experiences, reflecting how expectations of "nature" have changed over time.

It is worth considering what it means to encounter and view these images in the form of a postcard. Postcards are material artifacts of exchange that were purchased and consumed, sometimes as a form of remembering, sometimes as a way of sharing that experience with others. Such images were not usually the result of a single experience but were produced for a mass audience and actively marketed to tourists. Their mobility through the mail at the cheapest possible rates allowed them to circulate far beyond the hands of individual tourists who were looking for an encounter with nature. While inexpensive to send, postcards documented a wide range of tourist experiences from modest daytrips to extravagant weeks- or months-long excursions.

1. What is the narrative about bears presented in these postcards, both in the captions and the composition of the images? How does this narrative relate to Colpitts's analysis?
2. What do these postcards indicate about the scale and nature of the tourist infrastructure that has developed in the national parks?

To what extent do these postcards allow us to think about the recreational elements of the park being gendered, classed, and racialized?

3. What is the broader message about the wilderness as a landscape of play that these images are trying to "sell" to actual and potential tourists? How have our contemporary perceptions of wilderness, national parks, and play changed (or not) since the interwar period?

Series 4: Consuming Sports

Today, the celebrity status of sports stars is taken for granted. However, the commodification of professional sports evolved in uneven stages throughout the twentieth century, fuelled by shifts in consumerism, leisure, and especially the rise of mass media, including radio and television. The five photographs in this series (Figures 13–17) reflect the public presentation of professional athletes to a wide audience in the 1950s, but they also tell us a great deal about the contested spaces of bodies and athletics in the post-war period.

Figures 13 and 14 are professional public relations photographs of two famous athletes. Barbara Ann Scott, an Ottawa-born figure skater, attracted worldwide attention when she became the first North American to win the European and World Championships and followed that feat with a gold medal at the 1948 Olympics. With her face on the cover of Life and Time magazines, Scott became known as "Canada's Sweetheart" and turned professional in 1949, travelling in a number of ice revue shows in the 1950s. Maurice "The Rocket" Richard led the Montreal Canadiens to eight Stanley Cups and was venerated by French-speaking Canadians, who rioted in Montreal when Richard was suspended for hitting an official in 1955.

The last three photographs offer a different visual perspective on the relationship between media and athletes. All three were taken by newspaper photographer Jack De Lorme for the Calgary *Albertan*. None of the athletes was famous, but all of them were professional: Barbara Baker was an American wrestler travelling through Calgary on tour; Gerry Musetti and Don Bailey, also American imports, played for the Calgary Stampeders football club; and Hiromi Uyeyama was a touring jockey described as a member of the "only Japanese trainer-jockey combination on the continent" and went by the nickname of "Spud." All three of these photographs were cropped and published in the *Albertan* in 1956 and offer a snapshot of how newspapers presented professional sports to their audience. These images, while made to appear spontaneous in nature, were just as carefully posed as the public relations shots of Scott and Richard.

1. Consider the various sports presented in these five images. Which are considered "rough" and which are considered "respectable"? How are athletes' bodies posed to reflect these differences?

2. In the article that accompanied Figure 15, Barbara Baker is described as an athlete who "packs her 130 pounds into her 5'2" frame with nary a muscle visible anywhere." Comparing Baker's portrayal with that of Scott (Figure 13), how and why are the two athletes presented differently?

3. How are masculinity and femininity constructed in these photographs? Where do these gendered constructions become ambiguous in the relationship between poses, bodies, and the sports involved?

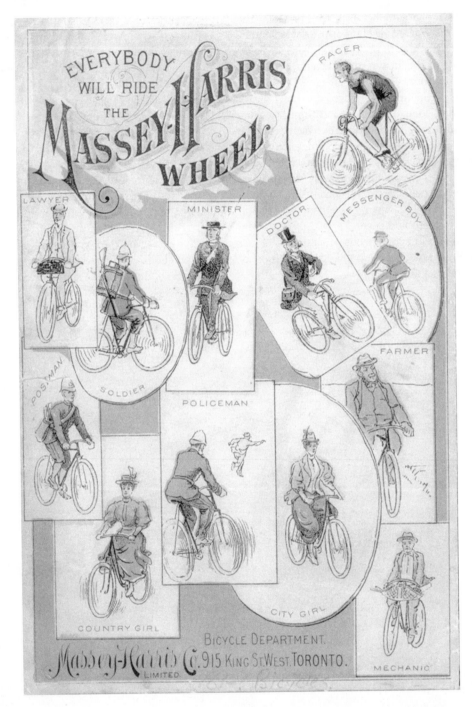

Figure 1. Massey-Harris Company, "Everybody Will Ride the Massey-Harris Wheel," Baldwin Room Broadsides and Printed Ephemera Collection, Toronto Public Library.

Figure 2. Dunlop Tires, "You Are Sure of . . ." *Massey Illustrated*, March 1897.

Figure 3. "Watching for Prey," *Pioneer* (Toronto), 26 December 1920.

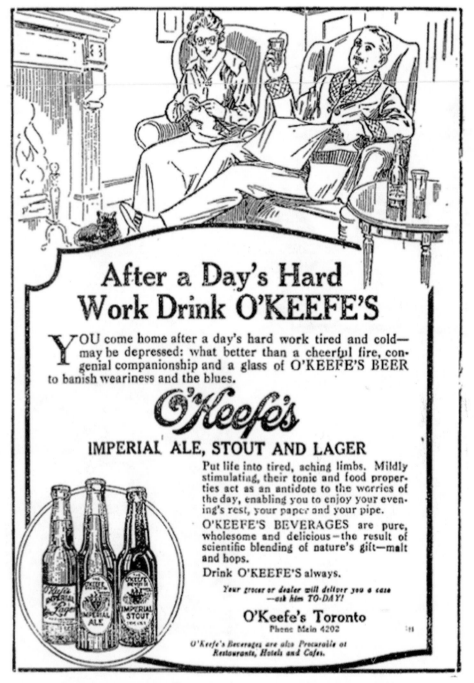

Figure 4. "After a Day's Hard Work, Drink O'Keefe's," *Toronto World*, 10 May 1920, 6.

Figure 5. "Big in the West," Calgary Brewing Advertisement, *Hotel News* 7, no. 5 (April 1934): 25.

Figure 6. "A-Hunting We Will Go," Drewry's Advertisement, *Hotel News* 11, no. 11 (October 1938): 14.

Figure 7. "Bill, It's Time for a Big Chief," Saskatoon Brewing Company Advertisement, *Hotel News* 12, no. 9 (August 1939): 27.

Figure 8. "Highest," Calgary Brewing Advertisement, *Hotel News* 11, no. 9 (August 1938).

Figure 9. Postcard of a bear looking into a tourist's car entitled "Tourists' Cars Are Subject to Inspection by Wild Game on the Auto Road Near Banff, Alberta," Banff National Park, Alberta (no date). Glenbow Archives, NA-4334-25.

Figure 10. Postcard of bears entitled "Four of a Kind," Jasper, Alberta (no date). University of Alberta, Peel's Prairie Provinces Postcard Collection, no. 8211. Image courtesy of Peel's Prairie Provinces (peel.library.ualberta.ca), a digital initiative of the University of Alberta Libraries.

Figure 11. Postcard of a bear cub with a toddler entitled "Hello You," photo by J. A. Weiss, 1945, Jasper, Alberta. University of Alberta, Peel's Prairie Provinces Postcard Collection, no. 8197. Image courtesy of Peel's Prairie Provinces (peel.library.ualberta.ca), a digital initiative of the University of Alberta Libraries.

Figure 12. Postcard of three bears entitled "Native Players on the Golf Course, Jasper Park, Canadian Rockies," c. 1940. University of Alberta, Peel's Prairie Provinces Postcard Collection, no. PC010585.16. Image courtesy of Peel's Prairie Provinces (peel.library.ualberta.ca), a digital initiative of the University of Alberta Libraries.

Figure 13. Barbara Ann Scott, Olympic and world champion figure skater, 1948.

Figure 14. Maurice "The Rocket" Richard. Courtesy of the Hockey Hall of Fame, Toronto, 000038–0094.

Figure 15. Barbara Baker, wrestler, 1956, by Jack De Lorme. Courtesy of Glenbow Archives, Calgary, NA–5600–8349a.

Figure 16. Gerry Musetti and Don Bailey, Calgary Stampeders football, 1956, by Jack De Lorme. Courtesy of Glenbow Archives, Calgary, NA–5600–8062a.

Figure 17. Hiromi "Spud" Uyeyama, jockey, 1956, by Jack De Lorme. Courtesy of Glenbow Archives, Calgary, NA–5600–8039d.

 *More online.*